Using Quattro Pro® 5.0 for Windows™, Special Edition

BRIAN UNDERDAHL

Using Quattro Pro 5.0 for Windows, Special Edition.

Library of Congress Catalog No.: 93-85248

ISBN: 1-56529-295-2

96 95 94 93   4 3 2

Interpretation of the printing code: the rightmost double-digit number is the year of the book's printing; the rightmost single-digit number, the number of the book's printing. For example, a printing code of 93-1 shows that the first printing of the book occurred in 1993.

Screen reproductions in this book were created by using Collage Plus from Inner Media, Inc., Hollis, NH.

This book is based on Quattro Pro 5.0 for Windows.

Publisher: David P. Ewing

Associate Publisher: Rick Ranucci

Managing Editor: Corinne Walls

Publishing Plan Manager: Thomas H. Bennett

Marketing Manager: Ray Robinson

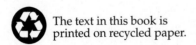 The text in this book is printed on recycled paper.

To Darlene, who's made my life very happy. Your faith in me and your hard work have given me a rare opportunity seldom available. May your opportunities be as precious.

CREDITS

Title Manager
Don Roche

Acquisitions Editor
Sherri Morningstar

Product Development Specialist
Joyce J. Nielsen

Production Editor
Cindy Morrow

Editors
Judy J. Brunetti
Christine Prakel
Brad Sullivan

Technical Editor
Ed Hanley

Formatter
Jill Stanley

Book Designer
Amy Peppler-Adams

Indexer
Craig Small

Production Team
Nick Anderson
Jeff Baker
Angela Bannan
Claudia Bell
Danielle Bird
Charlotte Clapp
Mark Enochs
Brook Farling
Heather Kaufman
Bob LaRoche
Beth Rago
Caroline Roop
Sandra Shay
Marc Shecter
Amy Steed
Suzanne Tully
Michelle Worthington
Lillian Yates

Composed in *Garamond* and *MCPdigital* by Que Corporation

Brian Underdahl is an author and independent consultant based in Reno, Nevada. He is the author of Que's best-selling books *Upgrading to MS-DOS 5*; *Upgrading to MS-DOS 6*; *Que's Guide to XTree*; *1-2-3 for DOS Release 3.1+ Quick Reference*; and *Easy Paradox for Windows*. He was also a contributing author to Que's *Using Symphony,* Special Edition; *1-2-3 Beyond the Basics*; *1-2-3 for DOS Release 3.1+ QuickStart*; *1-2-3 Power Macros*; *Using 1-2-3 Release 3.1*; *Using 1-2-3 for DOS Release 3.1+,* Special Edition; *Using 1-2-3 for Windows*; and *Using 1-2-3 Release 2.4,* Special Edition. He has also served as technical editor for Que on *Using 1-2-3 Release 2.3*; *Batch Files and Macros Quick Reference*; and *Computerizing Your Small Business*.

ACKNOWLEDGMENTS

Using Quattro Pro 5.0 for Windows, Special Edition, is the result of long hours and hard work by many individuals. The efforts of each of these people have earned them my deepest gratitude, and I'd like to thank all of them:

Don Roche, title manager, who worked on the front end of this project and helped me form the scope of the book.

Joyce Nielsen, senior product development specialist, for her many long days, late nights, and lost weekends dedicated to making this the best book possible. Joyce has been far more understanding and hard working than any author has the right to expect.

Sherri Morningstar, acquisitions editor, for arranging schedules to allow me the opportunity to take on this project.

Debbie Abshier, acquisitions coordinator, for coordinating the technical editing schedule and the many details necessary to keeping projects on track.

Cindy Morrow, production editor, for superior and thorough editing, which greatly improved the resulting book.

Judy Brunetti, **Christine Prakel**, and **Brad Sullivan**—editors who contributed much time and effort during the editing stage of this project.

Ed Hanley, technical editor, for making sure that the book is technically correct.

David Ewing, publisher, and **Rick Ranucci**, associate publisher, for having enough faith to believe in me through a long project. These two gentlemen have made it possible for me to find my place as an author.

The professionals in the **Que Production Department** for their unbelievable efforts in producing the highest quality book.

Nan Borreson and **Karen Giles** of Borland for their valuable support during the development of this book.

CONTENTS AT A GLANCE

II Building the Spreadsheet

III Creating Graphics and Printing Reports

IV Managing Databases

VI Analyzing Data

VI Quattro Pro 5.0 for Windows Command Reference

Introduction

In the late 1970s and early 1980s, personal computers were often considered to be toys—not the tools of successful businesses. Few real business applications were available, and the computers of the era were difficult to use. Both situations had to change before personal computers could become as popular with business as they are today. One early development that brought forth a substantial change was the invention of the electronic spreadsheet. The first available spreadsheet program was VisiCalc, and its introduction meant that the personal computer was at last considered a serious tool in the business world. Later, when IBM introduced the IBM PC, a new electronic spreadsheet, Lotus 1-2-3, became the star of the spreadsheet programs.

After the highly visible success of Lotus 1-2-3 came several excellent competitors. One of these, Quattro, offered more features and better value than 1-2-3. Quattro drew many fans, and the race to improve the spreadsheet programs began. Quattro Pro 5.0 for Windows represents the latest and most sophisticated result of this development effort.

For many years, DOS has been the major operating system for personal computers. The limitations of DOS have, however, limited the ability to provide easier-to-use and more powerful software programs. As the computer industry has grown and matured, several factors have made it possible to finally provide for the ever-expanding needs of today's computer users. More powerful hardware has allowed advanced operating environments such as Microsoft Windows and more sophisticated programs such as Quattro Pro for Windows to finally become available.

Whether you are new to spreadsheets, an experienced Quattro Pro user, or interested in Quattro Pro for Windows, this book is for you. *Using Quattro Pro 5.0 for Windows*, Special Edition, follows in the Que tradition of leading you from the basics of spreadsheets into the intermediate and advanced features of Quattro Pro for Windows.

Who Should Read This Book?

Using Quattro Pro 5.0 for Windows, Special Edition, is written and organized to meet the needs of a wide range of readers, from those for whom Quattro Pro 5.0 for Windows is their first spreadsheet product to those who are experienced with Quattro Pro or Lotus 1-2-3 and are upgrading to Quattro Pro 5.0 for Windows.

If Quattro Pro 5.0 for Windows is your first electronic spreadsheet program, this book helps you learn the basics so that you can quickly begin using Quattro Pro 5.0 for Windows. The first part of the book teaches you the fundamental concepts for understanding Quattro Pro 5.0 for Windows. The basic commands, the use of the keyboard and mouse, the Quattro Pro 5.0 for Windows screen, and the methods of creating and modifying Quattro Pro 5.0 for Windows spreadsheets are covered.

If you are an experienced Quattro Pro or Lotus 1-2-3 user and are upgrading to Quattro Pro 5.0 for Windows, this book describes all the new features in Quattro Pro 5.0 for Windows and how to apply them. As a true Windows product, Quattro Pro 5.0 for Windows offers many features not included in the DOS versions of Quattro Pro or Lotus 1-2-3.

Using Quattro Pro 5.0 for Windows, Special Edition, provides tips and techniques to help new users become experienced users and to help experienced users get the most from Quattro Pro 5.0 for Windows. As you continue to use Quattro Pro 5.0 for Windows, you will find this book a helpful guide, reminding you of the steps, tips, and cautions for using the program.

The Organization of This Book

As you browse through this book, you will get a better sense of its organization and layout. *Using Quattro Pro 5.0 for Windows*, Special Edition, is organized to follow a natural path of learning and using Quattro Pro 5.0 for Windows.

Part I—Getting Started

Chapter 1, "An Overview of Quattro Pro 5.0 for Windows," covers the uses, features, and commands in Quattro Pro 5.0 for Windows that are the same as, or similar to, commands in other versions of Quattro Pro and Lotus 1-2-3. This chapter introduces the general concepts for understanding Quattro Pro 5.0 for Windows as a spreadsheet program and introduces the program's major use: creating spreadsheets, databases, graphics, and macros. Finally, this chapter details the hardware and software requirements for using Quattro Pro 5.0 for Windows.

Chapter 2, "Understanding Quattro Pro for Windows Basics," helps you begin using Quattro Pro 5.0 for Windows and includes starting and exiting the program; learning tricks of the keyboard and mouse; understanding features of the screen display; and getting context-sensitive, on-screen help.

Chapter 3, "Using the Graphical User Interface," teaches you to use what may be a familiar program in a new environment. You learn how to manipulate and display windows, as well as how to use menus, dialog boxes, SpeedBars, SpeedButtons, and the mouse to improve your efficiency.

Chapter 4, "Learning Spreadsheet Basics," introduces the concepts of spreadsheets, notebooks, and files, and teaches you how to move the cell pointer around the spreadsheet, enter and edit data, and use the Undo feature. You also learn to create formulas that link cells in different notebook files, and how to use the Quattro Pro 5.0 for Windows Interactive Tutors to quickly learn basic tasks.

Part II—Building the Spreadsheet

Chapter 5, "Using Fundamental Commands," teaches you how to use the most fundamental commands for building spreadsheets. You also learn to save your notebook and workspace files and to temporarily leave Quattro Pro 5.0 for Windows in order to return to the operating system.

Chapter 6, "Changing the Format and Appearance of Data," shows you how to change the way data appears on-screen, including the way values, dates, formulas, and text are displayed. You also learn how to suppress the display of zeros and to control the fonts, colors, and shading used to display spreadsheet information.

Chapter 7, "Using Functions," describes all the built-in functions available in Quattro Pro 5.0 for Windows: Boolean, database, date and time, engineering, financial, logical, mathematical, miscellaneous, statistical, and string.

Chapter 8, "Managing Files," covers those commands related to saving, erasing, and listing files, as well as the commands for combining data from several files, extracting data from one file to another, and opening more than one file in memory at a time. This chapter also teaches you how to transfer information between different programs and how to use Quattro Pro 5.0 for Windows in a multiuser environment.

Chapter 9, "Using the Optimizer and Solve For," introduces powerful tools for what-if analysis. The Optimizer and Solve For tools provide linear and nonlinear optimization, as well as goal seeking and other problem-solving capabilities.

Part III—Creating Graphics and Printing Reports

Chapter 10, "Creating Presentation Graphics," teaches you to create graphs from spreadsheet data. This chapter covers all the options available to create a graph; change the type of graph; enhance a graph by adding titles, lines, and labels; as well as change the fonts, colors, and shading used. You learn how to add graphs to a spreadsheet, create slide shows using the Quattro Pro 5.0 for Windows Light Table, and preview your graphs. You also learn how to use analytical graphs to examine data relationships.

Chapter 11, "Printing Reports," shows you how to preview and print reports, change printing options, and selectively print desired blocks of data. You learn how to print a basic report by using only a few commands, and to enhance a report for producing more professional-looking output.

Part IV—Managing Databases

Chapter 12, "Creating Databases," introduces the Quattro Pro 5.0 for Windows database and shows you how to create, modify, and maintain data records, including sorting, locating, and extracting data.

Chapter 13, "Understanding Advanced Data Management," covers special commands and features of Quattro Pro 5.0 for Windows data management. These features include data tables, data regression, and using data from external sources.

Part V—Customizing Quattro Pro for Windows

Chapter 14, "Understanding Macros," is an introduction to the powerful macro capability in Quattro Pro 5.0 for Windows. This chapter teaches you to create, name, and run simple macros. You also learn to create macros by recording keystrokes, and to avoid some common errors in building macros.

Chapter 15, "Using the Advanced Macro Commands," explains the powerful, advanced macro commands in Quattro Pro 5.0 for Windows. You learn how to use the advanced macro commands, how to find and correct errors in macro programs, and how to document your macros. Finally, you find a complete reference to the advanced macro commands, as well as examples that use many of these macro commands.

Chapter 16, "Using SpeedButtons and Custom Dialog Boxes," shows you how to use an exciting new feature of Quattro Pro 5.0 for Windows: SpeedButtons. You learn how to use and create custom SpeedButtons and dialog boxes. You also learn how to use the SpeedBar Designer to create custom SpeedBars.

Part VI—Analyzing Data

Chapter 17, "Using Analysis Tools and Experts," shows you how to use the powerful new data analysis tools and Experts in Quattro Pro 5.0 for Windows. You learn to perform sophisticated data analysis by simply responding to the prompts.

Chapter 18, "Using the Data Modeling Desktop," shows you how to use dynamic crosstab analysis to view your data in new ways. You learn to quickly produce new views that provide different perspectives on the relationships between data items.

Chapter 19, "Consolidating Data and Managing Scenarios," introduces two powerful new features that enable you to quickly combine data from several sources, and to try different combinations of data. You learn to create several different data sets within a single notebook, enabling you to examine several possibilities.

Chapter 20, "Sharing Data Using the Workgroup Desktop," shows you how to share data between several Quattro Pro 5.0 for Windows users. You learn how to mail, publish, or subscribe to notebooks using a LAN or services such as MCI Mail.

Part VII—Quattro Pro 5.0 for Windows Command Reference

The Quattro Pro 5.0 for Windows command reference is a comprehensive guide to the procedures for using nearly every command from the Quattro Pro 5.0 for Windows menus. The command reference also provides many reminders, tips, and cautions that greatly simplify and expedite your day-to-day use of Quattro Pro 5.0 for Windows.

Appendixes

Appendix A, "Installing Quattro Pro 5.0 for Windows," shows you how to install Quattro Pro 5.0 for Windows so that the program runs with your hardware and operating system.

Appendix B, "Upgrading to Quattro Pro 5.0 for Windows," provides an introduction to Quattro Pro 5.0 for Windows for those who are familiar with other versions of Quattro Pro or Lotus 1-2-3.

Other Titles to Enhance Your Personal Computing

Although *Using Quattro Pro 5.0 for Windows*, Special Edition is a comprehensive guide to Quattro Pro 5.0 for Windows, no single book can fill all your Quattro Pro 5.0 for Windows and personal computing needs. Que Corporation publishes a full line of books that complement *Using Quattro Pro 5.0 for Windows*, Special Edition.

Several Que books can help you learn and master your operating system and environment. *Using Windows 3.1*, Special Edition, covers the Microsoft Windows operating environment in detail, and *Windows 3.1 QuickStart* shows you how to quickly learn the basics of Windows. *Using MS-DOS 6*, Special Edition, is an excellent comprehensive guide to the MS-DOS operating system. *Upgrading to MS-DOS 6*, written by the author of *Using Quattro Pro 5.0 for Windows*, Special Edition, is directed at users who are upgrading to the latest version of MS-DOS. Que's *MS-DOS 6 QuickStart* also is available for users who prefer a quick-and-easy approach to learning DOS fundamentals.

If you find your computer hardware is not up to the requirements of today's more powerful Windows-based software, consider Que's *Upgrading and Repairing PCs*, 2nd Edition. This book provides the information you need to get the most from your current equipment, as well as how to upgrade your system when necessary.

All these fine Que books can be found in better bookstores and computer stores worldwide. In the United States, you can call Que at 1-800-428-5331 to order books or obtain further information.

Conventions Used in This Book

Several conventions are used in *Using Quattro Pro 5.0 for Windows*, Special Edition, to help you learn the program. Examples are provided for these conventions to help you distinguish the different elements in Quattro Pro 5.0 for Windows.

When an action explained in the text can also be accomplished by clicking a SpeedButton, that button appears in the margin next to the paragraph that pertains to it. For example, text might explain how to choose menu options to print a spreadsheet; because you can also print by clicking the Print SpeedButton, the Print SpeedButton would appear in the margin next to the text.

Special typefaces used in *Using Quattro Pro 5.0 for Windows*, Special Edition, include the following:

Type	Meaning
italic	New terms or phrases when they are initially defined; function and advanced macro command syntax

(continues)

Type	Meaning
boldface	Information you are asked to type, including the Quattro Pro 5.0 for Windows menu and dialog box options that appear underlined on-screen
`special type`	Direct quotations of words that appear on-screen or in a figure; menu command prompts

Elements printed in uppercase include block names (SALES), functions (@SUM), mode indicators (READY), and cell references (A1..C10 and A:A1).

References to keys are as they appear on the keyboard of the IBM Personal Computer and most compatibles. The function keys, F1 through F12, are used for special situations in Quattro Pro 5.0 for Windows. In the text, the function key name and the corresponding function key number usually are listed together, such as Edit (F2).

When two keys appear together with a plus sign, such as Shift+Ins, press and hold down the first key while you then press the second key. When two keys appear together without a plus sign, such as End Home, the first key is pressed and released before the second key is pressed.

The following conventions pertain to macros:

- Single-character macro names appear with the backslash (\) and single-character names in lowercase: \a.

- Quattro Pro 5.0 for Windows menu keystrokes in a macro line appear in lowercase: {ALT}bc.

- Block names within macros appear in uppercase.

- Representations of direction keys, such as {DOWN}; function keys, such as {CALC}; and editing keys, such as {DEL}, appear in uppercase letters and are surrounded by braces.

- Advanced macro commands are enclosed within braces, such as {GETLABEL}, when used in a syntax line or within a macro, but appear without braces in the text.

- The Enter key is represented by the tilde (~).

Getting Started

An Overview of Quattro Pro 5.0 for Windows

Since personal computers first became popular business tools, electronic spreadsheets have been some of the most well-known software programs. Millions of people use packages like Quattro Pro and Lotus 1-2-3 to solve business problems, analyze financial transactions, perform statistical analyses, and handle countless other tasks. These programs offer their users an electronic spreadsheet, a database manager, business graphics, and a presentation-level report generator all in one convenient package.

Quattro Pro 5.0 for Windows provides a new level of performance and capability to the personal computer user. It offers WYSIWYG (what-you-see-is-what-you-get) capabilities and many advanced features that take full advantage of the latest versions of the Microsoft Windows operating environment.

This chapter presents an overview of Quattro Pro 5.0 for Windows. It covers features, commands, and functions common to all releases of Quattro Pro as well as those that are new to Quattro Pro 5.0 for Windows. If you are upgrading from another release of Quattro Pro (or Lotus 1-2-3), this chapter serves as a general introduction to the new features and commands of Quattro Pro 5.0 for Windows. Topics covered here include the following:

- General capabilities of Quattro Pro 5.0 for Windows (an overview for readers new to Quattro Pro, electronic spreadsheets, or personal computers)

- New features (directed at readers upgrading from a previous Quattro Pro or Lotus 1-2-3 release)

- Types of functions and commands

- File-management capabilities

- Security features

- New and greatly enhanced graphics and report presentation capabilities

- Ways of automating Quattro Pro 5.0 for Windows using the powerful advanced macro commands

- System requirements

Understanding Quattro Pro 5.0 for Windows Capabilities

Quattro Pro 5.0 for Windows is similar in its basic functions to other electronic spreadsheet programs like Quattro Pro for DOS, but it also offers many powerful and important features that the other programs lack. Quattro Pro 5.0 for Windows can be used for everything from very simple applications to complex financial planning. It brings a new level of database power to the spreadsheet user by enabling direct access to dBASE and Paradox relational database files. It also includes sophisticated presentation graphics capabilities with which you can create graphic representations of financial and scientific data for use in presentation-quality reports or on-screen slide shows.

Quattro Pro 5.0 for Windows combines all the traditional features of Quattro Pro with the increased power of Microsoft Windows. New features of Quattro Pro 5.0 for Windows include the following:

- The capability to link to other Windows applications, such as word processors and graphics programs

- The capability to share data with other Windows applications by way of the Windows Clipboard

- Object Inspectors, which provide direct access to all actions available for the selected item

- SpeedBars, which enable you to perform common commands and procedures by pointing at an icon and clicking the mouse button

- SpeedButtons and custom dialog boxes, which enable you to create your own user interface

- Powerful methods of finding optimal solutions to complex what-if problems

- Support for any printer or display used by Windows

- Multitasking through Windows

- Powerful new data analysis tools, which enable you to quickly solve complex problems

- Interactive Tutors, which teach you how to use Quattro Pro 5.0 for Windows using your data

- Experts, which rapidly guide you through complex tasks

- Data Modeling Desktop, which enables you to develop new relationships in your data

- Consolidator and Scenario Manager, which provide a simple way to combine and test different combinations of information

- Workgroup Desktop, which makes it easy to share notebook data with other users

Many of the significant changes that occurred between earlier versions of Quattro Pro and Quattro Pro 5.0 for Windows were made possible by the Windows environment. As a graphical user interface (GUI), Microsoft Windows offers your programs a wide variety of fonts and colors. This feature enables you to organize your data graphically for easy identification; with it you can create presentation-quality graphics much more easily than you could with most non-Windows programs. Full mouse support gives you the ability to manipulate objects directly. You can, for example, size and move windows, select blocks, and execute commands with the mouse. A WYSIWYG display enables you to see data as it will appear on paper in its final printed form. Pull-down and cascade menus enable you to keep track of where you are in the menu structure at all times.

The Windows environment gives Quattro Pro 5.0 for Windows speed, power, and flexibility. Its multitasking capabilities enable you to print one spreadsheet while you're working on another at the same time. With Dynamic Data Exchange (DDE) and Object Linking and Embedding (OLE), you can link Quattro Pro 5.0 for Windows spreadsheets to other Windows applications. Multiple windows enable you to view several spreadsheets at the same time, to display the Help window while you work, and to display graphs and spreadsheets simultaneously.

Quattro Pro 5.0 for Windows can best be described as an electronic accountant's pad or an electronic spreadsheet. When you start the program, your computer screen displays a grid of columns and rows into which you can enter text, numbers, or formulas in the same way as an accountant would record figures on a columnar pad. Quattro Pro 5.0 for Windows extends this analogy by offering three-dimensional spreadsheet notebooks, in which you can move from page to page or view several pages on-screen at the same time.

In Quattro Pro 5.0 for Windows, the notebook with its spreadsheet pages is the basis of the whole product. Whether you are working with a database application or creating a graph, you must work within the structure of the notebook. Figure 1.1 shows the Quattro Pro 5.0 for Windows screen.

Each notebook file contains 257 pages. The first 256 pages are spreadsheet pages; the last page is always the Graphs page. By default, each notebook page is identified by a letter. The first page is labeled *A*, the second page is labeled *B*, and so on. You can add descriptive names to page if you like. You could, for example, give pages *A* and *B* the more informative names *Sales* and *Expenses*. Each notebook page is made up of 256 columns, labeled A through IV, and 8192 rows, numbered consecutively.

The intersections of rows and columns form *cells*, in which you enter data. Each cell is identified by an address, which consists of a page name, column letter, and row number. If, for example, you are entering data in the first page, the fourth column, and the ninth row, you are entering information in cell *A:D9* (see fig. 1.2).

As you work in the spreadsheet, Quattro Pro 5.0 for Windows indicates the *active cell*—the cell in which you can enter data—with a rectangular outline. This outline is called the *cell selector*. You can use the direction keys or the mouse to move the cell selector. See Chapter 4, "Learning Spreadsheet Basics," for more information on moving the cell selector.

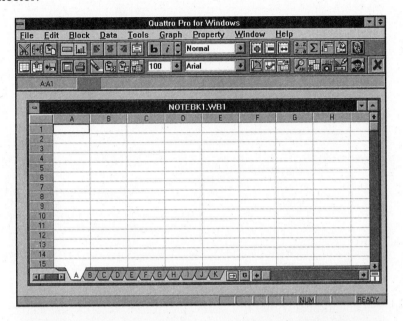

Fig. 1.1

The Quattro Pro for Windows screen.

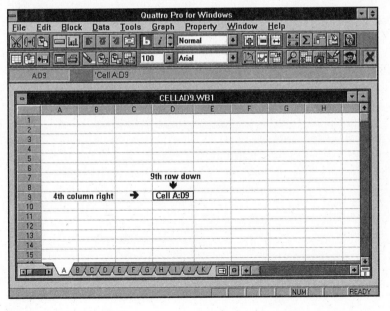

Fig. 1.2

Data entered in cell A:D9.

Potentially you can fill over two million cells on one spreadsheet page—and each notebook contains 256 spreadsheet pages. Most users, however, never need to handle this much data or have the necessary computer equipment. Your system memory and disk requirements for using Quattro Pro 5.0 for Windows depend on many factors, including the number and types of Windows applications running at the same time, the size of your spreadsheets, and the types of data contained in each cell. Refer to the section, "Understanding Quattro Pro 5.0 for Windows System Requirements," later in this chapter for more information on minimum system requirements.

Creating Formulas

Because electronic spreadsheet programs like Quattro Pro 5.0 for Windows primarily were designed for financial and scientific applications, their handling of formulas is both sophisticated and easy-to-use. You can create a simple formula that adds the values in two cells on the same spreadsheet page as follows:

+A1+A2

This formula indicates that the value displayed in the current cell is the sum of the values stored in cells A1 and A2 on the current page. Each time you enter a new value in A1 or A2, the formula in the current cell recalculates and displays the new sum. If, for example, A1 originally contains the value 2 and A2 contains the value 7, the formula results in the value 9. But if you change the value in A2 to 8, the value in the cell containing the formula is recalculated to 10.

Formulas are created using symbols called *operators,* which give Quattro Pro 5.0 for Windows instructions for combining, manipulating, or relating values. Some familiar operators used to combine or manipulate numbers include + (addition), – (subtraction), * (multiplication), / (division), and ^ (exponentiation). *Logical operators*, which are used to judge the relationship between two values, include < (less than), > (greater than), and = (equal to). Formulas that use logical operators are true/false formulas. That is, the value of the formula is true (or 1) if the expressed relationship is true. The value of the formula is false (or 0) if the expressed relationship is false. For example, the logical formula 1<2 is true, while 1=2 and 1>2 are both false.

The power of Quattro Pro 5.0 for Windows formulas, however, is best illustrated by the program's capability to link data across spreadsheet pages and notebook files. By referencing cells in other spreadsheet pages and notebook files, formulas can calculate results from multiple spreadsheet applications. To create a formula that accesses data on another spreadsheet page, specify the spreadsheet page on which the data is located (indicated by letter label *A* through *IV* or by a name you have assigned to that page), enter a colon (:), and then enter the cell address. The following example shows a formula that links data across three spreadsheet pages:

+A:B3+B:C6+D:B4

If you have named the spreadsheet pages, you might use a formula similar to this one:

+Sales:B3+Expenses:C6+Overhead:B4

To access data from another notebook file, simply include the notebook name—surrounded by square bracket—sin the formula. Note the following examples:

+A:C6+[SALES1.WB1]A:C5

+Sales:D20+[EXPENSE]Reps:G15

FOR RELATED INFORMATION

▶▶ "Learning Spreadsheet Basics," p. 85.

▶▶ "Linking Notebooks Using Formulas," p. 282.

Playing "What If" with the Optimizer and Solve For

Because Quattro Pro 5.0 for Windows remembers the relationships between cells and does not merely calculate values, you can change a cell value and observe what happens when your formulas are recalculated. This what-if capability makes Quattro Pro 5.0 for Windows an incredibly powerful tool for many types of analysis. You can analyze, for example, the effect of an expected increase in the cost of goods, determining the product price increases required to maintain your current profit margins.

The Quattro Pro 5.0 for Windows Optimizer tool is similar to the 1-2-3 Solver, and its Solve For tool is similar to the 1-2-3 Backsolver.

The Optimizer revolutionizes Quattro Pro's capability to perform what-if analysis. If you have a problem involving a number of variables, the Optimizer can explore all possible options and find an answer that satisfies the conditions you impose.

To solve a what-if problem manually, you enter the necessary numbers and formulas into the spreadsheet and then change various numbers until you reach the desired result. The Optimizer does this work for you by performing all possible calculations within limits you specify. It uses symbolic (algebraic) and numeric analysis to solve both linear and nonlinear problems.

The Solve For utility provides a means to solve goal-seeking problems that have only one variable. To find out how large a loan you can obtain at a specified term, interest rate, and monthly payment amount, for example, you would use the Solve For utility.

Chapter 9, "Using the Optimizer and Solve For," describes these two utilities in more detail.

Using Quattro Pro 5.0 for Windows Functions

Building useful applications in Quattro Pro 5.0 for Windows would be quite difficult if you had to generate complex mathematical, statistical, logical, financial, and other types of formulas from scratch. To make things easier, the program provides several hundred built-in formulas—called *functions*—that are tailored for business, scientific, and engineering applications, among others. You can use these functions as shortcuts instead of entering complicated formulas containing many operators and parentheses.

Functions in Quattro Pro 5.0 for Windows are labeled by the @ sign followed by the name of the function. Some commonly used functions, for example, include @SUM, @RAND, and @ROUND. Many functions require you to enter an *arguments*—pecifications needed to calculate the results of a formula—after the function name. To add the values contained in block A2 through H2, for example, you can enter

@SUM(A2..H2). Or you can use block names to specify arguments. If block A2 through H2 is named SALES, for example, you can enter **@SUM(SALES)**.

Quattro Pro 5.0 for Windows includes 10 main categories of functions: Boolean, database, date and time, engineering, financial, logical, mathematical, miscellaneous, statistical, and string. Chapter 7, "Using Functions," describes Quattro Pro 5.0 for Windows functions in detail.

Using Quattro Pro 5.0 for Windows Command Menus

The *command menus*, which appear at the top of the screen, offer several groups of related commands. The *SpeedBars*, which are located just below the menu bar, include icons that provide shortcut methods for performing common spreadsheet tasks. In addition, Quattro Pro 5.0 for Windows offers *Object Inspectors*—object-oriented dialog boxes containing commands and actions relating to the selected object. In many instances, you have several different ways to select the same commands. As you use Quattro Pro 5.0 for Windows, you will find some of these ways easier to use than others. This book, however, concentrates on demonstrating effective procedures rather than suggesting a particular method of command selection.

The *notebook* is the basis for all applications you create, modify, and print in Quattro Pro 5.0 for Windows. You can enter data in the form of text, numbers, or formulas. Menu commands enable you to format, copy, move, and print your data; they also enable you to create graphic representations and to perform database operations on your data. In addition, you can use menu commands to save and retrieve your notebook and workspace files, to manage and change the files, and to read and write files in formats different from the Quattro Pro 5.0 for Windows spreadsheet file format.

The term *workspace* refers to the area of the Quattro Pro 5.0 for Windows screen that contains all open notebooks. Each time you save a *workspace file*, you save the current layout of all open notebooks in the workspace (but not their contents). When you later retrieve a workspace file, the same notebooks are opened. They are sized and positioned as they were when the workspace file was saved.

The menu commands often lead to further levels of commands or dialog boxes. Press the *Alt* key to access the command menu. You will use some commands frequently whenever you create or modify a notebook application. Other commands, such as specialized database commands, you might use rarely (or never). The following sections introduce the commands you probably will use most frequently—those related to creating and modifying notebook applications.

Using File Commands

The File commands help you organize and maintain files, print files, and open multiple files at once. Using File commands, you can create a new blank notebook, open an existing notebook, or close all files in the current workspace. You can save a notebook file, save the current workspace, or load a group of notebooks that you saved earlier as a workspace file.

You also print your notebooks using these commands. The File commands enable you to preview reports before printing, change page layouts, and make printer selections.

Using Edit Commands

The Edit menu includes commands that enable you to copy and move the data in a cell or group of cells from one location to another in a notebook, from one Quattro Pro 5.0 for Windows notebook to another, and from a Quattro Pro 5.0 for Windows notebook to another Windows application. Some Edit commands create DDE and OLE links between Quattro Pro 5.0 for Windows notebooks and other Windows applications. Other Edit commands provide means for you to move to a specified location and to search for and optionally replace values.

The Edit Copy command can save you hours of manually copying text, numbers, and formulas. Copying formulas is one of the most important functions of this command. If you copy a formula to another part of a spreadsheet, the formula remains the same but the cell addresses and block names change positionally to reflect the move (so the formula results in a different value). Edit Copy uses the Windows Clipboard, and can be used when you want to make multiple copies of the same data.

Edit Cut moves data from the spreadsheet to the Windows Clipboard; after it has been placed on the Clipboard, the data can be pasted into another area of the current notebook, another notebook, or another Windows application. Edit Clear and Edit Clear Contents delete data from the spreadsheet. Edit Search and Replace enables you to find and replace characters in both labels and formulas.

Edit Paste Link and Edit Paste Special are used to create and maintain dynamic links between Quattro Pro 5.0 for Windows spreadsheets and other Windows applications, such as Word for Windows.

Edit Undo reverses the effects of most Quattro Pro 5.0 for Windows actions. After you undo an action, Edit Undo becomes Edit Redo until you perform another action that can be undone.

Edit Define Style enables you to create and name a group of cell formatting options that you then can apply quickly to any spreadsheet cell.

Edit Insert Object enables you to insert an OLE object into a notebook.

Using Block Commands

The Block commands affect single cells or blocks. If you are used to Lotus 1-2-3, you recognize that *blocks* are very similar to 1-2-3 *ranges*. Because they can contain groups of noncontiguous cells, however, Quattro Pro 5.0 for Windows blocks are more like 1-2-3's *collections*.

A Copy command appears on both the Edit and Block menus. Although similar, the two commands are different in one important respect. Edit Copy uses the Windows Clipboard; Block Copy does not. If you need to make several copies of data at different places in a spreadsheet or to copy data to another Windows application, use Edit Copy and Edit Paste. If you need to make a single copy and do not want to move the cell selector to the destination cell, use Block Copy. In most cases, however, you can select either command with equal results.

The Block Move command enables you to move the contents of one cell or a large block of cells to another area of the spreadsheet page or to another spreadsheet page.

Block Insert and Block Delete are used to add or delete complete or partial rows, columns, and spreadsheet pages, or to insert files into the current notebook. These commands enable you to create room for additional data and to remove sections of your spreadsheets that no longer are needed. Block Insert Break causes Quattro Pro 5.0 for

Windows to add a page break at the current cell selector location. If you print a spreadsheet containing a page break, data below the break appears on a new page.

The **B**lock **F**ill command has many uses. You can use it to add a series of dates, create database record numbers, or fill a block with a series of numbers, incrementing by a growth factor or by an exponential factor.

One of the most useful **B**lock commands, **N**ames, enables you to attach a name to a single cell or group of cells. Naming a group of cell values *SALES*, for example, makes it easier to create a formula to total the numbers; simply enter the function @SUM followed by the *block name* of the group in parentheses: **@SUM(SALES)**. Block names are also useful for printing. If you name an area, you can avoid the hassle of specifying exact cell addresses each time you want to print that area. Just enter the name instead. You can also use this command to name parts of a single notebook page or parts of many notebook pages so that you can move the cell selector quickly and easily from one area to another. As you become accustomed to using block names, you will find many occasions when they save you time and simplify your work. Block names are even more important if you use macros, because they help ensure proper functioning of your macros even if the notebook layout is changed.

Block **R**eformat adjusts (or justifies) a block of text to fit a given column range. Although Quattro Pro 5.0 for Windows is clearly not intended to replace a word processor, this command enables you to produce short notes and memos.

Using Data Commands

Quattro Pro 5.0 for Windows provides true database management commands and functions so that you can sort, query, extract, and perform statistical analysis on your data. You can even access and manipulate that data from an external database! Using the Quattro Pro 5.0 for Windows **D**ata commands instead of independent database programs gives you an important advantage, however. Because these commands are similar to the other commands used in Quattro Pro 5.0 for Windows, you can learn to use and manage databases as you learn the rest of the program.

After building a database in Quattro Pro 5.0 for Windows (which is similar to building any other notebook application), you can perform a variety of operations on that database. Some of these tasks can be accomplished with standard Quattro Pro 5.0 for Windows commands. Other database operations require the use of **Data** commands such as **Data S**ort and **Data Q**uery.

With Quattro Pro 5.0 for Windows you can easily access data in files created and maintained by an external data manager such as dBASE or Paradox. These data management capabilities are covered in detail in Chapter 12, "Creating Databases," and Chapter 13, "Understanding Advanced Data Management."

With the **Data Data M**odeling Desktop command, you can create many different cross-tabulation views of your data. This feature enables you to examine complex relationships in your data with ease. **Data Data Modeling** Desktop is covered in Chapter 18, "Using the Data Modeling Desktop."

Data Workgroup Desktop enables you to share data with other Quattro Pro 5.0 for Windows using the electronic mail capabilities of a LAN or a service such as MCI Mail. **Data Workg**roup Desktop is covered in Chapter 20, "Sharing Data Using the Workgroup Desktop."

Using Tools Commands

The **Tools** commands run Quattro Pro macros. They also enable you to extract and combine notebook data, control links, execute the advanced data regression and matrix math commands, perform advanced data analysis, and use the Optimizer and Solve For tools.

One of the most powerful **Tools** commands, UI **B**uilder, enables you to create your own dialog boxes that execute command sequences you specify and to customize the Quattro Pro 5.0 for Windows user interface.

Using Graph Commands

The **Graph** commands provide users the advantage of using a single program both to analyze data and to create instant graphs. With Quattro Pro 5.0 for Windows, you can create many types of graphs quickly, add special effects, and even create a slide show from a series of graphs.

The **G**raph commands open a Graph window and help you create graphs. With the **G**raph commands, you can add a new graph, import a graph from another file, change the size of a graph, or select a graph to view. When the Graph window is the active window, the SpeedBar displays icons used to create and enhance graphs. You can specify graph types, ranges, legends, and titles. In addition, you can enhance graphs by adding text, lines, arrows, and freehand drawings, using fonts and color, and moving graph elements. Quattro Pro 5.0 for Windows **G**raph commands can also import graphics files in eight different formats and export graphics in six different formats. The **S**lide Show command enables you to create, edit, and run on-screen slide shows using named graphs.

Using Property Commands

The **P**roperty commands provide users with a means to access the Object Inspectors, or object-oriented dialog boxes that enable you to control all the properties associated with a selected object. When a notebook block is selected, for example, the **P**roperty **C**urrent Object command displays a dialog box that includes settings for numeric format, font, shading, alignment, line drawing, protection, text color, data entry input, row height, column width, and hide or reveal.

Object Inspectors is one of the features that makes Quattro Pro 5.0 for Windows so much easier to use than any other spreadsheet program. Instead of struggling through several different menus to find all the actions appropriate for a selected object, you simply use the Object Inspectors to show the settings currently available.

Using Window Commands

The **W**indow commands control the display of all open windows. Quattro Pro 5.0 for Windows enables you to open many windows in order to display different spreadsheet pages, different notebook files, different graphs, or even different views of the same spreadsheet page. The **W**indow commands help you place, size, split, and move windows for optimum versatility. If several windows are open, selecting **W**indow also enables you to activate a window by choosing its name from a list.

Using Help Commands

Quattro Pro 5.0 for Windows includes an extensive on-line help system. The **Help** commands provide quick access to this information. Quattro Pro 5.0 for Windows, like all other applications designed for Windows, enables you to copy help text to the Clipboard and then paste it into a spreadsheet. You can copy macro command examples from the help text into your spreadsheet, for example, or incorporate portions of the sample macros into your own macros.

Managing Quattro Pro 5.0 for Windows Files

The type of file you create most often in Quattro Pro 5.0 for Windows is a *notebook file*. A notebook file saves all the data, formulas, and text you enter into a spreadsheet notebook, as well as the format of cells, the alignment of text, block names, and graph names and settings. Quattro Pro 5.0 for Windows notebook files are saved with a WB1 extension. *Workspace files*, which contain the settings for all open notebooks, are saved with a WBS extension. Quattro Pro 5.0 for Windows can also read many other file formats, including the following:

- WQ1 (Quattro Pro)
- WKS, WK1, WK3, and WKE (Lotus 1-2-3 worksheets)
- WRK and WR1 (Lotus Symphony)
- ALL, FMT, and FM3 (Lotus 1-2-3 Allways, Impress, and WYSIWYG formatting information)
- XLS (Excel)
- DBF, DB4, and DB2 (dBASE)
- DB (Paradox)
- BMP, CGM, CLP, EPS, GIF, PCX, PIC, and TIF (Graphics file formats)

Protecting Spreadsheets and Files

Quattro Pro 5.0 for Windows enables you to assign passwords when you save notebook files in order to protect those files from unauthorized users. It also enables you to protect individual cells, blocks of cells, and complete notebook pages from inadvertent changes. Chapter 5, "Using Fundamental Commands," provides more information on protecting your Quattro Pro 5.0 for Windows files.

Printing Reports and Graphics

The process of printing reports and graphics has also changed in Quattro Pro 5.0 for Windows. The most visible difference is that the Windows **F**ile menu is used to select printing commands. The **F**ile **P**rint commands enable you to print a spreadsheet on a printer, create an encoded file on disk, or preview a selection on-screen before printing it.

The **F**ile **P**rint commands take advantage of additional Windows print functionality by enabling you to use the Windows Print Manager and any print device supported by Windows.

File Printer Set**u**p enables you to specify a printer, using the Windows printer installation and configuration system.

With **F**ile Page Set**u**p, you can specify headers, footers, and margin size.

The **F**ile Print Preview utility, a major enhancement to Quattro Pro 5.0 for Windows, enables you to see a spreadsheet report before you print. The margins, fonts, headers, footers, fonts, and graphics on each page display exactly as they will print. You can cycle through all pages of the report before redisplaying the notebook.

Using Macros and the Advanced Macro Commands

One of Quattro Pro 5.0 for Windows most exciting features is its macro capability, which enables you to automate and customize Quattro Pro 5.0 for Windows for your applications. With Quattro Pro 5.0 for

Windows macro and advanced macro commands, you can create, inside the Quattro Pro 5.0 for Windows notebook, programs to use for a variety of purposes. At the simplest level, these programs are typing-alternatives that reduce the number of keystrokes—from any number to two—for a Quattro Pro 5.0 for Windows operation. At a more complex level, Quattro Pro 5.0 for Windows advanced macro commands give you a full-featured programming capability.

With Quattro Pro 5.0 for Windows, creating simple macros can be very easy. Quattro Pro automatically records keystrokes in macro-instruction format. You can then edit the commands, if necessary.

Whether you use Quattro Pro macros as alternatives to typing or as a programming language, macros can simplify and automate many of your Quattro Pro applications. When you create typing-alternative macros, you group together and name a series of Quattro Pro commands, text, or numbers. After you create and name a macro, you can easily repeat the commands contained in the macro. Depending on the macro name you selected, executing a macro may be as simple as pressing two keys: Ctrl and a letter key. You can also execute any macro by using the **Tools Macro Execute** command.

> **NOTE**
>
> If you have used Quattro Pro macros in previous releases, be aware that the macro key for Quattro Pro 5.0 for Windows is now the Ctrl key instead of the Alt key.

When you use Quattro Pro 5.0 for Windows macro commands, you will discover the power available for your applications. For the applications developer, the advanced macro commands are much like a programming language (such as BASIC). But the programming process is simplified significantly by the powerful features of Quattro Pro 5.0 for Windows spreadsheet, database, and graphics commands. Whether you want to create typing-alternative macros or complex programs, Chapter 14, "Understanding Macros," and Chapter 15, "Using the Advanced Macro Commands," give you the necessary information to get started.

Using Advanced Data Management

Several of the features new to Quattro Pro 5.0 for Windows provide advanced data management capabilities well beyond those of ordinary spreadsheet programs. But in spite of their power, you will find these features very easy to use. The *Data Modeling Desktop*, for example, provides extremely flexible cross-tabulation analysis similar to that offered by Lotus Improv for Windows. You can easily access notebook or database data, analyze its many relationships, and create a presentation-quality report of the results.

Other new advanced data management capabilities include *Experts*, which lead you through complex tasks one step at a time. You simply answer a few questions and the Experts produce graphs, manage scenarios, consolidate data, increase notebook performance levels, or create powerful analysis templates. If you prefer to work at your own pace, you can also use these tools without invoking the Experts.

Finally, Quattro Pro 5.0 for Windows makes it easy to share data with other users. Whether you are connected by a LAN or use a service such as MCI Mail, you can make certain every notebook user is working with current data. The *Workgroup Desktop* makes it easy to share notebook data with other users.

The advanced data management features of Quattro Pro 5.0 for Windows are covered in Part VI, "Analyzing Data."

Understanding Quattro Pro 5.0 for Windows System Requirements

Because Quattro Pro 5.0 for Windows has been completely rewritten and contains many features not included in previous Quattro Pro releases, it places much greater demands on computer hardware. Because of the system architecture that Quattro Pro 5.0 for Windows requires, many users might find that their current systems are unable to run the program. And Quattro Pro 5.0 for Windows requires much more memory than was required for other versions of Quattro Pro. Table 1.1 lists the system requirements to run Quattro Pro 5.0 for Windows.

Table 1.1 System Requirements for Quattro Pro 5.0 for Windows

Published by:	Borland International 1700 Green Hills Road Scotts Valley, CA 95066

System requirements:	System with 80286, 80386, 80486, or Pentium architecture
	EGA, VGA, or IBM 8514 monitor
	Available hard disk storage:
	    7M to 13M (depends on options installed)
	Random-access memory (RAM):
	    4M

Operating system:	DOS Version 3.11 or later and Microsoft Windows 3 or later
Optional hardware:	Mouse (highly recommended) Any printer supported by Microsoft Windows 3 or later

Summary

Quattro Pro 5.0 for Windows is an impressive addition to the selection of electronic spreadsheet programs, which revolutionized computing during the 1980s. It runs under DOS and Windows and takes full advantage of the graphical user interface and the multitasking capability of Windows. The program supports many new features including external data access, three-dimensional spreadsheets, network support, and file linking. Quattro Pro 5.0 for Windows additionally provides improved graphics, WYSIWYG display, full mouse support, and powerful new utilities.

Understanding Quattro Pro for Windows Basics

This chapter helps you to begin using Quattro Pro 5.0 for Windows. If you are familiar with Quattro Pro or Lotus 1-2-3, but new to Quattro Pro 5.0 for Windows, you might find that the introductory material presented here is too basic. If you want to begin using the Quattro Pro 5.0 for Windows spreadsheet immediately, read through the tables in this chapter and then skip to Chapter 3 or 4. The tables include important new reference information.

This chapter covers the following topics:

■ How to start and exit from Quattro Pro 5.0 for Windows.

■ How Quattro Pro 5.0 for Windows uses the keyboard.

■ How Quattro Pro 5.0 for Windows uses the Windows Desktop.

■ How to get on-screen help and use its examples in your spreadsheets.

Understanding the Basics of Microsoft Windows

Microsoft Windows is a powerful, easy-to-use extension to the MS-DOS operating environment. If you are new to Windows, the following basic information can help you get started.

Windows is a *Graphical User Interface* (GUI) that offers new levels of power and ease of use compared to older, non-GUI operating environments (if it is run on a PC with an 80286, 80386, 80486, or Pentium processor). Windows has three operating modes: *real mode*, *standard mode*, and *386-enhanced mode*. Windows 3.1 (the latest version) drops real mode and offers standard mode and 386-enhanced mode only.

Quattro Pro 5.0 for Windows only runs in Windows standard or 386-enhanced modes.

A mouse is highly recommended (although not specifically required) for use with Quattro Pro 5.0 for Windows. A mouse makes using Windows and Quattro Pro 5.0 for Windows much easier. And a number of exciting new features, such as Object Inspectors and SpeedBars, have been designed for use with a mouse.

Windows can run both *DOS programs* and *Windows programs* such as Quattro Pro 5.0 for Windows, ObjectVision for Windows, Word for Windows, and PageMaker (which cannot run without Windows). Windows programs offer many advantages, including the capability to access much more memory than the 640K available to DOS-based programs.

The GUI itself is one feature that makes Windows programs easier to use. Instead of typing a command to start and run a Windows program, you simply select the program's *icon* (a small picture that represents the program). Figure 2.1 shows several typical Windows program icons displayed in several program group windows.

To use a mouse to select an icon and run the program associated with that icon, move the mouse pointer to the icon and double-click the left mouse button.

Selecting an icon with the keyboard is slightly more complex. First, make certain the program group window containing the icon is the active window—the window with a highlighted border. If it is not the active window, press Ctrl+Tab until it is highlighted. Next, highlight the desired program icon using the direction keys. (When an icon is selected, its program title is displayed in reverse video.) Finally, press Enter to run the program.

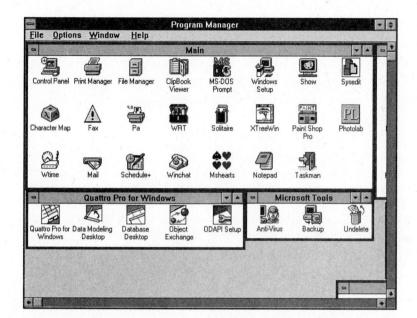

Fig. 2.1

Typical Windows
program icons.

Starting Quattro Pro 5.0 for Windows

If you have installed Quattro Pro 5.0 for Windows according to the directions in Appendix A, the program is stored in the C:\QPW5 drive and directory. The Quattro Pro 5.0 for Windows icon might be in a separate program group or it might be located in an existing program group.

Although you can have as many program groups as you like, too many groups clutter the Windows Desktop. Reducing group windows to icons helps, but you must open a group window before you can select its application icons. If you place your major Windows applications in the Main group window and do not reduce this group window to an icon, finding and running these programs is easier.

The method you use to move application icons depends on whether you use a mouse or the keyboard.

To move the Quattro Pro 5.0 for Windows icon to the Main program group window using a mouse, follow these steps:

1. Start Windows by entering **WIN** at the DOS prompt.

2. Activate the program group containing the Quattro Pro 5.0 for Windows icon by pointing to the icon with the mouse pointer, and then pressing (and holding down) the left mouse button.

3. Continuing to hold down the left mouse button, drag the icon to an open position in the Main program group window. Release the mouse button.

4. Delete the now-empty program group that contained the Quattro Pro icon by clicking the mouse in the group window, pressing Del, and then pressing Enter to confirm the deletion.

To move the Quattro Pro 5.0 for Windows icon to the Main program group window using the keyboard, follow these steps:

1. Start Windows by entering **WIN** at the DOS prompt.

2. Activate the program group window containing the Quattro Pro 5.0 for Windows icon by pressing Ctrl+Tab.

3. Select the Quattro Pro 5.0 for Windows icon using the direction keys.

4. Select **F**ile **M**ove by pressing Alt+F and then M. The Move Program Item dialog box appears (see fig. 2.2). If the suggested destination is not the Main program group, use the up- and down-arrow keys to correct the destination; then press Enter.

Fig. 2.2

The Move Program Item dialog box.

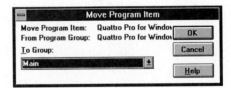

5. Make certain the now-empty program group is still highlighted (repeat step 2 if necessary). Press Del, and then press Enter to confirm the deletion.

Starting Quattro Pro 5.0 for Windows from the Program Manager

Regardless of where the Quattro Pro 5.0 for Windows icon is located, you can start the program by double-clicking the icon or by highlighting the icon using the direction keys and pressing Enter. If the Quattro

Pro 5.0 for Windows icon is contained in a program group that itself is an icon, you must first open the program group window icon before you can select the Quattro Pro 5.0 for Windows icon.

Before you can start Quattro Pro 5.0 for Windows from the Program Manager, the program group window that contains the Quattro Pro 5.0 for Windows program icon must be active.

To activate a group window, press Alt+Esc repeatedly until the Program Manager is in the foreground; then press Ctrl+Tab (or click anywhere inside the window with the mouse) to highlight the window.

If you don't want to start the program by selecting its icon—perhaps because its program group window has been reduced to an icon—the Program Manager's **F**ile **R**un command provides you with another option. To start Quattro Pro 5.0 for Windows using this second method, follow these steps:

1. Press Alt, and then select **F**ile to activate the Program Manager File menu. If you are using a mouse, click **F**ile **R**un to activate the dialog box.

2. Select **R**un, and the Run dialog box appears. Enter **C:\QPW5\QPW.EXE** in the text box (see fig. 2.3), and then press Enter to start Quattro Pro 5.0 for Windows.

Run
Command Line:
C:\QPW2\QPW.EXE
☐ Run Minimized
OK
Cancel
Browse...
Help

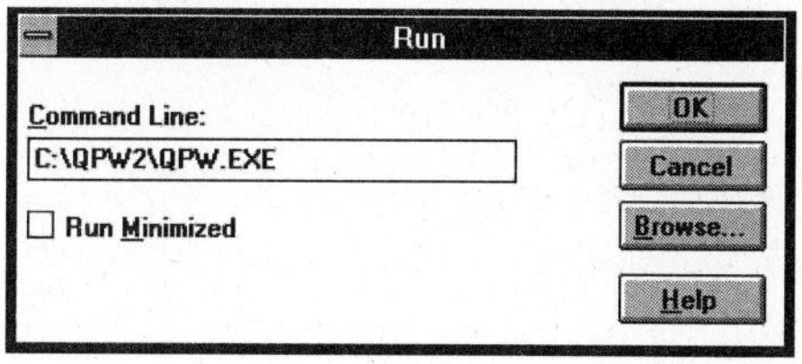

Fig. 2.3

The Run dialog box can be used to start Quattro Pro 5.0 for Windows.

Starting Quattro Pro 5.0 for Windows from DOS

Although you must run Quattro Pro 5.0 for Windows in Windows, you can start it directly from the DOS command line by passing the proper parameters to the Windows command. The basic syntax for starting any Windows program from the DOS command line is as follows:

WIN /*mode drive*:*path**program.extension*

To start Quattro Pro 5.0 for Windows from the command line using the default Windows mode (which depends on your system), enter the following:

CD \QPW5
WIN QPW.EXE

These examples assume that the Windows program directory is included in the PATH command issued in AUTOEXEC.BAT.

If you often start Quattro Pro 5.0 for Windows from the command line and you use MS-DOS 5 or MS-DOS 6, you might want to create a DOSKEY macro that enters the proper commands. To create a macro called QP4W, enter the following:

DOSKEY QP4W=C: $T CD \QPW5 $T WIN QPW.EXE

After creating this macro, you can start Quattro Pro 5.0 for Windows by entering the following command at the DOS prompt:

QP4W

If you have not yet upgraded to MS-DOS 5 or MS-DOS 6, you can create a small batch file to start Quattro Pro 5.0 for Windows from the command line. Enter the following at the DOS prompt:

COPY CON QP4W.BAT
C:
CD \WINDOWS
WIN C:\QPW5\QPW.EXE

After entering the final line press the F6 key, and then press Enter. QP4W.BAT must be located in a directory included in the PATH statement of your AUTOEXEC.BAT file.

After creating this batch file, you can start Quattro Pro 5.0 for Windows by entering **QP4W** at the DOS prompt.

Exiting Quattro Pro 5.0 for Windows

Windows applications can open multiple document windows. In Quattro Pro 5.0 for Windows, for example, you can have several different notebook files open at the same time. You have the option of closing individual notebooks or of exiting Quattro Pro 5.0 for Windows entirely, closing all open windows.

To exit Quattro Pro 5.0 for Windows and close all open windows at the same time, use the **File Exit** command (see fig. 2.4). Quattro Pro 5.0 for Windows commands and their menus are explained extensively throughout this book. At this point, however, you only need to know how to access the **File** menu and to use one simple command.

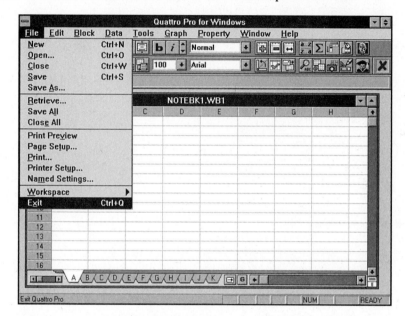

Fig. 2.4

The **F**ile menu with E**x**it selected.

To quit Quattro Pro 5.0 for Windows and return to the Program Manager using the keyboard, use this procedure:

1. Press the Alt key to activate the menu bar.

2. Select **File Exit**. If you have made any changes in the notebook, the File Exit confirmation box shown in figure 2.5 appears.

3. Choose **Yes** to save the file before exiting, **No** to exit without saving the file, or **Cancel** to cancel the exit command and return to Quattro Pro 5.0 for Windows; then press Enter.

4. If additional notebooks are open, the dialog box reappears for each notebook that contains unsaved changes. In each case, choose **Yes** to save the file, **No** to bypass saving the file, or **Cancel** to return to Quattro Pro 5.0 for Windows.

Fig. 2.5

The File Exit confirmation box.

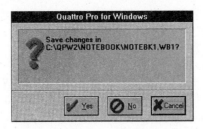

You also can use the Windows shortcut method of exiting Quattro Pro 5.0 for Windows. Press Alt+F4 and the File Exit confirmation box appears. Make your choices as outlined in steps 3 and 4.

To quit Quattro Pro 5.0 for Windows and return to the Program Manager using the mouse, click the Control menu box (the box in the upper left corner of the active window containing a long horizontal bar), select **C**lose, and the File Exit confirmation box appears. Make your choices as outlined in steps 3 and 4.

Closing Spreadsheet Notebooks

You can also close the active notebook without exiting Quattro Pro 5.0 for Windows. Suppose that you have completed work on a particular notebook and want to close it, but you want to keep Quattro Pro 5.0 for Windows loaded so that you can work on other projects later. Although Quattro Pro 5.0 for Windows enables you to have several notebooks open at the same time, you might be working on a sensitive notebook (such as a notebook containing a payroll database) that you don't want anyone else to be able to access.

In standard Windows terminology, an open Quattro Pro 5.0 for Windows notebook window is called a *document window*. In many Windows applications, including Quattro Pro 5.0 for Windows, you can close a document window without closing the application window.

To close a single open notebook using the keyboard, follow this procedure:

1. Press Ctrl+F4.

   A confirmation box like the one shown in figure 2.5 appears.

2. Select **Y**es to save the file before closing the window, **N**o to close it without saving the file, or **C**ancel to cancel the close command and return to the window; then press Enter.

To close a document window with the mouse, click the document window's Control menu box (the box in the upper left corner of the active window containing a short horizontal bar), select **C**lose, and the confirmation box appears. (You also can double-click the window's control menu box to close without having to select **C**lose.) Make your choice as outlined in step 2.

You can also use the **File Save** command to save your work before selecting **File Exit**.

▶▶ "Saving Notebook Files," p. 124.

▶▶ "Saving Files," p. 273.

FOR RELATED INFORMATION

Learning the Quattro Pro 5.0 for Windows Keys

The most common keyboard configurations for IBM and IBM-compatible personal computers are shown in figures 2.6 and 2.7. The enhanced keyboard is now the standard keyboard on all new IBM personal computers and most compatibles. Some compatibles, especially laptops, have different keyboards.

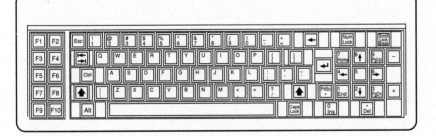

Fig. 2.6

The original IBM AT keyboard.

Keyboards generally are divided into four or five sections. The alphanumeric keys are located in the center, the numeric keypad is on the right, and the function keys are located at the left side or across the top. The special keys appear in various locations. The direction keys are in a separate section on the enhanced keyboard.

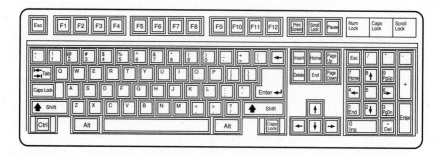

Most keys in the alphanumeric section match the keys on a typewriter, and most maintain their usual functions in Quattro Pro 5.0 for Windows. Several keys, however, have new and unique purposes or are not found on typewriter keyboards.

The keys on the numeric keypad (on the right side of the keyboard) are used to enter numbers or to move the cell selector around the screen. The keys on the numeric keypad are also used (with the Alt key) to enter international characters such as £, ¥, æ, and è.

The function keys produce special actions. You can use these keys, for example, to access Quattro Pro 5.0 for Windows editing functions, calculate a spreadsheet, and call up Help messages. A large number of functions are available because function keys can be used alone or in conjunction with the Alt, Ctrl, or Shift keys.

The special keys include Del (Delete), Ins (Insert), Esc (Escape), Num Lock, Scroll Lock, Break, and Pause. These keys, which produce special actions, are located in different places on different keyboards. Like function keys, special keys often can be used either alone or in combination with the Alt, Ctrl, or Shift keys.

Only the enhanced keyboard has a separate section for the direction keys: Home, End, PgUp (Page Up), PgDn (Page Down), and the four arrow keys (up, down, left, and right). On the enhanced keyboard, you can use the numeric keypad to enter numbers and the separate direction keys to move around the notebook.

The following sections list the Quattro Pro 5.0 for Windows special functions provided by the different key sections. The meanings of these keys will become clearer as they are explained in later chapters.

The Accelerator Keys

The accelerator keys provide shortcuts for executing common Windows and Quattro Pro 5.0 for Windows commands (see table 2.1).

Table 2.1 Accelerator Keys

Key(s)	Action(s)
Alt+F4	Same as File Exit; ends the Quattro Pro session, prompts you to save any unsaved files, and returns you to the Program Manager.
Ctrl+Esc	Displays the Task List that enables you to switch from one Windows application to another.
Ctrl+F4	Same as File Close; closes the current window and prompts you to save the file if it contains unsaved changes.
Ctrl+F6	Same as selecting Next from the Control menu of a Notebook window; makes the next open Notebook window active.
Ctrl+*letter*	Same as Tools Macro Execute; executes a macro in Quattro Pro 5.0 for Windows (the replacement for Alt+*letter* in earlier DOS releases).
Del	Same as Edit Clear; deletes selected data and related formatting without moving it to the Clipboard.

The Editing Keys

The editing keys are used to make changes in a cell or in a dialog box (see table 2.2).

Table 2.2 Editing Keys

Key(s)	Action(s)
→ or ←	Moves the cursor one character to the right or left.
↑ or ↓	If the current entry is on one line in the control panel, completes the entry and moves the cell selector up or down one cell; if the entry is on more than one line in the control panel, moves the cursor up or down one line.
Backspace	Erases the character to the left of the cursor.
Ctrl+←	Moves the cursor five character positions to the left.

(continues)

Table 2.2 Continued

Key(s)	Action(s)
Ctrl+→	Moves the cursor five character positions to the right.
Ctrl+PgUp or Ctrl+PgDn	Completes editing and moves the cell selector forward or back one notebook page.
Del	Erases the character above the cursor or erases the highlighted selection.
F2 (Edit)	Switches Quattro Pro 5.0 for Windows between EDIT and READY mode.
End	Moves the cursor to a position following the last character in the entry.
Enter	Completes editing and places the entry in the current cell.
Esc	Erases all characters in the entry.
Home	Moves the cursor to a position prior to the first character in the entry.
Ins	Switches between insert and overstrike modes.
PgUp or PgDn	Completes editing and moves the cell selector up or down one screen.

The Direction Keys

The direction keys (also called pointer-movement keys) move the cell selector around the notebook when Quattro Pro is in READY mode. In POINT mode, these keys move the cell selector and specify a block in the notebook. Table 2.3 shows a list of the direction keys.

Table 2.3 Direction Keys

Key(s)	Action(s)
→ or ←	Moves right or left one column.
↑ or ↓	Moves up or down one row.
Ctrl+← or Shift+Tab	Moves left one screen.
Ctrl+→ or Tab	Moves right one screen.

Key(s)	Action(s)
Ctrl+F6	Makes the next open notebook window active.
Ctrl+PgUp	Moves to the notebook page immediately above the current page.
Ctrl+PgDn	Moves to the notebook page immediately below the current page.
End+→ or End+←	Moves right or left to a cell that contains data and is next to a blank cell.
End+↑ or End+↓	Moves up or down to a cell that contains data and is next to a blank cell.
End+Home	Moves to the lower right corner of the active area on the current page.
Ctrl+End+Home	Moves to the lower right corner of the active area on the last active page.
Home	Moves to cell A1 on the current notebook page.
Ctrl+Home	Moves to cell A1 on the first notebook page.
PgUp or PgDn	Moves up or down one screen.

The Alphanumeric Keys

Most of the alphanumeric keys act the same way in Quattro Pro 5.0 for Windows as they would on a typewriter, but a few have special meanings. These keys are listed in table 2.4.

Table 2.4 The Alphanumeric Keys

Key(s)	Action(s)
. (period)	Used in a block address to separate the address of the cell where the block begins from the address of the cell where the block ends.
Alt	Used alone to activate the command menu; used with the function keys to provide additional functions.
Backspace	Erases the preceding character during data entry or editing; erases a block address from a prompt that suggests a block.

(continues)

Table 2.4 Continued

Key(s)	Action(s)
Caps Lock	Shifts the letter keys to uppercase. Unlike the shift-lock key on a typewriter, Caps Lock has no effect on numbers and symbols. Press Caps Lock again to return to lowercase.
Ctrl	Used with function keys to provide additional functions; used with letter keys to invoke macros.
Enter	Used in a spreadsheet to enter typed data into a cell; used in a dialog box to confirm and execute commands.
Shift	Used with a letter to produce an uppercase letter unless Caps Lock is toggled on; used with a number or symbol to produce the shifted character on that key; used with the numeric keypad (and Num Lock on) to produce a direction key.

The Numeric Keypad and the Direction Keys

The keys on the numeric keypad, located on the right side of IBM AT-style keyboards, are used mainly to move the cell selector around the spreadsheet and through menus (see fig. 2.6). With Num Lock off, these keys serve as direction keys. With Num Lock on, these keys function as number keys. The enhanced keyboard has separate keys for movement (see fig. 2.7). The functions of the direction keys are explained in Chapter 4, "Learning Spreadsheet Basics."

If you do not have an enhanced keyboard, you can use a macro to move the cell selector every time you press Enter. This technique enables you to keep Num Lock on and use the numeric keypad to enter numbers. You can use different macros to move the cell selector in different directions. (For information about creating and using macros, see Chapters 14 and 15.)

The Function Keys

The 12 function keys, F1 through F12, are used for special actions in Quattro Pro 5.0 for Windows. These keys are located across the top of the enhanced keyboard and on the left side on other keyboards (see figs. 2.6 and 2.7). Some keyboards have 12 function keys, but others have 10. Function keys can be used alone or with the Alt, Shift, and Ctrl keys. Table 2.5 lists the uses of the function keys in Quattro Pro 5.0 for Windows.

Table 2.5 The Function Keys

Key(s)	Action(s)
F1 (Help)	Displays a Help topic.
F2 (Edit)	Places Quattro Pro 5.0 for Windows in EDIT mode so that you can edit an entry.
Alt+F2 (Execute)	Displays the Run Macro dialog box.
Shift+F2 (Step)	Enters macro DEBUG mode.
F3 (Name)	Displays block names in EDIT mode in a formula.
Alt+F3 (Functions)	Displays a list of functions.
Shift+F3 (Macros)	Displays a list of macro commands.
Ctrl+F3 (Block)	Enables user to create block names.
F4 (Abs)	Toggles formulas from relative to absolute and vice versa.
Alt+F4 (Exit)	Closes Quattro Pro 5.0 for Windows or a dialog box.
Ctrl+F4 (Close)	Closes the active notebook file.
F5 (Goto)	Moves the cell selector to a cell, spreadsheet, or active file.
Alt+F5 (Group)	Enters Group mode.
Shift+F5 (SpeedTab)	Displays the graph page.
F6 (Pane)	Moves the cell selector between panes.
Ctrl+F6 (Window)	Displays the next open window.
F7 (Query)	Repeats the last **Data Query** command.
Shift+F7 (Select)	Extends the selection.

(continues)

Table 2.5 Continued

Key(s)	Action(s)
F8 (Table)	Repeats the last **D**ata **W**hat-if command.
F9 (Calc)	In READY mode, recalculates formulas. In EDIT or VALUE mode, converts a formula to its current value.
F10 (Menu)	Activates the menu bar.
F11 (Graph)	Displays the current graph.
F12 (Inspect)	Displays Object Inspector for the selected object.
Alt+F12 (Inspect Applications)	Displays application Object Inspector.
Shift+F12 (Inspect Window)	Displays active window Object Inspector.

Learning the Quattro Pro 5.0 for Windows Screen

The Quattro Pro 5.0 for Windows screen display is divided into several parts: the title bar, the menu bar, the SpeedBar, the input line, the status line, and the notebook. Together, these parts enable you to work with and display spreadsheets and graphs. Figure 2.8 shows the Quattro Pro 5.0 for Windows screen with many of its components labeled.

The Title Bar

The *title bar*, which is the top line of the Quattro Pro 5.0 for Windows screen, contains several parts. At the far left is a small box that activates the Control menu. Press Alt+space bar (or click the box) to display the Control menu; press Esc to close it. This menu enables you to size, close, and move the Quattro Pro 5.0 for Windows screen; it also enables you to switch to other Windows applications. Chapter 3, "Using the Graphical User Interface," describes the Control menus in more detail.

The middle of the title bar displays the name of the program: *Quattro Pro for Windows*.

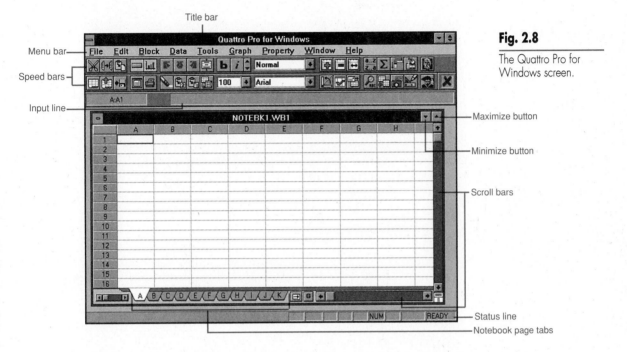

Fig. 2.8

The Quattro Pro for Windows screen.

At the far right of the title bar are boxes containing a down triangle (the *Minimize button*) and an up triangle (the *Maximize button*). If the Quattro Pro 5.0 for Windows screen has already been maximized, the Maximize button is replaced with the *Restore button*—a box containing an up triangle on top of a down triangle. If you click the Minimize button (or select the Minimize command from the Control menu), Quattro Pro 5.0 for Windows shrinks to an icon on the Program Manager screen. If you click the Maximize button (or select the Maximize command from the Control menu), Quattro Pro 5.0 for Windows enlarges to fill the screen. If you select the Restore button, (or select the Restore command from the Control menu), Quattro Pro 5.0 for Windows returns to its former size. The Minimize, Maximize, and Restore buttons are discussed in more detail in Chapter 3, "Using the Graphical User Interface."

The Menu Bar

The *menu bar*, which is the second line of the screen, always displays the Quattro Pro 5.0 for Windows command menu (including the **Help** command). To use this menu from the keyboard, you first must activate it by pressing the Alt key. A reverse video highlight, called the *menu pointer*, appears on the menu bar to indicate that the command menu is active. When the menu is active, a description of the highlighted menu selection is displayed at the left side of the status line. Press Esc to return to READY mode.

If you use the mouse to access menu commands, you do not need to activate the menu first. Clicking the command you want automatically activates the menu and displays the menu pointer.

The SpeedBars

The SpeedBars, which are the third and fourth lines of the screen, contain buttons that serve as shortcuts for many common tasks. One button, for example, automatically sets column widths to accommodate the length of data entries. Another button quickly sorts a block of data. Chapter 3, "Using the Graphical User Interface," covers the SpeedBars in more detail.

The Input Line

The *input line*, which is the fourth line of the screen, displays information about what you are working on. The section at the left of the input line, called the *address box*, displays the address of the currently selected cell or block. A *cell address* is made up of the notebook page letter (or name) followed by a colon, the column letter, and the row number. For example, the address of the top left cell in the first page is A:A1.

The right side of the input line is the *contents box*. When you enter information in a Quattro Pro 5.0 for Windows spreadsheet, the information appears first in the contents box. If you press Enter, the information is entered into the notebook cell. Each time you highlight a cell, that cell's contents are displayed in the contents box.

The Status Line

Quattro Pro 5.0 for Windows displays *status indicators* in the *status line* at the bottom of the screen. These indicators, such as CIRC and NUM, give you information about the state of the system (see table 2.6).

Table 2.6 The Status Indicators

Indicator	Description
BKGD	Quattro Pro 5.0 for Windows is calculating in the background.
CALC	You need to recalculate formulas by pressing F9 (Calc).
CAP	You pressed Caps Lock to type uppercase letters without using Shift.
CIRC	You entered a formula that contains a circular reference. Choose **Help** **A**bout Quattro Pro to identify the cell that contains the circular reference.
DEBUG	Quattro Pro 5.0 for Windows is in DEBUG mode; it steps through macros one instruction at a time.
END	You pressed End to use the End key with a direction key.
EXT	You pressed Shift+F7 and are extending a block selection.
MACRO	Quattro Pro 5.0 for Windows is executing a macro.
NUM	You pressed Num Lock to use the numeric keypad to type numbers.
OVR	You pressed Ins to edit data in overstrike mode instead of insert mode. In *overstrike mode*, each character you type replaces the character above the cursor. In *insert mode*, each character you type is inserted into the text at the cursor position.
REC	Quattro Pro 5.0 for Windows is recording a macro.
SCR	You pressed Scroll Lock so that ↑, ↓, ←, and → move the spreadsheet as well as the cell selector.

The *mode indicator* that appears on the right side of the status line informs you of the current mode of Quattro Pro 5.0 for Windows. If the program is waiting for your next action, the mode indicator displays READY. Table 2.7 lists the mode indicators and their meanings.

Table 2.7 The Mode Indicators

Mode	Description
COPY	You are using Drag and Drop to copy a block.
DATE	You are entering a date value.
EDIT	You pressed F2 (Edit) to edit an entry or made an incorrect entry.
FIND	Quattro Pro 5.0 for Windows is searching for matching database records.
FRMT	You are editing a format line during a **Data Parse** operation.
INPUT	You are inputting data using the **Data Restrict Input** command.
LABEL	You are entering a label.
MOVE	A block has been highlighted, and you have clicked and held the left mouse button on that block.
NAMES	You pressed F3 to display block names.
POINT	You are pointing to select a cell or block.
PREVIEW	You are previewing a report before printing.
READY	Quattro Pro 5.0 for Windows is ready for you to enter data or choose a command.
VALUE	You are entering a value.
WAIT	Quattro Pro 5.0 for Windows is completing a command or process, such as saving a file.

The Error Message Box

If Quattro Pro 5.0 for Windows encounters an error it displays an error message box (see fig. 2.9). Errors can be caused by many circumstances. You might have specified an invalid cell address or block name in response to a prompt, for example, or you might have tried to open a file that doesn't exist. Press Esc or Enter to clear the error and return to READY mode.

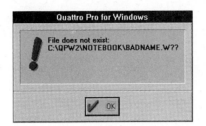

Fig. 2.9

An error message box.

The Notebook Window

The *notebook window* is the large white area that displays spreadsheet notebooks. You can open several notebooks at once in the work area. Figure 2.9 shows a single spreadsheet displayed in the notebook window.

At the bottom edge of each open notebook are several page tabs. When you open a new notebook, each page is identified with a letter; you are free to give the pages descriptive names. Clicking a tab with the mouse makes its corresponding page the *active* page. Chapter 4, "Learning Spreadsheet Basics," covers spreadsheet notebooks in detail.

Using the Quattro Pro 5.0 for Windows Help System

Quattro Pro 5.0 for Windows provides on-line, context-sensitive help at the touch of a key. Whatever operation you are involved in, you can press Help (F1) to get one or more screens of explanation and advice concerning what to do next. To display a Help screen with the mouse, click **Help** on the menu bar. After entering the Help system, you can select a particular topic. Figure 2.10 shows a typical Quattro Pro 5.0 for Windows Help screen.

The Help feature appears in a window that you can move and size like any other window. Occasionally, you might want to continue displaying the Help window while you work. To move back and forth among windows, click the window you want to work in or press Alt+Tab.

Fig. 2.10

A Quattro Pro 5.0 for
Windows Help screen.

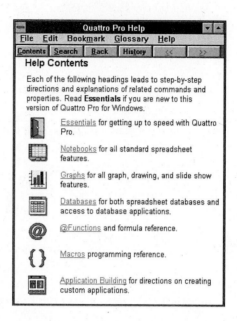

You can press Help (F1) at any time—even while executing a command
or editing a cell. The help you receive is context-sensitive.

Certain Help topics are displayed in a color different from the rest of
the Help screen. To get more information about one of these topics,
move the menu pointer to that topic and press Enter. If you move the
mouse pointer to a colored topic, the shape of the mouse pointer
changes from an arrow to a hand with a pointing index finger. Click
the topic to get more detailed help information.

Other options (such as **F**ile and **S**earch) are displayed at the top of the
Help window. One of these options is **C**ontents, which returns you to
the main Help index.

Two of the most useful options displayed at the top of each Help window are **F**ile **P**rint Topic and **E**dit **C**opy. The first of these commands
prints the text of the current help topic; the second copies the topic to
the Windows Clipboard.

For further details on Quattro Pro 5.0 for Windows features and commands, refer to other appropriate sections of the book.

Questions and Answers

Q: I installed Quattro Pro 5.0 for Windows, but now I can't find the program icon so that I can start the program. What's wrong?

A: In Windows, program icons are contained in program groups. Each program group can itself be reduced to an icon, making the individual program icons disappear. To restore a program group window so that you can see its program icons, click the program group icon and select **R**estore. By default, Quattro Pro 5.0 for Windows is installed in a program group called Quattro Pro for Windows, so you probably can find the program's icon in that group.

If you cannot locate the Quattro Pro 5.0 for Windows program icon, use the Windows Program Manager **F**ile **N**ew Program **I**tem command to add the icon to an existing program group such as Main or Applications. Adding a program icon to more than one program group does not create a new copy of the program, so you can add the same program icon to several program groups if you like.

Q: Why does my computer beep and display a warning message when I try to exit Quattro Pro 5.0 for Windows?

A: The program is warning you that you have made changes that you have not saved. This prevents you from accidentally losing work by forgetting to save your changes. Choose **Y**es to save the changes.

Q: How do I find help on a specific subject if the Help Contents screen doesn't show the topic I need?

A: Use the **S**earch command (available on all help screens) to display a dialog box that allows you to specify the topic to display. As you enter your topic, the selection list displays topics that match the characters you have entered so far. Select the topic that suits your need when it appears on-screen, and then choose **G**o To to see the appropriate help screen.

Summary

This chapter presented the information you needed to use Quattro Pro 5.0 for Windows for the first time. It provided instructions for starting and exiting from Quattro Pro 5.0 for Windows. It described the use of keys in Quattro Pro 5.0 for Windows and explained the different areas of the screen. It also gave you an introduction to the Help system.

Now you are prepared to use Quattro Pro 5.0 for Windows constructively. The next chapter familiarizes you with the graphical user interface, the mouse, and the Control menus.

Using the Graphical User Interface

Quattro Pro 5.0 for Windows supports graphics and runs under the *graphical user interface* (GUI) of Microsoft Windows. GUIs ("gooeys") are much easier to use than character-based interfaces; they also provide better printed and on-screen graphics. The Windows graphical user interface brings many advantages to Quattro Pro. In particular, it helps you to accomplish the following tasks:

- Linking to and using data from other Windows applications, employing either Dynamic Data Exchange (DDE) or the new Windows 3.1 Object Linking and Embedding (OLE)

- Displaying graphs and spreadsheets at the same time, either in the same window or in separate windows

- Using SpeedBars, SpeedButtons, and custom dialog boxes to automate common operations

- Using several spreadsheet notebooks at one time

- Running Quattro Pro 5.0 for Windows and other Windows applications at the same time

- Incorporating graphics images from other Windows applications in spreadsheets

- Executing other Windows applications using Quattro Pro for Windows advanced macro commands

This chapter presents the components of the Quattro Pro 5.0 for Windows graphical user interface and shows you how to use these components effectively. It covers tasks such as

- Using the mouse

- Changing the size, position, and arrangement of windows

- Changing global settings

- Using pull-down and cascade menus

- Using Object Inspectors

- Using dialog boxes

- Using SpeedBars and SpeedButtons

Customizing Your Spreadsheets

Quattro Pro 5.0 for Windows offers many new options for customizing spreadsheets. Several Quattro Pro 5.0 for Windows commands enable you to use colors and fonts to customize spreadsheets and graphs in a *WYSIWYG* (what-you-see-is-what-you-get) display.

Quattro Pro 5.0 for Windows makes all customization features easily accessible by way of *Object Inspectors*—context-sensitive dialog boxes specific to the selected item. When customizing, you can decide whether to display zeros, set the default label alignment (which format to use to display numbers), choose the fonts to use in a spreadsheet, and set font options (such as bold, italic, and underline). Figure 3.1 shows examples of some of these options.

Applying the same set of customization options to different blocks can be tedious, so Quattro Pro 5.0 for Windows provides an easy way to save a group of options as a named style. You can define a style using **E**dit **D**efine Style and then apply that style to spreadsheet blocks as needed.

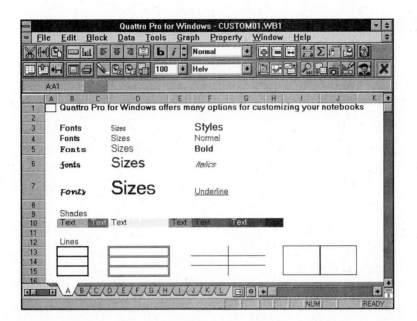

Fig. 3.1

Different font and style options can improve the appearance of reports.

You can make your spreadsheet data easier to see and understand by using color. Quattro Pro 5.0 for Windows enables you to apply colors to entire blocks of data and to highlight individual cells with a different color whenever the value of their contents falls outside a specified value range. You also can display positive values in one color and negative values in another color throughout the spreadsheet. This strategy is especially useful when a spreadsheet recalculation causes some values to become negative and, therefore, to change color.

Although Quattro Pro 5.0 for Windows uses a maximum of 16 colors in a spreadsheet notebook, you can change those colors to suit your purposes. The program enables you to replace each of the available colors with one of 16.7 million palette colors. Most of the choices are patchwork colors created from the colors the system can display. If you use a color printer, you might want to experiment with color selections to determine the combinations that produce the best results.

▶▶ "Enhancing the Appearance of Data," p. 201.

FOR RELATED INFORMATION

Using the Mouse

Mouse capability is one of the most exciting new features in Quattro Pro 5.0 for Windows. Like the keyboard, the mouse enables you to select commands and manipulate objects on-screen. But with the mouse you can perform tasks (such as moving through windows, setting column widths, and moving in dialog boxes) more quickly. Several Quattro Pro 5.0 for Windows features, such as SpeedBars and SpeedButtons, can be activated only with a mouse.

You move the *mouse pointer* around the screen by moving the mouse on a flat surface with your hand (see fig. 3.2). The mouse pointer, which first appears in the shape of an arrow, moves in the same direction as your hand. The pointer changes shape as you perform different tasks in Quattro Pro 5.0 for Windows. Table 3.1 explains the various shapes of the mouse pointer.

Fig. 3.2

The mouse pointer moves in the same direction as the mouse.

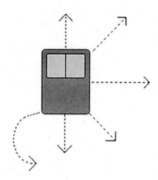

Table 3.1 Mouse Pointers

Shape	Meaning
Arrow	You can perform normal operations, such as selecting blocks and menu commands.
White double arrow	You can resize the window.
Black double arrow	You can create or resize a window pane. If the mouse pointer is in a row or column heading and close to a grid line, you can widen a column or heighten a row.
Hourglass	Quattro Pro 5.0 for Windows is in the middle of an operation, and you can do nothing with the mouse.

Shape	Meaning
Hand pointing up	The pointer is over a highlighted Help topic.
Open Hand	You can move the contents of the selected block by dragging and dropping. Hold down the Ctrl key to copy the contents of the selected block by dragging and dropping.
I-beam	The pointer is over data in the edit line; you can edit or enter data.

Most mouse devices have left and right buttons. Use the left button to select cells and blocks, use menus, and enter information in dialog boxes. Use the right button to activate the Object Inspectors and Object Help features.

Table 3.2 describes some mouse terminology that you need to know when reading this book and using Quattro Pro 5.0 for Windows.

Table 3.2 Mouse Terms

Term	Meaning
Click	Quickly press and release the mouse button. When activating Object Inspectors, click the right mouse button; otherwise, click the left mouse button.
Double-click	Quickly press and release the left mouse button two times.
Drag	Press and hold down the left mouse button while moving or *dragging* the mouse. Use this technique to handle tasks like highlighting a block or moving an object.
Grab	Move the mouse pointer to the object you want to move; press and hold down the left mouse button to *grab* the object (which you can then *drag* to another location).
Point	Position the mouse pointer over the object you want to select or move.
Select	Highlight cells or blocks or select graph objects.
Drag and drop	Point to a selected block, hold down the left mouse button, and move the selected block to a new location. To copy the selected block, hold down Ctrl while you press the left mouse button, move the mouse pointer to the target cell, and release the mouse button.

Using the Control Menus

The Quattro Pro window is used to display and work with Quattro Pro 5.0 for Windows notebooks and graphs. The small rectangle in the upper left corner of the screen is the *Control menu box*, which can be used to open the Quattro Pro 5.0 for Windows *Control menu*. This menu, which is similar to the Control menu in other Windows applications, enables you to manipulate the size and position of the Quattro Pro window, to close Quattro Pro 5.0 for Windows, and to switch to other Windows applications (see fig. 3.3).

Fig. 3.3

The Quattro Pro for Windows Control menu.

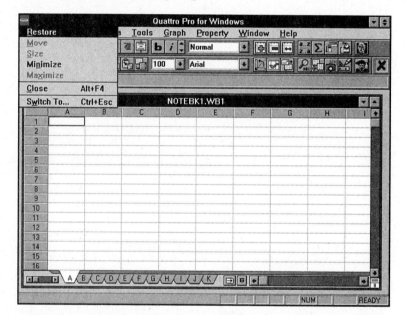

Although the menu shown in figure 3.3 offers seven options, three are *dimmed* to indicate that they are currently unavailable. If you run Quattro Pro 5.0 for Windows in a partial-screen window or reduce the screen to an icon, different choices may be dimmed and unavailable.

To access the Control menu with the keyboard, press Alt+space bar. Use the arrow keys to highlight a command name (or type its underlined letter); then press Enter.

To access the Control menu with the mouse, click the Control menu box, and then click the command you want to execute.

NOTE

Remember that double-clicking the Control menu box closes Quattro Pro 5.0 for Windows.

The *Notebook Control menu* controls a single notebook window in much the same way as the Control menu controls the Quattro Pro window. This menu is accessed by way of the *Notebook Control menu box* in the upper left corner of the current notebook window; it controls the current window's size and position. The Switch To option that appears on the Quattro Pro 5.0 for Windows Control menu is replaced here by the Next option, which simply switches between notebook windows. Figure 3.4 shows the Notebook Control menu.

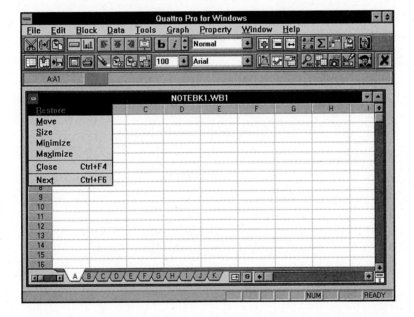

Fig. 3.4

The Notebook Control menu.

To access the Notebook Control menu with the keyboard, press Alt+- (hyphen). To choose a command, use the arrow keys to highlight it (or type its underlined letter), and then press Enter. Shortcut keys enable you to close the notebook window (Ctrl+F4) or to activate the next notebook window (Ctrl+F6) without having to access the Notebook Control menu.

To access the Notebook Control menu with the mouse, click the Notebook Control menu box, and then click the command you want to execute.

Changing the Size and Position of a Window

You can change the size and position of the Quattro Pro window or a notebook window by using either the mouse or the keyboard. You can enlarge a window to fill the entire screen, reduce a window to a smaller but still active size, or shrink the window to icon size.

Maximizing and Restoring a Window

When maximized, the Quattro Pro window fills the screen. If you maximize a notebook window, it fills the work area of the Quattro Pro window. The Control menu of every window has a Maximize command.

To maximize a window using the keyboard, choose the Maximize command from the appropriate menu.

To maximize a window using a mouse, you don't need to use the Control menus at all. At the top right corner of each window, you see a down triangle (the *Minimize button*) and an up triangle (the *Maximize button*). Simply click a window's Maximize button to enlarge it.

If you maximize a window, the up triangle that appears on the Maximize button changes to an up-and-down triangle. This change, which occurs only when a window is maximized, indicates that the button is now the *Restore button*. (When you first load Quattro Pro 5.0 for Windows, the Quattro Pro window is maximized and the Restore button appears instead of the Maximize button.)

If you choose the **R**estore command or click the Restore button, Quattro Pro 5.0 for Windows restores the window to its previous size.

Minimizing a Window

To turn the Quattro Pro window into an icon that appears in the Program Manager, select the Minimize command from the Quattro Pro 5.0 for Windows Control menu or click the Minimize button. If you are using other Program Manager applications and you want to run Quattro Pro 5.0 for Windows in the background, you either can minimize the Quattro Pro window or use Ctrl+Esc or Alt+Tab to switch to the other application.

You can shrink a notebook window in the Quattro Pro window to icon size by selecting the Minimize command from the spreadsheet's Control menu or by clicking the window's Minimize button. The ability to minimize notebook windows can be useful if you are working with several notebooks at once. Each kind of window within Quattro Pro is identified by a special icon. A notebook icon shows a grid, for example, and a graph icon shows a graph (see fig. 3.5).

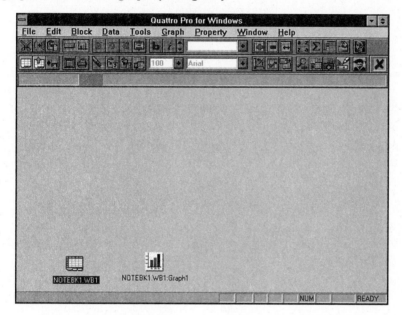

Fig. 3.5

Windows reduced to icons in the Quattro Pro window.

Sizing a Window

To change the size of a window, use the **Size** command from the appropriate Control menu and the direction keys, or use the mouse. Either method enables you to control the exact size of a window. You also can control the display of notebook windows by using the **Window Tile** and **Window Cascade** commands. The **Window Tile** command places all active notebook windows on-screen in positions that do not overlap. The **Window Cascade** command displays active notebook windows in an overlapping format with the current window in front and the title bar of every other active notebook window displayed above and behind the current window. For more information on the **Window Tile** and **Window Cascade** commands, see the section of this chapter called "Manipulating Windows."

To change the size of a window using the keyboard, follow these steps:

1. Press Alt+- (hyphen) to activate the window Control menu.

2. Select **S**ize.

3. Press the arrow key that points to the window border you want to adjust.

4. Move the edge of the window using the arrow keys.

5. Press Enter.

To size a window with the mouse, first move the mouse pointer to the border you want to move. When the mouse pointer changes to a thick white double arrow, press and hold down the left mouse button to grab and drag the border to the desired location.

 If you reduce the Quattro Pro window to less than a full screen before starting to print a long report, you then can switch to another Windows application while the report prints in the background. Simply reduce the size of the Quattro Pro window after you finish preparing a report, select the **F**ile **P**rint command, and begin the printing. When the hourglass appears, move the mouse pointer outside the Quattro Pro window and click the left mouse button to access the Program Manager or another application. Quattro Pro 5.0 for Windows continues printing the report while you work in other applications.

Moving a Window

You can use the keyboard or the mouse to move icons or windows that aren't maximized.

With the keyboard, choose the **M**ove command from the appropriate Control menu, use the direction keys to relocate the window, and then press Enter.

Moving a window or an icon is easier with the mouse. Click the title bar or icon and drag the object to the new location; then release the left mouse button.

Closing a Window

Each Control menu contains a **Close** command that enables you to close Quattro Pro 5.0 for Windows or a notebook window. But the standard Windows keyboard shortcuts provide a quick and easy way to close windows. Press Alt+F4 to close Quattro Pro 5.0 for Windows (or any Windows application window); press Ctrl+F4 to close a notebook window (or any Windows document window).

To close a Quattro Pro window using the mouse, double-click the appropriate Control menu box or choose the **Close** command from the Control menu itself.

If files were created or changed during the current session, a dialog box prompts you to save those files when you close the Quattro Pro window or a notebook window. Figure 3.6 shows a dialog box similar to the one you see on-screen.

Fig. 3.6

The File Exit dialog box.

▶▶ "Saving Notebook Files," p. 124.

FOR RELATED INFORMATION

Accessing the Task List

The **Switch To** command on the Quattro Pro 5.0 for Windows Control menu enables you to switch to the *Task List*, a Program Manager utility that manages multiple applications. You then can use the Task List to switch to the Print Manager to pause or resume printing, assign a priority level to the printer, or remove print jobs from the print queue. To switch to the Task List without using the Quattro Pro 5.0 for Windows Control menu, press Ctrl+Esc.

Figure 3.7 shows the Task List window. To learn more about the Task List, refer to the Windows Program Manager documentation.

Fig. 3.7

The Windows Task List.

You also can switch from one Windows application to another by pressing Alt+Tab. If the first application that appears in the foreground is not the correct application, hold down the Alt key and continue to release and press Tab until the desired application title appears. To switch to the new application, release Alt.

Quattro Pro 5.0 for Windows doesn't allow you to access the Task List while a report is being sent to a printer or to the Print Manager. To get instructions for switching to another application while Quattro Pro 5.0 for Windows is printing, refer to the previous section of this chapter called "Sizing a Window."

Changing Global Settings

If you are an experienced user of an earlier Quattro Pro release, you might not immediately recognize the correct Quattro Pro 5.0 for Windows default setting commands. In Quattro Pro 5.0 for Windows, default settings are known as *properties* and are set using Object Inspectors.

Some properties apply to Quattro Pro 5.0 for Windows in general. Others apply to specific spreadsheet notebooks, to specific notebook pages, or to selected blocks of cells. Table 3.3 summarizes the properties used to set the Quattro Pro 5.0 for Windows defaults.

Table 3.3 Setting the Quattro Pro 5.0 for Windows Defaults

Setting	Type of Property
Auto-Execute macros	Application Startup Startup Macro
Auto-Load file	Application Startup Autoload File
Beep on error	Application Startup Use Beep
Borders	Active Page Borders
Clock	Application Display Clock Display
Column width	Active Page Default Width
Currency position	Application International Currency
Currency symbol	Application International Currency
Date format	Application International Date Format
Default directory	Application Startup Directory
File extension	Application Startup File Extension
Format	Current Object Numeric Format
Grid lines	Active Page Grid Lines
Label alignment	Active Page Label Alignment
Lics conversion	Application International Conversion
Macro suppress redraw	Application Macro Suppress-Redraw
Palette	Active Notebook Palette
Punctuation	Application International Punctuation
Recalculation	Active Notebook Recalc Settings
SpeedBar	Application Display Display Options
Time format	Application International Time Format
Undo	Application Startup Options Undo
Worksheet protection	Active Page Protection
Zero display	Active Page Display Zeros
Zoom factor	Active Notebook Zoom Factor

Manipulating Windows

The **Window** command on the Quattro Pro 5.0 for Windows menu leads to other commands that enable you to size and arrange open windows in the application window and to make another notebook window active (see fig. 3.8).

Fig. 3.8

The Window menu.

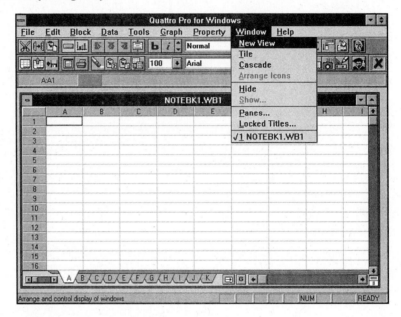

Cascading Windows

The **Window Cascade** command arranges open notebook windows in an overlapping format with the active notebook window on top and only the title bars of other open notebook windows showing (see fig. 3.9).

Tiling Windows

The **Window Tile** command sizes and arranges all open notebook windows side-by-side, like floor tiles (see fig. 3.10). The active notebook window's title bar has a dark background.

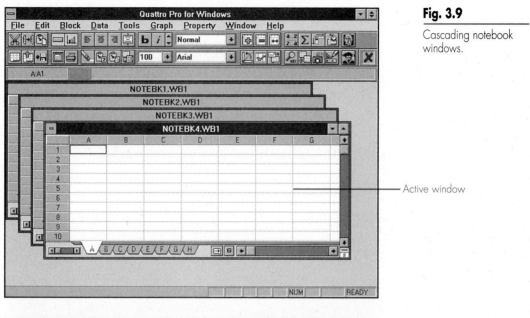

Fig. 3.9

Cascading notebook windows.

Active window

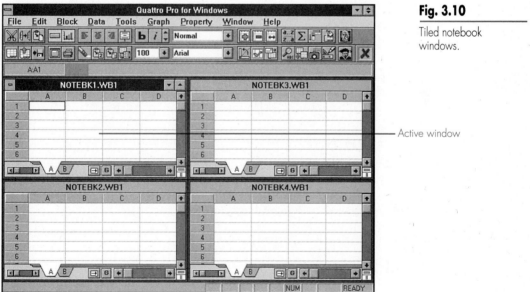

Fig. 3.10

Tiled notebook windows.

Active window

Choosing a Window Display Mode

Quattro Pro 5.0 for Windows offers some other display options in addition to the cascade and tile display modes. You can display a new view of a single notebook, split a spreadsheet notebook window vertically or horizontally into two panes, or maximize a spreadsheet notebook window to fill the entire workspace. If you find choosing the best display mode difficult, the following guidelines can help you make your choice.

- Maximizing the window provides the largest visible work area.
- Tiling the windows enables you to view portions of several notebooks at the same time.
- Cascading the windows provides a large visible workspace (although not as large as maximizing a window) and makes switching between windows easy.
- To display two views of the same notebook, use **W**indow **N**ew View or the mouse to split the notebook window. This choice enables you to view two notebook pages at the same time.

Making Another Window Active

If you choose the **W**indow command from the main menu, the menu shown in figure 3.8 appears. The bottom part of this menu displays a list of open windows, using a check mark to indicate the active window. To make a different window active, press the number to the left of the appropriate window name or click the name with the mouse.

Other options enable you to activate windows without using the **W**indow command. To cycle through the open windows, activating each window in turn, press Ctrl+F6. You also can activate a window by clicking inside its borders with the mouse.

Using Command Menus

Almost every task you perform in Quattro Pro 5.0 for Windows is part of a command. Commands help you analyze and organize data effectively, copy and move data, graph and format data, sort and manipulate databases, open and close spreadsheet notebooks, and use colors and fonts to customize spreadsheets.

Using the Quattro Pro 5.0 for Windows Main Menu

The Quattro Pro 5.0 for Windows main menu always appears on the horizontal menu bar at the top of the screen.

To access a command on the menu bar with the keyboard, you must first activate the menu by pressing the Alt key. A reverse video high-light, the *menu pointer*, appears in the menu bar. Use the left- and right-arrow keys to move the menu pointer from one command to another.

You can choose a command by highlighting it with the direction keys and pressing Enter or by simply typing the underlined letter—usually the first letter—of the command name. (In this book, the underlined letter of the command appears in boldface.) You cannot access menus by typing an underlined letter. After the menus are activated and ap-pear on-screen, however, you can type the underlined letters of the commands on the menus.

If you use the mouse to select commands, you don't need to activate the main menu first. Just click the command you want to use.

Using Pull-Down Menus and Cascade Menus

The commands on the menu bar lead to pull-down or cascade menus. Quattro Pro 5.0 for Windows uses *pull-down menus* to organize its first level of commands. If a command offers a second level of command choices, a *cascade menu* appears at the side of the pull-down menu (see fig. 3.11). Cascade menus look and function just like pull-down menus.

Menu items appear with a triangle, an ellipsis (...), or nothing beside them. If the menu item includes a triangle, a cascade menu appears when the item is selected. If the menu item includes an ellipsis, Quattro Pro 5.0 for Windows needs more information to complete the command and displays a dialog box when the item is selected. If the menu item has no marker, the item is the last selection in the command sequence. If you press Enter, Quattro Pro 5.0 for Windows executes the command. Figure 3.11 shows all three kinds of menu items.

To move the menu pointer through the pull-down and cascade menus, first click the top-level command; then use the up- and down-arrow keys or press the appropriate underlined letter of the command you want to select.

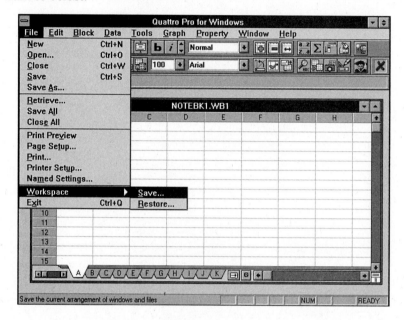

By pressing Esc, you can cancel a command at any time. Depending on the selected command, the Esc key either cancels the command completely or steps back through your previous keystrokes one menu level at a time. To cancel a command by using the mouse, click anywhere outside the menu. If a dialog box is displayed on-screen, click the Cancel button to cancel the command.

Occasionally, a menu item is *dimmed*. A dimmed command is currently unavailable. When the graph page is active, for example, all **B**lock commands are dimmed and unavailable. If you attempt to choose one of these commands with the keyboard or the mouse, nothing happens.

Using Object Inspectors

The Object Inspectors are an exciting feature of Quattro Pro 5.0 for Windows. *Object Inspectors* are dialog boxes that appear when you point at an object with the mouse and click the right mouse button or select the appropriate Object Inspector from the **P**roperty menu.

These pop-up menus or dialog boxes include all of the major options that apply to the selected object. If you point to a cell or a block, for example, the Active Block dialog box shown in figure 3.12 appears. This dialog box enables you to set label alignment, numeric format, row height, column width, and data entry type; to activate block protection; to choose line drawing and shading options; to select fonts and text colors; and to reveal or hide the block on-screen.

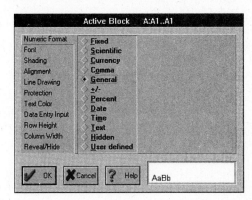

Fig. 3.12

The Active Block Object Inspector dialog box.

Quattro Pro 5.0 for Windows provides Object Inspectors for several types of objects. Table 3.4 provides a list of the correct locations to click in order to activate these Object Inspectors.

Table 3.4 Object Inspector Locations

Menu	Location to Click
Application	Quattro Pro 5.0 for Windows title bar
Active Notebook	Notebook window title bar
Active Page	The page tab below the spreadsheet page
Active Block	Within the selected block
Graph Window	Graph page title bar
Graph Objects	Within the selected object
Floating Graph	Within the floating graph
SpeedButton	Within the SpeedButton

FOR RELATED INFORMATION

▶▶ "Choosing Commands from Menus," p. 120.

Using Object Help

If you are unsure how to use a Quattro Pro 5.0 for Windows object, you often can obtain information using Object Help. This feature displays a description of the object and usually includes a help button that you can use to get more detailed information. To activate Object Help, point to the object, hold down the Ctrl key, and click the right mouse button.

Figure 3.13, for example, shows the Object Help that appears when you click the notebook title bar. Other objects that provide Object Help include the application title bar, icons on the SpeedBars, notebook blocks, page tabs, and so on.

Fig. 3.13

Object Help for the
Active Notebook
Title Bar.

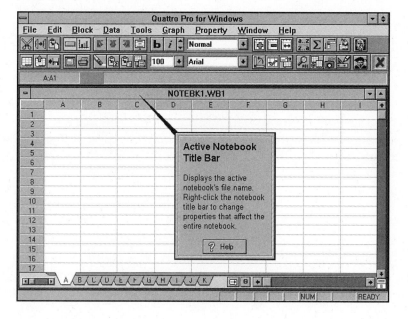

Using Dialog Boxes

If Quattro Pro 5.0 for Windows needs more information about a command, it displays a *dialog box*. To execute the command, you must complete the dialog box and either confirm the information by choosing OK or cancel it by choosing Cancel. The following sections explain how to use dialog boxes.

Navigating within a Dialog Box

A dialog box is composed of *fields*, which organize *choices*. Before you can specify a choice, you must first select a field. Using the keyboard, you can select a field either by pressing Alt and then the underlined letter of the field or by using the Tab and Shift+Tab keys to move the highlight to the field. The highlight functions much like a menu pointer: when you highlight a field in a dialog box, you can make a corresponding choice. Some fields do not have an underlined letter or cannot be surrounded by the highlight. These fields act as labels for the choices below them; don't worry about selecting them. When you select an option, the markers and the highlight move to show you the next choices. Figure 3.14 shows a dialog box that contains several different kinds of fields.

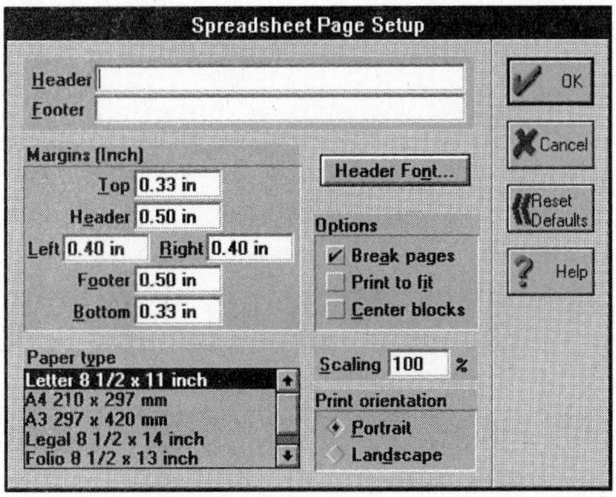

Fig. 3.14

A Quattro Pro for Windows dialog box.

If a button name is followed by an ellipsis (see the Header Font button in the Spreadsheet Page Setup dialog box shown in the figure), an additional dialog box appears if you select that button.

Using a dialog box is usually a straightforward process, especially using a simple dialog box that contains a limited number of selections. Table 3.5 describes the keys you use to navigate within a dialog box.

Table 3.5 Direction Key Actions in a Dialog Box

Key(s)	Action(s)
←	Moves to the preceding choice in a field
→	Moves to the following choice in a field
↑	Moves to the preceding choice in a field; in a list box, highlights the item one level up
↓	Moves to the following choice in a field; in a list box, highlights the item one level down
End	Moves to the last choice in a list box
Enter	Completes the command and closes the dialog box; toggles a selection in a check box
Esc	Closes the dialog box without completing the command; equivalent to selecting Cancel
Home	Moves to the first choice in a list box
PgDn	Scrolls down a list box
PgUp	Scrolls up a list box
Shift+Tab	Moves to the preceding field
Tab	Moves to the next field
Alt+letter	Moves to an option with the underlined letter that you pressed

Use Tab and Shift+Tab to move from field to field, use the direction keys to move from choice to choice, and press Enter to finalize your choices.

If you use a mouse, you don't need to select the field first; simply click the choice you want to make. Moving in a dialog box also is easier with the mouse. Complete all sections of the dialog box before you confirm the choices by clicking OK.

Entering Information in a Dialog Box

A dialog box often contains many sections, but you rarely need to fill in every field. The Spreadsheet Page Setup dialog box shown in figure 3.13, for example, displays 15 different options. If you want to set just the page header, fill in only the page header part of the dialog box and click OK or press Enter to confirm the dialog box.

Every dialog box has a *title bar* and *command buttons*. The title bar displays the command name or a description of the dialog box. When you choose a command button, you execute or cancel the command. Command buttons usually are labeled OK or Cancel.

To confirm the selections in a dialog box and execute the command, choose the OK button. To cancel a command and close the dialog box, choose the Cancel button or press Esc (or Ctrl+Break).

Option buttons are diamonds that indicate choices within a field. Option buttons are also known as *radio buttons*, because they function in a manner similar to the buttons on an automobile radio. If you select an option button, any other option button in the same field is deselected—you can select only one option button in a field at a time. The Print Orientation field in the Page Setup dialog box, for example, enables you to choose only one of two possible settings: **P**ortrait or Lan**d**scape (see fig. 3.14).

Using the keyboard, you can select an option by pressing the Alt key and the appropriate underlined letter or by using the Tab key. Use the direction keys to move through and select options. If you select a different option button, Quattro Pro for Windows deselects the previously selected option button.

Check boxes are square boxes that turn choices on or off. If a choice is turned on, a check mark appears in the box. To change the contents of a check box using the keyboard, first select the field using the Tab key; then use the direction keys to move through the choices to the check box. Press the space bar to put a check mark in the check box. If the check box already contains a check mark and you press the space bar, the check mark disappears and the choice is turned off. If you use the mouse, click a check box to turn it on or off.

List boxes display lists of choices. You can make only one choice per list box. With the keyboard, use the direction keys to highlight the choice you want; then press Enter. With the mouse, simply click the choice. A list box often has a *text box* on top that displays the currently selected choice.

If a list box contains more choices than appear on-screen, you can see the hidden choices by using the direction keys, including the PgUp, PgDn, Home, and End keys (see table 3.5), to scroll through them. If you use the mouse, you can click the *scroll boxes* (the up and down arrows) or drag the *elevator box* in the scroll bar to move through the contents of the list box.

Drop-down boxes are similar to list boxes. They are used if a dialog box cannot display a list box without covering other information. To see the choices in a drop-down box, click the down arrow or press the down-arrow key.

Text boxes can appear with or without list boxes. If a text box appears alone, you must enter information. In most cases you must type this information, but sometimes you can use the mouse to enter it. Quattro Pro 5.0 for Windows, for example, often uses text boxes to ask for the block that a command is supposed to affect. You can specify a block by pointing with the mouse or by using the keyboard, before or after you issue the command.

Sometimes Quattro Pro 5.0 for Windows fills in a text box with a suggested cell address, file name, or path. If you select a cell or block before issuing a command, that cell or block address appears in the text box. The suggested information appears in reverse video. To accept the suggestion, press Enter. To erase it and make another entry, simply begin typing; the suggested information is replaced by the information you type.

To correct errors in text boxes by using the mouse, move the mouse pointer to the mistake, click to display the cursor, use Del or Backspace to erase the incorrect characters, and type the correct information. Characters you highlight before you begin typing are replaced by the new characters you type.

Moving a Dialog Box

Occasionally, a dialog box covers data that you need to see before you can complete the command.

You cannot move a dialog box using the keyboard. To move the dialog box by using a mouse, move the mouse pointer to the dialog box title bar, grab the title bar by pressing and holding the left mouse button, and drag the dialog box to another location.

If you specify a block in a dialog box by pointing to the block, the dialog box temporarily shrinks so that you can see data and select cells freely.

If a dialog box requires you to enter two blocks (see the **B**lock **C**opy dialog box shown in figure 3.15, for example), and you have prespecified the first block, be sure to press Tab or to highlight the text in the second block text box with the mouse pointer before specifying the second block. You can streamline many Quattro Pro 5.0 for Windows procedures by prespecifying a block; doing so enables you to issue several commands pertaining to that block without having to reselect it multiple times.

Fig. 3.15

A dialog box with the first block prespecified.

Completing Input Line Prompts

When you begin typing a cell entry, Quattro Pro 5.0 for Windows displays the entry on the *input line*. As you begin an entry, two buttons—the Confirm button (a check mark) and the Cancel button (an X)—appear on the input line above column B (see fig. 3.16). These buttons are the mouse equivalents for Enter and Esc. These two buttons also appear—and function in the same manner—when you edit a cell entry.

Using SpeedBars and SpeedButtons

SpeedBars are groups of buttons that appear on the third and fourth lines of the screen and serve as mouse shortcuts to many Quattro Pro 5.0 for Windows features. (You cannot access SpeedBars using the keyboard.) Different SpeedBars appear, depending on the current task.

When you work with a spreadsheet notebook, for example, the standard notebook SpeedBar appears. Usually, the Productivity Tools SpeedBar appears on the fourth line directly below the standard notebook SpeedBar. You can use the SpeedBar Object Inspector to add, replace, or remove optional SpeedBars. Figure 3.17 shows the result of displaying the optional Productivity Tools, Analysis Tools, Consolidator, Scenario Manager, and Spell Checker SpeedBars below the standard notebook SpeedBar.

Fig. 3.16

The Confirm and Cancel buttons on the input line.

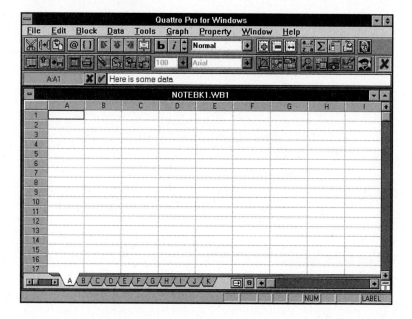

To use the Quattro Pro 5.0 for Windows SpeedBars, first select the object, cell, or block you want to affect; then point to the appropriate button and click the left mouse button. To adjust the column widths within a block to fit the data in its cells, for example, select the cell with the longest entry, and then click the Fit button on the SpeedBar.

SpeedButtons are buttons you create and place on a notebook page. They execute macros that you associate with them. Figure 3.18 shows several SpeedButtons added to a notebook.

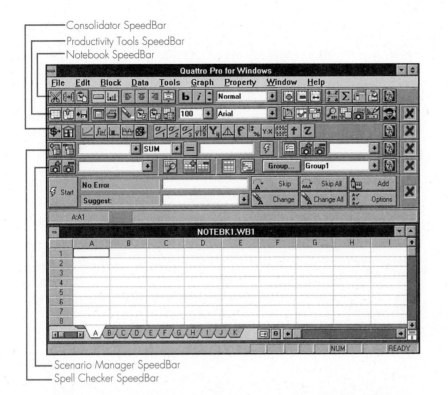

Fig. 3.17

The optional SpeedBars displayed below the standard notebook SpeedBar.

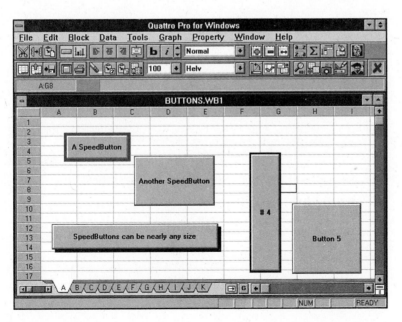

Fig. 3.18

A notebook with several added SpeedButtons.

FOR RELATED INFORMATION

▶▶ "Using SpeedButtons and Custom Dialog Boxes," p. 634.

Questions and Answers

Q: When I select a block, the mouse pointer changes to a hand and the block moves when I move the mouse. What should I do?

A: Quattro Pro 5.0 for Windows has a new feature—*single-cell drag and drop* (see Chapter 5)—that enables you to move or copy a block as small as a single cell. Unfortunately, you might find that the mouse pointer changes from the selector arrow to the drag-and-drop hand too quickly. To allow more time, change the **P**roperty **A**pplication Delay Time setting to a larger value. The 500 ms default allows you half a second. To increase the delay setting to three-quarters of a second, for example, use 750 ms.

Q: I upgraded from Quattro Pro for Windows Version 1, but now my notebooks are too large to fit the page. Why?

A: Quattro Pro 5.0 for Windows has a new SpeedBar—the Productivity Tools SpeedBar—that is displayed by default below the standard notebook SpeedBar. This additional SpeedBar reduces the room that is available to display your notebooks. Either resize your existing notebooks or remove the Productivity Tools SpeedBar to create additional notebook display space.

Q: Why do dialog boxes close before I make all of my entries?

A: You are probably pressing Enter after you make an entry. Pressing Enter confirms the dialog box, and uses the existing entries. Use Tab or click the next field to move from field to field in a dialog box; press Enter only if you are finished making all your entries.

Q: There are so many buttons on the SpeedBars. How do I tell what they do?

A: When you point to a SpeedBar button, the button's description is displayed on the status line at the lower left of the screen. For additional information, you can use Object Help. Point to a button, hold down Ctrl, and then click the right mouse button.

Summary

This chapter discussed the use of Quattro Pro 5.0 for Windows within the Windows graphical user interface. It showed you how to use the mouse; how to change the size, position, and arrangement of windows; how to access global settings; how to use the pull-down and cascade menus; how to use dialog boxes; and how to use SpeedBars and SpeedButtons. Because Quattro Pro 5.0 for Windows was designed as a Windows application, you can apply many of these skills to other Windows programs.

Chapter 4 introduces you to spreadsheet basics, providing instructions for moving the cell selector in a spreadsheet, entering and editing data, and using the Undo feature.

Learning Spreadsheet Basics

This chapter builds upon the skills you learned in the preceding chapters by presenting information you need to use Quattro Pro 5.0 for Windows notebooks. If you are new to electronic spreadsheets, this chapter helps you learn to use a spreadsheet for basic data analysis. If you are familiar with previous versions of Quattro Pro or Lotus 1-2-3, this chapter is valuable for learning the conventions and features of Quattro Pro for Windows.

You use Quattro Pro 5.0 for Windows to analyze and manipulate numbers, data, and formulas of different types. This program enables you to organize these elements into a format that helps you report results in an effective manner.

In Quattro Pro 5.0 for Windows, a single spreadsheet is called a *page*—a two-dimensional grid of columns and rows. A file that contains 256 spreadsheet pages and 1 graph page in a three-dimensional arrangement is called a *notebook*. Besides working with several pages in a notebook, you also can work with several notebooks at the same time; you can link notebooks by writing formulas in one notebook that refer to cells in another notebook. You also can assign descriptive names to individual pages and use these names in formula references—making formulas much easier to understand.

This chapter shows you how to perform the following tasks:

- Work with single and multiple notebook pages

- Link notebooks

- Move the cell selector around the spreadsheet and between pages

- Enter and edit data

- Document formulas, numbers, and data by adding descriptive notes to cells

- Add labels and headings to make notebooks more understandable

- Use the Undo feature

- Use Interactive Tutors and your data to learn Quattro Pro 5.0 for Windows

Understanding Spreadsheets, Notebooks, and Files

When you start Quattro Pro 5.0 for Windows, an empty notebook (with the name NOTEBK1.WB1) appears on-screen, as shown in figure 4.1. This notebook consists of 257 pages—256 spreadsheet pages and 1 graph page. Each spreadsheet page is identified initially by a letter—A through IV—that appears on the page tab at the bottom of the page. When you include a page reference in a formula or block specification, you type a colon after the page letter or page name. To refer to the upper left cell in notebook page C, for example, you use the formula reference C:A1.

You can choose the syntax used to specify 3D blocks by activating the Application Object Inspector and making a selection in the 3D Syntax field. To make this selection, point to the Quattro Pro 5.0 for Windows title bar and click the right mouse button, or choose the **P**roperty **A**pplication command. In the Display selections, choose **A**..B:A1..B2 or A:A1..**B**:B2. If you choose the first selection, **A**..B:A1..B2, you specify 3D blocks by first naming the pages, and then the cell addresses. If you choose the second selection, A:A1..**B**:B2, you specify 3D blocks by naming the first page and cell address, and then the second page and cell address.

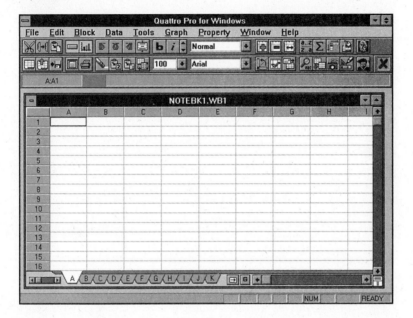

Fig. 4.1

A blank Quattro Pro for Windows notebook.

You can enter data in one or more pages of a notebook, and then save the notebook on disk with a single file name. When you retrieve the notebook file, the contents of each page remain exactly as you saved them. See Chapter 8, "Managing Files," for more information about files and saving work. After you save a notebook, the title bar displays the notebook's file name. In figure 4.2, the notebook file CONSRPT.WB1 is displayed.

Using Multiple-Page Notebooks

Usually, you need only a single page to analyze and store data. You can organize simple reports effectively with limited sets of data on a single page without the added complication of including page references in your formulas. These page references are necessary for accessing data that spreads across several pages.

Fig. 4.2

The CONSRPT.WB1
notebook.

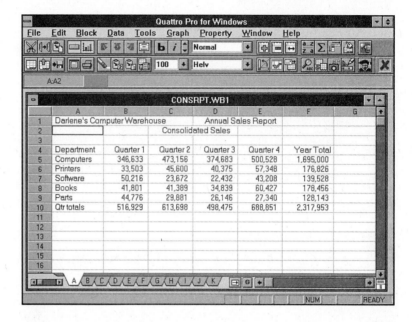

In other situations, however, you may need to use multiple pages to most effectively organize data. Some cases are well-suited to multiple notebook pages. Reports that consolidate data from several departments often work well as multiple-page reports—especially if one person produces the entire report. You can use a separate page for each department and store the consolidated report as a single notebook. You can put a formula on one page that refers to cells on other pages.

Don't assume, however, that a single notebook is always the best solution in producing consolidated reports. Multiple notebook files linked by formulas often are a better solution than a single, multiple-page notebook. Consolidating data from several departments or company locations may be easier when using multiple notebooks, for example, if several people are producing the individual reports. The person producing the consolidated report can create a notebook that uses formula links to consolidate the data from each notebook. A following section of this chapter, "Linking Notebooks with Formulas," explains the techniques involved in consolidating multiple notebooks. In addition, Chapter 19, "Consolidating Data and Managing Scenarios," shows you how to use the Consolidator, a powerful new tool for automatically consolidating data from different sources.

One good use of multiple notebook pages is to place each month's data on a separate page and use a 13th page for the yearly totals. Because Quattro Pro 5.0 for Windows enables you to name individual pages, you can name one page for each month so that you easily can locate the correct page.

You also can use multiple pages to effectively separate different kinds of data. You can place data input areas on one page, macros on another, constants on another, and the finished report on yet another page. Because you can apply protection on a page-by-page basis, this technique can provide some assurance that a spreadsheet masterpiece isn't damaged by an inadvertent error. For example, a data entry error can write over formulas, or the insertion or deletion of a row or column can destroy macros or data tables contained on the same page.

Displaying Multiple Pages

Quattro Pro 5.0 for Windows offers several methods of viewing multiple notebook pages; you choose the method that best suits you. The default screen shows part of one notebook page (again see fig. 4.2). In Chapter 3, "Using the Graphical User Interface," you learned that you can display notebooks in several ways: a single notebook maximized to cover the entire notebook workspace, multiple notebooks cascaded in an overlapping fashion, or multiple notebooks tiled side-by-side. Occasionally, however, you may want to view different areas of the same page or different pages in the same notebook at the same time. Quattro Pro 5.0 for Windows provides several options to handle these requests.

Splitting a single notebook display into two independent window panes enables you to see different parts of the same page or different pages in each of the two panes. Quattro Pro 5.0 for Windows enables you to split the window horizontally or vertically, and you can adjust the size of each pane as necessary—the two panes don't need to be the same size.

TIP

Using split windows may help you when entering formulas that refer to distant areas of the same notebook page. Suppose that you are entering a formula in cell Z87 that refers to several cells in the block BC200..BD215. If you create a vertical split and display Z87 in one pane and BC200..BD215 in the other, you easily can identify the correct cells as you enter the formula.

Often, locking titles on-screen is more useful than splitting the window into two panes. Locked titles remain synchronized with the cell selector, always displaying the same row or column as the cell selector (depending on the direction you move the selector). This action usually is more appropriate than the unsynchronized split window display. Chapter 5, "Using Fundamental Commands," describes the commands for splitting windows and locking titles.

Quattro Pro 5.0 for Windows gives you another option when you want a second, independent view of the same notebook. The **W**indow **N**ew View command provides a new window that displays the same notebook. This window can display the same page, a different area of the same page, or a completely different page. Figure 4.3 shows two views of the same notebook, CONSRPT.WB1. The two windows are shown tiled, but they can be displayed full-screen, tiled, cascaded, or overlapping in any manner you want.

Fig. 4.3

Two windows displaying views of the same notebook.

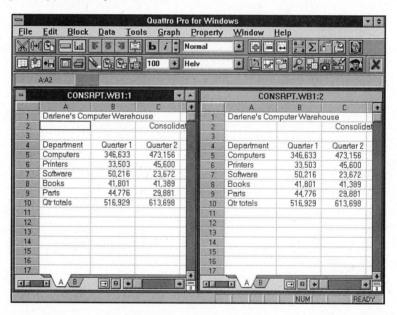

When two or more windows show views of the same notebook, the title bar for each window includes the view number after the notebook file name. In figure 4.3, the right window shows CONSRPT.WB1:2, indicating this window is the second view of the same notebook. The left window shows CONSRPT.WB1:1 in the title bar.

Whether you split a single notebook window into two panes or create multiple windows that display the same notebook, changes you make in one view are reflected in the other views. If you modify the formula in cell A:B5 of the CONSRPT.WB1:1 window, the same modifications appear in cell A:B5 of the CONSRPT.WB1:2 window.

When you no longer require multiple views of the same notebook, you can close all views (except one) of the notebook without closing the notebook. To close a window, use the notebook Control menu and choose **C**lose or press Ctrl+F4.

Linking Notebooks with Formulas

Besides working with multiple pages in a single notebook, you can work with data from several notebook files. You can enter a formula in one notebook cell that refers to cells in another notebook. This technique is called *linking*.

With this capability, you easily can consolidate data from separate notebook files. You may, for example, receive data in notebooks from several departments or locations. A consolidation notebook can use formulas to combine the data from each notebook. You also can apply this process in reverse; you can supply each department or location with a master notebook that contains data you provide. The individual department or location files can contain formulas that refer to the data tables in the master notebook. Chapter 20, "Sharing Data Using the Workgroup Desktop," shows you how to use the power of Quattro Pro 5.0 for Windows to share live data automatically across the room or around the world.

In figure 4.4, the notebook CONSRPT.WB1 is used to consolidate data from three other notebooks: CARSRPT.WB1, SPARRPT.WB1, and RENORPT.WB1. Formulas link the notebooks. The formula in cell A:B5 of CONSRPT.WB1, for example, is shown on the following line:

```
+[CARSRPT]A:B5+[RENORPT]A:B5+[SPARRPT]A:B5
```

This formula tells Quattro Pro 5.0 for Windows to add together the values in cell A:B5 of CARSRPT.WB1, cell A:B5 of RENORPT.WB1, and cell A:B5 of SPARRPT.WB1.

You can use linking formulas to create links to open or closed notebooks. Quattro Pro 5.0 for Windows maintains the formula links even after the supporting notebooks are closed.

Fig. 4.4

Linking notebooks with formulas.

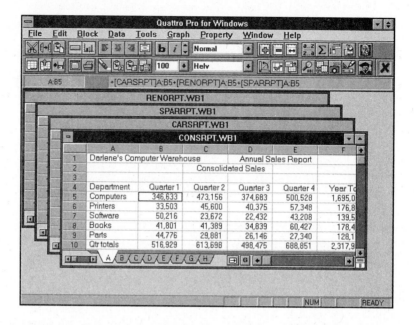

You also can use the **Edit Paste Link** and **Edit Paste Special** commands to link Quattro Pro 5.0 for Windows notebooks to each other or to other Windows applications. Chapter 8, "Managing Files," contains more detailed information on linking files, using the Windows Clipboard, and using linking formulas.

FOR RELATED INFORMATION

▶▶ "Saving Files," p. 273.

▶▶ "Linking Notebook Files," p. 282.

◀◀ "Changing the Size and Position of a Window," p. 62.

Using linked notebooks rather than one large notebook has several advantages:

■ When you create formula links between notebooks, these links remain even after you close the source files. Therefore, you can create linked notebooks using much more data than memory can store at one time.

■ You easily can link notebooks created by several people in different locations.

■ You can create links to sources of data other than Quattro Pro 5.0 for Windows notebooks.

Moving Around the Spreadsheet

You can enter data only at the location of the cell selector. This requirement, and the fact that you can display only a small portion of a spreadsheet notebook at a time, stresses the importance of knowing how to move the cell selector to other parts of the notebook. The following sections focus on moving the cell selector within a notebook and among open notebook files. Moving the cursor on the input line is covered in "Entering Data in the Notebook," a following section of this chapter.

Using the Direction Keys

The four arrow keys that move the cell selector are located on the numeric keypad (or on a separate pad of enhanced keyboards). When you press an arrow key, the cell selector moves to the next cell in the direction of the arrow. If you hold down an arrow key, the cell selector continues to move in the direction of the arrow key. When the cell selector reaches the edge of the screen, the spreadsheet page scrolls in the opposite direction to enable the cell selector to continue moving in the direction of the arrow. When the cell selector reaches the edge of the notebook (or the boundary of locked titles—see Chapter 5, "Using Fundamental Commands"), the cell selector stops moving even if you continue to hold down the arrow key.

You can use several other direction keys to move around the current notebook page one screen at a time. Press the PgUp or PgDn key to move up or down one screen at a time. Press the Tab key or Ctrl+→ to move one screen to the right, and press Shift+Tab or Ctrl+← to move one screen to the left. The size of one screen depends on the size of the notebook window; if the notebook window is full-screen, these direction keys move the cell selector much farther than if the notebook window occupies a small area.

Pressing the Home key moves the cell selector directly to the home position on the current notebook page. The home position is normally cell A1, but home can be different if the current page has locked titles (see Chapter 5, "Using Fundamental Commands"). Pressing End Home moves the cell selector to the last cell of the current page. The last active cell of the current page may not be in use, but this cell is at the intersection of the last column and last row in use. Therefore, if cells J1 and A200 on the current page contain data, the last active cell is cell

J200. You also can use Ctrl+Home to move to the home position on the first notebook page, or End Ctrl+Home to move to the last active cell on the last active notebook page.

Two direction keys are especially important for moving around a notebook. Ctrl+PgDn moves the cell selector to the next spreadsheet page, and Ctrl+PgUp moves the cell selector to the preceding spreadsheet page.

Pressing Ctrl+F6 moves the cell selector to the next open notebook window. The next open notebook window can be showing a different notebook or a different view of the same notebook. To move the cell selector between panes within the same notebook window, press F6. The notebook window or window pane that contains the cell selector is the active window, and all data you type enters the active window.

Using the Scroll Lock Key

The Scroll Lock key toggles the scroll feature on and off. When you press Scroll Lock, you activate the scroll feature and Quattro Pro 5.0 for Windows displays SCR on the status line at the bottom of the screen. When you press an arrow key with the scroll feature active, the cell selector stays in the current cell and the entire page scrolls in the opposite direction of the arrow. If you keep pressing the same arrow key when the cell selector reaches the edge of the screen, the cell selector remains beside the spreadsheet frame as the entire page scrolls. If you press an arrow key when the scroll feature is active and you cannot scroll the page farther, the cell selector moves in the direction of the arrow.

If the cell selector does not move as you expect, check to see whether you accidently turned on Scroll Lock. If the SCR indicator appears on the status line, press Scroll Lock again to turn off the scroll feature.

To use the mouse to scroll the spreadsheet page without moving the cell selector, drag the elevator box in the scroll bars at the right and bottom edges of the notebook. As you move the elevator box, the cell selector remains in the same cell even after the elevator scrolls this cell off-screen.

Using the End Key

When you press and release the End key, the END status indicator appears in the status line. Then if you press an arrow key, the cell selector moves in the direction of the arrow. The cell selector continues in the same direction until it reaches one of these cells: the first cell that contains data (if the cell next to the current cell in the direction of the arrow *didn't* contain data) or the last cell that contains data (if the cell next to the current cell in the direction of the arrow *did* contain data). If no cell in the direction of the arrow contains data, the cell selector stops at the edge of the spreadsheet page.

Figure 4.5 shows the cell selector in cell B8. If you press the End key and then the down-arrow key, the cell selector moves to cell B10. If you press End and the down arrow again, the cell selector moves to cell B8192, because the spreadsheet page contains no data in lower rows.

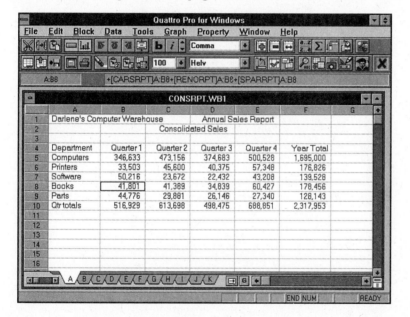

Fig. 4.5

The END indicator in the status line.

> You can use the End and Home keys to find the limits of the active area. You always can add data in the column to the right or the row below the active area without disturbing existing data. You also can use these keys when you specify a print block.

TIP

After you press the End key, the END indicator stays on until you press an arrow key, the Home key, or the End key again. If you press End by mistake, you can press End again to turn off the END indicator.

Using the Goto Feature

The Goto feature enables you to jump directly to a cell on the current notebook page, on other pages of the notebook, or to other open notebooks. You can use the Goto feature in two ways: press F5 (GoTo), or choose the **E**dit **G**oto command. When you press F5 (GoTo) or choose **E**dit **G**oto, the Goto dialog box prompts you for a destination (see fig. 4.6). After you type a cell address in the Reference text box, the cell selector moves directly to this address. If you type a block name, the cell selector moves to the upper left corner of the block.

Fig. 4.6

The Goto dialog box.

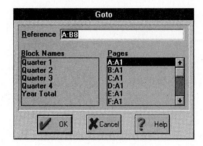

To move to a cell on another page, type the page letter or page name, followed by a colon and the cell address. If the cell selector is in cell A20 on page A and you want to move to cell J13 on page C, type the destination as **C:J13**.

To move the cell selector to another open notebook, precede the destination address with the notebook name enclosed in square brackets. For example, you could move the cell selector from B:B8 in notebook CONSRPT.WB1 to A:B2 in notebook CARSRPT.WB1 by typing the destination as **[CARSRPT]A:B2**.

Using the mouse is an easier way to move to another page or another notebook. To move to another page in the current notebook, click the page tab for the page where you want to move. If the page tab isn't displayed, use the tab scroller (to the left of the page tabs) to display the tab. To move to another notebook, click the mouse pointer anywhere in the new notebook's window. If the notebook is hidden behind other notebooks, press Ctrl+F6 or choose the **W**indow command and select the destination window from the displayed list.

You can use the Goto feature to select a block starting at the current cell and ending with the cell you specify in the Goto dialog box. Press Shift+Enter (or press Shift and choose OK) to confirm the Goto dialog box. Quattro Pro 5.0 for Windows selects a rectangular block using the current cell and the cell you specify as two corners. If the second cell is on another page, Quattro Pro 5.0 for Windows selects a three-dimensional block. The selected block must be in a single notebook; you cannot select a block across notebooks.

Using the Num Lock Key

The Num Lock key toggles the numeric keypad between numbers and direction keys. If you have an enhanced keyboard with a separate set of direction keys, you can use the numeric keypad to enter numbers and use the separate direction keypad to move the cell selector. Quattro Pro 5.0 for Windows displays the NUM indicator when the numeric keypad is toggled for entering numbers. Pressing the Num Lock key toggles the indicator on or off. If you find that the keys on the numeric keypad move the cell selector instead of entering numbers, press Num Lock to display the NUM indicator on the status line.

FOR RELATED INFORMATION

▶▶ "Locking Titles On-Screen," p. 147.

▶▶ "Using Blocks," p. 126.

◀◀ "Learning the Quattro Pro 5.0 for Windows Keys," p. 39.

Entering Data in the Notebook

To enter data in the notebook, move the cell selector to the appropriate cell, type the entry, and press Enter. As you type, the entry appears in the input line. After you press Enter, the entry also appears in the current cell. If you enter data in a cell that already contains an entry, the new data replaces the existing entry.

If you plan to make entries in more than one cell, you do not need to press Enter after each entry. Instead, you can enter the data, and then move the cell selector to the new cell with a direction key. Moving the cell selector completes the entry and moves the cell selector in a single step.

You can create two kinds of cell entries: labels or values. A *label* (or string) is a text entry, and a *value* is a number or formula. Unless you set the active block's properties to restrict data input to labels or dates, Quattro Pro 5.0 for Windows determines the kind of entry from the first character you type. (The following section, "Limiting the Type of Data Input," explains how to set this block property.) The program treats the entry as a value (a number or a formula) if you begin with one of the following characters:

0 1 2 3 4 5 6 7 8 9 + – (@ # . $

If you begin by typing any other character, Quattro Pro 5.0 for Windows treats the entry as a label. After you type the first character, the mode indicator in the status line changes from READY to VALUE or LABEL.

Limiting the Type of Data Input

Usually, when you begin a cell entry with one of the characters shown in the preceding section, Quattro Pro 5.0 for Windows treats the entry as a value. Although this guess usually is correct, certain types of label entries, such as addresses, telephone numbers, or Social Security numbers, also begin with numeric characters. To enter a label that begins with a numeric character, you must begin the entry with a label prefix (see the following section, "Entering Labels"). Quattro Pro 5.0 for Windows, however, enables you to instruct the program to treat all entries in a block as labels. Even if you begin an entry with a numeric character, the entry goes in the cell with a label prefix.

Dates are another kind of data that can be difficult to enter in a cell. If you type **6/26/94**, Quattro Pro 5.0 for Windows assumes that you are entering the formula +6/26/94 and places the result 0.0024549918166939 in the cell. To enter the date June 26, 1994, you can type **@DATE(94,6,26)** or **@DATEVALUE("26-JUN-94")**. Unfortunately, both methods are more difficult than typing **6/26/94**.

To restrict a block of cells to label or date entries, select the block and click the right mouse button, or choose the **P**roperty Current **O**bject command, to open the Object Inspector Active Block dialog box. Choose Data Entry Input; then in the Data Input Constraints box, check the **L**abels Only or **D**ates Only option (see fig. 4.7). If you check **L**abels Only, Quattro Pro 5.0 for Windows treats all future entries in the block as if you entered these entries with a label prefix. If you check **D**ates Only, Quattro Pro for Windows treats entries in the block as date entries if you type the entries in a date format. Entries that don't fit a date format produce the error message Invalid date or Invalid time.

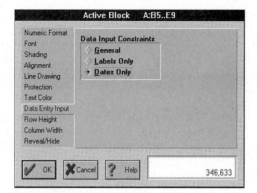

Fig. 4.7

Restricting the kind of data input in the active block.

Entering Labels

Labels make the numbers and formulas in a notebook understandable. Without labels to identify the data, understanding most spreadsheet reports would be difficult if not impossible. In figure 4.2, labels identify the departments and the time periods that generated the displayed results. Without labels, the numbers are meaningless.

In Quattro Pro 5.0 for Windows, a label can be a string of up to 1,022 characters. Labels can include titles, headings, explanations, and notes, all of which can make the spreadsheet easier to understand.

When you enter a label, Quattro Pro 5.0 for Windows adds a label prefix to the cell entry. The label prefix is not displayed in the spreadsheet, but the prefix appears in the input line as shown in figure 4.8. By default, Quattro Pro 5.0 for Windows adds an apostrophe ('), the label prefix for a left-aligned label. You can change the way a label appears by using one of the following label prefixes:

'	Left-aligned (default)
"	Right-aligned
^	Centered
\	Repeating
|	Nonprinting (if the label is in the leftmost column of the print block)

Regardless of the label prefix you enter, any label longer than the column width is displayed as a left-aligned label, as shown in cell B9 of figure 4.8.

Fig. 4.8

The label prefix appears in the input line but not in the spreadsheet.

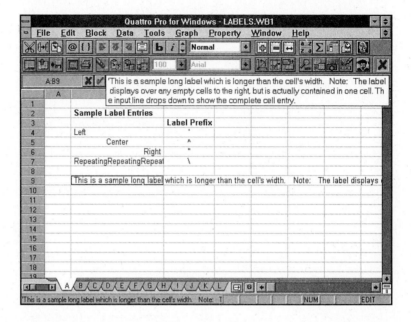

To use a different default label prefix, you can open the Active Page or Active Block dialog box, depending on whether you want to set the default for the entire page or for a specified block. To open the Active Page dialog box, point to the page tab and click the right mouse button or choose **P**roperty Active **P**age. To activate the Active Block dialog box, select the block and click the right mouse button or choose **P**roperty Current **O**bject. If you open the Active Page dialog box, choose Label Alignment. If you open the Active Block dialog box, choose Alignment. Choose **G**eneral to reset the alignment to the default; or choose **L**eft, **R**ight, **C**enter, or Center across **b**lock to specify a new default.

In figure 4.8, cell B7 contains a repeating label, which fills the width of the cell. If you change the column width, the repeating label adjusts to fill the new width.

If you want to use a label prefix as the first visible character of a label, you must precede the prefix with another label prefix. For example, if you type **\012** as a cell entry, Quattro Pro 5.0 for Windows treats this entry as a repeating label that appears in the cell as 012012012012. If you want \012 to appear in the cell, you first must type another label prefix, such as an apostrophe ('), and then type **\012**.

If a typed label results in an invalid formula, such as the address 17935 Texas Avenue, Quattro Pro 5.0 for Windows refuses to accept the entry and displays the error message box shown in figure 4.9.

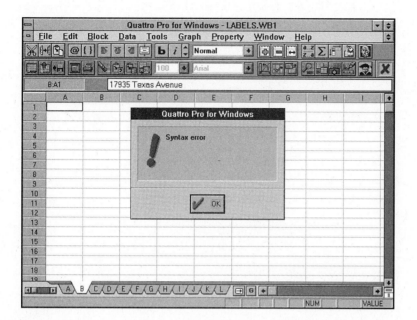

Fig. 4.9

An error message displays if a typed label results in an invalid formula.

Press Enter to confirm the error message and return to EDIT mode. If the label entry is accidentally evaluated as a formula, press Home, type the label prefix, and press Enter.

If a label is longer than the cell width, as shown in cell B9 of figure 4.8, the label appears across empty cells to the right. Even a label too long to display on-screen appears in its entirety in the input line when the cell selector rests on the cell that contains the long entry and F2 (Edit) is pressed.

If the cells to the right of a cell that contains a long label are not blank, Quattro Pro 5.0 for Windows cuts off the entry display at the nonblank cell border. The complete entry still is stored, however, and appears in the input line when the cell selector is on the cell. To display more of the label in the spreadsheet, you can insert new columns to the right of the cell that contains the long label, or you can widen the column.

TIP

To widen the column easily with the mouse, move the cell selector to the cell that contains the long label and click the Fit button on the SpeedBar. The column width adjusts to fit the length of the label.

Entering Numbers

To enter a number in the spreadsheet, type any of the ten numeric characters (0 through 9) and certain other characters, according to the following rules:

- You can start a number with a plus sign (+); the plus sign is not stored when you press Enter.

  +456 is stored and displayed as 456.

- You can start a number with a minus sign (–); the number is stored as a negative number.

  –456 is stored and displayed as –456.

- You can include one decimal point.

  .456 is stored and displayed as 0.456.

- You can end a number with a percent sign (%); unless the cell is formatted as Percent, the number is divided by 100, and the percent sign is dropped.

  456% is stored as +4.56 and displayed as 4.56.

- You can type a number in scientific notation.

  456E3 is stored and displayed as 456000.

  4.56E30 is stored and displayed as 4.56E+30.

  4.56E4 is stored and displayed as 0.000456.

  4.56E30 is stored and displayed as 4.56E–30.

- If you enter a number with more than 14 digits, the number is rounded and stored in scientific notation.

  12345678901234 is stored as 12345678901234 and displayed as 1.23E+13 if the column remains at the default width of 9, or 12345678901234 if column width is automatic.

  123456789012345 is stored as 1.2345678901235E+14 and is displayed as 1.2E+14 if the column remains at the default width of 9, or 1.2345678901235E+14 if column width is automatic.

The appearance of a number in the notebook depends on the cell's format, font, and column width. If the number is too long to fit in the cell, Quattro Pro 5.0 for Windows tries to show as much of the number as possible. If the cell uses the default General format and the integer portion of the number does not fit in the cell, Quattro Pro 5.0 for Windows displays the number in scientific notation. If the cell uses a format other than General or Scientific, or if the cell width is too narrow to display in scientific notation and the number cannot fit in the cell width, Quattro Pro 5.0 for Windows displays asterisks instead of the number.

Entering Formulas

The capability of calculating formulas is the real power of a spreadsheet program like Quattro Pro 5.0 for Windows. This capability makes the program an electronic spreadsheet, not just an electronic notepad. Formulas enable the program to calculate results and analyze data. As you change or add new data to a spreadsheet, Quattro Pro 5.0 for Windows recalculates the new results. You quickly can see the effects of changing information on the end results.

You can enter formulas that operate on numbers, labels, or the results of other formulas in the spreadsheet. Like a label, a formula can contain up to 1,022 characters. A formula can include numbers, text, operators, cell and block addresses, block names, and functions. A formula cannot contain spaces except in a block name, a quoted text string, or a note (see "Adding Notes to a Cell," a following section of this chapter).

Quattro Pro 5.0 for Windows uses four kinds of formulas: numeric, string, logical, and function. The following sections cover numeric, string, and logical formulas; function formulas are covered in Chapter 7, "Using Functions."

Although you can use Quattro Pro 5.0 for Windows as a calculator by typing numbers directly into a formula, as in **123+456**, doing so ignores the real power of Quattro Pro 5.0 for Windows formulas. A more useful formula uses cell references or block names in the calculation. Figure 4.10 demonstrates this capability.

In this figure, the values 123 and 456 are placed in cells A1 and A2, respectively. The formula +A1+A2, which refers to these two cells, produces the same result as the formula 123+456—the value 579. Suppose, however, that the data changes and you discover the first value should be 124, not 123. If you used the cell reference formula, you just type **124** in cell A1 and the formula recalculates the new value of 580. If you used the formula with numeric values rather than the cell reference formula, you must edit or retype the formula to change the data and obtain the new result. Now imagine that instead of adding two numbers, the formula added a group of ten numbers. This example clearly demonstrates the power of using cell references rather than data values in formulas.

Fig. 4.10

Formulas that use cell references are more flexible than formulas that contain numbers.

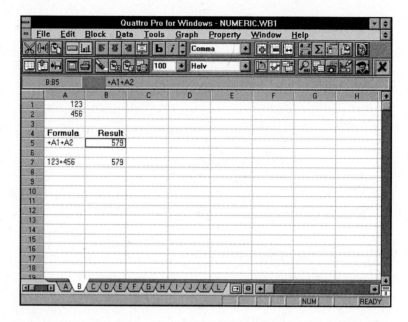

Notice that the formula in row 5 begins with a plus sign (+A1). If the formula begins with A1 (no plus sign), Quattro Pro 5.0 for Windows assumes that you are entering a label and performs no calculations.

Formulas are instructions to Quattro Pro 5.0 for Windows to perform calculations. You use *operators* to specify the calculations and in what order to perform the calculations. Table 4.1 lists the operators Quattro Pro 5.0 for Windows recognizes and the order of precedence—the order in which Quattro Pro 5.0 for Windows uses these operators.

Table 4.1 The Operators and Their Order of Precedence

Operator	Operation	Precedence
^	Exponentiation	1
− +	Negative, positive value	2
* /	Multiplication, division	3
+ −	Addition, subtraction	4
= <> < > <= >=	Equal to, not equal to, less than, greater than, less than or equal to, greater than or equal to	5

Operator	Operation	Precedence
#NOT#	Logical NOT	6
#AND# #OR#	Logical AND, logical OR	7
&	String concatenation	7

Using Operators in Numeric Formulas

You use operators for addition, subtraction, multiplication, division, and exponentiation (raising a number to a power). Quattro Pro 5.0 for Windows breaks down formulas and calculates results using the order of precedence shown in table 4.1. If a formula includes the exponentiation operator (^), Quattro Pro 5.0 for Windows calculates this exponentiation first. The balance of the formula is calculated according to the precedence of the operators. If the formula includes two operators of the same precedence, this portion of the equation is evaluated left to right. The order of precedence affects the result of many formulas. To override the order of calculation, you use parentheses. Operations within a set of parentheses always are evaluated first. Figure 4.11 shows several examples that demonstrate how operator order of precedence and parentheses affect calculations.

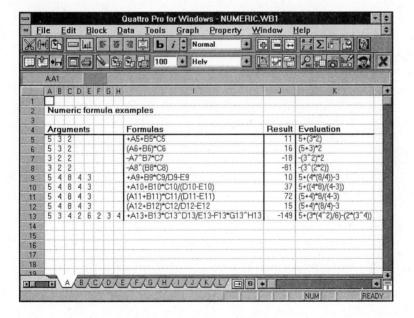

Fig. 4.11

Order of precedence and parentheses affect calculations.

A complex formula may contain many sets of parentheses, and you must have an equal number of left and right parentheses. Quattro Pro 5.0 for Windows helps you complete complex formulas by displaying unmatched parentheses in red, and then turning the matching pair green when you add the second parenthesis. If you have difficulty determining which parenthesis is missing its match, press F2 (Edit) and move the insertion point through the formula. When you highlight an unmatched parenthesis, it turns red. Add the missing member of the pair, and both parentheses turn green. Quattro Pro 5.0 for Windows uses this technique also to help you find unmatched square brackets [ ] in linking formulas and unmatched braces { } in macros.

Using Operators in String Formulas

A *string* is a label or the result of a string formula. String formulas use different rules than numeric formulas. Only two string formula operators exist: the plus sign (+), which repeats a string, and the ampersand (&), which *concatenate*s (joins) two or more strings.

String formulas always begin with the plus sign but cannot include more than one occurrence of the operator. To add two strings, you concatenate them using the ampersand. Figure 4.12 shows several examples of string formulas.

Fig. 4.12

Use string formulas to concatenate labels.

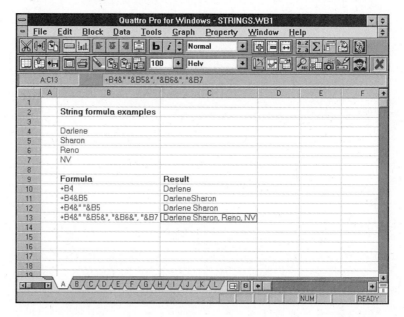

In figure 4.12, row 10 shows the plus sign used to repeat a string value. The formula to repeat a string or a numeric value is the same. Row 11 shows the result of concatenating two strings. Notice that no spaces exist between the two concatenated values. Rows 12 and 13 demonstrate how to include spaces and commas in quoted strings to produce more attractive results.

If you attempt to add two strings using the plus sign rather than the ampersand, Quattro Pro 5.0 for Windows treats the formula as a numeric formula rather than a string formula. A cell that contains a label has a numeric value of 0 (zero), so if you place the formula +B4+B5 in the spreadsheet shown in figure 4.12, the formula returns a value of 0.

You can use the ampersand only in string formulas. Also, if you use any numeric operators (after the plus sign at the beginning) in a formula that contains an ampersand, the formula results in ERR.

Quattro Pro 5.0 for Windows offers a number of powerful string functions, which are discussed in Chapter 7, "Using Functions."

Using Operators in Logical Formulas

Logical formulas are true/false tests. A logical formula returns a value of 1 if the test is true and a value of 0 if the test is false. Logical formulas often are used in database criteria tables and also to construct the tests used with the @IF function, discussed in Chapter 7, "Using Functions."

Logical formulas provide a shortcut method of performing conditional calculations. Suppose that you want to include the value contained in cell A1 only if this value is greater than 100. The logical formula +A1*(A1>100) returns the result you want. In this formula, the logical test, A1>100, evaluates as 0 unless the value in A1 is greater than 100. If A1 contains a value over 100, the logical test evaluates to 1. Because any value multiplied by 0 equals 0, and any value multiplied by 1 is the original value, the logical formula returns the result you want.

Pointing to Cell References

Formulas consist mainly of operators and cell references. As you enter a formula, you can type the cell address or you can point to the cell by moving the cell selector to the cell. When Quattro Pro 5.0 for Windows expects a cell address, you can use the direction keys or the mouse to point to the cell or block. When you move the cell selector as you are entering a formula, the mode indicator changes from VALUE to POINT, and the address of the cell selector appears in the input line.

If the formula requires additional terms, type the next operator and continue entering arguments until you finish. Press Enter or click the Confirm button to place the formula in the notebook. As you enter formulas, you can combine pointing and typing cell addresses—the result is the same.

To enter a block argument while pointing (using the direction keys), anchor the cell selector at one corner of the block by pressing the period (.), and then use the direction keys to highlight the block. You also can press and hold down the Shift key and use the direction keys to highlight a block in READY and POINT modes. Type the next operator to enter the block address or press Enter if the formula is complete.

You also can press Shift+F7 to extend the selection. After you press Shift+F7, Quattro Pro 5.0 for Windows displays the EXT indicator. Use the direction keys to highlight the block you want and press Enter to complete the selection.

If you use the mouse to point to a block, move the mouse pointer to the first cell of the block, press and hold down the left mouse button, drag the mouse pointer to highlight the block, and release the mouse button.

To refer to a cell on another notebook page, include the page letter or name, followed by a colon and the cell address. To include the value of cell A13 from a page named EXPENSES, for example, type **+EXPENSES:A13**. To point to a cell on another page, type +, and then use the direction keys, including Ctrl+PgDn and Ctrl+PgUp, to move the cell selector to other pages. You also can click the page tab with the mouse, and then point to the cell.

Pointing to a cell usually is faster and more accurate than typing a cell address in a formula. If the cell you are referencing is far from the current cell, however, you may find typing the cell's address an easier method. You also may want to consider using the **W**indow **N**ew View command (discussed previously in this chapter) to create a new view of the notebook, especially if you are entering several formulas that refer to distant cells.

Block names often are much easier to remember than cell addresses, and you can use block names in place of cell addresses in formulas. Chapter 5, "Using Fundamental Commands," covers the creation and use of blocks in spreadsheets.

Using Array Formulas

Notebooks often contain repetitive formulas, because you often want to perform the same calculation on related data. Quattro Pro 5.0 for Windows offers a new and powerful method of performing these types of repetitive calculations. Using *array formulas*, you enter a single formula, and Quattro Pro 5.0 for Windows automatically performs the same calculation on an entire array of values.

To create an array formula, you enter in the first result cell a formula that defines the array. Quattro Pro 5.0 for Windows then enters the corresponding values in the remaining result cells. In figure 4.13, each cell in row 7 contains the total of the two cells in rows 5 and 6 of the same column. A single array formula entered in cell B7 can replace five formulas in cells B7 through F7.

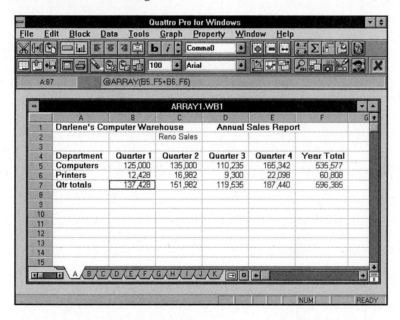

Fig. 4.13

Array formulas simplify repetitive calculations.

To enter the array formula in cell B7, type the following formula:

+B5..F5+B6..F6

When you press Enter, Quattro Pro 5.0 for Windows enters the array formula in B7 as:

```
@ARRAY(B5..F5+B6..F6)
```

Although cells C7 through F7 do not contain formulas, Quattro Pro 5.0 for Windows recalculates the results in these cells if any values in C5 through F6 change.

You can use array notation to enter the arguments for any function that accepts blocks of values as arguments, but you must consider how Quattro Pro 5.0 for Windows calculates values in array formulas. In figure 4.14, cells B2..D3 contain a set of values used in several calculations that demonstrate how array formulas differ from standard formulas.

Fig. 4.14

Array arguments may produce unexpected results.

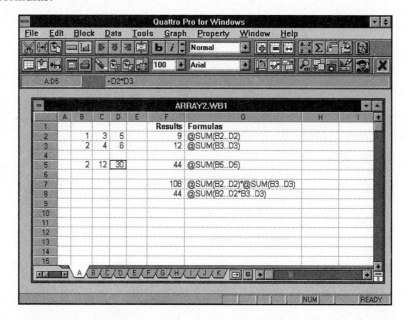

The formula in F7, @SUM(B2..D2)*@SUM(B3..D3), is evaluated as the sum of B2..D2 (9) times the sum of B3..D3 (12), resulting in the value 108. The array formula in F8, @SUM(B2..D2*B3..D3), is evaluated somewhat differently. This formula, which is evaluated as the sum of B2 times B3 (2) plus the sum of C2 times C3 (12) plus the sum of D2 times D3 (30), results in the value 44. Both formulas produce a correct result, but each serves a different purpose. If you use array arguments in formulas, make certain you understand these differences.

Changing Cell Formats

Quattro Pro 5.0 for Windows uses the default General format to display values in a spreadsheet. To improve the appearance of reports, however, you can control the numeric formats used. You can assign a currency format to monetary values, a percent format to percentage values, or a format that displays a specified, fixed number of decimal digits. If you create notebooks dealing with international matters, such as currency exchange rates, you may want to use an international format to display dates and times. Chapter 6, "Changing the Format and Appearance of Data," discusses the available numeric formats in Quattro Pro 5.0 for Windows and shows you how to apply these formats to notebooks.

Adding Notes to a Cell

As notebooks become more complex, documentation gains in importance. Quattro Pro 5.0 for Windows makes documenting formulas and values easy by adding notes to cell entries. These notes don't appear when you print a report, but as figure 4.15 shows, the notes appear on-screen in the input line when you move the cell selector to a cell that contains a note. If the note is too long to appear fully on-screen, press Edit (F2) to display the entire note.

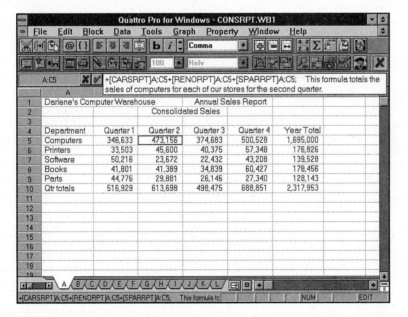

Fig. 4.15

Notes added to formulas and values provide valuable documentation.

The note attached to the formula in cell C5 in figure 4.15 clearly states the purpose of the formula. To attach a note to a formula or a value, type a semicolon immediately following the formula or value; then type the note. You can include up to 1,022 characters in a cell, including the length of the formula or value and the note.

FOR RELATED INFORMATION

▶▶ "Using String Functions," p. 261.

▶▶ "Using Blocks," p. 126.

▶▶ "Applying the Available Formats," p. 190.

◀◀ "Using the Mouse," p. 58.

Editing Data in the Notebook

As you enter data or formulas in the notebook, you may want to make changes to the data or formulas. A label spelling error, an incorrect numeric value, or a syntax error made while entering a formula are common mistakes you can correct. You can change an existing cell entry in two ways. You can replace the entire contents of the cell by retyping the complete entry, or you can edit the cell contents to change a part of the entry.

To replace the entire contents of a cell, move the cell selector to the cell, type the new entry, and press Enter. To edit the existing contents, move the cell selector to the cell and press F2 (Edit) to enter EDIT mode. Use the direction keys to move the cursor, press Del or Backspace to remove existing characters, press Ins to toggle between insert and overwrite, and type the corrections. Press Enter to complete the edits.

To use the mouse to edit cell contents, click the mouse pointer on the cell, point to the position of the proposed changes in the input line, and click the left mouse button. To replace a section of the entry, highlight in the input line the characters you want to replace. All new characters you type replace the highlighted characters.

After you finish editing a cell's contents, press Enter or click the Confirm button to add the contents of the input line to the spreadsheet cell. To discard the changes, press Esc or click the Cancel button. The content of the spreadsheet cell doesn't change until you press Enter or click the Confirm button.

If you make an error while entering a formula, Quattro Pro 5.0 for Windows displays a message box that describes the error. If you misspell one of the built-in functions, for example, the message box states that you typed an unknown function. If you forget to include a required argument, the message box states that you made a syntax error. Press Enter to confirm the message box and correct the error. If you are unsure of the exact error, convert the formula into a label by pressing the Home key, typing an apostrophe ('), and pressing Enter.

Using the Undo Feature

When you type an entry, edit a cell, or issue a command, you change the notebook. If you make a change in error, you can choose the **Edit** **Undo** command to reverse the previous change. If you type over an entry in error, you can undo the new entry to restore the previous entry. The Undo feature undoes only the last action performed, whether you were entering data, using a command, running a macro, or using Undo.

To ensure that the Undo feature is available, use the **P**roperty Application command to open the Application Object Inspector dialog box. Make sure that the **U**ndo enabled check box in the Startup section of the dialog box is marked. Choose OK to confirm the dialog box.

The Undo feature is powerful and can be tricky, so you must use care when invoking this command. To use Undo properly, you must understand what Quattro Pro 5.0 for Windows considers a change. A change occurs between the time Quattro Pro 5.0 for Windows is in READY mode and when the program returns to READY mode. If you press F2 (Edit), Quattro Pro 5.0 for Windows enters EDIT mode. After you press Enter to confirm the edits, Quattro Pro 5.0 for Windows returns to READY mode. If you choose **Edit Undo**, Quattro Pro 5.0 for Windows restores the cell contents that existed before you pressed Edit. To restore the last change, choose **Edit Redo** (which replaces **Edit Undo** until you make another change that can be undone).

If a single command makes the change, the Undo feature can undo changes made to an entire block of cells or even a complete notebook.

NOTE
> You cannot undo some commands. Moving the cell selector, saving a notebook, and the effects of recalculating formulas are commands you cannot undo. You also cannot undo commands that affect external database tables. Before you make a serious change to an important file, always save the work to protect against errors that Undo may not reverse.

Using Interactive Tutors

Learning the basics of Quattro Pro 5.0 for Windows is easier when you use the Interactive Tutors feature. This feature uses Computer Based Training (CBT) to step you through simple tasks. Unlike the simple tutorials found in many other programs, the Interactive Tutors use real data that you supply. Using real data creates a more lasting example that helps you learn faster.

NOTE
> While the Interactive Tutors teach you how to perform simple tasks, another new feature of Quattro Pro 5.0 for Windows, Experts, helps you perform more complex operations. Chapter 17 shows you how to use Experts.

 To activate the Interactive Tutors feature, choose the **Help** Interactive Tutors command or click the Interactive Tutors button on the Productivity Tools SpeedBar. The Interactive Tutor Catalog appears (see fig. 4.16).

After you choose a topic, the Interactive Tutors guide you through the subject one step at a time, explaining exactly how to continue. After you complete a step, click the Next button to go to the next step (see fig. 4.17). To review a step, click the Previous button.

As you complete each topic, a check appears in the box to show that you completed the topic. For an overall tutorial covering the basics of Quattro Pro 5.0 for Windows, complete each topic. You also can wait until you first need to use a feature in Quattro Pro 5.0 for Windows, and then use the appropriate Interactive Tutors topic to quickly gain a basic understanding of the subject.

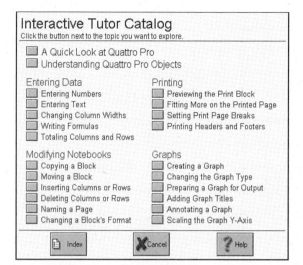

Fig. 4.16

The Interactive Tutor Catalog.

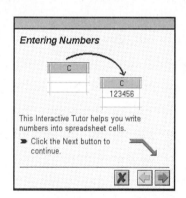

Fig. 4.17

Interactive Tutors guide you step by step through the basics.

Questions and Answers

Q: Why does the cell selector jump to an empty cell when I press End Home?

A: When you press End Home, Quattro Pro 5.0 for Windows moves the cell selector to the last active cell in the notebook. This cell is always at the intersection of the last column and last row used. For example, if you place an entry in cell E1 and another entry in A10, the last active cell is E10 because column E is the last column used and row 10 is the last row used.

Q: When I try to enter a formula, it does not calculate any values. Instead, the text of the formula appears in the notebook. What's wrong?

A: You may have one of two problems. First, you may be forgetting to begin the formula with an operator (such as +), which Quattro Pro 5.0 for Windows recognizes as the beginning of a formula. To add the values contained in A1 and A2, for example, you must type **+A1+A2**. If you type **A1+A2**, Quattro Pro 5.0 for Windows assumes that you are entering a label.

If you are entering formulas correctly but Quattro Pro 5.0 for Windows still places them in the notebook as labels, the active block's properties probably are set to restrict data input to labels. See the section, "Limiting the Type of Data Input," in this chapter for information on this property.

Q: When I try to enter a more complex formula, Quattro Pro 5.0 for Windows beeps and turns one of the formula's parentheses red. What does this mean?

A: You can create formulas and easily lose track of all the matching parentheses. Quattro Pro 5.0 for Windows is showing you a parenthesis that lacks its partner. Take a closer look at the formula and determine where you need to add another parenthesis to complete the formula.

Summary

This chapter covered the basic skills you need to use Quattro Pro 5.0 for Windows. You learned how to organize your work into notebooks and use multiple pages effectively. You learned how to move around notebook pages and between notebook pages. This chapter explained how to enter and edit labels, numeric values, and formulas, including formulas that refer to other notebook pages. You became familiar with adding notes to document formulas and value entries. The chapter also discussed how to use the Undo feature to reverse incorrect entries and commands. Finally, you learned how to use the Interactive Tutors to quickly acquire basic skills using real data.

In Chapter 5, you learn the fundamental commands that provide the tools you need to create and use Quattro Pro 5.0 for Windows notebooks effectively.

Building the Spreadsheet

PART II

OUTLINE

Using Fundamental Commands

Almost everything you do in Quattro Pro 5.0 for Windows involves commands. You use *commands* to tell Quattro Pro 5.0 for Windows to perform a specific task or a series of grouped tasks. Commands can change the basic operation of Quattro Pro 5.0 for Windows, or commands can operate on a notebook, a notebook page, a block of cells, or individual cells. You use commands to control data appearance, print reports, access database files, graph information, open and save notebooks, move and copy data, and perform many other tasks.

Quattro Pro 5.0 for Windows includes many commands. Some commands you use every time you run Quattro Pro 5.0 for Windows; other commands you rarely, if ever, use. Some commands are general enough to apply to all notebooks; other commands are specialized and apply to individual objects such as blocks or cells. This chapter covers the most fundamental commands used in Quattro Pro 5.0 for Windows. Later chapters cover more specific commands.

In this chapter you learn about the capabilities of these commands and also their limitations. You also learn that Quattro Pro 5.0 for Windows cannot perform certain actions—such as formatting a disk. For these types of tasks you must access the Windows Program Manager or the operating system, another subject covered in this chapter.

For additional information about the Quattro Pro 5.0 for Windows commands, refer to the command reference in Part VII of this book.

This chapter shows you how to do the following tasks:

- Choose commands from menus
- Save notebook and workspace files
- Use blocks and block names
- Control column widths and row heights
- Erase data from cells, blocks, rows, columns, and pages
- Insert and delete rows, columns, and pages
- Split the notebook window and display several pages at a time
- Lock titles on-screen
- Protect and hide data
- Control recalculation
- Move, copy, find, and replace data
- Verify spelling
- Fill blocks with data
- Access the Windows Program Manager or the operating system without quitting Quattro Pro 5.0 for Windows

Choosing Commands from Menus

The Quattro Pro 5.0 for Windows main command menu includes nine options (see fig. 5.1). Each option leads to a *drop-down menu*. A similar menu that appears when the graph window is active is covered in Chapter 10, "Creating Presentation Graphics." This chapter focuses on the commands of the Quattro Pro 5.0 for Windows main menu.

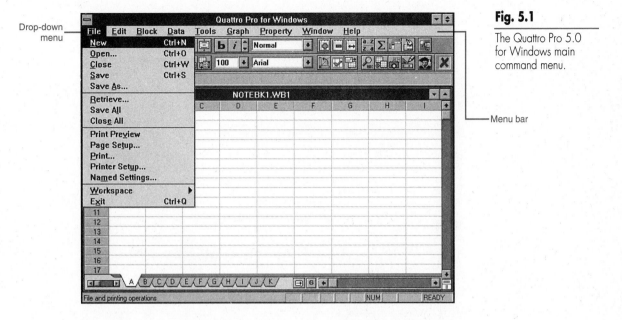

Fig. 5.1

The Quattro Pro 5.0
for Windows main
command menu.

The **F**ile commands enable you to save, open, and manage notebook
and workspace files. The commands on this menu also enable you to
set up your printer and page specifications, preview reports before
printing, and print reports and graphics. The **F**ile E**x**it command enables you to quit Quattro Pro 5.0 for Windows.

The **E**dit commands enable you to do the following tasks:

- Undo commands
- Use the Windows Clipboard to copy, cut, and paste information
- Create DDE (Dynamic Data Exchange) and OLE (Object Linking
  and Embedding) links to other Windows applications
- Move the cell selector to specified locations
- Perform search and replace operations
- Create and modify styles

The **B**lock commands enable you to copy, move, and fill blocks; insert
and delete rows, columns, and pages; work with named blocks; transpose data; reformat text; and insert hard page breaks.

The **D**ata commands enable you to query and sort databases, perform
what-if analyses, parse imported data, analyze frequency distributions,

and use the Database Desktop, the Data Modeling Desktop, and the Workgroup Desktop.

The **Tools** commands enable you to do the following tasks:

- Create, run, and debug macros
- Import and export data
- Perform data regression and matrix manipulation
- Use the Optimizer and Solve For utilities
- Create your own dialog boxes
- Create and control application links
- Use Scenario Manager
- Use the Analysis Tools utilities

The **Graph** commands enable you to create, view, and modify graphs; insert graph objects on notebook pages; and create on-screen slide shows.

The **Property** commands enable you to access the Object Inspectors. With Object Inspectors, you can control default settings for the active notebook, the active page, and the currently selected object in Quattro Pro 5.0 for Windows.

The **Window** commands enable you to create additional views of your notebooks, control the display of open windows, and select a window.

The **Help** commands enable you to access the Quattro Pro 5.0 for Windows Help system and determine available memory.

To issue a command from the keyboard, you must activate the main menu by pressing the Alt key. Use the arrow keys to move the menu pointer to the name of the command group and press Enter or the down arrow to activate the drop-down menu. Then move the menu pointer to the command and press Enter. You also can activate a menu group by pressing the underlined letter of the group. Then activate the menu option by pressing the underlined letter of the command.

If you use a mouse, just click the command group then click the command you want; Quattro Pro 5.0 for Windows automatically activates the menu.

If a drop-down menu option has another level of commands, the commands appear in a *cascade menu*. These drop-down menu options always are followed by a solid triangle marker. Figure 5.2 shows the cascade menu that appears when you choose **B**lock **N**ames.

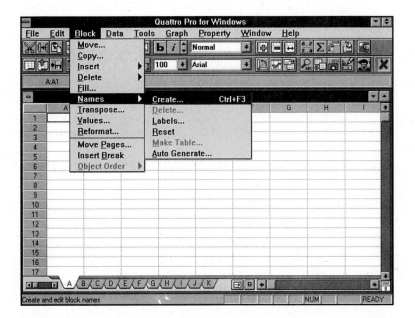

Fig. 5.2

Quattro Pro 5.0 for Windows uses drop-down and cascade menus.

When Quattro Pro 5.0 for Windows needs more information about a command, the selected menu option opens a *dialog box*. A dialog box is a window that enables you to read and enter information about a command. Menu options that lead to a dialog box always are followed by an ellipsis (...). Figure 5.3 shows the dialog box that appears when you choose **F**ile Save **A**s. Chapter 3, "Using the Graphical User Interface," explains how to move through the dialog boxes and enter information in them.

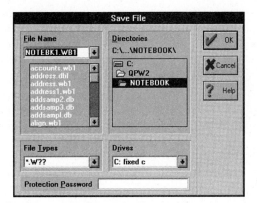

Fig. 5.3

The Save File dialog box.

TIP

Choosing a command may be faster if you press the Alt key and type the underlined letter of the command. For example, to choose **F**ile Save **A**s, you press Alt+FA. The Alt key activates the menu, F chooses the **F**ile command group, and A chooses Save **A**s. The underlined letter often is the first letter of a command, but not always. In this book, the entire command name always appears; the underlined letter you can type appears in boldface.

If you make a mistake while choosing menu commands, press Esc to return to the preceding menu. If you press Esc at the main menu, you return to READY mode. Click the Cancel button to close a dialog box without executing the command.

Quattro Pro 5.0 for Windows displays a description of most menu choices on the left side of the status line at the lower edge of the screen. As you move the menu pointer among choices, the description changes to reflect the highlighted choice.

If you execute a command accidentally, you usually can undo it. If you erase a block by mistake, for example, you can choose **E**dit **U**ndo Clear to recover the erased block. See Chapter 4, "Learning Spreadsheet Basics," for more information on the Undo feature.

Saving Notebook Files

When you build a new notebook or make changes to an existing notebook, all the work exists only in the computer's memory. If you do not save the notebook before you exit Quattro Pro 5.0 for Windows or before you close all open notebooks, you lose any new work. Quattro Pro 5.0 for Windows provides a warning if an open notebook has unsaved changes, asking whether you want to save the notebook. When you save a notebook, you give it a name and copy the notebook in memory to a disk file. The notebook file remains on disk after you quit Quattro Pro 5.0 for Windows or turn off the computer.

To save changes to an existing notebook, choose File from the Quattro Pro 5.0 for Windows main menu and choose **S**ave from the drop-down menu.

When you want to name a new notebook or save an existing notebook using a different name (keeping the old notebook file), use the **F**ile Save

As command. Quattro Pro 5.0 for Windows displays a dialog box that enables you to specify a new name as well as a different file format. If you specify the name of an existing file, Quattro Pro 5.0 for Windows displays the dialog box shown in figure 5.4. This dialog box asks whether you want to replace the existing notebook file, create a backup of the existing notebook file and then save the changed notebook, or cancel the **F**ile Save **A**s command.

Fig. 5.4

Quattro Pro 5.0 for Windows warns if a notebook file with the same name already exists.

▶▶ "Saving Notebook Files," p. 274.

FOR RELATED INFORMATION

Saving Workspace Files

The arrangement of notebooks in the Quattro Pro 5.0 for Windows notebook window is called a *workspace*. The workspace includes the position and size of notebook windows. You use the **F**ile **W**orkspace **S**ave command to save a workspace file. You then can load the file later with **F**ile **W**orkspace **R**estore to use the same arrangement of notebooks.

NOTE

Saving the workspace does not save changes to the individual notebooks. You still must use the **F**ile **S**ave command or answer **Y**es to the prompt to save changes when you close Quattro Pro 5.0 for Windows if you want to save your work.

▶▶ "Saving Workspace Files," p. 275.

FOR RELATED INFORMATION

Using Blocks

A *block* is usually a rectangular group of cells in a notebook. In Quattro Pro 5.0 for Windows, a block also can contain several groups of cells, defined by collections of rectangular blocks. Figure 5.5, for example, shows one rectangular block in cells A1..B3; a nonrectangular block including B5..B6, B7..D9, and E7..F7; and a noncontiguous block that includes C14..D15 and E17..F18.

Fig. 5.5

Different Quattro Pro 5.0 for Windows blocks on one page.

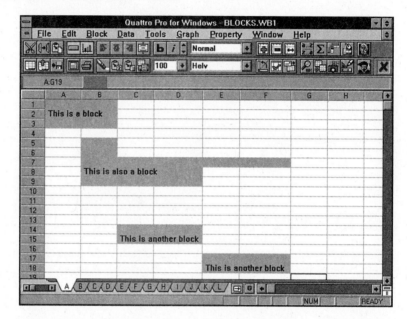

When you specify a block address, you define each rectangular block by marking cell addresses of any two diagonally opposite corners of the block. You separate the cell addresses with one or two periods and separate each rectangular block with commas. You can specify the nonrectangular block shown in figure 5.5 by typing **B5..B6,B7..D9,E7..F7**, for example. You also can specify this block in several other ways, as long as you separate each rectangular block with commas.

A block also can be *three-dimensional*, spanning two or more notebook pages. A three-dimensional block includes the corresponding cells on each page. When you use a three-dimensional block, you must include the page letter or page name with the cell addresses. To specify a block containing cells A1..C4 on pages A, B, and C, for example, you type the block address as **A:A1..C:C4**.

Many commands act on blocks. The **B**lock **C**opy command, for example, displays a dialog box asking for a **F**rom and a **T**o block. When Quattro Pro 5.0 for Windows prompts you for a block, you can respond in one of three ways:

- Type the address of the block.

- Highlight the block with the keyboard or the mouse before or after you choose the command.

- Type the block name if you have created a name.

Typing the Block Addresses

Typing the address is one method of specifying blocks. With this method, you type the addresses of cells diagonally opposite in a rectangular block, separating each cell with one or two periods. Quattro Pro 5.0 for Windows automatically inserts a second period if you type only one period. If the block is nonrectangular, you must specify each rectangular block and separate each block with a comma.

To specify the block A1..C4, for example, you type **A1..C4**, **A1.C4**, **A4..C1**, or **A4.C1**. Quattro Pro 5.0 for Windows regards each of these addresses the same as A1..C4.

This address method is most prone to error due to typing mistakes, so you may want to use one of the other two methods described in the following sections.

Selecting Blocks by Highlighting

Highlighting a block by pointing is usually the easiest method of specifying cell addresses. You highlight blocks in commands, dialog boxes, and formulas the same way. You can highlight a block with the keyboard or the mouse before or after you issue a command. In a formula, however, you must highlight the block after you begin typing the formula.

If you are highlighting a block with the keyboard, the End key often can help you make the selection faster. To highlight the block B5..F10 in figure 5.6, move the cell selector to cell B5. Press Shift+F7 (Extend) to anchor the block at this point. Press End and press the right arrow. Then press End and press the down arrow. Press Enter to complete the selection.

Fig. 5.6

A block of selected data.

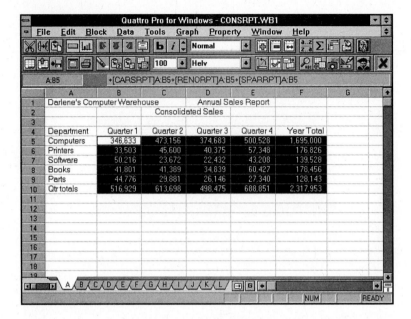

Quattro Pro 5.0 for Windows provides Shift+F7 as a method of anchoring a block selection. You also can anchor a block selection by pressing and holding down the Shift key while you move the cell selector.

As you use the End key with the arrow keys, the highlight expands from the anchor cell. In figure 5.6, the highlighted block is A:B5..F10. This block address is the address that appears in dialog boxes; this block also is affected by selections you make using the Active Block dialog box (described in a later section).

Highlighting a Block before You Issue a Command

With Quattro Pro 5.0 for Windows, you easily can work with large or three-dimensional blocks by highlighting the block before you issue a command. When you preselect a block, the address automatically appears in the dialog box.

Figure 5.7 shows the dialog box that appears after you select the block A:B5..F10 in figure 5.6, and then choose the **B**lock **C**opy command. Notice that both the **F**rom and **T**o text boxes show the same block: A:B5..F10. You can press Tab and Shift+Tab or use the mouse to move the highlight between the text boxes. Then enter the second block by typing its address or block name, or by pointing. Chapter 3, "Using the Graphical User Interface," covers the use of dialog boxes in detail.

Fig. 5.7

The preselected block address appears in the dialog box.

Highlighting a Block after You Issue a Command

When a dialog box requires two block arguments, you must select at least one of the blocks after you issue the command. If you forget to preselect a block before issuing the command, you must select both blocks after you issue the command. To select a block after a dialog box appears, move the highlight to the proper text box and specify the block.

Follow these steps to use the keyboard for selecting a block after issuing a command:

1. Use the Tab or Shift+Tab keys to select the text box. The selected text box contains the highlight.

2. Use the direction keys to move the cell selector to the beginning of the block.

3. To expand the selection, press the period (.) key or Shift+F7. Then use the direction keys (including Ctrl+PgUp and Ctrl+PgDn to select a three-dimensional block) to highlight the block.

4. Press Enter to complete the selection.

Follow these steps to use the mouse for selecting a block after issuing a command:

1. If the dialog box is hiding the first cell of the block, move the dialog box by pointing to its title bar and dragging the dialog box.

2. Point to the text box and double-click the left mouse button to highlight the text box.

3. Point to the beginning of the block, hold down the left mouse button, and drag the mouse to highlight the entire block.

4. Release the mouse button; the selected block now appears in the text box of the dialog box.

Extending Block Selections

Extending a block selection to include a three-dimensional block or a group of blocks allows you to include more than a single two-dimensional block in a command or a block name. These extended blocks make some operations easier and faster because one command can replace a series of commands.

Suppose that you want to copy the titles, department names, and summary formulas on the page shown in figure 5.6 to another page, but you do not want to copy the sales results or the store name. Because the information you want to copy and the information you do not want to copy are mixed together, you would need to use several steps to copy your information correctly if you do not use extended blocks.

You can select noncontiguous blocks using the mouse before or after you choose a command. To select noncontiguous blocks using the keyboard, you must select the block after choosing a command.

To use the keyboard to extend a block selection that includes noncontiguous blocks, perform the following steps:

1. Choose the command in which you want to use the noncontiguous blocks, such as **B**lock **C**opy.

2. Select the text box by pressing the Tab key or, if the text box has an underlined letter, by pressing Alt plus the letter. For example, in the Block Copy dialog box, choose the **F**rom text box by pressing Alt+F.

3. Enter the block addresses by typing the addresses of rectangular blocks and separating each block with a comma. You also can point to the first cell of each rectangular block, press the period key to anchor the highlight, and use the direction keys to highlight the block. Enter a comma and continue selecting rectangular blocks until you have selected each block.

If you use the mouse to extend a block selection that includes noncontiguous blocks, you can select the blocks before or after you choose a command. Use the following procedures:

1. Press and hold down the Ctrl key.

2. Select the first rectangular block.

3. Select each additional rectangular block.

4. Release the Ctrl key.

If you do not preselect the block and instead select a noncontiguous block to fill a text box in a dialog box, Quattro Pro 5.0 for Windows minimizes the dialog box. After you have completed the selection of the noncontiguous block, click the dialog box maximize button to restore the dialog box.

Figure 5.8 shows how the screen appears after you select the titles, department names, and summary formulas. Figure 5.9 shows the result of using **Block Copy** to copy the extended block selection to B:A1.

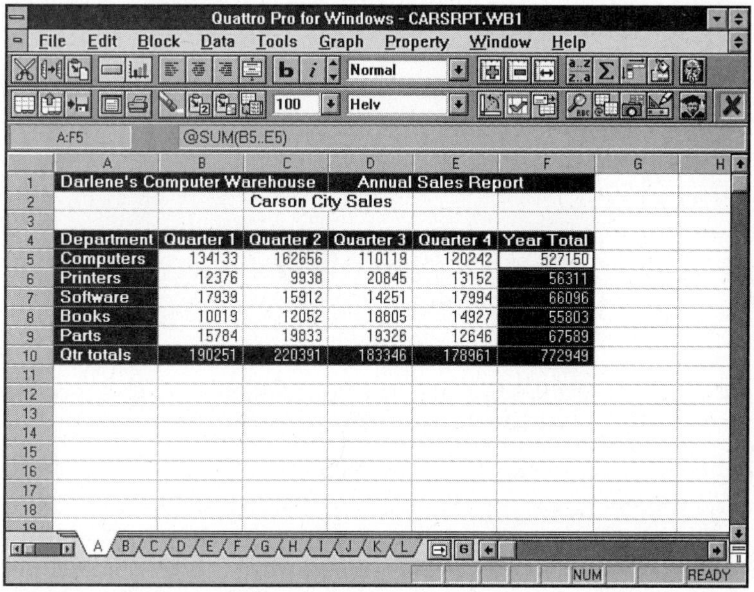

Fig. 5.8

Quattro Pro 5.0 for Windows enables you to select noncontiguous blocks.

For you to extend a block selection to create a three-dimensional block, the block address must include the page letters or page names. The three-dimensional block that includes cells B5..F10 on pages A and B, for example, can be specified as A:B5..B:F10 or A..B:B5..F10, depending on the application display 3-D syntax setting. You use the Ctrl+PgUp and Ctrl+PgDn key combinations to extend a block selection three-dimensionally while pointing. If you are selecting the block with the mouse, you can click a page tab to move the selector to the final page

in the block. Before you can extend the selection by clicking the page
tab, you must press and hold down Shift or press Shift+F7.

Fig. 5.9

The result of copying
a noncontiguous block
in one step.

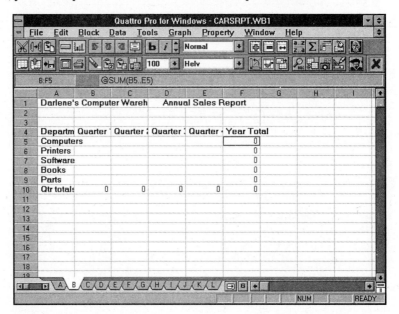

Specifying a Block with a Name

You also can specify a block in a dialog box using a name you assign to
the block. You can use up to 15 characters to name a block, and you
should use a descriptive name. You can use block names in formulas,
functions, commands, and macros.

You gain a number of advantages by using block names. First, block
names are easier to remember than block addresses—especially if a
block is noncontiguous. Second, typing a block name usually is easier
than pointing to a block in another part of the notebook. Third, macros
that use block names rather than cell addresses automatically adjust
after you move a block. Finally, block names also make formulas easier
to understand. The formula +QTR_1_TOTAL is easier to understand
than the formula +B10.

Whenever Quattro Pro 5.0 for Windows expects the address of a cell or
a block, you can specify a block name. You can enter a block name in
the Goto dialog box, for example, and Quattro Pro 5.0 for Windows
moves the cell selector to the upper left corner of the named block.

Creating Block Names with Block Names Create

You can use the **B**lock **N**ames **C**reate command to assign a name to a cell or a block. To create a block name, follow these steps:

1. Select the cell or block you want to name.

2. Choose **B**lock **N**ames **C**reate. The Create Name dialog box shown in figure 5.10 appears.

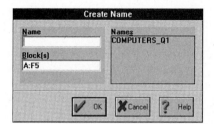

Fig. 5.10

The Create Name dialog box is used to create block names.

3. Type the block name and press Enter or click OK.

NOTE

If you type an existing block name after you preselected the block, Quattro Pro 5.0 for Windows replaces the existing block definition with the new name without warning you. If you have created formulas that contain this block name, the formulas automatically refer to the new block address and may produce results you don't expect.

Quattro Pro 5.0 for Windows does not distinguish between uppercase and lowercase letters; Block_1, block_1, and BLOCK_1 are equivalent block names. Follow these rules and cautions when creating block names:

■ Do not use spaces or the following characters in block names:

, ; + - * / & > < @ #

■ Do not start block names with numbers.

■ Do not create block names that also are cell addresses, column letters, or row numbers (such as A1, AA, or 199), names of keys (such as Edit), function names (such as @AVG), or advanced macro commands (such as WRITE).

■ Use descriptive block names and join parts of block names with the underscore (such as QTR_1_TOTALS).

Creating Block Names with Block Names Labels

You also can use the **Block Names Labels** command to create block names. With this command, you use labels already typed on a notebook page as block names for adjacent cells.

After you choose the **Block Names Labels** command, the Create Names From Labels dialog box shown in figure 5.11 appears. The Directions check boxes determine which cells are named using the labels. To name the cells to the right of the labels, choose **R**ight. To name the cells below the labels, choose **D**own. **U**p and **L**eft name cells above and to the left of the labels, respectively.

Fig. 5.11

The Create Names From Labels dialog box.

The Block Names Labels command ignores blank cells in the label block, so you can select several groups of labels at one time without harm. You should remember, however, that the **B**lock **N**ames **L**abels command creates single-cell blocks. If you need to create multiple-cell blocks, you must use the **B**lock **N**ames **C**reate command.

Creating Block Names with Block Names Auto Generate

 Quattro Pro 5.0 for Windows has another command you can use to generate block names automatically—**Block Names Auto Generate**. This command can generate block names for a row, a column, or for every cell in a selected block, using labels in the block.

After you choose the **Block Names Auto Generate** command, the Generate Block Names dialog box shown in figure 5.12 appears. The check boxes determine which cells the labels identify. To name the cells to the right of the labels, choose **R**ight of the leftmost column. To name the cells below the labels, choose **U**nder the top row. **A**bove the bottom row and **L**eft of rightmost column name cells above and to the left of the labels, respectively. The **Name** cells at intersections option names all cells in the block using the label cells in combination.

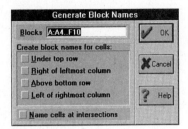

Fig. 5.12

The Generate Block Names dialog box.

In figure 5.12, the **Name** cells at intersections option creates the block name QUARTER 1_BOOKS for cell B8. The block names are created by concatenating (joining) the column label, an underscore, and the row label. If the existing labels are too long, Quattro Pro 5.0 for Windows cannot use the entire text of the intersecting labels to create the block names, because block names cannot contain more than 15 characters. Cell F7, for example, is named YEAR TO_SOFTWAR. Even with this limitation, you easily can understand the location of the named cells.

Deleting Block Names

Quattro Pro 5.0 for Windows has two commands that delete block names from the notebook. Use the **Block** Names **Delete** command to delete a single block name. You delete all block names at one time using the **Block** Names **Reset** command.

Deleting block names you no longer need allows you to select a name more easily from the now shorter list. You also save a small amount of memory when you delete unnecessary block names.

Listing All Block Names

A table of block names serves as important notebook documentation. Quattro Pro 5.0 for Windows creates a two-column table of block names and addresses using the **Block** Names **Make** Table command.

Be sure to select an area with enough room for the block name table, because the table overwrites any existing data without warning. A separate notebook page, which you may entitle *BlockTables*, is a good destination for the block name table. If you change the definition of a block name, or add or delete block names, the block name table is not updated automatically. You must issue the **B**lock **N**ames **M**ake Table command again to update the table.

Setting Column Widths

When you start a new notebook, all the columns on each spreadsheet page are set to the default column width of approximately nine characters. If columns are too narrow to display numeric data, asterisks appear rather than the numbers. If columns are too narrow for the length of labels and the cell to the right contains data, the labels are truncated. If columns are too wide, you may not see all the columns necessary to view the complete data, and you may not be able to print reports on the number of pages you want.

Whether a number fits in a cell depends on the column width, the numeric format, the font type, and font size. If a number appears as a series of asterisks, you need to change the column width, numeric format, font type, font size, or some combination of these factors.

Setting the Column Width for an Entire Notebook Page

You can change the default column width for an entire notebook page by using the Active Page Properties dialog box. You access the Active Page Properties dialog box by clicking the right mouse button while pointing to the page tab or by choosing **P**roperty Active **P**age. Select Default Width and enter the new default width in characters, inches, or centimeters—depending upon which Unit check box you choose.

Each page in a notebook has its own default column width setting. You set each page individually.

Setting the Column Width for One or More Columns

You can change the width of a single column or a group of columns. Explicitly setting a column width overrides the default width set for the page, so if you change the default column width for the page after you have set individual column widths, the columns you explicitly set do not change to the new page default.

To change a *single* column width with the mouse, follow these steps:

1. Point to the column border to the right of the column letter (in the spreadsheet frame). The mouse pointer changes to a horizontal double arrow.

2. Press and hold the left mouse button.

3. Drag the column border left or right until the column is the width you want. Release the mouse button.

When you are adjusting the column width, Quattro Pro 5.0 for Windows displays a dashed line to indicate the position of the new column border. If you move the right column border to the left of the left border, you hide the column.

To change the width of a *group* of columns at one time by using a mouse, follow these steps:

1. Highlight the columns you want to adjust by pointing to the column letter in the notebook frame and clicking the left mouse button (drag the mouse pointer to select adjacent columns).

    If the columns are not adjacent, hold down the Ctrl key as you select the columns. (See "Extending Block Selections" earlier in this chapter for more information on selecting noncontiguous blocks.)

2. With the mouse pointer in the highlighted column, press the right mouse button to activate the Active Block properties dialog box.

3. Select Column Width.

4. If you want to enter the column width in inches or centimeters, choose the appropriate check box under Unit.

5. If you want to reset the column width, select **R**eset Width to return the selected columns to the page default column width.

6. If you want to set the column width automatically based on the length of data, select Auto Width. If you select Auto Width, you can specify (in the Extra Character text box) that the column should be 0 to 40 characters wider than the data.

7. If you want to specify the column width, type the value in the Column width text box.

8. Choose OK to confirm the dialog box.

To change column widths using the keyboard, perform the following steps:

1. Be certain that the cell selector is in the column you want to adjust. If you want to adjust the width of adjacent columns, place the cell selector in the first column you want to adjust, hold down the Shift key, and move the cell selector to highlight each of the columns you want to adjust.

2. Choose **Property Current Object.**

3. Follow steps 3 through 8 in the preceding section.

 You also can click the Fit button on the SpeedBar to adjust the widths of columns automatically. Column widths that were set using the Auto Width setting or the Fit button remain at the current setting even when the length of data in the column changes. If you want the column width adjusted to fit new data, you must select the Auto Width setting or the Fit button again.

The width of columns set using the Auto Width setting or the Fit button depends on the number of rows that are selected when you adjust the width. If you select a single row, the column width adjusts to fit the longest data below the cell selector in the entire column. If you select more than one row, the column width adjusts to fit the cell with the longest data below the cell selector in the same column.

FOR RELATED INFORMATION

▶▶ "Applying the Available Formats," p. 190.

Setting Row Heights

You can adjust row heights in Quattro Pro 5.0 for Windows to make notebook entries easier to understand and more attractive. As you change fonts and point sizes, Quattro Pro 5.0 for Windows automatically adjusts row heights to fit, but you can override the default to create special effects or to add emphasis.

You can set the row height for an individual row or a group of rows at one time. You also can hide rows by setting their height to zero.

To adjust the height of a *single* row with the mouse, follow these steps:

1. Point to the row border just below the row number (in the spreadsheet frame). The mouse pointer changes to a vertical double arrow.

2. Press and hold down the left mouse button.

3. Drag the row border up or down until the row is the height you want. Release the mouse button.

When you are adjusting the row height, Quattro Pro 5.0 for Windows displays a dashed line to indicate the position of the new row border. If you move the lower row border above the top border, you hide the row.

To change the height of a *group* of rows at one time by using the mouse, follow these steps:

1. Highlight the rows you want to adjust. If the rows are not adjacent, hold down the Ctrl key as you select the rows. (See "Extending Block Selections" earlier in this chapter for more information on selecting noncontiguous blocks.)

2. Press the right mouse button to activate the Active Block properties dialog box.

3. Select Row Height.

4. If you want to enter the row height in inches or centimeters, select the appropriate check box under Unit.

5. If you want to reset the row height, choose **R**eset Height to return the selected rows to automatic.

6. If you want to specify the row height, type the value in the Row **H**eight text box.

7. Press Enter or click OK to confirm the dialog box.

To adjust row height using the keyboard, perform the following steps:

1. Be certain that the cell selector is in the row you want to adjust. If you want to adjust the width of adjacent rows, place the cell selector in the first row you want to adjust, hold down the Shift key, and move the cell selector to highlight each of the rows you want to adjust.

2. Choose **P**roperty **C**urrent Object.

3. Follow steps 3 through 7 in the preceding section.

▶▶ "Enhancing the Appearance of Data," p. 201.   **FOR RELATED** INFORMATION

Erasing and Deleting

You can remove part or all of a notebook in several ways. Any data that you remove is cleared from the notebook in memory but does not affect the notebook file on disk until you save the notebook file (see Chapter 8, "Managing Files"). Although the removed data is cleared from the notebook in memory, the **E**dit **U**ndo command can restore the data if you use the command before making any other changes. Also, because the on-disk notebook file is unaffected, you can recover deleted data if you do not save the changed notebook to disk.

Erasing Cells and Blocks

 You can use any of three commands to erase a cell or block: **E**dit **C**lear, **E**dit **C**ut, or **E**dit **C**lear Contents. The Del key functions as a keyboard shortcut for **E**dit **C**lear, the Cut button on the SpeedBar functions as a shortcut for **E**dit **C**ut, and Ctrl+B functions as a shortcut for **E**dit **C**lear Contents.

The **E**dit **C**lear command removes all data, attributes, and formats from the highlighted cell or block. To clear a cell or a block, you highlight the cell or block and press Del (or choose **E**dit **C**lear). If you accidentally clear a cell or block, immediately choose the **E**dit **U**ndo command before issuing any additional commands.

The **E**dit **C**ut command is similar to **E**dit **C**lear, except the data is placed on the Windows Clipboard. You can add data on the Clipboard to a notebook page using the **E**dit **P**aste command (covered later in this chapter) or to other Windows applications (see Chapter 8, "Managing Files").

Edit **C**lear Contents also is similar to **E**dit **C**lear, except this command affects only the data in the selected block. **E**dit **C**lear Contents does not remove attributes and formats from the highlighted cell or block.

Use **E**dit **C**lear when you want to quickly remove data that is no longer necessary. Use **E**dit **C**ut when you want to remove data from one area of a notebook and add the same data to other notebook locations or other applications. Use **E**dit **C**lear Contents when you want to remove data and later add new data that uses the existing attributes and formats.

Deleting Entire Rows, Columns, and Pages

After you erase cells using **E**dit Cut, **E**dit Clear, or **E**dit Clear Contents, the cells remain, but they are blank. In contrast, after you delete a row, column, or page, Quattro Pro 5.0 for Windows deletes the row, column, or notebook page and moves remaining data to fill the gap created by the deletion. The program also updates cell addresses in formulas (but not addresses in macros).

To delete a row, column, or page, use the **B**lock **D**elete command. Quattro Pro 5.0 for Windows displays the cascade menu from which you choose **R**ows, **C**olumns, or **P**ages. The Delete Rows, Delete Columns, or Delete Pages dialog box appears. Figure 5.13 shows the Delete Pages dialog box.

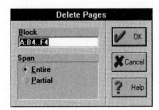

Fig. 5.13

The Delete Pages dialog box.

In the **B**lock text box, specify the block you want to delete. You can type the address, highlight cells, or preselect the block. Choose OK to confirm the dialog box and delete the block.

When you delete an area, Quattro Pro 5.0 for Windows moves data to fill the gap created by the deletion. If you delete a row, data below the deletion moves up on the current page. If you delete a column, data to the right of the deleted column moves to the left. If you delete a page, data on following pages moves forward in the notebook.

Formula references adjust to reflect the new addresses of the data. If you delete rows 5 and 6, for example, the formula @SUM(A1..A10) becomes @SUM(A1..A8). If a formula refers specifically to a deleted cell, however, the formula returns ERR.

If you delete rows, columns, or pages that are part of a named block, the block becomes smaller. If you delete a row, column, or page that contains one of the block borders, the block becomes undefined and any references to the block return ERR.

Deleting Partial Rows, Columns, and Pages

Sometimes when you want to delete a block of data, you want to delete only part of a row, column, or page. In other words, you want to delete specified data and move remaining data to fill the gap, but you do not want to remove data from surrounding rows, columns, or pages. Quattro Pro 5.0 for Windows enables you to specify the span of the deletion—whether the deletion affects the entire spreadsheet page or only the selected block.

Figure 5.14 shows a sample notebook page. Suppose that you want to delete the data in the highlighted block, C7..D9, and move the remaining data in columns C and D up to fill the gap without deleting data in rows 7, 8, or 9 in other columns. To accomplish this task you use a **B**lock **D**elete **R**ows **P**artial command.

Fig. 5.14

A single **B**lock **D**elete **R**ows **P**artial command can delete several partial rows in one step.

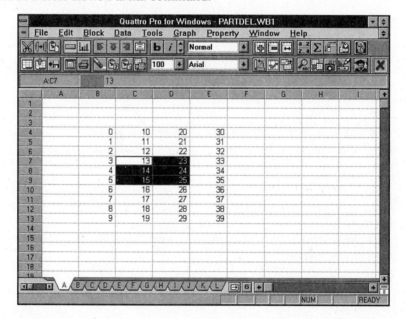

The Delete Rows, Delete Columns, and Delete Pages dialog boxes each include a Span field. To delete a partial row, column, or page, choose the **P**artial radio button (see fig. 5.15). Choose OK to confirm the dialog box and delete the partial row, column, or page. Figure 5.16 shows the result of deleting rows 7 through 9 in columns C and D.

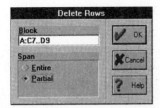

Fig. 5.15

Choose the **P**artial radio button in the Delete Rows dialog box to delete a partial row, column, or page.

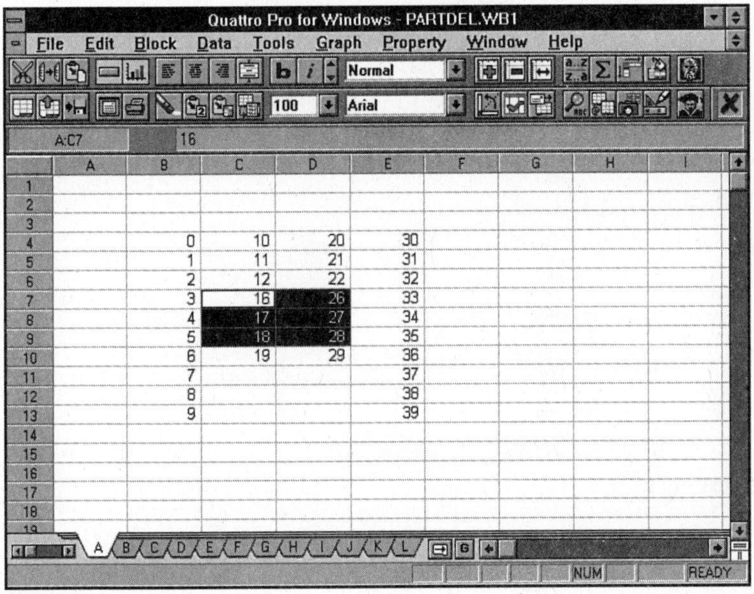

Fig. 5.16

The result of a partial row deletion.

◄◄ "Using the Undo Feature," p. 113.

►► "Saving Files," p. 273.

FOR RELATED INFORMATION

Inserting Rows, Columns, and Pages

Just as you can delete rows, columns, or pages, you also can insert them anywhere in the notebook with the **B**lock **I**nsert command. After you choose this command, Quattro Pro 5.0 for Windows displays a cascade menu with **R**ows, **C**olumns, **P**ages, and **F**ile selections. You choose which element you want to insert.

After you insert a row, column, page, or file, all existing data below, to the right, or on subsequent notebook pages moves to create room for the new data. Cell references in formulas and block names adjust automatically, but explicit cell addresses in macros do not adjust.

If you make an insertion in the middle of a block, the block expands to include the new rows, columns, or pages. Formulas referring to that block automatically include the added cells.

Row numbers, column letters, and page letters also adjust to reflect the insertions. If a formula refers to column D, for example, and you insert a new column to the left of column D, the formula adjusts to refer to column E.

To insert a row, column, page, or file, perform the following steps:

1. Move the cell selector to the cell where you want to begin inserting.

2. Highlight the number of rows, columns, or pages you want to insert.

3. Choose the **B**lock **I**nsert command and choose **R**ows, **C**olumns, **P**ages, or **F**ile.

4. To insert a partial row, column, or page, check the **P**artial check box.

5. To insert a file, specify the name of the file in the **F**ile name text box. In the **B**efore page text box, specify the notebook page that you want to follow the insertion.

6. Choose OK to confirm the dialog box and make the insertion.

Changing the Notebook Display

You can change the display of notebook windows in several ways. You can view notebook pages and graphs at the same time, compare data in two or more open notebooks, or view two different notebook pages or portions of the same notebook page. Chapter 3, "Using the Graphical User Interface," has more information on different ways to display multiple notebook windows. The following sections describe how you can split a single notebook window and view several pages of the same notebook.

Splitting a Window

Each open spreadsheet notebook appears in its own window. You can split a notebook window into two *panes* (sections) with the **W**indow **P**anes command. After you choose this command, the Panes dialog box appears (see fig 5.17). This technique is useful if you want to see parts of the notebook that do not fit in the window at the same time.

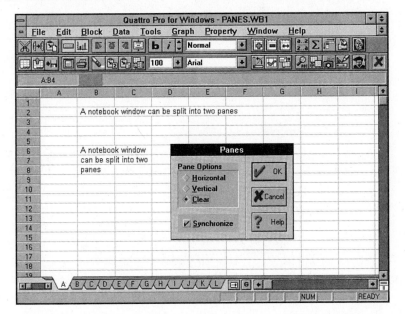

Fig. 5.17

The Panes dialog box.

To split a window with the mouse, point to the splitter box in the lower right corner of the window. The mouse pointer changes to a black, double vertical arrow when the pointer is positioned to create a horizontal split. If you move the pointer down slightly, it changes to a black, double horizontal arrow to indicate the pointer is positioned to create a vertical split. Hold down the left mouse button and move the pointer up to split the window horizontally or move the pointer left to split the window vertically. Release the mouse button when the dashed line is where you want the split.

A split window has two borders, two sets of page tabs, and two sets of scroll bars. Because of these elements, you cannot display as much data in a split window. Figure 5.18 shows a notebook window split into two horizontal panes.

Fig. 5.18

A notebook window split into two horizontal panes.

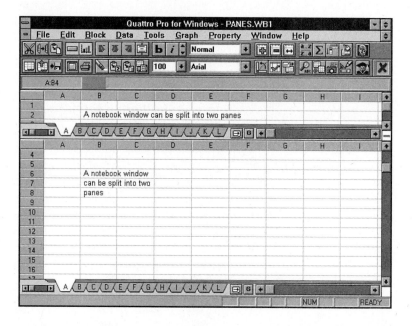

In a split window, you can change data in one pane and see how the change affects formulas in the other pane. A split window also is quite useful when you write macros, because you can write the macro in one pane and see the data the macro affects in the other pane.

Another common use for split windows is to display totals that normally are off-screen while you are entering data. You can split the window to see the totals in one pane and the data entry area in the other pane. You split the window vertically or horizontally depending on whether the two areas you want to see are in the same rows or columns.

At times, you may want to see two unrelated views of the notebook. Use the **W**indow **P**anes command to display the Panes dialog box. To enable the two panes to scroll separately, make sure that the **S**ynchronize check box is *not* checked. The two panes then are *unsynchronized*, which enables you to scroll to different areas in each pane without moving the display in the other pane.

To move between panes, press the F6 (Pane) key or point to the other window with the mouse pointer and click the left mouse button.

To remove the split and return the window to a single pane, use **W**indow **P**anes and choose the **C**lear radio button. Or you can point to the splitter box with the mouse, hold down the left mouse button, drag the box back to the lower right corner of the window, and release the button.

Displaying Several Pages

You can display different pages of the notebook by splitting the window into two panes and clicking the page tab or pressing Ctrl+PgUp or Ctrl+PgDn. Each pane can display a different page than the other pane displays.

You can split a single notebook window into two panes only and can display only two pages at one time as a result. If you need to see additional notebook pages at the same time, use the **W**indow **N**ew View command to display additional views of the same notebook.

FOR RELATED INFORMATION

◄◄ "Changing the Size and Position of a Window," p. 62.

Locking Titles On-Screen

Your notebook pages often are too large to display at one time. As you move the cell selector to display more areas of the page, data scrolls off the opposite edge of the display. Understanding data then can be difficult because the raw numbers appear without the accompanying labels. You no longer can tell which data belongs with which label.

To prevent titles from scrolling off the screen, you use the **W**indow **L**ocked Titles command. After you choose this command, the Locked Titles dialog box shown in figure 5.19 appears. You can lock the rows above the cell selector by choosing the **H**orizontal radio button. To lock the columns left of the cell selector, choose the **V**ertical radio button. You can lock both horizontal and vertical titles by choosing the **B**oth radio button. The **C**lear radio button unlocks titles.

Before you use the **W**indow **L**ocked Titles command, you need to position the cell selector. If you are locking horizontal titles, place the cell selector in the row below the last row you want locked. If you are locking vertical titles, place the cell selector in the column to the right of the last column you want locked. If you are locking both horizontal and vertical titles, place the cell selector in the row just below and the column just right of the intersection of the rows and columns you want to lock. Figure 5.20 shows the result of placing the cell selector in cell B2 before issuing the **W**indow **L**ocked Titles command and choosing **B**oth. The cell selector then moves to cell H25, the last cell in the database.

Fig. 5.19

The Locked Titles dialog box.

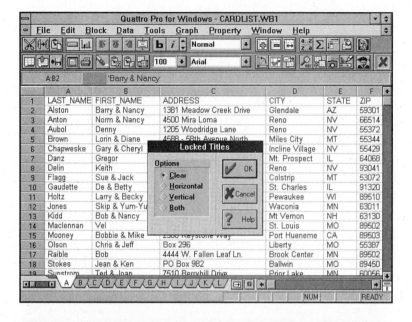

Fig. 5.20

Titles locked on-screen.

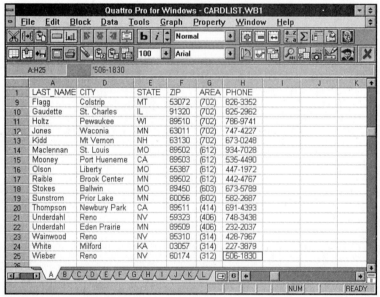

When titles are locked, pressing the Home key moves the cell selector to the position below and to the right of the titles rather than to cell A1. When you move the mouse pointer into the titles area, the mouse pointer becomes a circle with a diagonal slash—indicating you cannot select any cells. You also cannot use the direction keys to move the cell selector into the locked titles. You can move the cell selector into the locked titles only by using GoTo (F5). When you use GoTo to move into the locked titles area, the title rows and columns appear twice. You can clear the duplicate title display by using the direction keys to move at least one screen right and down.

Protecting and Hiding Spreadsheet Data

A typical Quattro Pro 5.0 for Windows notebook contains numbers, labels, formulas, and sometimes macros. When you build a notebook file, you often include data that you should not change after entering. After you set up a notebook, for example, you probably do not want the titles and captions to change. When you implement the final procedure for calculating a report, you probably do not want someone to make changes in formulas, either.

Because notebooks usually contain both the data input areas and the formulas used to calculate results, you run the risk of damage or changes to your formulas whenever someone enters data. If a formula changes, all the calculated results may be wrong. Finding the source of errors in results can be difficult, especially because most Quattro Pro 5.0 for Windows reports show only the results of calculations, not the formulas used to calculate the results.

If different people add data to the notebook, one person may want to change a formula that he or she feels is incorrect. For example, a formula may use factors to adjust for growth or inflation. If each department manager decides on factors favorable to his or her department instead of using the company-wide factors supplied by the Accounting Department, comparing reports accurately from different departments is impossible.

Quattro Pro 5.0 for Windows offers a number of features that protect data from accidental or deliberate change. You also can password-protect a file when you save it. Anyone who does not know the password cannot open or retrieve the file.

Protecting Cells from Change

Every notebook has areas containing formulas and labels that do not change over time. Other areas contain data that can change. You can protect areas that do not change and still allow changes to other cells by setting the Active Page Protection property to Enable and setting the Active Block Protection property to Unprotect for areas that can change.

You enable protection for the active page with the mouse by pointing to the page tab and clicking the right mouse button. With the keyboard, choose **P**roperty Active **P**age. Select Protection and check **E**nable. After you enable protection, no one can make changes to the data on the page unless the user disables protection for the page or a specified block. To allow changes to a specified block on a protected notebook page, highlight the block, point to the block, and click the right mouse button to activate the Active Block dialog box. With the keyboard, choose **P**roperty **C**urrent Object. Select Protection and check the **U**nprotect check box.

TIP

As you build a spreadsheet notebook, you probably do not want any protection enabled so that you can make entries without specifically unprotecting a cell. After you finish your model, enable protection for any pages that contain formulas, macros, or other data that must not change. Unprotect data entry cells and any cells that a macro must change, such as counter variables.

If you need to change a protected cell, you can unprotect the cell, change it, and then protect the cell again. You also can turn off protection for the page, make your changes, and then turn protection on again.

If you use the protection features in Quattro Pro 5.0 for Windows, remember that anyone can disable page and block protection. You should not depend on these features to hide confidential or sensitive data. You should save notebook files containing confidential or sensitive data using a password to prevent unauthorized persons from retrieving the file.

For greater protection, consider setting the notebook Password Level property. This property sets security limits so that only users who know the correct password can view formulas, show hidden notebooks, or open a notebook. To apply password protection, choose **P**roperty Active **N**otebook Password Level. Choose **N**one to use no password protection, **L**ow to require a password before displaying formulas,

Medium to require a password before displaying hidden notebooks, or **H**igh to require a password before opening a notebook. If you choose **L**ow, **M**edium, or **H**igh, the user is prompted to enter the same password twice after pressing Enter or clicking OK. Users must remember the exact password (including whether each character is uppercase or lowercase), otherwise they are unable to view formulas, show hidden notebooks, or open the notebook.

> **NOTE**
>
> If you save and then later reopen a notebook that has **L**ow or **M**edium level password protection, you cannot access the notebook Password Level property unless you supply the password and notebook name when you open Quattro Pro 5.0 for Windows. To perform this step, you must start Quattro Pro 5.0 for Windows using the Windows Program Manager **F**ile **R**un command. In the Command Line edit field, enter the command to start Quattro Pro 5.0 for Windows, a space, the notebook name, another space, and **/S** followed immediately by the password.

Hiding a Block of Data

If you do not want to use password protection to hide formulas or notebooks, you can hide data so it's not easily visible. You cannot use the following method to hide data from someone who knows Quattro Pro 5.0 for Windows, but you at least can make the data difficult to find.

To hide a block of data, you apply the Hidden numeric format to the block. A cell with the hidden format appears as a blank cell in the notebook, but the cell's contents still display when the cell selector is on the cell. If you place the block in a remote area of a page far back in the notebook and then apply the Hidden format, your chances of keeping the data hidden are somewhat better.

To apply the Hidden format, highlight the block to select it; click the right mouse button while pointing to the block or choose **P**roperty **C**urrent Object. Select Numeric Format Hidden and choose OK to confirm the dialog box and apply the format.

Hiding Columns and Rows

Quattro Pro 5.0 for Windows enables you to hide entire columns and rows. Hidden columns and rows retain their column letters and row numbers. Formulas that reference cells in hidden columns or rows produce the same results whether the cells are hidden or not.

To hide columns or rows, perform the following steps:

1. Highlight the block containing the columns or rows you want to hide.

2. Click the right mouse button while pointing to the highlighted block or choose **P**roperty **C**urrent Object.

3. In the Active Block dialog box, select Reveal/Hide.

4. Check **C**olumns or **R**ows, depending on what you want to hide, and check **H**ide as the operation (see fig. 5.21).

Fig. 5.21

Hiding columns using the Active Block dialog box.

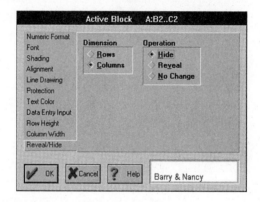

5. Choose OK to confirm the dialog box.

Figure 5.22 shows the notebook page with columns B and C hidden. The notebook frame clearly shows a jump from column A directly to column D. You can make the missing columns or rows less obvious by removing the column borders or row borders from the page. To remove these borders, point to the page tab and click the right mouse button or choose **P**roperty Active **P**age. Select Borders and uncheck **R**ow Borders to remove row borders; uncheck **C**olumn Borders to remove column borders.

When you print a report, Quattro Pro 5.0 for Windows does not print any data contained in hidden rows or columns. Hidden rows and columns remain hidden when you are in POINT mode.

FOR RELATED INFORMATION

▶▶ "Preventing Areas from Printing," p. 396.

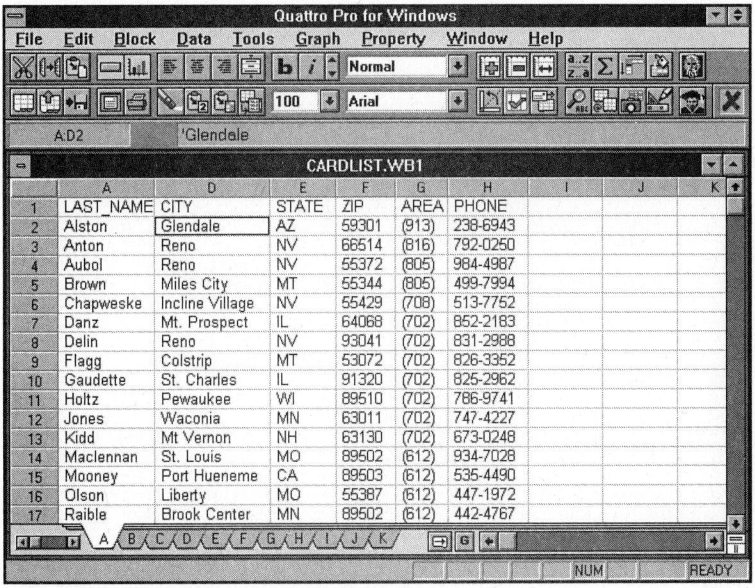

Fig. 5.22

Columns B and C are hidden on this notebook page.

Recalculating Data

When a value in a cell changes, Quattro Pro 5.0 for Windows automatically recalculates any other cell that depends on the changed value. This automatic recalculation of formulas represents a major difference between electronic spreadsheets such as Quattro Pro 5.0 for Windows and manual calculation methods. Although this recalculation normally is automatic, you can tell Quattro Pro 5.0 for Windows that you want to control recalculation manually.

Quattro Pro 5.0 for Windows has two methods of calculating results automatically. The default method performs background calculations, which occur between keystrokes. Background calculation enables you to continue working with Quattro Pro 5.0 for Windows while calculations occur. The Automatic recalculation setting, on the other hand, performs recalculations in the foreground and prevents you from using Quattro Pro 5.0 for Windows until the calculation finishes.

To change the recalculation setting for a notebook, perform the following steps:

1. Point to the notebook title bar and click the right mouse button or choose Property Active Notebook. The Active Notebook dialog box shown in figure 5.23 appears. The first notebook property, Recalc Settings, is selected by default.

Fig. 5.23

The Active Notebook dialog box.

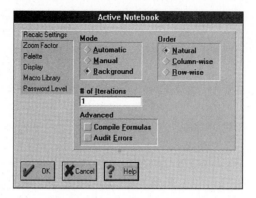

2. Choose the recalculation mode by checking **A**utomatic, **M**anual, or **B**ackground.

3. Choose the order of recalculation by checking **N**atural, **C**olumn-wise, or **R**ow-wise.

4. To change the number of iterations—the number of times formulas are recalculated—specify a value in the # of **I**terations text box.

5. To compile the notebook formulas—making formula recalculation faster in some cases—check Compile **F**ormulas.

6. To highlight the source of errors that cause cells to display ERR or NA, check Audit **E**rrors.

7. Choose OK to confirm the dialog box.

If you choose manual recalculation, Quattro Pro 5.0 for Windows recalculates formulas only when you press Calc (F9) or when a macro executes a {CALC} command.

Quattro Pro 5.0 for Windows normally uses *natural order* recalculation. Natural order recalculation causes formulas that depend on other formulas to recalculate after the formulas they depend upon. If the formula in cell B10 depends on the results of a formula in cell G99, for example, B10 recalculates after G99.

You also can instruct Quattro Pro 5.0 for Windows to use **C**olumn-wise or **R**ow-wise recalculation. **C**olumn-wise recalculation starts at cell A:A1 and continues down the column, then column B, and so on. **R**ow-wise recalculation starts in cell A:A1 and continues across row 1, then row 2, and so on.

Generally, you should leave Quattro Pro 5.0 for Windows set for **N**atural order recalculation. Usually, the only instance when **C**olumn-wise or

Row-wise is necessary occurs when you create an intentional *circular reference*. A circular reference is a formula that depends, directly or indirectly, on its own value. Quattro Pro 5.0 for Windows advises you when a circular reference exists by displaying the CIRC indicator in the status line. Circular references almost always are errors, and you should correct the circular reference instead of changing the recalculation order.

You use the # of **I**terations option in the Recalc Settings selection in the dialog box to specify the number of iterations to perform—the number of times to recalculate. Unless a circular reference exists, the default setting of 1 is sufficient. When a circular reference exists, however, you often need to recalculate several times to reach the point where values become stable—if they ever do. Generally, an erroneous circular reference, such as an @SUM function that includes its own cell address in the list of values to sum, continues to change regardless of the number of iterations. You should design a deliberate circular reference so that each recalculation produces a smaller change in value. Chapter 7, "Using Functions," has more information on proper use of the Quattro Pro 5.0 for Windows functions.

The Compile **F**ormulas option can result in faster notebook recalculations, especially on systems that have a Pentium or 80486DX processor, or an 80386 processor combined with an 80387 numeric coprocessor. Systems with an 80486SX processor, an 80386 processor without an 80387 numeric coprocessor, or an 80286 processor probably do not benefit much from this option. If you select the Compile **F**ormulas option, the first recalculation is somewhat slower as the formulas compile. Subsequent recalculations likely are faster. If you use the default **B**ackground recalculation mode, you may not notice much difference because you can continue to work while the notebook recalculates.

You use the Audit **E**rrors option to help locate the sources of errors that cause cells to display ERR or NA. After you check this option, the cell displays the address of the cell that is causing the error instead of displaying ERR or NA. You may need to adjust column widths to display the address rather than a row of asterisks.

> **NOTE**
>
> If a cell displays its own address when the Audit **E**rrors option is checked, the formula contained within the cell—rather than another cell—is the source of the error.

Moving Data

Quattro Pro 5.0 for Windows provides two sets of commands to move data: the **B**lock **M**ove command and the combination of the **E**dit **C**ut and **E**dit **P**aste commands. You use **B**lock **M**ove to move a block of data or a block of formulas to a single destination anywhere in the notebook. You use the **E**dit **C**ut command to move data from a notebook to the Windows Clipboard. Use the **E**dit **P**aste command to copy data from the Clipboard to a different location in the notebook, to another notebook, or to another Windows application. You can copy the same data many times with the **E**dit **P**aste command as long as you do not copy other information to the Clipboard.

Quattro Pro 5.0 for Windows also provides a very convenient method of moving data with the mouse: *drag-and-drop*. To move data using the drag-and-drop method, perform the following steps:

1. Select the block of data you want to move. The block can be any size, including a single cell.

2. Point at the selected block and hold down the left mouse button until the mouse pointer changes to a hand.

3. Move the mouse pointer to the upper left corner of the destination block. As you move the mouse pointer, Quattro Pro 5.0 for Windows displays an outline the size of the selected block.

4. Release the mouse button to drop the block of data in the new location.

To copy—rather than move—the selected block of data, hold down the Ctrl key when you point to the block in step 2.

When you move data, it overwrites any existing data in the destination location. Be sure the destination has enough room to accommodate the data you're moving.

TIP

If the mouse pointer changes to a hand too quickly when you are selecting a block, adjust the **P**roperty **A**pplication Delay Time property. The default delay time is 500 ms—one-half second. Try a slightly higher setting, such as 750 ms.

You also can use the Cut and Paste buttons on the SpeedBar to move data. The Cut button is the equivalent of the **E**dit **C**ut command, and the Paste button is the equivalent of the **Edit Paste** command. See Chapter 3, "Using the Graphical User Interface," for more information on using the SpeedBar.

Moving a Single Cell or a Block

When you create a notebook, you often need to move data or formulas from one place to another. As you create the notebook, for example, you may concentrate on developing formulas that produce the results you want; later you may give more concern to the layout and appearance of reports you intend to print.

You should understand how moving data and formulas in Quattro Pro 5.0 for Windows differs from copying data and formulas. When you move data, any formulas that refer to the moved data update automatically to refer to the same data in its new location. When you copy data, formulas referring to the original data location continue to refer to the same location. When you move formulas, the formulas do not change. When you copy formulas, the formulas may or may not change, depending on the types of references the formulas contain. See a following section, "Copying Data," for more information on copying data.

When you use the **B**lock **M**ove command, the moved data includes the same formulas and values, as well as the same alignment, fonts, and numeric formats. Column widths and row heights do not move, however. The source cells still exist after the move, but they are empty.

To move data and formulas with the **B**lock **M**ove command, follow these steps:

1. Select the cell or block you want to move.

2. Choose the **B**lock **M**ove command. The Block Move dialog box shown in figure 5.24 appears.

3. Press Tab or use the mouse to move the highlight to the **To** text box. Use the direction keys or the mouse to select the destination for the data, or type the destination address in the text box.

4. Press Enter or click OK to confirm the dialog box and move the data.

To specify the **F**rom and **T**o blocks, you can type the cell addresses, highlight the blocks, or enter block names. After you preselect a block, as you just did in step 1, the address appears in both the **F**rom and **T**o text boxes. You can use the preselected block as the source or destination of the move.

Fig. 5.24

The Block Move dialog box.

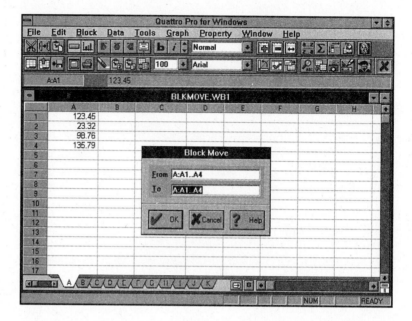

You also can move data with the **Edit Cut** and **Edit Paste** commands. You cannot use these commands to move formulas, because the formulas change to reflect their new location—unless the formulas use absolute rather than relative addressing. (See "Copying Formulas" later in this chapter for information on absolute and relative addressing.)

To move data with the **Edit Cut** and **Edit Paste** commands, follow these steps:

1. Highlight the cell or block containing the data you want to move.

2. Choose **Edit Cut** or click the Cut button on the SpeedBar.

3. Position the cell selector in the cell where you want to move the data.

4. Choose **Edit Paste** or click the Paste button on the SpeedBar.

The following guidelines determine the number and type of copies these commands create:

■ If the data moved to the Clipboard with the **Edit Cut** command was from a single cell, one copy of the data will be added to each highlighted cell after you choose **Edit Paste**.

■ If the data moved to the Clipboard with the **Edit Cut** command was from several rows in a single column, one copy of the data will be added to each highlighted column after you choose **Edit Paste.**

■ If the data moved to the Clipboard with the **Edit Cut** command was from several columns in a single row, one copy of the data will be added to each highlighted row after you choose **Edit Paste.**

■ If the data moved to the Clipboard with the **Edit Cut** command was from several rows and several columns, one copy of the data will be added to the spreadsheet page starting at the highlighted cell after you choose **Edit Paste.**

Three-dimensional data always creates a three-dimensional copy. If the source or destination data block includes more than one page, the same rules that apply to rows and columns also apply to the page dimension.

If you want additional copies of the same data, do not use any additional **Edit Cut** or **Edit Copy** commands. **Edit Paste** makes a copy of the data from the Clipboard, and the Clipboard holds only the most recent **Edit Cut** or **Edit Copy** contents.

> **NOTE**
>
> If you move data to a block that already contains data, Quattro Pro 5.0 for Windows replaces the existing data with the moved data. In some cases you may want to replace the data, but usually you do not. Use care when moving data to avoid moving data to cells that contain formulas or are used in a formula.

Suppose that you want to replace the numbers in D3..D10 with the numbers in A3..A10. Figure 5.25 shows the result of using the **Block Move** command to move A3..A10 to D3..D10. The formula in D12 changes from @SUM(D3..D10) to @SUM(ERR).

You must reenter the formula in D12 unless you immediately use **Edit Undo** to reverse the **Block Move** command. You must correct every formula in the notebook that refers to cells in the block D3..D10. A large notebook can have hundreds of formulas that refer to the same cells; finding and correcting each of these formulas can be a time-consuming project.

If you move one corner of a block used in a formula, the block expands or contracts, and the formula adjusts. A common use of the **Block Move** command is to move data and formulas to make room for additional data.

Fig. 5.25

The result of moving cells A3..A10 to D3..D10.

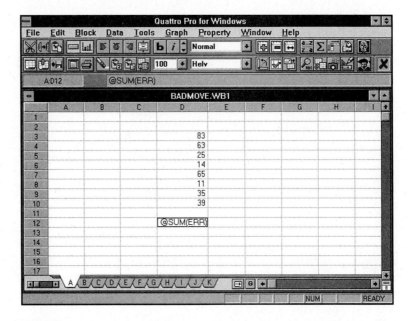

Figure 5.26 shows two blocks that contain data and formulas. (The formulas were formatted with Text format to show the contents rather than the results of the formulas.) The upper block, cells B3..E5, shows formulas that sum the block of columns from B through D. The lower block, cells B8..F10, shows the result of using the **B**lock **M**ove command to move the data and formulas from columns D and E to columns E and F. Each of the formulas in the lower block adjusted automatically to include the new, expanded data block.

> **NOTE**
>
> Inserting or deleting partial rows or partial columns often is an attractive alternative to using the **B**lock **M**ove command to expand or contract a block. The commands for inserting or deleting partial rows or partial columns are covered in earlier sections of this chapter.

Moving Formats and Data Types

Sometimes you may want to move the formatting and style properties from one cell or block to another without adding any data. You also may want to clear the data from a cell or a block but retain the formatting and style properties. To move the formatting and style properties, you use the **E**dit C**u**t and **E**dit Paste Special commands.

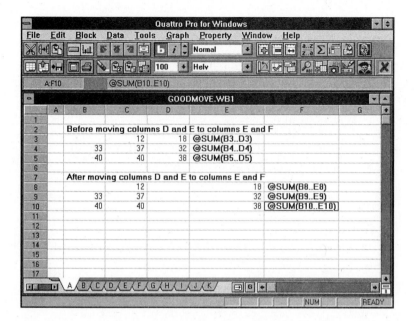

Fig. 5.26

Formulas adjust automatically when **B**lock **M**ove expands or contracts a block.

The **Edit Cut** command removes all data, formatting, and style properties from the highlighted block and places the information on the Clipboard. The **E**dit Paste Special command enables you to control which information is pasted back into the notebook. Figure 5.27 shows the Paste Special dialog box.

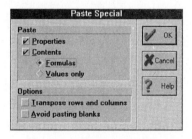

Fig. 5.27

The Paste Special dialog box.

The **E**dit Paste Special command is available only when the Clipboard contains data from Quattro Pro 5.0 for Windows. If the Clipboard contains data from another Windows application, the **E**dit Paste Special command is dimmed.

NOTE

The **Properties** check box controls whether to copy the formatting and style properties to the spreadsheet. The **C**ontents check box controls whether to copy formulas, values, or no data. If you choose the

Contents check box, you then can choose **Formulas** or **Values** only to specify whether to use formulas or the current values of formulas.

To move the formatting and style properties from one cell or block to another without adding any data, or to clear the data from a cell or block and retain the formatting and style properties, follow these steps:

1. Highlight the source cell or block.

2. Choose **Edit Cut** or click the Cut button on the SpeedBar.

3. Highlight the destination cell or block.

4. Choose **Edit Paste Special**. The Paste Special dialog box appears.

5. Uncheck the **Contents** check box.

6. Choose OK to confirm the dialog box and paste the formatting and style properties into the highlighted block.

FOR RELATED   INFORMATION

▶▶ "Applying the Available Formats," p. 190.

Copying Data

Quattro Pro 5.0 for Windows has two primary sets of commands for copying data and formulas. The **Block Copy** command and the combination of the **Edit Copy** and **Edit Paste** commands perform nearly the same function. The combination of the **Edit Copy** and **Edit Paste** commands uses the Windows Clipboard, which makes the task of creating multiple copies slightly easier. Also, both **Edit Copy** and **Edit Paste** have shortcut buttons on the SpeedBar, which makes their use a little easier.

Quattro Pro 5.0 for Windows provides the convenient drag-and-drop method of copying data with the mouse. To copy data using the drag-and-drop method, perform the following steps:

1. Select the block of data you want to move.

2. Point at the selected block, hold down the Ctrl key, and then hold down the left mouse button until the mouse pointer becomes a hand.

3. Move the mouse pointer to the upper left corner of the destination block. As you move the mouse pointer, Quattro Pro 5.0 for Windows displays an outline the size of the selected block.

4. Release the mouse button to copy the block of data at the new location.

Cell contents as well as formatting and style properties copy to the destination block. When you copy data, the duplicate cells replace everything that was in the destination block before the copy. To copy the formatting and style properties but not the cell contents, use the Edit Paste Special command rather than Edit Paste. See the preceding section, "Moving Formats and Data Types," for more information on the Edit Paste Special command.

Copying is one of the most frequent operations in Quattro Pro 5.0 for Windows, and the copy operation can be simple or complex. The following sections describe the commands and procedures you use to copy formulas and data.

Deciding Which Copy Command to Use

Although you can copy data and formulas with the Block Copy command or the combination of the Edit Copy and Edit Paste commands, deciding which method to use can be difficult.

If you want to make multiple copies of the same formulas or data in several notebook locations, you probably want to use the Edit Copy/ Edit Paste commands. After you place data on the Clipboard with Edit Copy, you can make as many copies as you like using Edit Paste.

If you want to make a single copy only, either command works well with one exception. Use Block Copy if you have other data on the Clipboard that you still want to use. Block Copy does not use the Clipboard, so using Block Copy does not change the Clipboard contents.

You even may find situations where you want to use Block Copy to copy data from one block to the destination block. Then you use a combination of Edit Copy and Edit Paste Special to copy the formatting and style properties from *another* block to the destination block.

Copying the Contents of a Single Cell or a Block

When you copy data, the copy contains the same labels, values, formatting, and style properties as the original data. Column widths and row heights do not copy, although row heights in the new location may adjust automatically to the incoming data if necessary. The data in the original location remains unchanged.

You can copy a single cell or a block to another part of the same notebook page, to another notebook page, or to another open notebook. You can make a single copy or multiple copies at the same time. To copy data with the **B**lock **C**opy command, follow these steps:

1. Highlight the cell or block you want to copy.

2. Choose the **B**lock **C**opy command. The Block Copy dialog box shown in figure 5.28 appears.

Fig. 5.28

The Block Copy dialog box.

3. Press Tab to highlight the To text box.

4. Type the destination address, or use the direction keys or the mouse to highlight the destination block.

5. Choose OK to confirm the dialog box and copy the block.

Quattro Pro 5.0 for Windows copies the data, overwriting existing data in the destination block.

You can specify both the **F**rom and **T**o blocks by typing cell addresses, entering block names, or highlighting the cells in the block. If you preselect a block, it appears in both the **F**rom and **T**o text boxes.

You can use the **M**odel copy option to make a copy that uses the **F**rom block as a model for the **T**o block. If you check **M**odel copy, formula references—even absolute references—adjust to fit the **T**o block (see "Copying Formulas" later in this chapter for more information on formula references). In addition, if you check **M**odel copy, you can specify whether to copy **F**ormula cells, **V**alue cells, **P**roperties, **O**bjects, or **R**ow/Column sizes.

You also can use the **E**dit **C**opy/**E**dit **P**aste commands to copy data. These commands use the Windows Clipboard to hold the data. Because they use the Clipboard, you can use these commands to copy data to and from other Windows applications. Neither command uses a dialog box; the commands execute as soon as you select them.

To copy data with the **E**dit **C**opy/**E**dit **P**aste commands, follow these steps:

1. Highlight the cell or block you want to copy.

2. Choose **E**dit **C**opy or click the Copy button on the SpeedBar.

3. Move the cell selector to the upper left cell of the destination block.

4. Choose **E**dit **P**aste or click the Paste button on the SpeedBar.

Copying Contents Multiple Times

When you copy data, the dimensions of both the source and destination blocks determine how many copies result. The following rules show how the sizes of the source and destination blocks affect the number of copies produced:

- If the source block is a single cell, a copy of the data will be added to each highlighted cell in the destination block.

- If the source block includes several rows in a single column, a copy of the data will be added to each highlighted column in the destination block.

- If the source block includes several columns in a single row, a copy of the data will be added to each highlighted row in the destination block.

- If the source block includes several rows and several columns, a copy of the data will be added to the spreadsheet page starting at the highlighted cell.

Three-dimensional data always creates a three-dimensional copy. If the source or destination data block includes more than one page, the same rules that apply to rows and columns also apply to the page dimension.

To create multiple copies of the contents of a single cell or a block of cells using the **E**dit **C**opy/**E**dit **P**aste commands, follow these steps:

1. Highlight the cell or block of cells you want to copy.

2. Choose **E**dit **C**opy or click the Copy button on the SpeedBar.

3. Highlight the entire destination block.

4. Choose **E**dit **P**aste or click the Paste button on the SpeedBar.

Copying Formulas

Copying formulas in Quattro Pro 5.0 for Windows is more complex than copying data because of the way the program stores addresses in formulas. Addresses may be *relative*, referring to column, row, and page offsets from the formula cell; *absolute*, always referring to a specific cell; or *mixed*, a combination of relative and absolute.

Copying a Formula with Relative Addressing

If you enter the formula **+B2** in cell C5, Quattro Pro 5.0 for Windows does not store the formula quite the way you may expect. The formula tells Quattro Pro 5.0 for Windows to add the value of the cell one column to the left and three rows above C5. When you copy this formula from C5 to D6, Quattro Pro 5.0 for Windows uses the same relative formula but displays the formula as +C3. This method of storing cell references is called *relative addressing*. After you copy a formula that uses relative addressing, Quattro Pro 5.0 for Windows automatically adjusts the new formula so its cell references are in the same relative location as they were in the original location.

Usually you want formulas to adjust to the new location. Relative addressing enables you to create a formula in one location and copy it to other locations to process different data.

Copying a Formula with Absolute Addressing

Sometimes you do not want a formula to address new locations after you copy the formula. You may, for example, create a formula that refers to data in a single cell, such as an interest rate or a growth factor percentage. Formulas that always refer to the same cell address, regardless of where you copy the formula, use *absolute addressing*.

To specify an absolute address, type a dollar sign ($) before each part of the address you want to remain absolutely the same. The formula +$B:$C$10, for example, always refers to cell C10 on notebook page B regardless of where you copy the formula.

You can enter dollar signs while you are typing a formula or while you are editing the cell. To return a formula to relative addressing, edit the formula and remove the dollar signs.

Copying a Formula with Mixed Addressing

You also can create formulas that use *mixed addressing*, in which some elements of the cell addresses are absolute and other elements are relative. You can create a formula, for example, that always refers to the same row but adjusts its column reference as you copy the formula to another column. Figure 5.29 shows an example of a notebook model that calculates loan payments for a series of different terms and interest rates.

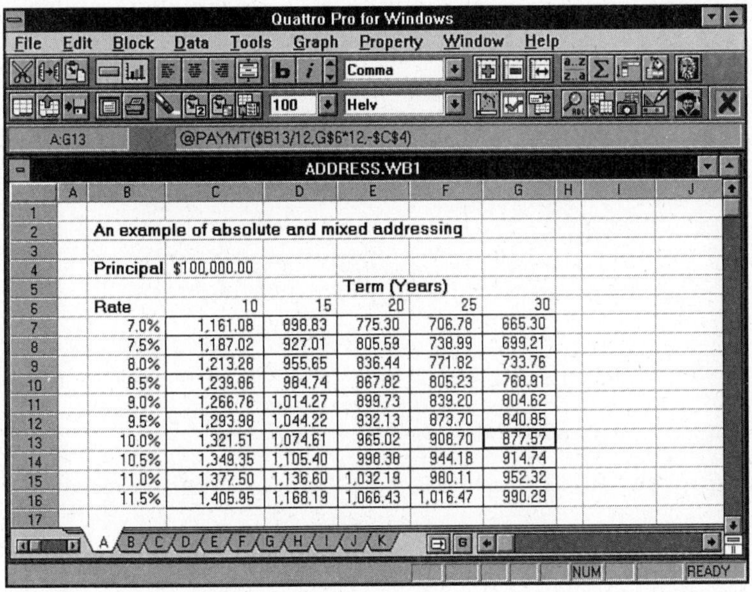

Fig. 5.29

Formulas with both absolute and mixed addressing.

In this example, a formula was created in cell C7 and copied to the block C7..G16. The first argument for the @PAYMT function is the interest rate, which is in column B. As the formula copies from column C to columns D through G, the first formula argument must continue to refer to column B. As the formula copies to rows 8 through 16, however, the first formula argument must adjust to refer to the same row as the new formula copy. Therefore, the argument must use mixed addressing that is column absolute and row relative. In cell G13, you can see the first argument is $B13/12, which divides the annual interest rate in column B by 12 to produce the monthly interest rate.

The second function argument always refers to the row of loan terms but adjusts to the correct column. Therefore, the argument must use mixed addressing that is row absolute and column relative. In cell G13, the second term is G$6*12, which multiplies the term in years in row 6 by 12 to produce the number of monthly payments.

The final argument, the loan principal amount, must be the same for all copies of the formula. This term uses both row and column absolute addressing and appears in the formula as -$C$4, which always refers to the principal amount in cell C4.

After you create a formula using the proper mix of relative and absolute addressing, you can copy the formula to create a table of formulas performing the same calculation using different terms, as shown in figure 5.29. For more information on Quattro Pro 5.0 for Windows functions, see Chapter 7, "Using Functions."

Figure 5.30 shows examples of the different addressing types in Quattro Pro 5.0 for Windows.

Transposing Data while Copying

At times, data may be in a more convenient format if you transpose the data from rows to columns or from columns to rows. Quattro Pro 5.0 for Windows provides two methods for transposing data, depending on whether you want to use the Windows Clipboard.

To transpose data using the Windows Clipboard, perform the following steps:

1. Place the data on the Windows Clipboard using the **Edit Copy** or **Edit Cut** command.

2. Choose **Edit Paste Special**.

3. Check the **Transpose rows and columns** check box.

4. Choose OK to confirm the dialog box.

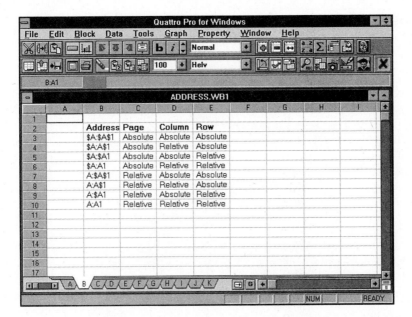

Fig. 5.30

Examples of the different addressing types in Quattro Pro 5.0 for Windows.

To transpose data without using the Windows Clipboard, perform the following steps:

1. Highlight the block you want to transpose.

2. Choose **B**lock **T**ranspose.

3. In the **T**o text box, specify the upper left corner of the destination block.

4. Choose OK to confirm the dialog box.

CAUTION

When you transpose rows and columns, Quattro Pro 5.0 for Windows attempts to adjust correctly cell addressing in any formulas. You may find, however, that formulas in a transposed block refer to cells other than what you intended. Use caution when transposing a block containing formulas and always verify the formulas after transposing the block.

Finding and Replacing Data

Edit **S**earch and Replace finds or replaces characters in a block of labels and formulas, much like the search-and-replace feature in most word processors. With **E**dit **S**earch and Replace, you can replace function arguments, modify a series of formulas by replacing a cell reference, or make global changes in a database.

When you choose **E**dit **S**earch and Replace, the Search/Replace dialog box shown in figure 5.31 appears. You can specify the block to search, what to search for or replace, what type of cell entries to search, whether to require a complete or partial match, the direction of the search, and whether the search should be case-sensitive (requiring an exact match of upper- and lowercase characters).

Fig. 5.31

The Search/Replace dialog box.

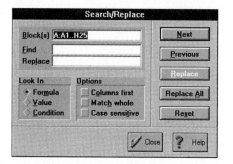

Suppose that you have a database containing names, addresses, phone numbers, and so on. The telephone company has created a new area code and has changed the former 718 area code to 818. The following steps show you how to search for and replace a label in the database block:

1. Highlight the area you want to search. In this case you highlight the database block.

2. Choose **E**dit **S**earch and Replace.

3. Enter the search string into the Find text box. In this case, type **(718)**.

4. Enter the replacement string in the Replace text box. In this case, type **(818)**.

5. Choose the type of search in the Look In field. Because you are looking in labels in this case, choose **V**alue.

6. Choose Replace **A**ll.

Instead of choosing Replace **A**ll in step 6, you may want to choose **Re**place to verify that the change is made correctly. If the change is correct, choose Replace **A**ll to replace the other occurrences. If you made an error, edit the appropriate fields in the dialog box and choose **R**eplace again.

If you choose **N**ext rather than Replace **A**ll, the cell selector moves to the first cell in the block with a matching string. You then can choose **N**ext to leave the first match unchanged, **R**eplace to change the highlighted cell, or Replace **A**ll to replace all occurrences.

Be very careful if you use **E**dit **S**earch and Replace to modify formulas. If your proposed changes result in a syntax error or an unknown function, Quattro Pro 5.0 for Windows displays an error message. Try your changes on a single copy of the formula before you choose Replace **A**ll.

Checking Spelling

When you create a business presentation, you want to make a good impression. A new feature of Quattro Pro 5.0 for Windows, the Spell Checker, quickly verifies that your notebooks are free of spelling errors.

To use the Spell Checker, first choose **T**ools Spell Check or click the Spell Check button on the Productivity Tools SpeedBar. This step adds the Spell Checker SpeedBar to the screen. You must use the mouse with Spell Checker; you cannot use the keyboard.

Before you begin using the Spell Checker, you may want to choose from its options:

- Click the Options button to display the Spell Check Options dialog box (see fig. 5.32).

- Choose Language to select the language to use.

- Select Choose New Dictionary to choose a different Personal Dictionary, a custom dictionary containing special terms such as names or technical terms unique to your business.

- Choose Remove Current Dict. to use the standard Quattro Pro dictionary only.

- Check Ignore Repeated Words to skip repeated words.

- Check Ignore Capitalization Errors to skip words with capital letters in the wrong places.

- Check Ignore Punctuation Errors to skip words with unusual punctuation.

■ Check Ignore Acronym Errors to skip acronyms and abbreviations that appear in the dictionary with different punctuation.

■ Check Ignore Words with Numbers to skip any words containing numbers.

■ Check Ignore UPPERCASE Words to skip any word in all upper-case letters.

Press Enter or click OK to confirm your selections and return to the notebook.

Fig. 5.32

The Spell Checker SpeedBar and the Spell Check Options dialog box.

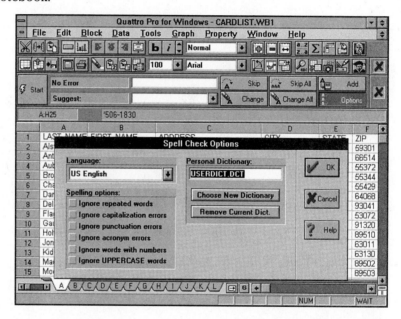

 To begin using the Spell Checker, select the block you want to check and click Start. The Start button becomes the Stop button. When Spell Checker finds a word it does not recognize, the word appears in the Misspelled text box and any suggestions appear in the Suggest text box. You also can type a replacement word in the Suggest text box. Choose one of the following options:

Skip	Bypass this occurrence of the misspelled word.
Skip All	Bypass all occurrences of the misspelled word.
Add	Add the word to your Personal Dictionary.
Change	Change this occurrence of the misspelled word to the word shown in the Suggest text box.

| Change All | Change all occurrences of the misspelled word to the word shown in the Suggest text box. | |

Click Stop to end Spell Checker. Click OK to confirm the Spell check halted message. Click the Close SpeedBar button at the right side of the Spell Checker SpeedBar to remove the SpeedBar from the screen.

Filling Blocks

When you build a new notebook, Quattro Pro 5.0 for Windows can fill a block automatically with a series of numbers, which is a handy function. For example, a notebook based on an incrementing time series, such as a loan amortization schedule, may require you to include dates in monthly intervals. You also can use an incrementing number series to number data records before sorting, enabling easy return to the pre-sort order.

You use the **B**lock **F**ill command to fill a block with numeric values. After you issue the command, the Block Fill dialog box appears (see fig. 5.33).

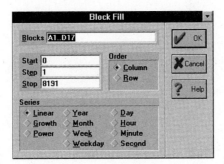

Fig. 5.33

The Block Fill dialog box.

Quattro Pro 5.0 for Windows offers a wide range of options for filling a block with numeric values. In addition to a simple **L**inear fill such as 1, 2, 3, 4..., you can choose a **G**rowth fill where you specify a factor by which each value is multiplied to produce the subsequent value. You also can choose a **P**ower fill, where you specify the exponential growth factor. Finally, you can choose a time-series block fill, such as **Y**ear, **M**onth, or Wee**k**.

Filling a Block with Numbers

The **B**lock **F**ill command is ideal for filling a block with an incrementing series of numbers, such as a series of interest rates or budget percentages. When you build a mortgage rate table, for example, you can use **B**lock **F**ill to create a list of evenly incrementing interest rates.

To use the **B**lock **F**ill command, follow these steps:

1. Highlight the block you want to fill.

2. Choose **B**lock **F**ill. The Block Fill dialog box appears.

3. Enter the **St**art, St**e**p (or increment), and **S**top values in the appropriate text boxes.

4. If the block spans multiple rows and multiple columns, choose **C**olumn to begin filling the block in the first column, then the second column, and so on; choose **R**ow to fill the first row, then the second row, and so on.

5. In the Series field, choose the type of fill. Table 5.1 summarizes the fill options.

6. Choose OK to confirm the dialog box and fill the block.

Table 5.1 Block Fill Types

Series	Type of Fill
Linear	Step value is added to start value.
Growth	Step value is used as a multiplier.
Power	Step value is used as an exponent.
Year	Step value is in years and is added to start value.
Month	Step value is in months and is added to start value.
Week	Step value is in weeks and is added to start value.
Weekday	Step value is in days with weekend days skipped and is added to start value.
Day	Step value is in days and is added to start value.
Hour	Step value is in hours and is added to start value.
Minute	Step value is in minutes and is added to start value.
Second	Step value is in seconds and is added to start value.

By default, Quattro Pro 5.0 for Windows uses 0 for the start number, 1 for the step (or increment), and 8191 as the stop number. Be sure to adjust these values to fit your needs. When filling a block, Quattro Pro 5.0 for Windows stops entering additional values when the specified block is filled or the stop number is reached. If you specify A1..A100 as the block to fill and you use the default start, step, and stop values, for example, cells A1..A100 fill with values 0 through 99. If you specify a start value of 8100, cells A1..A91 fill with values 8100 through 8191 and cells A92..A100 do not fill. If you specify a start value larger than the stop value, no values enter the block. Figure 5.34 shows the result of filling the block A1..D17 using the default values.

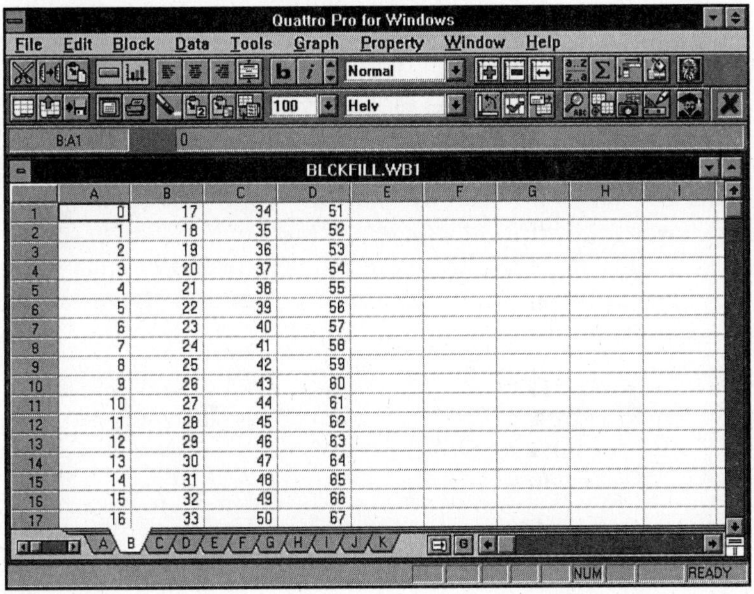

Fig. 5.34

Block **F**ill fills blocks with numeric values.

Filling a Block with Dates or Times

Block **F**ill enables you to fill a block with a sequence of dates or times without using values, formulas, or functions. Because the command enters the dates or times as serial numbers, Quattro Pro 5.0 for Windows formats the block with a date or time format to make the serial numbers understandable as dates or times. (Chapter 6, "Changing the Format and Appearance of Data," has more information on formatting data in the notebook.)

Quattro Pro 5.0 for Windows offers a very broad date value range: January 1, 1600, through December 31, 3199. The earliest date Quattro Pro

5.0 for Windows accepts, January 1, 1600, has a date serial number of -109571. The highest date Quattro Pro 5.0 for Windows accepts, December 31, 3199, has a date serial number of 474816.

For compatibility with Lotus 1-2-3, Quattro Pro 5.0 for Windows uses the value 61 for March 1, 1900. Dates prior to March 1, 1900, and dates after December 31, 2099, are correct in Quattro Pro 5.0 for Windows but are incorrect or not allowed in Lotus 1-2-3.

Date serial numbers increment by one for each day. You cannot use **B**lock **F**ill to enter a date such as June 26, 1994, which has a serial number of 34511, unless you remember to increase the stop value to a number at least as high as the serial number of the ending date you want.

Figure 5.35 shows a notebook that uses **B**lock **F**ill to create a series of dates in column B and monthly sales budget figures in column C. In this example, **M**onth was selected as the series for column B, the start value was 34511, and the step value was 1, producing a series of dates one month apart starting with June 26, 1994. Next, **G**rowth was selected as the series for column C, 1250 was specified as the start value, and the step value was set to 1.05, producing the budgeted growth in sales of 5% per month. To make the data easier to understand, column B was formatted with a date format, and column C was formatted to show commas and two decimal places.

Fig. 5.35

A sample budget produced using **B**lock **F**ill.

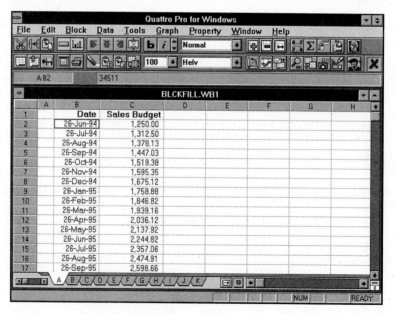

You can create the same budget notebook shown in figure 5.35 using formulas and functions in Quattro Pro 5.0 for Windows, but the **B**lock **F**ill command provides an easier and faster method of entering incrementing values into a notebook.

▶▶ "Applying the Available Formats," p. 190.   **FOR RELATED** **INFORMATION**

Accessing the Operating System

In this chapter, you learned how to use many different commands in Quattro Pro 5.0 for Windows to build and modify your spreadsheet notebooks. At times, however, you may need to perform a function you cannot do in Quattro Pro 5.0 for Windows. Suppose, for example, that you want to save a file on a disk but you have no formatted disks available. Or, while you are working on a report, you want to use a scanner to create a graphics image to use in a Quattro Pro 5.0 for Windows report.

A major benefit of working in the Windows environment is the ability to switch to other applications without closing and saving all the notebooks you have open in Quattro Pro 5.0 for Windows. If your computer has enough memory and hard disk space, you can leave Quattro Pro 5.0 for Windows without quitting the program and use the operating system or other Windows or DOS applications.

To leave Quattro Pro 5.0 for Windows without exiting the program, press Ctrl+Esc to access a Task List window displaying other Windows applications currently open; one of these selections is always the Windows Program Manager. If you choose Program Manager and click the **S**witch to button (or press Alt+S), you then can choose the DOS prompt icon that usually is in the Windows Main program group. After you are in the operating system, you can copy files, format disks, or execute other system functions. After you finish using operating system commands, type **exit** and press Enter to return to the Program Manager.

You also can leave Quattro Pro 5.0 for Windows temporarily by holding down the Alt key and pressing Tab until Program Manager appears on-screen. When you release the Alt key, you leave Quattro Pro 5.0 for Windows and access the Program Manager. In addition, you can choose the minimize button or the **Mi**nimize command from the Control menu in Quattro Pro 5.0 for Windows to reduce the program to an icon. You then can choose Program Manager to lead you to the DOS prompt icon.

Using another Windows application, such as the program that controls a scanner, is just as easy as using the operating system. Instead of selecting the DOS prompt icon, select the icon for the program you want to execute.

To return to Quattro Pro 5.0 for Windows, press Ctrl+Esc to activate the Task List. Then double-click the Quattro Pro 5.0 for Windows entry. You return to Quattro Pro 5.0 for Windows in the same status in which you left. The same notebook is active, and all settings remain the same as you left them.

NOTE

Before leaving Quattro Pro 5.0 for Windows to access the operating system, be sure to save any open notebooks. This step protects your files from being lost in case a program you run at the DOS prompt conflicts with Windows.

Questions and Answers

Q: What should I do when Quattro Pro 5.0 for Windows tells me a file already exists when I try to save a new notebook?

A: You can save the notebook using a different name, choose **B**ackup to rename the old notebook with a BAK file extension, or choose **R**eplace to lose the old notebook file. Be careful about choosing **B**ackup, though, because if you already have saved a backup notebook file using the same name, the old backup file is lost without further warning.

Q: What should I do if I cannot remember all the block names and addresses in my notebook?

A: Use the **B**lock **N**ames **M**ake Table command to create a listing of all the block names and addresses. Print a copy of the list and retain the printout as part of the notebook's documentation.

Q: When I use the Fit button, some columns become far too wide. What should I do?

A: The Fit button uses the width of the longest entry in a multirow selection or the longest entry at or below the cell selector if a single row is selected. Make certain you select the proper cell or block to set the column to the width you want.

Q: My old three-dimensional spreadsheet program could display three pages in perspective. How can I see three pages at the same time in Quattro Pro 5.0 for Windows?

A: Choose **W**indow **N**ew View to display as many different views of the notebook as you like. You also can split each view into two horizontal or vertical panes. Use **W**indow **T**ile or **W**indow **C**ascade to arrange the views of all open notebooks (except hidden notebooks).

Q: Why does the cell selector move to cell C3 rather than A1 when I press Home?

A: Your notebook has locked titles. Use **W**indow **L**ocked Titles **C**lear to remove the restriction on cell selector movement.

Q: Every time I use Spell Checker, it asks me about the same terms that are unique to my profession. How can I teach Spell Checker our special terms?

A: Next time you use Spell Checker, choose the Add button when one of your terms is suggested as a misspelling. This step adds the term to your personal dictionary, and Spell Checker stops asking about the term.

Q: Why does **B**lock **F**ill stop before completely filling the block I selected?

A: Check the **S**top value to make certain it is large enough. If you are certain you want the entire block filled, add a zero to the end of the **S**top value to make the value 10 times larger—**B**lock **F**ill should fill the rest of the block.

Summary

Learning all the commands in Quattro Pro 5.0 for Windows is a large task. Fortunately, however, you probably don't need to learn all the commands because some commands rarely, if ever, apply to your application of Quattro Pro 5.0 for Windows. In this chapter, you learned to use the fundamental commands in Quattro Pro 5.0 for Windows to build and work with notebooks. In particular, you learned how to use command menus; save notebooks; use blocks; change row heights and column widths; insert, delete, protect, copy, and move data; search for and replace data; verify spelling; automatically fill blocks with incrementing numeric values; and access the Program Manager and operating system.

In Chapter 6, you learn how to change the format and appearance of cell contents so that cells are clear and easily understood. You should find this information extremely useful as you begin to use Quattro Pro 5.0 for Windows to produce high-quality reports with the data in your notebooks.

Changing the Format and Appearance of Data

Manipulating data with Quattro Pro 5.0 for Windows is only the first step in using spreadsheet notebooks effectively. Turning raw data into clearly understandable information can be as important as calculating correct answers. In this chapter you learn to use the commands that control the appearance of data—both on-screen and in printed reports. The commands covered in this chapter enable you to control the *format*, the *style*, and the *alignment* of data.

The commands for formatting affect the display of data—how the numbers, dates, times, and labels display. These commands change only the way data appears. You do not change the value of data when you customize its format.

After you learn how to control the format and appearance of data, Quattro Pro 5.0 for Windows enables you to define *named styles*, incorporating all the formatting elements. Named styles can be applied quickly to blocks of data, enhancing the appearance of the data using your predetermined settings. In this chapter, you learn how to create named styles by applying basic techniques for changing the format and appearance of data.

This chapter shows you how to perform the following tasks:

- Change the default notebook settings

- Apply the available formats to change the appearance of data

- Enhance the appearance of data using fonts, label alignment options, lines, colors, and shading

- Create and modify named styles to quickly control many aspects of spreadsheet notebook data

Changing Default Notebook Settings

Quattro Pro 5.0 for Windows has a number of settings that define how the program operates or how the screen looks. The International selection in the Application dialog box controls the display of currency symbols, punctuation, and date and time formats for all notebooks. Each notebook page has its own Active Page Object Inspector, which controls such items as the display of zeros, default label alignment, borders and grid lines, and the color of data based on conditional values.

You can open the Application dialog box in one of two ways: by choosing the **P**roperty **A**pplication command from the main menu or by pointing to the Quattro Pro 5.0 for Windows title bar and clicking the right mouse button. Select International to display the settings shown in figure 6.1.

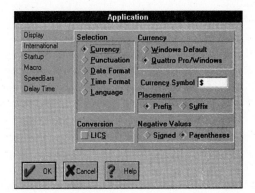

Fig. 6.1

The International settings in the Application dialog box.

Setting Currency, Punctuation, Date, and Time Formats

The options in the International section enable you to specify formatting conventions that vary from country to country. At times you may want to change some or all of the International settings. If you work with international currency, for example, you may want to change the currency symbol. If you work for an international company, you also may want to change the punctuation conventions and date and time formats used in your reports. The following section describes how to change these settings.

As you choose each option in the Selection field, the right side of the dialog box displays the choices available with the selected option. Figure 6.1, for example, shows the choices available when you choose the **C**urrency option, and then the **Q**uattro Pro/Windows option.

Setting Currency Defaults

The first International option, **C**urrency, controls the currency symbol and its position. You can type a dollar sign ($) directly from the keyboard, but other currency symbols require you to type the ANSI character code for the currency symbol you want to use. To type the ANSI character code, first make certain the keypad at the right side of the keyboard is set to enter numbers. If the NUM indicator does not appear at the bottom of the screen, press Num Lock. Next, press and hold down the Alt key while you enter the appropriate code (see below). Release the Alt key to enter the currency symbol in the text box. The following examples show you the ANSI character code to enter for some common currency symbols:

- To enter ¢ (cent sign), press Alt+0162

- To enter £ (British pound), press Alt+0163

- To enter ¥ (Yen), press Alt+0165

- To enter ¤ (general currency), press Alt+0164

For other currencies that do not have a currency symbol supported by the Microsoft Windows character set, Quattro Pro 5.0 for Windows enables you to enter descriptive text, such as DM. The currency symbol you specify appears along with any values in cells you format as currency. (See "Using the Format Commands" later in this chapter.) Because the currency symbol increases the display width of values formatted as currency, you may need to increase column widths to prevent cells from displaying asterisks. See Chapter 5, "Using Fundamental Commands," for information on setting column widths.

In addition to specifying the currency symbol, you can mark check boxes to control the positioning of the currency symbol. Check **P**refix to place the symbol before the value or **S**uffix to place the symbol after the value.

Setting Punctuation Defaults

The **P**unctuation option in the Selection field enables you to select the symbol used as the decimal point, the symbol to separate thousands in values, and the symbol to separate arguments in statements. Some countries use the period (.) as the decimal point and the comma (,) as the thousands and argument separator, and some countries use other conventions. Figure 6.2 shows the nine choices (including Windows Default) you can select from in Quattro Pro 5.0 for Windows.

Setting Date Defaults

The **D**ate Format option in the Selection field enables you to select the international format for displaying dates. When you check one of the option buttons, you choose both the long and short international format in one step. If you choose MM/DD/YY as the long international date format, for example, MM/DD is the corresponding short international date format. Figure 6.3 shows the international **D**ate Format selections.

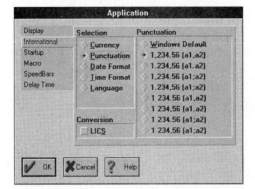

Fig. 6.2

The international **P**unctuation options available in Quattro Pro 5.0 for Windows.

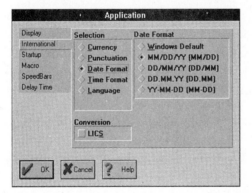

Fig. 6.3

The international **D**ate Format options available in Quattro Pro 5.0 for Windows.

Setting Time Defaults

The **T**ime Format option in the Selection field enables you to select the international format for displaying times. When you check one of the option buttons, you choose both the long and short international formats in one step. If you choose HH.MM.SS as the long international time format, for example, HH.MM is the corresponding short international time format. Figure 6.4 shows the international **T**ime Format selections.

Fig. 6.4

The International **T**ime Format options available in Quattro Pro 5.0 for Windows.

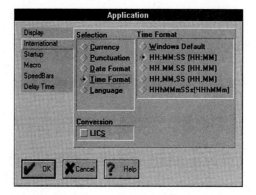

The remaining settings in the International section of the Application dialog box do not affect the format and appearance of data. These settings are covered in the appropriate chapters of this book.

Changing the Display of Zeros

Displaying zeros as blanks can be useful in spreadsheet notebooks where zeros represent missing or meaningless information. Making these cells appear blank can improve the appearance of the notebook and any reports you produce. Sometimes, however, making zeros appear blank can be confusing if you cannot tell whether the cell is blank because of missing data.

You use the **P**roperty Active **P**age menu command *or* the Active Page Object Inspector to control the display of zeros. You can set each notebook page independently of the other pages in the notebook. Choose **P**roperty Active **P**age from the main menu or access the Active Page Object Inspector menu by pointing to the page tab and clicking the right mouse button. From the resulting menu, select Display Zeros. Then click **N**o to suppress the display of zeros on the current page or **Y**es to display zeros on the current page.

FOR RELATED **INFORMATION**

◄◄ "Setting Column Widths," p. 136.

Setting Block Formats

A cell has two characteristics: contents and appearance. The *input line* displays the actual contents of the current cell. The formatting applied to the current cell controls the way the contents appear in the cell. Figure 6.5 shows examples of the different numeric formats available in Quattro Pro 5.0 for Windows.

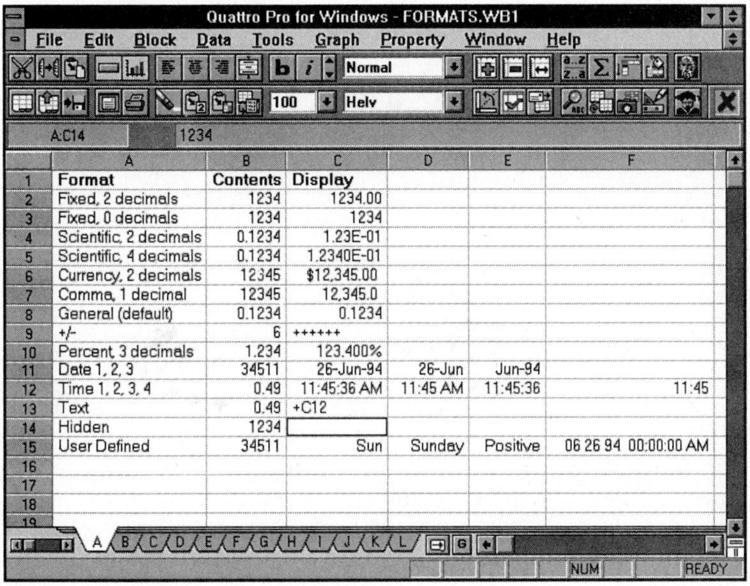

Fig. 6.5

Examples of Quattro Pro 5.0 for Windows numeric formats.

The Available Formats

You can display data in a cell in a variety of different formats. Quattro Pro 5.0 for Windows includes the following formats: Fixed, Scientific, Currency, Comma, General, +/–, Percent, Date, Time, Text, Hidden, and User Defined.

Most formats apply only to numeric data (numeric formulas and numbers). If you format a cell as Currency, for example, the format has no effect on any label you may add to the cell. Two formats, Text and Hidden, can apply to string formulas, and Hidden can apply to labels as well.

No matter what the format, numeric data usually is right-aligned. The rightmost digit usually appears in the second position from the right edge of the cell. The extreme right position is reserved for a percent sign, a right parenthesis, or an international currency symbol. Labels and the results of string formulas usually are left-aligned, even if the formula refers to a label with another alignment.

To change the alignment of numbers, labels, or formula results, use the Alignment selection in the Active Block dialog box. See the section "Aligning Labels and Values" later in this chapter.

If you have applied a numeric format to a cell, the column width must be wide enough to display the cell's data in the assigned format. Otherwise, Quattro Pro 5.0 for Windows displays asterisks in the cell rather than the formatted value. If the cell has not been formatted, Quattro Pro 5.0 for Windows attempts to display data that is too wide in Scientific format. To change the display, you must change the format or the column width. (See Chapter 5, "Using Fundamental Commands," for more information on changing the column width.)

The Contents versus the Format of a Cell

Formatting changes the appearance but not the value of data. The number 7892, for example, can appear in the format 7,892, $7,892.00, or 789200.0%, as well as many other formats. No matter how Quattro Pro 5.0 for Windows displays the number in a cell, the number remains the same.

Some formats display a number in rounded form. Even when the displayed number appears rounded, however, Quattro Pro 5.0 for Windows still stores and uses the exact value in calculations. If you format the value 1.5 as Fixed with zero decimal places, Quattro Pro 5.0 for Windows displays the number as 2 in a cell but uses the actual value of 1.5 in calculations.

In figure 6.6, the total in cell C7 appears to be an addition error. The sum of 2+2+2+2 should be 8, but the formula result displays as 6 because the numbers in cells C3..C6 are formatted as Fixed with zero decimal places. This apparent error is caused by rounding the display but not rounding the values.

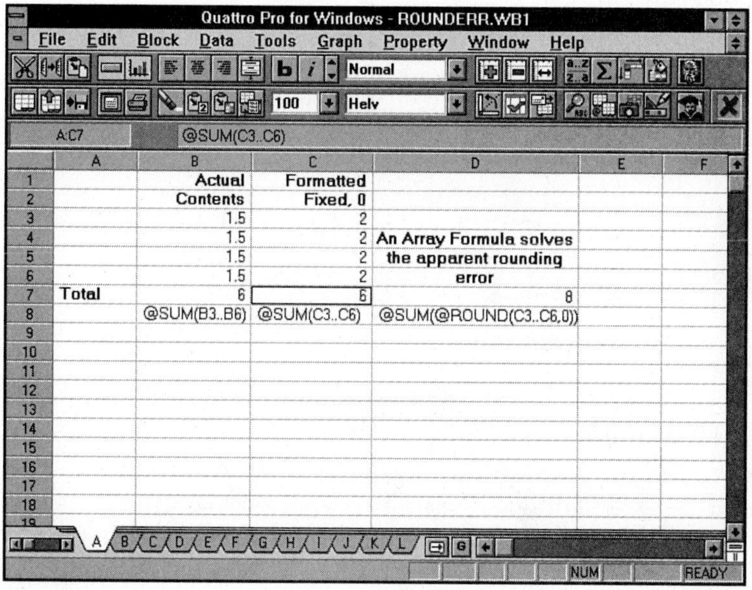

Fig. 6.6

Cell formatting can appear to cause rounding errors.

You easily can create apparent rounding errors—especially when you produce cross-tabulated reports. To avoid apparent rounding errors, you need to round the actual value of the numbers used in formulas, not just their appearance or format. To round the values used in a formula, use the @ROUND function to round each value before the value is used in the formula. In the example shown in figure 6.6, for example, one method of rounding the values is to change the formula to the following example:

@SUM(@ROUND(C3,0),@ROUND(C4,0),@ROUND(C5,0),@ROUND(C6,0))

This formula result displays as 8. Although the shorter formula, @ROUND(@SUM(C3..C6),0), may seem reasonable, this shorter version returns a value of 6. The reason is that the @SUM(C3..C6) portion of the formula, which uses the values stored in the cells rather than the displayed values, is calculated first.

In place of the longer formula shown above you can use this array formula:

@SUM(@ROUND(C3..C6,0))

This formula also returns a value of 8. The array formula returns the result you expect because each cell's value is rounded before the total is summed. Be aware, however, that array formulas do not produce correct results if you export the notebook to another spreadsheet program that does not support array formulas.

TIP

The best insurance against apparent rounding errors is to make certain the stored values match the displayed values. Use the @ROUND function to round calculated results to the same precision as the display format.

FOR RELATED INFORMATION

▶▶ "Using Mathematical Numerical Functions," p. 245.

Applying the Available Formats

To change the display format of a cell or block, first highlight the cell or block. Then choose **P**roperty **C**urrent Object or click the right mouse button inside the cell or block to open the Active Block dialog box. Select Numeric Format. If no numeric format has been assigned, the default **G**eneral format is checked, as shown in figure 6.7.

Fig. 6.7

Selecting Numeric Format from the Active Block dialog box.

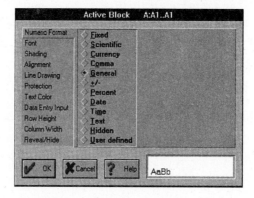

If you choose **F**ixed, **S**cientific, **C**urrency, C**o**mma, or **P**ercent, type the number of decimal places in the text box that appears after you choose one of these formats. Quattro Pro 5.0 for Windows suggests a default of 2 decimal places, but you can type another number between 0 and 15. Choose OK to confirm the dialog box and apply the format to the highlighted cell or block.

Figure 6.8 shows how the same number appears using the **F**ixed display format and 0 to 15 decimal places.

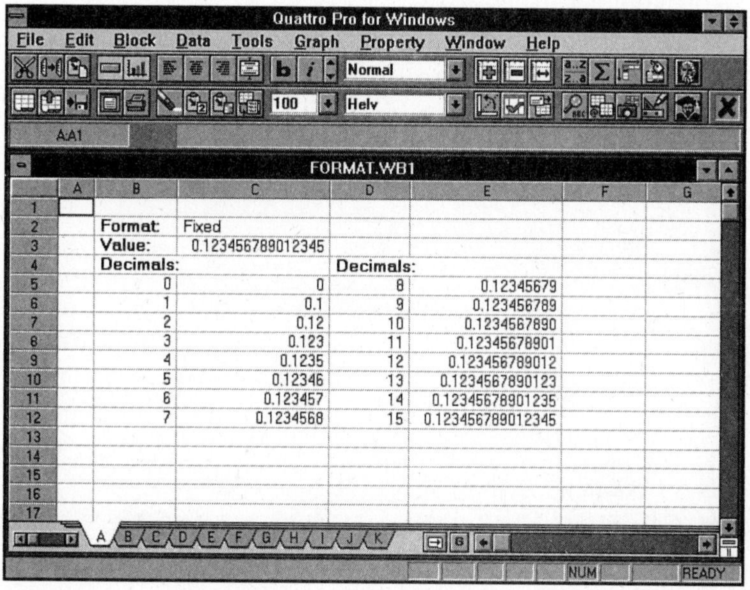

Fig. 6.8

The same number displayed in **F**ixed format with 0 to 15 decimal places.

When you start a new notebook, the default display format is **G**eneral. To change the format for an entire page, follow these steps:

1. Select the page. To select the entire page with the mouse, click the Select All button—the upper left corner of the spreadsheet frame where the row and column borders intersect.

To select the entire page with the keyboard, press Home to place the cell selector in cell A1. Then hold down the Shift key, press End and the down arrow, and then press End and the right arrow.

2. Choose the **P**roperty **C**urrent Object command or click the right mouse button to open the Active Block dialog box.

3. Select Numeric Format.

4. Choose a default display format.

5. Choose OK to confirm the dialog box.

If you choose a numeric format that prevents Quattro Pro 5.0 for Windows from displaying values in the selected format because the column width is too narrow, asterisks display rather than the formatted value. The program still uses the stored value in calculations, however. To display the value rather than asterisks, adjust the column width, select a different display format, or choose a different font or point size.

The following sections describe each display format in detail. You can apply a different numeric format to individual cells or blocks even if you have selected a default format for the entire page.

Fixed Format

You use the Fixed format when you want to display values with a specified, fixed number of decimal points. Quattro Pro 5.0 for Windows displays values with up to 15 decimal places. Negative numbers have a minus sign, and decimal values have a leading zero. No punctuation is used to denote thousands. Table 6.1 shows several examples of numbers displayed using the Fixed format.

Table 6.1 Examples of Fixed Display Format

Typed Entry	Number of Decimal Places	Display Result
100.99	0	101
100.99	1	101.0
−100.99	2	−100.99
100.99	5	100.99000

Scientific Format

You use the Scientific format to display very large or very small numbers. Such numbers usually have a few significant digits and many zeros.

A number in scientific notation has two parts: a *mantissa* and an *exponent*. The mantissa is a number from 1 to 10 that contains the significant digits. The exponent tells you how many places to move the decimal point to get the actual value of the number.

Quattro Pro 5.0 for Windows displays numbers in Scientific display format in powers of 10, with 0 to 15 decimal places, and an exponent from 308 to +308. If a number has more significant digits than the cell can display using the specified number of decimal places, the displayed value is rounded but the stored value is used in calculations.

The value 456,000,000 appears as 4.56E+8 in **S**cientific display format with two decimal places. E+8 signifies that you must move the decimal point eight places to the *right* to get the actual number. The value 0.00456 appears as 4.6E-3 in **S**cientific display format with one decimal place. E-3 means that you must move the decimal point three places to the *left* to get the actual number.

Values in cells using the **G**eneral display format appear in **S**cientific display format if the values are too large to display in **G**eneral display format.

Table 6.2 shows several examples of **S**cientific display format.

Table 6.2 Examples of Scientific Display Format

Typed Entry	Number of Decimal Places	Display Result
100.99	0	1E+2
10000.99	1	1.0E+4
−100.99	2	−1.01E+2
100.99	5	1.00990E+2

Currency Format

Currency format displays values with a currency symbol, such as a dollar sign ($) or the British pound sign (£), and thousands punctuation—depending on the current international settings. (See "Setting Currency, Punctuation, Date, and Time Formats" earlier in this chapter.) If you specify a currency symbol, the column width needs an extra position to display each character in the currency symbol. Values formatted as **C**urrency can have from 0 to 15 decimal places. Thousands are separated by commas, periods, or spaces according to the current international settings. Negative numbers appear in parentheses.

If you format a cell or a block with the **C**urrency display format, the current currency symbol appears along with the value. If you work with notebooks that use several different international currencies, you may find the **C**omma display format (discussed in the next section) more convenient. Table 6.3 shows several examples of **C**urrency display format with different currency symbols.

Table 6.3 Examples of Currency Display Format

Typed Entry	Number of Decimal Places	Display Result
100.99	0	¥101
10000.99	1	£10,001.0
−100.99	2	($100.99)
100.99	5	100.99000

Comma Format

Like the Currency display format, the Comma format displays data with a fixed number of decimal places and thousands punctuation. The thousands separator and the decimal point depend on the current international settings. Negative numbers appear in parentheses, and positive numbers less than 1000 appear the same as Fixed display format.

If a value has more decimal digits than the cell can display using the specified number of decimal places, the displayed value is rounded but the stored value is used in calculations.

Large numbers are easier to understand in Comma display format than in Fixed display format. The number 1,500,000 is easier to read than 1500000. Table 6.4 shows several examples of Comma display format.

Table 6.4 Examples of Comma Display Format

Typed Entry	Number of Decimal Places	Display Result
100.99	0	101
10000.99	1	10,001.0
100.99	2	(100.99)
100.99	5	100.99000

General Format

General format is the default format for all new notebooks. Numbers in General display format have no thousands separators and no trailing zeros to the right of the decimal point. A minus sign precedes negative numbers. If a number contains decimal digits, it contains a decimal point. If a number contains too many digits to the right of the decimal point to display in the current column width, the decimals are rounded in the display. If a number is too large or too small, it appears in **Scientific** display format.

If you do not explicitly apply a numeric format to a cell or a block, Quattro Pro 5.0 for Windows uses the **General** display format. Table 6.5 shows several examples of **General** display format.

Table 6.5 Examples of General Display Format

Typed Entry	Display Result
100.99	100.99
10000.99	10000.99
–100.99	-100.99
1234567890123	1.235E+12

+/- Format

The +/– format displays numbers as a series of plus signs (+), minus signs (-), or as a period (.). The number of signs equals the integer portion of the value. A positive number appears as a row of plus signs, a negative value appears as a row of minus signs, and a number between 1 and +1 appears as a period.

Table 6.6 shows several examples of +/– display format.

Table 6.6 Examples of +/- Display Format

Typed Entry	Display Result
5	+++++
1.99	+
5.5	- - - - -
.75	.

Percent Format

Percent format is used to display values as percentages with 0 to 15 decimal places. The number appears with its value multiplied by 100, followed by a percent sign (%). The number of decimal places you specify is the number displayed in the percent—not the number of decimal places in the value.

The displayed value is multiplied by 100, but the value used in calculations is not. To display 98% in a cell formatted with the **Percent** display format, you type **.98**.

If a value has more decimal digits than the cell can display using the specified number of decimal places, the displayed value is rounded but the stored value is used in calculations. Table 6.7 shows several examples of **Percent** display format.

Table 6.7 Examples of Percent Display Format

Typed Entry	Number of Decimal Places	Display Result
.99	0	99%
.99	1	99.0%
1.99	2	199.00%
100.99	5	10099.00000%

Date Format

Date formats display date serial numbers as dates rather than numbers. Quattro Pro 5.0 for Windows stores dates as serial numbers starting with January 1, 1600, (which is 109571) and increases the number by one for each whole day. December 31, 1899 is counted as 1. The latest date Quattro Pro 5.0 for Windows can display is December 31, 3199, with a serial number of 474816.

If the number is less than 109571 or greater than 474816, a date format appears as asterisks. Date formats ignore decimal fractions; 34511.55 with a short international date format appears as 6/26/94. The decimal portion of a date serial number represents the time as a fraction of a 24-hour clock.

> **NOTE**
>
> Quattro Pro 5.0 for Windows date serial numbers between December 31, 1899, and March 1, 1900, differ by one from the numbers in Lotus 1-2-3. The 1-2-3 date serial numbers during that time period contain an error because 1-2-3 accepts February 29, 1900, as a valid date, even though the year 1900 was not a leap year. Date serial numbers in Quattro Pro 5.0 for Windows and 1-2-3 agree for dates March 1, 1900, and later (up to December 30, 2099, the latest date 1-2-3 can display). 1-2-3 cannot use negative date serial numbers.

Quattro Pro 5.0 for Windows gives you a choice of five different **Date** display formats. Both Long Date Intl. and Short Date Intl. depend on the current international date format set using the **Property Application** menu. (See "Changing the Default Setting," earlier in this chapter.) Table 6.8 shows several examples of **Date** display formats.

Table 6.8 Examples of Date Display Formats

Typed Entry	Date Format	Display Result
34511	DD-MMM-YY	26-Jun-94
34511	DD-MMM	26-Jun
34511	MMM-YY	Jun-94
34511	Long Date Intl.	Sunday, June 26, 1994
34511	Short Date Intl.	6/26/94

Time Format

You use the **Time** formats to display date serial numbers as times. The decimal portion of a date serial number is a *time fraction*. The time fraction represents a fraction of a 24-hour day. For example, the time fraction for 8 a.m. is .33333..., the time fraction for noon is .5, and the time fraction for 3 p.m. is .675. When you use a **Time** format, Quattro Pro 5.0 for Windows displays the fraction as a time.

If a date serial number is greater than 1, the time formats ignore the integer portion. Both .5 and 33781.5 display 12:00:00 PM. Table 6.9 shows several examples of **Time** display format.

Table 6.9 Examples of Time Display Format

Typed Entry	Time Format	Display Result
.56	HH:MM:SS AM/PM	01:26:24 PM
.56	HH:MM AM/PM	01:26 PM
.56	Long Time Intl.	13:26:24
33781.56	Short Time Intl.	13:26

Text Format

You use **T**ext format to display the text of formulas rather than their results. Numbers in cells formatted as **T**ext appear in **G**eneral format. Unlike long labels that appear in blank cells to the right, formulas formatted as **T**ext are truncated if they are too long to display in the column width.

Quattro Pro 5.0 for Windows continues to use the value of formulas when you format them as **T**ext. You can apply **T**ext format to formulas in database criteria tables to make record selection criteria more understandable. **T**ext format also is useful when you are building an educational model.

Hidden Format

A cell or block formatted as **H**idden always appears blank. You use **H**idden format for intermediate calculations that you don't want to appear in a final report or for sensitive formulas you don't want displayed. The contents of a **H**idden cell appear in the input line when you highlight the cell, however, so **H**idden format offers little security.

User-Defined Format

Quattro Pro 5.0 for Windows enables you to define and apply your own numeric formats. **U**ser-defined formats can include many different elements. To create and apply user-defined formats, perform the following steps:

1. Highlight the block you want to format.

2. Open the Active Block dialog box by pointing to the block and clicking the right mouse button or by choosing **P**roperty **C**urrent Object.

3. In the Numeric Format section of the dialog box, choose **U**ser defined.

4. In the Formats defined text box, type the format you want by using the symbols and syntax shown in table 6.10.

5. Choose OK to confirm the dialog box and apply the format.

Table 6.10 User-Defined Format Symbols

Symbol(s)	Description
N or n	Defines numbers
0	Always displays a digit or a zero if the number does not include a digit in this position
9	Suppresses the display of leading zero
%	Displays number as a percentage
,	Inserts a comma (or the defined thousands separator)
.	Inserts a period (or the defined decimal separator)
;	Separates different formats for positive and negative numbers, or for positive numbers, zero, and negative numbers
E– or e–	Displays number in scientific notation, using a minus sign to precede negative exponents
E+ or e+	Displays number in scientific notation, using a minus sign to precede negative exponents and a plus sign to precede positive exponents
T or t	Defines dates and times
D or d	Displays day of month in one or two digits
DD or dd	Displays day of month in two digits
WDAY	Displays three-letter day of week in uppercase
Wday	Displays three-letter day of week with first letter capitalized

(continues)

Table 6.10 Continued

Symbol(s)	Description
wday	Displays three-letter day of week in lowercase
WEEKDAY	Displays day of week in uppercase
Weekday	Displays day of week with first letter capitalized
weekday	Displays day of week in lowercase
M or m	Displays one- or two-digit month number; if preceded by H, h, HH, or hh, displays one- or two-digit minute number
MM or mm	Displays two-digit month number; if preceded by H, h, HH, or hh, displays two-digit minute number
Mo	Displays one- or two-digit month number
MMo	Displays two-digit month number
MON	Displays three-character month name in upper-case
Mon	Displays three-character month name with first letter capitalized
mon	Displays three-character month name in lower-case
MONTH	Displays full month name in uppercase
Month	Displays full month name with first letter capitalized
month	Displays full month name in lowercase
YY or yy	Displays two-digit year number
YYYY or yyyy	Displays four-digit year number
H or h	Displays one- or two-digit hour number
HH or hh	Displays two-digit hour number
Mi	Displays one- or two-digit minute number
MMi	Displays two-digit minute number
S or s	Displays one- or two-digit second number
SS or ss	Displays two-digit second number
AMPM or ampm	Displays time in 12-hour format
\	Displays next character
*	Fills empty positions with character following the asterisk
'text'	Displays text

Enhancing the Appearance of Data

The display format options provide the basics for determining the appearance of data, but Quattro Pro 5.0 for Windows enables you to apply many more enhancements to improve the appearance of your data. The following sections describe how to perform these tasks:

- Use different fonts and point sizes to display your data

- Change the alignment of labels to match numeric data

- Use line-drawing options to create borders around cells and blocks

- Add color and shading to cells and blocks

Using Different Fonts

You use the Font selection in the Active Block dialog box to choose different *typefaces*, *point sizes*, and *attributes* (see fig. 6.9). A typeface is a type style, such as Arial, Courier New, or Times New Roman. Typefaces are available in a number of point sizes that represent character height. A standard 10 character-per-inch size usually is considered equivalent to a 12-point type size. Typefaces also have different attributes, such as weight (normal or **bold**) and *italic*.

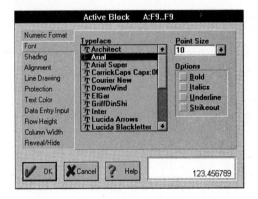

Fig. 6.9

The Font selection in the Active Block dialog box.

Several factors determine which font options are available. If you are using Windows 3.1 or a font manager program such as Adobe Type Manager, many additional fonts and point sizes are available (compared to Windows 3.0 without a font manager program). These additional fonts generally are higher resolution than the standard Windows fonts, and they greatly improve the quality of your reports.

A typeface of a given size with a given set of attributes is called a *font*. Although typeface and font have different meanings, users often interchange the two terms.

To change the font, choose **Property Current** Object or highlight the cell or block and click the right mouse button. Select Font. Choose an installed font from the list of typefaces. To change the point size, choose a size from the drop-down Point Size box. You can select check boxes for **Bold**, *Italics*, Underline, and ~~Strikeout~~. As you make selections, the sample box to the right of the Help button displays the data in the current cell using your choices. Choose OK to confirm the dialog box and apply the font changes.

If necessary, Quattro Pro 5.0 for Windows enlarges the row height to fit the selected fonts. Column widths do not adjust automatically, however, so numeric data may not fit in a cell after you change the font, and the data may display as asterisks. Adjust the column widths as needed to display the data correctly. Figure 6.10 shows how several different typefaces, point sizes, and attributes change the appearance of your data.

Use the Fit button on the Quattro Pro 5.0 for Windows SpeedBar to adjust column widths to the correct size after you make font selections. Highlight a single notebook row to adjust column widths to fit the longest cell entry below the highlighted row. Highlight a multiple-row block to adjust column widths to fit the longest cell entry in the specified block.

Aligning Labels and Values

You can align labels and values to the left side of cells (the default for labels), center labels and values in a cell or across a block, or align labels and values to the right side of the cell. Values (numbers and formulas) align with the right side of cells by default.

Quattro Pro for Windows
File Edit Block Data Tools Graph Property Window Help
Normal
100
Helv
A:F9
123.456789
FONTS.WB1
Examples of using different fonts
If necessary, Quattro Pro for
Windows enlarges the row height to
fit the selected fonts. Column widths
are not automatically adjusted,
however, so numeric data may not fit
in a cell after you change the font,
and may display as asterisks.
Adjust the column widths as needed
to correctly display the data.
NUM
READY

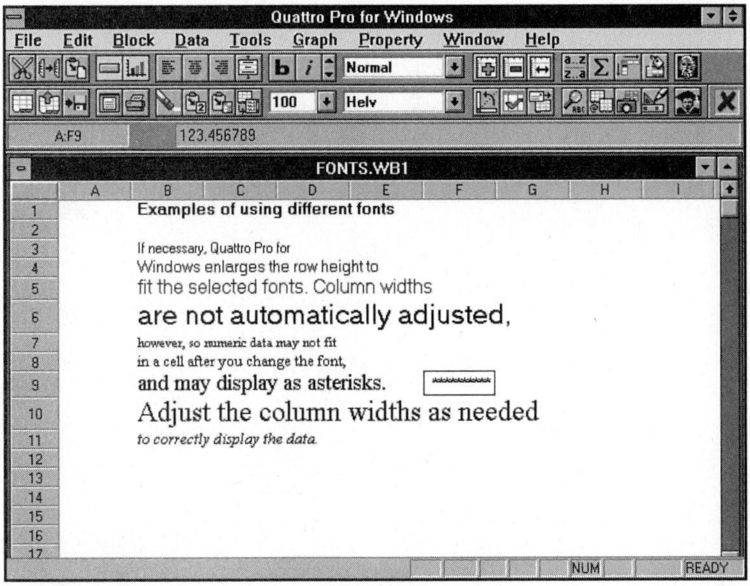

Fig. 6.10

You can use many different fonts in your spreadsheet notebooks.

To change the default label alignment for a notebook page, use the Label Alignment selection on the Active Page Object Inspector menu. To open the Active Page dialog box, choose the **P**roperty Active **P**age command or point to the page tab and click the right mouse button. Select Label Alignment and choose **L**eft, **R**ight, or **C**enter. Changing the default has no effect on existing labels.

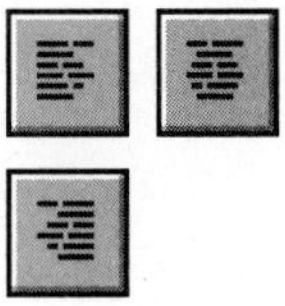

To change the label alignment for existing labels or values, use the Alignment selection in the Active Block dialog box. To open the Active Block dialog box, first highlight the block. Then choose **P**roperty **C**urrent Object or click the right mouse button inside the cell or block. Select Alignment. Choose **G**eneral to reset the alignment to the page default; or choose **L**eft, **R**ight, **C**enter, or Center across **b**lock.

Label alignment is relative to the column width. If a label's length is equal to or greater than the column width, the label aligns left unless you choose Center across **b**lock.

When you use labels as column headings over values, right-alignment of the labels often produces a better appearance because the column headings align with the data. Figure 6.11 demonstrates how labels aligned left, center, and right appear as headings over columns of values.

Fig. 6.11

Column headings with left, center, and right alignment.

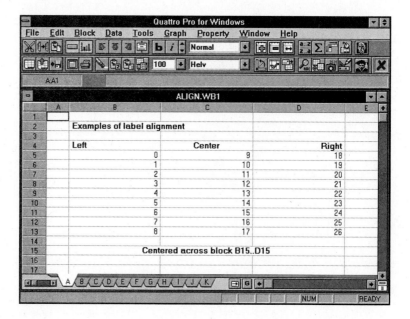

Formatting Cells with Borders

You can use the Line Drawing selection in the Active Block dialog box to draw lines above, below, on the sides, and around cells and blocks. Borders can be single lines, double lines, or thick lines. Figure 6.12, which has the spreadsheet grid turned off for clarity, shows several examples of cell and block borders.

To draw borders within or around a cell or block, follow these steps:

1. Highlight the cell or block.

2. Open the Active Block dialog box by choosing **Property Current Object** or by clicking the right mouse button inside the cell or block.

3. Select Line Drawing (see fig. 6.13).

4. Select the placement options you want.

5. Select the Line **Types** you want.

6. Choose OK to confirm the dialog box and add the selected borders.

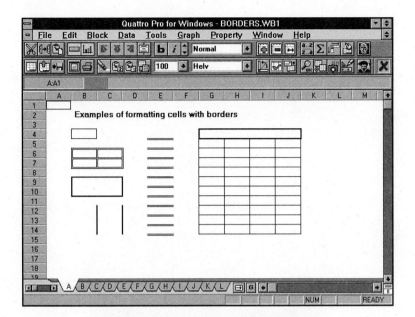

Fig. 6.12

Examples of different types of cell and block borders.

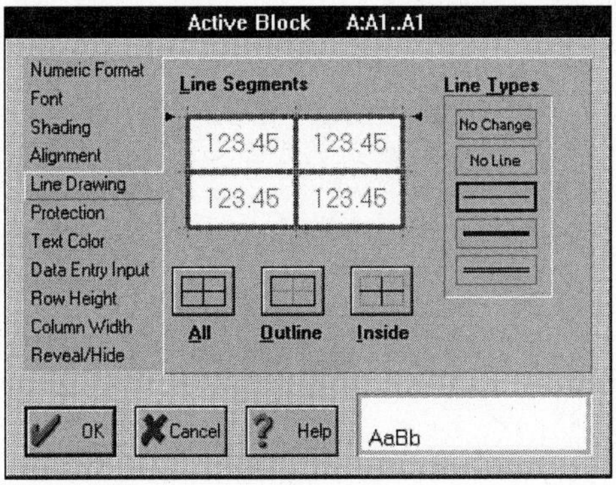

Fig. 6.13

Line Drawing options in the Active Block dialog box.

Any borders you add to cells or blocks print with the labels and values in a report. Quattro Pro 5.0 for Windows also can print spreadsheet grid lines (see Chapter 11, "Printing Reports").

Setting Color, Shading, and Display Options

You can change the appearance of the overall display in a number of ways. You can change the colors used for parts of the display and individual cells. You can show or hide the spreadsheet grid and frame. You also can zoom in or out to see more of the notebook at one time.

Setting the Color Palette

Quattro Pro 5.0 for Windows enables you to select object colors from a palette of 16 colors. You can adjust the palette to include any 16 colors from an almost unlimited range of pure and mixed colors. You adjust the color palette for a notebook by opening the Active Notebook properties dialog box and selecting Palette.

To adjust the color palette, choose **P**roperty Active **N**otebook or point to the notebook title bar and click the right mouse button. Select Palette. The Palette section of the Active Notebook dialog box shown in figure 6.14 appears. Point to the color you want to adjust and click the left mouse button to select the color.

Fig. 6.14

The Palette section of the Active Notebook dialog box.

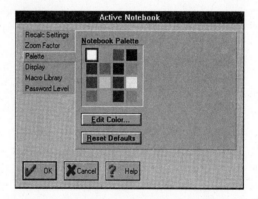

Choose **E**dit Color to display the Edit Palette Color dialog box shown in figure 6.15. Quattro Pro 5.0 for Windows enables you to adjust the color palette using your choice of three color models: **H**SB refers to Hue, Saturation, and Brightness; **R**GB refers to Red, Green, and Blue; and **C**MY refers to Cyan, Magenta, and Yellow. If you are adjusting colors for the best display on your monitor, the **R**GB model usually is the best option. If you are adjusting colors for printing on a color printer, the **C**MY model usually is most appropriate.

Adjust the color bars until the color meets your preference. Choose OK to confirm the dialog box. Select another color to edit in the Palette dialog box. Choose OK to confirm your selections and exit the dialog box.

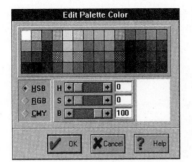

Fig. 6.15

The Edit Palette Color
dialog box.

Setting the Line-Drawing Color

You can select the color used to draw lines around cells and blocks for
each notebook page. To select the line-drawing color for a notebook
page, use the Line Color selection on the Active Page properties dialog
box. The Line Color section of the Active Page dialog box shown in
figure 6.16 appears when you make this selection.

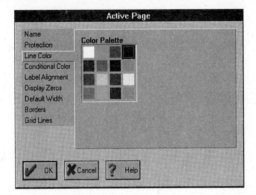

Fig. 6.16

The Line Color section of
the Active Page dialog
box.

To select the line-drawing color, choose **Property Active P**age or point
to the page tab and click the right mouse button. Select Line Color,
point to the color for line drawing, and choose OK.

Setting the Conditional Color

You can use color to emphasize values that are above or below specified values and to emphasize cells that return ERR. This step can make
data easier to understand at a glance, and the contrasting colors can

act as flags or warnings. If a formula recalculates to an out-of-range value, the color of the cell contents can change automatically, attracting attention immediately.

To specify conditional colors, open the Active Page properties dialog box by choosing **P**roperty Active **P**age or by pointing to the page tab and clicking the right mouse button. Select Conditional Color (see fig. 6.17).

Fig. 6.17

The Conditional Color section of the Active Page dialog box.

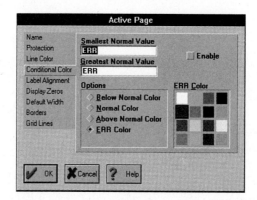

In the **S**mallest Normal Value text box, type the lowest number that should display in the color of in-range or normal values. To display negative numbers in a different color, for example, type **0**. In the **G**reatest Normal Value text box, type the highest number that should display in the color of in-range or normal values. To display numbers more than 1000 in a different color, for example, type **1000**. Choose the appropriate Options button and select the corresponding color. After you have set all the options you want, check the E**n**able check box and choose OK.

Setting the Text Color in a Block

You can add emphasis to text within a block by selecting any of the 16 colors on the current notebook palette. You use the Text Color selection in the Active Block dialog box to choose the text display color.

To choose the text display color for a block, follow these steps:

1. Highlight the cell or block.

2. Open the Active Block dialog box by choosing **Property Current Object** or by clicking the right mouse button inside the cell or block.

3. Select Text Color.

4. Select the text color you want to use and choose OK.

Setting the Shading Color

You can draw attention to cells or blocks by adding shading, a special effect that changes the background from white to a solid color. When you select shading, you also can select the foreground (text) color. Quattro Pro 5.0 for Windows enables you to select from 16 colors for both the background and the foreground (see fig. 6.18).

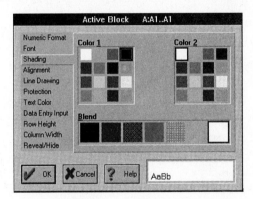

Fig. 6.18

Selecting block shading options.

To add shading, first select the cell or block, and then select Shading from the Active Block dialog box. Select the Color **1** (data), the Color **2** (background), and the **B**lend (shading pattern). Choose OK to confirm the dialog box and apply the shading.

Controlling the Display of Gridlines, the Worksheet Frame, and the Zoom Factor

You can control several other display options using the Object Inspectors. To control the display of gridlines, for example, right-click the page tab (or choose **Property Active Page**). Then select Grid Lines.

To control the display of the worksheet frame, right-click the page tab (or choose **P**roperty Active **P**age). Then select Borders.

To zoom in or out, right-click the notebook title bar (or choose **P**roperty Active **N**otebook). Then select Zoom Factor.

Chapter 3 shows you how to change many other global settings.

Using Named Styles

Named styles combine the following options into an easy-to-use group: alignment, format, protection, line drawing, shading, font, and text color. Named styles appear in the drop-down Style box on the SpeedBar and provide a shortcut method of applying attributes to cells and blocks.

To apply an existing named style, highlight the cell or block and choose the style you want from the drop-down style box.

To create or modify a named style, you can define the style settings using the Define/Modify Style dialog box options—or you can use an existing cell or block as a template. Figure 6.19 shows the Define/Modify Style dialog box.

Fig. 6.19

The Define/Modify Style dialog box.

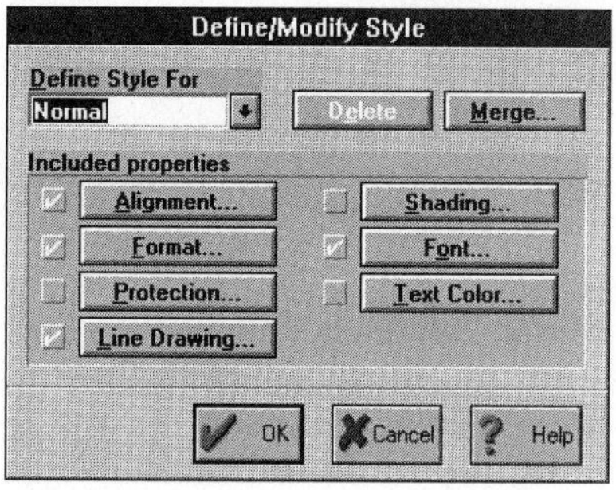

To use the Define/Modify Style dialog box options, choose **E**dit **D**efine Style. Type the style name in the **D**efine Style For text box. Choose and modify the properties you want to define. Press Enter or click OK.

To create or modify a named style using an existing cell or block as a template, choose **E**dit **D**efine Style. Type the style name in the **D**efine Style For text box. Choose **M**erge and type the name or cell address of the template in the Merge Style dialog box. Check the options to merge. Choose OK twice.

To remove an existing named style, in the **D**efine Style For text box, highlight the name of the style you want to delete. Choose De**l**ete, and then choose OK to confirm the dialog box.

Questions and Answers

Q: When I try to change the currency options in the Object Inspector Application dialog box, the options for currency symbol, placement, and negative values don't appear. What's wrong?

A: Make sure you choose **Q**uattro Pro/Windows rather than **W**indows Default, and the options should appear.

Q: Why did Ñ appear rather than ¥ when I tried to change the currency symbol to Yen?

A: You must include the leading 0, as in Alt+0165. Alt+165 displays the N with a tilde.

Q: Why doesn't my font list match what I see in the book?

A: The list of fonts displayed in your font list depends on several factors, including the version of Windows installed on your system, the fonts you have installed, and any font manager software you may have. If you are using Windows 3.1, you can obtain TrueType fonts from many sources and use them to enhance all your Windows documents.

Summary

This chapter presented a number of techniques you can use to make your data appear clearer and easier to understand. Turning raw data into clearly understandable information can be as important as calculating correct answers. In this chapter you learned to use the commands that control the appearance of data—both on-screen and in printed reports. The commands covered in this chapter enable you to change the default notebook settings. You also learned to apply the available formats to perform the following tasks: change the appearance of data; enhance the appearance of data using fonts, label-alignment options, lines, colors, and shading; and create and modify named styles.

You now can build and format spreadsheet notebooks. The next chapter extends your skills by showing you how to use the extensive library of functions in Quattro Pro 5.0 for Windows. Using these functions, you can access the vast power of Quattro Pro 5.0 for Windows to perform sophisticated data analysis.

Using Functions

Although you can construct your own spreadsheet formulas from scratch, developing the correct formulas for very complex equations can be daunting. Fortunately, Quattro Pro 5.0 for Windows provides a large variety of preconstructed formulas in the form of built-in *functions*. These functions handle a broad range of calculations and greatly ease the burden of developing your spreadsheet applications.

Quattro Pro 5.0 for Windows functions are available in several categories. Sections in this chapter discuss the following topics:

- Boolean functions
- Database functions
- Date and time functions - Business
- Date and time functions - Generation
- Date and time functions - Interpretation
- Engineering functions - Bessel
- Engineering functions - Complex number
- Engineering functions - Conversion
- Engineering functions - Test
- Financial functions - Annuity
- Financial functions - Bill
- Financial functions - Bond

- Financial functions - CD
- Financial functions - Cash Flow
- Financial functions - Conversion
- Financial functions - Depreciation
- Financial functions - Stock
- Logical functions
- Mathematical functions - Numerical
- Mathematical functions - Transcendental (logarithmic)
- Mathematical functions - Trigonometric
- Miscellaneous functions - General
- Miscellaneous functions - Cell Attribute
- Miscellaneous functions - Cell and Table
- Miscellaneous functions - Status
- Miscellaneous functions - Table Lookup
- Statistical functions - Descriptive
- Statistical functions - Inferential
- String functions - Modify
- String functions - Substring
- String functions - Value

The next section describes the generic steps for using Quattro Pro functions. Following sections provide descriptions for each of the Quattro Pro functions.

Entering a Quattro Pro 5.0 for Windows Function

Entering a Quattro Pro function requires the following four steps:

1. Type the @ sign to tell Quattro Pro that you want to enter a built-in function.

2. Type the function name.

3. If the function requires one or more arguments, type within parentheses any information, or arguments, that the function needs.

4. Press Enter.

An example of a function is @SUM. If you type the function **@SUM(1,3,5)**, Quattro Pro returns the calculated value 9—the sum of the numbers 1, 3, and 5.

All functions begin with—and are identified by—the @ sign. By typing @, you tell Quattro Pro that you are entering a function.

With the large number of functions available, you may not remember every function's name. Quattro Pro 5.0 for Windows functions, fortunately, use short names that are 1 to 14 character abbreviations indicating their purpose. The name of the function that calculates the sum, for example, is SUM. The name of the function that calculates the average is AVG, and the function that calculates the number of rows in a block is ROWS. Pressing the Help (F1) key enables you to access an index of the Quattro Pro functions. When in the input line, you also may click the @ symbol in the SpeedBar for a list of available @ functions.

After typing @ and the function name, enter any arguments the function needs to perform its calculations. Enter a function's arguments inside parentheses that immediately follow the function's name; be sure that you don't leave a space between the function name and the opening parenthesis. If the function has multiple arguments, separate the arguments with commas.

Following these guidelines, entering functions is simple and straightforward. Suppose, for example, that you want to calculate the total monthly sales from three branch offices. The function to calculate a sum is SUM, so you can easily write a Quattro Pro formula to make the calculation by typing

@SUM(500,450,525)

Quattro Pro returns the result 1475—the sum of the three numbers entered as arguments. The function begins with the @ sign, followed first by the function name SUM, and then by the arguments inside parentheses and separated by commas.

In this example, actual numeric values were entered as the function arguments. Although this might seem the easiest and most straightforward method, placing the data in spreadsheet cells and referring to those cells as the function's arguments offers several distinct advantages. Suppose, for example, that the manager of your second store phoned in late results indicating sales were actually $550, not $450 as reported earlier. If each store's sales were placed in a spreadsheet cell, correcting the calculation would be a simple matter of entering the correct data; Quattro Pro would automatically recalculate the correct result. With the sales figures stored in cells A1, A2, and A3, your formula could be entered as

@SUM(A1,A2,A3)

In addition, you can name each of the three cells that contain the sales results. You could then enter your formula in the following manner:

@SUM(STORE_1,STORE_2,STORE_3)

Some functions do not require arguments, so you do not enter any parentheses following the function name. The function @RAND, which returns a random number, is an example of one of the functions that do not require arguments.

FOR RELATED INFORMATION

◄◄ "Using Blocks," p. 126.

◄◄ "Entering Data in the Notebook," p. 97.

Using Boolean Functions

The *Boolean* functions enable you to perform binary, octal, decimal, and hexadecimal number manipulations. Boolean functions join, compare, and shift values at the bit level. These powerful functions provide capabilities for mathematical operations formerly available only in sophisticated programming languages. The Boolean functions perform bit manipulations on binary and hexadecimal numbers. You can use these functions in operations that apply digital logic to set, test, or shift bits in a number. Table 7.1 describes the Boolean functions.

Table 7.1 Boolean Functions

Function	Description
@ADDB(*Binary1*,[*Binary2*], [*BitIn*],[*Bits*])	Sums two binary numbers, or counts the bits in *Binary1* that are set to 1. If *BitIn* is 1, adds one extra bit to the result.

Function	Description
@ADDBO(*Binary1*,*Binary2*, [*BitIn]*,[*Bits*])	Returns the overflow bit of the sum of two binary numbers.
@ADDH(*Hex1*,[Hex2],[*BitIn*], [*Bits*])	Sums two hexadecimal numbers, or counts the bits in *Hex1* that are set to 1. If *BitIn* is 1, adds one extra bit to the result before returning the overflow.
@ADDHO(*Hex1*,*Hex2*,[BitIn*]*, [*Bits*])	Returns the overflow bit of the sum of two hexadecimal numbers. If *BitIn* is 1, adds one extra bit to the sum of the two numbers before returning the overflow.
@ANDB(*Binary1*,[*Binary2*], [*Bits*])	Performs a logical AND of *Binary1* and *Binary2*, or performs an AND reduction on *Binary1*.
@ANDH(*Hex1*,[*Hex2*],[*Bits*])	Performs a logical AND of *Hex1* and *Hex2*, or performs an AND reduction on *Hex1*.
@BITRB(*Binary*,*Position*)	Sets to 0 the bit at *Position* of a binary value.
@BITRH(*Hex*,*Position*)	Sets to 0 the bit at *Position* of a hexadecimal value.
@BITSB(*Binary*,*Position*)	Sets to 1 the bit at *Position* of a binary number.
@BITSH(*Hex*,*Position*)	Sets to 1 the bit at *Position* of a hexadecimal number.
@BITTB(*Binary*,*Position*)	Returns the value of the bit at *Position* of a binary number.
@BITTH(*Hex*,*Position*)	Returns the value of the bit at *Position* of a hexadecimal number.
@CATB(*Binary1*,[*HiBit1*], [*LoBit1*],[*Binary2*],[*HiBit2*], [*LoBit2*],[*Bits*])	Joins together two binary numbers or extracts selected bits from one binary number.
@CATH(*Hex1*,[*HiBit1*], [*LoBit1*],[*Hex2*],[*HiBit2*], [*LoBit2*],[*Bits*])	Joins together two hexadecimal numbers or extracts selected bits from one hexadecimal number.
@CATNB(*n*,*Binary1*,[*Binary2*], [*Binary3*],..., [*BinaryN*],[*Bits*])	Joins together *n* binary numbers.

(continues)

Table 7.1 Continued

Function	Description
@CATNH(*n*,*Hex1*,[*Hex2*], [*Hex3*],...,[*HexN*],[*Bits*])	Joins together *n* hexadecimal numbers.
@INVB(*Binary*,[*Bits*])	Inverts the bits of a binary number.
@INVH(*Hex*,[*Bits*])	Inverts the binary bits of a hexadecimal number.
@ORB(*Binary1*,[*Binary2*], [*Bits*])	Performs a logical OR of *Binary1* and *Binary2*.
@ORH(*Hex1*,[*Hex2*],[*Bits*])	Performs a logical OR of *Hex1* and *Hex2*.
@SHLB(*Binary*,[*ShiftBits*], [*BitIn*],[*Bits*])	Shifts the given binary number left by *ShiftBits* bits, and inserts the *BitIn* bit at the least significant bit (LSB).
@SHLBO(*Binary*,[*Bits*])	Returns the overflow bit of the given binary number after it has been shifted left by one bit.
@SHLH(*Hex*,[*ShiftBits*], [*BitIn*],[*Bits*])	Shifts *Hex* left by *ShiftBits* bits, and inserts the *BitIn* bit at the least significant bit (LSB).
@SHLHO(*Hex*,[*Bits*])	Returns the overflow bit of *Hex* after it has been shifted left by one bit.
@SHRB(*Binary*,[*ShiftBits*], [*BitIn*],[*Bits*])	Returns the result of shifting *Binary* right by *ShiftBits* bits, and inserts the *BitIn* bit at the most significant bit (MSB).
@SHRBO(*Binary*,[*Bits*])	Returns the overflow bit of *Binary* after it has been shifted right by one bit.
@SHRH(*Hex*,[*ShiftBits*], [*BitIn*],[*Bits*])	Returns the result of shifting *Hex* right by *ShiftBits* bits, and inserts the *BitIn* bit at the most significant bit (MSB).
@SHRHO(*Hex*,[*Bits*])	Returns the overflow bit of *Hex* after it has been shifted right by one bit.
@SUBB(*Binary1*,*Binary2*, [*BitIn*],[*Bits*])	Returns the difference of two binary numbers.

Function	Description
@SUBBO(*Binary1*,*Binary2*, [*BitIn*],[*Bits*])	Returns the overflow bit of the difference of two binary numbers.
@SUBH(*Hex1*,*Hex2*,[*BitIn*], [*Bits*])	Returns the difference of two hexadecimal numbers.
@SUBHO(*Hex1*,*Hex2*,[*BitIn*], [*Bits*])	Returns the overflow bit of the difference of two hexadecimal numbers.
@XORB(*Binary1*,[*Binary2*], [*Bits*])	Performs a logical exclusive OR of *Binary1* and *Binary2*.
@XORH(*Hex1*,[*Hex2*],[*Bits*])	Performs a logical exclusive OR of *Hex1* and *Hex2*.

Use two's complement notation to add or subtract negative numbers with the Boolean functions. The sign bit (the leftmost bit of the word) of two's complement notation is 0 for positive numbers, and 1 for negative numbers. Negative numbers are converted to two's complement by inverting each bit and adding 1.

The *Bits* argument defines the word size, and defaults to the number of bits in the largest input number. Each hexadecimal digit equals 4 bits.

The *BitIn* argument represents either the binary bit inserted during a shift, the carry bit for addition, or the borrow bit for subtraction; the default is 0.

Using Database Functions

The database functions enable you to perform statistical calculations and queries on a Quattro Pro 5.0 for Windows database or an external database. Each of the database functions has an equivalent statistical function. Database functions calculate values in a field that meet criteria you specify. Statistical functions calculate all values in a block. You use @DAVG, for example, to find the average value in a field in a database; you use @AVG to find the average value in a block. You also use database functions when you want to analyze cells in a block, if you want to consider only cells that meet specified criteria. Table 7.2 lists the functions and the database statistical functions they perform.

Table 7.2 Database Functions

Function	Description
@DAVG(*block,column,criteria*)	Averages the values of selected values in a field that meet the criteria.
@DCOUNT(*block,column, criteria*)	Counts the number of values of selected values in a field that meet the criteria.
@DMAX(*block,column,criteria*)	Finds the largest value of selected values in a field that meet the criteria.
@DMIN(*block,column,criteria*)	Finds the smallest value of selected values in a field that meet the criteria.
@DSTD(*block,column,criteria*)	Calculates the population standard deviation of selected values in a field that meet the criteria.
@DSTDS(*block,column,criteria*)	Calculates the sample standard deviation of selected values in a field that meet the criteria.
@DSUM(*block,column,criteria*)	Calculates the sum of selected values in a field that meet the criteria.
@DVAR(*block,column,criteria*)	Calculates the population variation of selected values in a field that meet the criteria.
@DVARS(*block,column,criteria*)	Calculates the sample variation of selected values in a field that meet the criteria.

The general format of these functions is

@FUNCTION(*block,column,criteria*)

Block and *criteria* are the same as those used by the **Data Query** command. *Column* indicates which field to select from the database. You do not need to specify *block* and *criteria* with the **Data Query** command before using the database functions.

Block specifies the database or part of a database to be used. It can be the name or address of a block that contains a database table, or the name of an external database table.

Criteria specifies which records are to be selected. *Criteria* can be a block name or an address.

Column is the column number of the field that the function is to select. The first field is in column 0, the second in column 1, and so on.

Database functions are similar to statistical functions (covered later in this chapter), but database functions process data items that meet only the criteria you specify. If, for example, you have a list of employees, their departments, and their annual salaries, @AVG calculates the average of all salaries, while @DAVG calculates the average salaries of a specified subgroup.

Using Date and Time Functions

The date and time functions enable you to convert dates and times to serial numbers; you then use the serial numbers to perform date and time arithmetic. These functions enable you to easily calculate differences between dates or times, sort by dates or times, and compare a range of dates or times. In addition, date and time functions are useful for documenting your spreadsheets and printed reports. You can, for example, type **@NOW** at the beginning of your spreadsheet to display the current date or time (depending on the cell format you assign). If you select the cells containing these functions when you print a report, the report shows the exact date and time you prepared the report for printing. There are three subcategories of date and time functions: business, generation, and interpretation.

Using Date and Time Business Functions

The date and time business functions perform calculations concerned with accounting for business days. With these functions, you can calculate the first or last business day in a given month, the number of business days between two dates, and whether a given date is a business day. Table 7.3 summarizes the date and time business functions and the calculations they perform.

Table 7.3 Date and Time Business Functions

Function	Description
@ABDAYS(*date,days,* [*holidays],[saturday],* [*sunday*])	Adds or subtracts business days to *date*.
@BDAYS(*startdate,enddate,* [*holidays],[saturday],* [*sunday*])	Returns the number of business days between *startdate* and *enddate*.
@BUSDAY(*date,[direction],* [*holidays],[saturday],* [*sunday*])	Returns *date* if it is a business day, or the closest business day before or after *date*.
@FBDAY(*date,[holidays],* [*saturday],[sunday*])	Returns the date of the first business day of the month in which *date* falls.
@ISBDAY(*date,[holidays],* [*saturday],[sunday*])	Returns 1 if *date* is a business day, or 0 if it is not.
@LBDAY(*date,[holidays],* [*saturday],[sunday*])	Returns the date of the last business day of the month in which *date* falls.
@NBDAY(*date,[holidays],* [*saturday],[sunday*])	Returns the date of the first valid business day after *date*.
@PBDAY(*date,[holidays],* [*saturday],[sunday*])	Returns the date of the first valid business day before *date*.

Date, startdate, and *enddate* are date serial numbers.

Days is an integer representing the number of days.

Direction is a flag specifying the direction of adjustment; 0 = forward (default); 1 = backward; 2 = forward if in same month as *date*, otherwise backward.

Holidays is the name or address of a block containing dates that are holidays, the date of a single holiday, or 0 to indicate no holidays.

Saturday is 1 if Saturday is a business day, 0 if it is not.

Sunday is 1 if Sunday is a business day, 0 if it is not. The default for *holidays, saturday,* and *sunday* is 0.

Using Date and Time Generation Functions

The date and time generation functions enable you to convert dates and times into serial numbers, which you can then use to perform date and time arithmetic. These functions offer a valuable aid when dates and times affect spreadsheet calculations or are used to control macros. Table 7.4 summarizes the date and time generation functions available in Quattro Pro 5.0 for Windows.

Table 7.4 Date and Time Generation Functions

Function	Description
@DATE(*year,month,day*)	Calculates the serial number representing the described date.
@DATEVALUE(*date_string*)	Converts a date expressed as a valid string into a serial number.
@NOW	Calculates the serial date and time number from the current system date and time.
@TIME(*hour,minute,second*)	Calculates the serial number representing the described time.
@TIMEVALUE(*time_string*)	Converts a time expressed as a valid string into a serial number.
@TODAY	Calculates the integer serial date number from the current system date.

Using Date and Time Interpretation Functions

The date and time interpretation functions convert a date/time serial number into a number. These functions are useful for calculations that deal with dates or time as units. Table 7.5 summarizes the date and time interpretation functions.

Table 7.5 Date and Time Interpretation Functions

Function	Description
@ACDAYS(*date*,*days*, [*calendar*],[*endmnth*])	Adds *days* to *date*.
@AMNTHS(*date*,*months*, [*endmnth*])	Adds *months* to *date*.
@CDAYS(*startdate*,*enddate*, [*calendar*],[*february*])	Returns the number of days between *startdate* and *enddate*.
@DAY(*datetimenumber*)	Returns the day of the month (1-31) represented by *datetimenumber*.
@EMNTH(*date*)	Returns the date of the last day of the month in which *date* falls.
@HOLS(*startdate*,*enddate*, *holidays*,[*saturday*],[*sunday*])	Returns the number of *holidays* between *startdate* and *enddate*, excluding *holidays* that fall on weekends.
@HOUR(*datetimenumber*)	Returns the number of hours past midnight (0-23) represented by *datetimenumber*.
@LWKDAY(*wkday*,*month*,*year*, [*auxwkday*])	Returns the date of the last *weekday* in *month* and *year*.
@MDAYS(*month*,*year*)	Returns the number of calendar days in *month* and *year*.
@MINUTE(*datetimenumber*)	Returns the number of minutes past the hour (0-59) represented by *datetimenumber*.
@MNTHS(*startdate*,*enddate*, [*endmnth*])	Returns the number of whole months between *startdate* and *enddate*.
@MONTH(*datetimenumber*)	Returns the month in number form (1-12) represented by *datetimenumber*.
@NWKDAY(*n*,*wkday*,*month*, *year*,[*auxwkday*])	Returns the date of the *n*th occurrence of *wkday* in *month* and *year*.
@SECOND(*datetimenumber*)	Returns the number of seconds past the minute (0-59) represented by *datetimenumber*.
@WKDAY(*date*)	Returns the day of the week that *date* falls on.

Function	Description
@YDAYS(*year*)	Returns the number of calendar days in *year*.
@YDIV(*date*,[*numdiv*], [*months*],[*anchor*],[*endmnth*])	Returns the date of the beginning of the year division in which *date* or *numdiv* always falls.
@YEAR(*datetimenumber*)	Returns the year number (-300 to 1299; 0 = 1900) represented by *datetimenumber*.
@YEARFRAC(*startdate*, *enddate*,[*calendar*])	Returns the year fraction representing the number of whole days between *startdate* and *enddate*.

Anchor is the date to anchor division boundaries on (the default is January 1, 1900).

Auxwkday is an auxiliary day of the week that must fall in the same week as *wkday*: 0 for no auxiliary day (default) or a number from 1 (Saturday) to 7 (Friday).

Calendar is a flag specifying which calendar to observe: 0 = 30/360 (default), 1 = actual/actual, 2 = actual/360, 3 = actual/365.

Date, startdate, and *enddate* are date serial numbers.

Days is an integer representing number of days to add.

Endmnth is a flag specifying whether to adhere to ends of months: 1 = yes (default), 2 = no.

February is a flag specifying whether to use 30-day treatment of February for 30/360 calendar: 0 = 30-day (default), 1 = use the actual-day treatment.

Holidays is a block containing dates that are holidays, the date of a single holiday, or 0 to indicate no holidays.

Month is a number from 1 (January) to 12 (December).

Months is the integer number of months per division, the default is 3.

N is a number from 1 to 5.

Numdiv is an integer representing number of divisions away from beginning of division in which *date* falls.

Saturday is a flag specifying whether Saturday is a business day: 0 = no (default), 1 = yes.

Sunday is a flag specifying whether Sunday is a business day: 0 = no (default), 1 = yes.

Wkday is a number from 1 (Saturday) to 7 (Friday).

Year is a number from 0 (1900) to 199 (2099), or a standard year like 1993.

Using Engineering Functions

The engineering functions enable you to perform calculations for solving complex engineering problems, work with imaginary numbers, convert between numbering systems, and test results. The engineering functions return modified Bessel functions, convert or modify a complex number (a number whose square is a negative real number), and return error functions or test the relationship of two numeric values. The engineering functions include four subcategories: Bessel, complex number, conversion, and test. The following sections describe the engineering functions.

Using Engineering Bessel Functions

The engineering Bessel functions return modified Bessel functions. Table 7.6 summarizes the engineering Bessel functions.

Table 7.6 Engineering Bessel Functions

Function	Description
@BESSELI(x,n)	Returns the modified Bessel function I$n(x)$.
@BESSELJ(x,n)	Returns the modified Bessel function J$n(x)$.
@BESSELK(x,n)	Returns the modified Bessel function K$n(x)$.
@BESSELY(x,n)	Returns the modified Bessel function Y$n(x)$.

x is a nonnegative numeric value at which to evaluate the function.

n is an integer representing the order of the Bessel function; if n isn't an integer, it's truncated to an integer.

Using Engineering Complex Number Functions

The engineering complex number functions convert or modify a complex number (a number whose square is a negative real number). Table 7.7 summarizes the engineering complex number functions.

Table 7.7 Engineering Complex Number Functions

Function	Description
@COMPLEX(*x*,*y*)	Converts real (*x*) and imaginary (*y*) coefficients into a complex number.
@CONVERT(*x*,*fromunit*,*tounit*)	Converts *x* from *fromunit* to *tounit*.
@IMABS(*complex*)	Returns the absolute value (modulus) of a complex number.
@IMAGINARY(*complex*)	Returns the imaginary coefficient of *complex*.
@IMARGUMENT(*complex*)	Returns the argument theta, an angle expressed in radians.
@IMCONJUGATE(*complex*)	Returns the complex conjugate of *complex*.
@IMCOS(*complex*)	Returns the cosine of *complex*.
@IMDIV(*complex1*,*complex2*)	Returns the quotient of *complex1* and *complex2*.
@IMEXP(*complex*)	Returns the exponential of *complex*.
@IMLN(*complex*)	Returns the natural logarithm of *complex*.
@IMLOG10(*complex*)	Returns the base-10 logarithm of *complex*.
@IMLOG2(*complex*)	Returns the base-2 logarithm of *complex*.
@IMPOWER(*complex*,*power*)	Raises *complex* to *power*.
@IMPRODUCT(*complex1*,*complex2*)	Returns the product of *complex1* and *complex2*.
@IMREAL(*complex*)	Returns the real coefficient of *complex*.

(continues)

Table 7.7 Continued

Function	Description
@IMSIN(*complex*)	Returns the sine of *complex*.
@IMSQRT(*complex*)	Returns the square root of *complex*.
@IMSUB(*complex1*,*complex2*)	Returns the difference of *complex1* and *complex2*.
@IMSUM(*list*)	Returns the sum of complex numbers.

Complex is a complex number in the format *x+yi, x+iy, x+yj,* or *x+jy.*

Complex1 is the complex numerator or dividend in the format *x+yi, x+iy, x+yj,* or *x+jy.*

Complex2 is the complex denominator or divisor in the format *x+yi, x+iy, x+yj,* or *x+jy.*

Fromunit is the unit type of the value *x.*

List is one or more complex numbers in the format *x+yi, x+iy, x+yj,* or *x+jy,* separated by commas.

Power is the power to which you want to raise *complex.*

Tounit is the units to convert the value *x* into.

X is a numeric value representing real coefficient of *complex.*

Y is a numeric value representing imaginary coefficient of *complex.*

Using Engineering Conversion Functions

The engineering conversion functions convert numbers from one number system to another. Table 7.8 summarizes the engineering conversion functions.

Table 7.8 Engineering Conversion Functions

Function	Description
@ASCTOHEX(*ASCII,*[*Places*])	Returns the hexadecimal string equivalent of an ASCII number.

Function	Description
@BASE(*Decimal*,[*Base*], [*Precision*])	Converts a base-10 number into another base.
@BINTOHEX(*binary*)	Returns the hexadecimal string equivalent of *binary*.
@BINTOHEX64(*binary*,[*places*])	Returns the hexadecimal string equivalent of *binary* (up to 64 bits).
@BINTONUM(*binary*)	Returns the decimal equivalent of *binary*.
@BINTONUM64(*binary*,[*signed*])	Returns the decimal equivalent of *binary* (up to 64 bits).
@BINTOOCT(*binary*)	Returns the octal string equivalent of *binary*.
@BINTOOCT64(*binary*,[*places*])	Returns the octal string equivalent of *binary* (up to 64 bits).
@HEXTOASC(*hex*)	Returns the ASCII equivalent of *hex*.
@HEXTOBIN(*hex*)	Returns the binary string equivalent of *hex*.
@HEXTOBIN64(*hex*,[*places*])	Returns the binary string equivalent of *hex* (up to 64 bits).
@HEXTONUM64(*hex*,[*signed*])	Returns the decimal equivalent of *hex* (up to 64 bits).
@HEXTOOCT(*hex*)	Returns the octal string equivalent of *hex*.
@HEXTOOCT64(*hex*,[*places*])	Returns the octal string equivalent of *hex* (up to 64 bits).
@NUMTOBIN(*decimal*)	Returns the binary string equivalent of *decimal*.
@NUMTOBIN64(*decimal*,[*places*])	Returns the binary string equivalent of *decimal* (up to 64 bits).
@NUMTOHEX64(*decimal*,[*places*])	Returns the hexadecimal string equivalent of *decimal* (up to 64 bits).
@NUMTOOCT(*decimal*)	Returns the octal string equivalent of *decimal*.
@NUMTOOCT64(*decimal*,[*places*])	Returns the octal string equivalent of *decimal* (up to 64 bits).

(continues)

Table 7.8 Continued

Function	Description
@OCTTOBIN(*oct*)	Returns the binary string equivalent of *oct*.
@OCTTOHEX(*oct*)	Returns the hexadecimal string equivalent of *oct*.
@OCTTONUM(*oct*)	Returns the decimal equivalent of *oct*.

ASCII is the ASCII character string to convert.

Base indicates the target number base.

Binary is a binary number to convert.

Decimal is any decimal value to convert.

Hex is the hexadecimal number to convert.

Oct is the octal number to convert.

Places is the number of characters to return.

Precision indicates the number of desired digits after the decimal point.

Signed is 1 if the most significant bit of *binary* is a sign bit, or 0 (default) if *binary* is positive.

Using Engineering Test Functions

The engineering test functions return error functions or test the relationship of two numeric values. Table 7.9 summarizes the engineering test functions.

Table 7.9 Engineering Test Functions

Function	Description
@DELTA(x,[y])	Tests whether two numbers are equal.
@ERF(*lower*,[*upper*])	Returns the error function.
@ERFC(*lower*)	Returns the complementary function.
@GESTEP(x,[y])	Tests whether a number is greater than a threshold value.

Lower is the lower bound.

Upper is the upper bound.

X and *y* are the numeric values to check. If *y* is omitted, it is assumed to be 0.

Using Financial Functions

The financial functions are powerful tools in many business spreadsheets. With these functions, you can discount cash flow, calculate depreciation, and analyze the return on an investment. These functions greatly ease the burden of complex financial and accounting calculations. They also provide tools allowing the average user to perform less complex, everyday financial computations. The financial functions include eight subcategories: annuity, bill, bond, CD, cash flow, conversion, depreciation, and stock. The following sections describe the financial functions.

Using Financial Annuity Functions

The financial annuity functions calculate values involving a series of periodic payments over a term. Table 7.10 summarizes the financial annuity functions.

Table 7.10 Financial Annuity Functions

Function	Description
@AMAINT(*principal,int,term, n,[part],[residual], [resoff],[adv],[odd],[simp]*)	Calculates the accumulated interest paid on an amortized loan after *n* payments.
@AMINT(*principal,term, payment,[residual],[resoff], [adv],[odd],[simp],[prec]*)	Calculates the periodic interest rate for an amortized loan.
@AMPMT(*principal,int,term, [residual],[resoff],[adv], [odd],[simp]*)	Calculates the periodic payment for an amortized loan.
@AMPMTI(*principal,int,term, n,[residual],[resoff],[adv], [odd],[simp]*)	Calculates the interest portion of the *n*th periodic payment of an amortized loan.

(continues)

Table 7.10 Continued

Function	Description
@AMPRN(*int,term,payment,* [*residual*],[*resoff*],[*adv*], [*odd*],[*simp*])	Calculates the initial principal of an amortized loan.
@AMRES(*principal,int,term, payment,*[*resoff*],[*adv*], [*odd*],[*simp*])	Calculates the end value of an amortized loan or the future value of an annuity.
@AMRPRN(*principal,int,term, n,*[*part*],[*residual*], [*resoff*],[*adv*],[*odd*],[*simp*])	Calculates the remaining balance of an amortized loan after *n* payments.
@AMTERM(*principal,int, payment,*[*residual*], [*resoff*],[*adv*],[*odd*],[*simp*])	Calculates the length of an amortized loan, expressed as number of payments.
@CTERM(*int,fv,pv*)	Returns the number of compounding time periods required to achieve *fv*, given *pv* and *int*.
@FV(*payment,int,nper*)	Returns the future value of an investment at the end of the term, given *payment*, *int*, and *nper*.
@FVAL(*int,nper,payment,* [*pv*],[*type*])	Returns the future value of an investment, given *int*, *nper*, *payment*, and optional *pv* and *type*.
@IPAYMT(*int,n,nper,pv,* [*fv*],[*type*])	Returns the interest portion of a single payment given *int*, *n*, *nper*, *pv*, and optional *fv* and *type*.
@IRATE(*nper,payment,pv,* [*fv*],[*type*])	Returns the interest rate given *nper*, *payment*, *pv*, and optional *fv* and *type*.
@MTGACC(*int,ttlper, principal,residual, extraprin,*[*fper*],[*lper*], [*rper*],[*option*])	Calculates the effects of paying extra monthly principal for amortized loans.
@NPER(*int,payment,pv,* [*fv*],[*type*])	Returns the number of periods given *int*, *payment*, *pv*, and optional *fv* and *type*.
@PAYMT(*int,nper,pv,*[*fv*], [*type*])	Returns periodic payments given *int*, *nper*, *pv*, and optional *fv* and *type*.
@PMT(*pv,int,nper*)	Returns the periodic payment required to fully amortize the principal during the term, given *pv*, *int*, and *nper*.

Function	Description
@PPAYMT(*int,per,nper,pv,* [*fv*],[*type*])	Returns the principal portion of a single payment.
@PV(*payment,int,nper*)	Returns the present value of an investment, given *payment*, *int*, and *nper*.
@PVAL(*int,nper,payment,* [*fv*],[*type*])	Returns the present value of an investment, given *int*, *nper*, *payment*, and optional *fv* and *type*.
@RATE(*fv,pv,nper*)	Returns the interest rate required to achieve a given *fv*, given *pv*, and *nper*.
@TERM(*payment,int,fv*)	Returns the number of periodic payments required to achieve a specified *fv*, given *payment* and *int*.

Adv is the number of advance payments made at loan inception; the default is 0.

Extraprin is the extra principal amount to be paid each period.

Fper is the number of the first period, relative to the starting point, in which extra principal is paid; the default is 1—the first period.

Fv is future value.

Int is the periodic interest rate.

Lper is the number of the last period, relative to the starting point, in which extra principal is paid; the default is until the end of the loan.

N is the number of payments made.

Nper is the number of periods.

Odd is the number of periods between loan inception and date of first payment (the default is 1).

Option specifies the output value type (the default is 0):

> 0 = number of periods to loan end, when balance equals *residual*.
>
> 1 = balance of loan at the *rper*.
>
> 2 = cumulative interest paid at *rper*.
>
> 3 = cumulative principal paid at *rper*.

10 = number of fewer periods in loan life, due to payment of extra principal

11 = balance reduction at *rper* due to payment of extra principal

12 = reduction in cumulative interest paid at *rper* due to payment of extra principal

13 = increase in cumulative principal paid at *rper* due to payment of extra principal

Part is the part of $(n+1)$th period passed; it must be from 0 to 1, and the default is 0.

Payment is the periodic payment.

Prec is the required precision of result; the default is 0.000001.

Principal is the initial loan principal.

Pv is present value.

Residual is the remaining balance on loan at the end of the loan term; the default is 0.

Resoff is the number of periods after last periodic payment that *residual* is to be paid; the default is 0.

Rper is the period for which the loan status is reported; the default is at loan end. *Rper* does not affect the value @MTGACC returns if *option* is 0 or 10.

Simp is 0 to specify compounded interest, or 1 to specify simple interest; the default is 0.

Term is the term of loan, expressed in number of total payments.

TtlPer is the total periods in the loan from start to finish, or the total periods remaining from the chosen starting period forward.

Type specifies whether payments are made at the beginning (1) or end (0) of the period.

Using Financial Bill Functions

The financial bill functions compute values for Treasury bills. Table 7.11 summarizes the financial bill functions.

Table 7.11 Financial Bill Functions

Function	Description
@DISC(*settle,maturity, price,*[*redemption*], [*calendar*])	Returns the discount rate for a security.
@INTRATE(*settle,maturity, investment,redemption,* [*calendar*])	Returns the interest rate for a fully invested security.
@PRICEDISC(*settle,maturity, discount,*[*redemption*], [*calendar*])	Returns the price per $100 face value of a security that pays periodic interest.
@RECEIVED(*settle,maturity, investment,discount,* [*calendar*])	Returns the amount received at maturity for a fully invested security.
@TBILLEQ(*settle,maturity, discount*)	Returns the price per $100 face value for a Treasury bill.
@TBILLPRICE(*settle, maturity,discount*)	Returns the price per $100 face value for a Treasury bill.
@TBILLYIELD(*settle, maturity,price*)	Returns the yield for a Treasury bill.
@YIELDDISC(*settle, maturity,price,*[*redemption*], [*calendar*])	Returns the annual yield for a discounted security.

Calendar is a flag specifying which calendar to observe: 0 = 30/360, 1 = actual/actual, 2 = actual/360, 3 = actual/365 (default is 0).

Discount is the rate of discount, and must be between 0 and 1.

Investment is the amount invested, and must be greater than 0.

Maturity is a number representing the maturity date, and must be greater than *settle*.

Price is the settlement price per 100 face value, and must be between 0 and 100.

Redemption is the redemption value per 100 face value, and must be greater than 0; the default is 100.

Settle is a number representing the settlement date, and must be less than *maturity*.

Using Financial Bond Functions

The financial bond functions compute values for bonds. Table 7.12 summarizes the financial bond functions.

Table 7.12 Financial Bond Functions

Function	Description
@ACCRINT(*settle*,*maturity*, *coupon*,[*issue*],[*firstcpn*], [*par*],[*freq*],[*calendar*])	Returns the accrued interest for a security that pays periodic interest.
@COUPDAYBS(*settle*,*maturity*, [*freq*],[*calendar*])	Returns the number of days from the beginning of the coupon period to the settlement date.
@COUPDAYS(*settle*,*maturity*, [*freq*],[*calendar*])	Returns the number of days in the coupon period that contains the settlement date.
@COUPDAYSNC(*settle*,*maturity*, [*freq*],[*calendar*])	Returns the number of days from the settlement date to the next coupon date.
@COUPNCD(*settle*,*maturity*, [*freq*],[*calendar*])	Returns the next coupon date after the settlement date.
@COUPNUM(*settle*,*maturity*, [*freq*],[*calendar*])	Returns the umber of coupons payable between the settlement date and maturity date.
@COUPPCD(*settle*,*maturity*, [*freq*],[*calendar*])	Returns the previous coupon date before the settlement date.
@DURATION(*settle*,*maturity*, *coupon*,*yield*,[*freq*], [*calendar*])	Returns the annual duration of a security with periodic interest payments.
@MDURATION(*settle*,*maturity*, *coupon*,*yield*,[*freq*], [*calendar*])	Returns the Macauley modified duration for a security with an assumed par value of $100.
@ODDFPRICE(*settle*,*maturity*, *issue*,*firstcpn*,*coupon*,*yield*, [*redemption*],[*freq*], [*calendar*])	Returns the price per $100 face value of a security with an odd first period.
@ODDFYIELD(*settle*,*maturity*, *issue*,*firstcpn*,*coupon*,*price*, [*redemption*],[*freq*], [*calendar*])	Returns the yield of a security with an odd first period.

Function	Description
@ODDLPRICE(*settle,maturity, lastcpn,coupon,yield, [redemption],[freq], [calendar]*)	Returns the price per $100 face value of a security with an odd last period.
@ODDLYIELD(*settle,maturity, lastcpn,coupon,price, [redemption],[freq], [calendar]*)	Returns the yield of a security with an odd last period.
@PRICE(*settle,maturity, coupon,yield,[redemption], [freq],[calendar]*)	Returns the price per $100 face value of a security that pays periodic interest.
@YIELD(*settle,maturity, issue,coupon,price, [calendar]*)	Returns the yield on a security that pays periodic interest.

Calendar is a flag specifying which calendar to observe: 0 = 30/360, 1 = actual/actual, 2 = actual/360, 3 = actual/365. The default is 0.

Coupon is the coupon rate between 0 and 1.

FirstCpn is a number representing the first coupon date.

Freq is the frequency of coupon payments in the number of payments per year: 1, 2, 3, 4, 6, or 12; the default is 2.

Issue is a number representing the issue date.

Lastcpn is a number representing the last coupon date.

Maturity is a number representing the maturity date.

Par is the par value; the default is 1000.

Settle is a number representing the settlement date.

Using Financial CD Functions

The financial CD functions compute values for certificates of deposit. Table 7.13 summarizes the financial CD functions.

Table 7.13 Financial CD Functions

Function	Description
@ACCRINTM(*issue*,*settle*, *coupon*,[*par*],[*calendar*])	Returns the accrued interest for a security that pays interest at maturity.
@PRICEMAT(*settle*,*maturity*, *issue*,*coupon*,*yield*, [*calendar*])	Returns the price per $100 face value of a security that pays interest at maturity.
@YIELDMAT(*settle*,*maturity*, *issue*,*coupon*,*price*, [*calendar*])	Returns the annual yield of a security that pays interest at maturity.

Calendar is a flag specifying which calendar to observe: 0 = 30/360, 1 = actual/actual, 2 = actual/360, 3 = actual/365. The default is 0.

Coupon is the coupon rate between 0 and 1.

Issue is a number representing the issue date.

Maturity is a number representing the maturity date.

Par is the par value; the default is 1000.

Price is the price per 100 face value.

Settle is a number representing the settlement date.

Yield is the annual yield between 0 and 1.

Using Financial Cash Flow Functions

The financial cash flow functions operate on tables of data that record income and expenditures. Table 7.14 summarizes the financial cash flow functions.

Table 7.14 Financial Cash Flow Functions

Function	Description
@DURAT(*discrate*,*flows*, [*initial*],[[*odd\periods*]], [*simp*],[*pathdep*],[*filter*], [*start*],[*end*])	Calculates the duration of a given cash flow structure.

Function	Description
@FUTV(*intrate,flows*, [[*odd*|*periods*]],[*simp*], [*pathdep*],[*filter*], [*start*],[*end*])	Calculates the future value of a given cash flow structure.
@IRR(*guess,flows*)	Returns the internal rate of return of an investment.
@NETPV(*discrate,flows*, [*initial*],[[*odd*|*periods*]], [*simp*],[*pathdep*],[*filter*], [*start*],[*end*])	Calculates net present value of a given cash flow structure.
@NPV(*rate,flows*,[*type*])	Returns the net present value of a future cash flow.
@PIRATE(*npv,flows*,[*initial*], [[*odd*|*periods*]],[*simp*], [*pathdep*],*guess*], [*precision*],[*maxiter*], [*filter*],[*start*],[*end*])	Calculates the internal rate of return of a given cash flow structure.
@SCMARG(*npv,discrate,flows*, [*initial*],[[*odd*|*periods*]], [*simp*],[*pathdep*],[*guess*], [*precision*],[*maxiter*], [*filter*],[*start*],[*end*])	Calculates the discount scenario margin—the margin to add to each discount rate in order to arrive at a given net present value.

Discrate is the discount rate or block containing discount rates corresponding to block of cash flows.

End is an ending cash flow amount to compare against individual flows.

Filter is a flag specifying filter type: 0 = no filter (default); 1 = cashflow less than *start*; 2 = cashflow less than or equal *start*; 3 = cashflow greater than *start*; 4 = cashflow greater than or equal to *start*; 5 = *start* less than cashflow less than *end*; 6 = *start* less than or equal cashflow less than or equal *end*.

Flows is a block containing cash flows.

Guess is an initial margin for numerical search.

Initial is the initial cash flow; the default is 0.

Intrate is the interest rate or a block containing interest (discount) rates.

Maxiter is the maximum number of iterations for search; the default is 50.

Npv is the net present value.

Odd | Periods is the delay between initial and first cash flow, in number of periods (the default is 1), or a block containing lengths of periods between cash flows.

Pathdep is a flag specifying whether to apply path-dependent compounding to each flow: 0 = no path (default), 1 = path.

Precision is the minimum required precision; the default is 0.000001.

Rate is the interest rate.

Simp is a flag specifying how to discount: 0 = compounded discounting (default), 1 = mixed compounded and simple discounting, 2 = simple discounting.

Start is a starting cash flow amount to compare against individual flows.

Type specifies whether payments occur at the beginning (1) or end (0) of period; the default is 0.

Using Financial Conversion Functions

The financial conversion functions change a value between a fraction to a decimal fraction, or change a given yield from one compounding frequency to another. Table 7.15 summarizes the financial conversion functions.

Table 7.15 Financial Conversion Functions

Function	Description
@DFRAC(*dec,denom*)	Converts a decimal number to a whole number and fractional component.
@FRACD(*frac,denom*)	Converts a number with a fraction component to a decimal.
@YLD2YLD(*y1,f1,f2,[q1],[q2]*)	Converts a yield expressed in one compounding frequency and time length to that in another frequency and/or time length.

Dec is the number to be converted, expressed as a decimal.

Denom is the denominator, and must be an integer.

F1 is the number of times a given yield is compounded per year.

F2 is the number of times a target yield is compounded per year.

Frac is the number to be converted.

Q1 is the number of periods for quoted yields; *f1* is the default.

Q2 is the number of periods for quoted yields; *f2* is the default.

Y1 is the given yield to be converted to another compounding frequency.

Using Financial Depreciation Functions

The financial depreciation functions compute depreciation over time. Table 7.16 summarizes the financial depreciation functions.

Table 7.16 Financial Depreciation Functions

Function	Description
@DDB(*cost,salvage,life, period*)	Returns the double-declining balance depreciation of an asset during the given period.
@SLN(*cost,salvage,life*)	Returns the straight-line depreciation of an asset over each period in its given useful life.
@SYD(*cost,salvage,life, period*)	Returns the sum-of-the-years' -digits depreciation of an asset during the given period.

Cost is the amount paid for an asset.

Life is the expected useful life in years.

Period is the time period for which you want to calculate depreciation.

Salvage is the value of an asset at the end of its useful life.

Using Financial Stock Functions

The financial stock functions return fee calculations from tables, and calculate values useful in evaluating stock options. Table 7.17 summarizes the financial stock functions.

Table 7.17 Financial Stock Functions

Function	Description
@FEETBL(*tu,ppu,*[*stdtbl*|*val*], [[*mintbl*|*val*]], [[*maxtbl*|*val*]],[*rndplcs*])	Returns fee calculations from tables.
@STKOPT(*optcode,optprem, undstkvalue,date,load, cmdstring*)	Calculates values useful in evaluating stock options.

Cmdstring is a command string enclosed in quotes specifying the operations to perform:

A = annualization ratio (365.25/D)

D = days from *DateTimeNum* until expiration of option specified

E = expiration date code of option specified

I = intrinsic value of option

L = load or fee to purchase or sell the option; can also be a general-purpose numeric constant

P = premium or market value of the option

S = strike or exercise price of the option

T = time value of the option

U = underlying value or price of the stock

+ = addition operator

– = subtraction operator

* = multiplication operator

/ = division operator

Date is a serial date number between 2 (January 1, 1900) and 73050 (December 31, 2099) representing the date on which to evaluate the stock option.

Load is the load or commission involved in the sale or purchase.

Maxtbl\val is a fee table or a single value that defines the maximum fee calculation; if omitted, *maxtbl* equals *stdtbl*.

Mintbl\val is a fee table or a single value that defines the minimum fee calculation; if omitted, *mintbl* equals *stdtbl*.

Optcode is an option code string with expiration month, strike-price, and put or call symbol enclosed in quotes.

Optprem is the option premium or price.

Ppu is the price per unit.

Rndplcs is the number of places—0 to 10—to which the final result is rounded; the default is no rounding.

Stdtbl\val is a fee table or a single value that defines the standard fee calculation.

Tu is the total units.

Undstkvalue is the value or price of the underlying stock.

Using Logical Functions

With the logical functions, you can add standard true/false logic to the spreadsheet. The logical functions evaluate Boolean expressions, which are either true (returning a value of 1) or false (returning a value of 0). Except for @IF, all the logical functions result in 1 or 0. These functions can help to prevent errors that may occur if a cell used in a formula contains the wrong data, to test for the values ERR (error) or NA (not available), or to determine whether a specified file exists. These functions are important for decision making when conditions elsewhere in the spreadsheet lead to different answers in the function results. Logical functions also control the operations of advanced macro programs. Table 7.18 summarizes the logical functions.

Table 7.18 Logical Functions

Function	Description
@FALSE	Returns 0, the logical value for false.
@FILEEXISTS(*filename*)	Tests whether the specified file exists.
@IF(*condition,true,false*)	Tests the *condition* and returns the result specified by *true* if the condition is true, and the result specified by *false* if the condition is false.
@ISERR(*cell*)	Tests whether the specified cell results in ERR.
@ISNA(*cell*)	Tests whether the specified cell results in NA.
@ISNUMBER(*cell*)	Tests whether the specified cell contains a number.
@ISSTRING(*cell*)	Tests whether the specified cell contains a string.
@TRUE	Returns 1, the logical value for true.

Using Mathematical Functions

With the mathematical functions, which include transcendental (logarithmic) and trigonometric operations, you can easily perform a variety of standard arithmetic operations, such as adding and rounding values or calculating square roots. For engineering and scientific applications, Quattro Pro 5.0 for Windows includes all standard trigonometric operations, such as functions to calculate sine (@SIN), cosine (@COS), and tangent (@TAN). The mathematical functions include three subcategories: numerical, transcendental, and trigonometric. The following sections describe the categories of mathematical functions.

Using Mathematical Numerical Functions

The mathematical numerical functions convert or modify a numeric value, or return a simple numeric value. Table 7.19 summarizes the mathematical numerical functions.

Table 7.19 Mathematical Numerical Functions

Function	Description
@ABS(*x*)	Returns the absolute value of a given number.
@CEILING(*x,y*)	Rounds a number up to the nearest integer.
@COMB(*r,n*)	Calculates the number of unordered subgroups of given size in a group.
@DEGREES(*x*)	Converts a given value from radians to degrees.
@EVEN(*x*)	Rounds a number up to the nearest even integer.
@FACT(*x*)	Calculates the factorial of a number.
@FACTDOUBLE(x)	Returns the double factorial of a number.
@FIB(*x*)	Calculates the *n*th term of a Fibonacci sequence.
@FLOOR(*x,y*)	Rounds a number down, toward zero.
@GCD(*x,y*)	Calculates the greatest common divisor of *x* and *y*.
@INT(*x*)	Returns the integer portion of a given value. In this function, the number is simply truncated, not rounded off.
@LCM(*x,y*)	Calculates the least common multiple of *x* and *y*.
@LINTERP(*knownx,knowny,x*)	Performs linear interpolation between sets of *xy* pairs.
@MDET(*array*)	Calculates the determinant of a matrix.
@MOD(*x,y*)	Returns the modulus of a given value with respect to another. (Modulus is the remainder when the first is divided by the second.)
@MROUND(*x,y*)	Returns a number rounded to the desired multiple.

(continues)

Table 7.19 Continued

Function	Description
@MULT(*list*)	Calculates the cumulative product of a set of numbers.
@MULTINOMIAL(*list*)	Returns the multinomial of a set of numbers.
@ODD(*x*)	Rounds a number up to the nearest odd integer.
@PI	Returns the value of pi.
@QUOTIENT(*x,y*)	Returns the integer portion of a division.
@RADIANS(*x*)	Converts a given value from degrees to radians.
@RAND	Returns a fractional random number between 0 and 1.
@RANDBETWEEN(*n,m*)	Returns a random number between the numbers you specify.
@ROUND(*x,num*)	Rounds off a given value (with up to 15 digits) to a given number of decimal places.
@SERIESSUM(*x,n,m, coefficients*)	Returns the sum of a power series based on a formula.

Array is a numeric array or a block of values specifying a square matrix; it must have an equal number of rows and columns, and cannot contain blank cells.

Coefficients is a block or array of one or more numeric values by which each power of *x* is multiplied.

Knownx is a one-dimensional block containing *x* values in increasing order.

Knowny is a one-dimensional block containing *y* values corresponding to the *x* values in *knownx*.

List is one or more numbers or blocks of numbers, separated by commas.

M, n, r, x, and *y* are numeric values.

Num is a number between –15 and 15.

Using Mathematical Transcendental Functions

The mathematical transcendental functions perform exponential, logarithmic, and square-root calculations. Table 7.20 summarizes the mathematical transcendental functions.

Table 7.20 Mathematical Transcendental Functions

Function	Description
@EXP(x)	Returns the exponential of x. X must be less than or equal to 709.
@LN(x)	Returns the natural logarithm of x.
@LOG(x)	Returns the logarithm of x to base 10. X must be greater than 0.
@SQRT(x)	Returns the square root of x. X must be greater than or equal to 0.
@SQRTPI(x)	Returns the square root of x multiplied by pi.

Using Mathematical Trigonometric Functions

The mathematical trigonometric functions perform calculations of angle values and triangle relationships. Table 7.21 summarizes the mathematical trigonometric functions.

Table 7.21 Mathematical Trigonometric Functions

Function	Description
@ACOS(x)	Returns the angle whose cosine is x.
@ASIN(x)	Returns the angle whose sine is x.
@ATAN(x)	Returns the angle whose tangent is x.
@ATAN2(x,y)	Returns the angle represented by x and y.
@COS(x)	Returns the cosine of x.
@SIN(x)	Returns the sine of x.
@TAN(x)	Returns the tangent of x.

Using Miscellaneous Functions

The miscellaneous functions return information about notebooks and cell attributes, current command settings, system memory, object properties, and Quattro Pro 5.0 for Windows' version number; they also perform table lookups. The miscellaneous functions include five sub-categories: general, cell attribute, cell and table, status, and table lookup. The following sections describe the miscellaneous functions.

Using Miscellaneous General Functions

The miscellaneous general functions return information on blocks and notebook pages. Table 7.22 summarizes the miscellaneous general functions.

Table 7.22 Miscellaneous General Functions

Function	Description
@ARRAY(*expression*, [*columns*],[*rows*])	Returns the result of *expression*.
@BLOCKNAME(*block*)	Returns the name of a cell or block specified by *block*.
@BLOCKNAME2(*notebooklink*, *block*)	Returns the block name created in the notebook specified by *notebooklink* that refers to *block*, which can be in another notebook.
@BLOCKNAMES(*block*)	Returns a two-column table showing the block names that intersect with *block*.
@BLOCKNAMES2(*notebooklink*, *block*)	Returns a two-column table showing the block names created in the notebook specified by *notebooklink* that refer to blocks that intersect with *block*.
@FIRSTBLANKPAGE(*block*)	Returns a string that contains the letters for the first unnamed blank page in a notebook.
@INDEXTOLETTER(*index*)	Returns a one- or two-character string equivalent for the *index* number of a page or column.

Function	Description
@LASTBLANKPAGE(*block*)	Returns a string that contains the letters for the last unnamed blank page in a notebook.
@LETTERTOINDEX(*letters*)	Returns the index number for column or page *letters*.
@PAGEINDEX(*name*)	Returns the index number for a specified page *name*.
@PAGEINDEX2(*notebooklink*, *name*)	Returns the index number for a specified page *name* in a note book specified by *notebooklink*.
@PAGENAME(*index*)	Returns the name of a page specified by *index*.
@PAGENAME2(*notebooklink*, *index*)	Returns the name of a page specified by *index* in a notebook specified by *notebooklink*.
@PAGENAMES	Returns a two-column table showing the page letters and corresponding page names for the active notebook.
@PAGENAMES2(*notebooklink*)	Returns a two-column table showing the page letters and corresponding page names for the notebook specified by *notebooklink*.

Block is a cell or block reference.

Columns is the number of columns in the output range.

Expression is a formula or @function using array syntax.

Index is an integer number from 0 to 255, inclusive.

Letters is a one- or two-character string enclosed in quotation marks.

Name is a string enclosed in quotation marks corresponding to the name of a page.

Notebooklink is a reference to a page, cell, or block in another note-book.

Rows is the number of rows in the output range.

Using Miscellaneous Cell Attribute Functions

The miscellaneous cell attribute functions return the attributes of a specified cell. Table 7.23 summarizes the miscellaneous cell attribute functions.

Table 7.23 Miscellaneous Cell Attribute Functions

Function	Description
@CELL(*attribute,block*)	Returns the requested *attribute* of the upper left cell in a given *block* of cells.
@CELLINDEX(*attribute, block,col,row,[page]*)	Returns the requested attribute of the cell at the intersection of a given *col*, *row*, and *page* in a *block* of cells.
@CELLPOINTER(*attribute*)	Returns the requested *attribute* of the active cell.

Using Miscellaneous Cell and Table Functions

The miscellaneous cell and table functions return simple information from a cell or block of cells. Table 7.24 summarizes the miscellaneous cell and table functions.

Table 7.24 Miscellaneous Cell and Table Functions

Function	Description
@@(*cell*)	Returns the contents of *cell*.
@CHOOSE(*number,list*)	Returns the *number* element from *list*.
@COLS(*block*)	Returns the number of columns in *block*.
@DDELINK([*appname|topic*] "*datatoreceive*",[*ncols*], [*nrows*],[*nsheets*])	Creates a "live" data link from another Windows application that supports DDE.
@ERR	Always returns ERR (the error indicator).

Function	Description
@NA	Always returns NA (not available).
@ROWS(*block*)	Returns the number of rows in *block*.
@SHEETS(*block*)	Returns the number of pages in *block*.

Using Miscellaneous Status Functions

The miscellaneous status functions return the current setting for commands, properties, and other elements. Table 7.25 summarizes the miscellaneous status functions.

Table 7.25 Miscellaneous Status Functions

Function	Description
@COMMAND(*commandequivalent*)	Returns current settings for *commandequivalent*.
@CURVALUE(*generalaction*, *specificaction*)	Returns the current value of a menu command setting.
@MEMAVAIL	Returns the number of bytes of available memory.
@MEMEMSAVAIL	Returns NA (included for compatibility with Quattro Pro for DOS).
@PROPERTY(*object*,*property*)	Returns current property settings for the given *object* and *property*.
@VERSION	Returns the version number of Quattro Pro.

Using Miscellaneous Table Lookup Functions

The miscellaneous table lookup functions are used to search for a value in a block of cells that has been specified as a data table. Table 7.26 summarizes the miscellaneous table lookup functions.

Table 7.26 Miscellaneous Table Lookup Functions

Function	Description
@HLOOKUP(*x,block,rows*)	Searches for *x* in the first row of *block*. Returns the value a given number of *rows* from the first row.
@INDEX(*block,column,row,* [*page*])	Returns the value at the intersection of *column* and *row* in *block*.
@VLOOKUP(*x,block,columns*)	Searches for *x* in the first column of *block*. Returns the value from a given number of *columns* from the first column.

Using Statistical Functions

The statistical functions enable you to perform all standard statistical calculations on your notebook data, such as aggregation, counting, and analysis operations on a group of values. The large number of statistical functions are separated into two subcategories:descriptive and inferential. The following sections describe the statistical functions.

Using Statistical Descriptive Functions

The statistical descriptive functions return a value that helps you summarize and describe a group of values. Table 7.27 summarizes the statistical descriptive functions.

Table 7.27 Statistical Descriptive Functions

Function	Description
@AVG(*list*)	Returns the average of all numeric values in *list*.
@COUNT(*list*)	Returns the number of nonblank cells in *list*.
@KURT(*list*)	Returns the kurtosis of *list*.
@LARGEST(*array,n*)	Returns the *n*th largest value in *array*.

Function	Description
@MAX(*list*)	Returns the largest numeric or last date value in *list*.
@MEDIAN(*list*)	Returns the median of *list*.
@MIN(*list*)	Returns the smallest numeric or earliest date value in *list*.
@MODE(*list*)	Returns the most common value in *list*.
@PERCENTILE(*array,x*)	Returns a number from *array* at the percentile indicated by *x*.
@PERCENTRANK(*array,y*, [*digits*])	Returns the percentage rank of *y* in *array*.
@QUARTILE(*array,z*)	Returns the quartile of *array*.
@SKEW(*list*)	Returns the skewness of a distribution.
@SMALLEST(*array,n*)	Returns the *n*th smallest value in *array*.
@STANDARDIZE(*xn,mean,sdev*)	Returns a normalized value.
@STD(*list*)	Returns the population standard deviation of all values in *list*.
@STDS(*list*)	Returns the sample standard deviation of all values in *list*.
@SUM(*list*)	Returns the total of all numeric values in *list*.
@TRIMMEAN(*array,fraction*)	Returns the mean of *array*, with a fraction of the points excluded.

Array is a numeric array or a block of values.

Digits is the number of significant digits for returned percentage value.

Fraction is the decimal fraction of data points to exclude.

List is one or more numeric or block values.

Mean is the arithmetic mean of a distribution.

N is a number that indicates the rank in size from the data set *array*.

Sdev is the standard deviation of a distribution.

X is a percentile value between 0 and 1, inclusive.

Xn is the number to normalize.

Y is the number to rank in *array*.

Z is a number signifying what quartile value to return: 0 = minimum value in *array*, 1 = 25th percentile, 2 = 50th percentile (median), 3 = 75th percentile, 4 = maximum value in *array*

Using Statistical Inferential Functions

The statistical inferential functions return a value (or values) that helps you draw conclusions about a group (or groups) of values. Table 7.28 summarizes the statistical inferential functions.

Table 7.28 Statistical Inferential Functions

Function	Description
@ANOVA1(*input block, output block,grouped*)	Performs single-factor analysis of variance.
@ANOVA2(*input block,output block,sample rows,alpha*)	Performs two-factor analysis of variance with replication.
@ANOVA3(*input block,output block,labels*)	Performs two-factor analysis of variance without replication.
@AVEDEV(*list*)	Performs the average of the absolute deviations of data points from their means.
@BETA(*z,w*)	Returns the beta function.
@BETADIST(*x,z,w,<a>,<b>*)	Returns the cumulative beta probability density function.
@BETAI(*z,w*)	Returns the incomplete beta function.
@BETAINV(*prob,z,w,<a>,<b>*)	Returns the inverse of the cumulative beta probability density function.
@BINOMDIST(*successes, trials,prob1,cumulative*)	Returns the individual term binomial distribution.
@CHIDIST(*x1,degfreedom*)	Returns the one-tailed probability of the chi-squared x2 distribution.
@CHIINV(*prob,degfreedom*)	Returns the inverse of the chi-squared x2 distribution.

Function	Description
@CHITEST(*actual,expected*)	Computes the probability that the actual and expected frequencies are similar by chance.
@CONFIDENCE(*alpha,sdev,size*)	Computes the confidence interval around the mean for a given sample size, using the normal distribution function.
@CORREL(*array1,array2*)	Returns a confidence interval for a population.
@COVAR(*array1,array2*)	Returns the covariance of two data sets.
@CRITBINOM(*trials, prob2,alpha1*)	Returns the smallest value for which the cumulative binomial distribution is less than or equal to a criterion value.
@DEVSQ(*list*)	Returns the sum of the squares of the deviations.
@EXPONDIST(*x1,lambda,cum*)	Returns the exponential distribution.
@FDIST(*x2,degfreedom1, degfreedom2*)	Returns the F probability distribution.
@FINV(*prob,degfreedom1, degfreedom2*)	Returns the inverse of the F probability distribution.
@FISHER(*x3*)	Returns the Fisher transformation.
@FISHERINV(*y*)	Returns the inverse of the Fisher transformation.
@FORECAST(*x4,knowny,knownx*)	Returns a value along a linear trend.
@FTEST(*array1,array2*)	Returns the result of the F-test.
@GAMMADIST(*x5,alpha2, beta,cum1*)	Returns the gamma distribution.
@GAMMAINV(*prob3,alpha2,beta*)	Computes the inverse of the cumulative gamma distribution function.
@GAMMALN(*x6*)	Returns the natural logarithm of the gamma function.
@GAMMAP(*a1,x1*)	Returns the incomplete gamma function.

(continues)

Table 7.28 Continued

Function	Description
@GAMMAQ(*a1,x5*)	Returns the complement of the incomplete gamma function.
@GEOMEAN(*list*)	Returns the geometric mean.
@HARMEAN(*list*)	Returns the harmonic mean.
@HYPGEOMDIST(*samplesuccess, samplesize,popsuccess, popsize*)	Returns the hypergeometric distribution.
@INTERCEPT(*knowny,knownx*)	Returns the intercept of the linear regression line.
@LOGINV(*prob4,mean,sdev1*)	Returns the inverse of the lognormal distribution.
@LOGNORMDIST(*x7,mean,sdev1*)	Returns the lognormal distribution.
@NEGBINOMDIST(*failures, successes1,prob5*)	Returns the negative binomial distribution.
@NORMDIST(*x8,mean,sdev2,cum2*)	Returns the normal cumulative distribution.
@NORMINV(*prob6,mean,sdev2*)	Computes the inverse of the cumulative normal distribution function.
@NORMSDIST(*x7,mean, sdev2,cum2*)	Computes the standard normal cumulative distribution.
@NORMSINV(*prob7*)	Returns the inverse of the standard normal cumulative distribution.
@PEARSON(*array1,array2*)	Returns the Peareson product moment correlation coefficient.
@PERMUT(*n,r*)	Returns the total number of arrangements of objects taken *r* at a time from a set of *n* objects.
@POISSON(*n1,mean1,cum3*)	Returns the poisson probability distribution.
@PROB(*xdata,probrange, lowerlimit,upperlimit*)	Returns the probability that values in a range are between two limits.
@RANK(*number,array,order*)	Returns the rank of a number in a list of numbers.
@RSQ(*knownx,knowny*)	Returns the value of the linear regression line through data points in known *x*s and known *y*s.

Function	Description
@SLOPE(*knownx,knowny*)	Returns the slope of the linear regression line.
@STEC(*knownx,knowny*)	Returns the standard error of a coefficient.
@STEYX(*knownx,knowny*)	Returns the standard error of a linear regression. The standard error is the deviation of the observed *y* values from the linear combinations.
@SUMPRODUCT(*block1,block2*)	The dot (scalar) product of the vectors corresponding to a block of cells.
@SUMSQ(*list*)	Returns the sum of the squares of the arguments.
@SUMX2MY2(*array1,array2*)	Returns the sum of the differences of the squares of the corresponding values in two arrays.
@SUMX2PY2(*array1,array2*)	Returns the sum of the squares of corresponding values in two arrays.
@SUMXMY2(*array1,array2*)	Returns the sum of squares of differences of corresponding values in two arrays.
@SUMXPY2(*array1,array2*)	Returns the sum of the sum of squares of corresponding values in two arrays.
@SUMXY(*array1,array2*)	Returns the sum of the products of the corresponding numbers in two arrays.
@SUMXY2(*array1,array2*)	Returns the sum of the product of values and the squares of the corresponding numbers in two arrays.
@TDIST(*x9,degfreedom,tails*)	Returns the Student's t-distribution.
@TINV(*prob8,degfreedom*)	Returns the inverse of the Student's t-distribution.
@TTEST(*array1,array2, tails,type*)	Returns the inverse of the cumulative two-tailed T distribution.
@VAR(*list*)	Returns the population variance of all values in a list.
@VARS(*list*)	Returns the sample variance of all values in a list.

(continues)

Table 7.28 Continued

Function	Description
@WEIBULL(*x10,alpha3, beta1,cum*)	Returns the Weibull Distribution.
@ZTEST(*array,x11,<s>*)	Returns the two-tailed P-value.

A is the optional lower bound to the interval of *x*; the default is 0.

A1 is a parameter to the function, and must be greater than 0.

Actual is a block containing actual values.

Alpha is the significance level, or percentage of the normal curve that is outside the confidence interval, and must be greater than 0 and less than 1.

Alpha1 is the critical probability to test, and must be greater than or equal to 0 and less than or equal to 1.

Alpha2 is a parameter to the gamma distribution, and must be greater than 0.

Alpha3 is a parameter to the distribution, and must be greater than 0.

Array is one or more numeric or block values.

Array1 is the first array of numeric values.

Array2 is the second array of numeric values.

B is the optional upper bound to the interval of *x*; the default is 1. *B* cannot equal *a* and must be greater than or equal to *x*.

Beta is a parameter to the gamma distribution, and must be greater than 0.

Beta1 is a parameter to the distribution, and must be greater than 0.

Cum is 1 to perform cumulative distribution function, or 0 to perform the probability density function.

Cum1 is any nonzero number to return the cumulative gamma distribution function, or 0 to return the probability density function.

Cum2 is 1 to return the cumulative normal distribution function, or 0 to return the probability density function; the default is 0.

Cum3 is 1 to return the cumulative Poisson probability distribution that the number of random events will be in the range from zero to *n*, or 0 to return the Poisson probability mass function that the number of events will be *n*.

Cumulative is 1 to return the cumulative distribution function, or 0 to return the probability that there are exactly *successes* successes.

Degfreedom is the integer number of degrees of freedom, and must be greater than or equal to 1.

Degfreedom1 is the numerator degrees of freedom, and must be greater than or equal to 1.

Degfreedom2 is the denominator degrees of freedom, and must be greater than or equal to 1.

Expected is a block containing expected values.

Failures is the number of failures.

Knownx is the independent range of values.

Knowny is the dependent range of values.

Lambda is the value to indicate, and must be greater than 0.

List is one or more numeric or block values.

Lowerlimit is the lower limit on the value for the desired probability.

Mean is the mean of *ln(x)* or of normal distribution.

Mean1 is the expected numeric value for the mean over the distribution, and must be greater than 0.

N is the number of different objects, and must be greater than or equal to 0.

N1 is the number of events, and must be greater than 0.

Number is a number from *array*.

Order is a flag indicating how to sort the list of numbers: any nonzero value = ascending order, 0 = descending order.

Popsize is the population size, and must be greater than or equal to 0.

Popsuccess is the number of successes in the population, and must be greater than or equal to 0 and less than or equal to *popsize*.

Prob is the cumulative probability value, and must be between 0 and 1.

Prob1 is the probability of a success on each trial run, and must be between 0 and 1.

Prob2 is the probability of success per trial, and must be between 0 and 1.

Prob3 is the probability associated with the gamma cumulative function, and must be between 0 and 1.

Prob4 is the probability associated with the lognormal cumulative distribution function, and must be between 0 and 1.

Prob5 is the probability of a success, and must be between 0 and 1.

Prob6 is the probability corresponding to the normal distribution, and must be between 0 and 1.

Prob7 is the probability corresponding to the normal distribution, and must be between 0 and 1.

Prob8 is the cumulative probability value, and must be between 0 and 1.

Probrange is a block or array of probability values associated with *xdata*, and must be between 0 and 1. The sum of *probrange* values must equal 1.

R is the number of objects taken at a time, and must be less than or equal to *n*.

S indicates that @ZTEST uses the sample standard deviation.

Samplesize is the sample size, and must be greater than or equal to 0 and less than or equal to *popsize*.

Samplesuccess is the successes in the sample, and must be greater than or equal to 0.

Sdev is the population standard deviation, and must be greater than 0.

Sdev1 is the standard deviation of *ln(x)*, and must be greater than 0.

Sdev2 is the standard deviation of the normal distribution, and must be greater than 0.

Size is the sample size, and must be greater than or equal to 1.

Successes is the number of successes in number of trial runs, and must be greater than or equal to 0.

Successes1 is the threshold of successes.

Tails is 1 to return a one-tailed distribution or 2 to return a two-tailed distribution.

Trials is the number of independent trial runs in the sample.

Type is a discrete variable specifying the type of test to conduct: 1 = a paired test, 2 = a two-sample equal variance test, 3 = a two-sample unequal variance test.

Upperlimit is the upper limit on the value for the desired probability.

W is the b parameter to the function, and must be greater than 0.

X is the value at which to evaluate the function over the interval *a* less than or equal to *x* less than or equal to *b*.

X1 is the value at which to evaluate the function, and must be greater than or equal to 0.

X10 is the function parameter to evaluate.

X11 is a value to test against the mean of the values in *array*.

X2 is a positive value at which to evaluate the function *degfreedom1*.

X3 is a numeric value, and must be greater than –1 and less than 1.

X4 is the numeric value at which to evaluate the function.

X5 is the value at which to evaluate the function, and must be greater than or equal to 0.

X6 is the value for which you want to calculate @GAMMALN, and must be greater than 0.

X7 is the value at which to evaluate the *function*.

X8 is the value to evaluate the function, and must be greater than 0.

X9 is the value at which to evaluate the distribution.

Xdata are values of *x* associated with the probabilities.

Y is a numeric value less than or equal to 354 for which you want the inverse of the Fisher transformation.

Z is a parameter to the function, and must be greater than 0.

Using String Functions

String functions help you manipulate text. You can use string functions to repeat text characters, convert letters in a string to upper- or lowercase, change strings to numbers, and change numbers to strings. You also can use string functions to locate, extract, or replace characters.

@PROPER, for example, converts to uppercase the first letter of each word in a string and converts the rest to lowercase. String functions can be important also when you need to convert data for use by other programs. They are invaluable when you need to read or write directly to ASCII text files. The string functions include three subcategories: modify, substring, and value. The following sections describe the string functions.

Using String Modify Functions

The string modify functions return a modified version of the original string. Table 7.29 summarizes the string modify functions.

Table 7.29 String Modify Functions

Function	Description
@CLEAN(*string*)	Returns *string* with any nonprintable ASCII codes removed.
@LOWER(*string*)	Returns *string* with all the alphabetic characters converted to lowercase.
@PROPER(*string*)	Returns *string* with the first letter of each word capitalized, and with all other letters lowercase.
@UPPER(*string*)	Returns *string* with all the alphabetic characters converted to uppercase.

Using String Substring Functions

The string substring functions compare two strings, or return a substring from a larger string. Table 7.30 summarizes the string substring functions.

Table 7.30 String Substring Functions

Function	Description
@EXACT(*string1*,*string2*)	Returns 1 if *string1* and *string2* are identical (including capitalization); otherwise returns 0.

Function	Description
@FIND(*substring,string, startnumber*)	Returns the position of *substring* in *string*, beginning with the character in *startnumber* position.
@LEFT(*string,num*)	Returns *num* characters from the beginning of *string*.
@MID(*string,startnumber,num*)	Returns *num* characters from *string*, starting with the character in *startnumber* position.
@REPEAT(*string,num*)	Returns a string made up of *num* repetitions of *string*.
@REPLACE(*string,startnum, num,newstring*)	Deletes *num* characters in *string*, beginning with *startnumber*, and replaces them with *newstring*.
@RIGHT(*string,num*)	Returns *num* characters from the end of *string*.
@TRIM(*string*)	Returns *string* without leading, trailing, or multiple spaces.

Using String Value Functions

The string value functions return basic value information from a string, or basic information to build up a string. Table 7.31 summarizes the string value functions.

Table 7.31 String Value Functions

Function	Description
@CHAR(*code*)	Returns the ANSI character that corresponds to *code*.
@CODE(*string*)	Returns the ANSI code of the first character in *string*.
@HEXTONUM(*string*)	Returns the decimal value of a given hexadecimal number *string*.
@LENGTH(*string*)	Returns the length of *string*, including spaces.
@N(*block*)	Returns the numeric value of the top left cell of *block*.

(continues)

Table 7.31 Continued

Function	Description
@NUMTOHEX(*x*)	Returns the hexadecimal value of *x*.
@S(*block*)	Returns the string value of the top left cell of *block*.
@STRING(*x*,*decplaces*)	Converts *x* into a string, rounding to *decplaces*.
@VALUE(*string*)	Returns the numeric value of *string*.

Questions and Answers

Q: Is there a shortcut method of entering @functions?

A: Press Alt+F3 to see a list of function categories. Choose the category, and then choose the function you need. Press F1 for additional help.

Q: Why do some functions seem to return incorrect values?

A: Make certain that you understand the correct syntax, and supply proper arguments. Remember, some functions count labels as zero, so you may need to adjust block addresses in formulas to only include numerical values.

Q: How can I make more easily remember how my complex formulas function?

A: Attach comments to the end of formulas. When you finish entering a formula, add a semicolon (;) and then include any necessary comments up to the 1022 character-per-cell limit.

Q: Why do my formulas that use financial functions display negative values instead of the positive results I expect?

A: Money paid out must be represented by negative numbers. Make certain that you use the proper sign for each argument.

Q: When I try to calculate a loan payment, the results don't seem to make sense. What's wrong?

A: Make certain that each argument correctly matches the desired period and the other arguments. To calculate a monthly payment, for example, be sure to divide an annual interest rate by 12. Also, if the loan term is expressed in years, make certain to multiply the term by 12 to find the number of monthly payments.

Summary

This chapter described all the functions that Quattro Pro 5.0 for Windows provides to make formula and spreadsheet construction easier and more error free. After you learn to use the functions built into Quattro Pro 5.0 for Windows, you can easily incorporate them into your spreadsheet models. As you gain more experience using Quattro Pro, continue to use this chapter as a reference to the functions.

Chapter 8 introduces you to managing files. You learn how to save, retrieve, and manage your files in Quattro Pro 5.0 for Windows.

Managing Files

Quattro Pro 5.0 for Windows provides a wide range of capabilities for file management, modification, and protection. Through commands on the main menu you can open and save individual notebooks, open and save groups of notebooks as a workspace, and combine data from several notebooks. You also use commands on the main menu to create links with other notebooks and other Windows applications, and to transfer files between different applications. This chapter discusses these topics and covers helpful file management techniques in Quattro Pro 5.0 for Windows.

In this chapter, you learn to perform the following tasks:

- Manage open files
- Name files
- Change directories
- Save files to disk
- Open existing files from disk
- Extract and combine data
- Link files
- Protect files with passwords
- Erase files
- Transfer files between programs

This introduction provides brief descriptions of the file management commands in Quattro Pro 5.0 for Windows; the balance of the chapter covers the commands in greater detail. Many of the basic commands for managing files are on the File drop-down menu (see fig. 8.1). Other file management commands, such as commands for combining, importing, and extracting files, are on the Tools drop-down menu (see fig. 8.2).

Fig. 8.1

The **F**ile drop-down menu.

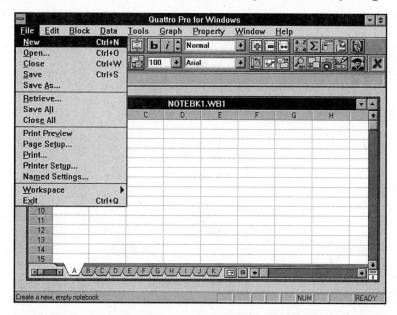

Fig. 8.2

The **T**ools drop-down menu.

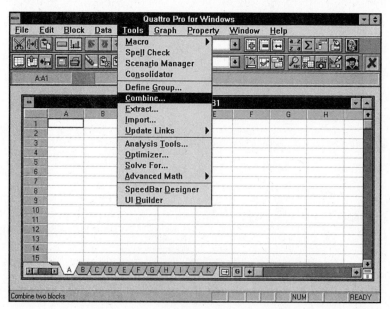

Use **File R**etrieve to read a notebook (file) from disk. The current file closes, and the new file replaces it. To open an additional notebook without closing already open notebooks, use **File O**pen (or click the Open Notebook button on the Productivity Tools SpeedBar).

To save notebooks, use **File S**ave, **File Save A**s, or **File Save All**. **File Save** (or the Save Notebook button on the Productivity Tools SpeedBar) saves the active notebook to disk. File Save **As** saves the active notebook using a name and location you specify. File Save **All** saves all open notebooks.

To save the current arrangement of open notebooks to disk as a workspace file, use **File W**orkspace **S**ave. Use **File W**orkspace **R**etrieve to retrieve a saved workspace file.

> **F**ile **W**orkspace **S**ave saves only the arrangement of the open notebooks—not the contents of the notebooks. To save the contents, be sure to use **F**ile **S**ave, **F**ile Save **A**s, or **F**ile Save A**ll** in addition to **F**ile **W**orkspace **S**ave.

NOTE

When you first start Quattro Pro 5.0 for Windows, a blank notebook appears on-screen. You can use this blank window to build a notebook, or you can use **File N**ew (or click the New Notebook button on the Productivity Tools SpeedBar) to start a new, blank notebook.

To combine information in a notebook on disk with the active notebook, use **Tools C**ombine. To save part of a notebook as a new notebook on disk, use **Tools E**xtract. You can read a text file into the active notebook by using **Tools I**mport.

Quattro Pro 5.0 for Windows does not provide a command for deleting files, so you must use the Windows File Manager or DOS to delete notebook files.

Managing Open Notebooks

In Quattro Pro 5.0 for Windows, a *notebook* consists of 256 spreadsheet pages and a graph page. These spreadsheet pages are an integral group in Quattro Pro 5.0 for Windows, even if you have not yet saved the notebook to a disk file. You can enter data on one or more pages. When you save the notebook, you save all the notebook's pages together. When you read a notebook file from disk, you read into memory all the notebook's pages.

After you create or modify notebooks in memory, you must save the information to disk or you lose the information. When you read a notebook file from disk, an exact copy of the disk file is created in the computer's memory. The existing file remains unchanged on disk until you save a new version of the file using the same name. When you save a notebook, you store on disk an exact copy of the notebook file in the computer's memory. The notebook remains unchanged in memory.

NOTE

> Unlike other three-dimensional spreadsheets, each Quattro Pro 5.0 for Windows notebook automatically has all 256 spreadsheet pages. You don't need to add the pages manually—you can use the pages as soon as you create the notebook.

Naming Notebook Files

The names you can assign to files depend on the operating system you use. In current versions of DOS, a file name can be up to eight characters long and can have an optional extension of up to three characters. The name can contain any combination of letters, numbers, and the following characters:

- ^ $ ~ ! # % & { } ( ) @ _ '

You cannot use any other special characters, such as spaces, commas, backslashes, or periods, except for a single period between the file name and the extension. DOS also reserves some names for its own use. You cannot use the following file names:

CLOCK$	LPT1	COM1
CON	LPT2	COM2
AUX	LPT3	COM3
NUL	LPT4	COM4
PRN		

The standard extension for Quattro Pro 5.0 for Windows notebooks is WB1. The standard extension for Quattro Pro 5.0 for Windows workspace files is WBS. When you type a notebook or workspace name to save, type only the descriptive part of the name. Quattro Pro 5.0 for Windows adds the appropriate file extension for you.

Quattro Pro 5.0 for Windows can read and save files in the following formats: Lotus 1-2-3 for DOS Releases 2.x and 3.x, Lotus 1-2-3 for Windows, Quattro Pro for DOS, Excel, and dBASE. If you want to save a Quattro Pro 5.0 for Windows notebook in another format, change the file's extension when you save the notebook. To save a notebook as a Lotus 1-2-3 for Windows file, for example, change the extension to WK3.

Quattro Pro 5.0 for Windows can read many other file formats including the following formats:

- WQ1 and WQ2 (Quattro Pro for DOS)

- WK1, WK3, WKE, and WKS (Lotus 1-2-3 worksheets)

- ALL, FMT, and FM3 (Lotus 1-2-3 Allways, Impress, and WYSIWYG formatting information)

- XLS (Excel)

- DBF, DB2, and DB4 (dBASE)

- BMP, CGM, CLP, EPS, GIF, PCX, PIC, and TIF (Graphics file formats)

- DB (Paradox)

When you choose **File O**pen or **File R**etrieve, Quattro Pro 5.0 for Windows lists all the files with extensions beginning with W. Quattro Pro 5.0 for Windows does not list files with other extensions. To open a file that has a nonstandard extension, you must type the complete file name and extension or use wild cards, such as ***.***.

You may want to save a file with a nonstandard extension so the file does not appear when Quattro Pro 5.0 for Windows lists the notebook files. You may, for example, want to assign a nonstandard extension to a file that is part of a macro-controlled system. This step prevents you from accidentally opening the file outside the macro. The nonstandard extension conceals the file from any list of notebook files. If you want to open the file, perhaps to make changes, you type the entire file name and extension.

Changing Directories

A hard disk usually is organized into several *directories* (also called *subdirectories*) that store related program or data files. The *path* or *path name* is the list of directories that leads from the root directory of the disk drive (usually C:\) to the file you want. When you perform file operations, Quattro Pro 5.0 for Windows displays the path name.

When you install Quattro Pro 5.0 for Windows, your program files are stored in a directory called QPW5, which the installation program creates under the root directory (unless you specified another directory). If you installed Quattro Pro 5.0 for Windows on your C drive, for example, the Quattro Pro 5.0 for Windows program directory is named C:\QPW5. By default, Quattro Pro 5.0 for Windows saves notebook and workspace files in this program directory. Managing your files is easier, however, if you create a separate directory for your data.

You cannot use Quattro Pro 5.0 for Windows to create a new directory—you must use the Windows File Manager or a DOS command to create directories. To use a DOS command to create a subdirectory called NOTEBOOK in the Quattro Pro 5.0 for Windows program directory, follow these steps:

1. From within Quattro Pro 5.0 for Windows, press Ctrl+Esc to activate the Windows Task List.

2. Select Program Manager and click **S**witch To (or press Alt+S). You also can double-click Program Manager.

3. Select the DOS Prompt icon in the Main group and press Enter or double-click the left mouse button on the icon.

4. Type the command **MD C:\QPW5\NOTEBOOK** and press Enter. (If you used a different drive or directory than C:\QPW5 to store the Quattro Pro 5.0 for Windows program files, substitute the correct drive letter and directory name.)

5. Type **EXIT** and press Enter to return to the Program Manager.

6. Press Ctrl+Esc to activate the Task List.

7. Select Quattro Pro 5.0 for Windows and click **S**witch To (or press Alt+S). You also can double-click Quattro Pro 5.0 for Windows.

Use the Startup section of the Application dialog box to change the default data directory to a different directory. To open the dialog box with the mouse, point to the Quattro Pro 5.0 for Windows title bar, click the right mouse button, and click Startup. To open the dialog box with the keyboard, choose **P**roperty **A**pplication, and then select Startup. Edit the **D**irectory text box to show the path to the data directory—such as the command C:\QPW5\NOTEBOOK shown in figure 8.3. Choose OK to confirm the dialog box.

You also can change directories temporarily when you open or save a file. In the Retrieve File dialog box shown in figure 8.4, for example, the **D**irectories list shows the directories on the current drive. The Drives box lists the available drives. To select a different drive or directory, use the mouse or direction keys to highlight the drive or directory you want. Choose OK to confirm the dialog box.

Fig. 8.3

The Startup section of the Application dialog box.

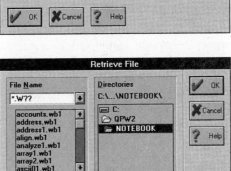

Fig. 8.4

The Retrieve File dialog box.

◄◄ "Using Dialog Boxes," p. 75.

FOR RELATED INFORMATION

Saving Files

When you build a new notebook or make changes to an existing notebook, all your work exists only in the computer's memory. If you do not save new notebooks or changes before you quit Quattro Pro 5.0 for Windows, you lose your work. When you save a notebook file, you copy the notebook in memory to a file on disk and give the notebook file a name. The file remains on disk after you quit Quattro Pro 5.0 for Windows or turn off the computer.

Saving Notebook Files

To save your work, use **File Save**, **File Save As**, or **File Save All**. If you have not yet saved the notebook, Quattro Pro 5.0 for Windows suggests a default name. The first notebook name Quattro Pro 5.0 for Windows suggests is NOTEBK1.WB1. When you use **File New** to open new blank notebooks, Quattro Pro 5.0 for Windows increases the numerical portion of the file name. The second new notebook is NOTEBK2.WB1, and so on.

If you already have saved the active notebook and assigned a name, **File Save** saves the active notebook to disk using the assigned name. If you choose **File Save As**, Quattro Pro 5.0 for Windows saves the active notebook using a name you specify in the Save File dialog box (see fig. 8.5). Choose **File Save All** to save all open notebooks.

Fig. 8.5

The Save File dialog box.

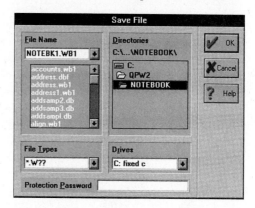

You also can apply a password to your notebook files when you save them. When a notebook is protected by a password, you must know the correct password before Quattro Pro 5.0 for Windows enables you to retrieve or open the notebook.

To apply a password to a notebook file you are saving, select the Protection **Password** text box and enter up to 15 characters. As you enter characters, Quattro Pro 5.0 for Windows displays graphics blocks rather than the password. After you choose OK to confirm the dialog box, Quattro Pro 5.0 for Windows displays the Verify Password dialog box shown in figure 8.6. Retype the password using the same combination of uppercase and lowercase characters—passwords are case-sensitive. Choose OK to confirm the dialog box.

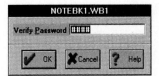

Fig. 8.6

The Verify Password
dialog box.

Saving Workspace Files

In Quattro Pro 5.0 for Windows, you can have several notebooks open in the workspace at the same time. You may, for example, consolidate notebooks from several different locations using a consolidation notebook. When you work with several open notebooks, you can arrange the notebooks on the desktop for convenient viewing. After you have the notebooks arranged, you can save the arrangement as a workspace file. When you later retrieve the workspace, the saved arrangement is restored, and each notebook opens in the position you saved it.

Use **File Workspace Save** to save the current arrangement of open notebooks to disk as a workspace file. To later retrieve a saved workspace file, use **File Workspace Retrieve**.

Although you use the **File Workspace Save** command to save the workspace, you still must save the open notebooks before quitting Quattro Pro 5.0 for Windows. The **File Workspace Save** command saves only the arrangement of the open notebooks—not the data in the notebooks.

Opening Files from Disk

The **File Open** and **File Retrieve** commands enable you to read a notebook file from disk into memory. You use **File Open** to read a notebook file from disk into memory without replacing the active notebook. You use **File Retrieve** to read a notebook file from disk into memory and replace the active notebook. When you use **File Retrieve**, the active notebook closes. When you use **File Open**, the active notebook remains open, but the newly opened notebook becomes the active notebook. Figure 8.7 shows four notebooks opened with the **File Open** command.

Fig. 8.7

Opening another
notebook leaves active
notebooks open.

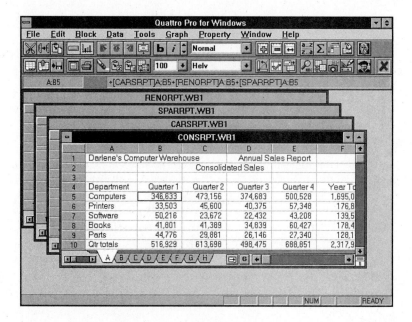

Besides opening several notebooks in different windows, you also can view the same notebook in two or more windows using the **W**indow **N**ew View command. Different views of the same notebook always contain the same data, although certain notebook settings may be different in each view. If you change the data in one view of a notebook—whether that view is a split pane or a totally separate window—Quattro Pro 5.0 for Windows changes the data in other views that display the same notebook.

To open a notebook by using the **F**ile **O**pen command, specify the name of the notebook in the **F**ile name text box of the Open File dialog box. (If you are using the **F**ile **R**etrieve command to replace the active file, the dialog box is identical except for its name: Retrieve File.) You can type or select the name from the list box. If all the notebook file names cannot appear in the list box, use the direction keys or the mouse to scroll the list box. If the notebook file you want to open is in another directory or on another drive, use the **D**irectories or D**r**ives list boxes to select the directory or drive.

By default, the **F**ile name list box displays all files in the current directory that have an extension starting with the letter W. You use the File **T**ypes list box to narrow the display to specific file types. For example, to display files created by Quattro Pro 5.0 for Windows only, select

*.WB1. The asterisk (*) serves as a wild card to match any number of characters. You also can use the question mark (?) as a wild card matching a single character. For example, to display all Quattro Pro 5.0 for Windows notebook files that have four characters followed by RPT, select ????RPT.WB1.

Using Files in Different Directories

When Quattro Pro 5.0 for Windows prompts you for a file name and gives you a default, the program shows the current directory and drive. To open or save a file in another directory, select the new directory in the **D**irectories list box or type a new path before the file name.

When Quattro Pro 5.0 for Windows lists the files in the current directory in the **F**ile Name list box, the dialog box lists existing subdirectories in the **D**irectories list box. To list the files in a subdirectory, highlight the subdirectory name and press Enter or double-click the left mouse button on the subdirectory name. Quattro Pro 5.0 for Windows lists the files and any subdirectories within the subdirectory you chose. To list the files in the parent directory—the directory above the displayed subdirectory—highlight the parent name and press Enter, or double-click the left mouse button on the parent name. You can move up and down the directory structure this way until you find the file you want.

To list the files on another drive, select the **D**rives list box. Highlight the drive letter and press Enter, or double-click the left mouse button on the drive letter.

Automatically Opening a Notebook at Startup

When you first start Quattro Pro 5.0 for Windows, a blank notebook appears. If you usually begin a work session with the same notebook, you can tell Quattro Pro 5.0 for Windows to retrieve this notebook automatically when the program starts. Use the **A**utoload File text box in the Startup section of the Application dialog box to tell Quattro Pro 5.0 for Windows the name of the notebook file to load when the program starts.

To instruct Quattro Pro 5.0 for Windows to load a notebook file by default when the program starts, follow these steps:

1. To activate the Startup section of the Application dialog box with the mouse, point to the Quattro Pro 5.0 for Windows title bar, click the right mouse button, and click Startup. To open the dialog box with the keyboard, choose **Property Application**. Highlight Startup, and press Enter.

2. Select the Autoload File text box and enter the name of the notebook file you want to load automatically when Quattro Pro 5.0 for Windows starts. The default setting opens QUATTRO.WB1.

3. Choose OK to confirm the dialog box.

If you work with macro-driven notebooks, you can create a notebook that provides the first menu of a macro-driven system or a menu of other notebooks to open. After you create and test the macro, you can tell Quattro Pro 5.0 for Windows to run the macro automatically when the program retrieves the notebook. Type the macro name in the **S**tartup Macro text box before you press Enter or click OK. If you include the macro in the autoload notebook file, your macro executes whenever you start Quattro Pro 5.0 for Windows.

Quattro Pro 5.0 for Windows also reserves two macro names, _nbstartmacro and _nbexitmacro, for macros that execute automatically when a file opens or closes, regardless of the Startup Macro setting.

FOR RELATED INFORMATION

▶▶ "Auto-Execute, Notebook Startup, and Notebook Exit Macros," p. 524.

Extracting and Combining Data

By using the **Tools Combine** command, you can combine data from several notebooks into a single notebook. If, for example, you are upgrading to Quattro Pro 5.0 for Windows from a two-dimensional spreadsheet program, you can combine several separate spreadsheets into a single notebook. If you receive notebook files from several departments, you can combine the notebook pages from each department into a single notebook.

By using the Tools Extract command, you can reverse the procedure and create notebooks that contain a specific data set only, such as the data for an individual department. This technique is useful when you need to work with the actual data in another notebook and not just refer to the data in formulas.

Extracting Data

Tools Extract copies data from a cell or a block to a new or existing notebook. You can use this command to create a partial file containing the specified block of data only. Tools Extract copies all formats and settings associated with the copied block.

To extract part of a notebook, highlight the cell or block and choose Tools Extract to open the File Extract dialog box (see fig. 8.8).

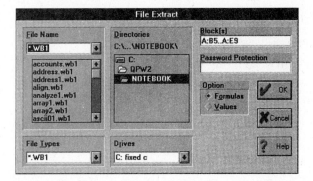

Fig. 8.8

The File Extract dialog box.

Choose the Formulas or Values option. When you choose Formulas, Quattro Pro 5.0 for Windows copies all data and extracts formulas, not values. When you choose Values, Quattro Pro 5.0 for Windows copies all data and extracts the current values of formulas, not the formulas themselves.

In the File name text box, enter the name of the file to which you want to extract. When you press Enter or click OK to confirm the dialog box, Quattro Pro 5.0 for Windows copies the data from the active notebook to the file specified. The data copies to cell A:A1 in the new notebook.

You also can apply a *password* to your notebook files before you extract them. If a notebook is password-protected, you must know the correct password before Quattro Pro 5.0 for Windows enables you to retrieve or open the notebook.

To apply a password to a notebook file you are extracting, select the **P**assword Protection text box and type up to 15 characters. Passwords are case-sensitive, so you must remember exactly how you type the password or you cannot retrieve or open the notebook later.

If you extract data to an existing notebook, Quattro Pro 5.0 for Windows overwrites the existing notebook, and you lose any existing data. Quattro Pro 5.0 for Windows first asks whether you want to back up or replace the existing notebook file before the data copies. Unless you are sure you don't want to keep the data, always choose Backup.

Quattro Pro 5.0 for Windows adjusts the addresses in formulas to reflect their new locations in the destination notebook. If you extract a formula, be sure that you also extract all the data the formula uses; otherwise, the formula calculates incorrectly. If you extract the values only, be sure that the CALC indicator is off before you issue the **Tools** Extract command. If necessary, press Calc (F9) before extracting the data. If you extract a named block, you should extract the entire block; otherwise, the block name in the destination notebook does not refer to the correct address.

Quattro Pro 5.0 for Windows also enables you to copy and move data between notebooks with the **E**dit Cut, **E**dit Copy, and **E**dit **P**aste commands (see Chapter 5, "Using Fundamental Commands").

Combining Data

The **T**ools **C**ombine command copies, adds, subtracts, multiplies, and divides values from notebooks on disk into the current notebook, beginning with the current cell. In the File Combine dialog box, you can combine information from any notebook or spreadsheet file on disk that Quattro Pro 5.0 for Windows can read—including Quattro Pro for DOS, Excel, and Lotus 1-2-3. You cannot combine information from dBASE or Paradox files.

When you use **T**ools **C**ombine, the source file is on disk, and you may have difficulty remembering block names or addresses. By opening the source file, you can refer to both notebooks and are less likely to make a mistake. Remember, though, that any changes you make in the source notebook are not in the combined data unless you save the changes before you use **T**ools **C**ombine.

These are the five **Tools Combine** options:

- **Copy** replaces data on all pages in the active notebook with data copied from all pages of a notebook on disk.

- **Tools Combine Add** adds the values of cells in the notebook on disk to numbers or blank cells in the active notebook. The incoming data does not overwrite active notebook cells containing formulas or labels; the data affects only blank cells or cells containing numbers.

- **Tools Combine Subtract** subtracts the values of cells in the notebook on disk from numbers or blank cells in the active notebook. The incoming data does not change active notebook cells containing formulas or labels; the data affects only blank cells or cells containing numbers.

- **Tools Combine Multiply** multiplies the values of cells in the active notebook by the numbers in cells of the notebook on disk. The incoming data does not change active notebook cells containing formulas or labels; the data affects only blank cells or cells containing numbers.

- **Tools Combine Divide** divides the values of cells in the active notebook by the numbers in cells of the notebook on disk. The incoming data does not change active notebook cells containing formulas or labels; the data affects only blank cells or cells containing numbers.

To combine data from another notebook on disk, first move the cell selector to the upper left cell of the block in which you want to start combining data. Next, choose **Tools Combine**. Select the source file and the combine operation you want to perform. In the Source field, choose Entire File to combine the entire active area of the notebook on disk with the active notebook. To combine a specified area of the notebook on disk with the active notebook, choose **B**lock(s) and type in the text box the name of the block to combine. Choose OK to confirm the dialog box and combine the data.

You also can combine data by using *linking* formulas. A formula can refer to data in other notebooks and offer the advantage of automatically updating the data when the source notebook changes. In some cases, however, you may not want to use formulas because you want to refer to static data. If you do not want the data updated every time you open the notebook, use **Tools Combine** to combine data. If you want the latest data revisions to appear automatically, use formulas to combine the data.

Quattro Pro 5.0 for Windows has another tool that makes combining data much easier—the Consolidator. Chapter 19, "Consolidating Data and Managing Scenarios," has more information on the Consolidator.

Linking Notebook Files

A *link* is a connection between two files that enables you to use data in one file to accomplish tasks in another. Quattro Pro 5.0 for Windows enables you to link files two ways. If you are creating links to other Quattro Pro 5.0 for Windows notebooks, you can use formula links—formulas that refer to cells in other notebooks. To link to other Windows applications, you can use **Edit Paste**, **Edit Paste Link**, or **Edit Paste Format** to create DDE (Dynamic Data Exchange) or OLE (Object Linking and Embedding) links.

When you link files, the file providing the data is the *source*, and the file receiving the data is the *destination*. If you create a link to an active notebook, the active notebook is the destination. If you use formula links, the source can be any other notebook file. If you use DDE or OLE links, the source can be any file created by a Windows application that supports DDE or OLE. DDE and OLE links are explained in greater detail later in this chapter.

Linking Notebooks Using Formulas

To link notebooks using formulas, you write in one notebook a formula that refers to data in a cell of another notebook. The formula can refer to data in an open notebook or in a notebook file on disk. The formula must contain the file reference enclosed in square brackets ([ ]). The cell or block address (or block name, if one exists) follows the square brackets.

Suppose that you want to calculate consolidated sales in a notebook called CONSRPT. Because sales in three stores are part of consolidated sales, you can write a formula to refer to the data located in three notebooks. The following formula links the three store notebooks—CARSRPT, RENORPT, and SPARRPT—to the notebook CONSRPT (see fig. 8.9):

```
+[CARSRPT]A:B5+[RENORPT]A:B5+[SPARRPT]A:B5
```

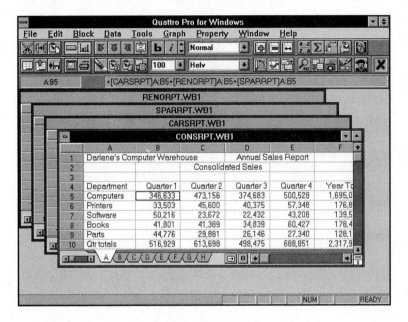

Fig. 8.9

Consolidating notebooks with formula links.

Quattro Pro 5.0 for Windows updates the formula result if the data in any of the three store notebooks changes.

If you move the data in the source notebook, the cell address in the linking formula adjusts. Formula links update automatically when you open the destination notebook.

If you delete a source notebook, the linking formula in the destination notebook results in NA. If you no longer need the source data in the calculation, edit the formula to remove the reference to the deleted notebook.

◄◄ "Entering Formulas," p. 103.

FOR RELATED INFORMATION

Linking to Other Program Manager Applications

Quattro Pro 5.0 for Windows takes advantage of the Windows Program Manager's DDE and OLE capabilities through the **E**dit **P**aste, **E**dit Paste **L**ink, or **E**dit Paste Format commands. Using these commands, you can link a Quattro Pro 5.0 for Windows notebook to any other Program Manager application, including word processors, spreadsheets, graphics programs, or database managers. Figure 8.10 shows an example of an OLE link between Quattro Pro 5.0 for Windows and a graphics image file.

Fig. 8.10

Quattro Pro 5.0 for Windows supports DDE and OLE links to other applications.

The image in figure 8.10, for example, was scanned and saved as a Windows bit-map file (BMP). The image then was loaded into Windows Paintbrush and modified to remove the background. The image was placed on the Clipboard using **E**dit **C**opy, then the image was added to the notebook using the Quattro Pro 5.0 for Windows **E**dit **P**aste command.

When you use the **E**dit **P**aste, **E**dit Paste **L**ink, or **E**dit Paste Format commands, the destination must be the active notebook window. Remember that the active window always contains the cell selector. If you have several windows open, you can move through them by selecting a window from the **W**indow drop-down menu, by pressing Ctrl+F6, or by clicking anywhere inside the window you want to activate.

Creating Links from Clipboard Data

If you use the **E**dit **C**opy command (or a similar command, depending on the application program) in a Windows application to copy data from an open file to the Clipboard, you can create a link between the active notebook in Quattro Pro 5.0 for Windows and the file from which you copied data.

When you use **E**dit **C**opy, the data and the *link reference* are stored on the Clipboard. If you then use **E**dit **P**aste, **E**dit Paste **L**ink, or **E**dit Paste **F**ormat, Quattro Pro 5.0 for Windows links the active notebook to the file and address from which you copied data to the Clipboard. In figure 8.10, for example, the Quattro Pro 5.0 for Windows notebook is linked to a graphics image produced by Windows Paintbrush.

Understanding DDE and OLE

DDE, *Dynamic Data Exchange*, and OLE, *Object Linking and Embedding*, are two methods of sharing data between Windows applications. Quattro Pro 5.0 for Windows supports both DDE and OLE, although OLE is available in Windows 3.1 only.

With DDE and OLE, applications share data to produce *compound documents*. Compound documents combine into a single document the best features of the different applications, such as a graphics program, a word processor, and a spreadsheet program. You can employ as many tools as you choose to complete a project and use the applications best suited to each task.

With DDE and OLE, you can paste data, such as a graphics image, into a Quattro Pro 5.0 for Windows notebook. The pasted data becomes a part of the notebook. If you print a report that includes the block containing the pasted data, the report looks like it was produced by a single application.

OLE is an extension of DDE. With OLE, data that can be displayed in a compound document and manipulated is an *object*. An object can be anything from a single cell to an entire report. When you incorporate an object produced by another Windows application in a Quattro Pro 5.0 for Windows notebook, the object maintains an association with the application that produced it. If you select the object (by double-clicking the object with the mouse), the application that produced the object starts. For example, if you select the graphics image shown in figure 8.10, the application that produced the image—Windows Paintbrush—starts, and you can edit the image. After editing the image (or other type of object), you then can exit the application that produced the object or use Alt+Tab to return to Quattro Pro 5.0 for Windows.

OLE offers two methods of adding data to a Quattro Pro 5.0 for Windows notebook. You can *link* or *embed* objects. The difference between linking and embedding is relatively minor. When you use Edit **P**aste, the object is embedded, and all the data associated with the object saves as part of the notebook. When you use Edit Paste Link, you link rather than embed the object; the data is stored in some other file and only a link to the data saves with the notebook. Embedding may slightly increase the size of the notebook file on disk. You can see no difference between linked and embedded objects in the notebook.

When you use Edit Paste **F**ormat, you choose whether you want to link or embed the object.

Edit Insert **O**bject is similar to **Edit P**aste except that instead of embedding an OLE object from the Clipboard, you embed the object directly from the Windows application that produces the object.

Erasing Files

When you create a file, you use space on your disk. Eventually, you run out of disk space if you occasionally do not erase old, unneeded files from the disk. Even if you have disk space left, too many files make searching through the file list to find a specific file difficult.

Before you erase old files, consider saving them to a floppy disk in case you need them again. Quattro Pro 5.0 for Windows notebook files are quite space efficient, and you can store a large number of files on a single floppy disk.

Quattro Pro 5.0 for Windows does not have a command for erasing files. You can use the Windows File Manager or DOS to erase old, unneeded files.

◀◀ "Accessing the Operating System," p. 177.

FOR RELATED INFORMATION

Transferring Files

Quattro Pro 5.0 for Windows provides several ways to transfer data to and from other programs. The Edit commands, covered earlier in this chapter and in Chapter 5, are the simplest way to pass data between Windows applications. Quattro Pro 5.0 for Windows also can read and write files in the most popular spreadsheet formats, including Lotus 1-2-3 Releases 2.x and 3.x, Excel, and earlier versions of Quattro Pro, as well as dBASE DBF and Paradox DB files. Finally, Quattro Pro 5.0 for Windows can import data from text files, as described in the following section.

Importing Text Files

The Tools Import command performs a function similar to Tools Combine. When you use Tools Import, you combine information with the active notebook, starting at the position of the cell selector. The new data overwrites any existing data. The source for these two commands is different; Tools Combine copies data from another notebook file, and Tools Import copies data from a text file.

When you choose Tools Import, a dialog box appears, enabling you to choose among importing a nondelimited ASCII Text File, a Comma and " Delimited File, and a text file delimited with Only Commas (see fig. 8.11). The fourth option, Parse Expert, is covered in Chapter 13, "Understanding Advanced Data Management."

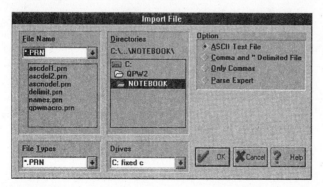

Fig. 8.11

The Import File dialog box.

By default, Quattro Pro 5.0 for Windows lists all the files with the PRN extension in the current directory. To list files with another extension—TXT, for example—type the appropriate characters, such as ***.TXT**, and press Enter.

Importing Unstructured Text Files

The typical text file contains lines of data with a carriage return at the end of each line. A text file has no structure except the carriage returns. To import a text file into a notebook, use **Tools Import** and choose **A**SCII Text File.

Figure 8.12 shows the result of importing a typical text file into a notebook. This data may have come from any software program. Each line in the text file becomes a long label in the cell, and all data is in one column. In most cases you probably want to split the incoming data into individual cells; you want numbers to be numbers and dates to be dates, not labels. To make this data usable, use the **Data Parse** command. See Chapter 13, "Understanding Advanced Data Management," for a complete discussion of **Data Parse**.

Fig. 8.12

The result of importing a typical text file into a notebook.

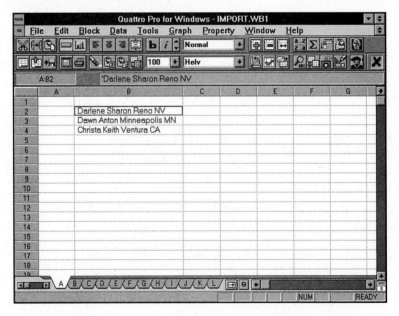

Importing Delimited Files

Some ASCII files are in *delimited* format, which enables you to import these files into separate cells without parsing. Quattro Pro 5.0 for Windows can import two kinds of delimited files: files that have commas between fields and quotation marks around labels; and files that use only commas between fields.

To import a delimited file, use **Tools Import** and choose **Comma and " Delimited File** or **Only Commas**. A typical delimited file contains lines of data similar to the following:

```
"Darlene Sharon",44.9,32000,"NV"

"Keith Daniel",21.4,21000,"CA"
```

Figure 8.13 shows the result of importing this data using **Tools Import** and choosing **Comma and " Delimited File**.

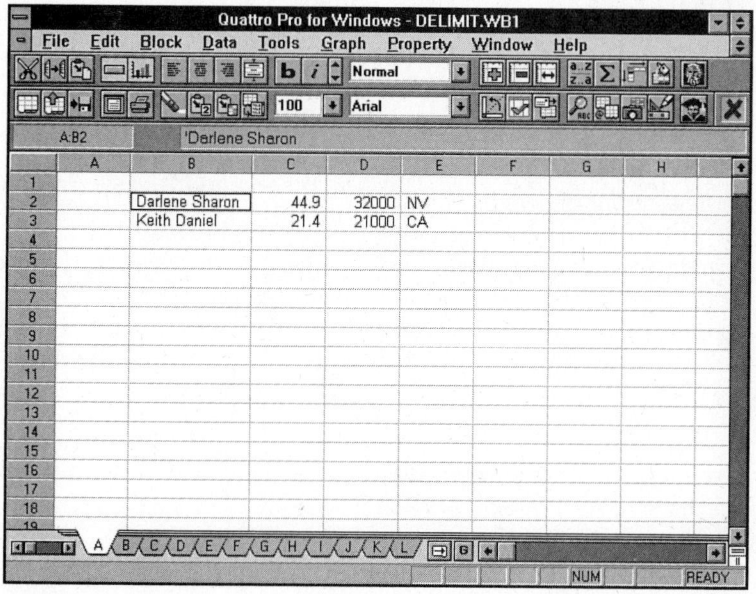

Fig. 8.13

The result of importing a delimited file into a notebook.

Using Files from Other Spreadsheets

Quattro Pro 5.0 for Windows can read files created by all earlier releases of Quattro Pro, Lotus 1-2-3, and Excel. By default, Quattro Pro 5.0 for Windows lists all files starting with W in the list box. You open a

Quattro Pro for DOS, Lotus 1-2-3, or Excel file the same way you open a Quattro Pro 5.0 for Windows file. Just select the name from the list box, and Quattro Pro 5.0 for Windows translates the file as the program opens it.

Quattro Pro 5.0 for Windows also can write files in these same formats. Of course, any features unique to Quattro Pro 5.0 for Windows are lost in the translation. 1-2-3 Release 2.x files, for example, cannot have multiple spreadsheet pages. Use **F**ile Save **A**s and specify a file name with the extension of the format you want to use. To save a notebook called BUDGET in 1-2-3 for Windows format, for example, type **BUDGET.WK3**.

Functions and macro commands new with Quattro Pro 5.0 for Windows do not work in files translated to another spreadsheet format.

Questions and Answers

Q: I have trouble remembering the names of my notebook files. What tricks can I use?

A: Several tricks may help you remember your file names.

First, try to be consistent. Don't name related files as BUDGET94.WB1 one time and 94PLAN.WB1 the next.

Next, develop a standard naming scheme. For example, if you do reports for several different departments, start each department's reports with a different letter. Use another letter to specify specific reports. Finally, use the same four-character positions for the month and year. AA0694.WB1 and AB0694.WB1 may be report one and report two for the sales department.

You also may consider storing related groups of files in their own directories.

Q: I used a password when I saved a file, and now I cannot retrieve the file although I'm certain I remember the correct password. What's wrong?

A: Passwords can be very tricky because they are case-sensitive. If you type **BRIAN** as the password when you save the file, you cannot type **brian** as the password when you retrieve the file.

If you're certain you entered the password correctly, including case, try entering the password again with the case reversed. You may have pressed the Caps Lock key accidentally before entering the password—maybe you thought you were entering **Brian**, but you really were entering **bRIAN**.

Q: I have hundreds of notebook files. May I use a shortcut way to display the file I want to retrieve?

A: After the File Retrieve dialog box opens, start typing the first characters of the file name in the text box. If you type an **M**, for example, the file list automatically jumps down to files that start with M. The next letter you type brings you even closer. Scroll to the file you want and select it.

Q: How can I decide whether to link or embed an object in my notebook?

A: Usually you don't need to decide. In most cases, either linking or embedding works just fine. If you intend to share the notebook with other users, however, embedding may be the better choice because the notebook file includes the embedded object.

Summary

In this chapter you learned to use the wide range of capabilities for file management, modification, and protection provided by Quattro Pro 5.0 for Windows. Specifically, you learned to open and save notebooks and workspaces; combine data from several notebooks; create links with other notebooks and other Windows applications; and transfer files between different applications.

The following chapter discusses two powerful Quattro Pro 5.0 for Windows utilities: the Optimizer and Solve For. These utilities revolutionize what-if analysis and spreadsheet problem solving.

Using the Optimizer and Solve For

The Optimizer and Solve For tools are powerful utilities that enhance the Quattro Pro 5.0 for Windows analytical abilities. Now that you learned the basics of creating and using Quattro Pro 5.0 for Windows notebooks, you can use these two tools to expand your capacity to analyze data.

These two tools help you create *what-if* scenarios with notebook data. What-if scenarios are a common way to analyze problems, using many different values for a set of variables to find optimal answers. What-if scenarios can be quite time-consuming, especially if done manually, because even problems with a limited number of variables have many possible solutions. When you use the Optimizer and Solve For tools to analyze what-if scenarios, Quattro Pro 5.0 for Windows searches out the answers for you, making an often difficult task much easier. For even more control over multiple scenarios, you may also want to try out the Scenario Manager tool, which is discussed in Chapter 19, "Consolidating Data and Managing Scenarios."

The Optimizer tool can analyze data to determine the best answer. A problem can have up to 200 variables and 100 constraints. The Optimizer tool finds sets of values for the variables that meet the defined constraints and produce the best available answer.

The Solve For tool modifies a single variable to find a specified answer to a problem. You use the Solve For tool when you have a specific goal in mind, such as finding the highest amount of principal you can borrow at a given loan payment and term.

This chapter shows you how to perform the following tasks:

- Set up what-if scenarios to use with the Optimizer
- Analyze Optimizer results
- Use functions with the Optimizer
- Use Solve For

Using the Optimizer

The Optimizer analyzes data to determine a series of possible answers to a specific problem. You can use the Optimizer, for example, to find the production mix that produces the highest profit. Other uses for the Optimizer include analyzing investment portfolios, determining the least costly shipping routes, and scheduling your staff.

Of course, you can solve these problems also by repetitively inserting different values into a notebook. The Optimizer does this automatically and uses advanced mathematical reasoning to select the best of all the possible answers.

Understanding Optimizer Terminology

Before you start using the Optimizer, you need to understand a few terms.

The Optimizer explicitly uses three types of values: *adjustable values*, *constraints*, and *solution cells*. The following sections explain each of these types.

Each Optimizer problem must have one or more adjustable cells. Adjustable cells contain the variables that the Optimizer changes in searching for the optimal answer. You can include up to 200 adjustable cells in a problem, but most problems are considerably less complex. Adjustable cells can contain numbers only, not formulas or text. As the Optimizer solves the problem, different sets of values are placed in the adjustable cells; therefore, the cells cannot be protected. Typical adjustable cells might include the production quantities for various parts, the number of employees working a certain shift, or the amount of capital invested in a project.

Constraints are conditions that serve as problem limits. Constraints are often used to specify the range of acceptable values for the variables, but you can specify constraints on calculated values also. Constraints are expressed as logical formulas that evaluate to true or false. When the Optimizer solves a problem, all constraints must be met before an answer is considered acceptable. Typical constraints might include upper and lower limits on production levels, a requirement that an endeavor produce a profit, or an obligation that at least one employee be on duty whenever a business is open.

Including a solution cell—the formula that defines the problem—in a problem is optional. When you use a solution cell, you specify whether its value should be maximized or minimized. If you do not include a solution cell, the Optimizer finds answers that meet all the defined constraints. Typical solution cells might include formulas that calculate total profits, the overall costs of complying with environmental regulations, or the amount that a nonprofit organization might earn from different combinations of fund-raising activities.

The Optimizer can solve *linear* and *nonlinear* problems. Linear problems are those in which variables change at a constant rate. The mathematical term for this is a *constant derivative*. Nonlinear problems, which are more complex, result when the relationships between variables are not additive. If a problem is truly linear, the Optimizer can solve the problem much more efficiently.

You determine if a problem is linear or nonlinear by examining the formulas that produce the end result. The problem is linear only if all variables are added or subtracted, or if they are multiplied or divided strictly by constants or by cells not involved in the problem itself. If any variable is multiplied or divided by itself or another variable, whether directly or indirectly, the problem is nonlinear. If a nonlinear function, such as @SIN or @LOG, is applied to a variable, the problem also is nonlinear. The Optimizer gives you the option of specifying a problem as linear. Unless you are certain it indeed is linear, however, you are safer using the default that assumes a nonlinear problem.

For example, a problem that states "the total production of three parts cannot exceed 25,000" has a linear constraint you can express as:

(Total part 1)+(Total part 2)+(Total part 3)<=25,000

On the other hand, a problem in which the variables are multiplied by each other is nonlinear. If both selling price and commission rate are variables, the net profit on a sale would be nonlinear:

Net profit=Selling price-(Selling price*commission rate)

A problem can be solved using one of two estimating methods. The default *Tangent* method uses linear extrapolation in estimating incremental values for variables. For most problems, this method is slightly faster and is usually suitable. Highly nonlinear problems sometimes are calculated faster using the *Quadratic* method, which uses quadratic extrapolation. In most cases the two methods produce very similar, if not identical, results.

The Optimizer approximates variable changes using a *finite difference* estimate—a method in which small changes are made in the values of variables and the Optimizer determines if the change was in the correct direction.

The Optimizer can use two distinct *differencing* methods. You can select whether the Optimizer uses *forward differencing* or *central differencing* to find partial derivatives. Forward differencing uses a single value slightly different from the current value of the variable, while central differencing uses two values in opposite directions. Central differencing is more accurate if the value is changing rapidly, but requires more calculations. The default forward differencing usually is acceptable.

The final method selection option controls the search method used to calculate improved values. The default *Newton* search uses a Newton method, and the *Conjugate* choice uses a conjugate gradient method. Unless your problem involves a very large number of variables and constraints, the default Newton method is the better selection because it is faster than the Conjugate method.

The constraints and the optimal cell are dependent on (are *functions* of) the variables. The first *derivative* of a function measures its rate of change. When a function has several variables, the function has several *partial derivatives*, which measure the rate of change with respect to each of the variables. Together, the partial derivatives form the *gradient* of the function. The gradient is a vector or *slope*. When the gradient is zero, the value is not changing.

An Optimizer Example Finding Optimal Production Levels

Finding optimal production levels to maximize profits is one type of problem well suited to solving with the Optimizer. Many factors may be involved in determining the best mix of products to utilize available production capacity fully. These factors include customer demand, material availability, differing profit rates based on individual production quantities, staffing levels, and so on. The following example shows how you can include some of these factors in an optimization problem.

Using a Production Scheduling Notebook

Figure 9.1 shows a sample notebook that represents the costs involved in producing three different products, such as camshaft bearings. In this example, it is assumed that the factory can produce 50,000 total parts per month and that the production can be divided among the three parts in the most profitable manner.

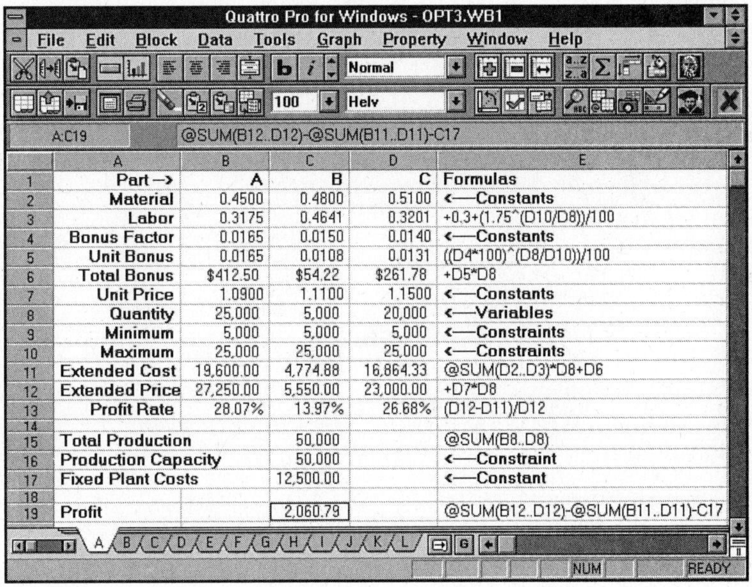

	A	B	C	D	E
1	Part —>	A	B	C	Formulas
2	Material	0.4500	0.4800	0.5100	<—Constants
3	Labor	0.3175	0.4641	0.3201	+0.3+(1.75^(D10/D8))/100
4	Bonus Factor	0.0165	0.0150	0.0140	<—Constants
5	Unit Bonus	0.0165	0.0108	0.0131	((D4*100)^(D8/D10))/100
6	Total Bonus	$412.50	$54.22	$261.78	+D5*D8
7	Unit Price	1.0900	1.1100	1.1500	<—Constants
8	Quantity	25,000	5,000	20,000	<—Variables
9	Minimum	5,000	5,000	5,000	<—Constraints
10	Maximum	25,000	25,000	25,000	<—Constraints
11	Extended Cost	19,600.00	4,774.88	16,864.33	@SUM(D2..D3)*D8+D6
12	Extended Price	27,250.00	5,550.00	23,000.00	+D7*D8
13	Profit Rate	28.07%	13.97%	26.68%	(D12-D11)/D12
14					
15	Total Production		50,000		@SUM(B8..D8)
16	Production Capacity		50,000		<—Constraint
17	Fixed Plant Costs		12,500.00		<—Constant
18					
19	Profit		2,060.79		@SUM(B12..D12)-@SUM(B11..D11)-C17

Fig. 9.1

A notebook for computing optimal product mix.

Several factors affect the final profit. Each bearing has a slightly different material cost and sells for a different price. Changing the machinery from one type of bearing to another results in lost machine time.

Longer runs of a single bearing are more efficient, resulting in reduced labor costs per bearing. Offsetting the reduced labor costs, however, is a bonus paid to the workers on longer runs.

In figure 9.1, the production manager has determined that bearing A produces the highest profit rate, thus the maximum number of type A bearings are scheduled—25,000 per month. Type C seems to produce the next highest profit rate, so 20,000 type C bearings are scheduled. The balance of the production, 5,000, is scheduled to produce the minimum acceptable number of type B bearings. The result of this production scheduling produces an operating profit of $2,060.79 for the month.

At first glance, it appears the production manager has determined the best method of allocating production capacity to produce the highest monthly profit. Of course, it would be possible to try other sets of values for each bearing's production quantity. Because each of the three values can vary between 5,000 and 25,000, however, the number of possibilities would be enormous.

Entering an Optimizer Problem

Figure 9.2 shows the Optimizer dialog box that appears when you select the **Tools O**ptimizer command.

Fig. 9.2

The Optimizer dialog box.

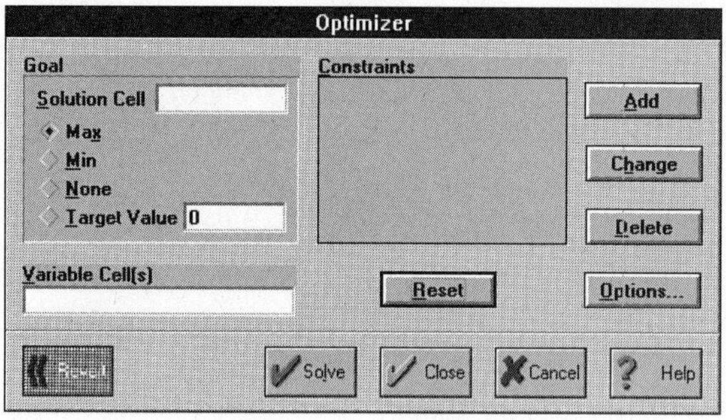

To make the production quantities of the three parts adjustable in the notebook, enter the cell addresses in the **V**ariable cells text box. In this example, you enter **B8..D8**.

You also must define the constraints that the Optimizer must satisfy in solving the problem. Add constraints by selecting the **C**onstraints text box. (Click **A**dd or use the direction keys to highlight **A**dd and press

Enter.) The Add Constraints dialog box shown in figure 9.3 appears. In this dialog box, you enter each of the problem constraints in turn.

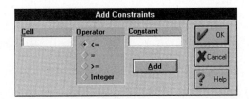

Fig. 9.3

The Add Constraints dialog box is used to enter problem constraints.

The quantity of part A (cell B8) must be equal to or greater than the minimum quantity shown in cell B9. Thus you need to enter **B8** in the **C**ell text box, select the >= (greater than or equal to) radio button in the Operator group box and **B9** in the Co**n**stant text box.

You can select <= (less than or equal to), = (equal to), >= (greater than or equal to), or Integer as the operator, depending on the constraint you wish to apply. If you want to use more than one condition, such as specifying that a constraint cell must be both an integer and greater than or equal to a value, you must add an additional constraint for each condition you wish to apply.

You can enter a cell address or a value in the Co**n**stant text box. Using a cell address, however, is preferable because it allows you to update the constraint values easily by entering new numbers in the constraint cells.

After you enter a constraint, select **A**dd to enter additional constraints or OK when all constraints have been entered. In this case, additional constraints are necessary. Cell B8 must be less than or equal to the value in B10, and similar constraints must be added for columns C and D. You can also specify array arguments for both **C**ell and Co**n**stant. Instead of entering three separate constraints, you could enter the single constraint **B8..D8 >= B9..D9**.

Finally, the total production, shown in cell C15, must be equal to the production capacity in cell C16.

Next you specify the cell that contains the formula the Optimizer will attempt to maximize or minimize. If you do not specify a formula cell, a solution to the problem that satisfies the specified constraints will be found. That solution, however, will be the first acceptable solution, not necessarily the optimal one. To enter the formula cell, select the **Solu**tion Cell text box in the Optimizer dialog box and enter the address of the formula cell. In this case, enter **C19**. Finally, specify the optimal condition for the formula cell. In this case, check the Max button in the Optimizer dialog box to specify that the value of cell C19 (profit) should be maximized. The dialog box should now appear similar to figure 9.4.

Fig. 9.4

The completed Optimizer dialog box.

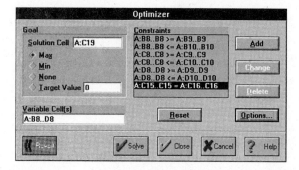

After you have defined the problem by indicating the variables, constraints, and optimal condition, select Solve to instruct the Optimizer to calculate the solution. Figure 9.5 shows the result in the production mix example.

Fig. 9.5

The optimal solution for the product mix example, as determined by the Optimizer.

Quattro Pro for Windows - OPT3.WB1

A:C19   @SUM(B12..D12)-@SUM(B11..D11)-C17

	A	B	C	D	E
1	Part →	A	B	C	Formulas
2	Material	0.4500	0.4800	0.5100	←——Constants
3	Labor	0.3229	0.3293	0.3201	+0.3+(1.75^(D10/D8))/100
4	Bonus Factor	0.0165	0.0150	0.0140	←——Constants
5	Unit Bonus	0.0140	0.0123	0.0131	((D4*100)^(D8/D10))/100
6	Total Bonus	$237.28	$160.60	$263.17	+D5*D8
7	Unit Price	1.0900	1.1100	1.1500	←——Constants
8	Quantity	16,910	13,006	20,083	←——Variables
9	Minimum	5,000	5,000	5,000	←——Constraints
10	Maximum	25,000	25,000	25,000	←——Constraints
11	Extended Cost	13,306.88	10,686.71	16,933.83	@SUM(D2..D3)*D8+D6
12	Extended Price	18,432.37	14,436.79	23,095.98	+D7*D8
13	Profit Rate	27.81%	25.98%	26.68%	(D12-D11)/D12
14					
15	Total Production		50,000		@SUM(B8..D8)
16	Production Capacity		50,000		←——Constraint
17	Fixed Plant Costs		12,500.00		←——Constant
18					
19	Profit		2,537.71		@SUM(B12..D12)-@SUM(B11..D11)-C17

A / B / C / D / E / F / G / H / I / J / K / L

NUM   READY

The Optimizer found a much different solution than the one proposed by the production manager. After redistributing production quantities to produce 16,910 pieces of bearing A, 13,006 pieces of part B, and 20,083 pieces of part C, the total monthly profit jumped from $2,060.79 to $2,537.71. The additional $476.92 represents an increase of more than 20% compared to the "best" product mix initially suggested.

This example, of course, did not take all possible factors into account. Even so, it clearly demonstrates the value of applying the Optimizer to a what-if scenario. Without using the Optimizer, you would have a difficult time finding a solution as favorable as the one calculated by the Optimizer.

The Optimizer can show you how it arrived at an answer. The reports generated by the Optimizer are discussed in the next section.

Interpreting Optimizer Results

Sometimes the Optimizer produces unexpected results. You may, for example, be greeted with a message box displaying `Objective function changes too slowly`. Quattro Pro 5.0 for Windows displays this message when it is unable to find a clear path to an answer because changing the values of the variables produces little change in the formula you want to optimize. If a problem is too large for the Optimizer, you may see a message box stating `No feasible solution`.

Even when the Optimizer produces an answer that seems acceptable, you may want to examine two reports that show how Quattro Pro 5.0 for Windows arrived at its solution.

To see the Optimizer's reports, select **T**ools **O**ptimizer **O**ptions **R**eporting. In the Report Output Blocks dialog box, shown in figure 9.6, type the addresses for the reports in the text boxes and press Enter or click OK to confirm the dialog box. Both the Detail report and the Answer report overwrite existing data in the notebook. Choose an area that is blank, such as an unused notebook page, and then choose So**l**ve to generate the reports. The following sections describe the two Optimizer reports.

Both the Detail report and the Answer report overwrite existing data in the notebook. Choose an area that is blank, such as an unused notebook page.

Fig. 9.6

The Report Output
Blocks dialog box.

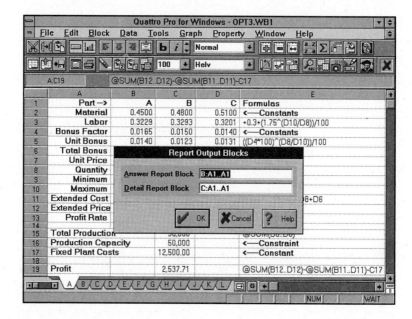

The Detail Report

The Detail report, shown in figure 9.7, shows the minimum and maximum values attained by the adjustable cells and the objective cell as the Optimizer attempted to find a solution. The range of objective cell values also is displayed for each set of adjustable cell values.

Fig. 9.7

The Detail report shows
the limits obtained
during problem solution.

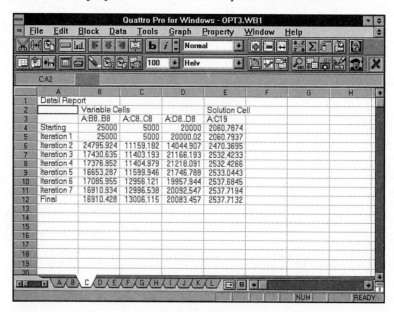

Quattro Pro 5.0 for Windows tries many values in attempting to find the optimal solution. By examining the values used, you may discover additional solutions that would be possible if you adjusted the constraints.

The Answer Report

The Answer report is generally more useful than the Detail report. The information displayed on the Answer report, shown in figure 9.8, includes the initial and final values of the objective cell, the initial and final values of the adjustable cells, and how the defined constraints were applied.

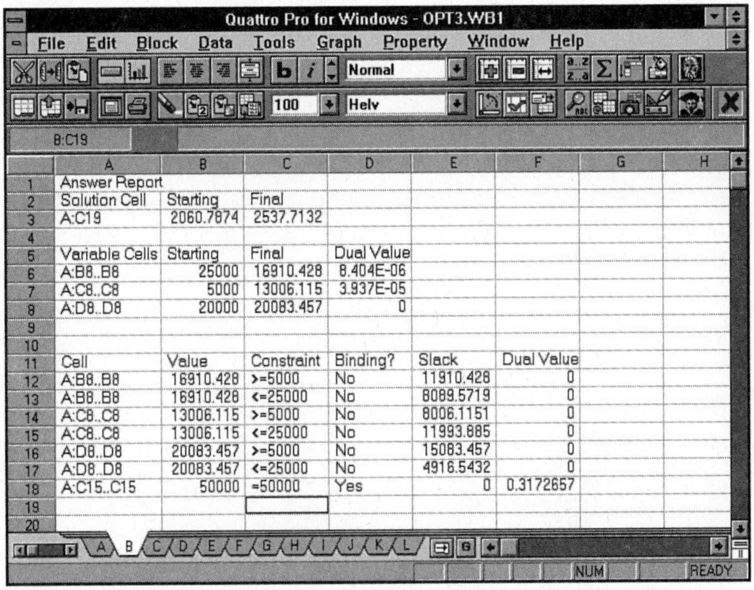

	A	B	C	D	E	F
1	Answer Report					
2	Solution Cell	Starting	Final			
3	A:C19	2060.7874	2537.7132			
4						
5	Variable Cells	Starting	Final	Dual Value		
6	A:B8..B8	25000	16910.428	8.404E-06		
7	A:C8..C8	5000	13006.115	3.937E-05		
8	A:D8..D8	20000	20083.457	0		
9						
10						
11	Cell	Value	Constraint	Binding?	Slack	Dual Value
12	A:B8..B8	16910.428	>=5000	No	11910.428	0
13	A:B8..B8	16910.428	<=25000	No	8089.5719	0
14	A:C8..C8	13006.115	>=5000	No	8006.1151	0
15	A:C8..C8	13006.115	<=25000	No	11993.885	0
16	A:D8..D8	20083.457	>=5000	No	15083.457	0
17	A:D8..D8	20083.457	<=25000	No	4916.5432	0
18	A:C15..C15	50000	=50000	Yes	0	0.3172657
19						
20						

Fig. 9.8

The Answer report shows how the problem was solved.

In figure 9.8 (row 18), you can see that only one of the defined constraints was *binding*. Total production was the binding constraint because it was limited to the plant's production capacity. None of the other constraints was binding in this problem. For each constraint that was not binding, Quattro Pro 5.0 for Windows shows the amount of *slack*—the difference between the defined constraint and the value actually obtained. The constraint that restricted cell B8 to a maximum of 25,000, for example, was never used. In fact, cell B8 was more than 8,000 below the point where the constraint would become binding.

Because only one constraint in this example actually was binding, you can infer that adjusting that constraint (production capacity) upward might result in an improved solution. If several constraints had bound the solution, improving the solution would be more difficult.

Using Functions with the Optimizer

You can include Quattro Pro 5.0 for Windows functions in the formulas in all the problem cells the Optimizer uses to determine solutions, provided you adhere to the following basic rules:

- *Functions in problem cells must use numbers as arguments.* Do not use functions that use strings, date or time values, or values from a database. For example, you can use the function @AVG in an Optimizer problem cell because @AVG uses only numbers to determine a numeric average. You cannot use a function such as @TRIM or @RIGHT.

- *Functions in problem cells must return numbers.* Do not use functions that return strings (such as @RIGHT), a date or time value (such as @TIME), or a value from a database (such as @DCOUNT). You can use functions that return Boolean values, such as @ISNA, because Quattro Pro 5.0 for Windows considers Boolean values to be regular numbers.

Some functions, although allowed in Optimizer problem cells, cause difficulties when the Optimizer is attempting to find its solutions. Functions that suddenly change value, such as @INT, can make it difficult to find a solution. Functions that suddenly change value are called *ill-behaved* functions because the derivative (or rate of change) of the function is *discontinuous*. Other functions that may exhibit this behavior include @IF, @CHOOSE, @ROUND, @HLOOKUP, and @VLOOKUP. You can use these functions in an Optimizer problem, but be aware of their potential to cause difficulties in finding solutions.

Chapter 7, "Using Functions," offers more details on using functions in formulas.

Using Solve For

The Solve For tool is a Quattro Pro 5.0 for Windows analysis utility that you use to find the value of a variable when you are seeking a specific goal. Rather than calculating an optimum answer by adjusting a block of variables, the Solve For tool adjusts a single variable to produce an answer you specify.

Figures 9.9 and 9.10 show a Quattro Pro 5.0 for Windows notebook that performs currency conversions among nine major currencies. This notebook converts specified amounts in one currency to the equivalent value in another currency. At a given exchange rate, for example, 1,142.80 Guilder convert to 3,463.51 French Francs.

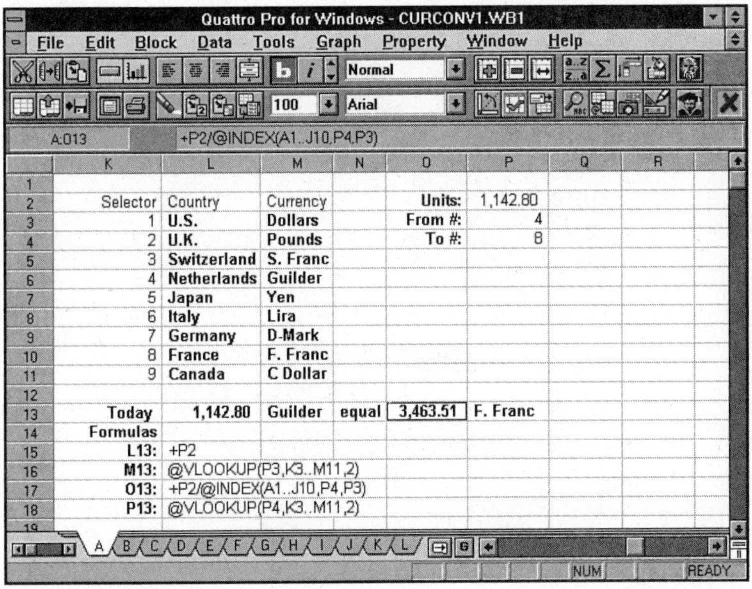

Fig. 9.9

The Exchange section of the currency conversion notebook.

When you select **Tools Solve For**, the dialog box shown in figure 9.11 appears. To use the Solve For tool, you first specify the **Formula Cell.** The Formula Cell is the cell that contains the formula whose value you want to specify. Next you specify the **Target Value,** or the value you want to achieve in the goal cell. Finally you must specify the **Variable Cell,** the cell whose value Solve For will adjust.

The Solve For tool calculates a numeric value using the formula in the goal cell. This value results from adjusting the variable cell, which must be blank or contain a numeric value.

In the example notebook, O13 is the Formula cell, and P2 is the Variable Cell. When you use Solve For, you specify a Target Value for the Formula Cell. In figure 9.11, 120 was specified as the Target Value. Figure 9.12 shows the result in the notebook after you press Enter or click OK to confirm the dialog box.

Fig. 9.10

The cross rates section of the currency conversion notebook.

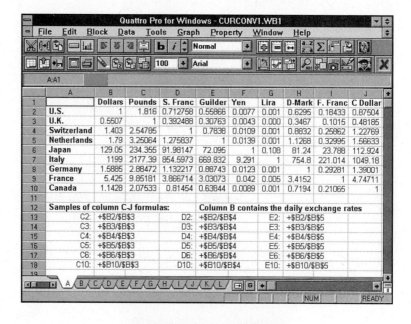

Fig. 9.11

The Solve For dialog box.

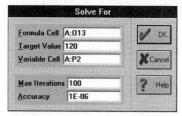

Because Solve For adjusts the value of a number in the notebook, you cannot tell whether Solve For entered the new value or if someone typed the value. This notebook was selected as an example because you can verify the result (although reversed) by specifying **120** as the adjustable value and changing the From # (cell P3) to **8** and the To # (cell P4) to **4**, shown in figure 9.13.

Most notebooks, of course, are not as able (as the currency conversion notebook) to perform reverse calculations and would therefore gain greater benefit from the Solve For tool. The currency conversion notebook, however, is unique in its ability to verify the Solve For results.

When you use Solve For, the adjustable value is permanently changed in the notebook. If you plan to use the Solve For tool to try several different values in a what-if analysis, make sure you save the notebook before you use Solve For. Then you always can return to the original notebook that contains the starting values. If you forget to save the notebook before using Solve For, you can return to the previous value if you immediately select **Edit Undo**. Remember, though, that **Edit Undo** can return you only to the last set of values used before you last used the Solve For tool. You can also use the Scenario Manager, discussed in Chapter 19, "Consolidating Data and Managing Scenarios," to keep a record of each different set of what-if values.

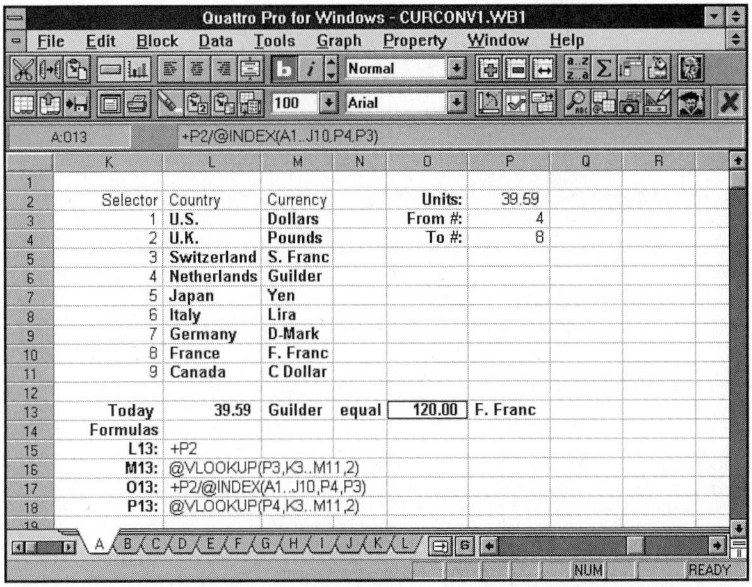

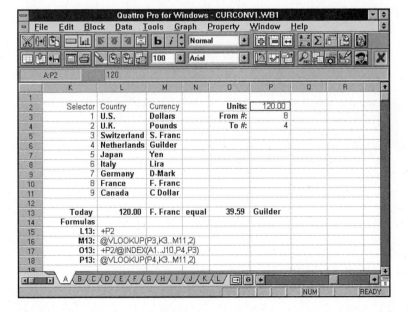

Fig. 9.12

The result of specifying a target value of 120.

Fig. 9.13

Reversing the conversion confirms the Solve For results.

Questions and Answers

Q: Optimizer is unable to find an optimal solution to my complex problem. What adjustments can I make to increase the likelihood of finding a solution?

A: First, try to supply initial values for the variables that you feel will be somewhat close to their final values. Optimizer usually has better success when it can start with a reasonable solution.

Try increasing the **M**ax. Time, Ma**x**. Iterations, **P**recision, and Tol**er**ance settings in the Optimizer Options dialog box. Optimizer's answer may take a little longer or be slightly less precise, but this may be just the edge Optimizer needs to find an answer.

Experiment with the other optional settings, such as Estimates, Derivatives, and Search, to see if these allow Optimizer to find a solution. Always do a "reality check" on your answers, though, to make certain they make sense.

Q: Why does Optimizer sometimes produce different results when solving the same problem again?

A: Some problems have more than one optimal solution. Different initial values for the variables might send Optimizer off in different paths toward a solution, resulting in different final results.

Q: How do I decide whether to use Optimizer or Solve For?

A: Use Solve For if your formula cell must reach a specific value, and there is a single variable cell. In such problems, Solve For is both easier to use and faster than Optimizer. If your problem does not meet these criteria, use Optimizer.

Summary

This chapter discussed the methods and commands you use to analyze data in what-if problems in notebooks. The Optimizer finds answers to problems with one or more variables and one or more constraints. The Solve For tool finds the value of a variable that will produce a desired result. The skills you learned in this chapter help you perform sophisticated analysis on data and give you powerful tools for solving difficult problems.

The next chapter introduces you to Quattro Pro 5.0 for Windows powerful presentation graphics capabilities. You learn how to create, modify, and enhance graphics. You also learn how to include graphics of any type in your notebooks, producing professional-looking reports from your data.

Creating Graphics and Printing Reports

PART

III

OUTLINE

Creating Presentation Graphics

Although Quattro Pro 5.0 for Windows spreadsheet capabilities may provide all the power you need for most data analysis, the presentation graphics features help you present data in an easier-to-understand manner. A well-executed graph can enable you to see and analyze large amounts of information quickly. Instead of trying to understand countless rows and columns of data, you can display the data in a graphical fashion.

Quattro Pro offers many types of business graphs. In fact, it includes many powerful graphic capabilities that previously required a dedicated graphics package or that were not available. Because the Quattro Pro graphics features are built in, you will find that creating sophisticated graphics within Quattro Pro is quite easy.

This chapter shows you how to do the following tasks:

■ Create graphs from data in a notebook

■ Select different types of graphs

- Select, edit, and move graph objects

- Enhance a graph using titles, data labels, and legends

- Import and export graphics in several different formats

- Add graphs to notebook pages

- Create on-screen slide shows

- Print graphs separately or with notebook data

- Use analytical graphs for advanced data analysis

Understanding Quattro Pro 5.0 for Windows Graphics

Quattro Pro 5.0 for Windows, like other versions of Quattro Pro, includes a **G**raph command on the main menu. The commands on the **G**raph menu enable you to create a graph, view a graph, add an existing graph to the notebook, copy a named graph, and view a slide show (see fig. 10.1).

Fig. 10.1

The **G**raph menu.

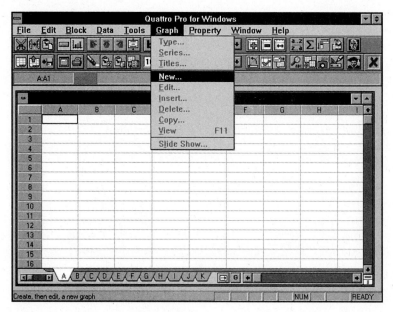

The Graph window gives you additional options for enhancing graphs.

Notice that most selections in the **G**raph menu shown in figure 10.1 are dimmed. These commands are not available when a Notebook window is the active window, but they become available when the Graph window is the active window.

In addition to providing **G**raph commands, Quattro Pro 5.0 for Windows provides a Graph window that gives you much more power and control over graphing. Before you can access the Graph window, however, you first must create a graph. Quattro Pro 5.0 for Windows provides a default name for the graph: the word GRAPH followed by an incrementing numeric suffix. In this case, the graph is named GRAPH1. In addition, Quattro Pro uses the currently highlighted spreadsheet block as the block to be graphed.

After the basic graph is defined, Quattro Pro displays a simple bar graph. Although Quattro Pro offers several different types of graphs, you must use the **G**raph **T**ype command to change the graph type.

The Graph window includes selections through which you can choose a different type of graph; add text, lines, arrows, rectangles, polygons, ellipses, and freehand objects to a graph; use fonts and colors; draw grid lines; and move graph objects.

Just as Quattro Pro 5.0 for Windows enables you to display several notebooks in different windows at the same time, the program also enables you to display graphs and notebooks in multiple windows. You can size, cascade, or tile the windows. See Chapter 3, "Using the Graphical User Interface," for more information about working with multiple windows.

Learning about Common Graphics Elements

When you create a graph, Quattro Pro automatically includes several *objects*. You can modify the display characteristics of these objects after you create the graph, but Quattro Pro uses default settings for the initial display.

Except for pie and doughnut graphs, all graphs have a *y-axis* (a vertical left edge) and an *x-axis* (a horizontal bottom edge). In horizontally oriented graphs, the y-axis is the bottom edge, and the x-axis is the left edge.

Quattro Pro automatically divides each axis with tick marks and scales the numbers on the y-axis, based on the minimum and maximum numbers in the associated data block.

The intersection of the y-axis and the x-axis is called the *origin*. The origin is zero unless you specify otherwise. Although you can plot graphs with a nonzero origin, using a zero origin makes a graph easier to compare and understand. Later in this chapter, you learn how to change the upper or lower limits of a scale.

A graph is made up of one or more *data series*, each of which reflects a category of data. The first category of data is always series 1, the second is series 2, and so on. Some graph types use a limited number of data series; for example, pie and doughnut charts use one data series, and XY graphs use two or more. Other graph types, such as line graphs, can graph multiple data series.

Legends are text placed beside or below a graph that explain the symbols, colors, or fill used to denote each data series. *Titles* are text placed above the graph and along the horizontal and vertical axis that provides information about the overall graph. *Labels* are text entries used to explain specific data items or entries in a graph.

Graphing Notebook Data

You use the **Graph** commands to create a graph that is linked to notebook data. With these commands, you can graph data from one notebook. To create a graph by using the **Graph** commands, you first must retrieve the notebook that contains the data you want to graph. Many of the examples in this chapter are based on the sales data notebook shown in figure 10.2.

To graph information from the sales data notebook, you need to know which data you want to plot and which data you want to use in labeling the graph. In figure 10.2, time-period labels are listed across row 4. Category identifiers are located in column A. The numeric entries in rows 5 through 9, as well as the formula results in row 10 and column F, are suitable for graphing as data points. For this example, however, the totals in row 10 and column F are not included in the graphed data. The column and row labels can be used to label the points on the graph.

To graph data and view it on-screen, first select the data block you want to graph. You can use either the keyboard or the mouse. To use the keyboard, move the cell selector to the first cell in the block, press and hold the Shift key, and use the arrow keys to highlight the block. In this case, highlight A4..E9.

Fig. 10.2

The sales data notebook.

Quattro Pro for Windows - RENORPT.WB1

File Edit Block Data Tools Graph Property Window Help

Normal   b i   Normal

100   Helv

A:A4   'Department

	A	B	C	D	E	F	G	H
1	Darlene's Computer Warehouse			Annual Sales Report				
2			Reno Sales					
3								
4	Department	Quarter 1	Quarter 2	Quarter 3	Quarter 4	Year Total		
5	Computers	125000	135000	110235	165342	535577		
6	Printers	12428	16982	9300	22098	60808		
7	Software	17932	3374	3719	21702	46727		
8	Books	26931	13970	8908	20682	70491		
9	Parts	13806	8138	4071	12471	38486		
10	Qtr totals	196097	177464	136233	242295	752089		
11								
12								
13								
14								
15								
16								
17								
18								
19								

A B C D E F G H I J K L   G

NUM   READY

To select a data block by using the mouse, click the first cell in the block with the left mouse button, and then hold down the button and drag the mouse pointer to the diagonally opposite corner of the block.

After you have selected a block to graph, choose **G**raph **N**ew from the Quattro Pro menu (refer to fig. 10.1). If you want, you can change the default graph name by typing a new name, such as **Sales 1**, in the Graph Name text box. If necessary, adjust the blocks shown in the Series range text boxes.

When you select **G**raph **N**ew, Quattro Pro attempts to determine whether your data is organized by rows or by columns. In some cases, as in this example, your data may be ambiguous. For instance, do you want to graph the data by quarter or by department? Either method could be useful, depending on your needs. In this case, Quattro Pro has decided to graph the data using quarterly data as the data series; the program assumes that your data is organized by columns. To switch to rows of data, which in this example would mean to graph by department, choose the Row/**c**olumn swap check box.

Press Enter or click OK to confirm the dialog box. By default, Quattro Pro displays a bar graph. You can change the graph type after the graph appears by using the **Graph Type** command. Figure 10.3 shows the **Graph New** dialog box, and figure 10.4 shows the default bar graph (graphed by quarters).

Fig. 10.3

The Graph New dialog box.

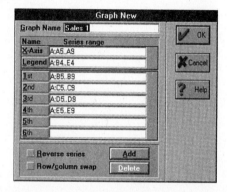

Fig. 10.4

The default bar graph of the sales data spreadsheet.

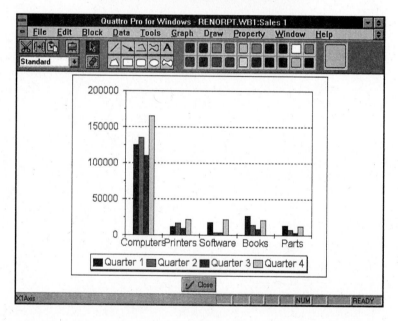

Suppose, for example, that you want to graph data from the spreadsheet in figure 10.2. Specifically, you want to compare the sales of equipment in the department's computers, printers, software, books, and parts. To create a basic graph, suitable for a quick on-screen look at the data, follow these steps:

1. Select the block A4..E9.

2. Choose **G**raph **N**ew.

3. Select the Graph Name text box and type **Sales 1**.

4. Press Enter or click OK.

Note in figure 10.4 that the command menu and the SpeedBar have changed. When you graph data from the notebook, Quattro Pro displays the graph in a separate Graph window and automatically uses the Graph window menu and the Graph window SpeedBar. If you press Next (Ctrl+F6) or select the notebook window from the **W**indow menu, the menu bar changes and displays the Quattro Pro 5.0 for Windows Notebook menu.

The Graph window menu includes a new menu item, **D**raw, that enables you to group and ungroup graph objects, change positions of graph objects so that they are in front of or behind others, control object alignment, and import or export graphics. In addition, the **G**raph and **P**roperty menus are slightly different when the Graph window is active. The options on the **G**raph menu are no longer dimmed as they were when the Notebook window was active, indicating that they now are available. The **P**roperty menu includes several new options that enable you to modify graph object properties: **G**raph Window, Graph **S**etup, Graph **P**ane, **L**egend, **X** Axis, **Y** Axis, and **S**eries.

> Quattro Pro 5.0 for Windows automatically updates your graphs to re-flect changes in notebook data.

TIP

When you create a graph in the notebook file by using the **G**raph commands, the graph is linked to the notebook file. When you change data in the graphed block, the graph is updated automatically to reflect the change.

Setting Up Graphs

Although the graph in figure 10.4 displays the data with visual impact, you probably would prefer to make several changes to improve its usefulness. If, for example, the graph lacks titles and should graph departmental rather than quarterly data, you may want to try another graph type to compare the data more clearly. Quattro Pro 5.0 for Windows offers several options for improving the appearance of your graphs and producing final-quality output suitable for business presentations.

After you have created the basic graph, you use the Graph window menu commands to change the selection of graph blocks, types and orientation; data labels and legends; x-, y-, and optional second y-axes; borders and grids; colors; hatch patterns; fonts; and lines.

After you choose the **Graph New** command, Quattro Pro creates as many data blocks as there are rows or columns in the specified block. It then creates a graph from the data in the block. Quattro Pro uses these data blocks in all subsequent Graph window menu commands until you change the data blocks.

Changing the Graph Orientation

TIP

If the x-axis labels display down a column, the data is in columns.

The Row/column swap check box in the Graph Series dialog box switches whether Quattro Pro assumes that the data series are in rows or columns. By default, Quattro Pro 5.0 for Windows assumes that the first row or column of your data with labels contains the x-axis labels (the labels along the bottom of the graph that group the data series in comparable sets). In the graph shown in figure 10.4, Quattro Pro could not determine whether the labels in row 4 or the labels in column A contained the x-axis labels, so it chose column A.

TIP

To change data series orientation, choose **Graph Series** Row/**column** swap.

To change the orientation of the data series, choose **Graph Series** Row/**column** swap. Figure 10.5 shows the Graph Series dialog box, and figure 10.6 shows the graph after the Row/**column** swap check box in the Graph Series dialog box is selected.

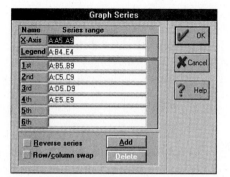

Fig. 10.5

The Graph Series
dialog box.

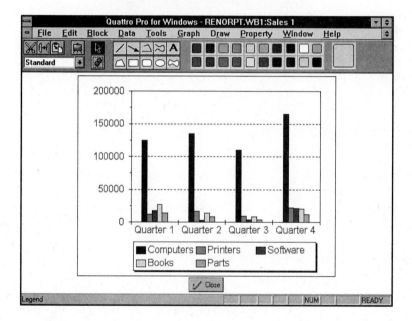

Fig. 10.6

The re-oriented graph
after Row/**c**olumn swap
is selected.

Specifying X-Axis Labels before You Create a Graph

When you graph a data block that contains labels in the first column or
row, Quattro Pro automatically uses the labels to label the x-axis. Sometimes, however, your data block may not include the x-axis labels as
the first column or row. The Graph Series dialog box (refer to figure
10.5) enables you to specify each of the data series manually.

Suppose, for example, that your data block includes a blank row between the row of x-axis labels and the first data series. If you included the row containing the x-axis labels and the empty row when you specified the block of data to graph, the empty row would appear as the first data series, and the row of x-axis labels would appear as the Legend labels. You then would have to correct each of the data blocks manually. Instead, include only the data series rows but not the row containing the x-axis labels or the empty row. You will have to add the x-axis series in the Graph Series dialog box.

If your data block includes the x-axis labels in the first column and a blank column before the first column of data, the x-axis labels would be correctly included, but the empty column would appear as the first data series. In this case, when you highlight the data block, include the x-axis label column, the empty column, and the columns of data. To remove the empty column, select the **1**st series range text box in the Graph New or Graph Series dialog box, and then choose **D**elete.

Specifying Legend Labels in the Data Block

When you graph a data block, Quattro Pro uses colors, symbols, or hatch patterns to identify data blocks. A *legend* is a key that identifies the data blocks in a graph. By default, Quattro Pro 5.0 for Windows places legend labels below the graph, but you can remove them or display them to the right of the graph.

You specify legend labels by specifying the cell addresses of the labels in the notebook. To add legend labels, choose **G**raph **S**eries from the Graph window menu. Select the Legend text box and enter the notebook block that contains the labels.

TIP

Include the legend labels in the data block.

If you prefer to enter legend labels automatically, make certain that the highlighted notebook data block contains the legend labels *before* you choose **G**raph **N**ew.

To change the position of the legend labels, select **P**roperty Graph **S**etup from the Graph window menu, or point to an area within the graph frame outside of the graph and click the right mouse button. The

Graph Setup and Background dialog box appears (see fig. 10.7). Select Legend Position and choose the left button to remove legends, the center button to display the legends below the graph, or the right button to display the legends to the right of the graph. Click OK or press Enter to confirm the dialog box. Figure 10.8 shows the graph after the legends are moved to the right side of the graph.

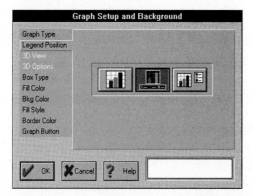

Fig. 10.7

The Graph Setup and Background dialog box.

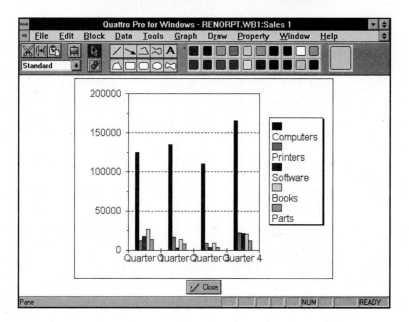

Fig. 10.8

Legends are easily moved to the right side of the graph.

Selecting and Changing Graph Types

By default, Quattro Pro 5.0 for Windows displays a bar graph when you use the **Graph New** command. To change the type of graph Quattro Pro displays, choose **Graph Type** after you use **Graph New**. When you choose the type of graph you want, Quattro Pro changes the display to reflect your choice.

Several types of graphs are available in Quattro Pro: **2**-D, **3**-D, **R**otate, **C**ombo, and **T**ext. Except for **T**ext graphs, each of the graph types also offers several variations. Table 10.1 shows the variations available with each graph type.

Table 10.1 Quattro Pro 5.0 for Windows Graph Types

Type	Options
2-D	Bar
	Variance
	Stacked Bar
	High Low
	Line
	XY
	Area
	Column
	Pie
	100% Stacked Bar
	Stacked Bar Comparison
	100% Stacked Bar Comparison
	Doughnut
	Radar
3-D	3-D Bar
	3-D Stacked Bar
	2.5-D Bar
	3-D Step
	3-D Unstacked Area
	3-D Ribbon

Type	Options
	3-D Area
	3-D Column
	3-D Pie
	3-D Surface
	3-D Contour
	3-D Shaded Surface
	3-D 100% Stacked Bar
	3-D Doughnut
Rotate	Rotated 2-D Bar
	Rotated 3-D Bar
	Rotated 2.5-D Bar
	Rotated Area
	Rotated Line
	Rotated 2-D Stacked Bar
	Rotated 2-D 100% Stacked Bar
	Rotated 2-D Comparison
	Rotated 2-D 100% Comparison
	Rotated 3-D Stacked Bar
	Rotated 3-D 100% Stacked Bar
Combo	Line-Bar
	High Low-Bar
	Area-Bar
	Multiple Bar
	Multiple Columns
	Multiple 3-D Columns
	Multiple Pies
	Multiple 3-D Pies
Text	Text

When you select **G**raph **T**ype, Quattro Pro displays the Graph Types
dialog box (see fig. 10.9). You can choose from all available graph
types. The same graph type options also are available in the Graph
Setup and Background dialog box, which appears when you choose
Property Graph **S**etup from the Graph window menu or point to the
graph (outside any objects in the graph but inside the frame) and click
the right mouse button (see fig. 10.10).

Fig. 10.9

The Graph Types
dialog box.

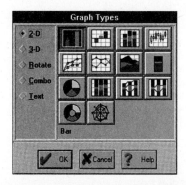

Fig. 10.10

The Graph Setup and
Background dialog box.

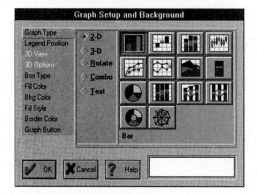

Choosing the best graph for a given application can sometimes be a matter of personal preference. Selecting a line-, bar-, or pie-type graph, for example, would be appropriate if you plan to graph only a single data block. At times, however, just one graph type will do the job. For instance, high low graphs are specialized for presenting certain types of stock market information. Table 10.2 lists and briefly explains each graph category. The sections that follow discuss each category in more detail.

Table 10.2 Graph Categories

Category	Description
100% Stacked Bar	Shows each bar as the same size, enabling you to compare percentages more easily.
Bar	Compares related data at a certain time or shows the trend of numeric data across time.

Category	Description
Combination	Mixes graph types to display different types of data together.
Comparison	Connects boundaries between data series with lines, enabling you to compare series values more easily.
Pie, Column, and Doughnut	Shows what percentage of the total each data point contributes. Do not use these types of graphs if the data contains negative numbers.
High Low	Shows fluctuations in data over time, such as the high, low, close, and open prices of a stock.
Line	Shows the trend of numeric data across time.
Radar	Shows data plotted around a common center, with x-axis values as spokes.
Stacked Bar and Area	Shows the relationship of values to the total.
Surface	Shows data points on a 3-D grid with variations plotted as elevation changes.
XY	Shows the relationship between one independent variable and one or more dependent variables.

When you use **Graph Type** to change the graph type, Quattro Pro uses the new graph type. If, however, you open another notebook file, Quattro Pro still uses the default bar graph type. Figure 10.11 shows the result of choosing **Graph Type 2**-D Stacked Bar—possibly a better choice for displaying the consolidated sales notebook data. In addition, each data series was assigned a fill style for better visibility.

Suppose that you want to display the graph in horizontal orientation. Choose **Graph Type R**otate and select the type of graph you want to use. Quattro Pro 5.0 for Windows displays the graph as shown in figure 10.12.

Using Two-Dimensional Graphs

Two-dimensional graphs are the most common type of business graphs. In this graph, data is plotted using an x-axis and a y-axis or, in the case of column and pie graphs, using no axis at all.

Fig. 10.11

A 2-D stacked bar graph of the sales data notebook.

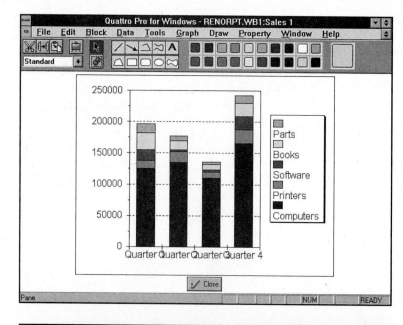

Fig. 10.12

A horizontal bar graph of the sales data notebook.

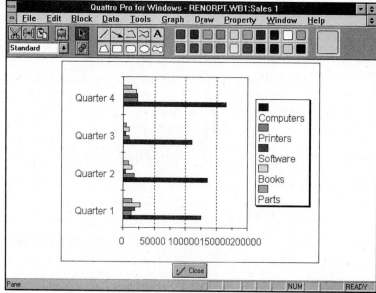

Using Bar Graphs

A *bar graph* shows data as a series of bars drawn next to each other. This type of graph is useful for showing how data categories compare over time. Figure 10.13 shows a simple, 2-D bar graph.

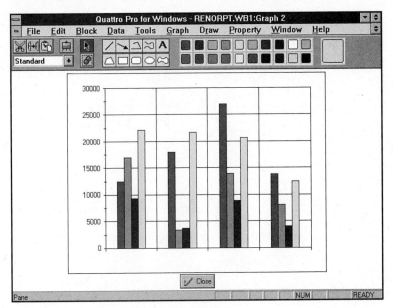

Fig. 10.13

A 2-D bar graph.

Using Variance Graphs

A *variance graph* is similar to a bar graph, except that the origin is adjustable to show how data varies from a specified value. Figure 10.14, for example, shows a variance graph of the same data as figure 10.13, but with the origin set to 15,000 instead of 0.

Initially, a variance graph has the origin set to 0, and so the graph appears identical to a standard 2-D bar graph. After you create the basic variance graph, adjust the origin by pointing to the graph y-axis and clicking the right mouse button, or by choosing **Property Y** Axis from the Graph window menu. The Y-Axis Properties dialog box appears (see fig. 10.15).

Select the Scale **Z**ero line at text box and enter a new value for the origin. In figure 10.14, the value was set to 15,000, so values smaller than 15,000 appear below the origin line.

Fig. 10.14

A variance graph shows how data varies from a specified baseline value.

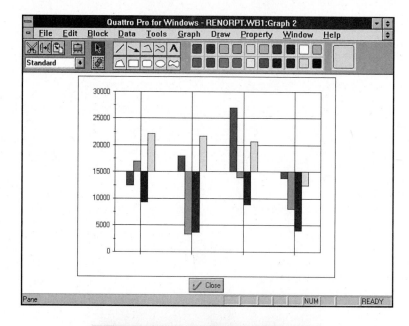

Fig. 10.15

The Y-Axis Properties dialog box.

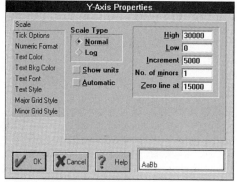

Using Stacked Bar Graphs

A *stacked bar graph* shows data as a series of bars stacked on top of one another. This type of graph is useful for showing the portion that data categories contribute to a whole, as well as comparing changes in those contributions over time. Stacked bar graphs not only show how each data item varies over time, but also how the total of all data items varies over the same time period. A *100% stacked bar graph* is a variation of the stacked bar graph; in this type of graph, the bar is always full height, and the individual data items are shown as their percentage of

100 percent. *Comparison* graphs and *100% stacked bar comparison* graphs are also variations of stacked bar graphs. For these graph types, the boundaries between the data segments in each bar are connected to the corresponding boundaries between the data segments in the next bar. These connecting lines can help you to spot trends more easily, but they may be difficult to understand if the bars contain too many data segments.

Figure 10.16 shows a simple stacked bar graph.

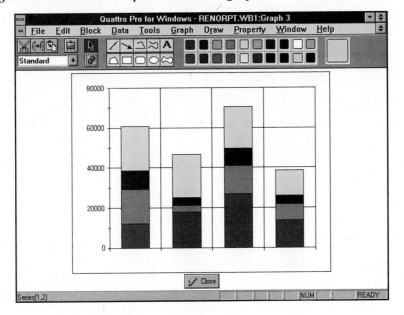

Fig. 10.16

A stacked bar graph.

Using High Low Graphs

High low graphs are sometimes called HLCO graphs, which stands for high-low-close-open. A high low graph is especially useful for graphing data about the price of a stock over time. Here are the meanings of the four values:

High	The stock's highest price in the given time period.
Low	The stock's lowest price in the given time period.
Close	The stock's price at the end, or close, of the time period.
Open	The stock's price at the start, or open, of the time period.

High low graphs are specialized for stock market information, but you also can use them to track other kinds of fluctuating data over time, such as daily temperature or currency exchange rates.

Each set of data consists of four figures representing high, low, close, and open values. The set of data is represented on the graph as a vertical line with tick marks. The line extends from the low value to the high value. The close value is represented by a tick mark extending to the right of the line, and the open value is represented by a tick mark extending to the left. The total number of lines on the graph depends on the number of time periods included.

Figure 10.17 shows a high low graph.

Fig. 10.17

A high low graph often is used to plot stock prices.

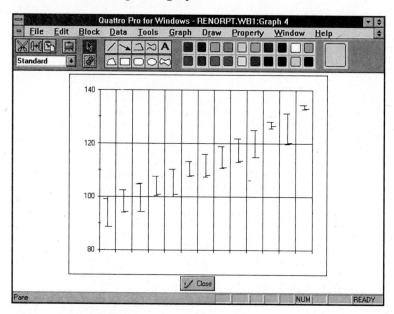

Using Line Graphs

Line graphs are the most common type of graph and one of the easiest to understand. Line graphs plot values using individual lines to connect the data points for each data series.

Figure 10.18 shows data plotted using a line graph.

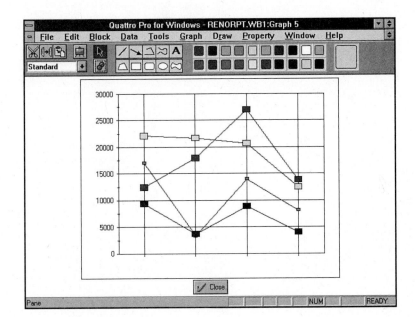

Fig. 10.18

A line graph plots data using lines to connect data points.

Using XY Graphs

The *XY graph*, often called a *scatter graph*, is a variation of a line graph. Like a line graph, an XY graph has values plotted as points in the graph. Unlike a line graph, an XY graph has its x-axis labeled with numeric values instead of labels.

XY graphs show the correlation between two or more sets of data. An XY graph, for example, can show the correlation between sales of hot chocolate and average daily temperature, or age and income.

To use XY graphs effectively, you need to understand two terms. One data block is called the *independent variable*, which is data you can change or control. The other data blocks, the *dependent variables*, are dependent on the independent variable; in other words, you cannot control or change the dependent variable.

Quattro Pro 5.0 for Windows always plots the independent variable on the x-axis, and the dependent variables on the y-axis; thus, the independent data should be in the first row or column, and the dependent data should be in the second and succeeding rows or columns.

Figure 10.19 shows an XY graph, based on a notebook that plots a trigonometric function (@SIN) as it relates to a specified angle. To find the correlation between angles and the values of the functions, you can create an XY graph.

Fig. 10.19

An XY graph of a trigonometric function.

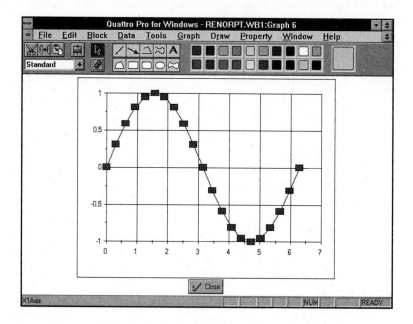

Using Area Graphs

An *area graph*, which emphasizes broad trends, is a combination of a line graph (which illustrates a change in data over time) and a stacked-bar graph (which illustrates individual sets of values). Area graphs plot the first data series closest to the x-axis, and stack additional data series above each other. Each data series line represents the total of the data series being plotted plus all lower data series.

Area graphs are filled between the origin and the plotted lines. Generally, you shouldn't use area graphs to plot negative data, especially when plotting several data series. If some data series are negative and others are positive, it is difficult to determine which is which. Figure 10.20 shows an area graph.

Using Column Graphs

A *column graph* compares values in a single set of data that contains only positive numbers. Each value appears as a section of the column and represents a percentage of the total. You can plot only one row or one column of numeric data in a column graph. Column graphs are very similar in function to pie graphs, but column graphs are more effective when you want to plot a large number of data items.

Figure 10.21 shows data plotted in a column graph.

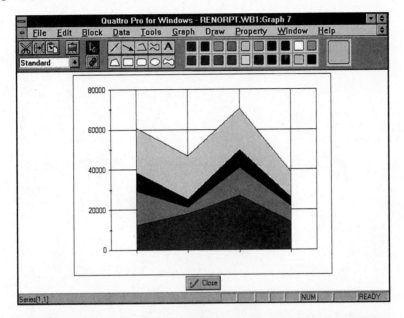

Fig. 10.20

Area graphs stack data series to show data totals.

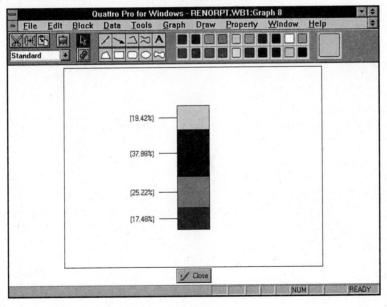

Fig. 10.21

A column graph plots data as a percentage of the total.

Using Pie Graphs

Like a column graph, a *pie graph* compares values in a single set of data that contains only positive numbers. Each value appears as a slice of the pie and represents a percentage of the total. You can plot only one row or one column of numeric data in a pie graph.

If you attempt to plot too many data items, the wedges of the pie graph become too small to understand easily. Use column graphs to plot data series with large numbers of individual items. Figure 10.22 shows data plotted as a pie graph.

Fig. 10.22

A pie graph plots data as a percentage of the total.

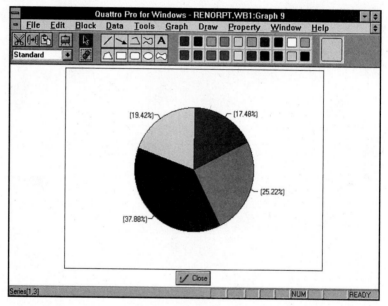

Using Doughnut Graphs

A *doughnut graph* is a variation of a pie graph; unlike a pie graph, however, a doughnut graph has a center ring cut out. You use a doughnut graph exactly as you use pie graphs. Figure 10.23 shows data plotted as a doughnut graph.

Using Radar Graphs

A *radar graph* plots data radiating out from a single center point. X-axis values appear as spokes in a wheel, and y-axis data is plotted on each spoke. Radar graphs may make spotting trends easier, depending on the type of data being graphed. Figure 10.24 shows data plotted as a radar graph.

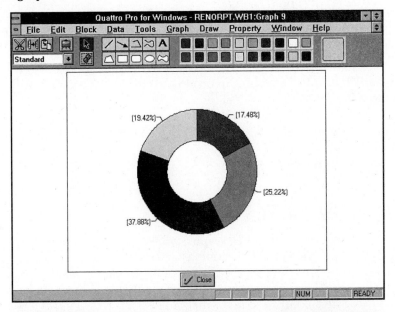

Fig. 10.23

A doughnut graph is a variation of a pie graph.

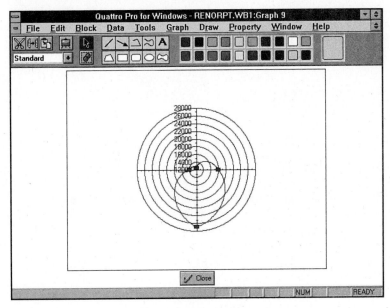

Fig. 10.24

A radar graph plots data around a central point.

Using 3-D Graphs

A 3-D graph plots data in three-dimensional perspective. Instead of just using an x-axis and a y-axis, a 3-D graph adds a z-axis. In some cases, 3-D graphs do a better job than 2-D graphs of showing the complex relationships between groups of data items.

Use restraint when deciding whether to choose a 3-D graph instead of a similar 2-D graph. Although Quattro Pro 5.0 for Windows offers 3-D versions of most graphs, don't fall for the trap of creating a graph type that obscures the data by being too entertaining. Remember, the purpose behind creating business graphs is to inform viewers, not to dazzle them. Make certain that the graph type you select appropriately displays your data.

Using 3-D Stacked Bar Graphs

Similar to regular stacked bar graphs, *3-D stacked bar* graphs work best with small amounts of data in comparing sets of data over time. A 3-D stacked bar graph shows data as a series of 3-D bars stacked on top of one another. This type of graph is useful for showing the portion that data categories contribute to a whole, as well as comparing changes in those contributions over time. 3-D stacked bar graphs not only show how each data item varies over time, but also how the total of all data items varies over the same time period.

Figure 10.25 shows a 3-D stacked bar graph.

Using 2.5-D Bar Graphs

2.5-D bar graphs show data as a series of deep bars drawn next to each other. This type of graph is useful for showing how data categories compare over time.

A 2.5-D bar graph is not a true 3-D graph, because it does not use depth to portray a z-axis value, but instead to add a third dimension to the bars. Figure 10.26 shows a 2.5-D bar graph.

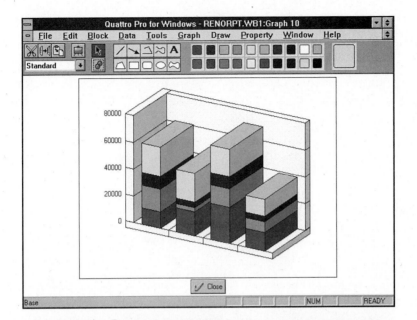

Fig. 10.25

A 3-D stacked bar graph shows data as a portion of the total.

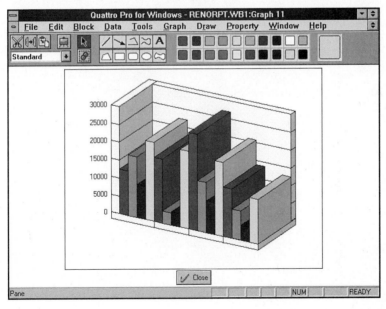

Fig. 10.26

A 2.5-D bar graph adds depth to its bars.

Using 3-D Bar Graphs

3-D bar graphs show data as groups of bars plotted on a three-dimensional grid. Often a 3-D bar graph provides an easier-to-understand display of the relationship between the plotted data series than a 2-D bar graph can.

If possible, arrange the data series with the largest values first and the smallest values last. This will help to prevent smaller values from being hidden by large values. If it is not possible to arrange the data series in this manner, consider using a 2-D graph to prevent data from being hidden.

Figure 10.27 shows a 3-D bar graph.

Fig. 10.27

3-D bar graphs show data on a three-dimensional grid.

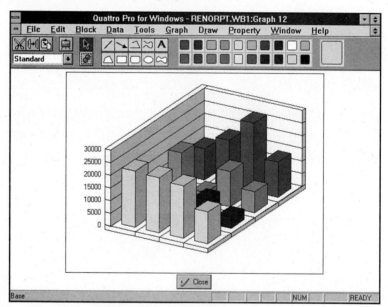

Using Step Graphs

Step graphs are nearly identical to 3-D bar graphs, except that the bars in a step graph touch. Step graphs are most useful for displaying data that changes in regular increments, rather than data that may change abruptly in either direction. Figure 10.28 shows a step graph.

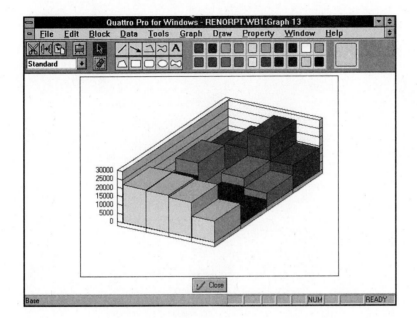

Fig. 10.28

Step graphs are 3-D bar graphs with bars touching each other.

Using 3-D Unstacked Area Graphs

3-D unstacked area graphs plot values using lines (which are stretched to add depth) to connect the data points for each data series, while filling the area between the lines and the origin. Because larger values in a 3-D unstacked area graph can hide lower values plotted behind them, this type of graph is best suited to displaying sorted data.

Figure 10.29 shows a 3-D unstacked area graph.

Using Ribbon Graphs

Ribbon graphs are similar to 3-D unstacked area graphs; they plot values using lines (which are stretched to add depth) to connect the data points for each data series. Ribbon graphs, however, do not fill the area between the lines and the origin.

Ribbon graphs are better than 3-D unstacked area graphs at displaying unsorted data because larger values are less likely to hide lower values plotted behind them in a ribbon graph. Figure 10.30 shows a ribbon graph.

Fig. 10.29

3-D unstacked area graphs are similar to 3-D step graphs.

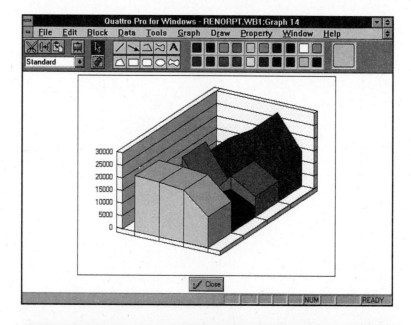

Fig. 10.30

Ribbon graphs are better than 3-D unstacked area graphs at displaying unsorted data.

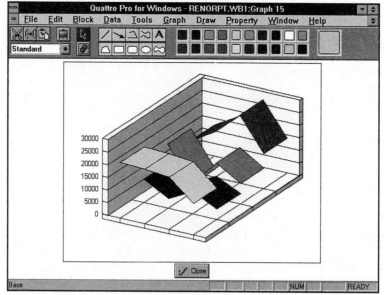

Using 3-D Area Graphs

3-D area graphs, which emphasize broad trends, are a combination of a line graph and a 3-D stacked-bar graph. 3-D area graphs plot the first data series closest to the x-axis, and stack additional data series above each other. Each data series line represents the total of the data series being plotted plus all lower data series. 3-D area graphs are filled between the origin and the plotted lines.

3-D area graphs usually should not be used to plot negative data, especially if plotting several data series. If some data series are negative while others are positive, it is difficult to determine which is which. Figure 10.31 shows a 3-D area graph.

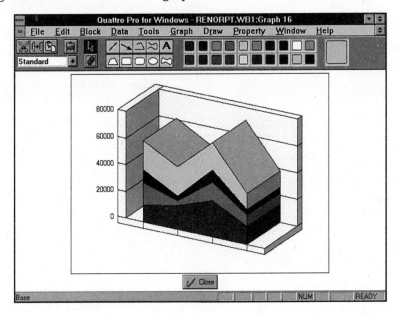

Fig. 10.31

3-D area graphs emphasize broad trends.

Using 3-D Column Graphs

A *3-D column* graph compares values in a single set of data that contains only positive numbers. Each value appears as a section of the column and represents a percentage of the total. You can plot only one row or one column of numeric data in a 3-D column graph.

3-D column graphs are very similar to 2-D column graphs, except that the column is displayed with a third dimension: depth. Figure 10.32 shows a 3-D column graph.

Fig. 10.32

A 3-D column graph.

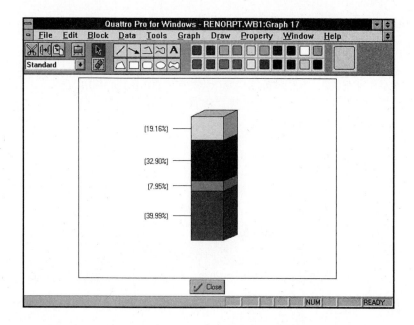

Using 3-D Pie and Doughnut Graphs

3-D pie graphs and *3-D doughnut* graphs, like 3-D column graphs, are extensions of the standard 2-D graphs—in this case the 2-D pie or doughnut graphs. Like a 2-D pie graph, a 3-D pie graph plots a single data series, showing each data item as a percentage of the total. A 3-D doughnut graph also plots a single data series, showing each data item as a percentage of the total. The data series cannot contain negative values. Figure 10.33 shows a 3-D doughnut graph.

Using Surface Graphs

Surface graphs display data as lines connecting the data items for each series. The line for each data series is connected to the line for the next data series, and the area between the lines are filled in with different colors. Figure 10.34 shows a surface graph.

Using Contour Graphs

Contour graphs are very similar to surface graphs, except in the method used to color the surface plot. Instead of coloring the segments between each set of lines with a distinct color, contour graphs apply color to show how far the surface lies above the origin. Contour graphs can be used to show elevations, as in contour maps. Figure 10.35 shows a contour graph.

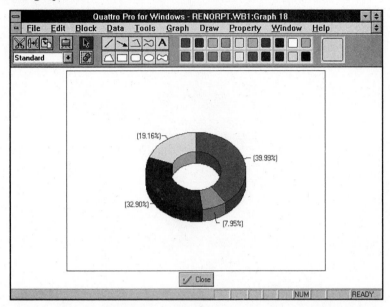

Fig. 10.33

A 3-D doughnut graph shows each data item as a percentage of the total.

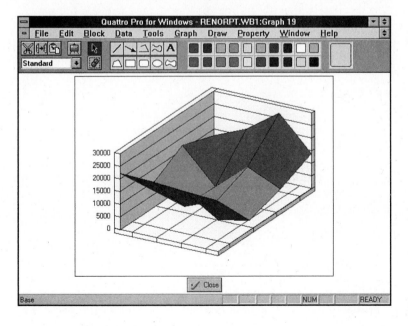

Fig. 10.34

Surface graphs plot data as lines connected by colored surfaces.

Fig. 10.35

Contour graphs can be used to create contour maps.

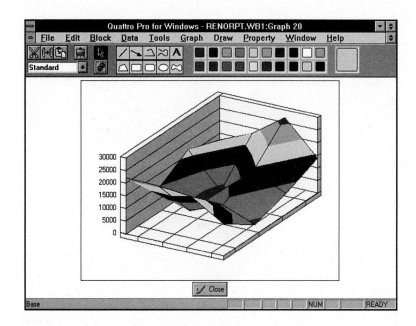

Using Shaded Surface Graphs

Shaded surface graphs are another variation on surface and contour graphs. The shaded surface graph uses a single color to create the surface, but applies different shading to show the slope of the surface between data points. Shaded surface graphs may reproduce better than surface and contour graphs on black-and-white printers. Figure 10.36 shows a shaded surface graph.

Using Text Graphs

Text graphs are a special type of Quattro Pro 5.0 for Windows graph. Instead of plotting notebook data, text graphs enable you to create graphics objects that you can place anywhere you like in a notebook.

TIP

Text graphs can contain more than just text.

Text graphs can contain text, objects you create using the drawing tools available in the Graph window, and imported graphics. The section, "Enhancing a Graph," later in this chapter shows you how to create and modify text and drawn objects, as well as how to import graphics images created by other programs.

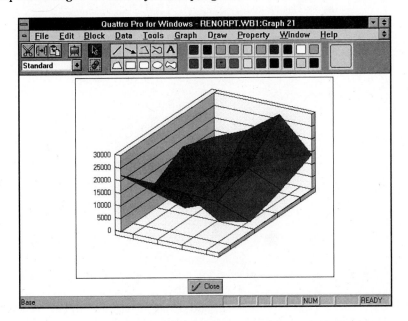

Fig. 10.36

Shaded surface graphs may be a better choice for black-and-white printing.

Figure 10.37 shows a text graph displayed in the Graph window. To create a text graph, make sure that no notebook data is highlighted and choose **G**raph **N**ew. You also can change an existing graph to a text graph by choosing **G**raph **T**ype from the Graph window menu and selecting **T**ext as the type. The graph of the data will no longer appear.

After you create a text graph, you can place it anywhere you like in a notebook (just as you can any other Quattro Pro graph). You can use text graphs to enhance the appearance of your notebooks, or simply to make them easier to use by providing dramatic visual clues instructing the user how to use the notebook.

Rotating Graphs

Sometimes you can create a more stunning visual effect by rotating a graph. *Rotated* graphs place the x-data series along the left vertical axis and the y-data series along the horizontal axis. Values are plotted as horizontal distances from the left axis instead of vertical distances from the lower axis.

Fig. 10.37

Text graphs can display text, drawn objects, and imported graphics.

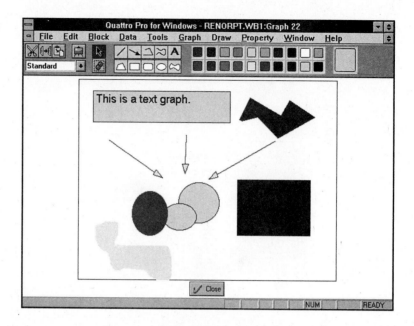

Quattro Pro 5.0 for Windows enables you to plot eleven of its standard graphs as rotated graphs: 2-D Bar, 3-D Bar, 2.5-D Bar, Area, Line, Stacked Bar, 2-D 100% Stacked Bar, 2-D Comparison, 2-D 100% Comparison, 3-D Stacked Bar, and 3-D 100% Stacked Bar. Figure 10.38 shows a rotated 2-D bar graph.

TIP

Be consistent when creating graphs; use the same type of graph to show similar data.

The choice of whether to use a standard or a rotated graph is usually a matter of personal preference. For the most effective presentation, and the highest level of understanding of the data you are presenting, most graphics presentation experts recommend using a few, well-planned graph types. Do not, for example, present similar data using two very different types of graphs and expect your audience to easily understand your point. Instead, use the same type of graph to show changes in the basic data.

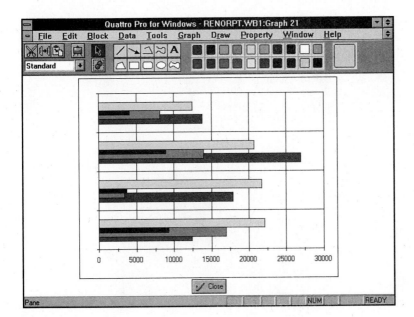

Fig. 10.38

A rotated bar graph.

Mixing Graph Types

Quattro Pro 5.0 for Windows enables you to mix graph types so that
you can compare different sets of data. The **Graph Type Combo** command enables you to select from several different combinations of
graph types. You can combine a bar graph and a line, area, or a high
low graph. You also can display multiple column, 3-D column, pie, 3-D
pie, or bar graphs.

Graphs that combine a bar graph and a line, area, or a high low graph,
are used to display data that is related, but that requires different types
of plotting to best show different data series. Suppose, for example,
that you are plotting temperature levels over the past three decades.
You might plot yearly temperatures as bars and show record highs,
record lows, and historical average temperatures as lines. Combined
bar and high low graphs often are used to track stock market data and
show individual stock performances. Figure 10.39 shows a combined
area-bar graph.

Graphs that show multiple columns, pies, or bars show several different data series plotted as individual graphs, but include each individual
graph within a single-named graph in the notebook. You might use
these types of combined graphs to show how different company offices

controlled their expense percentages, even if their overall expenditures were widely different. Figure 10.40 shows a multiple 3-D column graph that has individual 3-D column graphs for four different data series.

Fig. 10.39

A combined area-bar graph.

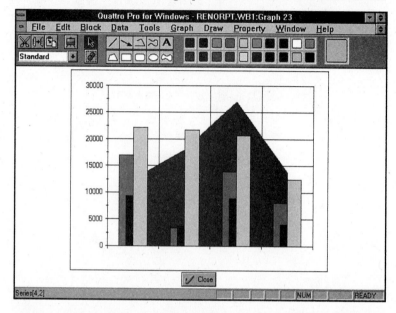

Fig. 10.40

A multiple 3-D column graph.

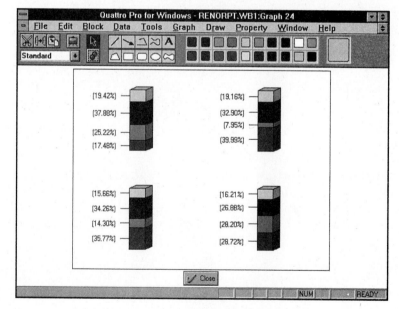

As this figure shows, each column is the same size. You can compare how the data items within each data series relate as a percentage of the total of the data series, but you cannot determine the relative values of data items between series. When selecting one of the Combo graph types, consider whether it will display the data in a meaningful manner.

Selecting Graph Objects

Most Graph window menu commands require that you select an object before you can choose the command. You must, for example, select an object or a graph before you can copy, delete, rearrange, or move the object or graph in the Graph window; adjust the object's line style or colors; and make other layout changes to the object or graph. You can select one or several objects at a time in a Graph window. When an object is selected, small squares, or *handles*, appear on the object.

To select graph objects, click them with the left mouse button.   **TIP**

You select or deselect an object by using the mouse. To select an object, point to the object and click the left mouse button. To select several objects, draw a box large enough to include all the objects you want to select by positioning the mouse pointer at one corner of this box. Then either drag the mouse until you surround all the objects, or hold down the Shift key when clicking subsequent items.

To deselect all selected items, position the mouse pointer anywhere in the Graph window—outside the selected objects—and click the mouse. To deselect one item when several items are selected, position the mouse pointer on the item; then press and hold down Shift while you click the mouse.

Editing Graph Text Objects

You can edit any object that contains text, such as titles, labels, and notations. The method you must use, however, depends on how the object was added to the graph. Text you add to a graph with the Text box tool, for example, can be edited by selecting the text and pressing Edit (F2). Text, such as data labels and legends, must be edited by changing the notebook cell that contains the label text.

Figure 10.41 shows text that was added by using the Text box tool. After editing the text, click outside the text box to deselect the text box.

Fig. 10.41

Editing text added with
the Text box tool.

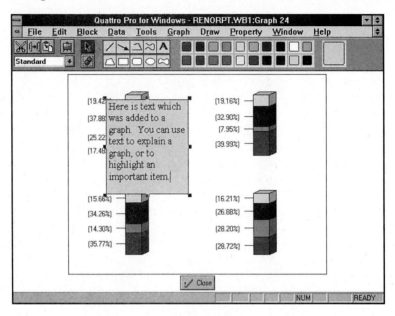

Graph titles are a special type of graph text. Titles include up to two lines of text that are displayed centered above the graph, as well as a single line of text to the left, below, or to the right of the graph that explains the purpose of each graph axis. You enter titles as text in the Graph Titles dialog box.

Moving Graph Objects

You occasionally may want to move graph objects within a graph or redesign the graph. The only objects you can move directly, however, are those added using one of the Graph window tools. You cannot, for example, move graph titles, but you can move text you added using the Text box tool.

TIP

You must use a mouse to move graph objects.

To move an object that was added using one of the Graph window tools, first select the object. When you begin to move an object, a dotted box appears around the object and the mouse pointer changes to a hand (see fig. 10.42). Hold down the left mouse button and drag the dotted box to the new location. Release the mouse button when you have positioned the dotted box where you want to move the object. The dotted box disappears, and the object is moved to the new location.

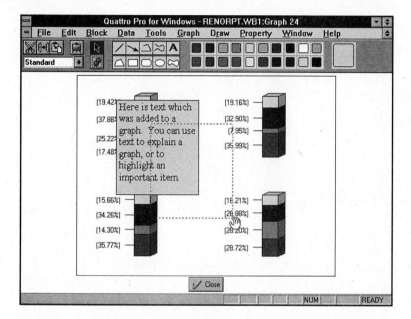

Fig. 10.42

Moving a graph object.

If you find that you cannot move an object, it most likely was added to the graph and positioned automatically. The titles shown in figure 10.42, for example, cannot be moved because Quattro Pro 5.0 for Windows automatically determines their position.

Changing the Size of Graph Objects

You can use the Graph window tools to change the size of objects you added to a graph. You cannot directly change the size of objects automatically added to a graph, although you can use the Object Inspectors to change the point size used to display titles, legends, and data labels. (See "Using Fonts and Attributes," later in this chapter.)

To change the size of an object by using the mouse, click the object whose size you want to change. To define the new size, drag one of the handles. When you begin to change the size of a drawn object, a dotted box or line appears around it and shows the changing size. When you finish moving, the dotted box disappears, and the object changes size. Release the mouse button when you are finished.

TIP

Graph text in text boxes automatically wraps to a new line.

When you change the size of a text box in a Quattro Pro graph, the point size of the text within the box does not change. If you change the length of the text box, the text automatically adjusts the position where words wrap to the next line—just as text automatically wraps to the next line in a word processor.

Enhancing a Graph

You enhance a graph in the Graph window. Quattro Pro 5.0 for Windows features for enhancing a graph's appearance are accessed through the commands of the Graph window menu and through the tools on the Graph window SpeedBar. Figure 10.43 shows the tools on the Graph window SpeedBar.

If the graph you want to enhance currently is displayed as a floating object or *frame* in a notebook window, first display the graph in the Graph window by pointing to the graph and double-clicking the left mouse button. If the graph is not currently displayed as a floating object in a notebook window, but has already been modified during the current session, you can use the **W**indow command and select the Graph window displaying the graph. You also can use the SpeedTab button to select the Graphs page, point to the icon for the graph you want to modify, and double-click the left mouse button. Finally, you can use the **G**raph **E**dit command to select a graph to modify.

As you work with these commands and tools to enhance graphs, Quattro Pro updates the graph automatically so that you can see the effects of your changes. The following sections show you how to use specific commands to enhance your graphs.

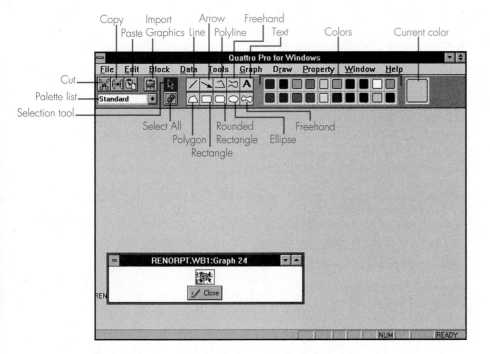

Fig. 10.43

The tools on the Graph window Speedbar.

Adding Descriptive Text, Lines, and Arrows

With Quattro Pro 5.0 for Windows, you can add descriptive numbers, labels, lines, and arrows to existing graphs. To add descriptive information to a graph, you first must determine the type of information you will be adding. You can, for example, add a title to the graph using either the **Graph Titles** command or the Text box tool.

If you use the **Graph Titles** command, you specify the exact text for the titles. The main title automatically is centered over the top of the graph. If you use the Text box tool, you can place the text anywhere you like on the graph—even on top of other graph objects.

All y-axis titles are automatically turned 90 degrees.

TIP

When you add 1st and 2nd Y-Axis titles, Quattro Pro automatically turns the titles 90 degrees and displays them vertically. Because you cannot rotate text that you add with the Text box tool, you should always add the y-axis titles by using **Graph Titles**.

Adding Descriptive Text to a Graph

Sometimes graph titles and labels aren't enough to describe adequately the contents of a graph. You may want to add a few words that point out a particular data block or that state a conclusion illustrated by the graph.

When you choose the Text box tool, Quattro Pro displays the text box on the graph. Type the text you want to add into the text box. The text box expands as necessary as you add additional text. You can move the text anywhere—even inside the graph or on top of a data block.

TIP

> You can change the font, point size, and attributes of any text on a graph.

You can use the **P**roperty **C**urrent Object command—or point to text on a graph and click the right mouse button—to change the font, point size, and attributes of any text on a graph. For more information on making such changes, see "Using Fonts and Attributes," later in this chapter.

Adding Lines, Arrows, and Objects to a Graph

To emphasize specific objects in a graph, you can use the tool icons to add lines, arrows, and other objects (refer to fig. 10.43). When you use a tool icon, Quattro Pro displays a line, arrow, or other object on the graph, with handles to indicate that the object is selected. As long as the object is selected, you can move it or change its size. Figure 10.44 shows a graph with both descriptive text and an arrow that emphasizes a data block.

If you add an arrow to a graph, you can use the **P**roperty **C**urrent Object command—or point to the arrow and click the right mouse button—to manipulate the arrow. The Arrow dialog box, shown in figure 10.45, enables you to change the colors and style used to display the arrow.

TIP

> When the mouse pointer changes to crosshairs, it is in position for resizing.

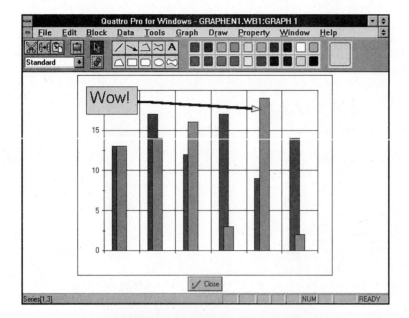

Fig. 10.44

A graph enhanced with text and an arrow.

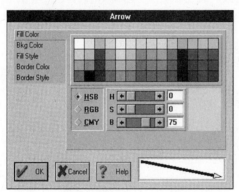

Fig. 10.45

The Arrow dialog box.

You can use the mouse to change the size and direction of a line or arrow. First, select the line or arrow, and then point to the end of the line or arrow you want to move. When the mouse pointer is on the handle at the end of the line or arrow, the pointer changes to crosshairs, indicating that you can manipulate the line or arrow. Hold down the left mouse button, move the end to its new position, and release the button.

To add other types of drawn objects to a graph, select the tool icon corresponding to the type of object you want to add. If, for example, you want to add a rectangle, select the Rectangle tool. Point to the location where you want the first corner of the rectangle, press and hold down the left mouse button, and drag the dotted box to the size you want. When you release the mouse button, Quattro Pro adds the object to the graph.

> **TIP**
>
> To remove an object added in error, click the Cut button.

If you make a mistake adding an object, click the Cut button or press the Delete key while the object is still selected to remove the object. You also can resize objects or change their properties by using the **P**roperty **C**urrent Object command or the Object Inspectors.

Adding Titles

After you create a graph, you can add titles to it in two ways: with the **G**raph **T**itles command on the Graph window menu, or with the Text box tool. The section, "Adding Descriptive Text to a Graph," earlier in this chapter showed you how to add text using the Text box tool. Next you see how to add titles using the **G**raph **T**itles command.

When you graph data from a notebook, you can specify the titles after you create and view the graph. With the **G**raph **T**itles command, you can create a **M**ain Title, a **S**ubtitle, an **X**-Axis Title, a Y**1**-Axis Title, and a Y**2**-Axis Title (see fig. 10.46).

You use the **M**ain Title and **S**ubtitle text boxes to create the first and second titles; they appear centered above the graph, with the first title in larger type above the second title. You use the **X**-Axis Title, Y**1**-Axis Title, and Y**2**-Axis Title text boxes to add titles for the graph axes. Figure 10.47 shows the graph with titles added.

To enter titles, first select the appropriate text box from the Graph Titles dialog box. You then type a title in the text box. You can edit the titles and notes by choosing the **G**raph **T**itles command and changing or editing the contents of the text boxes. When you have finished entering or editing the titles, click OK or press Enter to confirm the dialog box.

You also can edit any single title, as well as control its use of color, font, and text attributes by using the **P**roperty menu or the Object Inspectors. See the section, "Using Fonts and Attributes," later in this chapter.

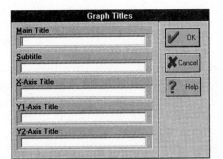

Fig. 10.46

The Graph Titles dialog box.

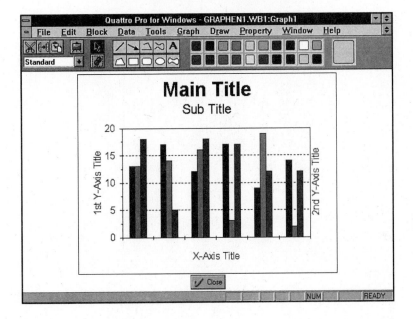

Fig. 10.47

The graph after adding titles.

Adding Data Labels

Knowing the exact value of a data block in a graph is sometimes helpful. You can only label data blocks by using the Object Inspectors. To add data labels, you must decide whether you want to use the actual data values as data labels.

If you want to use text as data labels, create a block of labels in the notebook equal in dimension with the data series you want to label. If, for example, the data series is located in cells A:C3..C8, the label series might be located in A:F3..F8.

If you want to use the actual data values as data labels, the label series can be the same block as the data series.

After you create the label series block, point to the data series in the graph you want to label and click the right mouse button. The Object Inspector displays a dialog box that is named according to the type of graph. Figure 10.48, for example, shows the Bar Series Properties dialog box because the current graph is a bar graph. Select Label series and enter the address of the data labels. Click OK or press Enter to confirm the dialog box. Figure 10.49 shows the graph after adding data labels for the second data series.

Fig. 10.48

The Bar Series Properties dialog box.

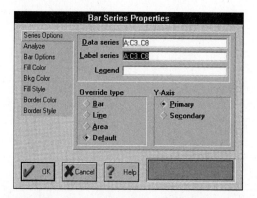

Fig. 10.49

The second data series now has data labels.

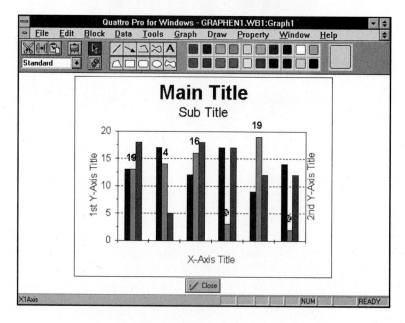

Data labels are often difficult to see, especially when they are displayed on top of a graph bar. You may find it more effective to include the graphed data as a table on the notebook page immediately below the graph. Your printed report will then show both the graph and the data in a more readable fashion.

Using Fonts and Attributes

You can change the font, point size, colors, and style of any text object on a graph. Quattro Pro 5.0 for Windows uses a wide variety of Windows fonts and point sizes that you can display on-screen and print onto paper.

> **NOTE**
>
> Quattro Pro 5.0 for Windows, like most Windows programs, benefits greatly from the increased flexibility offered by font manager programs, such as Adobe Type Manager and the TrueType font manager built into Windows 3.1. Although you can use Quattro Pro 5.0 for Windows without the scalable fonts that these font managers provide, they greatly enhance the output of nearly all Windows programs.

Before you change the font or other attributes of a text object, you need to select that text by pointing to the text block and clicking the right mouse button. Figure 10.50 shows the Graph Title Properties dialog box that the Object Inspector displays when you point at the main title text, click the right mouse button, and select Text Font.

To change the font used to display the text, select Text Font; then select a font name from the **T**ypeface list box. (The selections available to you depend on your printer and whether you have a font manager installed.) Select the size of the font from the **P**oint Size list box. Select the **B**old, **I**talics, **U**nderline, or **S**trikeout check boxes to apply any of these attributes to the text.

To change the color of the text, select Text Color. The dialog box changes to display the color palette selections as shown in figure 10.51. You can use one of the defined color choices by pointing to the small color boxes and clicking the left mouse button on the color you want. You also can create your own color by using the slide bars to select exactly the mix you desire. See "Setting Color, Shading, and Display Options" in Chapter 6 for more information on Quattro Pro 5.0 for Windows' color selections.

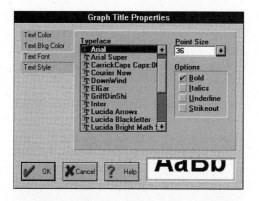

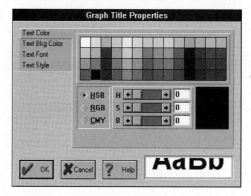

To change the color of the text shadow, select Text Bkg Color. The dialog box displays color palette selections as shown in figure 10.51, but the color you select changes the text shadow, not the text.

Finally, select Text Style to control how the text is displayed. Select **S**olid to display the letters using solid colors, **W**ash to fade the colors, or **B**itmap to use a Windows Bitmap image as the pattern. Select **Sh**adow to add a drop shadow to the letters. Figure 10.52 shows the Main Title Line dialog box showing **W**ash selections.

Click OK or press Enter to confirm the dialog box. Figure 10.53 shows the effects of changing several title attributes for each of the titles. The main title, for example, has a different typeface as well as a wash pattern, the subtitle is in italics, the x-axis title is underlined, and the 2nd Y-Axis title uses strikeout.

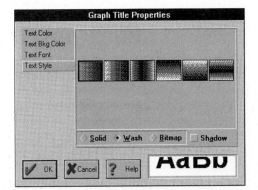

Fig. 10.52

The Graph Title Properties dialog box showing **W**ash selections.

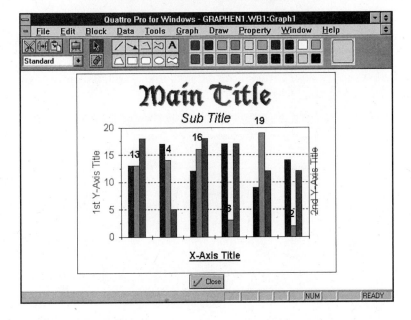

Fig. 10.53

The effects of changing several title attributes for each of the titles.

Customizing Graph Display Options

In addition to changing text colors, Quattro Pro 5.0 for Windows enables you to select colors, patterns, and styles for many of the other objects shown on a graph. Remember, though, that unless your printer can print in color, you may be better off using hatch patterns or symbols to differentiate data series.

Quattro Pro has several different dialog boxes that are used to customize graph display options. The dialog box that is activated when you invoke the Object Inspectors (by pointing to an object in the graph and clicking the right mouse button), depends on the object. If, for example, you point to a data bar, the Bar Series Properties dialog box appears (see fig. 10.54).

Fig. 10.54

The Bar Series Properties dialog box.

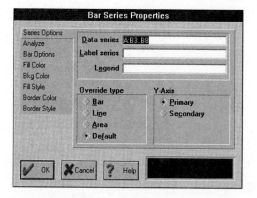

If you point to a line representing a data series, the Line Series Properties dialog box appears (see fig. 10.55).

Fig. 10.55

The Line Series Properties dialog box.

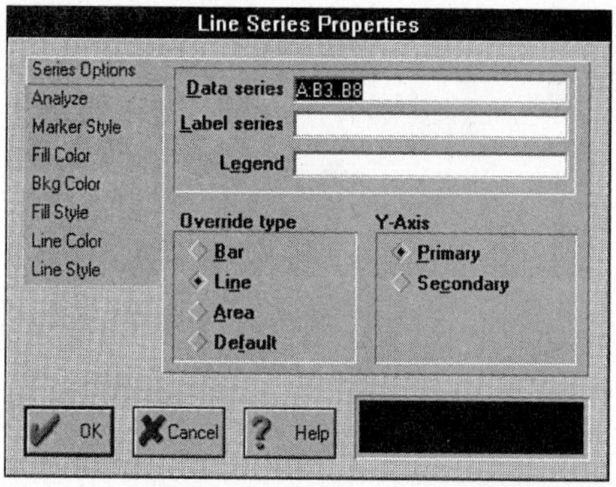

In each case, you select the graph object you want to customize by pointing to the object and clicking the right mouse button. Quattro Pro also enables you to activate some Object Inspector dialog boxes by using the Graph window **P**roperty menu. These include the Graph Window dialog box, the Graph Pane dialog box, the Graph Setup and Background dialog box, the X-Axis dialog box, and the Y-Axis dialog box.

In addition to the Object Inspector dialog boxes already mentioned, you can activate several others to customize graph objects by pointing and clicking the right mouse button. These include the Area Series dialog box, the Pie Graph dialog box, the Column Graph dialog box, and the Legend Series dialog box. Also, each type of object you can draw, such as lines, arrows, rectangles, ovals, and so on, has an Object Inspector dialog box.

Each Object Inspector dialog box offers the range of options available for the selected object. The Bar Series dialog box, for example, provides the Bar Width option, which enables you to specify the width of the bars in the graph. The Line Series dialog box provides a different option, Marker Style, that enables you to select the symbol used to represent data points.

The Object Inspector dialog boxes provide a nearly limitless array of customization options for your Quattro Pro graphs. As you experiment with the possibilities, you may want to make notes to remind yourself of object properties that display your data most effectively. That way you can easily apply these same properties as you create new graphs.

Importing and Exporting Graphics

In the past, it often was difficult to share graphics images created by one program with another program, especially if the programs were from different manufacturers. The reason for such difficulty has been the large number of graphics file formats, each unique to specific programs.

Quattro Pro 5.0 for Windows has the capability of importing and exporting graphics images in many formats. Whether you create a graphics image with Windows Paintbrush, scan a photo, or download graphics from an on-line service such as CompuServe, Quattro Pro 5.0 for Windows probably will be able to import the image. In addition, you can export images in nearly as many formats. You can, in fact, use Quattro Pro to convert images from one format to another by first importing the image, and then exporting it in another format. Table 10.3 shows the graphics file formats supported by Quattro Pro 5.0 for Windows.

Table 10.3 Quattro Pro 5.0 for Windows Graphics File Formats

Format	Import	Export	Description
BMP	Yes	Yes	Windows 3 Bitmap; used by Windows paint programs
CGM	Yes	Yes	Computer Graphics Metafile; vector-based clip art

(continues)

Table 10.3 Continued

Format	Import	Export	Description
CLP	Yes	No	Quattro Pro for DOS
EPS	Yes	Yes	Encapsulated PostScript; commonly used by typesetters, also Macintosh
GIF	Yes	Yes	CompuServe Graphics Interchange Format
PCX	Yes	Yes	Bitmap paint format
PIC	Yes	No	Lotus PrintGraph files
TIF	Yes	Yes	Tag Image File format; scanners

To import a graphics image, the Graph window must be active. If you want to add an imported graphic to a notebook page, create a new, blank text graph. From the Graph window menu, choose **D**raw **I**mport. The Import graphics file dialog box appears (see fig. 10.56). Select the graphics image **F**ile Name you want to import. If necessary, select from lists of different File **T**ypes, **D**irectories, or **D**rives. Click OK or press Enter to confirm the dialog box and import the image. Depending on the size of the graphics image file, some types of file formats may require considerable time to convert as they are being imported.

Fig. 10.56

The Import graphics file dialog box.

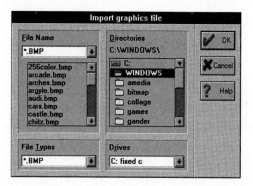

To export graphics images, select **D**raw **E**xport. Quattro Pro 5.0 for Windows displays the Export graphics file dialog box (see fig. 10.57). When you are exporting a graphics image, you have some additional options. Selecting the **B**itmap gray scale check box instructs Quattro Pro to save the image as a gray scale rather than as a color image.

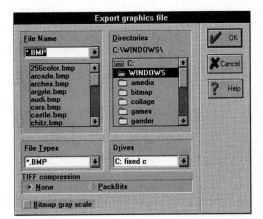

Fig. 10.57

The Export graphics file dialog box.

TIP

When exporting TIFF files, use the compression method that the destination application understands.

If you are exporting an image as a TIFF file (with the TIF extension), you can select the type of file compression to use. The default, **N**one, saves an uncompressed image, which can be quite large due to the format of TIFF files. The other option, **P**ackBits, is a method of compressing the image. You choose the method supported by the program that will later use the file.

Viewing Graphs

Quattro Pro 5.0 for Windows displays graphs in windows just as it displays notebook files. You can resize and move Graph windows, change the display to **T**ile or **C**ascade windows, and add graphs to a notebook so that they can be printed as part of a notebook report.

Displaying Graphs in a Graph Window

When you first create a new graph, it appears in a Graph window. In a Graph window, Quattro Pro normally composes the graph to fit the Graph window, and the size of the graph may be different from its size when printed. If you intend to create a graph for a specific purpose other than for screen display, you may want to adjust the graph's aspect ratio property before modifying the graph. Figure 10.58 shows the Graph Window Object Inspector dialog box, which you access by choosing **P**roperty **G**raph Window or by pointing to the Graph window title bar and clicking the right mouse button (when the graph window is not maximized).

Fig. 10.58

The Graph Window Object Inspector dialog box.

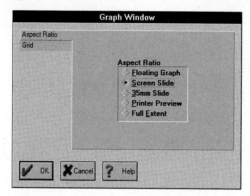

When the Graph Window Object Inspector dialog box is displayed, select the correct aspect ratio for your application. Select **F**loating Graph to retain the proportions of the floating graph. Select **S**creen Slide (the default) for graphs that will be part of an on-screen slide show. Select **3**5mm Slide for graphs that will be sent to a slide service for processing into 35mm slides. Select **P**rinter Preview to show a graph as it will look when printed with the current page setup. Select Full **E**xtent to adjust the graph to fill the graph window and fit the area designated for the floating graph.

To modify a graph, you must display it in a Graph window. If the graph currently is displayed on a notebook page, you can display it in a Graph window by pointing to the graph and double-clicking the left mouse button. If the graph is not displayed in the notebook, use **G**raph **E**dit to select and display it in a Graph window.

Displaying Graphs in the Notebook

Before you can print a graph as part of a notebook-based report, you must add it to a notebook by using the Notebook menu **G**raph **I**nsert command. Quattro Pro can print a graph from the Graph window or as part of a notebook report.

To add a graph to the notebook, choose **Graph Insert**. In the Insert named graph text box, select the name of the graph. Click OK or press Enter to confirm the dialog box. Then select the notebook block where you want the graph displayed. Figure 10.59 shows a graph added to the notebook.

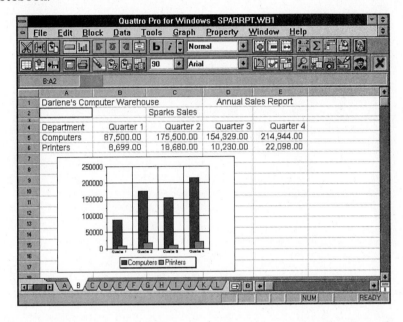

Fig. 10.59

A graph added to a notebook block.

File Print Preview changes the appearance of the notebook to printer preview mode and displays the notebook as it will appear when printed. Figure 10.60 shows the notebook in preview mode. To return to the notebook, click End or press Esc.

Whenever you plan to print a notebook, you should first view it in File Print Preview mode. You might, for example, find that you need to adjust the size of graphs added to the notebook. Or you might need to use the File Page Setup Print to fit command in order to make the printed graph fit on one sheet of paper.

Creating Slide Show Graph Displays

You can use Quattro Pro 5.0 for Windows to create a slide show from any graphs you create. This capability enables you to create presentations that display graphs in a specified order and that use any combination of special effects to move from one graph to the next.

Fig. 10.60

The notebook in **F**ile Print Pre**v**iew mode.

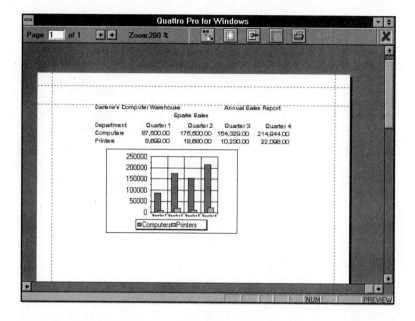

The first step in creating a slide show is to create and name each of the graphs you want to include. While running a slide show, Quattro Pro displays your graphs full-screen—just as they appear when you view a graph by using the **Graph V**iew command.

As you create the graphs, consider where they will appear. Whether you are creating a slide show that will be viewed by an audience on a large-screen monitor or one that will be viewed on a small monitor by one or two people, make certain that all graph objects are large enough to be understandable. Text should be displayed in a large, bold font for easy reading. Keep slide show graphs simple enough so that viewers have time to understand each screen fully in the length of time they are displayed.

After you have created the graphs you want to use in your slide show, move to the Graphs page—the last page of the notebook. To move quickly to the Graphs page, click the SpeedTab button.

The Graphs page has three icons (or buttons) you use to create, edit, and run slide shows. Figure 10.61 shows the Graphs page with labels showing the Create Slide Show, Edit Slide Show, and Run Slide Show icons.

Cut   Paste   New SpeedBar
Copy   New Graph   Edit Slide Show

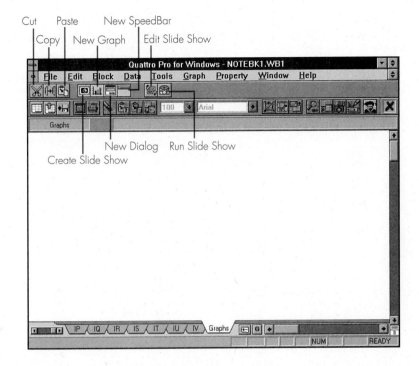

New Dialog   Run Slide Show

Create Slide Show

Fig. 10.61

The slide show icons on the Graphs page.

To begin assembling your graphs into a slide show, click the Create Slide Show icon. The Create Slide Show dialog box appears (see fig. 10.62). Enter the name of your slide show in the text box and click OK or press Enter. Quattro Pro creates a new icon on the Graphs page and names it with the title you entered in the dialog box.

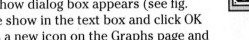

Fig. 10.62

The Create Slide Show dialog box.

Next, add graphs to the slide show by dragging the graph icons over the Slide Show icon. When the Slide Show icon is highlighted, release the mouse button. Graphs appear in the slide show in the order you add them, but you can change their order after you create the slide show.

After you add the graphs to the slide show, you can edit the slide show to control how the graphs display. To edit a slide show, select the Slide Show icon and click the Edit Slide Show icon; or just double-click the

Slide Show icon itself. Quattro Pro displays the Light Table dialog box, which shows small images of each graph in the slide show (see fig. 10.63).

Fig. 10.63

The Light Table dialog box enables you to edit slide shows.

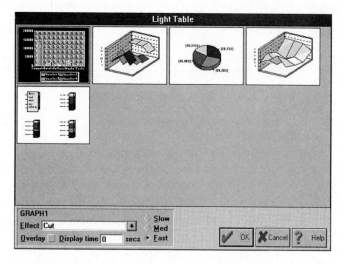

The Light Table shows the graphs in the order they appear when the slide show is run. You can move a graph to a different position by pointing to the small graph image, pressing and holding down the left mouse button, and dragging the image to its new position. Release the mouse button to drop the image in the new position.

The options at the bottom of the Light Table dialog box enable you to control how each graph is displayed. To cause a graph to paint the screen left to right as it overlaps the previous graph, for example, choose the Wipe Right option from the **E**ffect list box. The **S**low, **M**ed, and **F**ast selections control how quickly the graph replaces the previous graph. The **D**isplay time option controls the length of time—in seconds—a graph is displayed. A **D**isplay time setting of zero displays the graph until a mouse button is clicked or a key is pressed. The **O**verlay check box causes the graph to paint over, rather than replace, the existing graph. After you finish editing the slide show, click OK or press Enter.

To run a slide show, select the Slide Show icon and click the Run Slide Show icon, or select **G**raph S**l**ide Show and select the name of the slide show you want to run. If you did not specify a duration for the graphs, click a mouse button or press a key to move from one graph to the next.

Saving Graphs and Graph Settings

Quattro Pro saves a graph the same way that a notebook file is saved. Using Quattro Pro to construct a graph from existing data in a notebook is easy, but rebuilding the graph whenever you want to print or display it on-screen may become tedious. You can name and use graph settings with the **G**raph **N**ew command. When you name graph settings, use **F**ile **S**ave to save those settings in the notebook file.

To display the graph associated with a name, choose **G**raph **E**dit, highlight the name, and then select OK. You can quickly access the Graph window to modify a graph displayed in the notebook by double-clicking the graph.

To delete a graph name, choose **G**raph **D**elete, highlight the name in the list box or enter the name in the text box, and press Enter or click OK.

◀◀ "Saving Notebook Files," p. 274.   **FOR RELATED** **INFORMATION**

Using Analytical Graphing

Quattro Pro has a powerful new tool—*analytical graphing*—that can perform sophisticated analysis of your data without changing data in your notebook or requiring you to enter complicated formulas. Analytical graphing can display aggregations, moving averages, linear fit lines, or exponential fit curves.

Analytical graphs display a new view of your existing data. This view replaces the standard view, such as a line or set of bars displaying the actual data, with a line or bar that displays trends in your data. For example, an aggregation might show a single weekly average of sales rather than the actual sales for each individual day of the week.

To display an analytical graph of your data, first create a graph of that data using the steps outlined earlier in this chapter. Although you can use any graph type, you will probably find one of the line or bar graph types best suited to analytical graphing.

If you want to display both an analytical and standard graph of your data on the same chart, specify the same data set for more than one data series. That is, if A3..A12 contains the data to analyze, and you want to see both the actual data graphed and the analytical graph of the same data, specify A3..A12 for both the 1st and 2nd data series. If you prefer, you can also simply duplicate the same data in two or more data sets.

After you have created your standard graph, make certain it is displayed in the Graph window so that you can modify the graph. Choose **P**roperty **S**eries to display the Select Series dialog box. Select the data series to modify, and press Enter or click OK to display the Series Properties dialog box. Select Analyze (see fig. 10.64). You can also display this dialog box by pointing to the data series in the graph and clicking the right mouse button.

Fig. 10.64

Perform analytical graphing with the Series Properties dialog box.

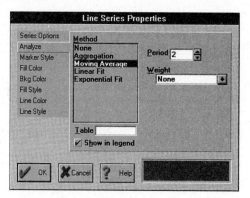

Select the type of analysis to perform:

- Choose None to display data normally.

- Choose Aggregation to summarize data in periodic form. If you select Aggregation, select the **S**eries period, the amount of data represented by each data item; **A**ggregation period, the method of grouping the data items; and **F**unction, the type of aggregation to perform.

- Choose Moving Average to show the general trend of data averaged over several data points. If you select Moving Average, specify **P**eriod, the number of data points to average; and **W**eight, whether or not to give later data points higher importance.

- Choose Linear Fit to generate a straight line that best fits the data.

- Choose Exponential Fit to generate a curve that follows the data.

Next, choose **T**able if you want to generate a table of the calculated analysis in the notebook. Specify a location that will not overwrite existing notebook data. Check **Sh**ow in legend to show the type of data analysis in the data legend. Press Enter or click OK to confirm the dialog box and display the analytical graph. Figure 10.65 shows a graph that displays each type of analytical graph for the same data set.

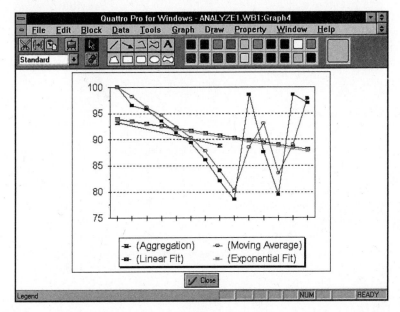

Fig. 10.65

Analytical graphs display trends in data.

Previewing and Printing Graphs

The first part of this chapter showed you how to create Quattro Pro graphs that are displayed on-screen. Screen graphs are useful for viewing by one or two people, but often you need to create printed copies that you can distribute to colleagues, use in business presentations, or file for future reference.

> **TIP**
>
> Use Print Manager to print while you continue working.

If you have Windows configured to use the Print Manager, Quattro Pro uses the background printing capability to enable you to continue working while a graph is printing.

Previewing a Graph

Before you print a graph, you can *preview* it. Previewing saves you time and paper and enables you to make all the adjustments and changes before you print.

 You can preview a graph by choosing the **F**ile Print Preview command. When you finish previewing the graph, press Esc to return to the notebook.

Changing the Size and Location of Printed Graphs

Most aspects of a graph's appearance are determined when you design the graph for screen display. You can specify other aspects of a graph's appearance when you are ready to print.

When you add a graph to a notebook, you specify the size of the graph and where it will appear on the page. By using the **F**ile Print Preview command, you determine whether it will fit on a single printed page. If it does not, you have two options available to help make it fit on the page.

Use **F**ile Page Setup Print to fit to keep the graph in the same proportion to the notebook data.

If you want the graph to maintain the same size in proportion to the notebook data as it currently shows in the notebook window, you can adjust the size of the printed page using the **F**ile Page Setup Print to fit command in the Spreadsheet Page Setup dialog box (see fig. 10.66).

Fig. 10.66

The Spreadsheet Page Setup dialog box.

Spreadsheet Page Setup

Header|
Footer|

Margins (Inch)
Top 0.33 in
Header 0.50 in
Left 0.40 in   Right 0.40 in
Footer 0.50 in
Bottom 0.33 in

Header Font...

Options
☑ Break pages
☐ Print to fit
☐ Center blocks

Paper type
Letter 8 1/2 x 11 inch
Legal 8 1/2 x 14 inch
Statement 5 1/2 x 8 1/2 inch
A4 210 x 297 mm
B5 182 x 257 mm

Scaling 100 %

Print orientation
◆ Portrait
◇ Landscape

✔ OK
✘ Cancel
Reset Defaults
? Help

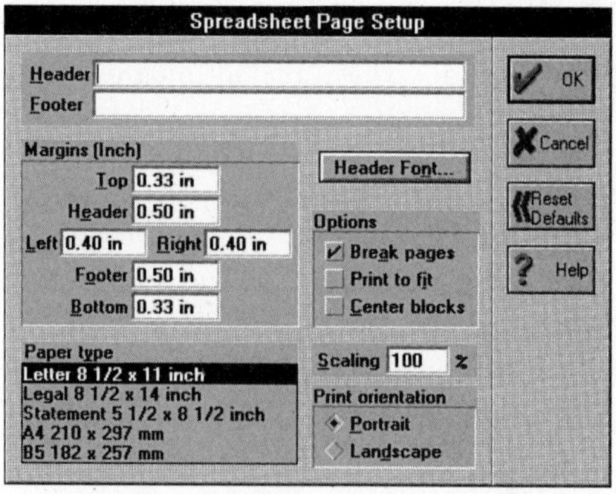

If you want to print the graph on a full page by itself, print the graph from the Graph window. Either double-click the graph when it is displayed on a notebook page, or choose **G**raph **E**dit and select the graph. When the Graph window is active, choose **F**ile **P**rint Pre**v**iew to preview the graph before printing or **F**ile **P**rint to print the graph on its own full page.

Printing Color Graphs on a Black-and-White Printer

If you have a color monitor, you probably are creating and viewing your graphs in color. If you are printing graphs on a black-and-white printer, however, you might have difficulty differentiating between areas that were easily discernible on-screen. Depending on your printer brand, model, and Windows printer driver, several possible solutions may be available.

Usually, you want to use hatch patterns instead of solid fills in graph areas that can be filled. Line graphs can include symbols instead of connectors to make lines easier to distinguish.

> If your printer model has a color option, try selecting color when printing black and white.

TIP

Some black-and-white printers offer a color option either as an add-on kit or simply by installing a multicolored ribbon. Even if you aren't using a color kit or color ribbon, you may find that your printer's Windows driver uses different shades of gray if you specify a color ribbon using the **F**ile Printer Set**u**p Set Up command.

▶▶ "Printing Graphics with Text," p. 406.

FOR RELATED **INFORMATION**

Questions and Answers

Q: I still have quite a number of Lotus 1-2-3 graph files in PIC format. How can I use them in Quattro Pro 5.0 for Windows?

A: You can import PIC files into the Graph window by using the **D**raw **I**mport command. After you have imported a graphics file, you can use it unchanged as part of your notebook presentations. Although you cannot directly modify imported graphics files in Quattro Pro 5.0 for Windows, you can change their appearance in several different ways.

First, you can add additional graphics elements in front of the existing image. These elements will hide parts of the existing image, but do not result in permanent changes to the existing image.

To make more extensive changes, use the **D**raw **E**xport command and save the file in BMP or PCX format. Use Windows Paintbrush to modify the actual image saved in the BMP or PCX file. For example, you can use Paintbrush to change colors, to cut and paste parts of the image, and so on. Save the modified image, and then use **D**raw **I**mport to reload the new file.

Q: How can I make it easier to see data in a 3-D graph?

A: 3-D graphs often obscure data because higher-valued data may be in front of lower-valued data. Sometimes you can make lower valued data easier to see by using the **G**raph **S**eries **R**everse series check box. If this does not work, you may want to consider reorganizing the data, if possible, so that lower-valued data displays in front of higher-valued data.

You may also want to experiment with the Elevation setting in the 3D View section of the Graph Setup and Background dialog box. Using a number higher than the default 30 displays the graph from a higher view point, and may make it easier to see all the data.

Q: When I create a graph, Quattro Pro displays the data I want, but reverses the rows and columns. How can I change this?

A: Use the **G**raph **S**eries Row/**c**olumn swap check box. When you create a graph, Quattro Pro makes its best guess about the layout of your data, but sometimes guesses incorrectly. The **G**raph **Se**ries Row/**c**olumn swap check box quickly swaps the rows and columns to display the graph correctly.

Q: How can I display all the X-axis labels I need without having them unreadable because of overlap?

A: You have several options. You can use the Tick Options Labels settings in the X-Axis Properties Object Inspector dialog box to specify the number of rows to use, whether to skip any labels, and the maximum length of labels. You can use the Text Font section in the same dialog box to specify a different point size, which will allow more characters in the same amount of space. Finally, you can create shorter descriptive labels.

Q: Is there an easy way to show a trend line in a bar graph?

A: This is actually a two-part question. You can easily show one or more sets of data using lines instead of bars (or bars instead of lines) by using the Series Properties Object Inspector dialog box and selecting an override type.

The method you use to show a trend line depends on several factors. If your notebook contains a data set that already performs the trend analysis, simply change the override type for the data set. If your notebook does not include a separate trend analysis data set, use one of the analytical graphing options to perform and display the desired analysis. Remember, though, that the analytical graphing options display the trend analysis instead of the actual data, so you may want to create a duplicate data set to use for the analytical graphing display.

Q: How can I add text, arrows, and other graphical objects to my notebooks without covering up existing data?

A: Set the graph fill style property to None in the Graph Setup and Background Object Inspector dialog box. This makes the graph background transparent, and allows notebook data under a floating graph to be displayed.

Summary

In this chapter, you learned how to create and enhance various graph types, save graphs with your notebooks, and use the Graph window tools and menu commands to produce attractive and informative graph displays. You learned how to print graphs and to modify graph orientation, size, and shape. Finally, you learned how to incorporate graphs and notebook data on the same page.

By experimenting with the techniques presented in this chapter and those covered in Chapter 11, you will be able to create printed reports that effectively present your data in tabular and graphical form. In Chapter 11, you learn more about printing reports.

Printing Reports

Printing the reports based on the Quattro Pro 5.0 for Windows note-books you create usually is as important as creating the notebooks themselves. Printed reports enable you to make good use of the data in your notebook and database files by sharing it with other people.

With Quattro Pro 5.0 for Windows, you are always in a *WYSIWYG* (what-you-see-is-what-you-get) environment. What you see on-screen closely resembles the printed output on paper. If you use different fonts, point sizes, or other attributes—such as bold, italics, or underlining on-screen—these same attributes appear in your printed reports. When you include graphics in your reports, Quattro Pro 5.0 for Windows includes these in your printed reports as well.

This chapter introduces the commands and procedures you use to print Quattro Pro 5.0 for Windows reports. After learning to use these commands, you can effectively use Quattro Pro 5.0 for Windows to print professional-appearing reports presenting your data dynamically. This chapter shows you how to perform the following tasks:

- Use the Quattro Pro 5.0 for Windows printing commands

- Preview reports before printing

- Select single- and multiple-block print areas

- Hide areas within a print block

- Enhance reports with headers and footers

■ Print the frame, grid lines, and cell formulas

■ Control print margins

■ Combine graphics and text on the same page

Understanding the Commands for Printing

While the Quattro Pro 5.0 for Windows printing commands are similar to the /Print commands from previous versions of Quattro Pro, they offer more functionality and ease of use. Printing involves a less complex menu structure than earlier versions.

Quattro Pro 5.0 for Windows has five main commands you can use to control printed output: File Print Preview, File Page Setup, File Print, File Printer Setup, and File Named Settings. These commands appear on the File menu, as shown in figure 11.1.

Fig. 11.1

The **F**ile menu contains the commands for printing.

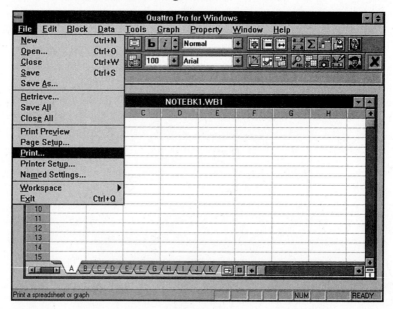

The File Print Preview Command

Use the File Print Preview command to preview how your printed output will appear. With File Print Preview, you can see how Quattro Pro 5.0 for Windows breaks up a large block over several pages and how multiple blocks may fit on one or more pages.

> You can also use the Print Preview button on the Productivity Tools SpeedBar to quickly display the print preview screen.
>
> **TIP**

File Print Preview enables you to use the Spreadsheet Page Setup dialog box and to see the print margins before printing. The next section of this chapter covers the File Page Setup command, which enables you to control many print options.

To see a screen preview, select the File Print Preview command. If you have not already selected a block, the active area of the current page is displayed as the print block. If a block is currently selected, or if you have previously specified one or more print blocks, Quattro Pro 5.0 for Windows displays the selected areas.

The *active area* of a notebook page is determined by the last column and the last row that contain data. If you make an entry in notebook cell Z10 and another entry in cell B200, the active area of the notebook page stretches from cell A1 to cell Z200. If your printed reports unexpectedly include several empty pages, press End and then Home to determine the size of the active area. You may need to explicitly define the print block if the active area is too large.

When you see the preview on-screen, you can zoom in to view an area in more detail by clicking the left mouse button or by pressing the plus key (+). Click the right mouse button or press the minus key (–) to return to the normal display. Press Esc or click the End button to return to the Quattro Pro 5.0 for Windows display. Using the mouse, you can print the report without returning to the Quattro Pro 5.0 for Windows display by clicking the printer button.

When you preview a report, the mouse pointer changes to resemble a magnifying glass, as shown in figure 11.2. This pointer shape reminds you that when you click the left mouse button, the area under the mouse pointer will be magnified.

Fig. 11.2

You can view reports before printing using **F**ile Print Pre**v**iew.

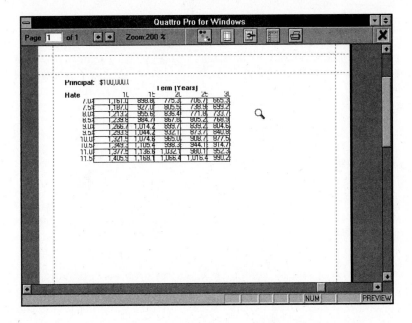

Figure 11.2 shows a mortgage payment notebook in the **F**ile Print Pre**v**iew window. The display is zoomed to 200 percent of normal size to enable closer examination of the report before printing.

The File Page Setup Command

You can select many printing options through the Spreadsheet Page Setup dialog box. You can select the File Page Setup command directly from the File menu or, if you are using a mouse, from the Print Preview page.

As shown in figure 11.3, the Spreadsheet Page Setup dialog box includes options for specifying a header and footer, margins, paper type, header font, compression, orientation, and for centering the print block.

The options that appear in the Spreadsheet Page Setup dialog box are discussed throughout later sections in this chapter.

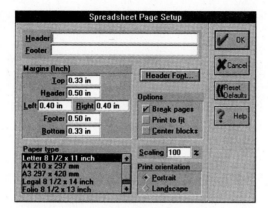

Fig. 11.3

The Spreadsheet Page Setup dialog box.

The File Print Command

The **File Print** command displays the Spreadsheet Print dialog box, which gives you the option to start the printing process, specify the print blocks, select the pages to be printed, and specify the number of copies to be printed.

> **TIP**
>
> You can also use the Print button on the Productivity Tools SpeedBar to quickly display the Spreadsheet Print dialog box.

If you select the **O**ptions button, a second dialog box enables you to specify which rows or columns to print on each page and whether to print the frame, grid lines, and cell formulas. You also use this box to specify whether to advance the paper between print blocks.

Figure 11.4 shows the Spreadsheet Print dialog box, and figure 11.5 shows the Spreadsheet Print Options dialog box.

When you select **File Print** and have not specified a print block or selected a block in the notebook, Quattro Pro 5.0 for Windows prints the active area of the current notebook page.

Fig. 11.4

The Spreadsheet Print
dialog box.

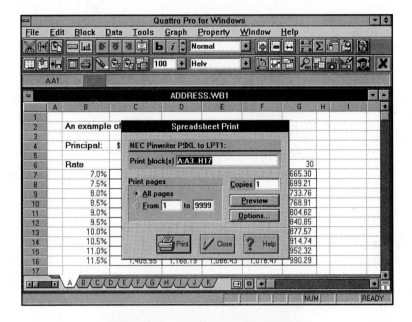

Fig. 11.5

The Spreadsheet Print
Options dialog box.

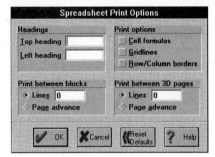

The File Printer Setup Command

You use File Printer Setup to specify a printer and use the Windows
printer configuration system, or to redirect print output to a file. Figure
11.6 shows the Printer Setup dialog box; remember that the printer and
port selections depend on your system configuration.

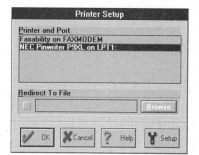

Fig. 11.6

The Printer Setup dialog box.

When you select the Setup button in the Printer Setup dialog box, Windows displays a dialog box specific to your printer. If, for example, you have an HP LaserJet IV, the dialog box displayed is different from the one seen if you have an NEC P9XL. Figure 11.7 shows the dialog box that appears if you have an NEC P9XL.

Fig. 11.7

Each different printer type has its own Setup dialog box.

Although each printer type offers different setup options, each Windows Printer Setup dialog box includes a **H**elp option. If you are unsure of the correct setting of any option available for your printer, select **H**elp to display information about the different options.

Use the Windows Print Manager to get information about print jobs in progress or in the print queue. (To access Windows Print Manager from Quattro Pro 5.0 for Windows, press Ctrl+Esc and select Print Manager.)

TIP

If your computer seems sluggish when the Print Manager is handling background print jobs, reduce the background printing priority setting in the Print Manager. The lower the setting, the faster your computer operates. Lower settings, however, reduce print speed.

The File Named Settings Command

Quattro Pro 5.0 for Windows enables you to save current print settings under a unique name, recall the settings with this name, and reuse the settings without specifying each setting individually. You use the **File Na**med Settings command to create or use named print settings (see fig. 11.8).

Fig. 11.8

The Named Print Settings dialog box.

To assign a name to the current print settings, select **File Na**med Settings **C**reate. You are prompted for a new print settings name. To change an existing named print setting, select **File Na**med Settings, highlight the setting you want to change, and select Update. To remove a named setting, select **File Na**med Settings, highlight the setting you want to remove, and select **D**elete. To use an existing named setting, select **File Na**med Settings, highlight the setting you want to use, and select OK to confirm the dialog box. Named settings are saved with the notebook; be sure to save your file after making any modifications.

Printing a File to Disk

You can delay the actual printing of a report or use a printer that is not connected to your system but still specify the print settings to be used. Select the **R**edirect To File check box in the Printer Setup dialog box to create a disk file containing the commands necessary to tell the printer how to print the report. To change the name of the print file, type a name for the print file in the text box. Press Enter or click OK to confirm the dialog box. When you select the **File P**rint command, Quattro Pro 5.0 for Windows creates the disk file.

The disk file created when you use the Redirect To File check box contains commands specific to the selected printer. To create an ASCII text file, you must first use the Windows Control Panel Printers setting to add the Generic/Text only printer selection as an installed printer. Select Generic/Text only before checking the Redirect To File check box. When you later print the report, you create an ASCII text file that does not contain printer-specific formatting commands.

Printing Quattro Pro 5.0 for Windows Reports

With the printing commands, you can print the simplest to the most complex notebooks. To quickly print a block, use the **File P**rint command.

To add headers and footers, to specify different margins, or to scale printing to fit the page, use the Spreadsheet Page Setup dialog box. To use top or left borders (repeating specific rows or columns—or both—on all pages), or to print the frame, grid lines, or cell formulas, use the Spreadsheet Print Options dialog box.

The following sections show you how to print reports quickly and efficiently. First you learn how to print a short report of a page or less. Then you learn how to print a multiple-page report. You also learn how to compress a report to fit on one page. In later sections of this chapter, you learn how to include headers and footers in reports, add grid lines, column letters, and row numbers, and print top or left headers (borders) on each page.

Printing Single-Page Reports

For most print jobs, when the defaults and the printer are set up, printing a report of a page or less involves only a few steps. To print a single-page report, follow these steps:

1. Make sure the printer is on-line and that the paper is properly positioned.

2. If you do not want to print the entire active area of the current page, select the block to print by highlighting the data with the mouse or the keyboard. (If you don't have a mouse, press Shift+F7 to anchor the corner of the block and use the direction keys to highlight the block.)

3. Choose the **File Print** command.

4. Select OK.

If you do not specify a block to print, Quattro Pro 5.0 for Windows automatically sets the entire active area of the current notebook page as the print block. If you preselect a block, the selected block becomes the print block. Once a print block has been specified, Quattro Pro 5.0 for Windows remembers the specified block and uses the same block as the print block unless you specify a different block.

If you forget to preselect the block to print, you can specify the block in the Print **b**lock(s) text box of the Spreadsheet Print dialog box. You can type the block addresses, or you can highlight the block with the keyboard or the mouse.

To highlight the print block by using the keyboard, perform the following steps:

1. First select the Print **b**lock(s) text box.

2. Use the direction keys to move the cell pointer to one corner of the block.

3. Press Shift+F7 to anchor the block, and then use the direction keys to highlight the block.

4. Press Enter to complete the selection.

To highlight the print block by using the mouse, perform the following steps:

1. First select the Print **b**lock(s) text box by pointing to the text box and clicking the left mouse button.

2. Point to one corner of the print block in the notebook, hold down the left mouse button, and drag the pointer to highlight the block.

3. Release the mouse button after the entire print block is highlighted.

For many reports, a two-dimensional block—a single rectangular area on one notebook page—is all you need to print. Later sections in this chapter show you how to print reports using multiple print blocks. Figure 11.9 shows how the loan amortization notebook appears when printed using the default settings.

Principal: $100,000.00	Term (Years)				
Rate	10	15	20	25	30
7.0%	1,161.08	898.83	775.30	706.78	665.30
7.5%	1,187.02	927.01	805.59	738.99	699.21
8.0%	1,213.28	955.65	836.44	771.82	733.76
8.5%	1,239.86	984.74	867.82	805.23	768.91
9.0%	1,266.76	1,014.27	899.73	839.20	804.62
9.5%	1,293.98	1,044.22	932.13	873.70	840.85
10.0%	1,321.51	1,074.61	965.02	908.70	877.57
10.5%	1,349.35	1,105.40	998.38	944.18	914.74
11.0%	1,377.50	1,136.60	1,032.19	980.11	952.32
11.5%	1,405.95	1,168.19	1,066.43	1,016.47	990.29

Fig. 11.9

The printed Loan Amortization Report.

Printing Multiple-Page Reports

If the print block contains more rows or columns than can fit on a page, Quattro Pro 5.0 for Windows uses multiple pages to print the report unless you instruct the program to compress the print. (See "Fitting a Report onto One Page" later in this chapter.) You follow the same steps for printing a multiple-page report as shown for printing a single-page report in the preceding section.

Figure 11.10 shows part of a Quattro Pro 5.0 for Windows notebook used to track customer accounts. In this example, the active area of page A extends from A1..L95 and is too large to print on a single page without being compressed. Figure 11.11 shows the result of selecting the File Print Preview command—Quattro Pro 5.0 for Windows is displaying page 1 of 4.

When you print a multiple-page report, you must pay attention to where Quattro Pro 5.0 for Windows splits the data between pages—both vertically and horizontally. Quattro Pro 5.0 for Windows can split the data at inappropriate locations, resulting in a report that is difficult to interpret. Use the File Print Preview command to see exactly how Quattro Pro 5.0 for Windows prints a large print block. Use the zoom option (left mouse button or plus key to enlarge, right mouse button or minus key to reduce) to make the display easier to understand.

Fig. 11.10

A customer accounts notebook extending from A1..L95.

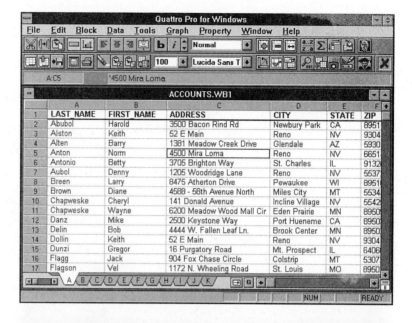

Fig. 11.11

Quattro Pro 5.0 for Windows will print the report on four pages.

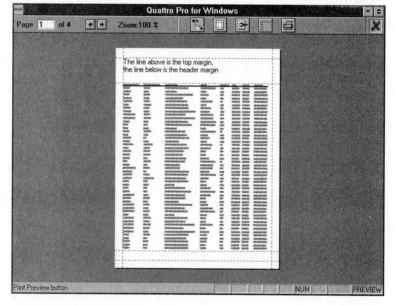

Printing Multiple Blocks

Although most reports use a single, two-dimensional print block, Quattro Pro 5.0 for Windows easily can incorporate several two- or three-dimensional blocks on one or more notebook pages.

You specify a three-dimensional print block by preselecting the block or by entering the block address or block name in the **File Print** dialog box—the same way you specify a two-dimensional block. Use Ctrl+PgDn and Ctrl+PgUp to move between notebook pages when you select three-dimensional blocks by pointing.

When you are selecting a three-dimensional block, you can press Shift+F7 to extend the block selection, or you can hold down the Shift key as you select the block. After you have highlighted the block on the first page, use Ctrl+PgDn or Ctrl+PgUp; or you can click the notebook page tabs to move to the final page of the block. When you have se-lected a three-dimensional block, Quattro Pro 5.0 for Windows draws a line under the page tabs to show the pages that are included in the block.

To specify multiple print blocks, press and hold down the Ctrl key while you are selecting the blocks. To type the names or addresses of multiple print blocks, enter the first block name or address in the Spreadsheet Print dialog box, type a comma, and type the next block.

When you specify multiple print blocks, previewing the printed output is always a good idea, so you may want to select **File Print Preview** or **File Print Preview**. If you are satisfied with the previewed printed out-put, click the printer button or press Esc to return to the notebook display and use the **File Print** command to print the report. If you se-lected the **File Print Preview** command, the program returns you to the Spreadsheet Print dialog box instead of to the notebook. Figure 11.12 shows the customer accounts notebook with four print blocks selected, and figure 11.13 shows the result of selecting **File Print Preview** to pre-view the printed output.

You can specify any combination of two- and three-dimensional print blocks. Quattro Pro 5.0 for Windows prints the blocks in the order in which you select the blocks or enter the block names or addresses.

Fig. 11.12

Four print blocks are
preselected.

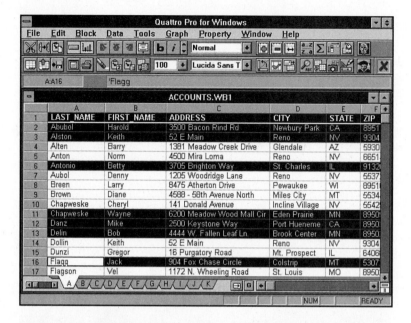

Fig. 11.13

Previewing the printed
report containing four
print blocks.

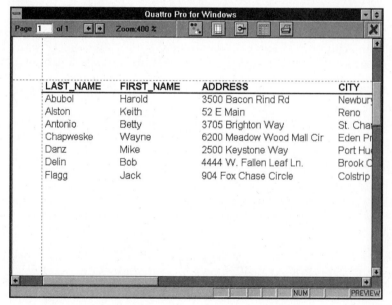

Fitting a Report onto One Page

To fit all the printed output on one page, use the File Page Setup command and select the Print to fit check box. Quattro Pro 5.0 for Windows attempts to reduce the size of the print enough to fit the entire report on a single page. If the report still does not fit a single page, Quattro Pro 5.0 for Windows uses the maximum compression on all pages.

If you use this command, select File Print Preview before printing to preview the printed report. The maximum level of compression may result in a report that is too small to read. In some cases, changing print orientation may improve the appearance of the report. Choose Portrait to print the report tall and narrow or choose Landscape to print the report wide and short.

To control the exact level of compression, enter a percentage in the Scaling text box of the Spreadsheet Page Setup dialog box. To reduce the size of print by one-half, for example, enter **50** in the Scaling text box. You can expand the print also by entering a number larger than 100. To print the report three times the normal size, enter **300**. Be sure the Print to fit check box is not checked, however, because the Print to fit option overrides any scaling factor you enter.

If you want to automatically reduce the size of the printed report without manually specifying an exact level of compression, select the Print to Fit check box on the Spreadsheet Page Setup dialog box before printing. When the report is printed, Quattro Pro 5.0 for Windows compresses the report to fit on a single page.

Inserting Manual Page Breaks

If you print a large block and Quattro Pro 5.0 for Windows uses several pages to print the report, you may be unhappy with the way the data is split. To control where Quattro Pro 5.0 for Windows splits the report, you can insert a page break.

To insert a page break, move the cell pointer to the first column of the print block and then to the row where you want the break to occur. Select the Block Insert Break command. Quattro Pro 5.0 for Windows inserts a row and places a page break symbol (::) in the cell selected. You also can type |:: to insert a page break.

When you print, Quattro Pro 5.0 for Windows advances the paper and begins printing data below the page break on a new page. The row that contained the cell selector before you issued the **B**lock Insert **B**reak command becomes the first row of data printed on the new page.

Be sure to position the cell selector in the first column of the print block before selecting the **B**lock Insert **B**reak command. Otherwise, Quattro Pro 5.0 for Windows inserts a row and places a page break symbol (::) in the cell selected but does not break the printed report at the row containing the page break symbol (::).

Use the **F**ile Print Preview command to view the printed output before printing to make certain that the page breaks are where you want them.

Preventing Areas from Printing

Sometimes you want to prevent areas of the notebook from being included when you print a report. The best way to accomplish this often is to design the notebook carefully, locating information not to be printed in different areas of the page or on different pages. You may not always be able to separate data you want to print from data you do not want to print, however. Quattro Pro 5.0 for Windows makes it easy to control which areas are or are not printed.

You can control which notebook areas are printed in several ways. One method, selecting multiple print blocks, was covered earlier in this chapter. You also can hide areas within a print block to prevent them from appearing in printed output. The following sections show you several methods of hiding data and explain when to use each method.

Excluding Rows or Columns from Printing

Hiding a row or column not only excludes the row or column from printing, but also prevents a gap from appearing in the printed output. Suppose, for example, that you want to print a report using information from the customer accounts notebook but want to exclude address and telephone number information. You can hide the columns containing this information, and they will not appear in the printed report. In addition, the printed report will not show a gap where the hidden columns should be.

You also can hide entire rows on a Quattro Pro 5.0 for Windows note-book page. Just as hiding a column excludes the column from the printed report, hiding a row excludes the row from the printed report and eliminates a gap in the printout.

Select the Reveal/Hide option in the Active Block dialog box to hide rows or columns and exclude them from printed output. To hide rows or columns, follow these steps:

1. Select the rows or columns you want to hide.

2. With the mouse, point to the selected block of rows or columns and click the right mouse button. With the keyboard, select **Prop**erty **C**urrent Object.

3. Select Reveal/Hide.

4. Choose the dimension you wish to hide, **R**ows or **C**olumns.

5. Choose Hide to hide the selected rows or columns, or choose Reveal to unhide any hidden rows or columns in the selected block (see fig. 11.14).

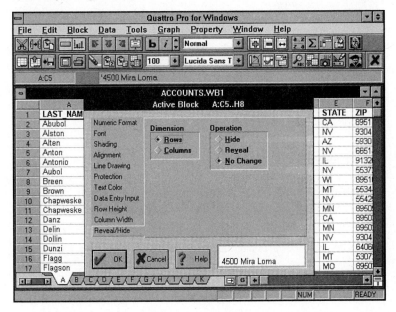

Fig. 11.14

Select Reveal/Hide in the Active Block dialog box to hide rows or columns.

6. Press Enter or click OK to confirm the dialog box.

Figure 11.15 shows the result of hiding columns C through H and rows 5 through 9 in the customer accounts notebook. As the spreadsheet frame shows, hidden rows and columns retain their row numbers and column letters. Formulas that refer to cells in hidden rows or columns continue to refer to the same cells even when they are hidden. Chapter 5, "Using Fundamental Commands," has more information on hiding rows and columns.

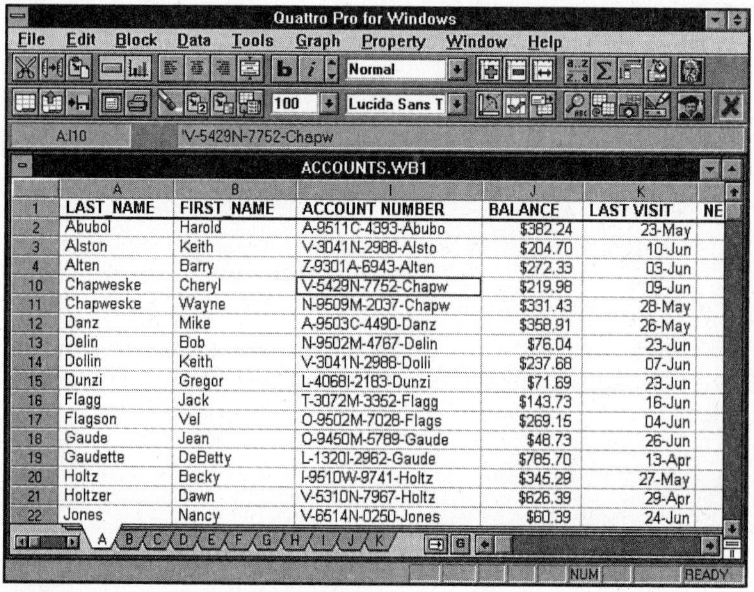

Fig. 11.15

The result of hiding rows 5 through 9 and columns C through H.

Hiding Cells or Blocks

To hide only part of a row or column or an area that spans one or more rows and columns, select the Numeric Format option in the Active Block dialog box and then select Hidden. Data formatted as hidden will not appear in printed output—an empty gap appears where the data is hidden. Figure 11.16 shows the result of applying hidden format to the block C5..H9 in the customer accounts notebook.

Although the data in cells formatted as Hidden does not appear in printed reports, the resulting gap may not be acceptable if it emphasizes the fact that data is missing. You may find that using Hidden format is more appropriate for hiding isolated data, such as copyright notices, than for hiding blocks of data in the middle of larger data blocks.

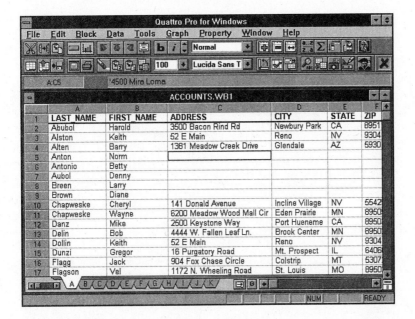

Fig. 11.16

The effect of hiding C5..H9 using Numeric Format **H**idden.

To apply the hidden format to a block of cells, follow these steps:

1. Select the cell or block you want to hide.

2. With the mouse, point to the selected cell or block and click the right mouse button. With the keyboard, select **P**roperty **C**urrent Object. The Active Block dialog box appears.

3. Select Numeric Format.

4. Choose Hidden.

5. Select OK to confirm the dialog box.

To unhide a hidden cell or block, select an appropriate numeric format for the cell or block using the Active Block dialog box. For more information on the numeric formats available in Quattro Pro 5.0 for Windows, see Chapter 6, "Changing the Format and Appearance of Data."

FOR RELATED INFORMATION

◄◄ "Protecting and Hiding Spreedsheet Data," p. 149.

◄◄ "Applying the Available Formats," p. 190.

Changing Printing Options

Descriptive text makes reports much easier to understand. In most cases, a printed report that contains numbers without descriptive headings is difficult if not impossible to interpret. Quattro Pro 5.0 for Windows has many features that you can use to make your reports easier to understand and less subject to misinterpretation. The following sections show you how to apply headers and footers, row and column headings, and other optional features to improve the appearance and readability of your reports.

Creating Headers and Footers

By default, Quattro Pro 5.0 for Windows reserves 0.5 inch at the top and at the bottom of each page. Any headers or footers you specify are printed in this space.

The Spreadsheet Page Setup dialog box contains six different text boxes you can use to set the page margins. The **T**op and **H**eader margins work together, as do the **B**ottom and **F**ooter margins. The Header margin, for example, specifies the total distance between the top of the page and the beginning of the report text. The **T**op margin specifies the distance between the top of the page and the beginning of the header text.

If you specify a Header margin of 1.25 inches, and a **T**op margin of 0.5 inches, the header text begins 0.5 inches from the top of the page and the report text begins 1.25 inches from the top of the page. The **B**ottom and **F**ooter margins function in the same manner.

In figure 11.17, the Header margin was specified as 1.25 inches and the **T**op margin was specified as 0.5 inch. The margin lines button also was selected so that the margins display as dotted lines.

You specify a header or footer in the Spreadsheet Page Setup dialog box. A header or footer can have up to three parts: a left-aligned, a centered, and a right-aligned section. When you enter header or footer text, separate the segments with a vertical bar (|). Segments that precede the first vertical bar are left-aligned, segments following the first vertical bar but preceding the second vertical bar are centered, and segments following the second vertical bar are right-aligned. You can use any combination of the three segments.

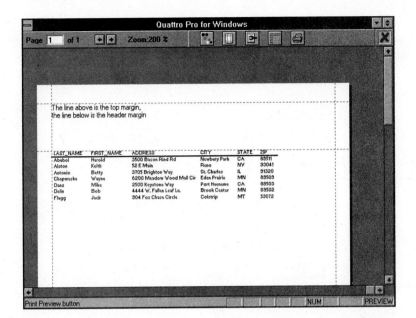

Fig. 11.17

Displaying margin settings.

You also can instruct Quattro Pro 5.0 for Windows to include the page number, the current date, or the contents of a cell in the header or footer. To include a page number, you include a number sign (#). To print the current date, type in the @ sign. To include the contents of a cell, enter a backslash (\ ) followed by the cell address or block name. If you specify a block name, Quattro Pro 5.0 for Windows includes the contents of the upper-left cell in the block only.

The following example produces a header or footer that has three segments: a left-aligned page number, the centered text *Customer Accounts*, and a right-aligned date:

```
#¦Customer Accounts¦@
```

To enter a header or footer, select **File Page Setup Header** or **File Page Setup Footer**. Type the header or footer in the text box and press Enter (or click OK) to confirm the dialog box. You can view the header or footer by selecting **File Print Preview**.

Quattro Pro 5.0 for Windows has a number of additional options for printing information in headers and footers. Table 11.1 describes the symbols you use to display information in headers and footers.

Table 11.1 Header and Footer Formatting Symbols

Symbol	Description
#	Current page number
@	Current date
|	Left, center, or right aligned text
#d	Current date in Short International format
#D	Current date in Long International format
#ds	Current date in standard Short format
#Ds	Current date in standard Long format
#t	Current time in Short International format
#T	Current time in Long International format
#ts	Current time in standard Short format
#Ts	Current time in standard Long format
#p	Current page number
#p+n	Current page number plus the number n
#P	Total number of pages in printout
#P+n	Total number of pages in printout plus the number n
#f	Notebook name
#F	Notebook name with path
#n	Prints balance of text on new line

Printing Row and Column Headings

Row or column headings often can make a multiple-page report easier
to understand. When you include row or column headings, each
printed page includes the descriptive text that explains the data being
presented.

To include row or column headings, select File Print, and then choose
the Options button to display the Spreadsheet Print Options dialog
box. For the Top heading, select one or more rows of labels to print
above each page of data. For the Left heading, select one or more columns of data to print at the left of each page of data. Setting headings
in a printout has an effect similar to freezing titles on a notebook page.

Any rows you designate as a **T**op heading and any columns you designate as a **L**eft heading should not be included in a print block. If you include them in the print block, Quattro Pro 5.0 for Windows prints these elements twice—first as part of the headings and then as part of the print block.

The customer accounts notebook provides a good example of how headings work. If you print the notebook at normal size (instead of compressed to fit on a single page), the printout requires four pages. The printed output is both too long and too wide to fit on a single page. When you try to understand the printed report, you find that it is difficult to match customer account numbers and balances with customer names because they are on different pages. The lower pages also lack the field name headings.

To make each page after the first easier to understand, you can designate columns A and B (which contain the customers' names) as left headings and row 1 (which contains the field names) as the top heading. To prevent double printing of the customers' names and the field names, adjust the address of the print block to exclude row 1 and columns A and B.

To modify the print settings for the customer accounts notebook to use columns A and B as left headings and row 1 as a top heading, follow these steps:

1. Select **F**ile **P**rint.

2. Edit the Print block(s) text box to adjust the print block to exclude the left headings columns and the top headings rows. In this case, enter **A:C2..L95** as the print block.

3. Select **O**ptions.

4. In the **L**eft heading text box, enter the block address of cells in the columns you want as left headings. In this case, enter **A:A1..B1**. You need enter cell addresses from a single row only; Quattro Pro 5.0 for Windows automatically uses the same columns as left headings for any rows in the print block.

5. In the **T**op heading text box, enter the block address of cells in the rows you want as top headings. In this case, enter **A:A1**. You need to enter cell addresses from a single column only, although you can include columns that span the entire print block if you want. Quattro Pro 5.0 for Windows automatically uses the same rows as top headings for any columns in the print block. The Spreadsheet Print Options dialog box should now look like figure 11.18.

Fig. 11.18

Top and Left headings
entered in the Spread-
sheet Print Options
dialog box.

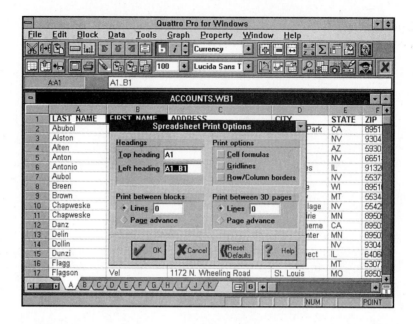

Fig. 11.18

Top and Left headings entered in the Spreadsheet Print Options dialog box.

6. Select OK to confirm the dialog box.

You can then select either **P**review in the File Print dialog box to view the printed output before printing or Print to print the report immediately. Figure 11.19 shows page 4 of the print preview. The data on this page is now as easy to understand as the data on page 1 because both left and top headings serve to identify the data.

To clear top and left headings, highlight the text box in the Spreadsheet Print Options dialog box, press **D**el to clear the text box, and select OK.

Printing the Spreadsheet Frame and Grid Lines

Printing the spreadsheet frame (which shows the row numbers and column letters) is useful particularly when you are developing a notebook. The printouts show the location of data on the notebook page. To include the spreadsheet frame in your printed report, check the **R**ow/Column borders check box in the Spreadsheet Print Options dialog box. You can also print the spreadsheet grid lines by checking the **G**ridlines check box.

You probably will want to remove the checks from both check boxes before preparing final printed reports.

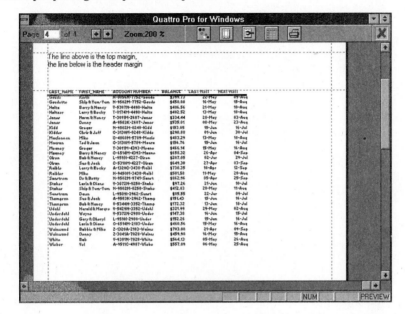

Fig. 11.19

Left and top headings make page 4 as easy to understand as page 1.

Printing Cell Formulas instead of Results

As you develop large or complex Quattro Pro 5.0 for Windows notebooks, you will find that a printout of cell formulas is a very important tool when locating calculation errors or defending assumptions made. A printout of cell formulas is a meaningful part of the documentation that should be created for each of your important notebooks. Fortunately, Quattro Pro 5.0 for Windows can produce this vital piece of documentation easily.

To print cell formulas instead of the calculated results, check the Cell formulas check box in the Spreadsheet Print Options dialog box.

When you select the **Cell Formulas** option, Quattro Pro 5.0 for Windows prints the contents of each cell on a separate report line. This procedure can result in a printed report that is much larger than you expect. The customer accounts notebook, for example, requires 17 pages when printed this way in standard, noncompressed print.

Setting Margins

The Spreadsheet Page Setup dialog box enables you to change margins. Select Top, Header, Bottom, Footer, Left, or Right. Enter the margin width in the text box.

The first line of printed data is offset from the top of the page by the dimension of the Header margin. The last line of printed data is offset from the bottom of the page by the Footer margin. Be certain the margins you specify allow enough room to print the data. (See "Creating Headers and Footers," previously in this chapter.)

Some printers, especially laser printers, cannot print to the edge of a sheet of paper. Consult the owner's manual for your printer to determine the minimum acceptable margin settings.

Naming and Saving Print Settings

Quattro Pro 5.0 for Windows enables you to save current print settings under a unique name, recall the settings with this name, and reuse the settings without specifying each setting individually. You use the File Named Settings command to create named print settings.

To assign a name to the current settings, select File Named Settings, and then choose Create. Enter a unique name in the text box. Press Enter or click OK to confirm the dialog box. To use a named print setting, select the setting you want in the Named Print Settings dialog box.

Printing Graphics with Text

If you add a graphic to a Quattro Pro 5.0 for Windows notebook page and include the graphic in the selected print block, the graphic prints along with any text. Quattro Pro 5.0 for Windows can print graphics separately also if the Graphs page is the current page.

In Quattro Pro 5.0 for Windows, graphics can be graphs created from notebook data, text graphs created in the Graph window, or a graphics image imported from another Windows application. Regardless of the source, Quattro Pro 5.0 for Windows can include any of these graphics on a notebook page.

To combine text and graphics on the same page, select **Graph Insert**. Choose the name of the graphic from the list box and select OK. Select the block for the graph with the mouse by pointing and dragging the selection box. See Chapter 10, "Creating Presentation Graphics," for more information on creating graphics with Quattro Pro 5.0 for Windows.

Stopping and Suspending Printing

After starting a print job, you may realize that you made a mistake in the notebook data or the print settings and need to correct the error before the report is printed. You can halt the current print job, clear the print queue, and temporarily suspend printing if your printer is using the Windows Print Manager. Press Ctrl+Esc and select Print Manager. Select **Pause** to suspend printing, and select **Resume** to resume printing. When the printer is paused, you can select **Delete** to cancel the current print job.

> **NOTE**
>
> If you use Quattro Pro 5.0 for Windows with Windows for Workgroups, you will find the correct command for pausing the printer is **P**rinter **P**ause Printer. The command to resume printing is **P**rinter **R**esume Printer.

If you cancel a print job, the printer is reset. You may need to adjust the top-of-form position to print the next job correctly, starting at the top of a new sheet of paper. Your Microsoft Windows manual has more information on using the Print Manager.

Questions and Answers

Q: Why are there always blank pages included in my report?

A: If you don't specify the print block, Quattro Pro 5.0 for Windows prints the entire active area of the current notebook page. To eliminate the problem, create a block name for the report area you want to print, and use the block name to specify the print block.

Q: When I use the Print to fit option, my report prints much too small. Instead of printing just small enough to fit on the page, the report is reduced to about one fourth of the page. What's wrong?

A: If you use the Print to fit option, but forget to specify the print block, Quattro Pro 5.0 for Windows shrinks the entire active area of the current notebook page to fit the printed page. Because the active area may be larger than the area you really want to print, make certain you specify the exact print block you want to include in the report.

If you specify the print block, but Print to fit still seems to shrink the printed output too much, you may not have a clear understanding of how this option functions. When Quattro Pro 5.0 for Windows shrinks the print block, it shrinks the block horizontally and vertically by the same percentage. Your report may be narrow enough to fit the page width without compression, but may require vertical compression to fit the page. In that case, you may want to deselect the Print to fit check box and print the report normal size.

Q: Why do the top two lines of my report print twice?

A: You have included the top two report lines in both the print block and the Top heading text box of the Spreadsheet Print Options dialog box. If you want to print those same two lines at the top of each page, make certain they are included in the Top heading text box but are not included in the print block.

Q: Why do some numbers print as asterisks even though they appear correctly on-screen?

A: Some typefaces are designed for the screen display, while others are optimized for the printer. You may be using a typeface that appears slightly different when printed than it does on-screen. You can either widen the column widths slightly to compensate, or select a different typeface.

Q: Why do my page headers only appear on the first page of my report?

A: To print headers and footers correctly, you must select the Break pages check box in the Spreadsheet Page Setup dialog box. If this box is not selected, only the first page header will print.

Summary

This chapter showed you how to create printed reports from your notebook data. It also showed you how to enhance the appearance of the printed output to make your reports easier to understand and more readable. You learned the specific commands for printing, changing print settings, and previewing reports before printing. This chapter also showed you how to exclude data from printed reports, how to use headers and footers, and how to print borders, grid lines, and the spreadsheet frame.

The next chapter introduces Quattro Pro 5.0 for Windows databases. You learn the basics of creating databases and how to use them to organize your data. You also learn how to locate database records that meet the criteria you specify.

Managing Databases

Creating Databases

Quattro Pro 5.0 for Windows has a third major element—*database management*—that, combined with its electronic spreadsheet and graphics capabilities, makes Quattro Pro 5.0 for Windows a powerful business and scientific-analysis tool.

Quattro Pro 5.0 for Windows provides many of the advanced database management features of programs like Paradox and dBASE. The Borland Database Engine, a built-in part of Quattro Pro 5.0 for Windows, enables you to use Paradox and dBASE database files without translation.

This chapter introduces the basics of Quattro Pro 5.0 for Windows database management. It shows you how to create and manage databases in a notebook. The next chapter expands on database management by showing you how to use advanced data management features.

Specifically, this chapter shows you how to do the following:

- Understand the terms that define a Quattro Pro 5.0 for Windows database

- Create and modify a database

- Sort data records

- Locate and extract data records
- Create and use database forms

Defining a Database

A *database* is a collection of related information, organized so that you can list, sort, or search its contents. The information contained in a database can be any type of data that can be organized. For example, a customer list, a telephone book, a series of measurements showing manufacturing quality, and historical listings of currency exchange rates are all typical databases.

Understanding the Database Block

In Quattro Pro 5.0 for Windows, the word *database* means a block of cells that spans at least one column and two or more rows. A database is actually an organized list, designed to enable easy access to the information it contains. Databases are made up of *fields* and *records*. A field is a single data item, such as the company name or last name of a customer. A record is a collection of associated fields, such as all related information about a single customer. When a database is contained in a Quattro Pro 5.0 for Windows notebook, each field is contained in a single column, and each record is contained in a single row.

The *database block* is a rectangular block of notebook cells that contains all the columns of fields and all the rows of records. The top row in the database block must contain the *field names* for each of the fields in the database. Field names are similar to Quattro Pro 5.0 for Windows block names and follow the same rules discussed in Chapter 5, "Using Fundamental Commands."

In Quattro Pro 5.0 for Windows, the database block can be contained in the notebook or it can be an external *database table*. Do not confuse database table with *data table*. A data table is the table of calculations created with the **D**ata **W**hat-if command. Database table is often used with relational databases because a single database may contain several tables of related information. The **D**ata **W**hat-if command is covered in more detail in Chapter 13, "Understanding Advanced Data Management."

Understanding the Criteria Table

In order for a database to be useful, you must be able to limit a search to records that meet specific conditions. If, for example, you want to find Joyce Nielsen's phone number, you don't want to search through every name in the phone book until you find her number. Instead, you want to find just those records where the last name is Nielsen and the first name is Joyce.

Quattro Pro 5.0 for Windows enables you to limit your database operations to records that meet the criteria you specify. To create such a limit, you create a *criteria table*. A criteria table is a block containing database field names and selection criteria. These selection criteria specify conditions that must be met before records are selected. In the example, you would enter selection criteria that tell Quattro Pro 5.0 for Windows to select only those records that contain Nielsen in the last name field and Joyce in the first name field.

The field names you enter in a criteria table must exactly match the field names in the database block, otherwise Quattro Pro 5.0 for Windows may not select the records you desire. Quattro Pro criteria tables are covered in more detail later in this chapter in the section titled "Entering the Criteria Table."

Understanding the Output Block

Many database operations process records in place. You may, for example, edit the records in a database to show new addresses when a customer moves. Other database operations require you to extract a series of database records to be processed externally from the database itself. Creating a list of unique ZIP codes to comply with postal regulations is one such example.

In Quattro Pro 5.0 for Windows, an *output block* is a separate database that can contain specified subgroups of records. The output block can contain as many or as few database fields as you want; the output block does not have to contain all the fields from the database.

You may, for example, want to create an output block to hold copies of the name, phone, balance due, and due dates for customers in your customer accounts database whose balance due is over $100 and whose payment is over 30 days past due.

Field names included in the output block must match exactly the corresponding field names in the database block. You need not include all field names from the database block, however. Quattro Pro 5.0 for Windows output blocks are covered in more detail in the section "Specifying the Output Block," later in this chapter.

Working with a Quattro Pro 5.0 for Windows Database

Quattro Pro 5.0 for Windows supports a database contained in a notebook. Databases contained in notebooks are easy to use because you can see the entire database and its structure on-screen. You learn how to access external databases with Quattro Pro 5.0 for Windows in Chapter 13.

A Quattro Pro 5.0 for Windows notebook database resides in the spreadsheet's row-and-column format. Figure 12.1 shows the general organization of a Quattro Pro 5.0 for Windows notebook database. Field names that describe the data items appear as column headings in row 2. Information about each specific field is entered in a cell in the appropriate column. In figure 12.1, cell A3 represents data (Add It Up Computing) for the first field (COMPANY) in the database's first record, which is in row 3.

In figure 12.1, the field names have a bold attribute applied to distinguish them visually from the database records. Although optional, this setting can be an important addition—one that makes your notebook database easier to understand.

A Quattro Pro 5.0 for Windows notebook database theoretically has room for 8,191 records (the number of rows in a notebook, 8,192, less one row for the field names). In reality, however, the number of records in a notebook database is limited by the amount of available memory: internal memory (RAM) plus disk storage allocated as virtual memory by Windows. You should consider creating an on-disk database, if your database will hold several hundred or more records.

Another possibility is to split a single, large database into several smaller ones. You can, for example, place different types of information in independent databases. You then use the cell and table functions to relate information in one database to that in another database.

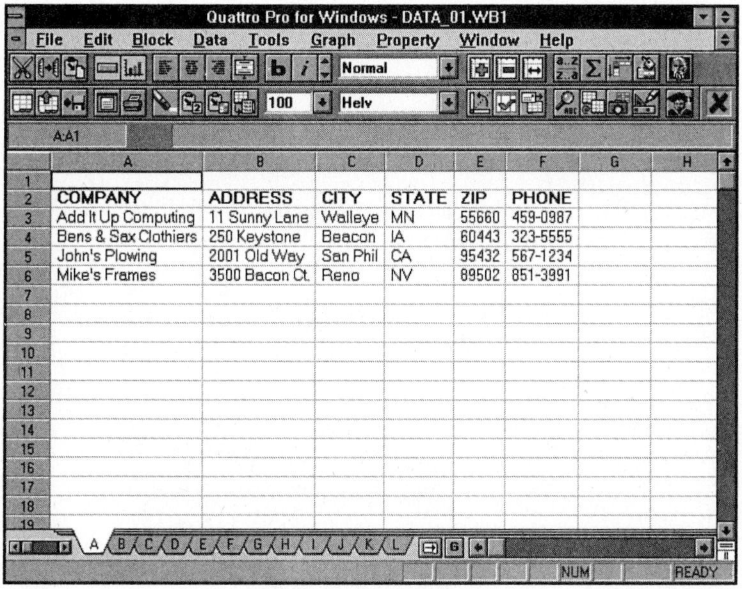

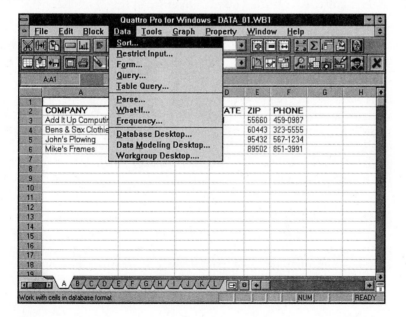

Fig. 12.1

Organization of a Quattro Pro 5.0 for Windows notebook database.

You access the **D**ata commands from the Quattro Pro 5.0 for Windows main menu. All the other options on the main menu work as well on databases as they do on spreadsheets, so you have the complete power of Quattro Pro 5.0 for Windows available for manipulating notebook databases. Figure 12.2 shows the **D**ata menu.

Fig. 12.2

The **D**ata pull-down menu.

The **S**ort, **F**orm, and **Q**uery (search) commands (covered in this chapter) are true data management operations. You use the **R**estrict Input, **P**arse, **W**hat-If, and **F**requency commands for data creation or data manipulation. The **T**able Query and **D**atabase Desktop commands (also covered in Chapter 13) access external database files using the Database Desktop. The Data **M**odeling Desktop command (covered in Chapter 18, "Using Data Modeling Desktop") performs sophisticated and flexible cross-tabulation analysis of data. You use the Work**g**roup Desktop command (covered in Chapter 20, "Sharing Data Using the Workgroup Desktop") for sharing data with other Quattro Pro 5.0 for Windows users.

FOR RELATED INFORMATION

◀◀ "Using Miscellaneous Cell and Table Functions," p. 250.

Creating a Database

You can create a database as a new notebook or as part of an existing notebook. If you decide to build a database as part of an existing notebook, choose an area, such as an unused notebook page, that is not used for anything else. This area should be large enough to accommodate the number of records you plan to enter in the database.

Because each Quattro Pro 5.0 for Windows notebook automatically has 256 spreadsheet pages, the best structure is usually to place each database table on its own page.

After you decide which area of the notebook to use, you create a database by entering field names across a row and entering corresponding data in the cells below the field names. Entering data in a notebook database is simple and is identical to entering data for any other Quattro Pro 5.0 for Windows application. The most critical step in creating a useful database is choosing the fields properly.

Determining Which Data to Include

Quattro Pro 5.0 for Windows retrieves database information by using field names. Before you create a database, consider the kind of output you expect from the database and the source of the data. Write down the types of information available and consider any source documents, such as order forms or customer information cards, already in use that can provide input to the database. You will probably find that designing the database to allow sequential input from the data source—rather than using a design that requires the user to jump around and backtrack—is more efficient.

Besides determining which information to include in the database, consider how the data is best used. Suppose that you established ORDERDATE as a field name to describe the date an order was placed. Then you entered record dates as labels in the general form, MMM-DD-YYYY, such as **Jun-26-1994**. Although you can search for an ORDERDATE that matches a specific date, you cannot perform a mathematical search for all ORDERDATEs within a specified period of time or before a certain date. To get maximum flexibility from Quattro Pro 5.0 for Windows **D**ata commands, enter dates in the databases in the following format:

@DATE(*year,month,day*)

You can use Ctrl+Shift+D to enter dates. You can also use the Active Block dialog box Data Entry Input property to restrict the field to accept dates only and enter dates in the following format:

MM/DD/YY

See Chapter 4, "Learning Spreadsheet Basics," for more information on setting the Data Entry Input property to restrict input to dates.

You then need to choose the level of detail needed for each item of information and determine whether you enter data as a number or a label. Enter telephone and social security numbers, for example, as labels and not as numbers. Use the Active Block dialog box Data Entry Input property to restrict the field to accept labels only to make entering labels that begin with numeric characters easier.

Certain types of information, such as telephone numbers and social security numbers, should be entered as labels to prevent Quattro Pro 5.0 for Windows from attempting to evaluate them as formulas. You want a telephone number to appear as 459-0987, for example, not as 528.

Be sure to plan the database carefully before you establish field names and enter data. Advance planning helps you create a database that is more efficient for data entry and easier to use in analyzing your data.

Entering Data

After you have planned the database, you can begin building it. To understand how the process works, create a Company database as a new database in a blank notebook. Enter the field names across a single row (A:A2..A:F2 in Fig. 12.1).

The field names must be labels, even numeric labels, such as '1, '2, and so on. Quattro Pro 5.0 for Windows uses a *single* row for the field names. If, for example, cell B1 contains the label STREET, and cell B2 contains the label ADDRESS, the field name for the second field of the Company database would be ADDRESS, not STREET ADDRESS.

All field names must be unique and they cannot duplicate existing block names in the same notebook. Only the first 15 characters in a field name are used, so field names that have the same first 15 characters are not considered unique even though they may differ in later characters.

To control the manner in which data is displayed on-screen, you use the Active Block dialog box and set the numeric format and column width. Remember, you can quickly select an entire column and set its properties by pointing to the column letter and clicking the right mouse button to activate the Active Block dialog box (or select **Prop**erty **C**urrent Object). You can also click the Fit button to quickly adjust column widths.

After you enter the field names and set all desired properties, you can add records to the database. To enter the first record, move the cell selector to the row directly below the field name row, and then enter the data across the row. To enter the first record, for example, type the following entries in these cells:

A:A3:	**Add It Up Computing**
A:B3:	**'11 Sunny Lane**
A:C3:	**Walleye**
A:D3:	**MN**
A:E3:	**'55660**
A:F3:	**'459-0987**

Notice that the contents of the ADDRESS, ZIP, and PHONE fields are entered as labels. If you did not restrict data input for columns B, E, and F to labels (through the Active Block dialog box), be sure to type a ' label character as shown in this example.

The sample Company database is used periodically throughout this chapter to demonstrate the results of using various **D**ata commands. In this book, the database is limited to a single screen for clarity. In real-life applications, however, you can track many more data items. You can, for example, maintain up to 256 fields (the number of columns in a notebook) in a single Quattro Pro 5.0 for Windows database table.

◄◄ "Entering Data in the Notebook," p. 97.

FOR RELATED **INFORMATION**

Modifying a Database

After you plan the database organization and collect the data, creating a notebook database is quite easy. Quattro Pro 5.0 for Windows also makes modifying and maintaining the database a simple task.

To add or delete database records, you use the same commands you already know for inserting and deleting rows on a notebook page. Because records correspond to rows, you can insert a record in a database by first inserting a new row and then entering the data for each database field. Figure 12.3 shows a row for a new record inserted into the middle of a database.

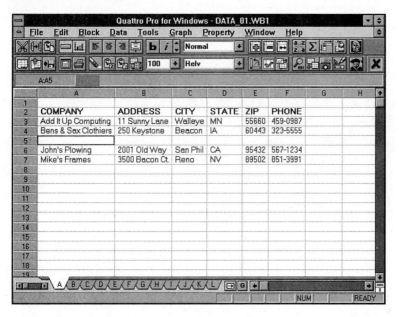

Fig. 12.3

A row inserted for a new record in the database.

Instead of inserting records into the middle of a database, you will probably find it more convenient to append records to the end of the database and then instruct Quattro Pro 5.0 for Windows to sort the database. Sorting the database records, which is covered in the next section, rearranges the records in the proper physical order.

You can delete database records by deleting the row containing the record, or by selecting the **Data Query** command and choosing Delete. To delete a record by deleting its row, move the cell selector to the row containing the record to delete and select the **B**lock **D**elete **R**ows command or the Delete button on the SpeedBar. Be extremely careful when you specify the records to be deleted. Unless you save the notebook before the deletion or use the **E**dit **U**ndo command immediately following the deletion, the records you delete are removed permanently. Rather than deleting records by deleting rows, you may want to consider using **Data Query** commands (discussed later in this chapter) and extracting the inactive records to a separate database before deleting them.

You modify fields in a notebook database the same way you modify the contents of any cells in a Quattro Pro 5.0 for Windows notebook. You change the cell contents by retyping the cell entry or by using the Edit (F2) key to edit the entry (see Chapter 4, "Learning Spreadsheet Basics," for more information on entering and editing data).

To add a new field to a database, you place the cell selector in the field name row of the field that you want to follow the new field. You use the **B**lock **I**nsert **C**olumns command (or the Insert button) to insert a column for the new field. Enter the new field name and fill the field with values for each record. To insert an AREA field between the ZIP and PHONE fields in the Company database, for example, position the cell selector in cell A:F2, issue the **B**lock **I**nsert **C**olumns command, and then type the new field name **AREA** in cell A:F2, as shown in figure 12.4.

To delete a field, position the cell selector in the column containing the field you want to remove, and then select the **B**lock **D**elete **C**olumns command (or the Delete button).

All other commands, such as those for moving and formatting cells, work the same in both database and spreadsheet applications.

Fig. 12.4

A column inserted for a new database field.

Quattro Pro for Windows - DATA_01.WB1

File   Edit   Block   Data   Tools   Graph   Property   Window   Help

Normal

100   Helv

A:F2   'AREA

	A	B	C	D	E	F	G	H
1								
2	COMPANY	ADDRESS	CITY	STATE	ZIP	AREA	PHONE	
3	Add It Up Computing	11 Sunny Lane	Walleye	MN	55660		459-0987	
4	Bens & Sax Clothiers	250 Keystone	Beacon	IA	60443		323-5555	
5								
6	John's Plowing	2001 Old Way	San Phil	CA	95432		567-1234	
7	Mike's Frames	3500 Bacon Ct.	Reno	NV	89502		851-3991	
8								
9								
10								
11								
12								
13								
14								
15								
16								
17								
18								
19								

A / B / C / D / E / F / G / H / I / J / K / L /

NUM   READY

Sorting Database Records

You can change the order of notebook database records by sorting them according to the contents of the fields. You use the **Data Sort** command to sort any block of data in a notebook. Selecting **Data Sort** displays the Data Sort dialog box shown in figure 12.5.

To sort the database, you start by specifying the block to sort. This block must include all fields for all the records to be sorted, but it must not include the field name row. If you do not include all fields when sorting, you destroy the integrity of the database because parts of one record end up with parts of other records. In figure 12.5, the data sort block includes the area A:A3..A:G6.

The data sort block must not include the field name row; otherwise, the field names would be sorted along with the database records.

The data sort block does not necessarily have to include all records, however. If part of the database already has the organization you want, or if you do not want to sort all the records, you can specify a data sort block that includes only those records you want to sort.

Fig. 12.5

The Data Sort dialog box.

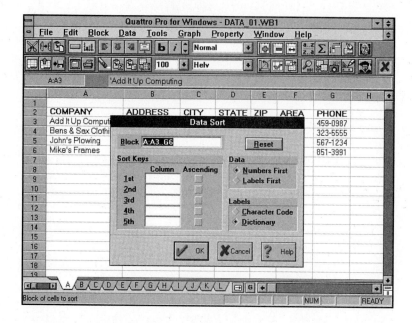

After choosing the data sort block, you must specify the *sort keys*. Sort keys are the fields used to sort the database records. You can specify up to five sort keys. The records are sorted first by using the 1st key. If the 1st key cannot uniquely sort the records, the 2nd key is used to break the tie. The 3rd, 4th, and 5th keys are each used to break a tie in the higher precedence keys. You must set a 1st key, but the other keys are optional.

For each specified sort key, you must specify whether the sort should be an ascending or descending sort. With an ascending sort, the number 1 comes before 2, and the letter B comes before C. A descending sort reverses the sort order.

Quattro Pro 5.0 for Windows offers several additional sort options. You can specify whether numbers or labels appear first when sorting data, and you can specify whether Quattro Pro 5.0 for Windows uses a dictionary or Character Code sort. A dictionary sort ignores the case of letters, so *apple* and *Apple* sort together before *ball* and *Ball*. A Character Code sort, however, places uppercase letters before lowercase letters. A Character Code sort would produce the sort order: Apple, Ball, apple, ball.

After you specify the data sort block, specify the sort key(s) on which to reorder the records, specify whether the key fields should be sorted in ascending or descending order, and select the appropriate additional options, you press Enter or click OK to confirm the dialog box and sort the records. You may also want to save the notebook before sorting the records so that you can retrieve the original database in case you make an error specifying the sort options.

Using the One-Key Sort

A common example of a database sorted according to a single key sort is a customer account database that sorts records according to a unique account number. Because each account number is used only once, sorting by account number always sorts the records in the same relative order.

In the Company database example, you can use the sorting capability to reorder records alphabetically on the STATE field. First select the data sort block (A:A3..A:G6); then select the **Data Sort** command.

Next, select **1**st key and type the address or point to any cell in the column containing the first key field. For example, enter **A:D2** (for STATE) as the **1**st key. Select a sort order (ascending or descending). For this example, choose ascending order. Finally, press Enter or click OK. Figure 12.6 shows the database sorted in ascending order by STATE.

You can add a record to the sorted database without having to insert a row manually to place the new record in the proper position. Add the new record to the bottom of the database, expand the data sort block, and then sort the database again using the same sort key. Because Quattro Pro 5.0 for Windows remembers the previous **Data Sort** settings, you can sort the new record into the proper position by pressing Enter or clicking OK after you expand the data sort block.

Using a Multiple-Key Sort

A multiple-key sort uses additional sort keys to break ties in the sort order. A common example of a double-key sort is the yellow page section of the telephone book. In the yellow pages, records are sorted first according to business type (the 1st key), and then by business name (the 2nd key). To see how a double-key sort works (first sorting by one key, and then by another key within the first sort order), you can add a new record to the end of the Company database, and then reorder the database, first by STATE, and then by CITY within STATE.

Fig. 12.6

The database sorted by STATE.

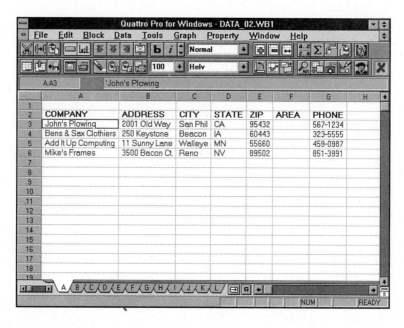

Place the cell selector in cell A:A7 and add the following entries to the indicated cells:

A:A7:	**Raoul's Bar**
A:B7:	**'10 Lillie Lane**
A:C7:	**Camel**
A:D7:	**CA**
A:E7:	**'95309**
A:G7:	**'369-2468**

After adding the new record, select **Data S**ort. Notice that the data sort block is still specified as A:A3..A:G6. To include the new record, edit the text box to show A:A3..A:G7 (you can also prespecify the block A:A3..A:G7 before you select **Data S**ort). The STATE field (column D) is still specified as the 1st key, so you do not have to respecify it. Select 2nd key, enter **A:C2**, and choose Ascending for the sort order by CITY. Press Enter or click OK. Figure 12.7 shows the database sorted by STATE and by CITY within STATE.

Records are now grouped first by STATE in alphabetical order (CA, IA, MN, and NV), and then by CITY within STATE (Camel, CA before San Phil, CA). When you determine the order to use sort keys, be sure to request a reasonable sort. For example, you probably don't want to sort first by CITY and then by STATE within CITY.

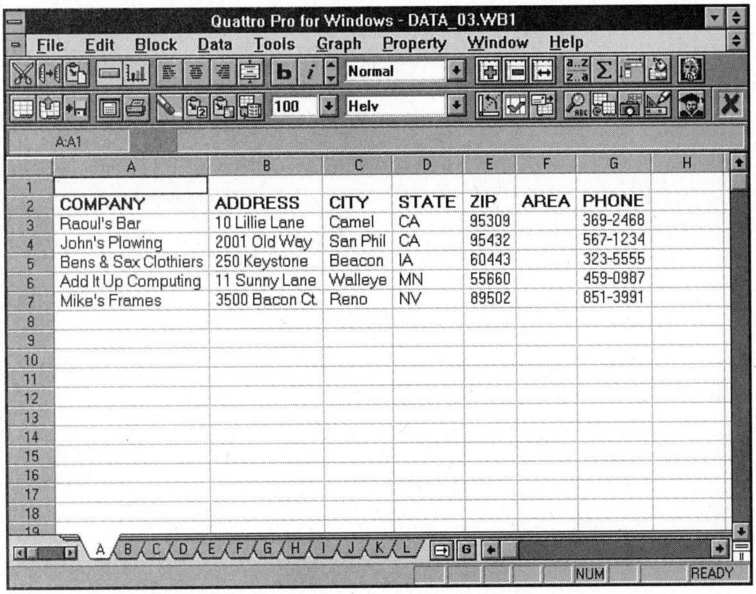

Fig. 12.7

The Company database sorted using two sort keys (STATE and CITY).

Determining the Sort Order

Sometimes it may appear that Quattro Pro 5.0 for Windows sorts records incorrectly. If, for example, you specified the ADDRESS field in the Company database as the **1st** key, the results would appear as shown in figure 12.8.

Although you might expect the record for Bens & Sax Clothiers at 250 Keystone to appear before the record for John's Plowing at 2001 Old Way, Quattro Pro 5.0 for Windows does not sort the records in that order. The reason for this is that the ADDRESS field is a label field, so the records are sorted character-by-character.

You probably would not sort the Company database by using the ADDRESS field as a key, but in some cases you may have to sort label fields that look like numbers. One method you can use to ensure that the records are sorted as you expect is to make all the labels that look like numbers the same length (as in the ZIP and PHONE fields) or add enough leading zeros (0) so that all the labels have the same format (0250 and 2001, for example). Figure 12.9 shows the result of sorting the Company database on the ADDRESS field after padding all the address numbers with leading zeros so that all are four characters long.

Fig. 12.8

The result of sorting by ADDRESS.

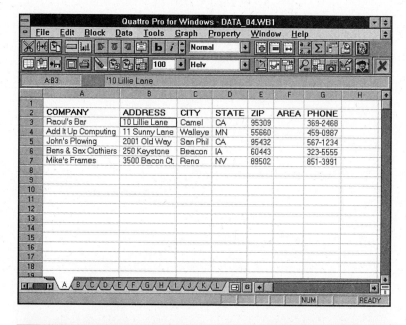

Fig. 12.9

The sort by ADDRESS after padding address numbers with leading zeros.

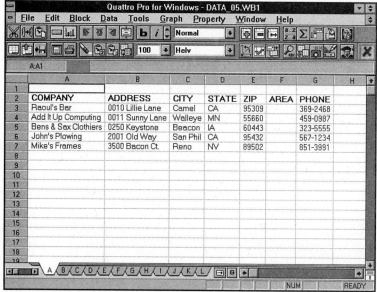

Restoring the Presort Order

If you sort a database, you cannot restore the records to their original order (unless you use the **E**dit **U**ndo command immediately after sorting the records, or save the file immediately before the sort and retrieve the file again after the sort). You can, however, add a record number field to the database, and use the record number to restore the original sort order after you have sorted the records on another field. You specify the record number field as the 1st key and select Ascending order to return the records to their original order.

To create a record number field, add an additional column to the data sort block. Use the **B**lock **F**ill command to add sequential record numbers in the new column. After sorting on another field, resort the database on the record number field to restore the original record order. See Chapter 5, "Using Fundamental Commands," for more information on using the **B**lock **F**ill command.

◄◄ "Filling Blocks," p. 173.

FOR RELATED INFORMATION

Searching for Database Records

In this section of the chapter, you learn how to use **D**ata **Q**uery to search for records, and then edit, extract, or delete the records you find. You can use the **D**ata **Q**uery commands with a Quattro Pro 5.0 for Windows notebook database. Looking for records that meet specified conditions is the simplest form of searching a Quattro Pro 5.0 for Windows database. To determine which companies in the Company database are in California, for example, you can use a search operation to find any records with CA as the value in the STATE field.

After you locate the information you want, you can extract it from the database and place it in another part of the notebook, separate from the database. You can, for example, extract all records with a California address and print the extracted records. You can also search for only the first occurrence of a specified field value to develop a unique list of field entries. You can, for example, search the STATE field to extract a list of the different states, or you can search the ZIP field to develop a list of the different ZIP codes to comply with postal regulations for reduced-rate mailings. Finally, if you no longer want to do business in a particular area, you can delete all records for a specified state.

After you select **Data Query**, the dialog box shown in figure 12.10 appears. To initiate any search operation, you need to make the appropriate selections from this dialog box. Table 12.1 describes the Data Query dialog box options.

Fig. 12.10

The Data Query dialog box.

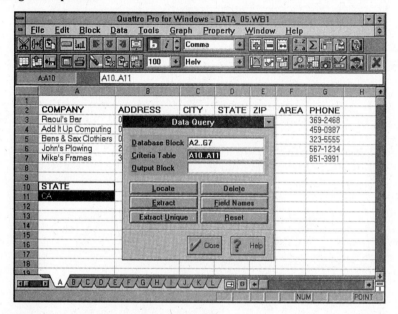

Table 12.1 Data Query Dialog Box Options

Option	Description
Database Block	The location of the search area, including the field name row; must be specified for all **Data Query** operations
Criteria Table	The location of the search conditions; must be specified for all **Data Query** operations
Output Block	A block in which a **Data Query** command copies records or parts of records to an area outside the database; must be specified for **Extract** and **Extract Unique** operations
Locate	Moves down through the database and positions the cell selector on records that match specified criteria
Extract	Creates copies, in the output block, of all or some of the fields in records that match specified criteria
Extract Unique	Creates a single copy, in the output block, of all or some of the unique fields in records that match specified criteria

Option	Description
Delete	Deletes from the database all records that match specified criteria
Field Names	Creates block names for every field name in the database
Reset	Erases the **D**atabase Block, **C**riteria Table, and **O**utput Block settings

Specifying the Database Block

The database block for the **Data Query** command is the group of records you want to search. The specified area must begin with the field name row and include all the records you want to search. Normally, the database block includes the entire database table.

Unlike the data sort block, the database block must always include the field name row. Although this may seem confusing, remember that the **Data Query** operations search the database by using the field names, so you must include the field names in the database block. On the other hand, you can use the **Data Sort** command to sort any block of data, whether it is a database or not. The **Data Sort** command does not use field names, and they should not be included when specifying a data sort block. In figure 12.10, the database block includes the area A:A2..A:G7; the data sort block starts one row lower and includes A:A3..A:G7.

Select the database block by preselecting the block or by typing the address in the **D**atabase Block text box in the Data Query dialog box. You do not have to specify the block again unless the search area changes. However, be careful not to highlight a different block because Quattro Pro 5.0 for Windows may assume you are highlighting another database block.

Entering the Criteria Table

When you want Quattro Pro 5.0 for Windows to search for records that meet certain criteria, you must establish a criteria table. The criteria table contains one or more conditions that records must satisfy before they are selected. Suppose, for example, that you want to search for all records in the Company database that contain CA in the STATE field. Place the cell selector in A:A10 and enter **STATE**; then enter **CA** in cell A:A11. (**Note:** You normally would place the criteria table to one side of the database block or on another notebook page, not directly below the database block. In this example, the criteria block was placed below the database block to enable the entire example to appear on one screen.)

Select **D**ata **Q**uery and specify A:A10..A:A11 in the Criteria Table text box. You can type the address or point to the block after selecting the text box.

You can use numbers, labels, or formulas as criteria. A criteria table can be up to 256 columns wide and two or more rows high. The first row must contain the field names of the search criteria, such as STATE, and must match the field names in the database block exactly.

If you misspell a field name in the criteria table, Quattro Pro 5.0 for Windows selects *all* records and ignores the specified criteria. To prevent this problem, copy the field names from the database block to the criteria table instead of retyping them.

If the second row of the criteria table is blank, Quattro Pro 5.0 for Windows selects all records. If you include more than one field in the criteria table, but do not specify conditions for some of those fields, Quattro Pro 5.0 for Windows ignores fields that do not have selection criteria when matching records. Only fields with specified selection criteria are considered when determining whether records should be selected.

Both the database block and the criteria table must be specified before you can use any of the **D**ata **Q**uery commands.

Specifying the Output Block

The output block is an area you designate to receive records copied by the **D**ata **Q**uery Extract or **D**ata **Q**uery Extract Unique commands. You do not have to specify an output block before you use the **D**ata **Q**uery Locate or **D**ata **Q**uery Delete commands.

The output block should be located to one side of or well below the database block if you place both on the same notebook page. A better idea is to place the output block on a separate notebook page so that you have room to add more records.

The first row of the output block contains the field names of those fields you want included in the copied records. The field names in the output block must match the field names in the database block exactly, but you need not include all the fields, and you can include them in any order you like. To avoid problems caused by mistyping, copy field names from the database block to the output block.

Quattro Pro 5.0 for Windows ignores label prefixes when matching field names. If, in the output block, you right-align a field name that is left-aligned in the database block, it is considered a matching field name.

You can specify two types of output blocks: one with a specified size, or an open-ended one. To specify an output block with a specified size, you include two or more rows (including the field name row) when you specify the address of the output block. An output block of a specified size can contain one fewer extracted record than the number of rows in the output block. That is, an output block of five rows can contain four records. If you do not include enough rows to hold the extracted records, Quattro Pro 5.0 for Windows displays a message box stating `Too many records for output block`.

To specify an open-ended output block, you include only the field name row when you specify the output block. An open-ended output block can contain as many extracted records as there are rows below the field name row on the notebook page. All data record rows in the output block are erased before new records are copied to the block by either the **D**ata **Q**uery **E**xtract or **D**ata **Q**uery Extract Unique command. If you have created an open-ended output block, all rows below the output block field name row (to the bottom of the page) are erased. Any nonrelated data you may have below an open-ended output block also is erased. Because of this, the best location for an open-ended output block is usually on its own notebook page.

To specify the output block, select **D**ata **Q**uery and enter the address of the block in the **O**utput Block text box. You can type the address or point to the block after selecting the text box.

Locating Records

When you select **L**ocate from the Data Query dialog box, a highlighted bar rests on the first record in the database block that meets the conditions specified in the criteria table. In the Company database example, the highlighted bar rests on the first record that contains CA in the STATE field, as shown in figure 12.11.

Fig. 12.11

The first record highlighted in a **D**ata **Q**uery **L**ocate operation.

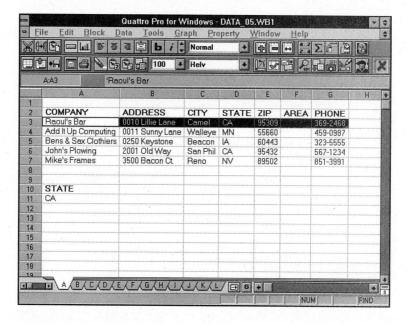

By using the down-arrow key, you can place the highlighted bar on the next record that meets the specified criteria. The up- and down-arrow keys move the highlighted bar through the database to only those records that meet the matching conditions. The mode indicator changes from READY to FIND during the search.

You can move the cell selector to different fields of a highlighted record using the right- and left-arrow keys. You can enter new values or use the Edit (F2) key to update the current values in any field, but if you change the record so that it no longer satisfies the specified criteria and then move to another record, you cannot return to the modified record during the **L**ocate operation.

To end the **L**ocate operation and return to the Data Query dialog box, press Esc or Enter. To return to READY mode, press Esc again or click OK.

Extracting Records

The **Data Query Locate** command has limited use, especially in a large database, because you must scroll through the entire database if you want to view each record that meets the specified criteria. As an alternative, you can use the **Data Query Extract** command to copy to the output block the records that meet the conditions. You can then view, print, or save the extracted records contained in the output block.

To execute a **Data Query Extract** command, you first must create and define the database block, the criteria table, and the output block.

In the Company database example, to extract the records that meet the criteria of containing CA in the STATE field, you first must create an output block. In this case, copy the field names from the first row of the database block (cells A:A2..A:G2) to the output block (cells A:A14..A:G14). (**Note:** In this example, the output block is placed on the same notebook page so that the entire operation is visible on a single screen.) Select **Data Query** and enter **A:A14..A:G14** in the **O**utput Block text box. You can type the address or point to the block after selecting the text box.

To extract the records, select the **Data Query Extract** command. The two records from California companies are extracted, as shown in figure 12.12.

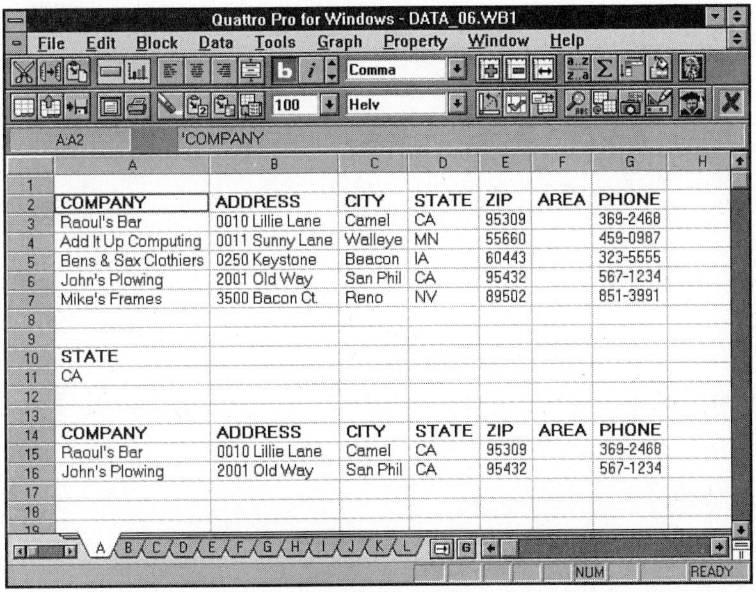

Fig. 12.12

A complete-record extract on an "exact match" label condition.

TIP

Be sure to check the **D**atabase Block setting in the Data Query dialog box. If the correct block is not specified, Quattro Pro 5.0 for Windows may display an error message such as **No records match criteria**.

You do not have to include all database fields in the output block. You might, for example, include only the COMPANY, AREA, and PHONE fields to create a telephone number listing.

Handling More Complicated Criteria

In addition to searching for an "exact match" to a single label field, Quattro Pro 5.0 for Windows permits a wide variety of record searches. You can search for exact matches to numeric fields, for partial matches of field contents, and for fields that meet formula conditions. You can also specify that fields meet all of several conditions or that fields meet either one condition or another.

Using Wild Cards in Criteria Tables

You can use wild cards for matching labels in database operations. The characters ?, *, and ~ have special meaning when used in the criteria table. The ? character instructs Quattro Pro 5.0 for Windows to accept any character in that specific position, and can be used only to locate fields of the same length. The * character, which tells Quattro Pro 5.0 for Windows to accept any and all characters that follow, can be used on field contents of unequal length. By placing a tilde (~) symbol at the beginning of a label, you tell Quattro Pro 5.0 for Windows to accept all values except those that follow. Table 12.2 shows how you can use wild cards in search operations.

Table 12.2 Using Wild Cards in Search Operations

Enter	To Find
N?	Any two-character label starting with the letter N, such as NC, NJ, NY, and so on
BO?L?	A five-character label, such as BOWLE, but not a shorter label like BOWL
BO?L*	A four-or-more character label, such as BOWLE, BOWL, BOLLESON, BOELING, and so on
SAN*	A three-or-more character label starting with SAN and followed by any number of characters, such as SANTA BARBARA and SAN FRANCISCO

Enter	To Find
SAN *	A four-or-more character label starting with SAN, followed by a space, and then followed by any number of characters, such as SAN FRANCISCO, but not SANTA BARBARA
~N*	Strings that do not begin with the letter N

Use the ? and * wild-card characters when you are unsure of the spelling or when you need to match several slightly different records. Always check the results by using **Data Query Locate** or **Data Query Extract** before you use wild cards in a **Data Query Delete** command. If you are not careful, you may remove more—or different—records than you intend.

Using Formulas in Criteria Tables

To set up formulas that query numeric or label fields in the database, you can use the following relational operators:

>	Greater than
>=	Greater than or equal to
<	Less than
<=	Less than or equal to
=	Equal to
<>	Not equal to

You create a formula that references the first field entry in the column you want to search. Quattro Pro 5.0 for Windows tests the formula on each record.

Because the criteria formula specifies which field is being tested, you can place the formula below any of the criteria table's field names. This is unlike label criteria, which must appear directly below the associated field name. You can, for example, use a formula to extract the records that have a ZIP code smaller than 90000. First, type the formula **+E3<="90000"** in cell A:A11, as shown in figure 12.13.

Fig. 12.13

A relational formula
condition to extract
records.

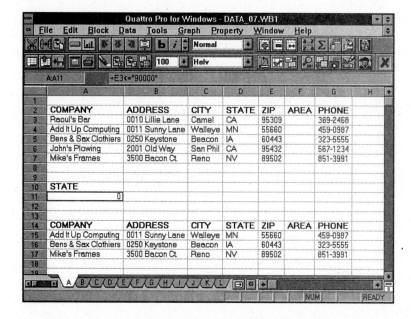

NOTE

When you specify a criteria formula that tests a field containing labels, be sure to enclose the matching value in quotes as shown in the formula in figure 12.13. If you forget to enclose the matching value in quotes, Quattro Pro 5.0 for Windows will not be able to correctly evaluate the query.

Although the formula is displayed in the control panel, notice that a zero (0) is displayed in cell A:A11. The formula checks whether the contents of cell A:E3 (in which ZIP equals '95309) is less than or equal to 90000 and returns the zero (0) to indicate a false condition. In this example, executing a **D**ata **Q**uery **E**xtract operation produces three records for which ZIP is less than or equal to 90000.

To reference cells outside the database, use formulas that include absolute cell addressing (see Chapter 5, "Using Fundamental Commands," for more information on relative, absolute, and mixed references). Suppose, for example, that immediately after you issue the preceding command, you decide to use 80000 instead of 90000 as the upper limit for extracted ZIP codes. Although you can just edit the existing formula, in this case you want to make it easier to make fast changes. To make it easier, you first must return to READY mode. Enter the value '80000 in cell A:E11, and then type the formula +E3<=$E$11 as the criterion in cell A:A11.

Repeat the **Data Query Extract** command. As you can see from figure 12.14, two records match and are extracted.

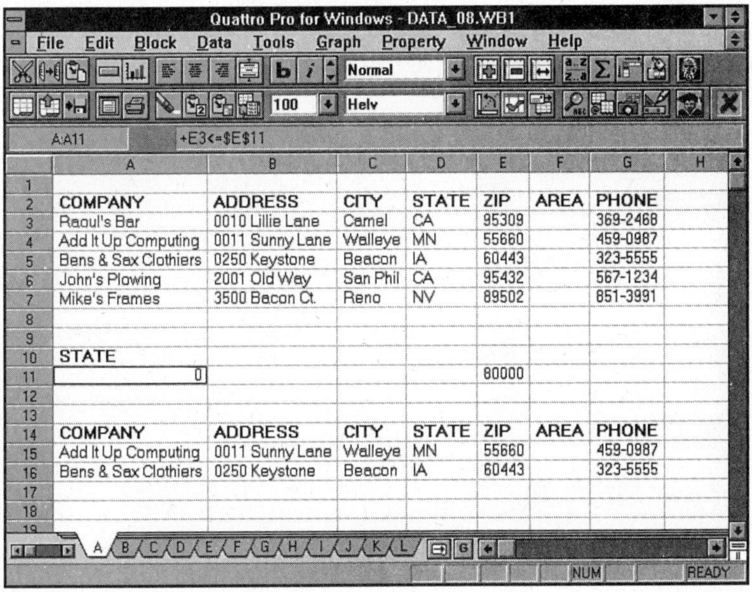

Fig. 12.14

A mixed formula condition to extract records.

Setting Up *AND* Conditions

Now that you have seen how to base a **Data Query Locate** or **Data Query Extract** operation on only one criterion, you learn how to use multiple criteria for your queries. You can set up multiple criteria as AND conditions (in which *all* the criteria must be met) or as OR conditions (in which any *one* criterion must be met). For example, searching a music department's library for sheet music requiring drums *and* trumpets is likely to produce fewer selections than searching for music appropriate for drums *or* trumpets.

You indicate two or more criteria, *all* of which must be met, by specifying the conditions on the criteria row immediately below the field names. First, though, you must adjust your criteria table to add another field. In this example, add the CITY field name to A:B10 by copying from A:C2 to A:B10. Finally, adjust the size of the criteria table; use the **Data Query Criteria Table** text box to indicate A:A10..A:B11. Now you can add the desired criteria to the criteria table.

For this example, suppose that you want only those records for companies not located in California and not in a city that starts with the letter B. In cell A:A11, enter the value criteria '~**CA** and in cell A:B11, enter the criteria ~**B***. Next, issue a **D**ata **Q**uery **E**xtract command, and Quattro Pro 5.0 for Windows extracts two records that meet both conditions. The results should look like figure 12.15.

Fig. 12.15

A logical AND search on two fields.

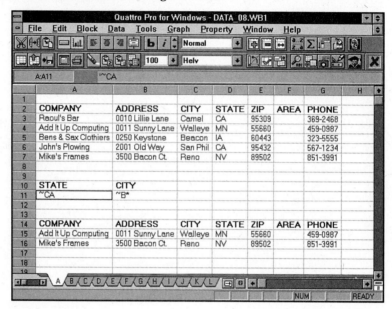

When you maintain a criteria table that includes many fields, you quickly can extract records based on an alternative condition. Enter the additional criteria only in the row immediately below the field name row.

Setting Up OR Conditions

Criteria placed on the same row have the effect of a logical AND; they tell Quattro Pro 5.0 for Windows to find or extract on this condition "AND" this one, and so on. Criteria placed on *different* rows have the effect of a logical OR; that is, find or extract on this condition "OR" that one, and so on. You can set up a logical OR search on one or more fields.

Searching a single field for more than one condition is the simplest use of an OR condition. You can, for example, extract those records where the STATE is MN or NV by placing MN in cell A:A11 and NV in cell A:A12 and expanding the criteria table to include the additional row.

You also can specify a logical OR condition on two or more different fields. Suppose, for example, that you want to search for records where either the state is not California or the city does not start with the letter S.

First, move the cell selector to A:B11 and press Del to erase the contents of that cell and to remove the AND condition. Next, enter ~**S*** in cell A:B12 to add the OR condition. Then adjust the criteria table to include the specified OR condition by expanding the criteria table down a row. When you issue the **Data Query Extract** command, four records are copied to the output block. Although Raoul's Bar does not meet the condition of not being in California, it does meet the condition of being in a city that doesn't start with S and is therefore extracted to the output block along with the records for companies who are not in California. Only one condition or the other had to be met before the copy was made. The results should look like figure 12.16.

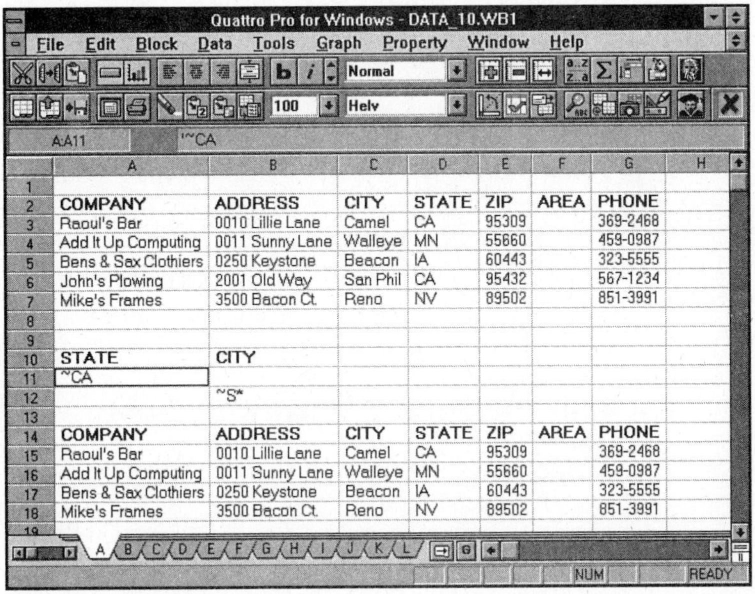

Fig. 12.16

A logical OR search on two fields.

To add additional OR criteria, drop to a new row, enter each new condition, and expand the criteria table. If you reduce the number of rows involved in an OR logical search, be sure to contract the criteria table. Remember, a blank row in the criteria table matches all records in the database.

Although no technical reason prevents you from mixing AND and OR logical searches, you may find it difficult to properly formulate such a mixed query. Follow the format of placing each AND condition in the row immediately below the criteria field name row, and each OR condition in a separate row below. Be careful, however, to ensure that each row in the criteria table specifies all the AND conditions that apply. If, for example, you want to search for records in which STATE equals CA and CITY starts with S or STATE equals NV and CITY starts with S, enter the AND and OR conditions in the following cells:

A:A11:	**CA**
A:B11:	**S***
A:A12:	**NV**
A:B12:	**S***

The criteria table remains unchanged. Repeating the *S** in cells A:B11 and A:B12 is critical because if Quattro Pro 5.0 for Windows finds a blank cell in a criteria table, the program selects all records for the field name above that blank cell.

You should test the logic of your search conditions on a small sample database in which you can verify search results easily by scrolling through all records and noting which of them should be extracted. If, for example, the database contains hundreds of records, you can test the preceding AND and OR search conditions on a small group or by using **Data Query Locate.**

Extracting a Unique Set of Records

Ordinarily, you use the **Data Query Extract Unique** command to copy into the output area only a small portion of each record that meets the criteria. If, for example, you want a list of the states in the database, set up an output block that includes only the STATE field (cell A14 in fig. 12.17). To search all records, leave blank the row below the field name row in the criteria table. Then, specify the output block as A14, and select **Data Query Extract Unique** to produce a list of the four different states in the database.

If you have a large mailing list database, you can produce a list of the ZIP codes to assist with preparing mailings. To do so, you specify in the output area only the field name ZIP, leave the row under field names in the criteria table blank, and select the **Data Query Extract Unique** command.

Fig. 12.17

The results of using the **D**ata **Q**uery Extract **U**nique command.

```
┌─────────────────────────────────────────────────────────────────┐
│ -         Quattro Pro for Windows - DATA_15.WB1          ▼│▲│
│ - File  Edit  Block  Data  Tools  Graph  Property  Window  Help  ▲│
│ ✕▐◀▐▒  □▐▦  ⊟▐▦▐▤  b │ i │▲  Comma      ▼  ⊞▐□▐⊞  ⋮⋮Σ▐▤▐▒▐▒ │
│ ▤▐▤◀▐  □▐▦▐▧  ▒▐▦▐▦▐▦ 100  ▼  Helv     ▼  ▐▤▐▦▐▧  ▒▒▐▦▐▦▐▒ ✕ │
│ ┌──────────┬─────────────                                        │
│ │ A:A14    │        'STATE                                       │
│ ┌──────────┴──────────────────────────────────────────────────┐ │
│ │      A            B          C       D     E    F     G    H ▲│ │
│ │ 1                                                            ││ │
│ │ 2 COMPANY      ADDRESS      CITY   STATE  ZIP  AREA  PHONE    ││ │
│ │ 3 Raoul's Bar  0010 Lillie Lane  Camel  CA  95309  369-2468  ││ │
│ │ 4 Add It Up Computing 0011 Sunny Lane Walleye MN 55660 459-0987││ │
│ │ 5 Bens & Sax Clothiers 0250 Keystone Beacon IA 60443 323-5555││ │
│ │ 6 John's Plowing 2001 Old Way San Phil CA 95432 567-1234    ││ │
│ │ 7 Mike's Frames 3500 Bacon Ct. Reno  NV 89502  851-3991    ││ │
│ │ 8                                                            ││ │
│ │ 9                                                            ││ │
│ │ 10 STATE        CITY                                         ││ │
│ │ 11                                                           ││ │
│ │ 12                                                           ││ │
│ │ 13                                                           ││ │
│ │ 14 STATE                                                     ││ │
│ │ 15 CA                                                        ││ │
│ │ 16 MN                                                        ││ │
│ │ 17 IA                                                        ││ │
│ │ 18 NV                                                        ▼│ │
│ │◀│▶│ ▲ A▕B▕C▕D▕E▕F▕G▕H▕I▕J▕K▕L▕ ⊟ 6 ◀       ▶ │ │
│ │                                      NUM         READY    │ │
│ └──────────────────────────────────────────────────────────────┘ │
└─────────────────────────────────────────────────────────────────┘
```

Deleting Records

As you learned in Chapter 5, you can use the **Block Delete Rows** command to remove rows from a notebook page. If you want a fast alternative to this one-by-one approach, use the **Data Query Delete** command to remove unwanted records from your database files. Before you select Delete from the Data Query dialog box, specify the block of records to be searched (database block) and the conditions for the deletion (criteria).

Suppose that you want to remove all records with a STATE field beginning with the letter N. To do so, enter the criterion **N*** in cell A:A11. Then issue the **Data Query Delete** command to delete the rows and remove all records for states that begin with N. The remaining records pack together and the database block automatically adjusts.

Be extremely careful when you issue the **Data Query Delete** command. If you accidently delete records, immediately select **Edit Undo** before issuing any additional commands.

Although the **Data Query Delete** command does not display the exact rows to be deleted, you can guard against deleting the wrong records by first saving the file or using the **Data Query Locate** (or **Data Query Extract**) command to examine the records before deleting them.

Using Database Forms

Quattro Pro 5.0 for Windows has a new feature—*database forms*—that make entering, editing, and searching for database records even easier. Database forms are dialog boxes that display one database record at a time and allow you to view and modify all of the database fields for a single record.

To display a database form for a database, highlight the database block, and then select **D**ata F**o**rm to display the Database Form dialog box shown in figure 12.18.

Fig. 12.18

The Database Form dialog box.

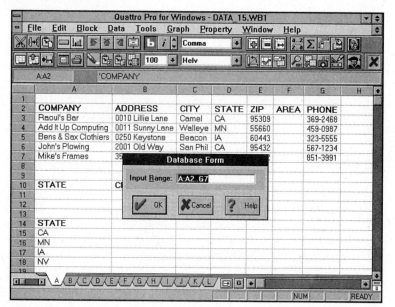

Make certain the Input **R**ange specifies the correct database block. The top row of the Input **R**ange must include the field names, and the entire database block should be included in the Input **R**ange so that any changes you make using the database form do not corrupt the database. Press Enter or click OK to confirm the dialog box and display the database form, as shown in figure 12.19.

When a record is displayed in the database form, you can enter or edit in any of the fields. Use the Tab key and the Shift+Tab key to move between fields. Use the scroll bar or the direction keys to move between records. In addition, you can use the following commands:

New adds a new, blank record at the end of the database.

Delete removes the currently displayed record from the database.

Revert cancels any change made to the current record.

Go Next displays the next record.

Go Previous displays the previous record.

Search displays a form on which you can specify record selection criteria. You use the same methods you learned earlier for entering criteria as you use in criteria tables.

Close enters any changes in the database and closes the database form.

Help displays help on database forms.

After you complete your entries, select Close to close the database form and return to the notebook.

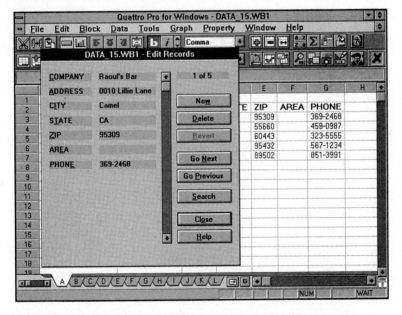

Fig. 12.19

The Database Form displays individual database records.

Using the Database Desktop

The Database Desktop is a companion program to Quattro Pro 5.0 for Windows. This application enables you to access information in existing dBASE and Paradox database files. Through the Database Desktop, you can query a database, add new records to a database, modify existing records in a database, or delete records from a database.

The Database Desktop isn't intended as a complete database management tool. You cannot use the application to create a new dBASE or Paradox database, nor can you use it to modify the structure of an existing database file.

Before using the Database Desktop, you must load the application into memory. Although the Database Desktop is a separate program from Quattro Pro 5.0 for Windows, the Quattro Pro 5.0 for Windows main menu includes a command that you use to load the Database Desktop.

 To load the Database Desktop into memory, select the **Data D**atabase Desktop command. Your system briefly displays a message informing you of its progress loading the program, and then displays the Database Desktop on top of the Quattro Pro 5.0 for Windows screen (see fig. 12.20).

Fig. 12.20

The Database Desktop on top of the Quattro Pro 5.0 for Windows screen.

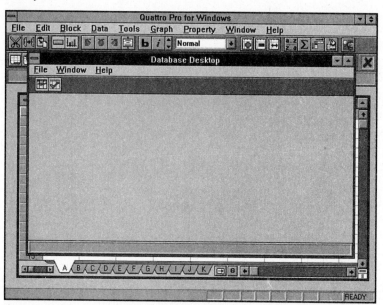

For convenience, click the Maximize button or select Maximize from the Database Desktop Control menu to provide the largest possible work area. Press Alt+Tab to switch between the Database Desktop and Quattro Pro 5.0 for Windows.

Understanding Database Desktop Terminology

To effectively use the Database Desktop, you must understand some special terminology. Table 12.3 summarizes the most important Database Desktop terms.

Table 12.3 Database Desktop Terms

Term	Definition
Alias	A name substituted for a complete drive and path specification. Using aliases makes working with database files more convenient.
Answer table	The group of records selected as a result of a query.
Edit view	An alternate view of a table, which enables you to edit field contents.
Example element	A variable used to represent values in a field. Example elements are used to join tables and to create complex queries.
Field view	The default view of a table. In field view, entries you type replace the entire contents of the field.
Index	A method used to sort database records in a particular order. The Database Desktop cannot create or modify a database index.
Join	The process of relating the information in two or more database tables.
Locked columns	A set of database fields (columns) that remain visible at the left edge of the screen as the view of the database is scrolled horizontally.
Private directory	A local directory used to store temporary files in a networked environment.
Query	A set of conditions that determines the database records that you select.
Query by example (QBE)	The Database Desktop method of selecting records by specifying a set of fields.

(continues)

Table 12.3 Continued

Term	Definition
Record locking	A method of preventing others from modifying or deleting the currently active record. In the Database Desktop, the currently highlighted record is locked automatically.
Set	A group of records.
Table	A collection of database fields and records. The Database Desktop uses several types of tables, including database tables, query tables, and answer tables.
Table query	A method of performing a predefined Database Desktop query from within Quattro Pro 5.0 for Windows.
Working directory	The directory where Database Desktop first looks for your files. Database Desktop uses the alias :WORK: for the working directory.

Opening a Table

The simplest way to use the Database Desktop is to open a database table without selecting specific records. When you open a database table in this manner, you can view all fields for all records in the database. Figure 12.21 shows a database table opened by using the File Open Table command.

When you issue the File Open Table command, the database files in your working directory appear in the Select File dialog box. If you want to open a database file in another directory, select Path or Browse and choose the directory that contains the database file you want to open.

After you open a database table, you can modify (or edit) existing records, insert new records, or delete complete records. You cannot change the structure of the database table—that is, you cannot add new fields, delete existing fields, or change a field definition.

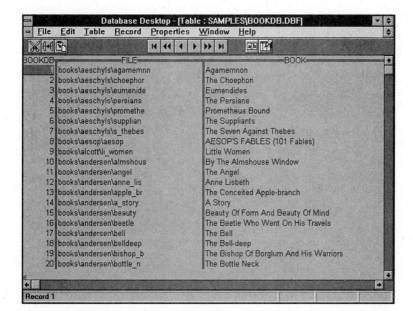

Fig. 12.21

A database table opened by using the **F**ile **O**pen **T**able command.

Changing the Table View

You can modify the current view of the database by rearranging the displayed order and width of the fields. Changing the view of a database doesn't modify the actual database table. Figure 12.22 shows the same BOOKDB.DBF database table as figure 12.21; in figure 12.22, however, the field (column) order and widths have been adjusted for a more meaningful display.

To rearrange the view of the database table by moving database fields, point to the top of the column you want to move. Then hold down the left mouse button and drag the column to the new location. When you release the mouse button, the column under the pointer and all columns to the right move to the right, and the selected column is inserted.

To move a column using the keyboard, select the column and press Ctrl+R. The selected column moves to the last position in the table. You cannot move columns to the left directly; instead, you must move columns indirectly by moving preceding columns to the right.

To change the width of a column, point to the right side of the column border, just below the top of the column. When the pointer changes to a white double-headed arrow, hold down the left mouse button and drag the column border to its new width. If the column contains numeric data and the column is too narrow to display the data, asterisks—rather than the data—appear in the column.

Fig. 12.22

A rearranged view of the BOOKDB.DBF database table.

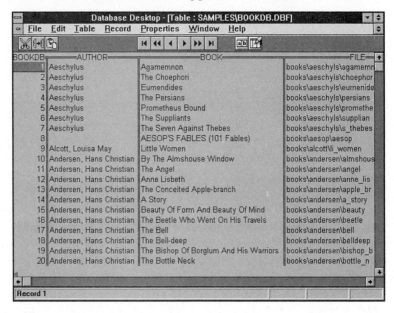

To change the height of the rows in the table view, point to the line that appears in the first column below the first record, and drag the line to the desired row height.

You cannot adjust column widths or row heights by using the keyboard.

Most database tables are too wide to display all fields on-screen at one time. To view additional fields, you must scroll the view by using the direction keys or the scroll bars. As you scroll the view, however, the displayed information may be difficult to interpret because important fields can scroll off screen to the left. To prevent this scrolling, lock the far left columns.

To lock columns, point to the left-pointing triangle that appears below the left edge of the first column, and use the mouse to drag the triangle under the column border you want to lock. When you release the mouse button, a right and a left triangle appear under the column border.

Saving the Table View

After you determine a table view that displays the database information most conveniently, you can save the view for future use. Use the **P**rop-erties **S**ave Properties command to save the current column-order and column-width settings. These settings are saved in a file that uses the same name as the database file, but adds TV as the extension.

To restore the last saved table view settings, select **P**roperties **R**estore Settings. If you reopen a table, any saved table view settings are re-stored.

Performing a Query

Rather than opening a database table and viewing the complete set of records, often you may want to view a subset of those records that you select by using specified criteria. You may want to search for records, for example, for a single customer, for records applying to sales over a specified amount, or for customers in a certain group of states. You use the Query commands in the Database Desktop to select specified records.

To create a new query, select **F**ile **N**ew Query. Choose the appropriate database table from the Select File dialog box. If the database table is not in the working directory, choose **P**ath or **B**rowse, select the correct directory, and select the database table you want to query. After you select a database table, the Database Desktop Query Editor appears (see fig. 12.23).

The Query Editor uses *Query by Example* (QBE) to build a database query; you place example values in the fields displayed in the Query Editor, and records are selected based on these values. The example values you include can be simple values for exact matching, or com-parison values to match a range of values. You also can instruct the Query Editor to perform calculations on the values in the database.

To build a query, you use certain symbols, operators, and reserved words. Query Editor *symbols* indicate the fields you want included in the answer table, whether to include duplicate values, and the default sort order. *Operators* select field values based on criteria you specify. The >= operator, for example, selects records that contain a value in the selected field greater than or equal to a specified value. *Reserved words* perform special database operations, such as inserting and delet-ing records.

Fig. 12.23

The Database Desktop
Query Editor enables
you to create database
queries.

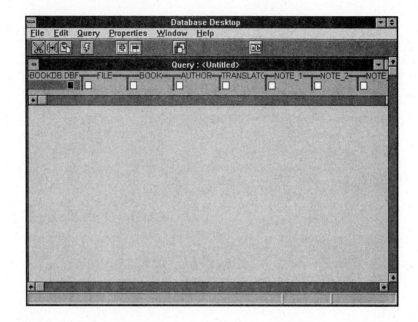

Tables 12.4, 12.5, and 12.6 summarize the symbols, operators, and reserved words you use to create a query with the Query Editor.

Table 12.4 Query Editor Symbols

Symbol	Function
Check mark	Displays all unique values for the selected field, sorting in ascending order.
Check plus	Displays all values (including duplicates) for the selected field.
Check descending	Displays all unique values for the selected field, sorting in descending order.
GroupBy check	Groups displayed records by the values in the selected field.
No check	Field does not display in answer table.

Table 12.5 Query Editor Operators

Operator	Meaning
=	Equal to
>	Greater than
<	Less than
>=	Greater than or equal to
<=	Less than or equal to
..	Matches any number of characters
@	Matches a single character
LIKE	Matches records similar to specified string
NOT	Matches records excluding specified value
BLANK	Matches records with no entry in the field
TODAY	Matches records with today's date
, (AND)	Enters multiple criteria, all of which must be satisfied
OR	Enters multiple criteria, only one of which must be satisfied
AS	Displays values in answer table using a specified field name
!	Creates an inclusive link that includes all records in the specified table
+	Adds values or concatenates strings
-	Subtracts values
*	Multiplies values
/	Divides values
( )	Groups expressions
AVERAGE	Averages selected record values in numeric fields
COUNT	Counts selected record values
MIN	Returns minimum value of selected records
MAX	Returns maximum value of selected records
SUM	Totals selected record values in numeric fields
ALL	Includes all values, including duplicates
UNIQUE	Discards duplicate values

(continues)

Table 12.5 Continued

Operator	Meaning
ONLY	Displays only members of a specified set
NO	Creates a set containing only records that *don't* match
EVERY	Creates a set containing only matching records
EXACTLY	Displays only members of specified set and no others
FIND	Locates records in a table

Table 12.6 Query Editor Reserved Words

Reserved Word	Meaning
CALC	Produces a calculated result
INSERT	Adds records from source tables to a target table
DELETE	Removes complete records from a table
CHANGETO	Changes all matching values to a specified value

To see how the Query Editor works, suppose that you want to search the BOOKDB.DBF database to see a listing of authors with 10 or more works in your library, and you want a count of the total number of works for each of these authors. Because you have a large number of anonymous works, you also want to exclude works that list no author. This query uses the three types of Query Editor elements: symbols, operators, and reserved words.

To begin building the query, you first must determine the fields to include in the answer table. Here, the only database field you want is the AUTHOR field. Although you want a count of titles by each author, you don't want all individual titles listed. You will use the reserved word CALC to create a calculated field in the answer table. Also, because you want to include a single listing for each author, the default check mark is the correct symbol to indicate how to display the field values. If you use the check plus symbol, one copy of each selected author's record is shown for each title included in the database. The check descending symbol produces the same listing as the default check mark, but sorted in descending order. The group by check symbol is used to create a set of records grouped according to the values in the selected field without displaying the values in the field. Unchecked fields do not display in the answer table.

To select a field by using the default check mark, point to the small box at the left of the column and click the left mouse button. To select another type of symbol, point to the selection box, hold down the left mouse button, and drag the highlight to the correct symbol. You cannot select a field with the keyboard. In this case, place a check mark in the AUTHOR field.

Next, to restrict the answer table to exclude records that do not list an author, add the operators NOT BLANK as arguments in the AUTHOR field. The BLANK operator selects records that *are* blank, but the NOT operator tells the Database Desktop to exclude records that meet the following criteria. Combining the two operators excludes records that don't list an author.

To produce a calculated column, you use the reserved word CALC. Here, the calculated value is the total number of book titles for each author, so you use the argument CALC COUNT, which you place in the BOOK field. Do not place a check in the BOOK field selection box, because you want the calculated field—not the BOOK field—included in the answer table.

One more step remains in building the query. Because you want to restrict the answer table to authors with 10 or more titles, you must add another argument in the BOOK field:

COUNT >= 10

As an additional argument, you must separate it from the first argument with the AND operator, which is specified by a comma (,). The complete set of BOOK field arguments now looks like this:

CALC COUNT, COUNT >= 10

NOTE

Arguments you add to a single line of the query are evaluated as AND arguments—all conditions must be met before a record is selected. To create OR arguments, use the OR operator or place the arguments on separate query lines. To add a new line to a query, press the down-arrow key.

To run the completed query, click the Run Query button, press F8, or select **Q**uery **R**un. A dialog box displays the progress of the query, and when the query is complete, the answer table displays the selected records (see fig. 12.24).

Fig. 12.24

The answer table displays the query results.

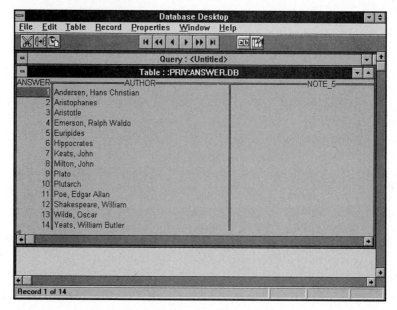

In this case, the answer table shows that the database contains 14 authors with 10 or more book titles. By changing the comparison value and rerunning the query, you can produce different sets of answers.

Sharing Results with Quattro Pro 5.0 for Windows

The Database Desktop stores the current answer in a temporary file called ANSWER.DB in your working directory. You can import this file into a Quattro Pro 5.0 for Windows notebook, but when you do, the imported information is static and is not updated when the database changes. Also, because the Database Desktop always stores the answer table in ANSWER.DB, only the latest answer table is retained. You can use the Windows File Manager to rename ANSWER.DB, but always use the DB file extension so that Quattro Pro 5.0 for Windows can recognize the file as a Paradox database file.

A better way to share database information between the Database Desktop and Quattro Pro 5.0 for Windows is to link the Database Desktop answer table to a Quattro Pro 5.0 for Windows notebook. In this way, the information in your notebook is updated to reflect changes in the database.

To create a link between the Database Desktop answer table and a Quattro Pro 5.0 for Windows notebook, follow these steps:

1. After you run the query and the answer table is generated, select **E**dit Select **A**ll to select all answer table records.

2. Next, select **E**dit **C**opy (or click the Copy button on the SpeedBar) to copy the selected records to the Windows Clipboard.

3. Press Alt+Tab to return to Quattro Pro 5.0 for Windows.

4. Move the cell selector to the upper left cell of the block where you want to add the selected records, and then select **E**dit Paste **L**ink.

> Use caution when selecting the location of the block, because the incoming records overwrite all existing notebook data.

Figure 12.25 shows the notebook after the Edit Paste Link command is executed.

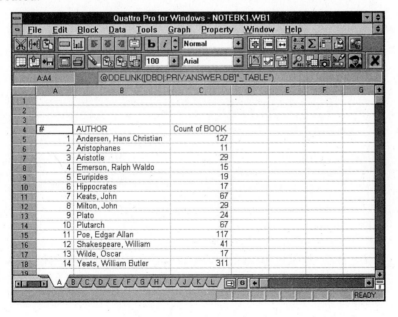

Fig. 12.25

The notebook is linked to the database, using the DDELINK function.

Quattro Pro 5.0 for Windows creates a link by using the following function:

@DDELINK([DBD|:WORK:ANSWER.DB]"_TABLE")

The @DDELINK function uses the following format:

@DDELINK(*source*,[*columns*],[*rows*],[*sheets*])

The *source* argument is the origin of the linked data. The *columns*, *rows*, and *sheets* arguments are optional. These arguments limit the number of columns, rows, or notebook pages used by the linked data.

You also can create a link in the opposite direction so that your notebook provides data to the Database Desktop. You may link a notebook cell to the Query Editor, for example, and enter selection values in this notebook cell. When you change the value, the notebook block that contains the data linked *from* the Database Desktop is updated to reflect the new selection.

To link a Quattro Pro 5.0 for Windows notebook cell to a field in the Database Desktop Query Editor, follow these steps:

1. Place a sample value in the notebook cell, and then select **E**dit **C**opy.

2. Press Alt+Tab to return to the Database Desktop (or use **D**ata **D**atabase Desktop to load the Database Desktop).

3. Select the field in the Query Editor.

4. Select **E**dit Paste **L**ink to create the link.

5. Select **Q**uery **W**ait for DDE to instruct the Database Desktop to run the query whenever the source notebook cell is changed.

6. Press Alt+Tab to return to the Quattro Pro 5.0 for Windows notebook.

Whenever you change the data in the cell linked to the Database Desktop, the query executes and updates the answer table. If the notebook is linked to the answer table as shown in figure 12.25, the notebook also is updated.

Using DDE links between Quattro Pro 5.0 for Windows and the Database Desktop, you can create complete database applications that enable notebook users to select exactly the group of records they want to view. Because you are working with the data in a Quattro Pro 5.0 for Windows notebook, you can use the Object Inspectors to control the complete range of properties for the displayed data.

Joining Tables

Two primary kinds of databases exist. The first, a *flat-file* database, is completely contained in a single file; all database fields and records are in this one file.

Relational databases split information into two or more smaller files, which are related in some way. One file, for example, may contain customer records, another file may contain inventory records, and a third file may detail sales orders. The customer file and the order file are related because both contain information on customers. The customer file has the detailed customer information, while the order file probably has a field that shows the customer ID for each order. Similarly, the inventory and order files are related, with the inventory file containing detailed information on each item in stock, while the order file probably has a field for only the part number.

Relational databases usually are more efficient than flat-file databases at tracking complex information because each file in a relational database is fairly small and is quickly searched and updated. The overall size of a relational database also is usually smaller, because less information has to be repeated.

The Database Desktop can handle both kinds of databases with ease. To create a relational database query, you open the different database tables (files) that make up the relational database, and then indicate how to join (relate) the files. The answer table can contain any combination of fields from the related database tables. In the following example, you see how to join two database tables, but you can have several different related tables in a relational database. To join two of the sample database files, follow these steps:

1. Select all the related tables after you issue the File New Query command. Select BOOKORD.DB and CUSTOMER.DB, for example, to join these two tables.

    All open database tables then are displayed in the Query Editor.

2. Perform the join by clicking the Join Tables button on the Query Editor SpeedBar and then clicking the related fields in the two tables. An *example element*—a variable or placeholder that represents the values in the field—is placed in the field. By default, the first example element used to join tables is EG01, the second is EG02, and so on.

Figure 12.26 shows the Query Editor after BOOKORD.DB and CUSTOMER.DB are joined by using the Cust and Cust ID fields of the files.

Fig. 12.26

Joining database tables by using example elements.

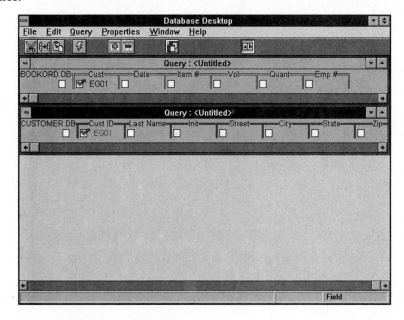

To join fields by using the keyboard, select the fields, press F5, and enter the example element.

After you join database tables, you can query the tables as though both were a single table. You can create a query, for example, that shows the date of each order and the address of the customer who placed the order. You also can restrict the query to include only certain records, such as orders over a specified amount.

Using Table Query

After you create a query by using the Database Desktop Query Editor, you can save and then run the query from within Quattro Pro 5.0 for Windows, using the **D**ata **T**able Query command. You can, for example, create and refine a database query, and then use macros to execute your fully developed query from within a notebook application.

To save a query for reuse, either within the Database Desktop or in a Quattro Pro 5.0 for Windows notebook, follow these steps:

1. Select **F**ile **S**ave or **F**ile Save **A**s when the Database Desktop Query Editor is active.

2. Enter a name for the query, but do not specify an extension. The extension QBE is used for query files.

3. Select OK to save the query.

To reuse a saved query in the Database Desktop, choose the **F**ile **O**pen **Q**uery command.

Database Desktop queries are saved in text files. You can import a query file into a Quattro Pro 5.0 for Windows notebook block, or you can run the query directly from the QBE file. Figure 12.27 shows a query imported into a notebook and formatted with the Courier font for easy viewing.

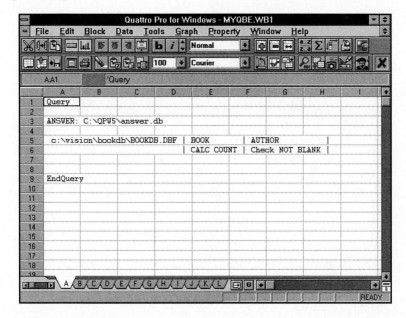

Fig. 12.27

A QBE query imported into a notebook.

To run a saved query from within a Quattro Pro 5.0 for Windows notebook, follow these steps:

1. To display the Table Query dialog box shown in figure 12.28, select **D**ata **T**able Query.

2. Select Query in **F**ile to execute a query in a QBE file, or Query in **B**lock to execute a query that you previously imported into a notebook block.

3. If you select Query in **F**ile, specify the name of the QBE file. If you select Query in **B**lock, specify the notebook block that contains the query.

4. Specify the **D**estination—the upper left corner of the notebook block where you want to place the database records.

5. Select OK to confirm the dialog box and execute the query. Figure 12.29 shows the result of running the query.

Fig. 12.28

The Table Query dialog box.

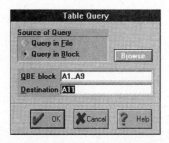

Fig. 12.29

The result of running the table query.

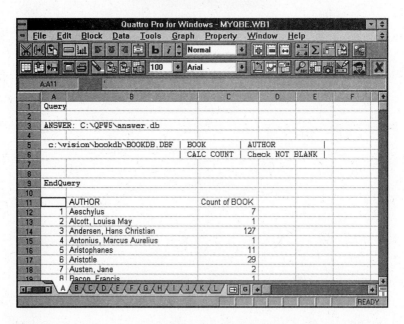

Although you cannot use the Database Desktop to create new databases, you can use this tool to access existing databases and to create queries. After you create a query, you can use DDE links to make sure that your Quattro Pro 5.0 for Windows application always has the latest data. You also can save queries and then execute them using macros. These features enable you to use the Database Desktop as a tool for creating more powerful Quattro Pro 5.0 for Windows applications that feature easy access to dBASE and Paradox database files.

Questions and Answers

Q: Why do the field names move when I sort my database?

A: You included the field name row in the data sort block. Don't forget that all rows in the data sort block are sorted and that the database block has one more row than the data sort block.

Q: Why does a blank row appear below the field names when I sort my database?

A: You highlighted an extra row below the last row of data. When you used **D**ata **S**ort, the empty row was sorted into the first position. Make sure you only include the actual rows you want to sort when you specify the data sort block.

Q: I need to find all the records in my database that have a value in a numeric field greater than the average of the values in the field. How can I find these records?

A: Use a formula of the form +*field_value*>@AVG($*all_values_in_field*). Make certain to use an absolute reference for the comparison values. For example, suppose that cell A2 has the field name SCORES and the records are contained in rows 3 through 20. Your criteria formula would be

> **+SCORES>@AVG($A$3..$A$20)**

Q: I know my database contains records that match my selection criteria, but I still get a message `No records match criteria`. What's wrong?

A: There are several possible reasons for receiving this message. It may be possible that no records really match your selection criteria. Check your selection criteria carefully.

You may have a misspelled field name in the criteria table or in a criteria formula. You may be trying to match numeric entries with a label criteria or a label entry with a numeric criteria.

Finally, check the **D**atabase Block specified in the Query dialog box. If a block is highlighted after you select **D**ata **Q**uery, it replaces the existing **D**atabase Block.

Summary

This chapter introduced the basics of Quattro Pro 5.0 for Windows database management. It showed you how to create and manage databases in a notebook. You learned the terms that define a Quattro Pro 5.0 for Windows database. You also learned how to create and modify a notebook database, sort data records, and to locate, extract, and delete data records. In addition, you learned how to access large external database files using the Database Desktop feature.

The next chapter expands on Quattro Pro 5.0 for Windows database management by showing you how to use advanced data management features.

Understanding Advanced Data Management

In addition to basic database management, Quattro Pro 5.0 for Windows has powerful features that enable you to perform advanced data management tasks. These capabilities enable you to work with data tables, analyze data frequency distribution, perform data regression analysis, multiply and invert matrices, and import data from other programs.

Many of the functions this chapter describes are highly specialized. Not long ago, performing these calculations required the services of very expensive, stand-alone programs or many hours of manual problem solving. Quattro Pro 5.0 for Windows makes it easy to perform advanced data analysis quickly.

This chapter shows you how to accomplish the following:

- Create and use data tables
- Use a frequency distribution to analyze your data
- Perform regression analysis

■ Use matrix arithmetic to invert and multiply matrices

■ Load data from ASCII files and other programs

In addition to the advanced data management techniques discussed in this chapter, you will also want to consider the new analysis tools and Experts which are covered in Chapter 17, "Using Analysis Tools and Experts." These new features make it even easier to use the power of Quattro Pro 5.0 for Windows to perform sophisticated and complex data analysis functions.

Creating Data Tables

TIP

Data what-if tables work with variables whose values you estimate.

Data what-if tables enable you to work with variables whose values are unknown. In many notebook models, the variables your formulas use are known quantities. For example, a sales summary deals with variables whose exact values are known. As a result, calculations performed using those values contain no uncertainties. Other notebook models, however, involve variables whose exact values are unknown. Models for financial projections often fall into this category. For example, next year's cash flow projection may depend on prevailing interest rates or other variable costs. You can make an educated guess at what costs may be, but you cannot predict them exactly.

With the **D**ata **W**hat-if commands, you can create tables that show how the results of formula calculations vary as the variables used in the formulas change. Quattro Pro 5.0 for Windows can show you the results of changing one variable in a problem or the combined effect of changing two variables simultaneously.

Here's a common example. You decide to purchase a new home that requires a mortgage loan. Area banks offer you several combinations of loan periods and interest rates. You can use a what-if table to calculate your monthly payment with each combination of period and interest rate. You also can use a what-if table to produce a table showing the principal and interest portion of each payment and the outstanding loan balance after each payment is made.

TIP

Use **D**ata **W**hat-if to analyze database information in cross-tabulation tables.

Another function of the **Data What-if** commands is to create *cross-tabulation tables.* A cross-tabulation table provides summary information categorized by unique information in two fields, such as the total amount of sales each sales representative makes to each customer.

The following sections show you how to use the **Data What-if** commands to perform "sensitivity" or "what if" analyses and to cross-tabulate information in what-if tables. First, however, you need to understand some terms and concepts.

General Terms and Concepts

A *what-if table* is an on-screen view of information in a column format with the field names at the top. A what-if table contains the results of a **Data What-if** command plus some or all of the information used to generate the results. A *what-if table block* is a notebook block that contains a what-if table.

A *variable* is a formula component whose value can change.

An *input cell* is a notebook cell used by Quattro Pro 5.0 for Windows for temporary storage during calculation of a what-if table. One input cell is required for each variable in the what-if table formula. The cell addresses of the formula variables are the same as the input cells.

An *input value* is a specific value that Quattro Pro 5.0 for Windows uses for a variable during the what-if table calculations. As Quattro Pro 5.0 for Windows calculates the what-if table results, the input values are substituted into the formulas as the values of the input cells.

The *results area* is the portion of a what-if table where the calculation results are placed. One result is generated for each combination of input values. The results area of a what-if table must be unprotected, as discussed in Chapter 5.

Do not use logical formulas such as +A1>A2 in what-if tables.

CAUTION

The formulas used in what-if tables can contain values, strings, cell addresses, and functions. You should not use logical (or Boolean) formulas because this type of formula always evaluates to 0 or 1. Using a logical formula in a what-if table does not cause an error, but the results generally are meaningless.

The Two Types of What-If Tables

After you select **D**ata **W**hat-if, the What-If dialog box appears, as shown in figure 13.1.

Fig. 13.1

The What-If dialog box.

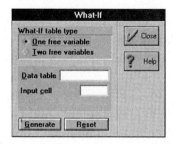

The Table selections correspond to the two kinds of what-if tables that Quattro Pro 5.0 for Windows can generate. These two table types differ in the number of formulas and variables each table can contain. Following are the two table types:

Data **W**hat-if **O**ne free variable   One or more formulas with one variable

Data **W**hat-if **T**wo free variables   One formula with two variables

CAUTION

What-if tables aren't recalculated when notebook data changes. To reflect the results of changed data, you must reissue the **D**ata **W**hat-if **G**enerate command.

Creating a What-If One-Variable Table

A what-if table created with the **D**ata **W**hat-if **O**ne free variable command shows the effects of changing one variable on the results of one or more formulas. Before using this command, you must set up the what-if table block and one input cell.

TIP

Label the input cell to provide notebook documentation.

The *input cell* can be a blank cell anywhere in the notebook. The best practice is to identify the input cell by entering an appropriate label above the input cell or to the left of the input cell. Quattro Pro 5.0 for Windows does not require that you label the input cell, but the documentation a label provides is valuable for understanding how the what-if table is calculated.

The what-if table block is a rectangular notebook area and can be placed in any empty notebook location. The size of the what-if table block can be calculated using the following information:

- The block has one more column than the number of formulas being evaluated.

- The block has one more row than the number of input values being evaluated.

The general structure of a what-if block is shown in the following listing:

- The top left cell in the what-if table block is empty.

- The formulas to be evaluated are entered across the first row. Each formula must refer to the input cell.

- The input values to be plugged into the formulas are entered down the first column.

- After the what-if table is calculated, each cell in the results block contains the result obtained by evaluating the formula at the top of that column with the input value at the left of that row.

Suppose, for example, that you plan to purchase a house with a 25-year mortgage of $100,000 and a 9.25 percent interest rate. For each monthly payment, you want to determine the interest and principal portions of the payment and the balance remaining.

For this example, you can use cell B5 as the input cell and identify it with the label *Period* in cell A5. You also need to add the following labels and data:

Cell	Label	Data
A2	**Principal**	**100000**
A3	**Term**	**25**
A4	**Rate**	**0.0925**

After you enter the labels in cells A2 through A5, highlight the label block and use the **B**lock **N**ames **L**abels **R**ight command to assign block names to cells B2 through B5.

Next, add one formula for each item you want to calculate. Enter the following formulas:

Cell	Formula
B11:	@PPAYMT($RATE/12,PERIOD,$TERM*12,-$PRINCIPAL)
C11:	@IPAYMT($RATE/12,PERIOD,$TERM*12,-$PRINCIPAL)
D11:	@PAYMT($RATE/12,$TERM*12,-$PRINCIPAL)
E10:	+$PRINCIPAL
E11:	+E10-B11

Because payments are monthly, each annual interest rate is divided by 12 to get the monthly interest rate. The term of the loan is in years, so the term is multiplied by 12 to get the term in months.

Next, enter the payment numbers down column A starting in A12. Use **B**lock **F**ill **B**locks to set the fill block to A12..A311, change Start to 1, and click OK or press Enter. This places the values 1 through 300, the payment numbers, down the column.

Finally, enter the following labels to document the what-if table:

Cell	Label
A9	Payment
A10	Number
B9	Principal
C9	Interest
D9	Total
E9	Balance

The what-if scenario is ready to go. Select **D**ata **W**hat-if, specify **A:A11..E311** as the Data Table, and enter **A:B5** as the Input cell **1**. Figure 13.2 shows the completed notebook and What-If dialog box.

Select **G**enerate. Quattro Pro 5.0 for Windows calculates the results and places them in the what-if table. Click Close or press Enter to confirm the dialog box and return to the notebook. The resulting table, which calculates the mortgage payments, is shown in figure 13.3.

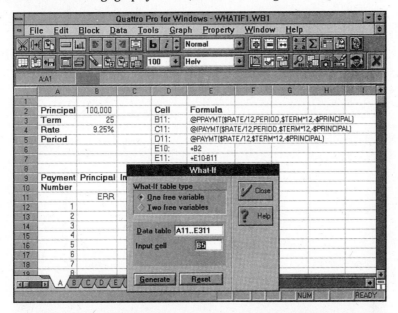

Fig. 13.2

The completed notebook and What-If dialog box for the mortgage calculations.

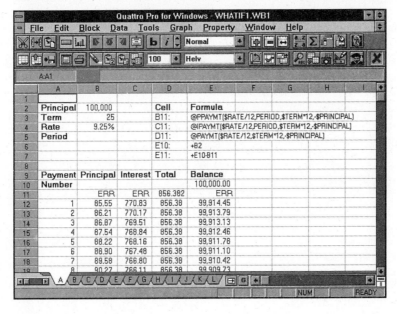

Fig. 13.3

The results of selecting **D**ata **W**hat-If **G**enerate to calculate mortgage payments.

TIP

Hide the what-if table formula row before printing the table.

In figure 13.3, the results area, cells B12 through E311 have been formatted as Comma, 2 decimal places. The formulas in row 11, however, have not been formatted to show that several of the formulas return ERR because they refer to the empty input cell, B5. Before printing the table, you may want to format cells B11..E11 using **H**idden numeric format or set the row height for row 11 to zero to prevent the ERR values from appearing in the printed table.

You can use **D**ata **W**hat-if **O**ne free variable to calculate many other types of information as well, as long as each formula is related to the variables located down the first column of the what-if table.

Creating a One-Variable Cross-Tabulated Table

TIP

Use **D**ata **W**hat-if **O**ne free variable to analyze database information in a cross-tabulation table.

You also can use**D**ata **W**hat-if **O**ne free variable with a database to create a cross-tabulation table. This type of analysis requires an input cell that can be anywhere in the notebook. For a cross-tabulation analysis, the cell immediately above the Input cell must contain the name of the what-if table field on which the analysis is based. (It might be easier to think of the Input cell as similar to a criteria table. The Input cell is where Quattro Pro 5.0 for Windows substitutes the unique values as it evaluates the formulas.)

NOTE

Quattro Pro 5.0 for Windows has a powerful new tool, the Data Modeling Desktop, which performs very flexible cross tabulation analysis of data. Chapter 18, "Using the Data Modeling Desktop," shows you how to use this exciting new tool to easily examine the many possible relationships contained in your data.

The structure of a what-if table block for a cross-tabulation analysis is similar to the structure for a what-if analysis. The upper left cell may be empty, and the top row contains the formula(s) that are to be evaluated. In most cases, these formulas contain one or more database functions.

> Cross-tabulation what-if tables use the values in the left column as selection criteria.

TIP

The left column of the what-if table block again contains input values. Rather than representing values that are plugged directly into the formulas, however, the input values for a cross-tabulation analysis are the values or labels that you can use as *criteria* for the analysis.

After the what-if table has been calculated, each cell in the results block contains the result of the formula at the top of the column. This formula has been applied to those database records that meet the criteria at the left of the row.

Imagine, for example, that you keep an address list showing customers in many different states. To help you understand where you get most of your business, and therefore, where you should plan to spend your advertising dollars, you need to total the number of customers and the amount of business you receive from each state. The database that handles this application is shown in figure 13.4.

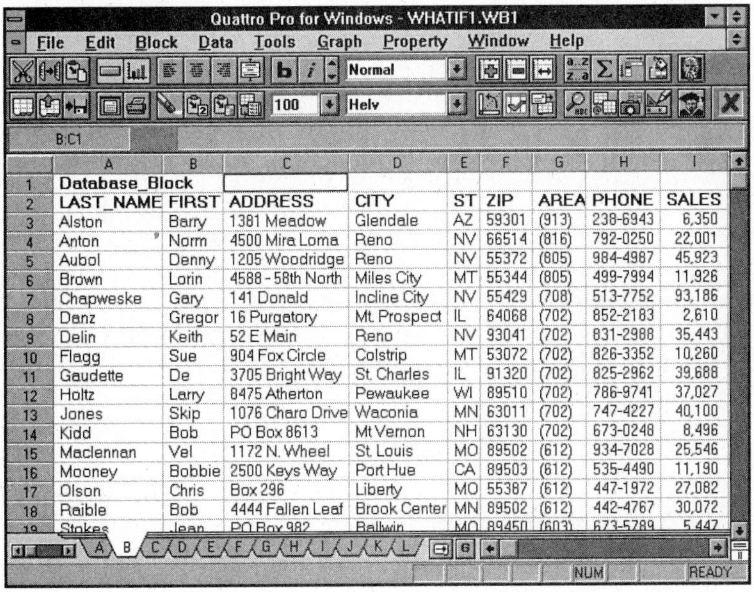

Fig. 13.4

A customer database showing sales in different states.

	A	B	C	D	E	F	G	H	I
1	Database_Block								
2	LAST_NAME	FIRST	ADDRESS	CITY	ST	ZIP	AREA	PHONE	SALES
3	Alston	Barry	1381 Meadow	Glendale	AZ	59301	(913)	238-6943	6,350
4	Anton	Norm	4500 Mira Loma	Reno	NV	66514	(816)	792-0250	22,001
5	Aubol	Denny	1205 Woodridge	Reno	NV	55372	(805)	984-4987	45,923
6	Brown	Lorin	4588 - 58th North	Miles City	MT	55344	(805)	499-7994	11,926
7	Chapweske	Gary	141 Donald	Incline City	NV	55429	(708)	513-7752	93,186
8	Danz	Gregor	16 Purgatory	Mt. Prospect	IL	64068	(702)	852-2183	2,610
9	Delin	Keith	52 E Main	Reno	NV	93041	(702)	831-2988	35,443
10	Flagg	Sue	904 Fox Circle	Colstrip	MT	53072	(702)	826-3352	10,260
11	Gaudette	De	3705 Bright Way	St. Charles	IL	91320	(702)	825-2962	39,688
12	Holtz	Larry	8475 Atherton	Pewaukee	WI	89510	(702)	786-9741	37,027
13	Jones	Skip	1076 Charo Drive	Waconia	MN	63011	(702)	747-4227	40,100
14	Kidd	Bob	PO Box 8613	Mt Vernon	NH	63130	(702)	673-0248	8,496
15	Maclennan	Vel	1172 N. Wheel	St. Louis	MO	89502	(612)	934-7028	25,546
16	Mooney	Bobbie	2500 Keys Way	Port Hue	CA	89503	(612)	535-4490	11,190
17	Olson	Chris	Box 296	Liberty	MO	55387	(612)	447-1972	27,082
18	Raible	Bob	4444 Fallen Leaf	Brook Center	MN	89502	(612)	442-4767	30,072
19	Stokes	Jean	PO Box 982	Ballwin	MO	89450	(603)	673-5789	5,447

To analyze the customer database, begin by creating a criteria table and an output block. Take advantage of the three-dimensional nature of the Quattro Pro 5.0 for Windows notebook and place the criteria table and output block on a separate page where they do not affect the existing database block.

To begin creating this model, copy the database field names from the top row of the database block to a blank area on an unused page. This page is where you place the criteria table. In this example, copy B:A2..I2 to C:A2. Create an output block to which you have Quattro Pro 5.0 for Windows extract a unique list of states. In this case, enter **ST** in cell C:A11. After creating the output block, use **D**ata **Q**uery commands to enter the following blocks:

Block	Address	Or Block Name
Database Block	**B:A2..I26**	**DATABASE_BLOCK**
Criteria Table	**C:A2..I3**	**CRITERIA_TABLE**
Output Block	**C:A11**	**OUTPUT_BLOCK**

TIP

Create a unique list of database values for what-if analyses using **D**ata **Q**uery Extract **U**nique.

Select **D**ata **Q**uery Extract **U**nique to create a unique list of states from the database in the output block. The output block is used as the left column of the what-if cross-tabulation table. After the list of states has been extracted, click OK or press Enter to confirm the Data Query dialog box and return to the notebook.

Next, enter the formulas that calculate the number of customers in each state and the total value of orders for each state. These formulas are placed in the top row of the what-if cross-tabulation table and use database functions to analyze the data based on the values in the first column of the table. As Quattro Pro 5.0 for Windows calculates each row's results, the value in the first column is used as the criteria value.

In cell C:B11, enter the following formula that calculates the number of customer records for each state:

@DCOUNT(DATABASE_BLOCK,0,CRITERIA_TABLE)

In cell C:C11, enter the formula that totals the sales for each state:

@DSUM(DATABASE_BLOCK,8,CRITERIA_TABLE)

Select **Data** **What-if** **D**ata table and specify **C:A11..C21** as the what-if table block. Select Input **c**ell and specify **C:E3** (the ST field in the criteria table) as the cell where Quattro Pro 5.0 for Windows substitutes the values from the first column of the what-if table. The dialog box now looks like figure 13.5.

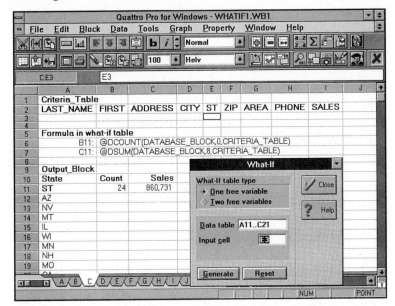

Fig. 13.5

The completed What-If dialog box.

Select **G**enerate to generate the cross-tabulation table. Click Close or press Enter to confirm the dialog box and return to the notebook. Select the block C12..C21, point to the block, click the right mouse button, and change the numeric format to C**o**mma, 0 decimals for easier reading. The notebook now appears as shown in figure 13.6.

TIP

Quattro Pro 5.0 for Windows analyzes database records if the what-if table uses database functions.

As the two preceding examples demonstrate, you can use **Data** **W**hat-if **O**ne free variable to produce a table of results using a column of values directly in formulas or as criteria to select database records for analysis. Quattro Pro 5.0 for Windows determines the type of analysis you are requesting by whether the formulas you include are database functions.

Fig. 13.6

The completed cross-tabulation table helps analyze database information.

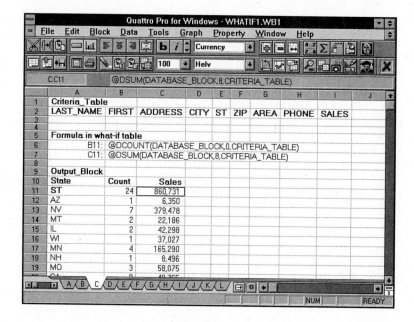

Creating a What-If Two-Variable Table

The what-if two-variable table enables you to evaluate one formula based on changes in two variables. To use **Data W**hat-if **T**wo free variables, you need two blank input cells, one for each variable. The cells can be located anywhere in the notebook and need not be adjacent to each other. The input cells can be identified with an appropriate label in a cell next to or above each input cell.

The size of the what-if table block depends on the number of values of each variable you want to evaluate. The block is one column wider than the number of values of one variable and one row longer than the number of values of the other variable.

TIP

The formula for a what-if two-variable table must be in the upper left corner of the table.

A major difference between **Data W**hat-if **O**ne free variable and **Data W**hat-if **T**wo free variables is the location of the formula to be evaluated. In **Data W**hat-if **O**ne free variable, the formulas are placed along the top row of the table, and the upper left corner is usually blank. With

Data What-if Two free variables, the upper left cell of the what if table block contains the formula to be evaluated. This formula must refer to the input cells.

The cells below the formula contain the various input values for one variable. These values are used for the **Column** input cell. The cells to the right of the formula contain the various input values for the other variable. These values are used for the **Row** input cell. Be sure that the formula correctly refers to the two input cells so that the proper input values are input into the correct part of the formula.

After the what-if table is calculated, each cell in the results block contains the result of evaluating the formula with the input values in that cell's row and column.

Suppose, for example, that you want to create a what-if table that shows the payments on a new car loan of $15,000. To allow the greatest flexibility, you want to know what effect interest rates between 8 percent and 13.5 percent and payment periods of 12 to 72 months have on your monthly payment. A what-if two-variable table easily can show you this broad range of options.

Use descriptive labels to document the input cells.   **TIP**

Decide on a location for the two input cells. You can use cells B2 and B3. For documentation purposes, place identifying labels in the adjacent cells A2 and A3. In this case, use **Interest rate** as the label in A2 and **Term** as the label in A3. If you prefer, you can use the less descriptive labels **Column Input** and **Row Input**.

Because you have twelve values of one variable and six values of the other, the what-if table block is 13 rows by 7 columns in size. You can use the block A5..G17. Enter the following @PMT formula in cell A5:

@PMT(15000,B2/12,B3)

Next, enter the values in the what-if table block. Enter the interest rates in the block A6..A17 and the loan terms in B5..G5. The easiest method for entering these incrementing values is to use the **Block Fill** command. For example, to enter the interest rates, highlight A6..A17 and select **Block Fill**. Select **Start** and enter **8%**. Select **Step** and enter **.5%**. Click OK or press Enter to confirm the dialog box and fill the block. To improve the appearance of the table, format A6..A17 as **Percent**, 1 decimal. You also can use **Block Fill** to enter the loan terms in B5..G5.

Now, highlight A5..G17 and select **Data What-if**. The **Data** table should show A:A5..G17. Select **Two** free variables. Enter **B2** as the **Column** input cell and enter **B3** as **R**ow input cell. Select **Generate**. Quattro Pro 5.0 for Windows calculates the what-if table, as shown in figure 13.7. Click Close or press Enter to confirm the dialog box and return to the notebook.

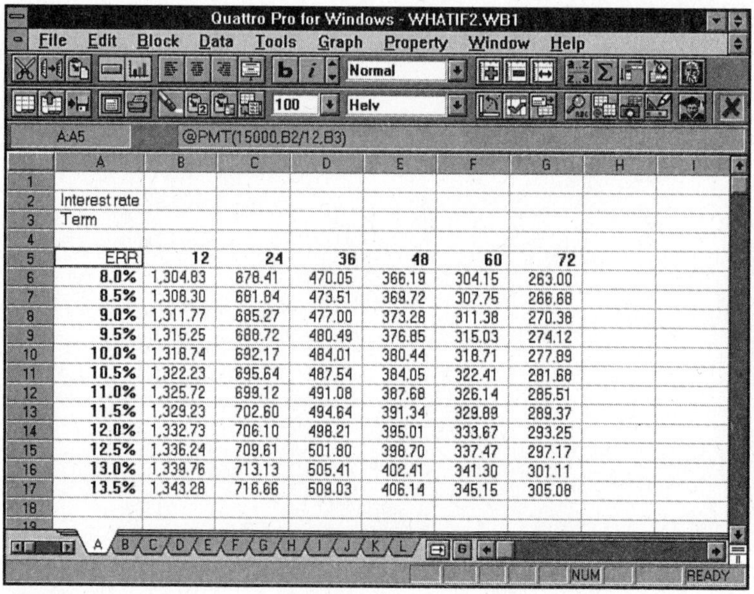

Fig. 13.7

The completed table of loan payment amounts created with **D**ata **W**hat-if 2 Way Table.

Quattro Pro for Windows screen showing WHATIF2.WB1

	A	B	C	D	E	F	G	H	I
1									
2	Interest rate								
3	Term								
4									
5	ERR	12	24	36	48	60	72		
6	8.0%	1,304.83	678.41	470.05	366.19	304.15	263.00		
7	8.5%	1,308.30	681.84	473.51	369.72	307.75	266.68		
8	9.0%	1,311.77	685.27	477.00	373.28	311.38	270.38		
9	9.5%	1,315.25	688.72	480.49	376.85	315.03	274.12		
10	10.0%	1,318.74	692.17	484.01	380.44	318.71	277.89		
11	10.5%	1,322.23	695.64	487.54	384.05	322.41	281.68		
12	11.0%	1,325.72	699.12	491.08	387.68	326.14	285.51		
13	11.5%	1,329.23	702.60	494.64	391.34	329.89	289.37		
14	12.0%	1,332.73	706.10	498.21	395.01	333.67	293.25		
15	12.5%	1,336.24	709.61	501.80	398.70	337.47	297.17		
16	13.0%	1,339.76	713.13	505.41	402.41	341.30	301.11		
17	13.5%	1,343.28	716.66	509.03	406.14	345.15	305.08		
18									

TIP

Format the formula cell as **H**idden to improve the appearance of the what-if table.

To further improve the appearance of the table before printing, format the results area using **C**omma, 2 decimal places, as shown in figure 13.7. Also, you may want to apply **H**idden format to the formula cell, A5, to prevent ERR from displaying.

TIP

Use **W**indow **L**ocked Titles to freeze the input values on-screen.

If you create a what-if table larger than the screen, you can use **Window Locked Titles** to freeze the input values (the top row and left column of the what-if table) on-screen as you scroll through the result cells.

Creating a Two-Variable Cross-Tabulated Table

You can use a **D**ata **W**hat-if **T**wo free variables table to create a cross-tabulation analysis of records in a what-if table. A two-variable cross-tabulation analysis requires a criteria table that has two blank input cells which can be anywhere in the notebook as long as they are in adjacent columns of the same row. The cell immediately above each input cell must contain the name of the database field for which that input cell serves as a criterion.

The structure of a what if table block for a two-variable cross-tabulation analysis is similar to that for a what-if two-variable analysis. The upper left cell contains the formula to be evaluated, and the formula must use a database function. The criteria block argument should refer to the two input cells and the field names above the cells. The top row and left column contain the values or labels that are used as criteria when database records are selected for the formula calculations. The contents of the cells in the left column of the what-if table block are used as criteria in the **C**olumn input cell, and the contents of the cells in the top row of the what-if table block are used as criteria in the **R**ow input cell. Be sure that the what-if table block input values correspond correctly with the input cells; otherwise, the analysis produces erroneous results.

Suppose that you want to create the two-variable cross-tabulation table shown in figure 13.8. To create a what-if table showing each sales representative's total sales of each item, you need a what-if two-variable table that is cross-tabulated based on the NAME and ITEM fields of the database table. Use cells E2 and F2 for the input cells, and place the field names above them in cells E1 and F1. For accuracy, copy the field names from the database.

Next, create the what-if table block. Down the first column of the block you need a listing of each sales representative's name. To create this list, enter the field name **NAME** in cell E10. Select **D**ata **Q**uery **D**atabase Block and enter the address of the database block, in this case **B:A1..C15**. Select **C**riteria Table and enter **B:E1..F2**. Select **O**utput Block and specify **B:E10**. Finally, select Extract Unique to create the column of names. Click OK or press Enter to confirm the dialog box and return to the notebook. The top row of the what-if table block must contain the names of the individual items from the ITEM field. You can type the item names, copy them from the database, or use another **Data Query Extract Unique** command to create a unique list that you then must place across the row. Enter the following formula in cell E10:

@DSUM(A1..C15,2,E1..F2)

The criteria for the **C**olumn input cell (the input cell under NAME) are the sales representatives' names. For the **R**ow input cell, the criteria are the items.

The next step is to select **D**ata **W**hat-if **T**wo free variables and specify E10..I14 as the **D**ata table, E2 as the **C**olumn input cell, and F2 as the **R**ow input cell. Select **G**enerate, and Quattro Pro 5.0 for Windows analyzes the data, placing the results in the what-if table. The results are shown in figure 13.8.

TIP

Include an extra column in the what-if table as a summary column.

Notice in figure 13.8 that the what-if table block includes one additional column to the right of the last item in the top row. By including an extra column (or an extra row), you tell Quattro Pro 5.0 for Windows to calculate the table formula using only one of the input values. In this case, for example, column I shows the total sales for each sales representative. If the table block had included an extra row below the list of names, sales for each item would have been totaled in the extra row.

◄◄ "Filling Blocks," p. 173.

◄◄ "Extracting a Unique Set of Records," p. 442.

FOR RELATED INFORMATION

Creating Frequency Distributions

The command for creating frequency distributions in Quattro Pro 5.0 for Windows is the **D**ata **F**requency command. A *frequency distribution* describes the relationship between a set of data classes and the frequency of occurrence of each class's members. Frequency distribution is used, for example, to show how much production varies from the norm. Statistical process control uses frequency distribution to show how well a production line is performing.

A list of measurements showing plus or minus variations from the nominal dimension illustrates the use of the **D**ata **F**requency command to produce a frequency distribution, as shown in figure 13.9. In this example, 20 samples, each measuring 7 pieces, are compiled. The manufacturer wants to know how far average production varies from the specified product dimensions.

To use the **D**ata **F**requency command, you first specify the Value Block(s), which correspond to the block of sample measurements in this example. After specifying **A:B2..H21** for the **D**ata **F**requency Value Block(s), you set up the block of intervals at A:J3..J13, in what Quattro Pro 5.0 for Windows calls the **D**ata **F**requency **B**in Block. If you have evenly spaced intervals, you can use the **B**lock **F**ill command to enter the values for the **B**in Block. If the intervals are not evenly spaced, you cannot use the **B**lock **F**ill command to fill the block. Figure 13.10 shows the completed Frequency Tables dialog box.

> The results column is always one row longer than the **B**in Block.   **TIP**

After you specify these blocks and click OK or press Enter, Quattro Pro 5.0 for Windows creates the results column (K3..K14) to the right of the **B**in Block (J3..J13). The results column, which shows the frequency distribution, is always in the column segment to the right of the **B**in Block and extends down an additional row.

Fig. 13.9

Data Frequency used to
analyze production
sampling data.

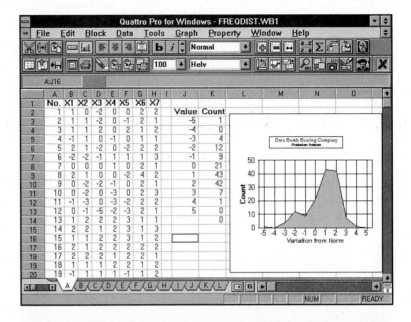

Fig. 13.10

The completed
Frequency Tables
dialog box.

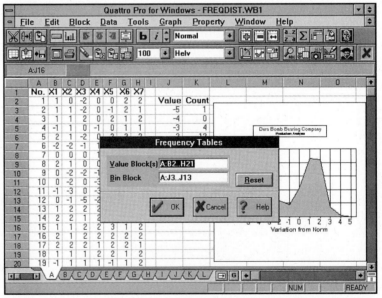

The values in the results column represent the frequency of distribution of the numbers in the Value Block(s) for each interval. The first interval in the Bin Block is for values less than or equal to the first value you specify; the second interval is for values greater than the first value you specify and less than or equal to the next value in the **B**in Block, and so on. The last value in the results column, in cell K14, shows the frequency of leftover numbers (the frequency of numbers larger than the highest specified value).

The **D**ata **F**requency command can help you create understandable results from a series of numbers. The results are graphed easily, as shown in figure 13.9. A manufacturer looking at this graph probably would feel that production was staying fairly close to design specifications. Figure 13.9 shows the data plotted as an area graph (use A:J3..J13 for the X graph block and A:K3..K13 for the first data block).

| **FOR RELATED** | **INFORMATION** |

◄◄ "Setting Up Graphs," p. 319.

◄◄ "Filling Blocks," p. 173.

Using the Tools Advanced Math Commands

The **T**ools **A**dvanced Math commands enable you to perform specialized mathematical analyses. Most Quattro Pro 5.0 for Windows users never have to use regression analysis, matrix inversion, or matrix multiplication. Most people don't need these advanced features; however, if you do need to use them, Quattro Pro 5.0 for Windows saves you the cost and inconvenience of buying stand-alone packages for performing these calculations.

Using the Tools Advanced Math Regression Command

TIP

Use **T**ools **A**dvanced Math **R**egression to determine the relationship between sets of values.

The **T**ools **A**dvanced Math **R**egression command gives you a multiple linear regression analysis package within Quattro Pro 5.0 for Windows. Use **T**ools **A**dvanced Math **R**egression when you want to determine the relationship between one set of values (the dependent variable) and one or more other sets of values (the independent variables). Regression analysis has a number of uses in a business setting, including relating sales to price, promotions, and other market factors; relating stock prices to earnings and interest rates; and relating production costs to production levels.

Think of linear regression as a way of determining the "best" line through a series of data points. Multiple regression accomplishes this for several variables simultaneously, determining the "best" line relating the dependent variable to the set of independent variables. Consider, for example, a data sample showing parts produced versus hours worked. Figure 13.11 shows the data, and figure 13.12 shows the data plotted as an XY graph (use A4..A14 for the X graph block and B4..C14 for the first graph block).

Fig. 13.11

Hours worked versus production data.

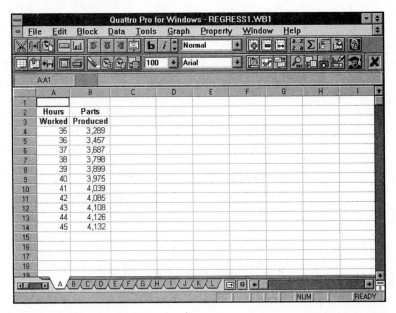

The Tools Advanced Math Regression command simultaneously can determine how to draw a line through these data points and how well the line fits the data. When you invoke the command, the Linear Regression dialog box shown in figure 13.13 appears.

Use the Independent text box to specify one or more independent variables for the regression. The Tools Advanced Math Regression command can use several independent variables, but they must be in adjacent columns. The variables in the regression are columns of values, which means that any data in rows must be converted to columns with **B**lock **T**ranspose before the **T**ools **A**dvanced **M**ath **R**egression command is issued. In this example, the **I**ndependent variables are specified as **A4..A14**.

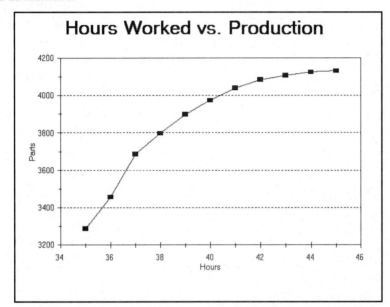

Fig. 13.12

A graph of hours worked versus production data.

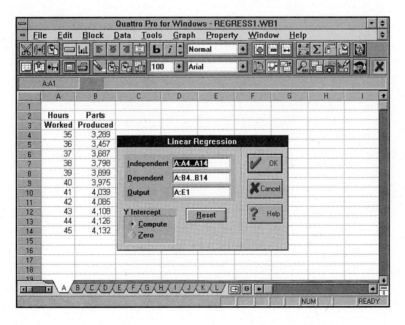

Fig. 13.13

The Linear Regression dialog box.

The **D**ependent text box specifies the dependent variable. The dependent variable must be in one column (in this example, **B4..B14**).

The **O**utput text box specifies the upper left corner of the results block. This should be an unused section of the notebook because the output is written over any existing cell contents. In this example, **E1** was specified as the output block.

The Y Intercept field enables you to specify whether you want the regression to calculate a constant value. Calculating the constant is the default; in some applications, however, you may need to exclude a constant. Select **C**ompute to allow Quattro Pro 5.0 for Windows to calculate the Y Intercept or **Z**ero to force it to use a Zero Y Intercept. **C**ompute is the default.

Figure 13.14 shows the results of using the **T**ools **A**dvanced Math **R**egression command in the hours worked versus production example. The results (in cells E1..H9) include the value of the constant and the coefficient of the single independent variable. The results also include many regression statistics that describe how well the regression line fits the data.

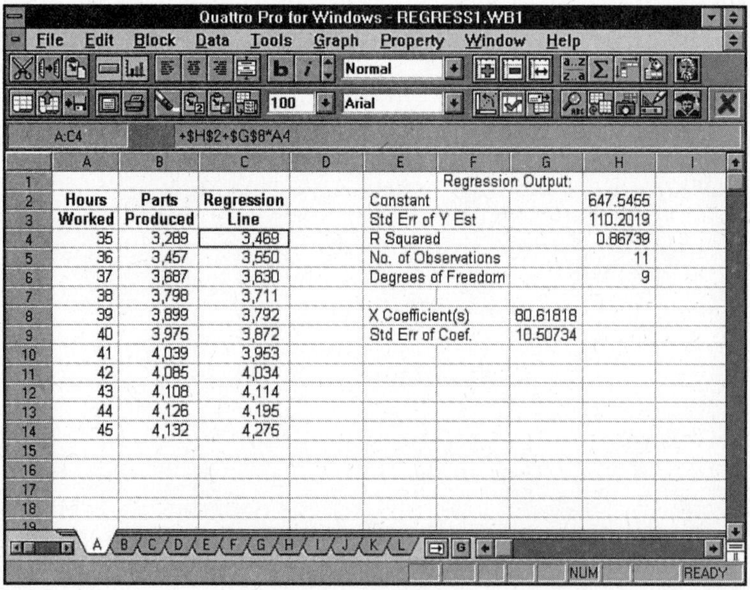

Fig. 13.14

The results of **T**ools **A**dvanced Math **R**egression on hours worked versus production data.

The new data in column C is the computed regression line. These values consist of the constant plus the coefficient of the independent variable multiplied by its value in each row of the data. To calculate the regression line, enter the formula +$H$2+$G$8*A4 in cell C4. Then copy the formula from C4 to C5..C14. This line can be plotted against the original data as graph block B, as shown in figure 13.15.

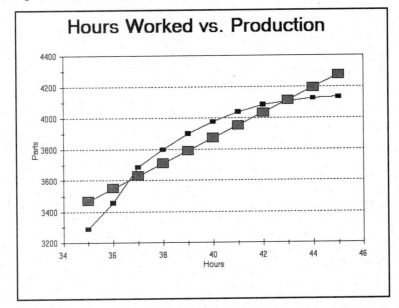

Fig. 13.15

A plot of hours worked versus production data, with a regression line.

> **TIP**
>
> Quattro Pro 5.0 for Windows does not automatically recalculate regression tables.

When you are working with **Tools Advanced Math Regression**, keep in mind that the results in the **Output** block are static values, and Quattro Pro 5.0 for Windows does not update them automatically if your data changes. To make certain you are working with the most recent values, including the calculated regression line, reissue the **Tools Advanced Math Regression** command before using the data in a critical analysis.

Using the Tools Advanced Math Invert and Multiply Commands

The **Tools Advanced Math Invert** and **Tools Advanced Math Multiply** commands are specialized mathematical commands that enable you to solve systems of simultaneous linear equations and manipulate the resulting solutions. These commands are powerful but have limited application in a business setting. If you are using Quattro Pro 5.0 for Windows for certain types of economic analyses or for scientific or engineering calculations, you may find these commands valuable.

TIP

A matrix must be square to be inverted.

The **Tools Advanced Math Invert** command enables you to invert a nonsingular square matrix of up to 90 rows and columns.

The **Tools Advanced Math Multiply** command enables you to multiply two rectangular matrices together in accordance with the rules of matrix algebra. The number of columns in the first matrix must equal the number of rows in the second matrix. The result matrix has the same number of rows as the first matrix and the same number of columns as the second matrix.

Normally, you use the **Tools Advanced Math Invert** and **Tools Advanced Math Multiply** commands together to solve problems. The following example shows how to combine the two commands to solve simultaneous systems of equations.

Suppose an airplane flies from airport 1 to airport 2, a distance of 630 kilometers, in exactly 3 hours. After a brief stop, the plane returns to airport 1 but requires 3.5 hours to travel. To complicate matters, imagine that the wind speed doubles between the first and second trips. The problem you must solve is to determine the air speed of the plane and the speed of the wind during each leg of each trip.

To solve this problem algebraically, you can use the following equations:

x = air speed of plane in still air
y = wind speed leg one
$2y$ = wind speed leg two

Therefore:

$x+y$ = ground speed leg one = 630/3 = 210 kph
$x-2y$ = ground speed leg two = 630/3.5 = 180 kph

You can now create the matrix problem for Quattro Pro 5.0 for Windows to solve. Figure 13.16 shows a notebook model created to solve this problem.

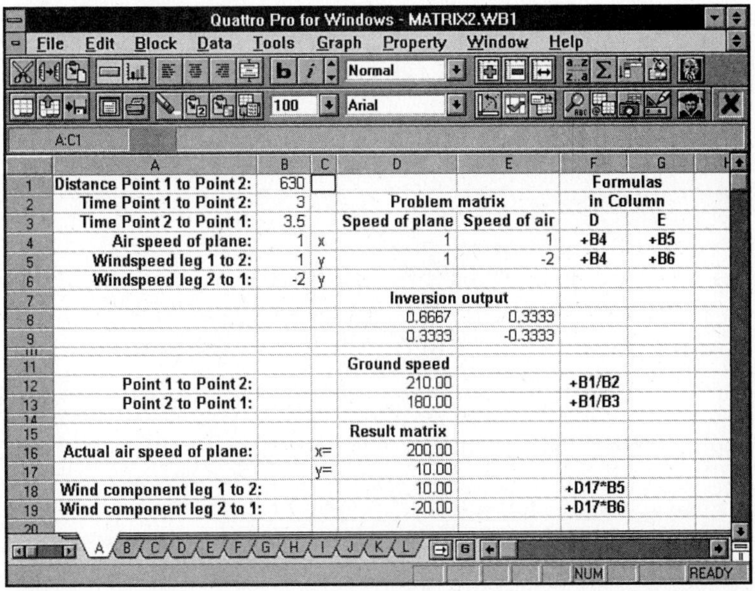

Fig. 13.16

Using **T**ools **A**dvanced Math **I**nvert and **T**ools **A**dvanced Math **M**ultiply to solve simultaneous equations.

In this figure, cells A1..B6 are used to describe the problem. Cells D4..E5 hold the matrix you want to invert. The matrix you invert contains the coefficients of the two equations you want to solve, x+y and x-2y. The labels above and to the right of the problem matrix serve as documentation and are not part of the problem.

To begin solving the problem, select **T**ools **A**dvanced Math **I**nvert. Select **S**ource and specify **D4..E5**. Select **D**estination and specify **D8**. The Matrix Invert dialog box now looks like figure 13.17. Click OK or press Enter to perform the inversion.

Next, you must multiply the inversion matrix by the distance matrix to determine the values of x and y. Select **T**ools **A**dvanced Math **M**ultiply. Select **M**atrix 1 and specify **D8..E9**. Select **M**atrix 2 and specify **D12..D13**. Select **D**estination and specify **D16**. The completed Matrix Multiply dialog box now appears as shown in figure 13.18. Click OK or press Enter to perform the multiplication.

The result matrix shows that *x* has a value of 200 and *y* has a value of 10. Therefore, the airplane has an airspeed of 200 kilometers per hour, the wind speed on the first leg is 10 kilometers per hour, and the wind speed on the second leg is 20 kilometers per hour.

Fig. 13.17

The completed Matrix
Invert dialog box.

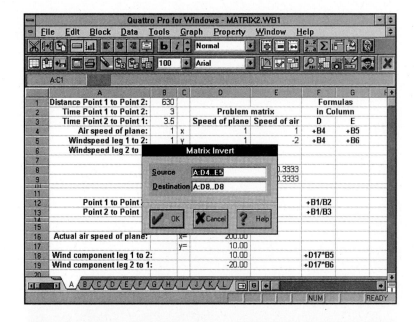

Fig. 13.18

The completed Matrix
Multiply dialog box.

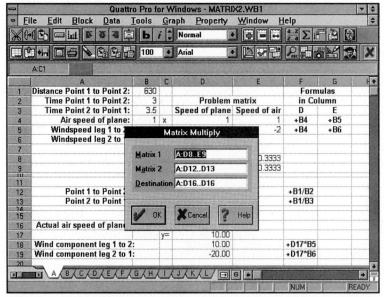

TIP

Quattro Pro 5.0 for Windows can solve matrix problems faster if you
have a math coprocessor.

Quattro Pro 5.0 for Windows can solve much larger systems of simultaneous linear equations, but because these problems can be quite complex, a math coprocessor may be a good investment if you need to solve these kinds of problems on a regular basis.

Importing Data from Other Programs

Quattro Pro 5.0 for Windows provides several means of importing data from other applications. You can access data directly in many different spreadsheet and database file formats by using the **File Open** or **File Retrieve** commands (see Chapter 8). You also can import data from many other Windows applications using **Edit Paste**, **Edit Paste Link**, and **Edit Paste Format** (see Chapter 5).

Sometimes, however, you want to import data created by a program that does not support a format Quattro Pro 5.0 for Windows can read directly and is not a Windows application. Data produced by a mainframe computer is seldom saved in a PC spreadsheet or database file format, for example. In these cases, you must use another Quattro Pro 5.0 for Windows capability: the capability to import data from a text file. The following sections show you how to import several different types of text files and how to convert them into notebook data Quattro Pro 5.0 for Windows can use.

Using the Tools Import Command

Use the **Tools Import** command to read data stored on disk as a text file into the current notebook. Depending on the format, these files can be read directly to a block of cells or a column of cells. Specially formatted "numeric" data can be read directly to a block of notebook cells. ASCII text can be stored as long labels in one column with one line of data per cell. You then must disassemble these labels into the appropriate data values or fields by using functions or the **Data Parse** command. You can also use the **Tools Import Parse Expert** command to combine the functions of importing and parsing text files. The **Tools Import Parse Expert** command is discussed in "Using the Parse Expert," later in this chapter.

TIP

Text files whose lines are too long to import using **T**ools **I**mport can be read using advanced macro commands, such as Read.

You also can use certain advanced macro commands (see Chapter 15) to read and write an ASCII sequential file directly from within Quattro Pro 5.0 for Windows advanced macro command programs. In some cases, a text file contains lines that are too long (over 1022 characters) for the Tools Import command to handle. These types of files can only be imported using advanced macro command programs.

Quattro Pro 5.0 for Windows can import three different types of ASCII text files using the **T**ools **I**mport command. Table 13.1 shows the three types of files and explains how the files differ.

Table 13.1 Types of ASCII Text Files Quattro Pro 5.0 for Windows Can Import

Type	Description
Nondelimited	Lines of text that are not broken down into individual data items
Comma and " delimited	Lines of text with commas between fields and labels surrounded by quotes
Comma only delimited	Lines of text with commas between fields

TIP

Use the Windows Courier typeface to display ASCII text in a fixed space font.

Figure 13.19 shows how these three different types of ASCII text files appear. For clarity, the data is displayed using a Courier 10-point typeface—a fixed space Windows font. Using fixed space fonts is important when importing ASCII text because these fonts make judging the character strings within text strings easier.

To import an ASCII text file, follow these steps:

1. Move the cell selector to a blank area of the notebook. Incoming text overwrites existing data, so it's usually a good idea to use a new, blank notebook page for the imported text.

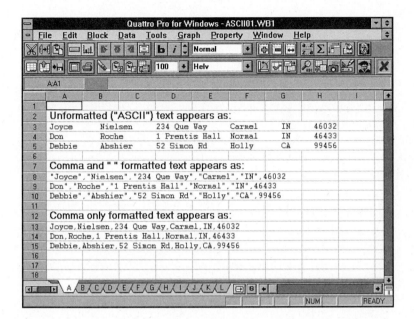

Fig. 13.19

Three types of ASCII text.

2. Select **Tools** Import. The Import File dialog box, shown in figure 13.20, appears.

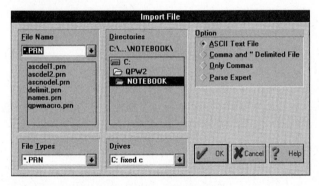

Fig. 13.20

The Import File dialog box.

3. If the ASCII text file you want to import is not in the current directory or not in the current drive, make the appropriate entries in the **Directories** and **Drives** fields.

4. By default, Quattro Pro 5.0 for Windows offers to import text from files with a PRN extension. If necessary, you can select another type of file in the File **Types** list box or simply enter a wild card (such as ***.TXT**) in the **File** name list box. Once the correct files are displayed, select the name of the file to import.

5. In the Option field, select the type of ASCII text file to import. Refer to figure 13.19 and table 13.1 to determine the type of file. If you are unable to determine which type of file you are importing, select **A**SCII Text File to import the file without regard to delimiters. After examining the imported data, you can decide whether you should attempt to reimport the file using a different selection.

6. Click OK or press Enter to confirm the dialog box and import the data. Figure 13.21 shows how each of the three types of text files appear after being imported using the appropriate Option selection.

Fig. 13.21

ASCII text after being imported using **T**ools **I**mport.

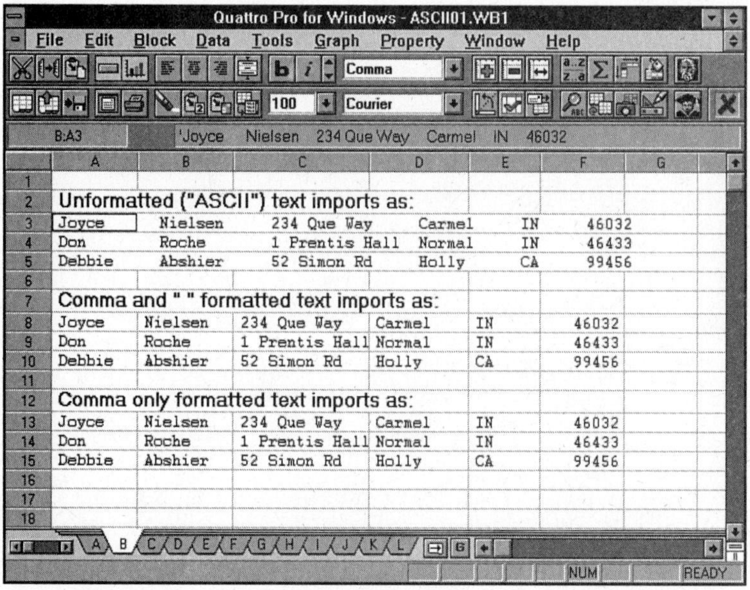

Delimited text is imported in a different manner than nondelimited text. As figure 13.21 shows, nondelimited text is imported as long labels that are placed in the first column of the block where the cell selector was located before **T**ools **I**mport was selected. Delimited text, on the other hand, is placed into individual cells. Each line of delimited text is placed in one row, but each delimited field within the line is placed in the cell to the right of the last field.

TIP

Nondelimited text usually must be processed with **D**ata **P**arse to be useful.

Because nondelimited text is imported as long labels in one column, you usually must process further such data before it is useful in a Quattro Pro 5.0 for Windows notebook. The next section describes the **Data Parse** command designed to help you break down nondelimited, imported text into useful data.

Using the Data Parse Command

> **TIP**
>
> Use **D**ata **P**arse to split long labels imported from text files into separate text, number, or date fields.

The **Data Parse** command is a flexible and easy method of extracting numeric, string, and date data from long labels and placing the data in separate columns. For example, suppose that you downloaded a disk file containing inventory data from your company's mainframe computer, and you want to load the ASCII file in Quattro Pro 5.0 for Windows. After you load the file by using the **Tools Import** command, you must reformat the data with the **Data Parse** command.

> **NOTE**
>
> The **D**ata **P**arse command does not require the use of a fixed space font, such as Courier, for proper operation but the examples of the **D**ata **P**arse command in this chapter use Courier 10 point for clarity. Quattro Pro 5.0 for Windows can create a format line and parse data properly regardless of the font used, but the examples are easier to understand if a proportional font is not used.

The **Tools Import** command loads the data into the block A2..A4, as shown in figure 13.22. Visually, the data is formatted in a typical note-book block, such as A2..H4, but the display is misleading. The current cell selector location is A2; the entire contents of the row exist only in that cell as a long label.

To break the long label columns, follow these steps:

1. Move the cell selector to the first cell to be parsed and select **Data Parse**. The Data Parse dialog box appears.

2. Select the Input text box and specify the column of labels. In this example, specify **A2..A4**.

Fig. 13.22

The results of a **T**ools **I**mport command.

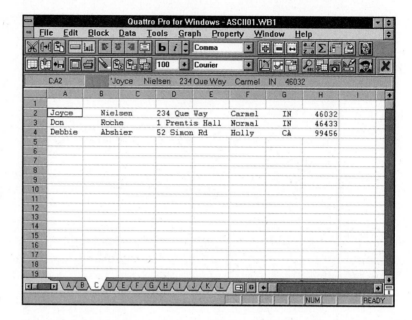

3. Select **O**utput and specify a cell below the last row of labels. In this example, specify **A10**.

4. Select **C**reate. Quattro Pro 5.0 for Windows inserts a new row at the top of the block you specify in the **I**nput text box and places a proposed format line in the new row. The format line is used to determine how the parsed data is broken down into individual fields. The notebook now appears as shown in figure 13.23.

In some cases, Quattro Pro 5.0 for Windows is unable to determine the correct field breakdown because multiple data items belong in one field. In figure 13.23, for example, the format line shows a V at the beginning of the address field, indicating the start of a numeric (or Value) field. Also, the format line proposes to break the address field into three separate data fields. In this case, you must edit the format line to correctly reflect the data being parsed. Table 13.2 shows the symbols you use in a format line.

Table 13.2 Special Symbols in Data Parse Format Lines

Symbol	Purpose
		Begins a format line
V	Begins a value (numeric) field

Symbol	Purpose
L	Begins a label field
T	Begins a time field (data must appear as a time serial number)
D	Begins a date field (data must appear as a date serial number)
>	Continues a field
*	Continues a field (used to indicate blanks that may be part of the same field)
S	Skips the character in the current position

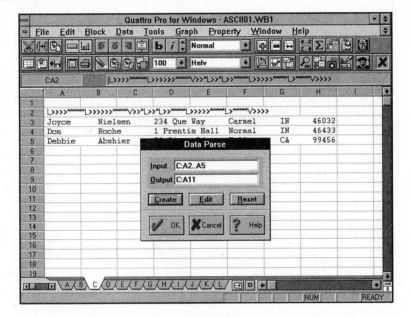

Fig. 13.23

The notebook after the proposed format line is inserted.

To edit the proposed format line, follow these steps:

1. If you click OK or press Enter to return to the notebook, select **D**ata **P**arse to return to the Data Parse dialog box.

2. Select the Input text box and specify the block containing the format line and the data to be parsed. Remember, the block is now one row longer than before due to the insertion of the format line. In this example, specify **A2..A5**.

3. Select **E**dit. The Edit Parse Line dialog box appears as shown in figure 13.24.

Fig. 13.24

The Edit Parse Line
dialog box.

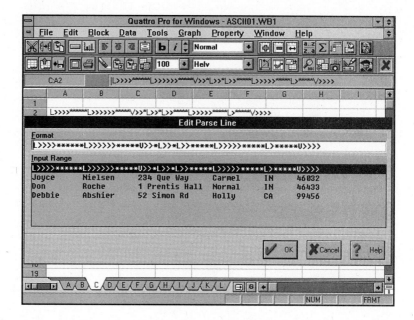

4. In the text box, edit the format line to reflect the data correctly, which is shown in the following line:

   L>>>>******L>>>>>>*****V>>*L>>*L>>*****L>>>>>*****L>*****V>>>>

   In this case, change the line to the following:

   L>>>>******L>>>>>>*****L>>>>>>>>>>*****L>>>>>*****L>*****V>>>>

   The Edit Parse Line dialog box now appears as shown in figure 13.25.

5. Click OK or press Enter to return to the Data Parse dialog box. To parse the data and return to the notebook, click OK or press Enter again. Figure 13.26 shows how Quattro Pro 5.0 for Windows breaks down the data into individual field entries in separate cells.

TIP

After using **D**ata **P**arse, adjust column widths to display the parsed data properly.

In figure 13.26, the cell selector is moved to cell C11 to show that even though the cell width is currently too narrow to display the entire contents of the field (234 Que Way), the data still is placed in the cell. After you use **D**ata **P**arse, you may want to adjust column widths to display the parsed data properly.

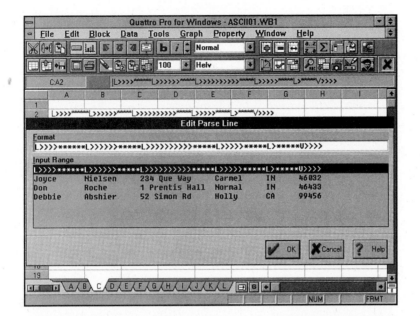

Fig. 13.25

The changed format line in the Edit Parse Line dialog box.

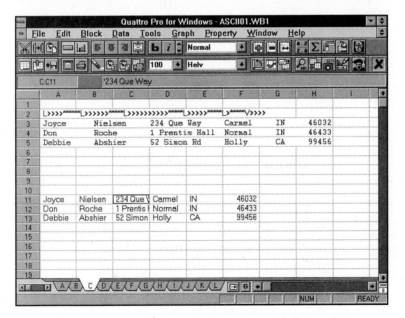

Fig. 13.26

The imported data after being parsed.

To create a Quattro Pro 5.0 for Windows database from the parsed data, add field names to the row above the parsed data.

TIP

If you want to save parsed data in another format, move the data to the top page of the notebook first.

Once you have imported and parsed ASCII text, you can save the data in any format Quattro Pro 5.0 for Windows supports. Be careful, however, when you save data in formats other than Quattro Pro 5.0 for Windows notebook or 1-2-3 Release 3.x (WK3). When you save files in one of the other formats supported by Quattro Pro 5.0 for Windows, only the top page of the notebook is saved. Be sure you move the parsed data to the top notebook page before saving the notebook in another format.

Using the Parse Expert

Instead of first importing ASCII text files and then parsing them, you can often use the **Tools Import Parse** Expert command to import and parse the file in one step. You may, in fact, want to try this command before you use one of the other options for importing a text file, because the Parse Expert can save considerable time and effort.

Figure 13.27 shows the result of using the **Tools Import Parse** Expert command to import and parse the text file shown in the previous examples. In this case, the Parse Expert was able to correctly identify each of the fields, and to separate the entries into individual columns. The Parse Expert was also able to adjust most of the column widths to correctly display the data. The only remaining manual task is to adjust the width of column F which holds the ZIP entries.

FOR RELATED INFORMATION

▶▶ "Using the Advanced Macro Commands," p. 542.

◀◀ "Defining a Database," p. 414,

◀◀ "Importing Text Files," p. 287.

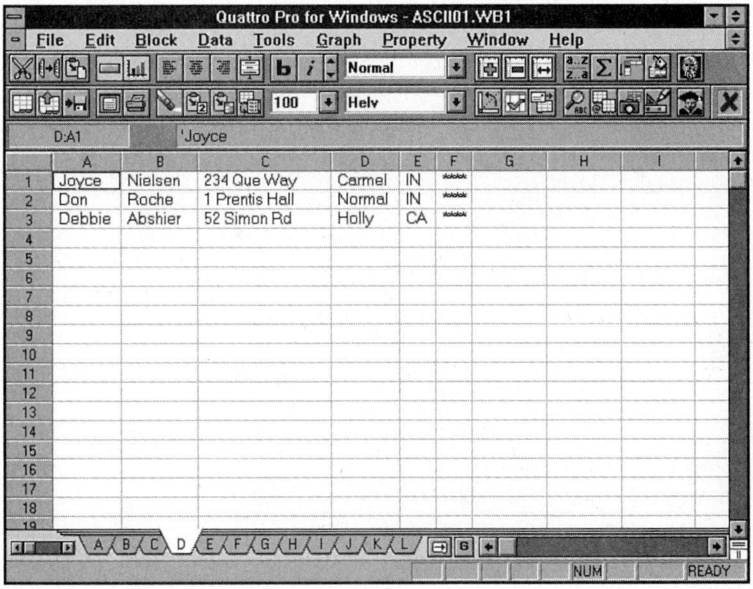

Fig. 13.27

The Parse Expert imports and parses text files in one step.

Questions and Answers

Q: My what-if table doesn't recalculate when I change data in the notebook. What's wrong?

A: What-if tables contain calculated data, not formulas, so they don't change when notebook data is changed. Either reissue the **D**ata **W**hat-If command to create an updated version of the table, or create a table containing formulas instead of a what-if table. If you create a table containing formulas, it will automatically be updated to reflect changes in the notebook.

Q: Although I can use the charts created by regression analysis, I'm not enough of an expert to be certain my figures are accurate. Isn't there an easier way to chart these types of trends?

A: If you don't require full-blown regression analysis, you may want to consider using analytical graphing instead (see Chapter 10, "Creating Presentation Graphics"). If your application does require this type of in-depth analysis, you may want to ask the Analysis Tools Experts for assistance (see Chapter 17, "Using Analysis Tools and Experts").

Q: How can I use the airspeed example with different data?

A: Make certain you create the model using the formulas shown in the figures. If you include these formulas, changing the problem to match new data is as simple as adjusting the variables in B1..B6, and then reissuing the **T**ools **A**dvanced Math **I**nvert and **T**ools **A**dvanced Math **M**ultiply commands.

Q: The text file I want to import contains several lines of extra information at the beginning of the file. How can I import this file?

A: First, use **T**ools **I**mport ASCII Text File to import the file. Next, move the cell selector down to the first row of actual data, and begin the parse block at that row, skipping the header information.

Don't forget, though, that Quattro Pro 5.0 for Windows can open many types of files, including both dBASE and Paradox files, without the extra steps involved in importing and parsing the file. If you can open the file directly, you will save quite a little time and effort.

Summary

This chapter addressed the advanced data management capabilities of Quattro Pro 5.0 for Windows. **D**ata **W**hat-If, **D**ata **F**requency, **T**ools **A**dvanced Math **R**egression, **T**ools **A**dvanced Math **I**nvert, **T**ools **A**dvanced Math **M**ultiply, and **D**ata **P**arse manipulate data and can be used in database or notebook applications.

Data management is one of the advanced capabilities of Quattro Pro for Windows. If you have mastered data management, you are a true "power user," and you probably already are using Quattro Pro for Windows macros. If not, be sure to continue your learning. Chapter 14 presents the creation and use of keyboard macros, and Chapter 15 introduces you to the powerful advanced macro commands.

Customizing Quattro Pro for Windows

PART

V

OUTLINE

Understanding Macros

You can use the Quattro Pro 5.0 for Windows spreadsheet, graphics, and database capabilities without ever using macros. You may feel that these three components provide all the functions you need. Quattro Pro 5.0 for Windows macros, however, provide a convenient method of automating many tasks that you repeat each time you use the program.

Quattro Pro 5.0 for Windows has two categories of macros. This chapter covers the first category, the simple command macros that you easily can create and use. The more advanced macro commands, which perform many of the functions of programming languages, such as BASIC, C, or COBOL, are covered in the following chapter. Don't worry if you've never written programs; the concepts covered in this chapter are simple and easy to understand.

Specifically, this chapter covers the following subjects:

- Defining a macro
- Developing and writing a simple macro
- Understanding command equivalents
- Guidelines for creating macros
- Creating macros by recording keystrokes
- Finding and avoiding errors in macros

Defining a Macro

A *macro* is a set of instructions that tells Quattro Pro 5.0 for Windows how to perform a task. The simplest macros are just short collections of keystrokes that duplicate an action you perform by pressing a series of keys, such as retrieving a file or formatting a cell. More complex macros may use advanced macro commands, but complex macros still are no more than instructions that tell Quattro Pro 5.0 for Windows how to perform a task.

As you use Quattro Pro 5.0 for Windows, consider how many times you repeat the same operations. You retrieve notebook files, print reports, enter text, and set numeric formats. Often, these tasks require a long series of keystrokes that you must repeat every time you use Quattro Pro 5.0 for Windows. By creating and running a macro, however, you can reduce a long series of keystrokes to a two-keystroke abbreviation.

A simple, straightforward example of a keystroke macro is one that enters text, such as your company name or your address. If you count the number of keystrokes required to enter this information at several locations in a notebook, you can easily see the advantage of simply pressing two keys to instruct Quattro Pro 5.0 for Windows to type the entry for you. If you create this type of macro, you only have to press the Ctrl key and the letter key you assign to the macro, and Quattro Pro 5.0 for Windows types the text entry for you—you don't have to retype the entire entry when you want to include the same label in your notebook. Macros that you execute in this manner—pressing Ctrl plus a letter key—are called Ctrl+*letter* macros. Later in this chapter, you learn to create this type of macro.

You name a Ctrl+*letter* macro by using the backslash key (\) and one letter of the alphabet. Previous versions of Quattro Pro (and Lotus 1-2-3) called these macros Alt+*letter* macros (or *instant macros*). Windows applications, however, usually reserve the Alt key for invoking the main menu, so the Ctrl key replaces the Alt key for starting macros named with the backslash key (\) and a letter.

The Ctrl+*letter* method is not the only way to name a macro. You learn about other methods for naming macros later in this chapter.

Developing Your Own Macros

The steps for creating any macro are simple. The steps outlined in this section show you the basic procedure, but the following sections expand on these steps. To create any Quattro Pro 5.0 for Windows macro, perform these steps:

1. Plan what you want the macro to accomplish. Write down all the tasks the macro will perform in the order that the tasks are to be completed.

2. Identify the keystrokes that you want the macro to enter. Write down each keystroke you enter as you manually step through the task.

3. Determine where you want the macros located. Macros execute instructions from the top cell of the macro and work down through lower cells. A macro ends when a blank cell, a cell with a numeric value, or a command that stops execution is reached. Consider placing macros on a separate notebook page. You learn how to place macros in a separate macro library notebook in a later section.

4. Enter the macro keystrokes, command equivalents, and commands into a cell or successive cells down one column. Be sure all cells in a macro contain labels or string formulas.

5. Name the macro in one of two ways:

   ■ Assign the macro a Ctrl+*letter* name, which consists of a backslash (\) followed by a character, such as \q.

   ■ Choose a descriptive name, such as CLEAN_UP, for a macro.

6. Document the macro.

> **NOTE**
>
> Always use block names rather than cell addresses in macros. Because you enter macros as labels in a notebook, cell addresses in macros do not adjust when you rearrange the notebook. Macros that use block names rather than cell addresses, however, refer to the correct locations even if the block has been moved.

Good planning and clear documentation of macros are always important. As the macros become more complex, you should continue to follow these same basic steps when creating macros.

Writing a Macro That Enters Text

In this section, you learn to create a macro that enters text in various locations in a notebook. The example uses a company name, *Darlene's Computer Warehouse, Inc.,* but you can easily substitute your name or your company's name in the exercises.

Before you begin creating a macro, plan what you want the macro to accomplish and identify the keystrokes the macro is to enter. With the macro that enters a company name in the notebook, you want the macro to enter the letters, spaces, and all punctuation included in the name. Then you want the macro to complete the entry by pressing Enter (or performing the equivalent action).

You begin building the macro by storing the keystrokes as text in a notebook cell. After entering the name, you complete the entry by adding a tilde (~), which in a macro is the equivalent of pressing Enter.

Cell B3 in figure 14.1 contains the keystrokes that you want to use as part of the macro:

```
Darlene's Computer Warehouse, Inc.~
```

Fig. 14.1

A simple macro for entering a company name.

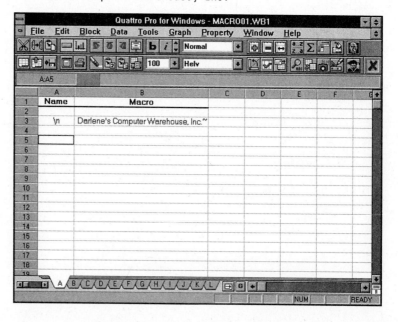

The tilde (~) is included at the end of the line. Remember that the tilde represents the pressing of the Enter key, which is an important step in ensuring that the macro executes correctly. Forgetting to include the tilde to complete an entry is a common mistake that often occurs during macro creation.

For better visibility, you can set the width of column B to include all the macro keystrokes, as shown in figure 14.1. The macro functions correctly, however, whether or not you adjust the column width. As you learn more about naming macros, you may find that setting the width of the column holding the macro names (here, column A) to 15 is helpful. Macro names, like other Quattro Pro 5.0 for Windows block names, can hold up to 15 characters, so setting the column width to 15 may provide a useful clue.

The next step in writing the macro is naming this sequence of keystrokes as a macro. The step is optional with Quattro Pro 5.0 for Windows because you can run macros whether or not the macros are named. You can execute any Quattro Pro 5.0 for Windows macro by using the Run Macro dialog box you access through the **Tools Macro Execute** command. Naming, however, makes a macro easier to run, especially if you name the macro with the backslash (\) and one letter (also known as Ctrl+*letter*). Naming macros also helps give each macro a convenient form of self-documentation.

> **TIP**
>
> Don't forget to place the apostrophe (') before the backslash so that Quattro Pro 5.0 for Windows recognizes the macro name as a label.

In this section, you learn to use the Ctrl+*letter* method of naming macros. In a following section of this chapter a second, more descriptive method of naming macros is covered.

The Ctrl+*letter* method of naming macros is convenient when the macro name is located in the column to the left of the macro keystrokes, like the name \n shown in figure 14.1. To name a macro by using this method, take the following steps:

1. Move the cell selector to the cell that contains the macro name. Here, move the cell selector to cell A3.

2. Select the **Block Names Labels** command, as shown in figure 14.2. The Create Names From Labels dialog box appears, as shown in figure 14.3.

Fig. 14.2

The **B**lock **N**ames **L**abels command used for naming a macro.

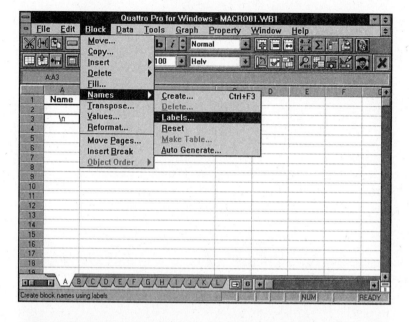

Fig. 14.3

The Create Names From Labels dialog box.

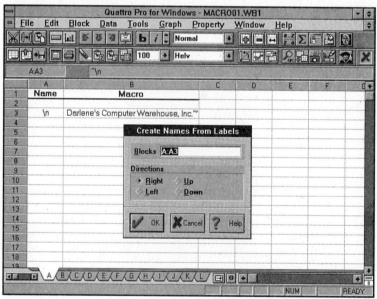

3. From the dialog box, select **R**ight as the direction of the adjacent cell to which you apply the name. This action assigns the name in cell A3, \n, to cell B3.

4. Press Enter or click OK.

By placing the macro's name to the left of the first cell of the macro, you document the macro's name. This technique also helps you to quickly remember the macro name for later use.

To *execute,* or run, this macro, move the cell selector to the cell in which you want the name to appear, hold down the Ctrl key, and press N. Quattro Pro 5.0 for Windows enters the sequence of characters identified as the macro \n.

Figure 14.4 shows the result of moving the cell selector to B10 and running the \n macro. The macro executes the same set of keystrokes regardless of the position of the cell selector. If you move the cell selector to a different page, the macro still functions in the same way.

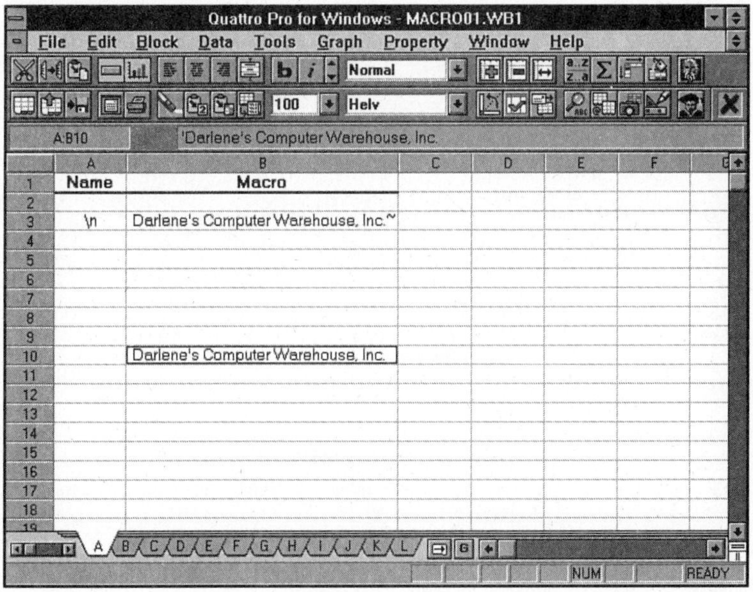

Fig. 14.4

The result of moving the cell selector to cell B10 and running the \n macro.

Because Quattro Pro 5.0 for Windows macros are contained in a notebook, you must save the notebook if you want to save the macros for future use.

Command Equivalents—A New Macro Language

Because Quattro Pro 5.0 for Windows has a replaceable user interface, the developers were faced with a unique problem. How do you create a macro command language that enables the user to modify or replace the menus and still remain easy to understand, but at the same time reliably performs the same actions regardless of any changes in the menus? The answer is to create a new macro language known as *command equivalents,* which are descriptive commands that function regardless of which menu is active.

Even if you remove the **F**ile commands from the menu, for example, you still need a way to save your work. Command equivalents provide the full set of commands usually available on the Quattro Pro 5.0 for Windows menus, and these commands are clear and easy to understand. Even if you have no interest in learning the advanced macro commands covered in Chapter 15, the Quattro Pro 5.0 for Windows command equivalents are easy to understand because the command equivalents look so much like the Quattro Pro 5.0 for Windows command menus.

The following sections show examples of simple command equivalent macros.

Understanding Command Equivalent Addressing

Quattro Pro 5.0 for Windows has two methods you can use to include block addresses in macros. Use the first method, *absolute addressing,* to show cell addresses (such as A:A1..B5) or to show block names (such as SALES_TOTAL). Absolute addressing has the advantage of being clear and easy to understand.

Unfortunately, absolute addresses always refer to the same addresses, making it difficult to create general-purpose macros that perform common tasks at any location. The second method of including block addresses in macros, *relative addressing,* enables you to create macros that function regardless of the current cell selector location. Relative addressing specifies addresses as an offset from the current cell selector location, using the following format:

$$[]P(pn):C(cn)R(rn)$$

The [] refers to the active notebook. If you do not include [], the relative reference refers to a cell offset from the cell containing the macro command, not the cell selector. Next, *pn* is the number of pages, plus or minus, from the cell selector. For macro actions that affect the current page, the P(*pn*): argument is optional.

The *cn* argument specifies the number of columns, plus or minus, from the cell selector. Finally, *rn* specifies the number of rows, plus or minus, from the cell selector.

If the cell selector is in A:A1 and you want the macro to perform some action on cell C:D3, use **[]P(2):C(3)R(2)**. If you want the macro to affect the current cell, enter **[]C(0)R(0)**.

When a command equivalent macro command specifies a *block* argument, you can use absolute or relative addressing, depending on the purpose of the macro.

Writing a Simple Command Equivalent Macro

Besides writing macros that repeat text, you can write macros that repeat commands. If you follow the same procedure each time, macro writing quickly becomes second nature. Remember that each command defined in a macro must tell Quattro Pro 5.0 for Windows to perform the same sequence of commands, as though *you* were typing the keystrokes.

Suppose that you want to create a macro that performs a task you perform often, such as naming macros. For this task, you usually enter the following commands:

1. Press the Alt key and select **Block** (or point to **Block** and click the left mouse button) to activate the **Block** menu.

2. Select the **Names** command, and then the **Labels** command to activate the Create Names From Labels dialog box.

3. Select **R**ight to name the cells to the right of the highlighted labels.

4. Click OK to confirm the dialog box.

The Quattro Pro 5.0 for Windows command equivalent for this sequence of steps is:

{BlockName.Labels *block*,Right}

Here, *block* is the label block. Because you want to create a general-purpose macro that uses the currently highlighted labels to name the cells to the right, you want to use relative addressing. The relative address designation for the current cell selector location is []C(0)R(0), so to create this macro, enter the following command in cell B3:

{BlockName.Labels []C(0)R(0),Right}

Move the cell selector to A3 and enter the name for the macro. Here, to make the macro name easy to remember, enter **^\r** (the caret (^) is a centering label prefix, but you can use an apostrophe (') to left align or a quote (") to right align if you prefer).

Because the macro isn't named yet, you cannot run the macro in typical Ctrl+*letter* fashion. You can, however, use the Run Macro dialog box to run the macro—even before naming—and have the macro perform the steps necessary to name itself.

Select **Tools Macro Execute** to display the Run Macro dialog box. Select the **Location** text box and enter **A:B3** as the address of the macro to execute, as shown in figure 14.5.

Fig. 14.5

The Run Macro dialog box.

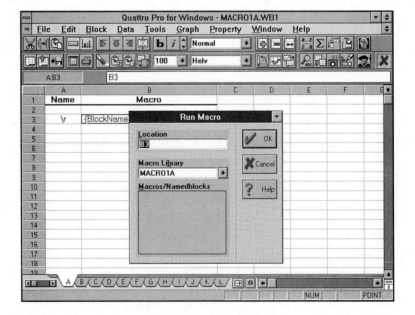

When you select OK to confirm the dialog box and run the macro, the macro in cell A:B3 executes and names itself \r. After you name the \r macro and assign the name to cell A:B3, you can easily use this macro to name other macros. You must first place the cell selector on the label that you enter one cell to the left of a macro's first cell, and then press the keystroke combination Ctrl+R.

Writing a More Complex Command Equivalent Macro

Many commands require only one step, but other Quattro Pro 5.0 for Windows commands require you to enter a series of information. The {BlockName.Labels} macro, for example, requires only one step because you can specify all arguments necessary with one command. Filling a block with incrementing numbers, on the other hand, requires you to specify a series of arguments. The next example shows you how to use the {BlockFill} command equivalent macro commands to fill a block.

The **B**lock **F**ill command can use many different options to fill a notebook block. Suppose that you want to fill a block with dates spaced a month apart, starting with today's date. Quattro Pro 5.0 for Windows can easily accomplish this task, and you can create a command equivalent macro that duplicates the steps. First, however, write down the steps you follow to fill the block when you use **B**lock **F**ill:

1. Select **B**lock **F**ill.

2. Select the **B**lock(s) text box and enter the block to fill. Here, enter **A:C13..C20**.

3. Select St**a**rt and enter the starting value. Here, enter the date serial number for today's date.

4. Select St**e**p and enter the step value. Here, you can use the default value of **1**.

5. Select **S**top and enter the stop value. Here, you can enter a date serial number equal to today's date plus a number large enough to fill the block completely, such as today's date serial number plus 1000.

6. Select the Series you want to use for the fill. Here, select **Month**.

7. Select OK to confirm the dialog box and fill the block.

Each manual step has a command equivalent. Figure 14.6 shows the macro created using Quattro Pro 5.0 for Windows command equivalent macro commands.

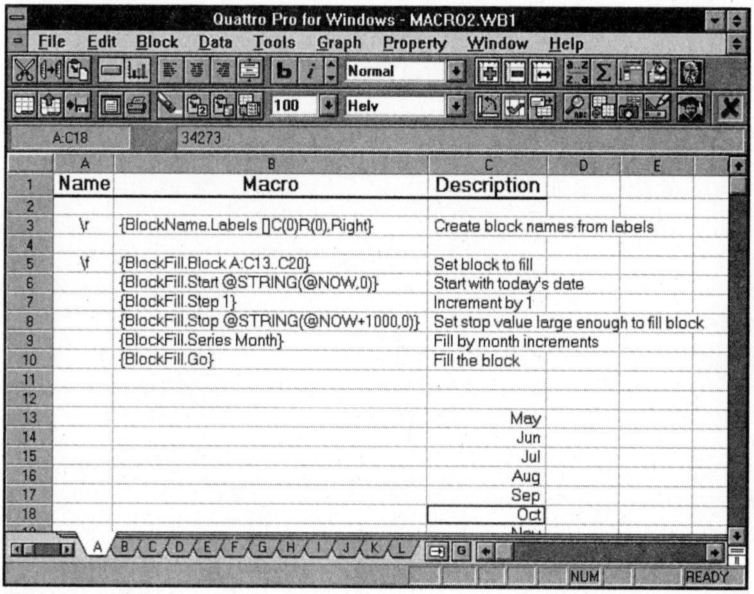

Fig. 14.6

The **B**lock **F**ill macro using command equivalents.

The macro, named \f, starts in cell A:B5 with the following statement:

{BlockFill.Block A:C13..C20}

This statement is the command equivalent of steps 1 and 2 and sets the block A:C13..C20 as the block to fill. The following statement, in A:B6, enters the Start value:

{BlockFill.Start @STRING(@NOW,0)}

Notice that the Start value is entered in the macro command as @STRING(@NOW,0). As you learn in the section, "Formatting Rules for Macros," later in this chapter, macro commands must be entered as strings (or labels). The @STRING function is used to convert the date serial number returned by @NOW to a string that looks like a number.

The macro next enters a St**e**p value. Here, the value entered is 1 (the default St**e**p value). If you enter the **B**lock **F**ill command manually, just look at the value in the St**e**p text box. If the value is 1, bypass this step. When you create a macro, however, you must consider whether a previous **B**lock **F**ill command may have entered a different St**e**p value. To be safe, include the following command, shown in A:B7, to set the St**e**p value:

> {BlockFill.Step 1}

You must change the default **S**top value, 8191, to allow the block to be completely filled. Because Quattro Pro 5.0 for Windows doesn't care if the **S**top value is much larger than necessary, this example just adds 1000 to the St**a**rt value to ensure the block is filled:

> {BlockFill.Stop @STRING(@NOW+1000,0)}

Because you want to fill the block with months, the following command selects **M**onth as the series:

> {BlockFill.Series Month}

Finally, the command in A:B10 executes the **B**lock **F**ill command:

> {BlockFill.Go}

In following sections of this chapter, you see how Quattro Pro 5.0 for Windows records macros using command equivalents. These recorded macros look identical to the command equivalent macros that you enter.

Understanding the Guidelines for Creating Macros

In previous sections, you learned to write simple macros. You learned the importance of planning the macro and identifying the keystrokes that you want the macro to perform. The following sections build on this knowledge and show you additional important elements of successful macro creation and execution. These elements include formatting macros, naming and running macros, planning the layout of macros, documenting macros, and protecting your macros.

Formatting Rules for Macros

You must follow certain rules in formatting Quattro Pro 5.0 for Windows macros to ensure successful operation. Several other conventions also simplify the task of reading and understanding macros. You find these points especially important when you need to debug or edit a macro or when you need to change or add a new operation to a macro. The following sections list certain rules to follow so that the macros run properly and can be maintained with minimum effort.

Enter Macro Cells as Text or String Formulas

When you type a macro into a notebook, you must enter each cell of the macro as text or as a string formula. Certain keystrokes, such as numbers, cause Quattro Pro 5.0 for Windows to change from READY mode to VALUE mode. Other keystrokes, such as the slash key (/), change Quattro Pro 5.0 for Windows to MENU mode. You must, therefore, place a label prefix—usually the apostrophe (')—before any of the following characters if you type the character as the first character in a macro cell:

   1 2 3 4 5 6 7 8 9 0 / + - @ # $. \ (

The apostrophe (') switches Quattro Pro 5.0 for Windows to LABEL mode from READY mode. Using an apostrophe before any of these characters and numbers ensures that Quattro Pro 5.0 for Windows doesn't misinterpret the text entry. If any character not in this list is the first keystroke in the cell, Quattro Pro 5.0 for Windows switches to LABEL mode and prefixes the entry with an apostrophe when you press Enter.

Use Command Equivalents to Represent Menu Commands

Because the Quattro Pro 5.0 for Windows menus are so easily modified or removed completely, menu commands always should be represented by the command equivalents. Command equivalents function whether the standard Quattro Pro 5.0 for Windows menus, modified menus, or no menus are displayed.

Macros that attempt to duplicate keystrokes rather than use command equivalents fail or execute the wrong command if the menu is changed.

Use Braces with Macro Commands

You must enclose macro commands in braces {} (whether the commands are the command equivalents or the advanced macro commands covered in Chapter 15. If you use parentheses () or square brackets [], Quattro Pro 5.0 for Windows cannot recognize the macro commands and halts the macro execution or enters the unrecognized string as text in the current cell selector location.

Use the Correct Syntax

The syntax for the command equivalents and the advanced macro commands must be correct. See Chapter 15 for the correct syntax for the advanced macro commands used in Quattro Pro 5.0 for Windows. You must place each command equivalent or advanced macro command within one cell. You cannot write a macro command that has the beginning brace on one line and the closing brace on another line.

As an example, see the \r macro shown in figure 14.5.

You must enter **{BlockName.Labels []C(0)R(0),Right}** in one cell. You cannot split the command so that **{BlockName.Labels** is in one cell and **[]C(0)R(0),Right}** is in another cell. If you attempt to split a command in this way, Quattro Pro 5.0 for Windows informs you that an error has occurred.

Use the Tilde to Represent the Enter Key

You use the tilde (~) in a macro to represent the action of pressing the Enter key. Among the most common errors made while creating macros that duplicate keystrokes is to forget to include the tilde to complete an entry.

Use Repetition Factors

Use repetition factors in macros when possible. Rather than entering **{RIGHT}{RIGHT}{RIGHT}** to move the cell selector three columns to the right, for example, type **{RIGHT 3}** or **{R 3}**. Not only is typing a command by using a repetition factor easier, this method also makes reading the macros easier.

When you use a repetition factor, be sure that you place a space between the true key name, such as **RIGHT**, and the number of repetitions, such as **3**. **{RIGHT 3}** is correct and **{RIGHT3}** is not.

Naming and Running Macros

You can start macros in several different ways, depending on how you name the macros. Consider the following examples:

- You execute a macro named with the backslash (\) and a letter by holding down the Ctrl key and pressing the designated letter, or by using the Run Macro dialog box. You invoke this dialog box by selecting **T**ools **M**acro **E**xecute from the Quattro Pro 5.0 for Windows menu.

- You can execute a macro with a descriptive name of up to 15 characters by using the Run Macro dialog box.

- You can launch an auto-execute macro, which by default is named \0 (backslash zero), in two ways. This macro starts (after any notebook startup macro is executed) when you load a notebook that contains the \0 macro. You also can initiate auto-execute macros with the Run Macro dialog box.

- You can execute any macro, whether named or not, by using the Run Macro dialog box. Specify the macro's first cell address in the **L**ocation text box of the Run Macro dialog box, and then select OK.

- If you name a macro _nbstartmacro, Quattro Pro 5.0 for Windows automatically executes the macro (before any auto-execute macro) whenever you load the notebook. Such macros are called *notebook startup macros.*

- If you name a macro _nbexitmacro, Quattro Pro 5.0 for Windows automatically executes the macro whenever you close the notebook. Such macros are called *notebook exit macros.*

A previous section of this chapter shows examples of the first method—naming and running a macro with the Ctrl+*letter* combination. In previous versions of Quattro Pro, you press Alt+*letter* to execute macros named with a backslash (\) and a letter. Because Windows reserves several Alt+*key* combinations for other uses, however, in Quattro Pro 5.0 for Windows you must press Ctrl+*letter*.

> **NOTE**
>
> Although several Quattro Pro 5.0 for Windows commands have Ctrl+*letter* keyboard shortcuts, if you like, you can use the same Ctrl+*letter* combinations to name your macros. After you press the Ctrl+*letter* combination that names your macro, Quattro Pro 5.0 for Windows runs your macro instead of executing the keyboard shortcut. For example, if you name a macro \n, Quattro Pro 5.0 for Windows runs your macro instead of executing the keyboard shortcut for **F**ile **N**ew.

With the second method, you assign a descriptive name to the first cell in the macro and then execute the macro from the Run Macro dialog box. With the third method, you create a macro named \0 that is executed when you load the notebook. With the fourth method, you can execute *any* macro by using the Run Macro dialog box. Invoking a macro in Quattro Pro 5.0 for Windows with the Run Macro dialog box enables you to test portions of macros because you don't always have to start at the first cell of a macro.

Use the \0 name only if you want Quattro Pro 5.0 for Windows to invoke a macro as soon you retrieve the notebook (but not until after any notebook startup macro is executed), but use the Ctrl+*letter* or descriptive name for any other macro. Both types of names have advantages. When you invoke a macro with a Ctrl+*letter* name, you use fewer keystrokes than when you invoke a macro with a descriptive name. One disadvantage to using a Ctrl+*letter* macro name, however, is that you may have difficulty remembering a macro's specific purpose, particularly when you have created many macros. You have a better chance of selecting the correct macro when you use descriptive names. Another disadvantage of Ctrl+*letter* macro names is that you can have only 26 macros named in this way. This requirement can be a difficult limitation, especially if you store a large number of common macros in a macro library notebook for use with your other Quattro Pro 5.0 for Windows notebooks.

You usually place macro names immediately to the left of the first cell of the macro, but you can use other placements if you prefer. You can, for example, place all macro names in the cell immediately above the first cell of the macro if you want to be certain the macro name stays with the macro itself if you move the macro.

The following sections describe the approaches of creating, naming, and running macros. The macros shown in figure 14.7 illustrate the methods.

Fig. 14.7

Macros that illustrate naming conventions.

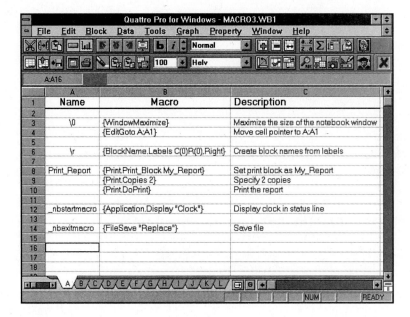

Ctrl+*letter* Macros

You can name a macro by using the backslash key (\) and a letter. This method is the Ctrl+*letter* method of naming a macro. Versions of Quattro Pro for DOS and Lotus 1-2-3 for DOS refer to these macros as Alt+*letter* macros because you invoke these macros by holding down the Alt key and pressing the designated letter. You start these macros in Quattro Pro 5.0 for Windows by holding down the Ctrl key and pressing the *letter* key.

The \r macro in figure 14.7 demonstrates the Ctrl+*letter* approach to naming a macro. You can use upper- or lowercase letters to name a macro. Quattro Pro 5.0 for Windows does not differentiate between upper- and lowercase letters for block names. You can have only 26 Ctrl+*letter* macros because \r and \R represent the same notebook block.

Macros with Descriptive Names

You can use up to 15 characters to name notebook blocks in Quattro Pro 5.0 for Windows. Named macros are considered to be identical to any other blocks, so you can also use up to 15 characters in a descriptive macro name. A descriptive macro name provides excellent documentation for your macros. The macro name Print_Report in figure 14.7 clearly shows the purpose of the macro.

When naming your macros with descriptive names, however, keep the following points in mind:

■ Don't use block names for macros that also are Quattro Pro 5.0 for Windows keystroke equivalents, such as CALC or RIGHT, or cell addresses, such as AA1.

■ Don't use block names that also are advanced macro commands or command equivalents, such as BlockCopy.

■ Don't create block names that combine two or more other block names using arithmetic operators. For example, if you have blocks named SALES and REPORT, don't create a block named SALES-REPORT or SALES+REPORT. You, however, can create a block named SALES_REPORT.

You can execute the macros you have named with descriptive names in one way only: from the Run Macro dialog box. Select **T**ools **M**acro **E**xecute to display this dialog box. Figure 14.8 shows how the screen appears after the Run Macro dialog box is invoked for the example in figure 14.7.

To start a macro, select the macro name in the **M**acros/Named Blocks list box, or enter the name in the **L**ocation text box and select OK.

The Run Macro dialog box displays all block names in the active notebook, including block names that aren't macro names. If you have other notebooks open in memory, you can select a different notebook in the Macro Li**b**rary list box and then select a macro name from that notebook.

Fig. 14.8

The Run Macro dialog box displays a list of block names in the notebook.

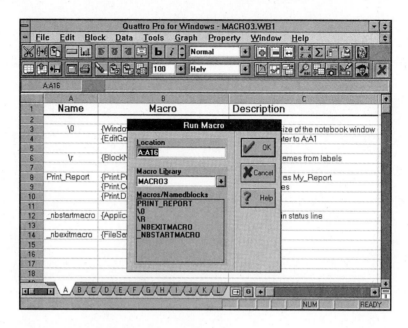

To start an unnamed macro, or to start macro execution in a cell other than at the beginning of a named macro, select the **L**ocation text box and point to the notebook cell where you want to begin execution. When you invoke the Run Macro dialog box, the **L**ocation text box displays the current cell selector location. You can also highlight the cell that contains the first macro instruction you want to execute before you invoke the Run Macro dialog box. When the correct notebook cell is shown in the **L**ocation text box, select OK to run the macro.

Auto-Execute, Notebook Startup, and Notebook Exit Macros

You may want some macros to run automatically when you retrieve the notebook that contains them. Quattro Pro 5.0 for Windows provides two slightly different methods of accomplishing this task. Notebook startup macros, which are named _nbstartmacro, are always executed first whenever a notebook containing them is opened. Auto-execute macros, which are usually named \0, are executed if the **A**pplication **S**tartup **S**tartup Macro property specifies the name of the auto-execute macro.

You may also want to make certain that a list of tasks, such as automatically saving the notebook, is performed whenever the notebook is closed. Notebook exit macros, which are named _nbexitmacro, are executed whenever a command to close the notebook is issued.

> **CAUTION**
>
> Use caution when creating notebook exit macros. If the notebook exit macro automatically saves the notebook, replacing the existing notebook on disk, you could destroy the existing notebook when you simply wanted to discard changes to the notebook and start over.

You can specify another name for your auto-execute macros using the Startup Macro text box in the Startup section of the Application dialog box. If you make a name change for your auto-execute macros, the new name is used to determine the auto-execute macro in all of your Quattro Pro 5.0 for Windows notebooks, not just the current notebook. If you later want to share a notebook with other Quattro Pro 5.0 for Windows users, your auto-execute macros probably won't execute automatically on their system—use notebook startup macros for macros that must be run regardless of the Startup Macro setting.

Suppose that when you retrieve a certain notebook, you always want its window maximized and the cell selector moved to cell A:A1, regardless of the size of the window or the cell selector location when you last saved the notebook. The auto-execute macro in figure 14.7 maximizes the notebook window and moves the cell selector to A:A1 when you retrieve the notebook.

You can also use this technique in advanced macro programs. When you construct your own menus and SpeedBars for a notebook model, for example, you may want an advanced macro program to execute automatically and place your custom menu and SpeedBar on-screen. You could also use a notebook exit macro to restore the standard Quattro Pro 5.0 for Windows appearance when the user closes the notebook.

Figure 14.9 shows another auto-execute macro. This macro moves the cell selector to the bottom of a column of labels or numbers (the macro assumes that at least two entries already are in the list).

Fig. 14.9

An auto-execute macro that moves the cell selector.

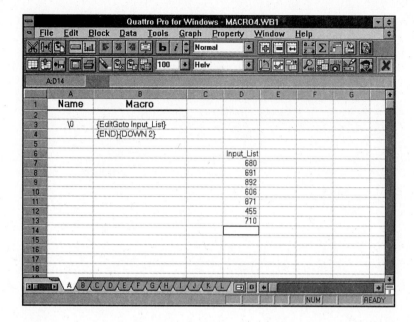

The macro tells Quattro Pro 5.0 for Windows to perform the following actions:

1. Press GoTo (F5).

2. Enter **Input_List** as the block to go to.

3. Select OK.

4. Press End.

5. Press the down-arrow key twice to move to the bottom of the column of entries and then move down to the next cell.

These steps are performed when you complete the macro, save the notebook, and then retrieve the notebook again later.

The actual contents of the macro cells are shown in the following example:

```
'{EditGoto Input_List}
'{END}{DOWN 2}
```

Because a macro is actually a text label, a label prefix must precede the macro text. In this example, the apostrophe (') precedes the macro instructions. You can also use the ^ and " label prefixes if you prefer. Quattro Pro 5.0 for Windows doesn't care which label prefix you use. The apostrophe is usually the easiest label prefix to use because Quattro Pro 5.0 for Windows enters an apostrophe automatically when you type the left brace ({).

To practice the method of creating and naming a macro described in the preceding text, type the numbers in column D and the label above them in cell D6. Use the **B**lock **N**ames **C**reate command to create the block name Input_List in cell D6. Type the keystrokes that the macro duplicates. Press F5, select Input_List, and select OK. Press the End key once. Now press the down-arrow key twice. You have entered the same steps the macro performs.

Move the cell selector to cell B3 and type the entries shown in cells B3 and B4 in figure 14.9.

Type '**\0** in cell A3. Then select **B**lock **N**ames **L**abels **R**ight and select OK. Save the notebook; when you retrieve the notebook again, the macro runs. If you want to run the macro again after you retrieve the notebook, select **T**ools **M**acro **E**xecute, choose \0 from the list of macro names, and select OK.

Planning Macro Layout

You can place a macro that contains as many as 1,022 characters in one cell, but you should divide a long macro. To break apart a long macro, place each part of the macro in consecutive cells down a column.

A good way to break a macro into parts is to divide in terms of small tasks. Limit each cell to one task or, at most, to a few related tasks. By limiting the number of keystrokes in a cell, you can more easily debug, modify, and document a macro. Using multiple cells down a column to store a macro makes the macro much easier to read and understand.

Figure 14.10 shows two macros that execute an identical sequence of keystrokes. Both macros type the company name in the current cell, move the cell selector down one row, type the street address, move the cell selector down one more row, and then enter the city, state, and ZIP code. In each case, the block name is assigned to one cell. The macro in B3 is named \a, and the macro in B5 is named \b.

Fig. 14.10

Using multiple cells
makes macros easier to
read.

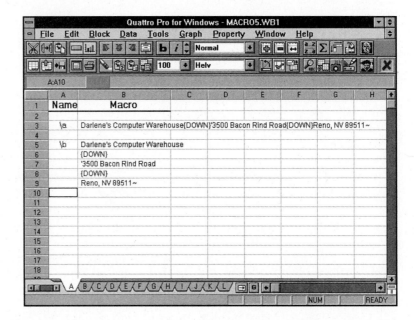

Macros execute the instructions in one column, working down from the
cell where execution begins. The \b macro, for example, starts executing in cell B5 and continues down through cell B9. The macro executes
properly whether the block name is defined as B5 or B5..B9.

Macros continue executing instructions down the column until the
macros encounter one of the following conditions:

- An empty cell

- A cell that contains a numeric value, ERR, or NA

- A cell that contains an advanced macro command that explicitly
  stops a macro (see Chapter 15 for more information on these
  kinds of commands)

Both macros perform the same tasks and enter the same keystrokes,
but the \b macro is much easier to read and understand because it
breaks the job into smaller tasks. You may not appreciate the difference in readability at the time you create a macro, but if you later have
to understand and modify the macro, you will be glad you separated it
into small, logical tasks.

Because all macro commands must be labels, the first label prefix in
the macro cell is ignored as the macro is executed. To make the macro
type a label that begins with a number, such as a telephone number or

an address, you must place an additional label prefix in the macro cell for Quattro Pro 5.0 for Windows to type.

Notice the apostrophes (') in front of the address entries 3500 Bacon Rind Road in cells B3 and B7 of figure 14.10. Because of the apostrophes, Quattro Pro 5.0 for Windows types the entries into the cells as labels when the macro runs. If you don't include the extra apostrophe, Quattro Pro 5.0 for Windows beeps and reports an error when the macro runs.

> You can repeat key names by including a repetition factor.

TIP

Quattro Pro 5.0 for Windows enables you to repeat certain key names by including a repetition factor. A *repetition factor* tells Quattro Pro 5.0 for Windows that you want a command repeated the number of times you specify. The \c macro, shown in figure 14.11, performs the same keystrokes as the \a and \b macros in figure 14.10. The \c macro then moves the cell selector down two rows and enters the phone number. The \c macro uses a repetition factor, {DOWN 2}, to repeat the {DOWN} key name. When you use a repetition factor, leave a space between the key name and the number.

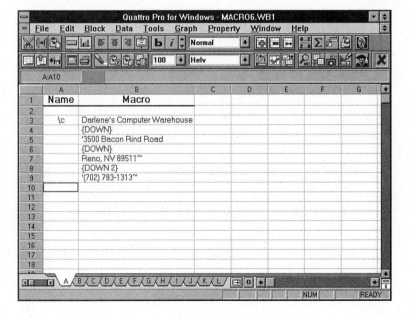

Fig. 14.11

The \c macro uses a repetition factor.

Documenting Macros

Documenting Quattro Pro 5.0 for Windows notebooks is an important part of the development process. Unless you take the time to document the notebooks properly as you create them, correcting problems or making necessary modifications becomes difficult, if not impossible.

Documenting your Quattro Pro 5.0 for Windows macros is especially important because you can easily forget exactly what a macro accomplishes. You can document macros by using many of the techniques you also use to document notebooks:

- Use descriptive names as macro names.
- Include comments within the notebook.
- Use command equivalents rather than simply repeating menu selection keystrokes.
- Keep and organize any notes you make as you create the notebook.

Using Descriptive Names

You have seen how you can use the backslash and a letter to name a macro, and then execute such Ctrl+*letter* macros by holding down the Ctrl key and pressing the assigned letter. A Ctrl+*letter* macro is easy to execute, but the macro name doesn't really describe the macro's purpose.

Use descriptive block names to name your macros. You can then execute these macros by selecting **T**ools **M**acro **E**xecute and choosing the macro name from the Run Macro dialog box.

Because you can assign more than one block name to the same block, you can also assign Ctrl+*letter* names to some of your macros that have descriptive names. For example, if a notebook includes a macro called Main_Menu, you can also assign \m as a block name to the macro. The descriptive name, Main_Menu, tells anyone looking at the macros what the macro's exact purpose is. The Ctrl+*letter* name, \m, makes it easy to execute the macro.

Including Comments in Your Notebook

In figure 14.7, a description of each macro's function is found in the column to the right of the macros. With these simple macros, you probably can identify the tasks the macros perform just by reading the macro code. If you are familiar with the Quattro Pro 5.0 for Windows menu structure or the command equivalents, the comments may seem redundant or unnecessary.

With longer and more complex macros, however, you not only may find such documentation helpful but also vital to understanding what a macro actually accomplishes. Later, when you want to verify that a macro is functioning properly, or when you want to make changes, this internal documentation provides valuable information about the macro's purpose and its intended action.

You may find that you do not necessarily need to add a comment for each individual macro line, especially when you create simple macros or use command equivalents. In these cases, the following guidelines may help you determine how much documentation is necessary:

- Always document the overall purpose of a macro or a subroutine. This documentation is especially important when you break your macros down into structures of general-purpose macro modules that you can reuse often.

- Document any individual macro lines when specific operations may be unclear. If you have used a special trick or shortcut, be sure that you document it fully.

- Budget your time and energy by concentrating your documentation efforts where they are most needed. Avoid spending too much time writing extensive documentation for very simple macros.

- Include all necessary steps, especially when creating command-equivalent macros, and you won't have to wonder when you later look at the macro how a missing step is accomplished. For example, don't leave out steps that set default values, such as the Step value in a **Block Fill** macro.

Keeping Design Notes

Keep a file to retain any paperwork you create, or paperwork you are given, as part of designing and constructing a notebook. Be sure that you include any notes you make that have helped you design the macros, as well as printed copies of all notebook formulas and a current listing of all block names. Your file should also include copies of any printed reports with notations telling which macros generate these reports.

This kind of external documentation is extremely valuable. This material not only makes it easier to understand your notebooks and their macros but also greatly eases the burden for someone who later has to make modifications. Without documentation, maintaining a notebook or the macros in a notebook is a daunting task indeed.

The documentation file always should include a complete hard-copy printout of all macros. This printout should include the row and column labels, which you can select with the **File Print** Options **R**ow/Column borders check box. For complex macros, you also may want to include a diagram showing the logical flow through the macro, especially when the macro branches based on conditional logic.

Finally, include references to any external materials, such as books or magazine articles, you have used. Include titles, dates, and page numbers so that you later can refer to the same materials if necessary.

Protecting Macros

Unlike many other types of programs, such as database management programs, in Quattro Pro 5.0 for Windows, the data and the programs (macros) are in the same files. Even if you place all of your macros in separate macro library notebooks, these notebooks still are just Quattro Pro 5.0 for Windows notebooks and can be changed by anyone who knows Quattro Pro 5.0 for Windows well enough.

Most users store macros customized for particular applications in the same notebook that contains the application's data. In these instances, place the macros together outside the area that the main model occupies. Storing the macros together makes it easier for you to find a macro for editing and also helps you avoid accidentally overwriting or erasing part of a macro as you create the model.

Because each Quattro Pro 5.0 for Windows notebook has 256 notebook pages, you may want to devote one page exclusively to the macros. If you use this approach, you can avoid some common problems. For example, suppose you use Quattro Pro 5.0 for Windows commands to insert or delete columns or rows. When you use these commands—manually or within macros—the macros may become corrupted if they are placed on the same page as your data rather than on their own page with the other macros.

You may want to consider using page IV for your macros. Using this page not only allows sufficient notebook pages in front of the macros page for your data but also makes page IV easily accessible. If you click the SpeedTab button, Quattro Pro 5.0 for Windows displays the Graphs page, which is right behind page IV. When the Graphs page is displayed, simply point to the page tab for page IV and click the left mouse button to make page IV the active page. You also may want to change the page name to Macros to remind you of the page contents.

Besides using a separate notebook page, you also may want to consider using a separate macro library notebook to hold your macros. Quattro Pro 5.0 for Windows can execute macros contained in open notebooks other than the active notebook, and your macro library notebook even can be a hidden notebook.

Macros that use cell addresses rather than block names can stop functioning properly when you insert or delete rows or columns in a notebook. Such macros, in fact, can do serious damage to the remaining formulas and data in the notebook when the macros act upon the incorrect block of cells. Always use block names rather than cell addresses in your macros to prevent this kind of potentially serious problem.

Recording Macros

In the examples presented previously in this chapter, you planned what actions you wanted the macros to perform, stepped through the keystrokes necessary to perform these actions manually, and then typed the keystrokes or command equivalents that instructed the macro to perform the same steps.

Quattro Pro 5.0 for Windows provides an easier method of creating simple macros. Quattro Pro 5.0 for Windows can record your keystrokes and mouse actions while you step through the commands, and then place the command equivalents or the keystrokes in the notebook. Later, when you want to perform the same task, you can use these recorded actions as macros.

The following sections show you how to choose the recording method Quattro Pro 5.0 for Windows uses to record your actions as macros, how to record simple macros, and how to play back recorded actions as macros.

Specifying the Recording Method

In a previous section, you learned that Quattro Pro 5.0 for Windows has a new macro language called command equivalents. These command equivalents are used for simple macros and do not depend on a particular Quattro Pro 5.0 for Windows menu being active.

When you use the macro recorder to record commands and actions, by default, Quattro Pro 5.0 for Windows records these commands and actions as command equivalents rather than as keystrokes. If necessary, you can instruct Quattro Pro 5.0 for Windows to record keystrokes rather than command equivalents. To change the recording method, select **T**ools **M**acro **O**ptions to display the Macro Options dialog box shown in figure 14.12.

Fig. 14.12

The Macro Options dialog box.

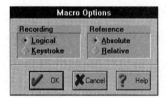

To record actions as keystrokes, select **K**eystroke. To return to recording command equivalents, select **L**ogical. Both methods are available, but you always should record actions as command equivalents if possible. This action ensures that the recorded actions function correctly when used as macros.

The other choice in the Macro Options dialog box, the Reference field, determines whether actual cell addresses or offsets from the current cell selector location are recorded. The default selection, **A**bsolute, records actual cell addresses or block names. **R**elative records the offsets from the current cell selector location. If you are recording a macro that always must act on the same notebook block, choose **Absolute**. If you are recording a macro that is more general in nature, such as one that uses the current cell selector location as its starting point, choose **R**elative.

Relative addresses are recorded as offsets from the current cell selector location. These offsets use the format []P(*pn*):C(*cn*)R(*rn*), where *pn* is the number of pages of offset (plus or minus) from the cell selector location, *cn* is the number of columns of offset, and *rn* is the number of rows of offset. For actions on the current page, the page offset is optional.

Beginning the Recording Process

After you select any necessary optional settings for recording macros, you can start the macro recorder. Decide where you want Quattro Pro 5.0 for Windows to place the recorded actions, and select **Tools Macro Record**. The Record Macro dialog box appears, as shown in figure 14.13.

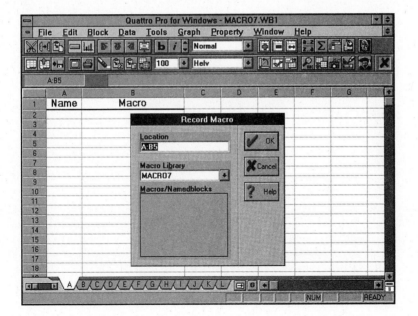

Fig. 14.13

The Record Macro dialog box.

Type the address in the **L**ocation text box in which you want to store the recorded actions. Select OK to begin the recording. Quattro Pro 5.0 for Windows displays the REC indicator in the status line to show you that the macro recorder is active.

Suppose that you want to duplicate the **B**lock **F**ill macro shown in figure 14.6. Select the **B**lock **F**ill command, and make each selection in the dialog box just as you usually would. Select OK to confirm the dialog box and fill the block.

After you complete the series of commands you want to record, select **T**ools **M**acro **S**top **R**ecord. Figure 14.14 shows how Quattro Pro 5.0 for Windows records the commands in the notebook.

Fig. 14.14

The **B**lock **F**ill commands recorded by Quattro Pro for Windows.

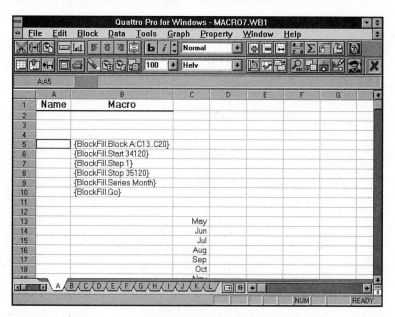

The recorded steps are similar to the manually entered macro in figure 14.6. A few differences, however, exist. In figure 14.6 the starting value for the block fill is entered in cell B6 as @STRING(@NOW,0), but in figure 14.14 the value is shown as 34120, a date serial number. Quattro Pro 5.0 for Windows records the value of the function, not the function itself. You must manually edit the recorded macro to change the date serial numbers in cells B6 and B8 to functions, as shown in figure 14.6.

Even if you followed all the steps necessary to create the block fill, Quattro Pro 5.0 for Windows may have recorded a slightly different sequence of commands. If the default value of 1 is already listed in the

Step list box, for example, the command recorded in cell B7 of figure 14.14 isn't included in your recording of the macro. Also, if you select the list boxes in a different order, Quattro Pro 5.0 for Windows records the actions in the order that you select each action.

Playing Back Your Recorded Macros

The macro recorded in figure 14.14 works as recorded, but you probably want to modify the macro slightly before you play it back. For one thing, the date serial numbers recorded in cells B6 and B8 may be fine today, but you may want to edit the macros to include functions, as shown in figure 14.6.

You may also want to assign a block name to recorded macros— to make the macros easier to execute and to provide some documentation.

Finally, examine carefully all macros Quattro Pro 5.0 for Windows records for you to make sure that all necessary steps are included. The Block Fill macro, for example, normally functions just fine without the {BlockFill.Step 1} command, but produces unexpected results if a previous Block Fill command changes the Step value to a value other than the default of 1.

After you complete any necessary corrections or modifications, execute a recorded macro the same way you execute any other Quattro Pro 5.0 for Windows macro. If you assign a Ctrl+*letter* name to the macro, hold down the Ctrl key and press the assigned letter. You can also select Tools Macro Execute and run the macro from the Run Macro dialog box.

Debugging Macros

Even a well-designed macro program can contain bugs, or errors, that prevent the macro from functioning correctly. Whether the error is a missing label prefix or tilde, a missing or incorrectly entered command equivalent, or a logical error that causes the macro to function incorrectly, macro errors can be very difficult to find. Because Quattro Pro 5.0 for Windows executes macros rapidly, you often cannot determine exactly why your macro is not accomplishing exactly what you expect. This section introduces you to some methods that help you find and correct errors in macros.

No matter how simple a macro is or how careful you are in designing a macro, it may not perform flawlessly the first time you try executing it. You can, however, take a careful series of precautions that help minimize the work necessary to eliminate macro errors.

Before you begin writing or recording a macro, always invest the time necessary to design the macro carefully. Just as you never start out on a long road trip without first making certain you have a good set of road maps, you never start out building a macro without a comprehensive plan showing the actions the macro is to perform. Take the time to plan the details, including each step or decision the macro makes. List the block names for any notebook blocks the macro manipulates and any other macros the macro uses.

After you have the macro documentation and have created the macro, plan to test and debug your macros thoroughly. Testing is necessary to verify that the macro functions exactly as you expect it to. Don't feel you safely can bypass the testing process—someone else who uses a macro you create probably will not be happy to find bugs that you could have prevented!

Quattro Pro 5.0 for Windows has a built-in macro debugger that you can use to test and debug your macros. This tool enables you to step through your macros and see the effects as the macro instruction is executed.

To test a macro, you must first activate the macro debugger tool. You can select **T**ools **M**acro **D**ebugger or press Shift+F2. When the macro debugger tool is activated, Quattro Pro 5.0 for Windows displays the DEBUG indicator in the status line.

When the macro debugger tool is active, execute the macro you want to test. Quattro Pro 5.0 for Windows displays the Macro Debugger window shown in figure 14.15.

In the Macro Debugger window, Quattro Pro 5.0 for Windows highlights each macro command before the command is executed. To execute the highlighted command and step to the next command, press the space bar. Continue pressing the space bar to step through the macro one instruction at a time.

Stepping through a macro one instruction at a time usually helps you find errors in the macro. Sometimes, however, you need more powerful methods to find macro errors. The options listed at the top of the Macro Debugger window give you important tools for these times.

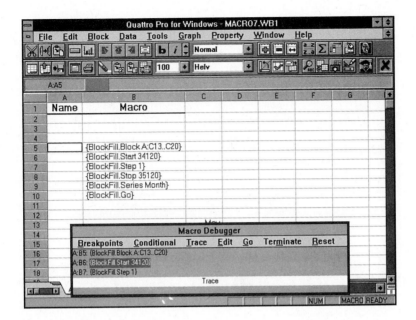

Fig. 14.15

The Macro Debugger window.

Table 14.1 summarizes the Macro Debugger window options.

Table 14.1 Macro Debugger Options

Option	Description
Breakpoints	Macro cells or blocks you specify. Macro execution proceeds at full speed until the macro reaches a breakpoint cell, and then the macro enters DEBUG step mode.
Conditional	Cells that contain logical (Boolean) formulas. Macro execution proceeds at full speed until the formula evaluates as TRUE, and then the macro enters DEBUG step mode.
Trace	Cells whose value you want to monitor while the macro steps through each instruction.
Edit	Enables you to modify the macro without leaving DEBUG mode.
Go	Causes a macro to resume executing instructions at full speed until a breakpoint or the end of the macro is reached.
Terminate	Halts the macro and closes the Macro Debugger window.
Reset	Removes any breakpoints and trace cells set with **B**reakpoints, **C**onditional, or **T**race.

You can use any combination of Macro Debugger window options necessary to test your macros. Suppose that a macro seems to work correctly most of the time but fails when a certain cell has a value larger than another cell. You can use the debugger Conditional option to run the macro full-speed until the first cell is larger than the second, and you can also use the Trace option to watch the values of the two cells after the execution returns to step mode.

Debugging macros can be a complex task. Often, the real problem with a macro exists several steps before the step that seems to produce the error. If you cannot find an error in a macro that fails, look at the steps that preceded the point of failure. You may find a logical error that alone is no problem but, when combined with later macro commands, is the real reason the macro failed.

Avoiding Common Macro Errors

Editing is a fairly regular part of creating macros, especially when macros are complex. Avoiding common macro creation errors in the first place is an important step in reducing the time you later must spend editing and debugging your macros.

If Quattro Pro 5.0 for Windows cannot execute a macro as written, the program displays an error message. Usually, the error message that reveals the type of error appears in a message box that shows where Quattro Pro 5.0 for Windows feels the error exists. Usually, this message accurately points you to the actual error, but occasionally the real error—the place where Quattro Pro 5.0 for Windows stops executing commands—precedes the error identified in the error message.

In the cell identified by the error message, look for the chronic macro errors almost everyone seems to make. If Quattro Pro 5.0 for Windows stops during a macro, you probably forgot to include the final step necessary to complete a command. In a macro that enters data, for example, forgetting to include a tilde to represent pressing the Enter key is a common error. Sometimes a macro halts because another command that executes a command, such as {BlockFill.Go}, is missing.

If you receive a message about an unknown key or command followed by an address, check the key or command name listed to be sure that the key or name is spelled correctly. Also, verify that you use braces {} rather than parentheses ( ) or brackets [ ], that arguments are correctly specified, and that no extra spaces are included in the macro.

The following list reviews the simple guidelines for preventing typical errors that can occur during the process of creating macros:

- *Check the syntax and spelling.* Incorrect grammar and spelling are common problems in macro key names, command equivalents, advanced macro commands, block names, and file names used in macros. All macro syntax and spelling must be exact.

- *Include all required tildes.* Remember to represent each required Enter keystroke in a macro.

- *Include all command steps.* If your macro lacks all necessary steps, such as explicitly setting values to the defaults, the macro may work some of the time and fail without warning at other times.

- *Erase the cell below the macro.* Remember that Quattro Pro 5.0 for Windows works down through the cells of a macro executing each command in turn. If the cell below the last macro command is not empty, Quattro Pro 5.0 for Windows can complete the macro commands and then beep or display an error message. Use Edit Clear or press Del to erase the cell below the last macro cell.

- *Use braces correctly.* Enclose key names, command equivalents, and advanced macro commands in braces rather than in brackets or parentheses. Symbols and words within braces {} are used to represent all the special keys on the keyboard. In all cases you must enclose a key's name in braces, such as {RIGHT}, for the right-arrow key or {EDIT}, for the F2 key. You must also enclose advanced macros commands in braces within a macro.

- *When possible, use descriptive block names.* Quattro Pro 5.0 for Windows macros are unlike Quattro Pro 5.0 for Windows formulas. Cell references in macros don't automatically adjust when you make changes to the notebook. Macros are labels, and labels don't change to reflect notebook changes in the way formulas change.

  If you always use block names rather than cell addresses in macros, these names continue to function correctly even when you rearrange the notebook. Block names adjust to the new addresses when you move blocks, so macros that use block names also adjust.

- *Use unique block names.* Do not use block names for macros that duplicate key names, command equivalents, or advanced macro commands. Never assign a name like BlockFill, EDIT, or QUIT to a block, whether a macro block or a notebook data block. Don't use a name that may be construed as a cell address.

- *Use valid cell references.* If you use string formulas to create cell addresses in macros, take extra care to design the formulas to produce only valid addresses.

- *Define all block names.* Forgetting to assign a block name is easy, especially if you included the block name label in the notebook. If you include the label TOTAL in the notebook, for example, you must also assign the block name TOTAL to a notebook cell if you want Quattro Pro 5.0 for Windows to recognize the name.

- *Use the backslash (\) in Ctrl+letter macro names.* Never use the forward slash (/); without a backslash, Quattro Pro 5.0 for Windows cannot recognize the macro as a valid Ctrl+*letter* macro.

Using the Advanced Macro Commands

The Quattro Pro 5.0 for Windows command equivalents provide a high degree of flexibility and power, but you may find that you are writing large and complex macros if you don't advance to using the advanced macro commands (described in Chapter 15). Many Quattro Pro 5.0 for Windows advanced macro commands serve as efficient replacements for the command equivalents, but other advanced commands perform tasks that have no command equivalents.

Advanced macro commands offer much of the power of programming languages, such as C++, Pascal, and BASIC, but at the same time, these macros function within Quattro Pro 5.0 for Windows. This capability gives you access to the power of Quattro Pro 5.0 for Windows and the flexibility of an advanced programming environment.

If the advanced macro commands sound like something more complex than you want to get involved with, you should at least look over the commands and examples in Chapter 15. You don't have to use the advanced macro commands; however, you may find the limitations of simple macro programs are overcome easily by the addition of a few of the advanced macro commands.

Questions and Answers

Q: I'm new to Quattro Pro 5.0 for Windows. What's the fastest way to learn the command equivalent macro language?

A: Try recording some macros. You'll quickly see how the command equivalents relate to standard Quattro Pro 5.0 for Windows commands and how command equivalent macro programs are much easier to read and understand than the old-style keystroke macros.

Q: I created a macro that seems to have a mind of its own. Why does my macro ignore the current cell selector location?

A: If your macro uses relative addressing, you must include the brackets ([ ]) at the start of the relative address to tell the macro to use the current cell selector location, rather than the location of the macro command, as the starting point for the relative address.

You may also encounter this problem if you have upgraded from the first release of Quattro Pro for Windows, which did not use the brackets in relative addressing.

Q: Why does my macro stop before it finishes the task it is supposed to perform?

A: There are many possible reasons for macros to stop too soon. The most common are missing instructions, such as {BlockFill.Go}, or missing keystrokes, such as a tilde (~). If the macro executes some of its steps but leaves a dialog box on-screen instead of confirming the dialog box, look for these types of missing steps.

If the macro stops and displays an error message, the error message dialog box usually attempts to explain the problem. Carefully examine your macros, trying each step in turn manually. You will usually be able to discover the problem if you try to accomplish the desired task without adding any steps not shown in the macro.

Q: I created a notebook masterpiece that produces a complex report, slices bread, and hums classical music while you're entering data. Even though this gem works perfectly every time on my computer, the auto-execute macro that performs this magic doesn't run on my friend's system. How can I convince them I'm not making this up?

A: Auto-execute macros only run if the **Startup Macro** setting is correct in the Application Object Inspector dialog box. If you want to make certain a macro runs whenever you open the notebook, use the notebook startup macro, _nbstartmacro, instead of \0. Sorry, I can't help with the bread slicing or humming, though.

Q: I created and tested a macro and verified that everything was working properly. Once I started using the notebook, though, the macro suddenly seemed to go crazy. Instead of selecting and modifying the correct notebook cells, the macro is destroying existing data. What's wrong?

A: Did you remember to use block names instead of cell addresses in your macro? If not, the macro does not adjust when you rearrange the notebook but continues to affect the same cell addresses.

If you did use block names, you may have inadvertently corrupted the macro by inserting or deleting rows that included the macro. To prevent this in the future, always use a separate notebook page for your macros.

Q: I inherited a notebook from someone who has left the company. Our procedures have changed, but I can't understand the macros in the notebook (the person who developed the macros didn't bother to document them). What can I do?

A: It can be difficult to understand complex macros, especially if they lack proper documentation. One trick you can use is to select **Tools Macro Debugger**, and then step through the macros one instruction at a time. That way you can see exactly what each instruction does to the notebook. Don't forget to make plenty of notes, and add documentation to the macros so they will be easier to understand next time someone needs to make a change.

Summary

The information in this chapter helps you learn the basics of creating Quattro Pro 5.0 for Windows macros. Creating macros is the first step toward customizing the way Quattro Pro 5.0 for Windows works, and simple macros provide tools that make everyday tasks easier.

This chapter also showed you how to document and test macros. You can use the important techniques presented in this chapter regardless of the complexity of your macro programs. As you learn more about the advanced macro commands in Chapter 15, you use these same techniques to create more complex macros.

Using the Advanced Macro Commands

In addition to the keystroke and command equivalent macro capabilities, Quattro Pro 5.0 for Windows provides a powerful set of advanced macro commands that offer many of the powerful features of full-featured programming languages, such as BASIC and C++. Although not quite as powerful as a stand-alone programming language, the Quattro Pro 5.0 for Windows advanced macro command language can perform high-level programming functions, such as looping, branching, and conditional control of program flow by testing for specified conditions. This advanced macro command language also can be used to share data with and execute other Windows applications.

The preceding chapter introduces you to the process of automating Quattro Pro 5.0 for Windows by using keystroke and command equivalent macros. Using macros to automate repetitive tasks, to perform a group of menu commands, or to type long labels into the notebook can greatly reduce the amount of time you spend creating or working with a notebook.

An *advanced macro command* is a macro instruction that tells Quattro Pro 5.0 for Windows to perform one of the built-in programming functions. Many of these advanced macro commands perform functions, such as reading and writing directly to files, that cannot be duplicated through keyboard operations. This chapter introduces you to these commands.

This chapter is not intended to teach you advanced programming theory and concepts but to introduce you to the advanced macro commands. The chapter serves as a reference to the power of the advanced macro commands and includes several useful examples you can incorporate in your Quattro Pro 5.0 for Windows notebooks.

Why Use the Advanced Macro Commands?

Programs created with advanced macro commands give you added control and flexibility in Quattro Pro 5.0 for Windows notebooks. With these commands, you can construct, customize, and control notebook applications created in Quattro Pro 5.0 for Windows. You can automate tasks, such as accepting input from the keyboard during a program, performing conditional tests, repeating a sequence of commands, and creating user-defined command menus.

You can use the advanced macro commands as a full-featured programming language to develop custom notebooks for specific business applications. You can ensure that data is entered correctly, and even guide novice users through complex applications. You can launch other Windows applications and link data between Quattro Pro 5.0 for Windows notebooks and files in other Windows applications.

After learning the concepts and the components of the advanced macro commands discussed in this chapter, you will be ready to develop programs that perform the following tasks:

- ■ Create menu-driven notebook models
- ■ Accept, control, and validate input from a user

- Manipulate data within Quattro Pro 5.0 for Windows notebooks and between Quattro Pro 5.0 for Windows and other Windows applications

- Execute tasks a predetermined number of times or until predetermined conditions exist

- Control program flow

- Make intelligent decisions based on user input or data values

- Launch other Windows applications based on decisions made within a Quattro Pro 5.0 for Windows notebook

As you become more experienced with the advanced macro commands, you can take full advantage of their power in order to develop a complete business system application—from order entry, to inventory control, to accounting. To take Quattro Pro 5.0 for Windows to its practical limits, the advanced macro commands are the proper tools.

Understanding the Elements of Advanced Macro Command Programs

The Quattro Pro 5.0 for Windows advanced macro commands are a set of commands that you cannot invoke from the keyboard. These commands add to the power of Quattro Pro 5.0 for Windows and provide many functions to greatly enhance your notebook applications.

The examples in this chapter show you how to incorporate advanced macro commands into macros to produce complete, efficient programs that take Quattro Pro 5.0 for Windows' macro capability far beyond automating keystrokes. These programs contain advanced macro commands and all the elements that can be included in macros.

Quattro Pro 5.0 for Windows macro programs can include the following:

- Keystrokes and command equivalents for selecting Quattro Pro 5.0 for Windows commands

- Block names and cell addresses

■ Keyboard macro commands for moving the cell selector, for function keys, for editing keys, and for other special keys

■ Advanced macro commands

Understanding Advanced Macro Command Syntax

Like the command equivalents in the simple macros introduced in Chapter 14, all advanced macro commands are enclosed in braces ({}). Just as you must represent the right-arrow key in a macro as {RIGHT} or {R}, you must enclose a command, such as QUIT, in braces: {QUIT}.

NOTE

When you write advanced macro command programs, press Shift+F3 to see a list of macro commands. Quattro Pro 5.0 for Windows lists all the macro commands grouped by category. To enter the desired command, select the category, highlight the command, and press Enter.

Some commands are just one command enclosed in braces. To quit a macro during its execution, for example, use the command {QUIT}; no arguments are needed. Many other commands, however, require additional arguments within the braces. The arguments that follow commands have a grammar, or syntax, similar to the syntax used in Quattro Pro 5.0 for Windows @functions. The general syntax of commands that require arguments is as follows:

{COMMAND *argument1,argument2,...,argumentN*}

An *argument* can consist of numbers, strings, cell addresses, block names, formulas, or functions. The command name and the first argument are separated by a space; for most commands, arguments are separated by commas (with no spaces). As you study the syntax for the specific commands presented in this chapter, keep in mind the importance of following the conventions for spacing and punctuation. Consider this example:

{BLANK *blockname*}

When you use the BLANK command to erase a specified notebook block, you must follow the command BLANK with the cell address or block name indicating the block to erase. In the macro command {BLANK *blockname*}, *blockname* is the argument.

Creating Advanced Macro Command Programs

Advanced macro command programs, like keystroke and command equivalent macros, must be efficient and error free. You begin a macro command program by defining the actions you want the program to perform and the sequence of those actions. Then you develop the program, test it, and make certain the program produces proper results under all possible conditions.

If you have created keystroke or command equivalent macros, you have a head start toward developing advanced macro command programs. These programs share many of the conventions used in the command equivalent macro programs presented in Chapter 14. If you haven't experimented with Quattro Pro 5.0 for Windows macros, take some time to review the examples in Chapter 14 before you try to develop advanced macro programs. Many of the concepts that Chapter 14 presents, especially the concepts related to testing and debugging macros, are very useful as you experiment with the advanced macro commands.

Like keystroke and command equivalent macros, advanced macro programs should be planned carefully and positioned in the notebook. Locating your macros on a separate notebook page (such as page IV) or in a separate macro library notebook is the best practice.

You enter advanced macro command programs just as you enter keystroke or command equivalent macros—as text cells. You must use a label prefix to start any line that begins with a nontext character (such as numbers or /) so that Quattro Pro 5.0 for Windows does not interpret the characters that follow as numbers or commands. Fortunately, Quattro Pro 5.0 for Windows recognizes the left brace ({) as a label character, so in most cases, you do not have to enter a label prefix.

After you decide where to locate your program and you begin entering program lines, keep several considerations in mind. Remember to document advanced macro command programs to the right of each program line. Because advanced macro command programs are usually more complex than keystroke or command equivalent macro programs, more complete documentation is very important. A well-documented program is much easier to debug and modify than an undocumented program.

As described in Chapter 14, you can invoke macro programs in one of the following ways:

■ Macros you named by using the backslash key (\) and a letter can be invoked by holding down the Ctrl key and pressing the appropriate letter key.

■ Macros you named using descriptive names can be invoked using the Run Macro dialog box. You activate the Run Macro dialog box by selecting **T**ools **M**acro **E**xecute or by pressing Alt+F2.

■ Macros you named using the backslash key and the number 0 are automatically executed when the notebook is retrieved (as long as the Application Startup **S**tartup Macro is set to \0, which is the default).

■ Macros you named _nbstartmacro are notebook startup macros, and are automatically executed first whenever the notebook is opened—regardless of the Application Startup **S**tartup Macro setting.

■ Macros you named _nbexitmacro are notebook exit macros, and are automatically executed whenever the notebook is closed.

You can give the same Quattro Pro 5.0 for Windows block more than one name. You, for example, can give an often-used macro both a descriptive name, such as Main_Menu, and a Ctrl+*letter* name, such as \m. By doing so, you gain the documentation benefit of the long, descriptive name and the ease of use of the Ctrl+*letter* name.

After you develop and run a program, you may need to debug it. Like keystroke and command equivalent macros, advanced macro command programs are subject to problems, such as missing characters, misspelled command and block names, and incorrect syntax. Another common problem is the use of cell addresses that have changed in a notebook application. You can eliminate this problem by always using block names in place of cell addresses.

To debug advanced macro command programs, use the Quattro Pro 5.0 for Windows macro debugger tool described in Chapter 14. Before you execute the program, press Shift+F2 to invoke the debugger tool; then execute your advanced macro command program. Press the space bar to continue with the next operation in the program. For more complex testing, you may need to use the more advanced debugger options, such as breakpoints and value tracing.

Introducing the Advanced Macro Commands

The Quattro Pro 5.0 for Windows advanced macro commands fit into several different categories. In any advanced macro command program, you can use commands from one category, or you can use commands from many different categories. The following sections examine each of the commands in each category and show several examples of advanced macro command programs you can incorporate in your Quattro Pro 5.0 for Windows notebooks.

Using Commands That Control the Screen

The commands listed in table 15.1 can sound the computer's speaker, control the message displayed in the indicator, and improve the performance of your programs.

Table 15.1 Screen Commands

Command	Description
{BEEP}	Sounds the computer's speaker
{INDICATE}	Resets the mode indicator to display a specified string
{PANELOFF}	Disables the display of menus and prompts
{PANELON}	Enables the display of menus and prompts
{WINDOWSOFF}	Disables screen updates
{WINDOWSON}	Enables screen updates
{ZOOM}	Maximizes or restores the size of the active window

The BEEP Command

The BEEP command activates the computer's speaker system to produce 1 of 10 different tones. The BEEP command is commonly used to alert the user to a specific condition in the program or to draw the user's attention. Use the following form for BEEP:

{BEEP *number*}

The tone represented by the optional *number* argument can be a number, formula, or location. The 10 different tones, represented by the numbers 1 through 10, are different pitches of the beep you usually hear when you have made an error.

Consider the following example:

```
{IF TOTAL_SALES<TOTAL_COSTS}{BEEP}
```

This statement produces a sound if the condition presented in the IF statement is TRUE. If the condition is not TRUE, the BEEP command is not executed.

For an even more attention-getting alert, use several different tones to draw the user's attention. The following macro, for example, produces a rising series of tones likely to be heard even in a noisy office:

```
{BEEP 1}
{BEEP 2}
{BEEP 3}
{BEEP 4}
{BEEP 5}
```

Because BEEP is an advanced macro command and not a keystroke equivalent, the optional *number* argument is not a repetition factor. To sound the speaker three times, for example, you must write {BEEP}{BEEP}{BEEP} rather than {BEEP 3}.

The INDICATE Command

The INDICATE command alters the mode indicator in the lower-right corner of the Quattro Pro 5.0 for Windows screen. This command commonly is used to provide custom indicators. The INDICATE command displays a string of up to seven characters. The format of the INDICATE command is as follows:

```
{INDICATE string}
```

The following INDICATE command displays the message START in the lower right corner of the screen:

```
{INDICATE START}
```

Unless cleared, the mode indicator displays the string set by the INDICATE command until you exit Quattro Pro 5.0 for Windows. To clear the string and return the mode indicator to the normal mode, use the following command:

```
{INDICATE}
```

To remove the mode indicator completely, use an empty string as in the following example:

```
{INDICATE ""}
```

One of the best uses for the INDICATE command is to inform the user of the progress of a long macro program. As each step in the macro is completed, change the mode indicator to show the current process number. This technique is especially useful in macro programs that do not frequently update the screen display, such as the programs that read and write to data files.

The PANELOFF Command

The PANELOFF command freezes the control panel and prevents the display of menus and prompts during macro execution. Macro programs that select commands from Quattro Pro 5.0 for Windows menus can benefit from the PANELOFF command because the screen does not have to be redrawn during macro execution. The format of the PANELOFF command is shown in the following line:

```
{PANELOFF}
```

TIP

The Quattro Pro 5.0 for Windows Application Object Inspector dialog box includes options for suppressing the redrawing of the screen during macro execution. If you select **N**one, the screen normally is redrawn during macro execution, and you should use the PANELOFF command for better performance.

The PANELON Command

The PANELON command enables the display of menus and prompts during macro execution. Macro programs that select commands from Quattro Pro 5.0 for Windows menus execute slower if the PANELON command is used because the screen must be redrawn during macro execution. The format of the PANELON command is as follows:

```
{PANELON}
```

PANELOFF and PANELON are provided primarily for compatibility with Lotus 1-2-3 macros.

When only one notebook window is open, the WINDOW command is ignored.

The following macro prompts the user to select a window number and then uses the WINDOW command to make the selected window the active window:

```
{GETLABEL "Which window number? ",ANSWER}
{WINDOW ANSWER}
```

The **WINDOWSOFF** Command

The WINDOWSOFF command freezes the main part of the screen but enables menus and prompts to display during macro execution. Most macros execute much faster when the screen is not updated during program execution. The format of the WINDOWSOFF command is shown on the following line:

```
{WINDOWSOFF}
```

The **WINDOWSON** Command

The WINDOWSON command unfreezes the screen, allowing the display of executing program operations. The format of the WINDOWSON command is as follows:

```
{WINDOWSON}
```

Like PANELOFF and PANELON, the WINDOWSOFF and WINDOWSON commands are included in Quattro Pro 5.0 for Windows primarily for Lotus 1-2-3 macro compatibility. In Quattro Pro 5.0 for Windows, use the Application Object Inspector dialog box to set the options for suppressing the redrawing of the screen during macro execution.

The **ZOOM** Command

The ZOOM command maximizes or restores the size of the active window. The format of the ZOOM command is as follows:

```
{ZOOM}
```

The ZOOM command is included primarily for compatibility with Quattro Pro for DOS.

Using the Interactive Commands

The commands listed in table 15.2 provide for all possible types of user input into a Quattro Pro 5.0 for Windows notebook. You can use these commands to provide a more user-friendly interface than that of Quattro Pro 5.0 for Windows standard commands and operations. For example, you can use these commands to create prompts and perform simple edit checks on the input before storing it in the notebook.

Table 15.2 Interactive Commands

Command	Description
{?}	Accepts any type of input until the user presses Enter
{ACTIVATE}	Makes a specified window active
{BREAKOFF}	Disables the Break key
{BREAKON}	Enables the Break key
{CHOOSE}	Displays a list of open windows for selection
{DODIALOG}	Displays a dialog box
{GET}	Accepts one character and places it into the specified location
{GETLABEL}	Displays a prompt and pauses macro execution while the user inputs a label
{GETNUMBER}	Displays a prompt and pauses macro execution while the user inputs a number
{GRAPHCHAR}	Returns the key the user pressed to leave a graph or message box
{IFKEY}	Branches based on the value of a key
{LOOK}	Places the first character typed into a specified location
{MENUBRANCH}	Prompts the user with a menu found at a specified location and branches based on user input
{MENUCALL}	Prompts the user with a menu found at a specified location and calls a subroutine based on user input
{MESSAGE}	Displays the contents of a block in a dialog box

(continues)

Table 15.2 Continued

Command	Description
{PAUSEMACRO}	Pauses macro execution while a dialog box is displayed
{STEPOFF}	Exits DEBUG mode
{STEPON}	Enters DEBUG mode so that the macro executes one step at a time
{UNDO}	Cancels the effects of the last command
{WAIT}	Pauses macro execution until the specified time
{WINDOW}	Makes a specified window active

The ? Command

The ? command pauses macro program execution so that the user can move the cell selector, complete part of a command, or enter any number of data keystrokes for the macro to process. The macro continues when the user presses Enter.

When the user presses Enter, Quattro Pro 5.0 for Windows ends the ? command and continues the macro; Quattro Pro 5.0 for Windows doesn't enter data or complete a menu command unless the next character in the macro is a tilde (~), {CR}, or a keyboard macro command, such as {RIGHT}. The following line shows the format of the ? command:

```
{?}
```

The following example moves the cell selector to the cell named ERROR_MSG and pauses to let the user read the message. When the user presses Enter, the macro continues.

```
{EditGoto ERROR_MSG}
{?}~
```

Because the ? command enables the user to move the cell selector, you cannot be certain that a macro containing this command always works precisely as you expect. Three other interactive commands, GET, GETLABEL, and GETNUMBER, are usually better choices, especially in notebooks designed for novice users.

The ACTIVATE Command

The ACTIVATE command makes a specified window the active window. The specified window can be any Quattro Pro 5.0 for Windows window. The following line shows the format of the ACTIVATE command:

    {ACTIVATE *window_name*}

Window_name must be enclosed in quotes.

The following example activates the named graph SALES in the notebook CONSRPT.WB1:

    {ACTIVATE "CONSRPT.WB1:SALES"}

To activate the only notebook, specify just the notebook name, as in the following example:

    {ACTIVATE "CONSRPT.WB1"}

The BREAKOFF Command

Usually, the easiest way to stop a macro program is to issue a Ctrl+Break command. By using the BREAKOFF command, however, Quattro Pro 5.0 for Windows can eliminate the effect of a Ctrl+Break command while a macro is running. BREAKOFF disables Ctrl+Break while a macro is running.

The format of the BREAKOFF command is shown in the following line:

    {BREAKOFF}

Use BREAKOFF to keep users from stopping a macro to alter data or to look at restricted data in a protected application. BREAKOFF stays in effect until Quattro Pro 5.0 for Windows executes a BREAKON command or until the macro ends.

Before you use a BREAKOFF statement, be sure that you have thoroughly tested and debugged your macro program. You may need to issue a Ctrl+Break to halt the program and correct errors while debugging a macro program. If BREAKOFF is in effect and the macro goes into a loop, the only way to stop the macro is to restart the computer. All data entered or changed since the last time the notebook was saved is lost.

The following macro disables Ctrl+Break before starting the File_Read subroutine, preventing the user from stopping the macro when the file is open. When the File_Read subroutine ends, BREAKON restores Ctrl+Break for the rest of the macro:

```
{BREAKOFF}
{File_Read}
{BREAKON}
```

The BREAKON Command

To restore the use of Ctrl+Break, use the BREAKON command. The format of this command is as follows:

{BREAKON}

When a macro program ends, the use of Ctrl+Break automatically is restored, so BREAKON is often unnecessary. In a large, complex macro-driven notebook application, however, you may want to include a "hidden" command that executes the BREAKON command. This way, you have the means to halt the macro program, even a macro that seems locked in an infinite loop.

The CHOOSE Command

The CHOOSE command displays a list from which you can select any currently open window. When you select a window from the list, Quattro Pro 5.0 for Windows makes a specified window the active window. The format of the CHOOSE command is shown on the following line:

{CHOOSE}

The CHOOSE command requires no arguments.

After you select a window, Quattro Pro 5.0 for Windows makes the specified window the active window, and then continues macro execution. Figure 15.1 shows how the CHOOSE command displays the list of open windows.

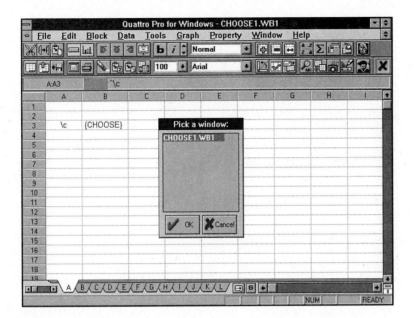

Fig. 15.1

The CHOOSE command displays a list of open windows.

The **DODIALOG** Command

The DODIALOG command displays a dialog box for the user or the macro to manipulate. You create dialog boxes with the UI Builder discussed in Chapter 16 by using the format shown on the following line:

> {DODIALOG *dialog_box,exit_cell,arg_block,user*}

Dialog_box is the name of the dialog box to display. *Exit_cell* is the cell where you want Quattro Pro 5.0 for Windows to store the value indicating how the dialog box was closed: 1 if OK was selected or 0 if Cancel was selected. *Arg_block* is the notebook block that contains the initial settings for the dialog box controls and is the place you want Quattro Pro 5.0 for Windows to store the values indicating the settings when the dialog box is closed. *User* specifies whether the user or the macro manipulates the dialog box. If *user* is 1, the user manipulates the dialog box; if *user* is 0, the Macro manipulates the dialog box.

Figure 15.2 shows how the DODIALOG command displays a custom dialog box called My Dialog 1.

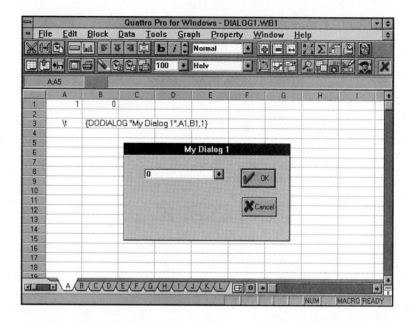

Each control in the dialog box whose Process Value property is set to Yes requires one cell in the *arg_block*. The first cell in the block is connected to the first control, the second to the second control, and so on. You use the UI Builder to set or change the order of dialog box controls. See Chapter 16 for more information on using the UI Builder to create custom dialog boxes.

The GET Command

The GET command suspends macro execution until you press a key, and then the command records the keystroke as a left-aligned label in a target cell. The keystroke then can be analyzed or tested in a number of ways, and the results of these tests can be used to change the flow of the program.

The format of the GET command is as follows:

{GET *location*}

where *location* is the address or name of a cell or block. If you specify a block, Quattro Pro 5.0 for Windows records the keystroke in the first cell of the block.

The keystroke can be any key except F1, which is not available within a macro, and Ctrl+Break, which halts the macro if BREAKOFF has not been used to disable Ctrl+Break. You have no time limit on a GET command because the macro waits indefinitely for a keystroke.

Because the GET command immediately records the keystroke and does not require the user to press Enter, GET can be used to create macro-driven menus that respond to one key press. Figure 15.3 shows a sample macro program that uses the GET command to store the user's response in a block named ANSWER and then transfers to the appropriate macro subroutine based on the keystroke stored in ANSWER.

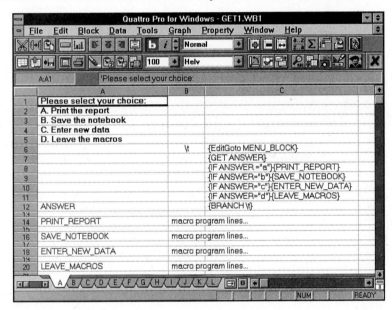

Fig. 15.3

The GET command allows a one-character input with a menu.

This example has the sample macro and the selection menu on one page for clarity, but place your selection menus on their own notebook page so that the user sees only the information you want displayed.

The GETLABEL Command

The GETLABEL command displays a prompt in a dialog box and accepts any type of alphanumeric entry from the keyboard. Macro execution is suspended until the user selects OK, at which point the keystrokes previously entered are stored as a left-aligned label in the specified location.

The format of GETLABEL is as follows:

{GETLABEL *prompt,location*}

GETLABEL displays the specified *prompt* and then stores the entry as a label in *location*. *Prompt* is any text enclosed in quotation marks (") or the address of a cell that contains a label. If you select OK without typing anything, Quattro Pro 5.0 for Windows enters the apostrophe (') label-prefix character in *location*.

You have no time limit on a GETLABEL command; the macro waits indefinitely for a response.

If you want the GETLABEL command to store the user's response at the current cell selector location, you can use the @CELLPOINTER function to supply the *location* argument. Figure 15.4 shows a sample macro that displays the prompt What is your name? and then enters the user's response into the current notebook cell.

Fig. 15.4

The GETLABEL command used to store an entry into the current cell.

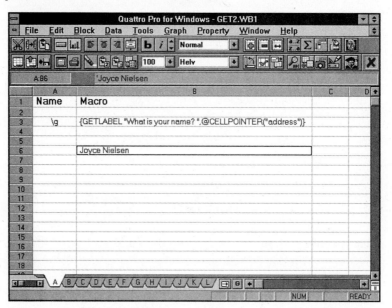

The GETNUMBER Command

The GETNUMBER command, like the GETLABEL command, displays a prompt in a dialog box and suspends macro execution until the user types a response and selects OK. When the user selects OK, Quattro

Pro 5.0 for Windows evaluates the response and stores the result in the specified location. The format for GETNUMBER is as follows:

{GETNUMBER *prompt,location*}

GETNUMBER displays the specified *prompt* and then stores the entry as a number in *location. Prompt* is any text enclosed in quotation marks (") or the address of a cell that contains a label. If you select OK without typing anything, or if you enter a label, Quattro Pro 5.0 for Windows enters ERR in *location*.

You have no time limit on a GETNUMBER command; the macro waits indefinitely for a response.

Because GETNUMBER returns ERR if the user enters a nonnumeric value, macros that contain the GETNUMBER command often include error-checking to ensure that the typed response was valid. In addition to checking for ERR, you also can include tests to ensure that the values entered are within an acceptable range.

Figure 15.5 shows a modification of the \g macro in figure 15.4.

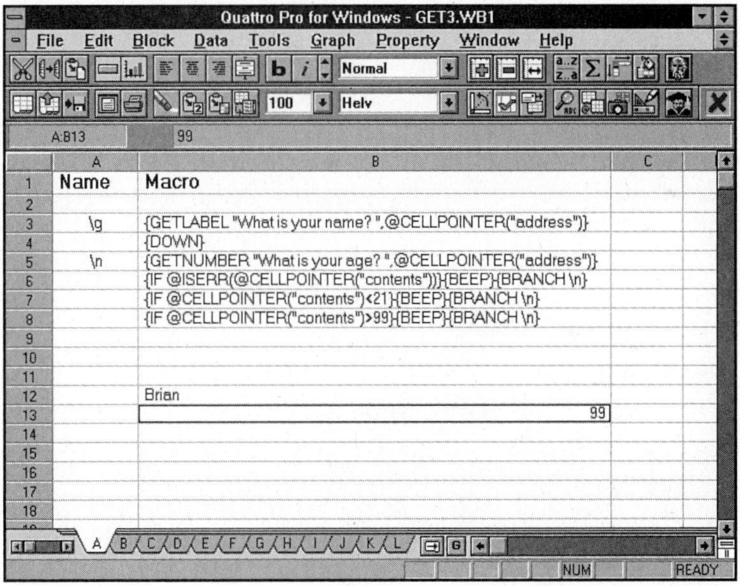

Fig. 15.5

The GETNUMBER command accepts only numeric entries.

In this example, after the macro uses the GETLABEL command to store the user's name in the current cell, the cell selector is moved down one row, and the GETNUMBER command requests the user's age, which is stored in the cell below the user's name. If the user doesn't enter an age, or if the user enters a value outside the acceptable range, Quattro Pro 5.0 for Windows beeps and branches back to the \n macro.

The GRAPHCHAR Command

The GRAPHCHAR command stores the key the user presses to close a message box or leave a graph. GRAPHCHAR is often used along with the MESSAGE command. The following line shows the format of the GRAPHCHAR command:

{GRAPHCHAR *location*}

Here, *location* is the cell address or block name in which you want the character stored.

GRAPHCHAR is very similar to GET. When the user presses a key, one character is stored in the specified location. Usually, the character is then evaluated, and the program branches based on the character that is entered. Like the GET command, GRAPHCHAR does not require the user to press Enter. Unlike GET, however, GRAPHCHAR does not halt macro execution.

Figure 15.6 shows a macro that uses the MESSAGE command to display a message box for five seconds. If the user presses a key while the message box is displayed, GRAPHCHAR stores the character in the cell named ANSWER. Whether the user presses a key or not, the macro continues after the five seconds have elapsed.

The IFKEY Command

The IFKEY command evaluates the argument and, depending on the value, branches. The following syntax shows the format of the IFKEY command:

{IFKEY *string*}

IFKEY determines whether *string* is the name of a keyboard macro command, such as Home or Edit, and executes the next command in the same cell if *string* is the name of a keyboard macro command. If *string* isn't the name of a keyboard macro command, IFKEY executes no additional commands in the same cell but continues to the next row of the macro.

Keyboard macro commands must appear in *string* without braces. That is, HOME is evaluated as TRUE, but {HOME} is not.

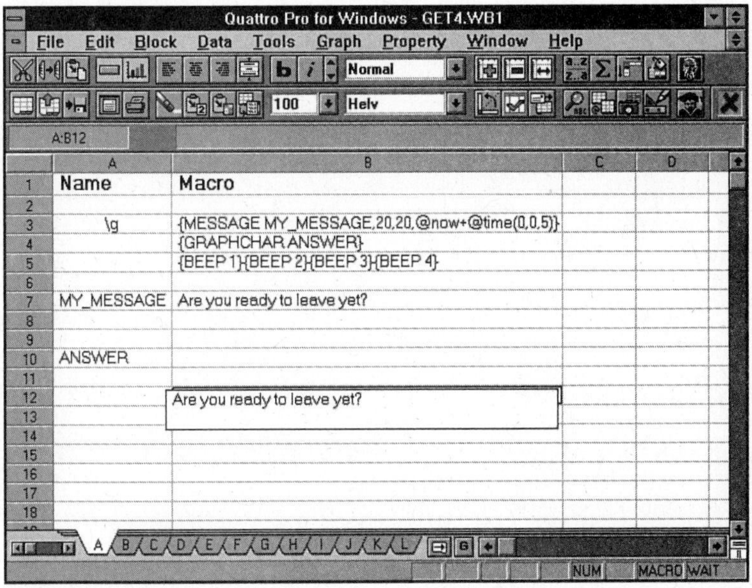

Fig. 15.6

The GRAPHCHAR command stores the response to a message box.

The LOOK Command

The LOOK command frequently is used to interrupt processing when the user presses a key. The LOOK command checks the Quattro Pro 5.0 for Windows type-ahead buffer. If any keys are pressed after program execution begins, a copy of the first keystroke is placed in the target-cell location. The LOOK command uses the following format:

{LOOK *location*}

When you include the LOOK command in a program, the user can type a character at any time. When the LOOK command is executed, the macro finds this character. An IF statement, therefore, can check the contents of *location* and process the user's input.

The *type-ahead buffer* is a small storage area in memory where the computer stores a small number of keystrokes. The computer stores the keystrokes until they can be processed by a program, such as Quattro Pro 5.0 for Windows.

Unlike the GET command, the LOOK command does not remove the character from the type-ahead buffer but places a copy of the character in the cell specified by *location*. Also, LOOK does not pause the program as does GET. Usually, the LOOK command is followed by an IF statement that checks for the user's response, and if a key has been pressed, a GET command is used to remove the character from the type-ahead buffer.

Figure 15.7 shows a test of the LOOK command. In this example, the macro waits for five seconds and if the user has not pressed a key, the macro sounds the speaker. The macro then branches back and starts over. If the user presses a key during the time the macro is waiting, the IF statement becomes TRUE and the program ends.

Fig. 15.7

The LOOK command examines the type-ahead buffer.

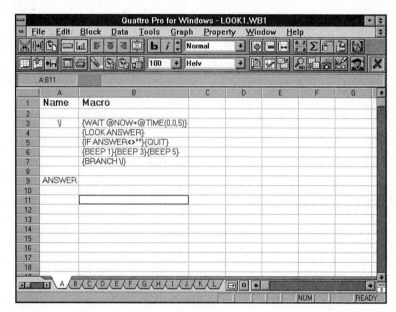

The LOOK command is very useful for creating self-running demonstrations. You, for example, can have the macro change screens at set intervals if no keys are pressed or allow the user to move through the demonstration at a faster pace by pressing specified keys.

The MENUBRANCH Command

The MENUBRANCH command defines and displays a menu from which individual macro programs can be executed. Menu item selection is identical to that of a Quattro Pro 5.0 for Windows command menu; you can highlight your choice and press Enter, or you can select an option by pressing the highlighted letter. The format of the MENUBRANCH command is as follows:

{MENUBRANCH *location*}

Location is a notebook block containing a menu block. The menu block consists of consecutive columns defining the menu. The top row of each column in the menu block contains the selections displayed in the menu. The second row contains the text that describes each selection. As a selection is highlighted, Quattro Pro 5.0 for Windows displays the description in the lower left corner of the screen. The third row of each menu block column contains the macro commands executed if the selection is chosen.

No empty columns can exist in the menu block, and the column to the right of the menu block must be blank.

Quattro Pro 5.0 for Windows displays the menu options with their first letter underlined, indicating the letter that you press to select the option. If more than one menu option uses the same first letter, both have the same letter underlined. Only the first option with a given underlined letter can be selected using this letter, however.

In Figure 15.8, Quattro Pro 5.0 for Windows displays a menu box created using the MENUBRANCH command. The menu structure begins in cell B5 and includes the entries in the block B5..D7.

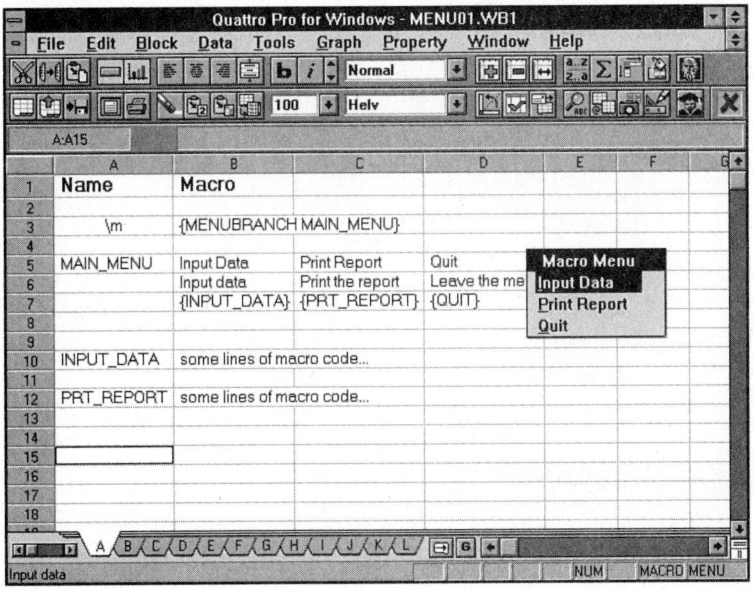

Fig. 15.8

A program that uses the MENUBRANCH command.

When the MENUBRANCH command is executed, Quattro Pro 5.0 for Windows displays a menu box that has the choices included in the top row of the menu block. As you highlight each option, the option description appears at the lower left corner of the screen.

You can select from the menu by moving the menu highlight, pressing the underlined letter, or pointing with the mouse. You can select the **P**rint Report option, for example, by moving the highlight down and pressing Enter, by pressing P (the underlined letter), or by pointing and clicking the left mouse button.

The MENUCALL Command

The MENUCALL command is identical to MENUBRANCH except that Quattro Pro 5.0 for Windows executes the menu program specified in MENUCALL as a subroutine. After individual menu programs have been executed, program control returns to the macro statement immediately following the MENUCALL statement. The format of the MENUCALL command is as follows:

> {MENUCALL *location*}

Location is a notebook block containing a menu block. The top row of the menu block contains the selections that appear in the menu. The second row contains the description that Quattro Pro 5.0 for Windows displays in the lower left corner of the screen as a selection is highlighted. The third row of each menu block column contains the macro commands executed if you choose a selection.

When you use MENUCALL, Quattro Pro 5.0 for Windows returns to the statement following the MENUCALL when a blank cell or a {RETURN} is encountered. The advantage of MENUCALL compared to MENUBRANCH is that you can call the same menu from several different places in a program and continue execution from the calling point after MENUCALL is finished. This procedure is, in fact, the big advantage of *calling* any subroutine over *branching* to a subroutine. A call continues with the next instruction after the call when the subroutine finishes, but a branch transfers program control completely.

The MESSAGE Command

The MESSAGE command displays a message in a dialog box for a specified period of time or until the user presses a key. The format of the MESSAGE command is as follows:

> {MESSAGE *block,left_col,top_line,time*}

Block is the block name or cell address that contains the text Quattro Pro 5.0 for Windows should display in the dialog box. Make certain the block is wide enough to display the text without truncating the display.

Left_col is the screen column number where the left edge of the dialog box should appear.

Top_line is the screen row number where the top edge of the dialog box should appear.

Time is the serial number of the time that the dialog box should be removed from the display. To display the dialog box until the user presses a key, use a value of 0. To display the dialog box for a specified period of time, such as 15 seconds, use the following *time* format:

```
@NOW+@TIME(0,0,15)
```

Substitute the desired display time as arguments to the @TIME function.

The MESSAGE command often is followed by the GRAPHCHAR command, which stores in a notebook cell the key that the user selected to close the dialog box displayed by MESSAGE.

The PAUSEMACRO Command

The PAUSEMACRO command pauses a macro to allow the user to complete the entries in a dialog box. The format of the PAUSEMACRO command is as follows:

{PAUSEMACRO}

Use the PAUSEMACRO command along with the DODIALOG command or a command equivalent invoked with the exclamation point (!), which activates a dialog box the user can complete. After the user completes the dialog box, the macro continues.

Figure 15.9 shows an example of a macro that fills a notebook block with dates, starting with today's date and incrementing by months. The macro starts by displaying the Block Fill dialog box and then places the value @NOW in the Start text box, 1 in the Step text box, and @NOW+1000 in the Stop text box. Next, the macro selects Month for the series, and then moves the highlight to the Blocks text box. At this point, the macro pauses to allow the user to specify the notebook block to be filled. When the user selects OK, the macro continues.

Fig. 15.9

The PAUSEMACRO
command pauses for
user input in a dialog
box.

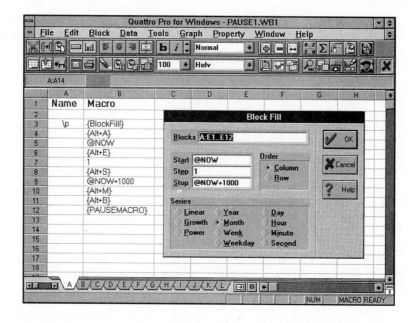

The STEPOFF and STEPON Commands

The STEPOFF and STEPON commands control whether macros execute at full speed or in single-step (DEBUG) mode for debugging and testing. The formats for these commands are as follows:

{STEPOFF}

{STEPON}

Use STEPOFF and STEPON when you need to debug a new section of macro programming added to an existing program. Place the STEPON command at the point that you want the macro to begin executing instructions one step at a time. Place the STEPOFF command at the point that you want the macro to return to executing instructions at full speed. Remove the STEPOFF and STEPON commands when the program has been tested and is operating properly.

The WAIT Command

The WAIT command causes the program to pause until a specified time. The format of the WAIT command is as follows:

{WAIT *time*}

The *time* argument is a Quattro Pro 5.0 for Windows date/time serial number and must include both the date and time portions of the serial number. *Time* is the serial number of the date and the time that macro execution should continue.

To specify a waiting period based upon the current date and time, use @NOW to return the current date/time serial number and add the delay using @TIME. For example, the following line causes the macro to delay for 1 minute and 15 seconds:

```
{WAIT @NOW+@TIME(0,1,15)}
```

Use WAIT to create self-running demonstrations or to create special effects, such as a timed series of beeps. Note, however, that very short delays of a few seconds or less may not be highly accurate.

The WINDOW Command

The WINDOW command switches to a specified open notebook window. The format of the WINDOW command is shown in the following line:

{WINDOW *number*}

Number can be the number (1-9) of any open notebook window. If you don't include the *number* argument, the WINDOW command switches to the next open notebook window.

Using the Macro Flow Commands

The commands listed in table 15.3 provide for program control and conditional branching in a Quattro Pro 5.0 for Windows macro program. These commands enable your programs to make intelligent decisions based on values in a notebook.

Table 15.3 Macro Flow Commands

Command	Description
{BRANCH}	Passes program control to another macro program
{DEFINE}	Defines the type and location of arguments passed to a subroutine

(continues)

Table 15.3 Continued

Command	Description
{DISPATCH}	Branches to a different macro
{FOR}	Executes a subroutine a specified number of times
{FORBREAK}	Terminates a FOR loop
{IF}	Branches based on conditional testing
{ONERROR}	Specifies macro to execute if an error occurs
{QUIT}	Stops macro execution
{RESTART}	Clears the command stack and treats the next instruction as the beginning of the macro program
{RETURN}	Returns control to the macro that called the current subroutine
{subroutine}	Executes a macro as a called subroutine

The BRANCH Command

The BRANCH command causes program control to pass unconditionally to the cell address or block name indicated in the BRANCH statement. Use the following format for the BRANCH command:

{BRANCH location}

The program begins reading commands and statements at the cell location indicated in the location argument. Program control does not return to the line from which it was passed unless directed to do so by another BRANCH statement.

BRANCH is an unconditional command unless preceded by another macro command such as IF, which directs program flow based on conditional testing. The macro command that performs the conditional testing must be in the same cell as the BRANCH command.

Because a BRANCH command does not return program control to the original program line, programs using the BRANCH command usually are not as efficient as programs that call subroutines (see the subroutine command discussion later in this section). A program can call a subroutine and therefore reuse the services of a specialized macro program, such as a printing routine several times; however, programs that branch usually require a copy of each routine for each separate use.

The DEFINE Command

The DEFINE command allocates storage locations and declares argument types for arguments passed to subroutines. A subroutine called with arguments must begin with a DEFINE statement that associates each argument with a specific cell location. The format of the DEFINE command is as follows:

{DEFINE *Cell_1(:type_1),Cell_2(:type_2),...,Cell_n(:type_n)*}

Cell_1 is the cell in which the first argument is stored, *Cell_2* is the cell in which the second argument is stored, and so on. If necessary, indicate the *type*:string or *:value* after each cell address. By default, Quattro Pro 5.0 for Windows stores arguments as literal strings. If you specify :value, the argument must be a value or a formula that produces a value. You also can use :s and :v to designate string and value arguments.

The number of arguments in the DEFINE statement must match the number of arguments passed in the subroutine call; otherwise, Quattro Pro 5.0 for Windows produces an error.

Suppose that you have a subroutine that calculates company profit-sharing contributions based on several factors. You can use a statement similar to the following to call the subroutine and pass the arguments:

```
{P_SHARE "J. Nielsen",27,36543,5}
```

You then can use a DEFINE command as the first statement in the P_SHARE subroutine, similar to the following example:

```
{DEFINE Name_Cell,Age_Cell:v,Sal_Cell:v,Yrs_Cell:v}
```

The DEFINE statement can pass information to a subroutine, but no equivalent statement is available for passing information back to the calling routine. Use one of the following methods to return information from the subroutine to the calling routine:

■ Always have the subroutine leave its answers in a known location, such as a named block, where the calling routines can find and use the information as needed.

■ Have the calling routine pass, as an argument, the cell address or block name in which the answer is to be placed.

■ Instead of using the DEFINE command to pass arguments, have both the calling and called routines use named blocks for storing all values. Then any routine or subroutine can use these values as global values available to all.

Passing arguments to and from subroutines is important to get the most out of Quattro Pro 5.0 for Windows macro programs. Subroutines that can use arguments, passed with the subroutine call or values stored in named blocks, simplify program coding and make the macros easier to trace. Subroutine arguments are essential when you are developing a subroutine to perform a common function you use repeatedly.

The DISPATCH Command

The DISPATCH command is a modified version of the BRANCH command. The DISPATCH command causes Quattro Pro 5.0 for Windows to transfer program control based on the contents of a specified notebook cell. The format of the DISPATCH command is as follows:

{DISPATCH *location*}

DISPATCH uses the contents of *location* to determine where the program branches. If *location* is the name of a multiple cell block or a text formula that results in the address or name of one cell block, program control is transferred to the first cell of the named block. If *location* is the address or name of one cell block, program control is transferred to the address stored in the block.

DISPATCH is most useful when you want the program to branch to one of several macros, depending on the value stored in a variable cell.

In figure 15.10, the DISPATCH statement selects a subroutine to be executed based on the value in the cell named ANSWER. This value is generated by the GETLABEL statement. The string formula in the DISPATCH command concatenates the word SUB_ and the menu selection label entered by the user.

The FOR Command

The FOR command is used to control the looping process in a program by calling a subroutine to be executed a specified number of times. FOR enables you to define the exact number of times a subroutine is executed. The FOR statement provides a loop capability (which is often called FOR-NEXT) similar to the loop capability provided by many other programming languages. The format of the FOR command is as follows:

{FOR *counter,start,stop,step,subroutine*}

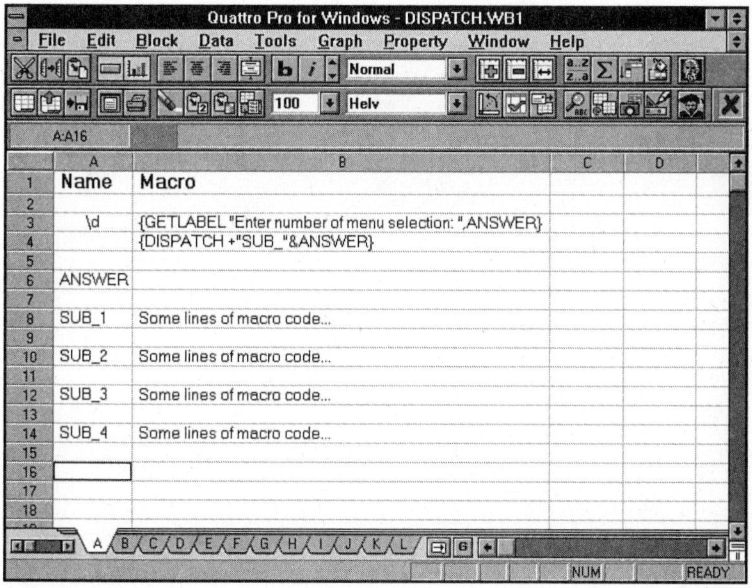

Fig. 15.10

An example of the DISPATCH command.

Counter is a notebook cell that the FOR statement can use to store the current count of the number of iterations (loops) of the *subroutine*. *Counter* must not be manipulated by the user or by any other macro command while the FOR statement is executing. *Start*, *stop*, and *step* are the values used to control the number of iterations. These values can be numeric values or formulas that result in numeric values. *Subroutine* is the block name or cell address of the macro program that is executed once for each iteration.

Figure 15.11 shows an example of how the FOR statement functions. When the \f macro is executed, the value in the cell named COUNTER is replaced with the value 1, and the subroutine BEEPER is called. BEEPER uses a string formula to determine how to sound the computer's speaker. As the program loops, the value of COUNTER is incremented, and BEEPER sounds a higher note with each pass through the loop. Finally, when COUNTER is incremented to 11, the program stops looping because the counter is now higher than the specified *stop* value.

The FORBREAK Command

The FORBREAK command terminates a FOR loop. Macro processing continues with the next command following the FOR command. The following line shows the format of the FORBREAK command:

    {FORBREAK}

Fig. 15.11

The FOR command executes a subroutine a specified number of times.

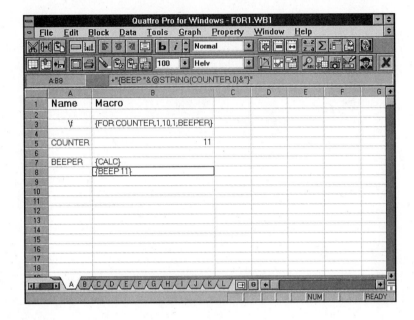

FORBREAK typically is used in conjunction with an IF statement. Use FORBREAK to terminate a FOR loop earlier than it otherwise would end. Suppose that you use a macro program FOR loop to perform calculations that must be limited to a maximum value. You include an IF test and a FORBREAK statement in the subroutine to cancel the FOR loop when the calculated value goes out of range.

Do not include FORBREAK any place other than in a subroutine called by a FOR loop. Otherwise, Quattro Pro 5.0 for Windows produces an error.

The IF Command

The IF command controls macro program flow by testing a specified condition. If the condition evaluates as TRUE, the next command in the same cell is executed. If the condition evaluates as FALSE, the rest of the commands in the same cell are ignored, and the macro continues with any instructions in the next cell down. The format of the IF command is as follows:

{IF *condition*}*instructions if condition=true*

Condition is a logical (Boolean) test that Quattro Pro 5.0 for Windows evaluates. The test is considered TRUE if *condition* evaluates as a nonzero, numeric value. If cell A1 contains the value 10, for example, a *condition* of A1<20 is TRUE because the logical formula A1<20 returns a value of 1 when cell A1 has a value less than 20. +A1 also is TRUE because the formula's value, 10, is both a number and nonzero. A1>10 is FALSE because the logical formula returns a value of 0.

When the test is considered TRUE, the next instruction following the IF statement in the same cell is executed. Unless this statement causes the program to branch or to terminate, the program continues by executing statements in the cells below the IF statement when no more instructions remain in the current cell.

You may experience unexpected results if you do not understand how the IF statement works. Because the statements in the cell below the IF statement also are executed if the statements following the IF statement do not cause the program to branch or to terminate, you must structure your program properly. If the statements below the IF statement should not be executed if *condition* is TRUE, make certain to include a BRANCH or QUIT statement following the IF statement.

The ONERROR Command

The ONERROR command is used to trap many errors that normally would halt program execution. The format of the ONERROR command is as follows:

> {ONERROR *branch_cell*,[*message_cell*],[*error_cell*]}

Branch_cell is the cell address or block name of the macro that Quattro Pro 5.0 for Windows should execute if an error that ONERROR can trap is encountered. *Message_cell* is an optional argument that specifies the cell address or block name of a cell where Quattro Pro 5.0 for Windows should store its error message indicating the type of error that occurred. *Error_cell* is an optional argument that specifies the cell address or block name of a cell in which Quattro Pro 5.0 for Windows should store the cell address indicating where the error occurred.

ONERROR cannot trap all macro errors. For example, ONERROR cannot trap programming or syntax errors. ONERROR is intended, instead, to trap operational and user errors, such as disk errors or a user pressing Ctrl+Break.

Figure 15.12 shows a macro that uses the ONERROR statement to determine if an error, such as the user's pressing Ctrl+Break, has occurred. The macro in this example just plays three tones on the speaker if Ctrl+Break is pressed, but ONERROR can be used to help a macro program recover from a user error. The error-trapping macro, which in this example is named ERROR_BRANCH, can examine the error message and decide on a course of action based on the message.

Fig. 15.12

The ONERROR statement traps user errors.

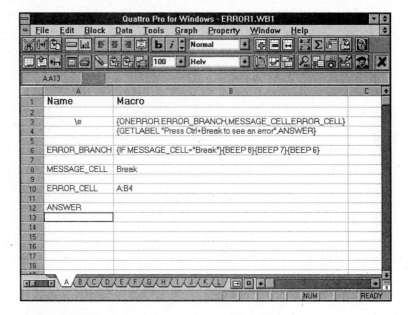

If ONERROR is included in a macro program and no errors occur, ONERROR is ignored. Only one ONERROR statement can be active. You can replace an existing ONERROR statement with a new ONERROR statement, but only the latest statement remains in effect. Rather than replace an existing ONERROR statement, structure the error-trapping macro to examine the error message and respond to the error that occurs.

The QUIT Command

The QUIT command terminates the macro program. The format of the QUIT command is as follows:

{QUIT}

The QUIT command forces the macro program to terminate unconditionally. Even without a QUIT command, the program terminates if it reaches an empty cell or a cell that contains a numeric value. The program also terminates if it is not currently executing a subroutine.

Never place a QUIT command at the end of a subroutine. The QUIT command prevents Quattro Pro 5.0 for Windows from continuing program execution at the statement following the subroutine call.

The most common use for the QUIT command is to terminate macro program execution if the user makes a menu selection to leave the macros. To use QUIT in this way, include the QUIT statement in a cell that performs a conditional test using the IF statement, as in the following example:

```
{IF ANSWER="q"}{QUIT}
```

The RESTART Command

The RESTART command clears the instruction stack and restarts the macro program at the next instruction. The format of the RESTART command is as follows:

```
{RESTART}
```

Quattro Pro 5.0 for Windows saves the return address when a subroutine call is executed. This technique is called *stacking* or *saving addresses on a stack.* By saving the addresses on a stack, Quattro Pro 5.0 for Windows can trace its way back through the subroutine calls to the main program.

The RESTART command can eliminate the stack to prevent Quattro Pro 5.0 for Windows from returning by the path from which it came, allowing a subroutine to be canceled at any time during execution. RESTART normally is used only when errors cause the stack to become invalid.

The RESTART command is different from the QUIT and RETURN commands. QUIT stops the macro immediately. RETURN tells Quattro Pro 5.0 for Windows to return immediately to the calling address, if any, or to quit if no address exists on the stack. RESTART, however, clears the stack but enables the subroutine to continue executing instructions. If the subroutine contains a RETURN statement, the macro stops when the RETURN is executed because no return address is on the stack. If a branch or subroutine call is encountered, processing continues and a new address stack is started.

The RETURN Command

The RETURN command indicates the end of subroutine execution and returns program control to the macro instruction immediately following the subroutine call. The format of the RETURN command is as follows:

{RETURN}

Do not confuse the RETURN command with QUIT, which ends the macro program completely.

Use RETURN in a subroutine called by a {*subroutine*}, MENUCALL, or FOR command. Quattro Pro 5.0 for Windows also ends a subroutine and returns to the calling routine when the program encounters a blank cell. RETURN is most useful when included in a conditional statement, such as a program line using an IF command, to cancel subroutine execution early.

Figure 15.13 shows an example of a macro that uses RETURN to end a subroutine early after performing a conditional test. This example performs the conditional test as the first statement of the subroutine, but most often a subroutine performs additional data processing before testing the results and performing an early return.

Fig. 15.13

A macro that uses the RETURN command.

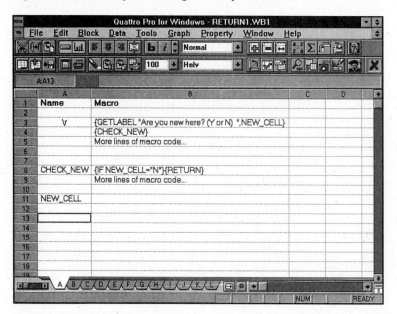

Subroutines

A *subroutine* is an independent program that can be run from within the main program. You call a subroutine by enclosing the name of the subroutine in braces: {PRINT_REPORT}. When Quattro Pro 5.0 for Windows encounters a name in braces, the program passes control to the named *subroutine*. Then, when the subroutine is finished or a RETURN command is executed, program control passes back to the next command following the subroutine call.

Using subroutines can decrease program creation time. Instead of including the same or very similar lines several places in a program, you create a subroutine that performs a specific group of commands. When you want the program to perform the same group of commands, include a call to the subroutine.

Subroutines also make problem isolation much easier. After you create and test a subroutine, you can be certain that the subroutine always performs the same group of commands.

One great advantage of subroutines is that any program in the notebook can use these subroutines. Create the subroutine once and then call it at any time from any program. When the subroutine ends, program execution control returns to the originating program.

Many of the macro program examples shown in this chapter use subroutines. Quattro Pro 5.0 for Windows macro programs that use subroutines are easy to create and understand. These programs tend to be much shorter than other types of macro programs, and because the subroutines perform specific tasks, program flow is usually very clear.

Using the Cell Commands

The commands listed in table 15.4 provide for manipulation of the data in Quattro Pro 5.0 for Windows notebook cells. With these commands, macros move, copy, and create new data.

Table 15.4 Cell Commands

Command	Description
{BLANK}	Erases a cell or a notebook block
{CONTENTS}	Copies cell contents as a label using a specified format

(continues)

Table 15.4 Continued

Command	Description
{GETDIRECTORYCONTENTS}	Lists the files in a specified directory
{GETWINDOWLIST}	Lists the open windows
{LET}	Places a numeric or string value in a specified cell
{PUT}	Places a numeric or string value in a specified cell in a block using column and row offset values
{PUTBLOCK}	Places the same value in all cells of a specified block
{PUTCELL}	Stores a value in the current cell
{RECALC}	Recalculates a block of formulas in row order
{RECALCCOL}	Recalculates a block of formulas in column order
{SPEEDFILL}	Fills a block with sequential data
{SPEEDFORMAT}	Applies a standard format to a block
{SPEEDSUM}	Calculates the numeric sum of a specified block

The BLANK Command

The BLANK command erases a cell or a block of cells in a notebook. The format of the BLANK command is as follows:

{BLANK *location*}

Location is the cell address or block name of the area to erase. BLANK is similar to the command equivalent EditClear except that EditClear erases the currently selected block, but BLANK clears the block specified in *location*.

Use BLANK to clear all existing data from a data input area before inputting new data. If the data cells in an input area have the block name INPUT_DATA, for example, use the following command:

{BLANK INPUT_DATA}

The CONTENTS Command

The CONTENTS command stores the contents of one cell in another cell as a label. The purpose of the CONTENTS command is to store a label that looks like a number. The CONTENTS command optionally assigns an individual cell width and/or cell format.

The format of CONTENTS command is as follows:

{CONTENTS *destination,source,*[*width*],[*format*]}

Destination is the cell in which CONTENTS places the new label. *Source* is a cell containing a numeric value that CONTENTS copies. *Width* is an optional argument specifying an apparent column width, from 1 to 72, to use in formatting the new label. *Format* is an optional argument specifying a numeric format used to create the new label.

Table 15.5 lists the numeric format codes you can use with CONTENTS.

Table 15.5 Numeric Format Codes for the CONTENTS Command

Code	Format of the Destination String
0-15	Fixed, 0 to 15 decimal places
16-31	Scientific, 0 to 15 decimal places
32-47	Currency, 0 to 15 decimal places
48-63	Percent (%), 0 to 15 decimal places
64-79	Comma (,), 0 to 15 decimal places
112	+/- (graph)
113	General
114	Date 1 (DD-MMM-YYYY)
115	Date 2 (DD-MMM)
116	Date 3 (MMM-YYYY)
117	Text
118	Hidden
119	Time 1 (HH:MM:SS AM/PM)
120	Time 2 (HH:MM AM/PM)
121	Date 4 (Long International)

(continues)

Table 15.5 Continued

Code	Format of the Destination String
122	Date 5 (Short International)
123	Time 3 (Long International)
124	Time 4 (Short International)
127	Notebook default

Figure 15.14 shows several examples of how the CONTENTS command stores values using different *width* and *format* settings.

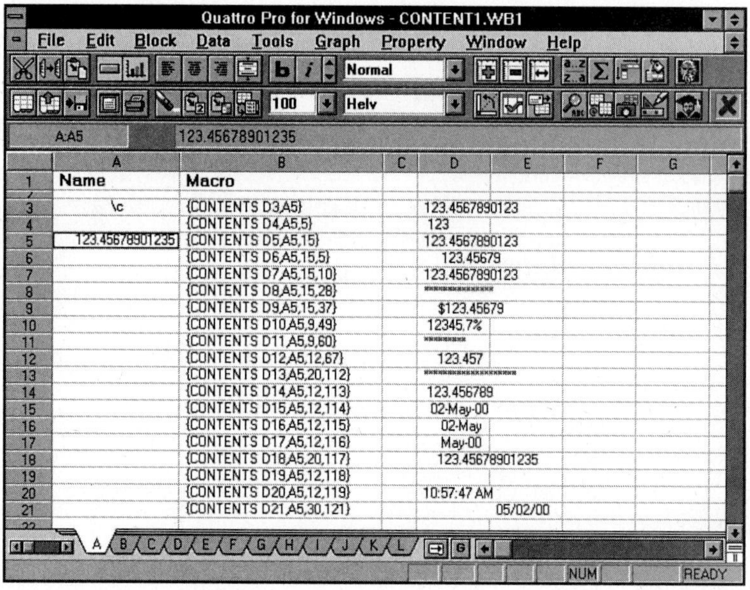

Fig. 15.14

The CONTENTS command stores values as labels.

The CONTENTS command is somewhat specialized, but this command is useful in instances that require converting numeric values to formatted strings. For example, you can use CONTENTS to build a header or footer string for printing on each page of a report.

The GETDIRECTORYCONTENTS Command

The GETDIRECTORYCONTENTS command stores a list of files in a specified notebook block. Use the following format for the GETDIRECTORYCONTENTS command:

{GETDIRECTORYCONTENTS *block*,[*path*]}

Block is the target cell or block in which you want to store the file list. If *block* is a single cell, GETDIRECTORYCONTENTS overwrites as many cells below *block* as necessary to list all the files. The optional *path* argument specifies the directory whose files you wish to list, and it can include file name and extension wild cards. If *path* is omitted, GETDIRECTORYCONTENTS lists the files in the current directory.

The GETWINDOWLIST Command

The GETWINDOWLIST command places a list of the open windows in a specified notebook block. Use the following format for the GETWINDOWLIST command:

> {GETWINDOWLIST *block*}

Block is the target cell or block in which you want to store the window list. If *block* is a single cell, GETWINDOWLIST overwrites as many cells below *block* as necessary to list all the open windows.

The LET Command

The LET command stores a numeric or string value in a specified notebook cell without moving the cell selector. Use the following format for the LET command:

> {LET *location,value,[:type]*}

Location is the target cell in which you want to store a value. The *value* argument specifies the numeric or string value you want to store. The *:type* argument is optional (shown in square brackets, which you do not type when entering the command) and is used to force Quattro Pro 5.0 for Windows to store *value* as a :string or as a :value. Otherwise, the value is stored as a string value.

The LET command copies values, not formulas. If the *value* argument is a formula, Quattro Pro 5.0 for Windows stores the displayed value of the formula, not the formula itself. If *:type* is specified as :string, Quattro Pro 5.0 for Windows stores the formula as text with a label prefix, not as a formula that can be evaluated.

Because it does not move the cell selector, the LET command provides a much faster method of entering values in cells than moving the cell selector to the target cell and making an entry.

Figure 15.15 shows several examples of how the LET command stores values. If possible, Quattro Pro 5.0 for Windows attempts to evaluate the *value* argument as a numeric value before storing the result in the target cell.

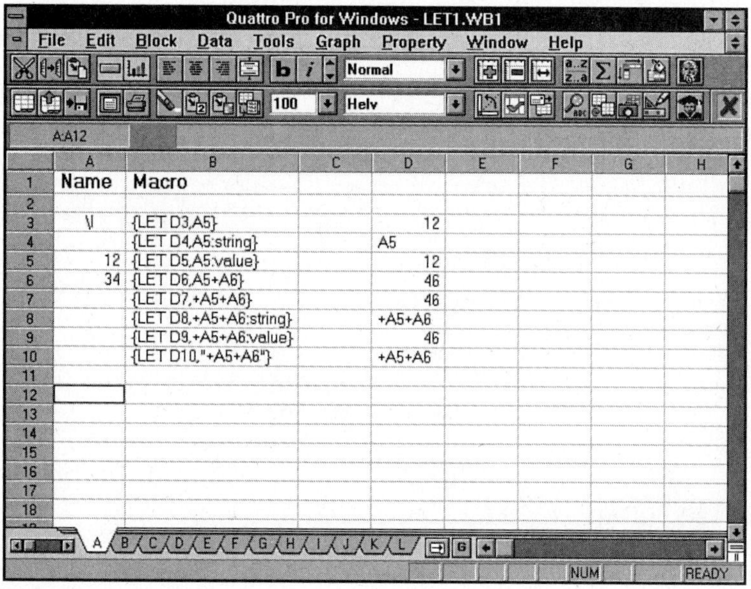

Fig. 15.15

Examples of the LET command.

The PUT Command

The PUT command stores an entry in a cell location. PUT is similar to LET, but instead of storing a value at a specified cell address, PUT stores a value in a cell determined by a column and row offset in a block. The format of the PUT command is as follows:

{PUT *block,col_offset,row_offset,value,[:type]*}

Block is the block name or cell addresses of the block that contains the cell in which the value is to be stored. *Col_offset* is the number of columns to the right of the first column of the block in which the target cell is located. If the target cell is in the first column of the block, *col_offset* is 0 (zero). *Row_offset* is the number of rows below the first row of the block in which the target cell is located. If the target cell is in the first row of the block, *row_offset* is 0 (zero). If *col_offset* or *row_offset* results in a cell outside the block, the macro stops with an error that cannot be trapped by ONERROR. The *value* argument specifies the numeric or string value you want to store. The *:type* argument is optional and is used to force Quattro Pro 5.0 for Windows to store *value* as a :string or as a :value. By default, the value is stored as a numeric value if possible; otherwise, the value is stored as a string value.

The PUT command is often used to update field values in a database block. For example, you can use the PUT command in a subroutine called by a FOR loop. The PUT command can be used to place updated values in a field indicating whether it is time to call on each customer in the database.

The PUTBLOCK Command

The PUTBLOCK command fills an entire specified block with the same value or function. The format of the PUTBLOCK command is as follows:

{PUTBLOCK *value*,[*block*]}

Value is the numeric, string, or function value you want to use to fill the block. The *block* argument is optional; if *block* is not specified, Quattro Pro 5.0 for Windows fills the currently selected block.

PUTBLOCK is useful for filling a block with a series of random numbers. Figure 15.16 shows an example of a macro that fills a single cell block, RAND_BLOCK, with random numbers between 0 and 100 each time this macro executes.

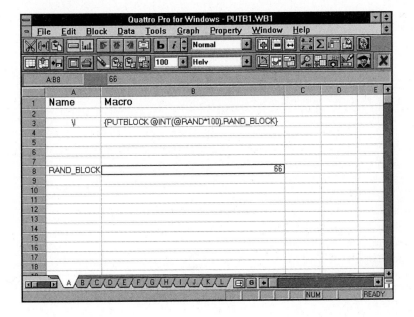

Fig. 15.16

PUTBLOCK fills a block with values.

The PUTCELL Command

The PUTCELL command stores a numeric or string value in the current cell. The format of the PUTCELL command is as follows:

{PUTCELL *value*}

Value is the numeric or string value to store in the current cell. PUTCELL is similar to LET except that PUTCELL does not use a *location* argument. The following LET statement is the equivalent to PUTCELL:

{LET @CELLPOINTER("address"),*value*}

The RECALC and RECALCCOL Commands

The RECALC and RECALCCOL commands enable you to recalculate a portion of the notebook without recalculating all formulas that may be changed. The format for these commands is as follows:

{RECALC *location*,[*condition*],[*iterations*]}

{RECALCCOL *location*,[*condition*],[*iterations*]}

Location is the notebook block containing the formulas that are recalculated. *Condition* is an optional formula that Quattro Pro 5.0 for Windows evaluates after each recalculation iteration. If *condition* is specified, recalculation continues until *condition* evaluates as TRUE (nonzero). *Iterations* is an optional limit to the number of iterations Quattro Pro 5.0 for Windows performs while attempting to cause *condition* to evaluate as TRUE.

The only difference between RECALC and RECALCCOL is the order in which the two commands recalculate the notebook. RECALC recalculates the notebook one row at a time, but RECALCCOL recalculates the notebook one column at a time.

Because Quattro Pro 5.0 for Windows performs background recalculation, it is usually better to allow Quattro Pro 5.0 for Windows to recalculate formulas as necessary rather than to use RECALC or RECALCCOL. After using some advanced macro commands, however, such as LET, GETLABEL, and GETNUMBER, the macro program might not see the updated values. In these cases, use CALC, RECALC, RECALCCOL, or follow the command that changes notebook data with a tilde, as in

```
{LET DATA_CELL,+NEW_DATA}~
```

Recalculating a portion of the notebook may cause formulas outside the recalculated block to fail to reflect current data. If you use RECALC or RECALCCOL, be sure to include a CALC command at some point before the macro ends in order to update all formulas.

The SPEEDFILL Command

The SPEEDFILL command fills the selected block with sequential data, based on entries in the upper left portion of the block, and is equivalent to the SpeedFill button on the SpeedBar. Use the following format for the SPEEDFILL command:

> {SPEEDFILL}

The SPEEDFORMAT Command

The SPEEDFORMAT command applies a named format to the selected block, and is the equivalent of the SpeedFormat button on the SpeedBar. Use the following format for the SPEEDFORMAT command:

> {SPEEDFORMAT *fmtname, numfmt?, font?, shading?, textcolor?, align?, linedraw?, autowidth?, colhead?, coltotal?, rowhead?, rowtotal?*}

The *fmtname* argument specifies the name of the format to apply. The *numfmt?, font?, shading?, textcolor?, align?, linedraw?, autowidth?, colhead?, coltotal?, rowhead?,* and *rowtotal?* arguments are Boolean arguments (1 or 0) that specify whether to apply (1) or skip (0) the corresponding format property.

The SPEEDSUM Command

The SPEEDSUM command sums rows and columns in a specified block. The SPEEDSUM command is the equivalent of selecting the SpeedSum button on the notebook SpeedBar. The following line shows the format of the SPEEDSUM command:

> {SPEEDSUM *block*}

Block includes the rows and columns you want to sum, plus the adjacent empty cells to hold the output.

Using the File Commands

The commands listed in table 15.6 provide the capability to open, read, write, and close a data file containing ASCII text data. These file manipulation commands provide a disk-file manipulation capability equal to the capability of the file commands of BASIC and other programming languages.

Table 15.6 File Commands

Command	Description
{ANSIREAD}	Reads a specified number of characters from the currently open data file without character mapping
{ANSIREADLN}	Reads a line of characters from the currently open data file without character mapping
{ANSIWRITE}	Writes characters to the currently open data file without character mapping
{ANSIWRITELN}	Writes a line of characters to the currently open data file without character mapping
{CLOSE}	Closes an open data file
{FILESIZE}	Calculates the size of the currently open data file
{GETPOS}	Stores the current file pointer location
{OPEN}	Opens a data file
{READ}	Reads a specified number of characters from the currently open data file; {ANSIREAD} performs the same function, without character mapping
{READLN}	Reads a line of characters from the currently open data file; {ANSIREADLN} performs the same function, without character mapping
{SETPOS}	Places the file pointer at a specified location
{WRITE}	Writes characters to the currently open data file; {ANSIWRITE} performs the same function, without character mapping
{WRITELN}	Writes a line of characters to the currently open data file; {ANSIWRITELN} performs the same function, without character mapping

The ANSIREAD, ANSIREADLN, ANSIWRITE, and ANSIWRITELN Commands

The ANSIREAD, ANSIREADLN, ANSIWRITE, and ANSIWRITELN commands perform the same functions as the READ, READLN, WRITE, and WRITELN commands, but without changing any character mappings. These commands are included primarily for international users who may be using an alternative character set. See the sections on the READ, READLN, WRITE, and WRITELN commands for more information.

The CLOSE Command

The CLOSE command closes an open data file and updates the operating system's file record. The CLOSE command should always be the last line of a macro associated with an open file. If you are writing to or modifying the file and you do not close it, you can lose the last data written to this file. The format of the CLOSE command is as follows:

{CLOSE}

The CLOSE command takes no arguments. Only one data file can be open at a time, and CLOSE closes whichever file is open.

Never leave data files open unnecessarily. If you experience a power loss or a system crash, the contents of any open files can be corrupted or lost. Always close open files as soon as the files no longer are needed.

The FILESIZE Command

The FILESIZE command calculates the length, in bytes, of the currently open file. The format of the FILESIZE command is as follows:

{FILESIZE *location*}

Location is the cell address or block name of the cell where Quattro Pro for Windows should place the value of the length of the open file.

Use FILESIZE to determine the current length of the open data file. If the data file contains fixed length records, the value returned by FILESIZE can be used to determine the number of records in the file by dividing the value by the length of each record.

If a data file is not separated into fixed length records but the macro always reads a fixed number of bytes from the file, use the value returned by FILESIZE to determine the number of READ commands necessary to read the entire file.

The GETPOS Command

The GETPOS command enables you to record the current position of the file pointer. The format of the GETPOS command is as follows:

{GETPOS *location*}

GETPOS records the current position of the file pointer in *location*. The GETPOS command is useful if you record in the notebook the location of file information you want to access again. You can use GETPOS to record your current place in the file before you use SETPOS to move the file pointer to another position.

Another common use for GETPOS is to record the current file pointer location in one file before you open a different data file. Because Quattro Pro 5.0 for Windows allows only one data file to be open at one time, opening a new data file closes the original data file. Unless you record the current file pointer location, you cannot return to the correct position if you later reopen the first data file.

The OPEN Command

The OPEN command opens a data file for processing. The format of the OPEN command is as follows:

{OPEN *file,mode*}

File is the name of the data file to open. *Mode* specifies the type of access that is allowed. The four types of access are shown in table 15.7.

Table 15.7 File Access Modes

Access Mode	Function
R (Read-Only)	Opens an existing file and enables access with the ANSIREAD, ANSIREADLN, READ, and READLN commands. You cannot write to a file opened with Read-Only access.

Access Mode	Function
W (Write)	Opens a new file with the specified name and enables access with the ANSIREAD, ANSIREADLN, ANSIWRITE, ANSIWRITELN, READ, READLN, WRITE, and WRITELN commands. Any existing file with the specified name is erased and replaced by the new file.
M (Modify)	Opens an existing file with the specified name and enables access with the ANSIREAD, ANSIREADLN, ANSIWRITE, ANSIWRITELN, READ, READLN, WRITE, and WRITELN commands. The file pointer is placed at the beginning of the file. Modify access cannot create a new file.
A (Append)	Opens an existing file with the specified name and enables access with the ANSIREAD, ANSIREADLN, ANSIWRITE, ANSIWRITELN, READ, READLN, WRITE, and WRITELN commands. The file pointer is placed at the end of the file. Append access cannot create a new file.

Only one data file can be open at a time. If a second OPEN command is encountered, the first open file is closed and the second file is opened. Open data files do not appear on-screen.

The OPEN command succeeds if it can open the specified file with the requested access mode. If the OPEN command succeeds, macro program execution continues with the cell below the OPEN command, and no more instructions in the same cell as the OPEN command are executed. If the OPEN command fails, instructions following the OPEN command in the same cell are executed. Note that this is the opposite of how an IF statement works.

An OPEN command with READ, MODIFY, or APPEND access fails if the file does not already exist. An OPEN command with WRITE access always succeeds unless a disk error occurs. An OPEN command with WRITE access also replaces any existing file that has the same name.

The following example shows a macro that opens a data file for APPEND access. If the file does not exist, the second OPEN command creates the file. If a disk error prevents the file from being created, the macro branches to an error-handling routine.

```
{OPEN "MYFILE",A}{OPEN "MYFILE",W}{BRANCH DISK_ERR}
```

The READ Command

The READ command reads a specified number of data bytes (or characters) from the currently open file, beginning at the present position of the file pointer. The characters that the command reads are placed in the notebook at the indicated cell location. The following line shows the format of the READ command:

> {READ *num_bytes,location*}

The *num_bytes* argument specifies the number of bytes to read, starting at the current position of the file pointer. *Location* is the notebook cell in which the characters are placed. READ places the specified number of characters into the location as a label. After the READ command executes, the file pointer is positioned at the character following the last character read.

The READ command is useful when you want to read a specific number of characters into a specified location in the current notebook. For example, data files, especially those created on mainframe computers, often have records too long to import into Quattro Pro 5.0 for Windows using the Tools Import command. If you know the record structure of the data file, you can use the READ and SETPOS commands to read the necessary portions of each record, regardless of the record length.

The READLN Command

The READLN command reads one line of information from the currently open data file, beginning at the current file pointer position. READLN strips out any carriage-return and line-feed sequences delimiting the lines. The format of the READLN command is shown in the following example:

> {READLN *location*}

READLN copies the current line from the file to the *location* specified.

Use READLN to read a line of text from a file whose lines are delimited by a carriage-return and line-feed sequence. You can use READLN, for example, to read the lines from an ASCII text file.

READLN suffers from the same limitation as the Tools Import command. If records in the data file are not delimited by carriage-return and line-feed sequences, READLN cannot read the data from the file. For most types of data files, the READ command is a better choice than READLN.

The SETPOS Command

The SETPOS command sets the position of the file pointer in the currently open data file. Use SETPOS when the file pointer must be set to an exact point within the file. The following syntax shows the format of the SETPOS command:

{SETPOS *position*}

Position is the offset from the first byte of the data file. Because position is an offset, not a character number, the first character in a file is at position 0 (zero), not 1.

SETPOS often is used when you need to work with two or more data files. Before the second data file is opened, the GETPOS command is used to save the current file pointer position in file one. When the first file later is reopened, SETPOS is used to return the file pointer to the position it was in before the file was closed.

Be careful using SETPOS. Quattro Pro 5.0 for Windows does not verify the file pointer position you specify. If you set the file pointer to a number past the end of the file and write to the file, Quattro Pro 5.0 for Windows attempts to expand the size of the file as necessary. If the number is large, considerable disk space may be wasted saving the file.

The WRITE Command

The WRITE command writes a string of text to the currently open file. The syntax of the WRITE command is shown in the following line:

{WRITE *string*}

You can specify a number of *string* arguments if the total number of characters doesn't exceed 1022. WRITE copies a string to the open file unless the file was opened for read-only access. The *string* argument can be a literal string, a block name or cell address that contains a string, or a string formula. WRITE does not place a carriage-return and line-feed sequence at the end of the string, so multiple WRITE statements can be used to concatenate text on one line. WRITE is well suited for creating or updating a file that contains fixed-length database records.

Be careful about where the file pointer is located before a WRITE command writes to a data file. If the file pointer is not at the end of the file, Quattro Pro 5.0 for Windows overwrites the existing characters in the file. If the file pointer is at the end of the file, Quattro Pro 5.0 for Windows extends the file by the number of characters written.

The WRITELN Command

The WRITELN command writes a string of text to the currently open file and appends a carriage-return and line-feed sequence at the end of the string. The format for the WRITELN command is as follows:

{WRITELN *string*}

The WRITELN command is identical to the WRITE command except that WRITELN appends a carriage-return and line-feed sequence at the end of the string.

Figure 15.17 shows a macro that uses all of the file commands except ANSIREAD, ANSIREADLN, ANSIWRITE, ANSIWRITELN, WRITE, and READLN. This macro reads text from an input file in 100-byte increments and writes the data to an output file in lines with a carriage-return and line-feed sequence appended at the end of the string. The macro in this example demonstrates an effective method of using advanced macro commands to break down a file that has lines too long to import into Quattro Pro 5.0 for Windows and create a new file that easily can be imported using the **Tools Import** command.

Fig. 15.17

A macro that uses the file commands.

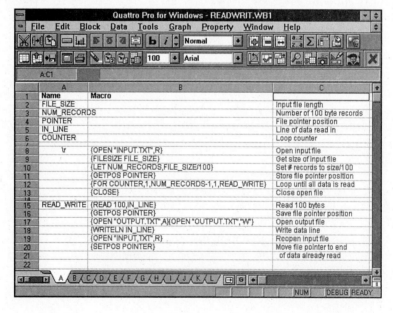

	A	B	C
1	**Name**	**Macro**	
2	FILE_SIZE		Input file length
3	NUM_RECORDS		Number of 100 byte records
4	POINTER		File pointer position
5	IN_LINE		Line of data read in
6	COUNTER		Loop counter
8	\r	{OPEN "INPUT.TXT",R}	Open input file
9		{FILESIZE FILE_SIZE}	Get size of input file
10		{LET NUM_RECORDS,FILE_SIZE/100}	Set # records to size/100
11		{GETPOS POINTER}	Store file pointer position
12		{FOR COUNTER,1,NUM_RECORDS-1,1,READ_WRITE}	Loop until all data is read
13		{CLOSE}	Close open file
15	READ_WRITE	{READ 100,IN_LINE}	Read 100 bytes
16		{GETPOS POINTER}	Save file pointer position
17		{OPEN "OUTPUT.TXT",A}{OPEN "OUTPUT.TXT","W"}	Open output file
18		{WRITELN IN_LINE}	Write data line
19		{OPEN "INPUT.TXT",R}	Reopen input file
20		{SETPOS POINTER}	Move file pointer to end
21			of data already read
22			

Using the DDE Commands

The commands listed in table 15.8 provide the capability to communicate with and execute other Windows applications that support DDE (Dynamic Data Exchange), a capability that enables the user to share data.

Table 15.8 DDE Commands

Command	Description
{EXEC}	Executes another Windows application or a DOS command
{EXECUTE}	Executes a macro in the specified Windows application
{INITIATE}	Opens a conversation between Quattro Pro 5.0 for Windows and another Windows application
{POKE}	Sends data from Quattro Pro 5.0 for Windows to another Windows application
{REQUEST}	Requests data from another Windows application
{TERMINATE}	Closes a conversation between Quattro Pro 5.0 for Windows and another Windows application

The EXEC Command

The EXEC command opens another Windows application or executes a DOS command. The format of the EXEC command is as follows:

{EXEC *application,window_size,*[*result*]}

Application is the name of the Windows application or the complete DOS command you want to execute. *Application* must be contained within quotes, as in the following example:

"WINWORD.EXE"

Window_size is the size for the application's window. Use 1 to allow the application to determine its own size, 2 to minimize the application, or 3 to maximize the window.

Result is an optional argument specifying the application ID for the operation.

Figure 15.18 shows a macro that uses most of the Quattro Pro 5.0 for Windows DDE macro commands.

Fig. 15.18

A macro using DDE macro commands.

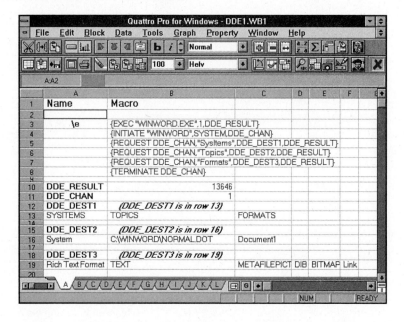

Here, the \e macro begins in B3 by using the following command to open Word for Windows:

```
{EXEC "WINWORD.EXE",1,DDE_RESULT}
```

The *window_size* is set to 1 to allow Word for Windows to determine its own window size. The block name DDE_RESULT is used as the optional argument specifying the application ID for the operation. The balance of the macro shown in Figure 15.18 is discussed in the following appropriate command sections.

Application can be any string you can type in the Windows Program Manager's File Run dialog box. To execute a DOS command, for example, use the following format:

```
{EXEC "COMMAND /C dos_command_string"}
```

To store the current DOS environment settings, such as the PATH and PROMPT, in a file called SET.TXT, use the following command:

```
{EXEC "COMMAND.COM /C SET > SET.TXT",1}
```

> **NOTE**
>
> In this example, **COMMAND.COM /C** is used to load the DOS command interpreter so that the command **SET > SET.TXT** can be executed, and then control returns to Quattro Pro 5.0 for Windows. The **/C** parameter tells the command interpreter to exit after completing the command that follows.

The EXECUTE Command

The EXECUTE command executes a macro in the specified Windows application. The application must support DDE, and the macro must use the syntax of the specified Windows application, not Quattro Pro 5.0 for Windows. The format of the EXECUTE command is as follows:

{EXECUTE *DDE_channel,macro_string,[result]*}

DDE_channel is the number of the DDE channel opened by the INITIATE command, which must precede the EXECUTE command.

Macro_string is a macro command supported by the Windows application in which the macro is to be executed. For details on appropriate *macro_string* arguments, see the documentation for the application.

Result is an optional argument specifying the application ID for the operation.

You can use several EXECUTE commands in a DDE conversation between Quattro Pro 5.0 for Windows and another Windows application. For example, you may tell an application to load a file, calculate a result, and then store the result in another file. The specific commands you pass to the other Windows application are determined by this program's capabilities and by the macro strings this program supports.

The INITIATE Command

The INITIATE command opens a DDE channel between Quattro Pro 5.0 for Windows and another Windows application that supports DDE. The format of the INITIATE command is as follows:

{INITIATE *application,file_name,DDE_channel*}

Application is the name of the Windows application with which you want to communicate. *Application* must support DDE.

File_name is the name of the file with which you communicate. *File_name* is sometimes referred to as *ProjectName*. If you do not want to communicate with a specific file, use the name System.

DDE_channel is the cell address or block name where Quattro Pro 5.0 for Windows stores the DDE channel number that then must be used with the EXECUTE, POKE, REQUEST, and TERMINATE commands. You can open more than one conversation between Quattro Pro 5.0 for Windows and another Windows application by using multiple INITIATE commands. If you do open more than one conversation, store each DDE channel number in a separate notebook cell.

In figure 15.18, the command in B4, shown in the following example, initiates the conversation between Quattro Pro 5.0 for Windows and Word for Windows:

```
{INITIATE "WINWORD",SYSTEM,DDE_CHAN}
```

The DDE channel number is stored in the block named DDE_CHAN for use by later commands.

You must use the INITIATE command before you can use the EXECUTE, POKE, REQUEST, and TERMINATE commands.

The POKE Command

The POKE command sends information from Quattro Pro 5.0 for Windows to another Windows application that supports DDE. The format of the POKE command is as follows:

{POKE *DDE_channel,destination,data_block,*[*result*]}

DDE_channel is the number of the DDE channel opened by the INITIATE command. The DDE channel must be open before you use POKE.

Destination is the location in the other Windows application where the data will be sent. *Destination* is determined by the other Windows application. In Word for Windows, for example, *destination* would be a bookmark.

Data_block is the Quattro Pro 5.0 for Windows notebook block containing the data to send to the other Windows application.

Result is an optional argument specifying the application ID for the operation.

The kind of data you can send to another Windows application is largely determined by the other Windows application. To send a block of notebook data called STORE_TOTALS to a Word for Windows document containing a bookmark named STORE_RESULTS (if the DDE channel number is stored in DDE_CHAN), you use the following command:

```
{POKE DDE_CHAN,"STORE_RESULTS",STORE_TOTALS}
```

The REQUEST Command

The REQUEST command requests data from another Windows application that supports DDE. The format of the REQUEST command is as follows:

{REQUEST *DDE_channel,data_to_receive,dest_block,[result]*}

DDE_channel is the number of the DDE channel opened by the INITIATE command. The DDE channel must be open before you use REQUEST.

Data_to_receive is the information in the other Windows application that is sent. If you haven't opened a conversation with a specific file in the other Windows application, *Data_to_receive* is determined by the other Windows application. For example, in Word for Windows, *Data_to_receive* can be "SysItems," "Topics," or "Formats." For all applications that support DDE, *Data_to_receive* can be "SysItems," which is a listing of the strings you can use for *Data_to_receive*.

Dest_block is the Quattro Pro 5.0 for Windows notebook block to receive the data from the other Windows application.

Result is an optional argument specifying the application ID for the operation.

In figure 15.18, three REQUEST commands are used. The first command, placed in cell B5, places a listing of all the strings you can use for *Data_to_receive* when communicating with Word for Windows in the block named DDE_DEST1 (which is in cells A13..C13). The following example shows an example of this format:

```
{REQUEST DDE_CHAN,"SysItems",DDE_DEST1,DDE_RESULT}
```

The next REQUEST command, in cell B6 places a list of all open files in Word for Windows in the block named DDE_DEST2 (which is in cells A16..C16):

```
{REQUEST DDE_CHAN,"Topics",DDE_DEST2,DDE_RESULT}
```

The final REQUEST command in cell B7 places a list of all Clipboard formats supported by Word for Windows in the block named DDE_DEST3 (which is in cells A19..F19), as shown in the following example:

```
{REQUEST DDE_CHAN,"Formats",DDE_DEST3,DDE_RESULT}
```

Do not use strings that the other Windows application doesn't support as the *Data_to_receive* argument or an error results. Use **SysItems** to determine the strings that the other Windows application supports.

The TERMINATE Command

The TERMINATE command closes the specified DDE conversation. The format of the TERMINATE command is as follows:

{TERMINATE *DDE_channel*}

DDE_channel is the number of the DDE channel opened by the INITIATE command. The DDE channel must be open before you use TERMINATE.

When you complete a DDE conversation, you use TERMINATE to close the conversation. In figure 15.18, the command in cell B8 closes the conversation between Quattro Pro 5.0 for Windows and Word for Windows, as shown in the following example:

```
{TERMINATE DDE_CHAN}
```

TERMINATE does not close the other Windows application, only the conversation between the two applications.

Using the User Interface Commands

The commands listed in table 15.9 provide the capability of changing the appearance of Quattro Pro 5.0 for Windows by modifying the menus and the SpeedBar.

Table 15.9 User Interface Commands

Command	Description
{ADDMENU}	Adds a menu to the menu tree
{ADDMENUITEM}	Adds a menu item to a menu

Command	Description
{DELETEMENU}	Removes a menu from the menu tree
{DELETEMENUITEM}	Removes a menu item from a menu
{SETMENUBAR}	Sets the active menu tree

The ADDMENU Command

The ADDMENU command adds a user-defined menu to the active menu tree. The format of the ADDMENU command is as follows:

{ADDMENU *menu_position,menu_block*}

Menu_position is the position in the currently active menu where you want to add a new menu. *Menu_position* must be enclosed in quotes. If *menu_position* is the name of a menu selection and is not followed by a slash, *menu_position* indicates the current menu selection that follows the new menu. For example, the following command adds a new menu that you defined in notebook block MY_MENU to the main Quattro Pro 5.0 for Windows menu immediately in front of **Help**:

{ADDMENU "/Help",MY_MENU}

If *menu_position* is followed by a slash and <-, *menu_position* indicates the current menu selection that includes the new menu as the first selection. For example, the following command adds a new menu that you defined in notebook block MY_MENU as the first item of the Quattro Pro 5.0 for Windows **Help** menu:

{ADDMENU "/Help/<",MY_MENU}

If *menu_position* is followed by a slash and ->, *menu_position* indicates the current menu selection that includes the new menu as its last selection. The following command adds a new menu that you defined in notebook block MY_MENU as the last item of the Quattro Pro 5.0 for Windows **Help** menu:

{ADDMENU "/Help/>",MY_MENU}

Menu_block is the name or cell address of the notebook block containing a menu definition. *Menu_block* must include the entire menu definition block, not just the upper left corner.

Figure 15.19 shows the result of using the ADDMENU command, which is defined in the notebook block MY_MENU, to add a new menu to the main Quattro Pro 5.0 for Windows menu immediately in front of **Help**. In this figure, the menu, whose title is Que, is selected and the first item is highlighted. The lower left corner of the screen displays the menu item description This is a new menu item.

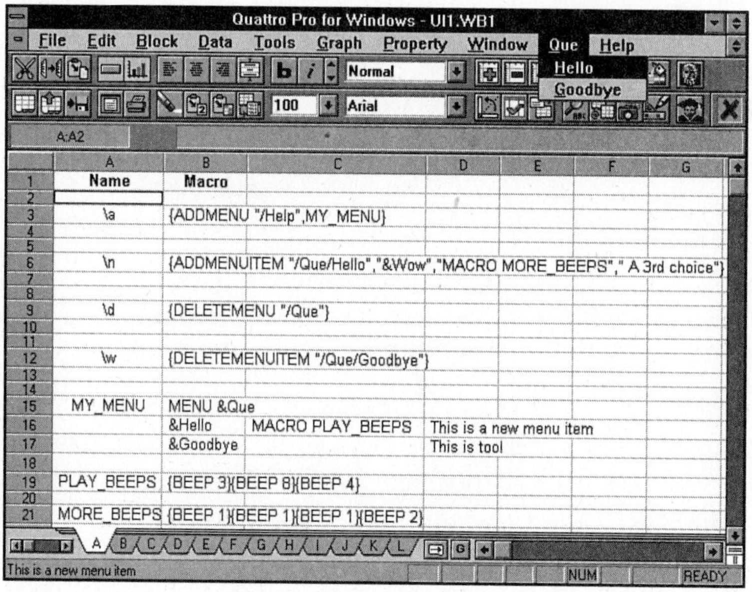

Fig. 15.19

ADDMENU adds new menus to the Quattro Pro for Windows menu.

The ADDMENUITEM Command

The ADDMENUITEM command adds a user-defined menu command to an existing menu on the active menu tree. The format of the ADDMENUITEM command is as follows:

{ADDMENUITEM
menu_position,name,command,[*message*],[*key*],[*area*],[*checked*]}

Menu_position is the position in the currently active menu where you want to add a new menu command. *Menu_position* must be enclosed in quotes.

Name is the command name to appear in the menu. Place an ampersand (&) in front of the character that will select the command and that will be underlined. *Name* must be enclosed in quotes.

Command is the command that executes when this menu item is selected. *Command* must be enclosed in quotes.

Message is an optional message that is displayed on the status line when the command is highlighted. *Message* must be enclosed in quotes.

Key is an optional shortcut key combination that the user can use to select the command. Separate each key in the shortcut key combination with a plus sign (+). *Key* must be enclosed in quotes.

Area is an optional argument specifying in which Quattro Pro 5.0 for Windows areas the command should be available. Enter **Yes** or **No** for each area, in the following order, and separate by commas: desktop, notebook, Graph window, Dialog window, and input line. The entire *area* argument must be enclosed in quotes.

Checked is an optional argument specifying whether the command should appear checked. Enter **Yes** or **No.** *Checked* must be enclosed in quotes.

ADDMENUITEM is very similar to ADDMENU except that ADDMENUITEM adds one command to an existing menu, and ADDMENU adds an entire menu.

In figure 15.20, the \n macro is executed after the \a macro, and a third choice, **W**ow, is added to the **Q**ue menu in front of the **H**ello selection.

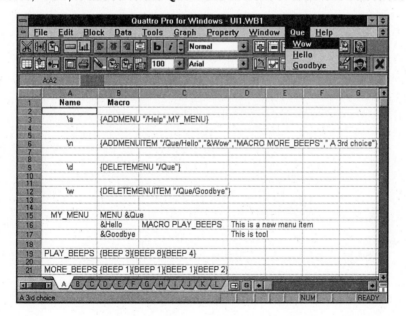

Fig. 15.20

The ADDMENUITEM command adds individual menu items.

The DELETEMENU Command

The DELETEMENU command removes a menu from the active menu tree. The format of the DELETEMENU command is as follows:

{DELETEMENU *menu_position*}

Menu_position is the menu in the currently active menu tree that you want to delete. *Menu_position* must be enclosed in quotes.

In figure 15.20, the \d macro shows an example of the DELETEMENU command. The macro deletes the **Q**ue selection from the active menu, and then redraws the menu to reflect the change. When this macro is executed, the active menu returns to the default Quattro Pro 5.0 for Windows notebook menu:

```
{DELETEMENU "/Que"}
```

The DELETEMENUITEM Command

The DELETEMENUITEM command removes one menu item from the active menu tree. The format of the DELETEMENUITEM command is as follows:

{DELETEMENUITEM *menu_position*}

Menu_position is the menu item in the currently active menu you want to delete. *Menu_position* must be enclosed in quotes.

In figure 15.21, the \w macro is used to remove the **G**oodbye option from the **Q**ue menu.

Use care with DELETEMENU and DELETEMENUITEM. These commands can remove menus and menu items that you have added and also can modify the standard Quattro Pro 5.0 for Windows menus. Be certain that you do not remove menus or menu items, such as **F**ile **S**ave, that prevent you from saving your work.

The SETMENUBAR Command

The SETMENUBAR command enables you to specify which menu tree is displayed on the menu bar. The format of the SETMENUBAR command is as follows:

{SETMENUBAR *menu_block*}

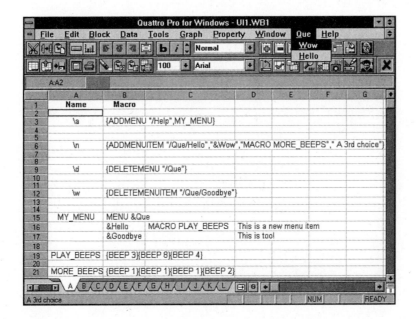

Fig. 15.21

DELETEMENUITEM removes one menu selection.

Menu_block is the name or cell address of the notebook block containing a menu definition. *Menu_block* must include the entire menu definition block, not just the upper left corner.

In figure 15.22, the following macro, named \s, is used to replace the complete Quattro Pro 5.0 for Windows notebook menu with the menu block, MY_MENU (shown in figures 15.18 through 15.20):

```
{SETMENUBAR "MY_MENU"}
```

You can use the following command, shown as the macro \t in figure 15.22, to restore the normal Quattro Pro 5.0 for Windows notebook menu:

```
{SETMENUBAR "QPW.MEN"}
```

Using the Miscellaneous Commands

The commands listed in table 15.10 provide documentation and scrolling capabilities.

Fig. 15.22

SETMENUBAR replaces the entire menu tree.

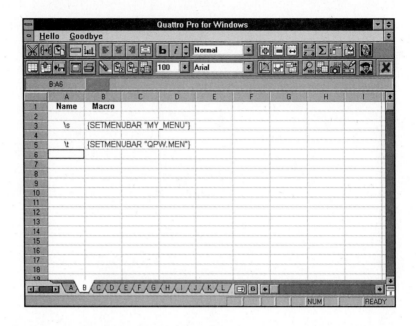

Table 15.10 Miscellaneous Commands

Command	Description
{}}	Inserts a right brace }
{{}	Inserts a left brace {
{~}	Inserts a tilde ~
{;}	Inserts a comment
{}	Inserts a blank line or prevents the current line from executing
{HLINE}	Scrolls the window horizontally by columns
{HPAGE}	Scrolls the window horizontally by pages
{VLINE}	Scrolls the window vertically by rows
{VPAGE}	Scrolls the window vertically by pages

The } and { Commands

These two commands enable you to embed a right brace (}) or a left brace ({) in a macro. The formats for these two commands are as follows:

> {}}
>
> {{}

The ~ Command

The ~ command enables you to embed a tilde (~) in a macro. The format for this command is as follows:

> {~}

Usually, when Quattro Pro 5.0 for Windows encounters a tilde in a macro, the tilde is interpreted as a press of the Enter key. By enclosing the tilde in braces, you tell Quattro Pro 5.0 for Windows to treat the tilde as an ordinary character, not as the Enter key.

Entering a Macro Comment Line

You enter a comment in a macro by using the following format:

> {;*comment text*}

Quattro Pro 5.0 for Windows ignores any comments you add to a macro. You use comments to provide documentation within a macro.

Entering a Blank Line in a Macro

You enter a blank line in a macro by placing a pair of empty braces ({}) at the beginning of the line. Quattro Pro 5.0 for Windows ignores any commands that follow a pair of empty braces. In the following example, a pair of empty braces prevent the STEPON command from executing:

> {}{STEPON}

Scrolling the Notebook Window

Quattro Pro 5.0 for Windows has four advanced macro commands that scroll the active notebook window horizontally or vertically. These commands do not move the cell selector but move the view of the notebook the same way the scroll bars move the view.

The formats for these four commands are shown in the following list:

{HLINE *distance*}

{HPAGE *distance*}

{VLINE *distance*}

{VPAGE *distance*}

The HLINE command scrolls the active notebook window horizontally the number of columns specified by *distance*. If *distance* is positive, the view scrolls right; if *distance* is negative, the view scrolls left.

The HPAGE command scrolls the active notebook window horizontally the number of screens specified by *distance*. If *distance* is positive, the view scrolls right; if *distance* is negative, the view scrolls left.

The VLINE command scrolls the active notebook window vertically the number of rows specified by *distance*. If *distance* is positive, the view scrolls down; if *distance* is negative, the view scrolls up.

The VPAGE command scrolls the active notebook window vertically the number of screens specified by *distance*. If *distance* is positive, the view scrolls down; if *distance* is negative, the view scrolls up.

Using the Object Commands

The commands listed in table 15.11 provide the capability to create, inspect, and control the properties of objects in the notebook.

Table 15.11 Object Commands

Command	Description
{COLUMNWIDTH}	Sets the width of columns in a block
{CREATEOBJECT}	Creates a graph or dialog object
{FLOATCREATE}	Creates a floating graph or SpeedButton

Command	Description
{FLOATMOVE}	Moves a selected floating object to specified coordinates
{FLOATSIZE}	Resizes a selected floating object
{GETOBJECTPROPERTY}	Gets a property setting
{GETPROPERTY}	Gets a property setting from the currently selected object
{MOVETO}	Moves selected objects to specified coordinates
{RESIZE}	Resizes selected objects
{ROWCOLSHOW}	Displays or hides rows or columns
{ROWHEIGHT}	Sets row heights
{SELECTBLOCK}	Selects a block of cells
{SELECTFLOAT}	Selects a floating object
{SELECTOBJECT}	Selects objects
{SETGRAPHATTR}	Sets graph object properties
{SETOBJECTPROPERTY}	Sets object properties
{SETPROPERTY}	Sets properties of selected object

The COLUMNWIDTH Command

The COLUMNWIDTH command changes the width of the columns in a specified block. Use the following syntax for the COLUMNWIDTH command:

> {COLUMNWIDTH *block,firstpane?,set/reset/auto,size*}

The *block* argument specifies the columns to set. *FirstPane?* is a Boolean argument (1 or 0) that specifies whether to resize the columns in the left or top pane (1) or in the right or bottom pane (0) if the active window is split into panes. The *set/reset/auto* argument is a numeric argument that specifies whether to set (0), reset (1), or use auto-width (2) in setting the column width. The *size* argument depends on the setting of the *set/reset/auto* argument. If *set/reset/auto* is 0, *size* is the new width of the column in twips (a twip is 1/1440th inch). The maximum width is 20 inches (28,800 twips). If *set/reset/auto* is 1, *size* is optional and is ignored. If *set/reset/auto* is 2, *size* is the number of characters to add on to the calculated width (the default is 1).

The CREATEOBJECT Command

The CREATEOBJECT command enables you to create objects in Dialog or Graph windows that you would normally add using the active window SpeedBar. In a Dialog window, for example, you can add dialog box items, such as radio buttons and labels. The format of this command is shown in the following line:

{CREATEOBJECT *object,x1,y1,x2,y2,[xn,yn]*}

Object is the type of object you want to add and must be enclosed in quotes.

In a Graph window you can create any of the following objects: line, arrow, rectangle, ellipse, roundedrectangle, text, polyline, polygon, freehandpolyline, or freehandpolygon.

In a Dialog window, you can create a button, checkbox, radiobutton, bitmapbutton, label, editfield, spinctrl, groupbox, rangebox, combobox, picklist, filectrl, colctrl, scrollbar, hscrollbar, or timerctrl.

x1,y1,x2,y2,[xn,yn] are the coordinates of the object. Each object must have *x1*, *y1*, *x2*, and *y2* coordinates specified. Some objects, such as polylines and polygons, may require additional sets of coordinates to specify additional points that define the object.

The following example creates a rectangle:

{CREATEOBJECT "Rectangle",50,50,150,100}

The FLOATCREATE Command

The FLOATCREATE command enables you to create a floating graph or SpeedButton in the active notebook window. The following line shows the format of this command:

{FLOATCREATE *object,upcell,x1,y1,lowcell,x2,y2,text*}

Object is the type of object you want to add. *Object* can be a SpeedButton or a graph.

Upcell is the upper left cell that contains the graph or SpeedButton.

x1 and *y1* are the offsets in pixels from the upper left corner of *upcell* to the left and top edge of *object*.

Lowcell is the lower right cell that contains the graph or SpeedButton.

x2 and *y2* are the offsets in pixels from the upper left corner of *lowcell* to the right and bottom edge of *object*.

Text is the named graph to display, or the label to appear on the SpeedButton.

In the following example, {FLOATCREATE} is used to display the named graph SALES_1 in the notebook block B2..E10:

```
{FLOATCREATE Graph,B2,4,4,E10,4,4,"SALES_1"}
```

The FLOATMOVE Command

The FLOATMOVE command enables you to move a floating object in the active notebook window. If the floating object is not already selected, you must first use the SELECTFLOAT command to select it. The format of this command is shown in the following line:

{FLOATMOVE *upcell,x1,y1*}

Upcell is the upper left cell that contains the graph or SpeedButton.

x1 and *y1* are the offsets in pixels from the upper left corner of *upcell* to the left and top edge of *object*.

The following example moves the selected object in the notebook so the object's upper left corner is over cell D4:

```
{FLOATMOVE D4,3,3}
```

The FLOATSIZE Command

The FLOATSIZE command enables you to resize a selected floating object in the active notebook window. If the floating object is not already selected, you must first use the SELECTFLOAT command to select it. The format of this command is shown in the following line:

{FLOATSIZE *upcell,x1,y1,lowcell,x2,y2*}

Upcell is the upper left cell that contains the graph or SpeedButton.

x1 and *y1* are the offsets in pixels from the upper left corner of *upcell* to the left and top edge of *object*.

Lowcell is the lower right cell that contains the graph or SpeedButton.

x2 and *y2* are the offsets in pixels from the upper left corner of *lowcell* to the right and bottom edge of *object*.

The GETOBJECTPROPERTY Command

The GETOBJECTPROPERTY command enables you to inspect specified objects. The format of this command is shown in the following line:

{GETOBJECTPROPERTY *cell,object.property*}

Cell is the notebook cell where you want to store the property setting.

Object is the object you want to inspect.

Property is the object property you want to examine.

The GETOBJECTPROPERTY command enables you to inspect any Quattro Pro 5.0 for Windows object, including those, such as the application title bar, that normally require a mouse for inspection.

The GETPROPERTY Command

The GETPROPERTY command inspects a specified property of the currently selected object. If the object is not already selected, you must first use the SELECTOBJECT command to select the object. The format of this command is shown in the following line:

{GETPROPERTY *property,cell*}

Property is the object property you want to examine.

Cell is the notebook cell where you want to store the property setting.

The following example inspects the selected object and stores the text color in cell A1:

```
{GETPROPERTY "Text Color",A1}
```

The MOVETO Command

The MOVETO command moves selected objects in the Dialog window or the Graph window to a specific position. This command can also move graph icons on the Graphs page. If the object is not already selected, you must first use the SELECTOBJECT command to select it. The format of this command is shown in the following line:

{MOVETO *x,y*}

x and *y* represent the new position, in pixels, of the upper left corner of the object.

The RESIZE Command

The RESIZE command enables you to change the size of selected objects in a Graph window or a Dialog window. If the object is not already selected, you must first use the SELECTOBJECT command to select it. The following line shows the format of this command:

{RESIZE *x,y,width,height,*[*vflip*],[*hflip*]}

x and *y* represent the new position, in pixels, of the upper left corner of the object.

Width is the new width, in pixels, for the selected object.

Height is the new height, in pixels, for the selected object.

Vflip is an optional argument that indicates whether the object is flipped vertically from its original orientation. To flip the object vertically, enter 1 for this argument.

Hflip is an optional argument that indicates whether the object is flipped horizontally from its original orientation. To flip the object horizontally, enter **1** for this argument.

The ROWCOLSHOW Command

The ROWCOLSHOW command hides or reveals rows and columns in a specified block. Use the following syntax for the ROWCOLSHOW command:

{ROWCOLSHOW *block,show?,row_or_col,firstpane?*}

Block specifies the block of rows or columns. *Show?* is a Boolean (0 or 1) argument that specifies whether to reveal (1) or hide (0) the rows or columns. *Row_or_col* is a numeric argument that specifies whether to affect rows (1) or columns (0). *Firstpane?* is a boolean (0 or 1) argument that specifies whether to affect the rows or columns in the upper or left pane (1) or the lower or right pane (0) if the window is split.

The ROWHEIGHT Command

The ROWHEIGHT command sets or resets row heights in a specified block. Use the following syntax for the ROWHEIGHT command:

{ROWHEIGHT *block,firstpane?,set/reset,size*}

Block specifies the block of rows or columns. *Firstpane?* is a Boolean (0 or 1) argument that specifies whether to affect the rows in the upper or left pane (1) or the lower or right pane (0) if the window is split. *Set/reset* is a numeric argument that specifies whether to set (0) or reset (1) the row heights. *Size* is a numeric argument that specifies the new row height, in twips (1/1400 inch). The maximum height is ten inches (14,400 twips).

The SELECTBLOCK Command

The SELECTBLOCK command enables you to select blocks within the active notebook. The following line shows the format of this command:

    {SELECTBLOCK *block*}

Block is the block of notebook cells you want to select. If you are selecting a noncontiguous block, you must separate the groups of cells with commas and enclose the block definition in parentheses.

In the following example, a single, contiguous block is selected:

    {SELECTBLOCK A1..C3}

To select a noncontiguous block, use the following format:

    {SELECTBLOCK (A1..C3,G10..H13)}

The SELECTFLOAT Command

The SELECTFLOAT command enables you to select floating objects in the active notebook window. If the floating object is not already selected, you must first use the SELECTFLOAT command to select it before you use the FLOATMOVE or FLOATSIZE command. The format of this command is shown in the following line:

    {SELECTFLOAT *object1*[,*objectn*]}

Object1 and *objectn* represent the object names for the objects you want to select. If you select more than one object, the FLOATMOVE or FLOATSIZE commands will process each equally.

In the following example, a SpeedButton is selected:

    {SELECTFLOAT Button1}

The **SELECTOBJECT** Command

The SELECTOBJECT command selects objects in the active Dialog window or Graph window. If an object is not already selected, you must use SELECTOBJECT to select it before using the GETPROPERTY, MOVETO, RESIZE, or SETPROPERTY commands. The format of this command is shown in the following line:

{SELECTOBJECT *object1*[,*objectn*]}

Object1 and *objectn* represent the object names or identification numbers for the objects you want to select. If you select more than one object, the GETPROPERTY, MOVETO, RESIZE, or SETPROPERTY commands will process each object equally.

The **SETGRAPHATTR** Command

The SETGRAPHATTR command sets the properties of selected objects in an active graph window. Use the following syntax for the SETGRAPHATTR command:

{SETGRAPHATTR *fillcolor,bkgcolor,fillstyle,bordercolor,boxtype*}

Fillcolor, bkgcolor, and *bordercolor* are colors in RGB format.

Fillstyle specifies one of the available fill styles for the selected objects.

Boxtype specifies the new border style for the selected objects.

The **SETOBJECTPROPERTY** Command

The SETOBJECTPROPERTY command changes a specified property for a specified object. The following line shows the format of this command:

{SETOBJECTPROPERTY *object.property,value*}

Object is the object for which you want to change a property.

Property is the object property you want to change. You must enclose the combined *object.property* argument in quotes.

Value is the new value for the property. *Value* must be enclosed in quotes.

The SETOBJECTPROPERTY command enables you to change properties for Quattro Pro 5.0 for Windows objects. The following example changes the text displayed in the title bar:

```
{SETOBJECTPROPERTY "Application.Title","Que's Title"}
```

The **SETPROPERTY** Command

The SETPROPERTY command enables you to change a property for the currently selected object. If the object is not already selected, you must first use SELECTBLOCK, SELECTFLOAT, or SELECTOBJECT to select it. The following syntax shows the format of this command:

> {SETPROPERTY *property,value*}

Property is the object property you want to change. You must enclose *property* in quotes.

Value is the new value for the property. You must enclose *value* in quotes.

The following example sets the color and shading for the selected block:

```
{SETPROPERTY "Shading","3,7,Blend4"}
```

Using the Analysis Tools Commands

The commands listed in table 15.12 provide the capability to perform sophisticated analysis functions.

Table 15.12 Analysis Tools Commands

Command	Description
{ANOVA1}	Performs a single-factor analysis of variance
{ANOVA2}	Performs a two-factor analysis of variance with replication
{ANOVA3}	Performs a two-factor analysis of variance without replication
{DESCR}	Creates a table of descriptive statistics
{EXPON}	Exponentially smooths values

Command	Description
{FOURIER}	Performs a Fourier transform
{FTESTV}	Performs an *F*-test
{HISTOGRAM}	Calculates probability and distributions
{MCORREL}	Returns a correlation matrix
{MCOVAR}	Returns a covariance matrix
{MOVEAVG}	Returns a moving average
{MTGAMT}	Generates an amortization schedule
{MTGREFI}	Generates refinancing information
{PTTESTM}	Performs a Student's *t*-test for means
{PTTESTV}	Performs a Student's *t*-test for unequal variances
{RANDOM}	Generates random values
{RANKPERC}	Computes rankings
{REGRESS}	Performs regression analysis
{SAMPLE}	Returns sample data
{TTESTM}	Performs a Student's *t*-test for equal variances
{ZTESTM}	Performs a *z*-test for means

The ANOVA1, ANOVA2, and ANOVA3 Commands

The ANOVA1, ANOVA2, and ANOVA3 commands perform analysis of variances. Use the following syntax for these commands:

{ANOVA1 *inblock,outblock,[grouped],[labels],[alpha]*}

{ANOVA2 *inblock,outblock*,samplerows,*[alpha]*}

{ANOVA3 *inblock,outblock,[labels],[alpha]*}

ANOVA1 performs a one-way analysis of variance. ANOVA2 performs a two-way analysis of variance, with more than one sample for each group of data. ANOVA3 performs a two-way analysis of variance, with only one sample for each group of data.

Inblock is the input block containing data arranged in rows or columns.

Outblock is the upper left corner of the block to place the results.

Grouped indicates whether to group results by column ("C") or row ("R"). Column is the default.

Labels indicates whether labels are located in the first row or column of the input block. Use 1 if the first row or column contains labels, or 0 (default) if there are no labels.

Alpha specifies the significance level at which to evaluate the *F*-statistic (default is .05).

Samplerows specifies the number of rows in each sample.

The DESCR Command

The DESCR command returns a table of descriptive statistics. Use the following syntax for the DESCR command:

> {DESCR*inblock*,*outblock*,*grouped*,[*labels*],
> [*summary*],[*largest*],[*smallest*],[*confidence*]}

Inblock is the input block containing data arranged in rows or columns.

Outblock is the upper left corner of the block to place the results.

Grouped indicates whether to group results by column ("C") or row ("R"). Column is the default.

Labels indicates whether labels are located in the first row or column of the input block. Use 1 if the first row or column contains labels, or 0 (default) if there are no labels.

Summary is a Boolean argument (0 or 1) that specifies whether to display (1) or omit (0) summary statistics.

Largest is a numeric argument that specifies reporting of the *n*th largest data point.

Smallest is a numeric argument that specifies reporting of the *n*th smallest data point.

Confidence is the confidence level of the mean (default .95).

The EXPON Command

The EXPON command performs exponential smoothing on a series of values. Use the following syntax for the EXPON command:

   {EXPON *inblock,outblock,[damping],[stderrs]*}

Inblock is the input block containing data arranged in a single row or column. *Inblock* must contain at least four numeric values and may not contain labels.

Outblock is the upper left corner of the block to place the results.

Damping is the damping factor and must be greater than or equal to zero (default .3).

Stderrs is a Boolean argument (0 or 1) that specifies whether to include (1) or omit (0) standard errors in *outblock*.

The FOURIER Command

The FOURIER command performs a fast Fourier transformation on a block of data. Use the following syntax for the FOURIER command:

   {FOURIER *inblock,outblock,[inverse]*}

Inblock is one or more numeric block values and must be a power of 2 between 2 and 1024.

Outblock is the upper left corner of the block to place the results.

Inverse is a Boolean argument (0 or 1) that specifies whether to perform a Fourier transformation (0) or the inverse Fourier transformation (1).

The FTESTV Command

The FTESTV command performs a two-sample *F*-test to compare population variances. Use the following syntax for the FTESTV command:

   {FTESTV *inblock1,inblock2,outblock,[labels]*}

Inblock1 is the first input block containing data arranged in a row or column.

Inblock2 is the second input block containing data arranged in a row or column.

Outblock is the upper left corner of the block to place the results.

Labels indicates whether labels are located in the first row or column of the input block. Use 1 if the first row or column contains labels, or 0 (default) if there are no labels.

The HISTOGRAM Command

The HISTOGRAM command calculates probability and distributions. Use the following syntax for the HISTOGRAM command:

> {HISTOGRAM *inblock,outblock,*[*binblock*],[*pareto*],[*cum*]}

Inblock is the input block containing data arranged in rows or columns. *Inblock* must not contain labels.

Outblock is the upper left corner of the block to place the results.

Binblock is a set of numbers (in ascending order) defining the bin range.

Pareto specifies whether to arrange the output table in both descending frequency and ascending *binblock* order (1), or just in ascending *binblock* order (0).

Cum specifies whether to include (1) or exclude (0) cumulative percentages in *outblock*.

The MCORREL and MCOVAR Commands

The MCORREL command computes the correlation matrix between two or more data sets. The MCOVAR command returns the covariance matrix between two or more data sets. Use the following syntax for these commands:

> {MCORREL *inblock,outblock,*[*grouped*],[*labels*]}

> {MCOVAR *inblock,outblock,*[*grouped*],[*labels*]}

Inblock is the input block containing data arranged in rows or columns.

Outblock is the upper left corner of the block to place the results.

Grouped indicates whether to group results by column ("C") or row ("R"). Column is the default.

Labels indicates whether labels are located in the first row or column of the input block. Use 1 if the first row or column contains labels, or 0 (default) if there are no labels.

The MOVEAVG Command

The MOVEAVG command returns a moving average. Use the following syntax for the MOVEAVG command:

> {MOVEAVG *inblock,outblock,*[*interval*],[*stderrs*]}

Inblock is the input block containing data arranged in a single row or column. *Inblock* must contain at least four numeric values and may not contain labels.

Outblock is the upper left corner of the block to place the results.

Interval is the number of values to include in the moving average (default is 3).

Stderrs is a Boolean argument (0 or 1) that specifies whether to include (1) or omit (0) standard errors in *outblock*.

The MTGAMT Command

The MTGAMT command generates an amortization schedule for a mortgage. Use the following syntax for the MTGAMT command:

> {MTGAMT [*outblock*],[*rate*],[*term*],[*origbal*],[*endbal*],[*lastyear*]}

Outblock is the upper left corner of the block to place the results.

Rate is the yearly interest rate (default is .12).

Term is the length of the loan in years (default is 30).

Origbal is the original loan balance (default is $100,000).

Endbal is the balance at loan completion (default is 0).

Lastyear is the last year through which to generate the amortization schedule (default is *term*).

The MTGREFI Command

The MTGREFI command generates information about refinancing a mortgage. Use the following syntax for the MTGREFI command:

> {MTGREFI [*outblock*],[*currbal*],[*currrate*],
> [*remterm*],[*candpctfees*],[*candrate*]}

Outblock is the upper left corner of the block to place the results.

Currbal is the remaining principal.

Currrate is the current yearly interest rate.

Remterm is the remaining term on the current loan.

Candpctfees is the number of points (or fees) on the candidate loan.

Candrate is the yearly interest rate on the candidate loan.

The PTTESTM and PTTESTV Commands

The PTTESTM command performs a paired two-sample Student's *t*-test for means. The PTTESTV command performs a Student's *t*-test for two independent samples with unequal variances. Use the following syntax for these commands:

> {PTTESTM inblock1,*inblock2,outblock,*[*labels*],[*alpha*],[*difference*]}

> {PTTESTV *inblock1,inblock2,outblock,*[*labels*],[*alpha*]}

Inblock1 is the first input block containing data arranged in a row or column.

Inblock2 is the second input block containing data arranged in a row or column.

Outblock is the upper left corner of the block to place the results.

Labels indicates whether labels are located in the first row or column of the input block. Use 1 if the first row or column contains labels, or 0 (default) if there are no labels.

Alpha specifies the significance level of the test (default is .05).

Difference is the hypothetical mean difference (default is 0).

The RANDOM Command

The RANDOM command generates random values drawn from several different types of distributions.

Use the following syntax to generate random values drawn from a uniform distribution:

> {RANDOM *outblock,columns,rows,distribution,*
> *seed,lowerbound,upperbound*}

Use the following syntax to generate random values drawn from a normal distribution:

> {RANDOM *outblock,columns,rows,distribution,seed,mean,sdev*}

Use the following syntax to generate random values drawn from a Bernoulli distribution:

> {RANDOM *outblock,columns,rows,distribution,seed,prob*}

Use the following syntax to generate random values drawn from a binomial distribution:

> {RANDOM *outblock,columns,rows,distribution,seed,prob,trials*}

Use the following syntax to generate random values drawn from a Poisson distribution:

> {RANDOM *outblock,columns,rows,distribution,seed,lambda*}

Use the following syntax to generate random values drawn from a patterned distribution:

> {RANDOM *outblock,columns,rows,distribution,*
> *seed,lowerbound,upperbound,step,repeatnumber,repeatsequence*}

Use the following syntax to generate random values drawn from a discrete distribution:

> {RANDOM *outblock,columns,rows,distribution,seed,inblock*}

Outblock is the upper left corner of the block to place the results.

Columns is the number of random sets to generate (default is the number of columns in *outblock*).

Rows is the number of rows of random numbers to generate.

Distribution is the type of random distribution to use:

1	uniform
2	normal
3	Bernoulli
4	binomial
5	Poisson
6	patterned
7	discrete

Seed is the starting number for the random number algorithm.

Lowerbound is the lower bound on the set of numbers to generate.

Upperbound is the upper bound on the set of numbers to generate.

Mean is the mean of the set of numbers to generate.

Sdev is the standard deviation of the set of numbers to generate.

Prob is the probability of success on each trail run, and must be between 0 and 1.

Trials is the number of trials.

Lambda is the expected number of events in each unit.

Step is the increment value.

Repeatnumber is the number of times to repeat each value.

Repeatsequence is the number of times to repeat each sequence of values.

Inblock is one or more numeric block values.

The RANKPERC Command

The RANKPERC command returns rankings of values in a block. Use the following syntax for the RANKPERC command:

> {RANKPERC *inblock,outblock,[grouped],[labels]*}

Inblock is the input block containing data arranged in rows or columns.

Outblock is the upper left corner of the block to place the results.

Grouped indicates whether to group results by column ("C") or row ("R"). Column is the default.

Labels indicates whether labels are located in the first row or column of the input block. Use 1 if the first row or column contains labels, or 0 (default) if there are no labels.

The REGRESS Command

The REGRESS command performs multiple linear regression analysis. Use the following syntax for the REGRESS command:

{REGRESS *inblocky,inblockx,yintzero,labels,*
confidence,outblock,residuals,stdresidual,residualoutblock,probability}

Inblocky is a single column of dependent variables (y values).

Inblockx is a block containing independent variables (x values).

Yintzero is a Boolean (0 or 1) argument specifying whether the y-intercept is 0 (1) or computed (0).

Labels indicates whether labels are located in the first row or column of the input blocks. Use 1 if the first row or column contains labels, or 0 (default) if there are no labels.

Confidence specifies the confidence level to apply.

Outblock is the upper left corner of the block to place the results.

Residuals is a Boolean (0 or 1) argument specifying whether to include (1) or exclude (0) residuals in the output table.

Stdresidual is a Boolean (0 or 1) argument specifying whether include (1) or exclude (0) standardized residuals in the output table.

Residualoutblock is the upper left corner of the block to place the residual table.

Probability is the upper left corner of the block to place the probabilities table.

The SAMPLE Command

The SAMPLE command returns a periodic or random sample of values. Use the following syntax for the SAMPLE command:

{SAMPLE *inblock,outblock,type,rate*}

Inblock is one or more numeric block values.

Outblock is the upper left corner of the block to place the results.

Type is "P" for a periodic sample or "R" for a random sample.

Rate is the periodic interval for a periodic sample or the number of samples for a random sample.

The TTESTM Command

The TTESTM command performs a Student's *t*-test using two independent samples with equal variances. Use the following syntax for the
TTESTM command:

{TTESTM *inblock1,inblock2,outblock,*[*labels*],[*alpha*],[*difference*]}

Inblock1 is one or more numeric block values representing the first
input block.

Inblock2 is one or more numeric block values representing the second
input block.

Outblock is the upper left corner of the block to place the results.

Grouped indicates whether to group results by column ("C") or row
("R"). Column is the default.

Labels indicates whether labels are located in the first row or column of
the input block. Use 1 if the first row or column contains labels, or 0
(default) if there are no labels.

Alpha specifies the significance level at which to evaluate the *F*-statistic
(default is .05).

Difference is the hypothetical difference in the means between *inblock1*
and *inblock2*.

The ZTESTM Command

The ZTESTM command performs a two-sample *z*-test for means, assum-
ing known variances for each sample. Use the following syntax for the
ZTESTM command:

{ZTESTM *inblock1,inblock2,outblock,*[*labels*],[*alpha*],
[*difference*],[*variance1*],[*variance2*]}

Inblock1 is one or more numeric block values representing the first
input block.

Inblock2 is one or more numeric block values representing the second
input block.

Outblock is the upper left corner of the block to place the results.

Grouped indicates whether to group results by column ("C") or row
("R"). Column is the default.

Labels indicates whether labels are located in the first row or column of the input block. Use 1 if the first row or column contains labels, or 0 (default) if there are no labels.

Alpha specifies the significance level at which to evaluate the *F*-statistic (default is .05).

Difference is the hypothetical difference in the means between *inblock1* and *inblock2*.

Variance1 and *variance2* are values indicating the variance of *inblock1* and *inblock2* (default is 0).

Questions and Answers

Q: How can I quickly find a listing of the macro commands?

A: Press Shift+F3 to see the macro commands broken down into their individual categories. When you select a macro command, it is automatically copied to the input line. If you need additional information, press F1 to see the help screen for the selected command.

Q: Many of the macro command arguments are listed as "Boolean" arguments. What does this mean?

A: Boolean arguments are those which have a value of 1 (for true) or 0 (for false). When an argument is a Boolean argument, you use either 1 or 0 to represent the argument.

Q: What are "self-modifying" macros?

A: The term "self-modifying" refers to a macro command that is the result of a string formula. The macro command that is executed depends on how the string formula is evaluated when the macro is run.

Self-modifying macros should be avoided because they are extremely difficult to understand and debug. Imagine how difficult it would be to understand a macro that changes as notebook data changes. You couldn't be certain how the macro might appear at runtime.

Instead of creating self-modifying macros, structure your macro programs using conditional logic so that different macro subroutines are executed depending on the needs of the program. You can use several macro commands, including {IF} and {OPEN} to create conditional tests.

Summary

In this chapter, you learned that macros can do much more than automate keystrokes. Macros also can be complete programs with processing features, such as loops, branching, and subroutines. Using the power of Quattro Pro 5.0 for Windows advanced macro commands, you can make notebook applications easier to use and customize Quattro Pro 5.0 for Windows for special notebook applications.

The Quattro Pro 5.0 for Windows macro programming language has many powerful capabilities that you can take advantage of. As you work with Quattro Pro 5.0 for Windows advanced macro commands, you discover that this modern spreadsheet program has a rich programming language that can solve many of your application problems.

In the following chapter, you learn to use the SpeedButtons and create custom dialog boxes, which you then can use to enhance notebook applications. SpeedButtons and custom dialog boxes make your applications much easier to use and appear more professional.

Using SpeedButtons and Custom Dialog Boxes

In previous chapters, you learned to create macros and use advanced macro commands. In this chapter, you learn about two exciting features in Quattro Pro 5.0 for Windows—SWSpeedButtons and custom dialog boxes.

Quattro Pro 5.0 for Windows is powerful and easy to use, but SpeedButtons and custom dialog boxes enable you to create notebook applications that are even easier to use. These two related features enable you to use the power of Quattro Pro 5.0 for Windows macro programming in ways never before available to the spreadsheet user.

SpeedButtons and custom dialog boxes are new to Quattro Pro 5.0 for Windows and enable you to customize the way the program functions. Instead of requiring a user to use keyboard commands to execute macros, for example, you can create SpeedButtons that execute macros.

Instead of relying on input line prompts, you can create dialog boxes that the user can manipulate. You can also create a special type of custom dialog box, a SpeedBar, which can combine standard SpeedBar controls with your own custom controls. Custom SpeedBars enable you to assemble exactly the set of tools you want.

The SpeedButtons and dialog boxes you create become a part of your Quattro Pro 5.0 for Windows notebook so when the notebook is opened, your SpeedButtons and dialog boxes are ready to use. If you create notebook applications for other people to use, SpeedButtons and dialog boxes give those applications a professional, finished appearance.

Learning the subjects discussed in this chapter enables you to perform the following tasks:

- Create your own SpeedButtons
- Modify the appearance and function of SpeedButtons
- Create custom dialog boxes
- Use dialog boxes to accept user input to macro programs
- Create custom SpeedBars

Understanding SpeedButtons and Custom Dialog Boxes

SpeedButtons are objects you place on a notebook page. When you select a SpeedButton, it executes a macro associated with the SpeedButton. You can place SpeedButtons anywhere in a notebook, and you can customize the appearance of SpeedButtons by changing their size and shape, the style and color of their borders, and the text displayed on the face of the SpeedButton.

Like SpeedButtons, you also use custom dialog boxes to enhance macro programs. Custom dialog boxes combine all the elements of Windows dialog boxes including push buttons, check boxes, radio buttons, text boxes, and so on. Custom dialog boxes can accept user input, allow the user to select options, and display lists.

You may find it useful to think of SpeedButtons as a simple form of custom dialog boxes. SpeedButtons and custom dialog boxes are used to enhance macro programs, but SpeedButtons perform one nonvarying task. As a result, SpeedButtons are somewhat easier to create. Once you understand the basics of creating SpeedButtons, you'll find that the task of creating custom dialog boxes, while slightly more involved, is still quite simple and straightforward.

Creating SpeedButtons

You use the Button tool on the Quattro Pro 5.0 for Windows SpeedBar to add SpeedButtons to a notebook. In figure 16.1, a new SpeedButton (with the default name of Button1) has been added to the notebook.

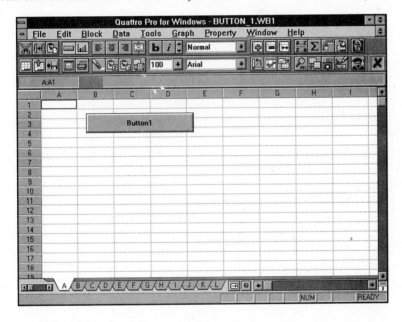

Fig. 16.1

Use the SpeedButton tool to add SpeedButtons to a notebook.

You need a mouse to create and to use SpeedButtons. If you are unsure whether the notebook user has a mouse, make certain you include a keyboard method of performing the tasks you assign to SpeedButtons.

To create a new SpeedButton, follow these steps:

1. Determine the proper notebook location for the SpeedButton. Select an area outside any report print blocks unless you want the SpeedButton to appear in the printout.

2. Select the SpeedButton tool on the Quattro Pro 5.0 for Windows SpeedBar.

3. Position the mouse pointer at the first corner of the area where you want the SpeedButton to appear and hold down the left mouse button.

4. Drag the mouse pointer to the diagonally opposite corner of the area where you want the SpeedButton to appear and release the mouse button. As you drag the mouse pointer, Quattro Pro 5.0 for Windows displays a dotted outline showing the size of the SpeedButton.

SpeedButtons remain in the same row and column position on the notebook page where they originally are placed when you move the cell selector to another part of the notebook. If you create a SpeedButton that covers cells B2..D4 on notebook page A, the SpeedButton disappears from the screen when you move to another notebook page or to another part of the same page.

SpeedButtons should be large enough to display text that describes the purpose of the SpeedButton but not so large that they cover important areas of the notebook. If you are creating several SpeedButtons from which the user can select a choice of actions, try to maintain a consistent size and alignment for a more uniform, professional appearance.

To create several SpeedButtons that have a consistent size and alignment, follow these steps:

1. Create a SpeedButton that has the desired size and shape.

2. Select the SpeedButton and use the Cut button to move the SpeedButton to the Clipboard.

3. Position the cell selector in the first cell that you want as the upper left corner of the new SpeedButton.

4. Click the Paste button to place a copy of the SpeedButton in the notebook.

5. Continue by positioning the cell selector in the next cell you want as the upper left corner of a new SpeedButton and by clicking the Paste button to place another copy of the SpeedButton in the notebook.

Repeat step 5 until you have placed in the notebook all the copies of the SpeedButton you want. Figure 16.2 shows three identical copies of the same SpeedButton spaced one row apart and aligned along the left edge of column B.

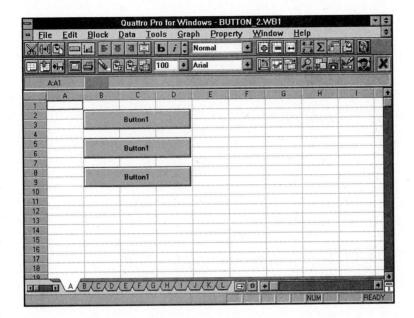

Fig. 16.2

Use consistent size and spacing to improve the SpeedButton's appearance.

Modifying SpeedButtons

Newly created SpeedButtons must be modified before they can serve a useful purpose. Each SpeedButton has five properties you can modify: the macro that the SpeedButton executes, the text that appears on the face of the SpeedButton, the color of the border around the Speed-Button, the type of the box around the SpeedButton, and the object name of the SpeedButton.

To modify any of the properties of a SpeedButton, point to the SpeedButton and click the right mouse button to activate the SpeedButton Object Inspector, which is called the *Button Object menu.* Figure 16.3 shows the Button Object menu.

The following sections describe each of the selections on the Button Object menu.

Assigning a Macro to a SpeedButton

New SpeedButtons must have a macro assigned to them before any actions can occur when you select them. To assign a macro to a SpeedButton, use the Macro Text option on the Button Object menu. Figure 16.4 shows the Macro Text dialog box that appears when you select the Macro Text option on the Button Object menu.

Fig. 16.3

The Button Object menu.

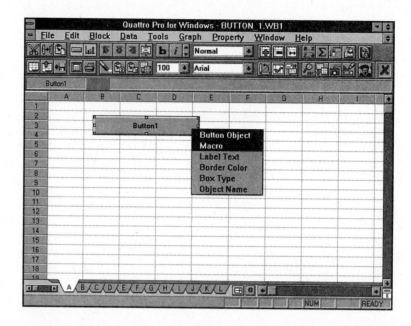

Fig. 16.4

The Macro Text dialog box.

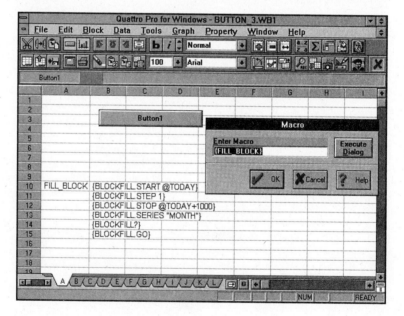

You can type macro instructions directly into the Macro Text dialog box, but it is much easier to enter the command to execute a notebook macro, such as **{FILL_BLOCK}**, as shown in Figure 16.4. Macros you enter in notebook cells are much easier to test, debug, and modify than macros you enter in the Macro Text dialog box.

In this example, a SpeedButton executes the FILL_BLOCK macro when the user selects OK. This macro uses Quattro Pro 5.0 for Windows command equivalents to display the Block Fill dialog box and to fill the highlighted notebook block with dates incremented by months.

Changing the Text on SpeedButtons

Use descriptive text on SpeedButtons to describe the function of the SpeedButtons. By default, the first SpeedButton in a Quattro Pro 5.0 for Windows notebook is named *Button1,* the second is named *Button2,* and so on. Unless you change the text displayed on your SpeedButtons, users will have a difficult task determining which SpeedButton executes the desired macro program.

The SpeedButton shown in figure 16.4, for example, should include descriptive text that informs the user of the SpeedButton's purpose— to fill a notebook block with dates. To change the label text displayed on a SpeedButton, follow these steps:

1. Point to the SpeedButton and click the right mouse button to display the Button Object menu.

2. Select Label Text, and the Label Text dialog box appears, as shown in figure 16.5.

3. Enter the new text you want to appear on the face of the SpeedButton.

4. Select OK to confirm the dialog box.

In this example, the text `Fill a Block with monthly dates` is entered as the descriptive text for the SpeedButton. A notebook user reading the text on the face of the SpeedButton clearly can see the purpose of the SpeedButton.

When selecting a label for the face of a SpeedButton, keep the text short but descriptive. Make certain that the notebook user can understand the purpose of the SpeedButton, but be concise.

Fig. 16.5

The Label Text dialog box.

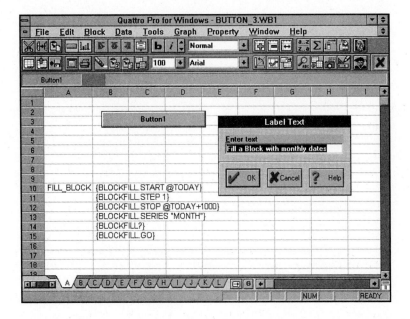

Changing the Border on SpeedButtons

You also can change the border color and box type of SpeedButtons to enhance their appearance. The border color and the box type don't affect how a SpeedButton functions, so any choices you make in these two areas are simply a matter of preference.

To change the border color on a SpeedButton, follow these steps:

1. Point to the SpeedButton and click the right mouse button to display the Button Object menu.

2. Select Border Color, and the Border Color dialog box appears, as shown in figure 16.6.

3. Select the new color you want for the border of the SpeedButton.

4. Select OK to confirm the dialog box.

To change the box type on a SpeedButton, follow these steps:

1. Point to the SpeedButton and click the right mouse button to display the Button Object menu.

2. Select Box Type, and the Box Type dialog box appears, as shown in figure 16.7.

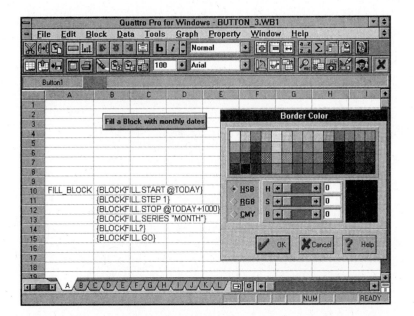

Fig. 16.6

The Border Color dialog box.

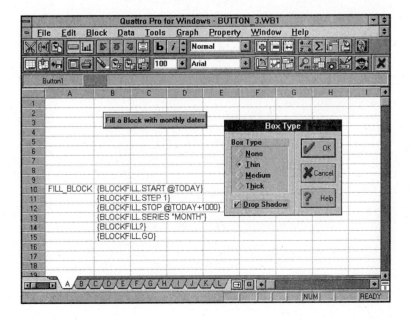

Fig. 16.7

The Box Type dialog box.

3. Select the new style you want for the border of the SpeedButton.

4. If you want the SpeedButton to appear as if it is on top of the notebook page, select the **D**rop Shadow check box.

5. Select OK to confirm the dialog box.

Changing the SpeedButton Object Name

Use the name of an object (such as a SpeedButton) when you create links between notebook objects or when you use advanced macro commands that manipulate objects. By default, each SpeedButton's name is the same as the default label text that appears on the SpeedButton's face. The SpeedButton's object name, however, does not change when you create new text to appear on the face of the button. The first SpeedButton you create in a notebook, for example, displays Button1 on its face, and Button1 is also the object name assigned to the button.

Because the default name isn't very descriptive, you may want to assign a new name to your SpeedButtons. To change the object name of a SpeedButton, follow these steps:

1. Point to the SpeedButton and click the right mouse button to display the Button Object menu.

2. Select Object Name, and the Object Name dialog box appears, as shown in figure 16.8.

Fig. 16.8

The Object Name dialog box.

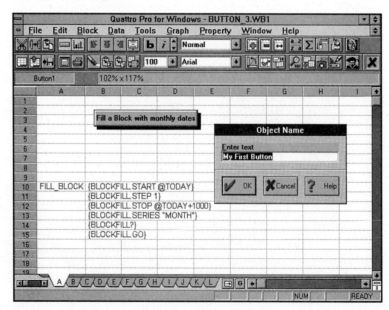

3. Type the new name you want for the SpeedButton.

4. Select OK to confirm the dialog box.

If you intend to change the names of SpeedButtons, always change the names before you create macros that use advanced macro commands to manipulate the SpeedButtons. When you change object names, macros that refer to those objects also must be changed to refer to the new names.

Creating Dialog Boxes

Now that you understand how to create SpeedButtons, you can create custom dialog boxes with a little extra effort. You may want to think of custom dialog boxes as slightly more complex and flexible SpeedButtons. A SpeedButton performs one predetermined action, but custom dialog boxes can present information, allow the user to make a selection from a series of choices, and execute actions when the dialog box is closed.

To create a dialog box, select **T**ools UI **B**uilder to display the Dialog window, as shown in figure 16.9. You also can display the Dialog window by selecting the New Dialog button from the Graphs page SpeedBar. When the Dialog window is active, the SpeedBar displays dialog building tools.

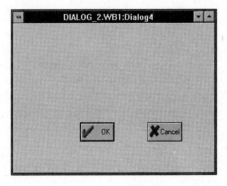

Fig. 16.9

In the Dialog window, the SpeedBar displays dialog building tools.

When you select **T**ools UI **B**uilder or the New Dialog button from the Graphs page SpeedBar, Quattro Pro 5.0 for Windows creates a new dialog box that contains two controls: an OK button and a Cancel button. You then use the tools on the Dialog window SpeedBar to add new elements to the Dialog box. Table 16.1 summarizes the tools on the Dialog window SpeedBar.

Table 16.1 Dialog Window SpeedBar Tools

Tool	Purpose
Cut	Deletes an object from the dialog box and places the object on the Clipboard
Copy	Copies an object from the dialog box to the Clipboard
Paste	Copies an object from the Clipboard to the dialog box
Test	Initiates dialog box test mode
Selection tool	Selects dialog box objects
Push button	Places a push button in the dialog box
Check box	Places a check box in the dialog box
Radio button	Places a radio button in the dialog box
Bitmap button	Places a bitmap button in the dialog box; bitmap buttons can display Windows bitmap images on their faces
Text	Places text in the dialog box
Edit field	Places a field that enables the dialog box user to modify its contents
Spin Control	Places an edit field that enables the dialog box user to select only integer numeric entries
Rectangle	Places a rectangle in the dialog box
Group box	Places a rectangle in the dialog box that is used to group check boxes and radio buttons
List box	Places a list box in the dialog box that enables the user to select from a list of items
Combo box	Places a combo box in the dialog box that combines an edit field and a list box
Pick list	Places a list box in the dialog box that enables the user to select from a list
File control	Places a list box in the dialog box that displays a list of files
Color control	Places an object in the dialog box that enables the user to select colors
Vertical scroller	Places a vertical scroller in the dialog box
Horizontal scroller	Places a horizontal scroller in the dialog box
Timer	Places a timer or alarm in the dialog box

Adding Dialog Box Objects

Depending upon the application, you may need to combine several objects in one dialog box. Related radio buttons, for example, should be placed in a group box. When a user selects one radio button, any other radio button already selected must be deselected.

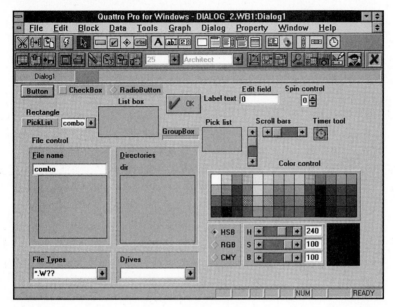

Fig. 16.10

The available dialog box objects.

Figure 16.10 shows a dialog box that contains samples of all the objects you can add to a dialog box.

A dialog box like the one in Figure 16.10 would not be very useful, but most of the objects displayed in the dialog box should be familiar to you. The objects you add to custom dialog boxes are identical to the objects used to build the standard Quattro Pro 5.0 for Windows dialog boxes.

Creating a Useful Dialog Box

To be useful, a dialog box must perform some function in your notebook. Standard Quattro Pro 5.0 for Windows dialog boxes, for example, perform such tasks as displaying lists of files you can retrieve enabling you to select the available options for filling a notebook block and to locate and extract database records.

Dialog boxes make Quattro Pro 5.0 for Windows notebooks easier to use because you can execute a complete set of instructions and make a complete set of option selections at once. Custom dialog boxes you add to your notebooks should be designed to allow the same method of operation. Include all the necessary elements, but keep the process as simple as possible.

Figure 16.11 shows a custom dialog box that provides the user with three options for filling a selected block with date values: Days, Weeks, or Months. Because the three options are radio buttons, only one can be selected at a time.

Fig. 16.11

A custom dialog box used to select Block Fill options.

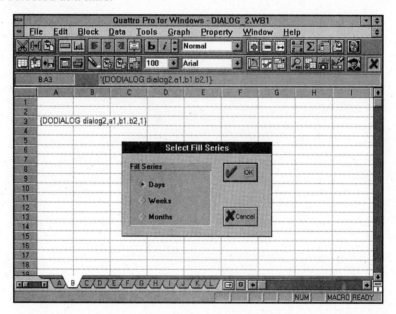

To create a dialog box like the one shown in figure 16.11, follow these steps:

1. Select **T**ools UI **B**uilder or click the New Dialog button on the Graphs page SpeedBar.

2. Select the Group box tool and place a group box that is large enough to hold the number of radio buttons you want to add in the dialog box.

3. Select the Radio button tool and add radio buttons to the group box. In this case, add three radio buttons.

4. Point to each radio button in turn and click the right mouse button. Change the Label Text for each button to reflect its purpose. In this case, name the three buttons **Days**, **Weeks**, and **Months** because you're going to use the radio buttons to select the fill series.

5. Select the top radio button, hold down the Shift key, and select the other two radio buttons.

6. Select Dialog Align Left to align the radio buttons.

7. Point to the group box title bar and click the right mouse button. Change the title shown at the top of the group box by selecting Group Text and entering the new text, in this case **Fill Series**.

8. If you want, move the OK and Cancel buttons. In this case, the OK button was aligned with the top of the group box, and the Cancel button was aligned with the bottom of the group box.

9. Point to the dialog box title bar and click the right mouse button. Select Title and enter the new text for the dialog box title. In this case, enter **Select Fill Series**.

Your dialog box is now ready to link to notebook cells and macros. See "Creating Object Links" later in this chapter for more information on linking dialog boxes to the notebook.

Use the DODIALOG macro command to display and use custom dialog boxes in your macro programs. The dialog box shown in figure 16.11, for example, can be used with a modification of the macro first shown in figure 16.4 to make the macro more flexible. Instead of always filling the block with dates separated by a month, the macro can display the Select Fill Series dialog box and enable the user to select the type of block fill.

Editing Dialog Box Objects

Each object in a dialog box, and the dialog box itself, has Object Inspectors available that you activate by pointing to the object and clicking the right mouse button. Figure 16.12 shows the Object Inspectors available for radio buttons, such as the buttons included in the Select Fill Series dialog box.

Fig. 16.12

The RadioButton Object Inspector.

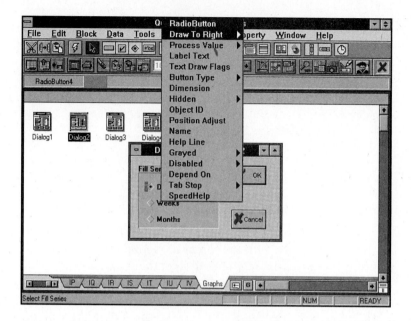

Each Object Inspector menu includes only those properties that apply to the selected object. A bitmap button Object Inspector menu, for example, includes the option of selecting a different bitmap image, but a radio button Object Inspector menu does not include this option. Several options are common to most dialog box Object Inspector menus. Table 16.2 lists options common to most dialog box Object Inspector menus.

Table 16.2 Common Dialog Box Object Inspector Options

Option	Purpose
Attach Child	Groups elements
Depend On	Specifies whether object should be displayed depending on window displayed
Disabled	Determines whether object can be selected but does not dim object
Frame	Specifies frame size and style
Grayed	Determines whether object can be selected and dims object
Help Line	Displays text when object is selected

Option	Purpose
Hidden	Specifies whether object is displayed
Label Text	Specifies text to display on object
Name	Displays the object's name
Object ID	Displays the object's identification number
Position Adjust	Specifies how object moves when dialog box is resized
Process Value	Enables DODIALOG to access object's value
Show Active	Shows black frame when selected
SpeedHelp	Specifies help text for the object
Tab Stop	Specifies whether Tab selects object
Terminate Dialog	Specifies whether Enter closes dialog box
Value	Displays initial value of the object

Use the dialog box Object Inspector to change any of the available properties. In figure 16.11, for example, the label each radio button displays is changed to describe the action of the button.

Creating SpeedBars

SpeedBars are a special type of dialog box you can use to add new push button controls to the top of your Quattro Pro 5.0 for Windows screen. In the following sections, you learn how to create SpeedBars and use the Dialog Links command to link dialog box objects.

SpeedBars can contain any of the available dialog box objects, but make certain that the objects you add to a SpeedBar fit in the default SpeedBar size. SpeedBars added to the Quattro Pro 5.0 for Windows screen reduce the available workspace because a notebook cannot share the space used by a SpeedBar.

Using SpeedBar Designer

The SpeedBar Designer enables you to quickly design a custom SpeedBar using standard or custom buttons. You can use nearly every button that is available on any of the standard Quattro Pro 5.0 for Windows SpeedBars, as well as creating your own buttons.

To create a new SpeedBar using the SpeedBar Designer, select **T**ools SpeedBar **D**esigner or click the SpeedBar Designer on the Productivity Tools SpeedBar. A new, blank SpeedBar is displayed, and the SpeedBar Designer SpeedBar replaces the Notebook SpeedBar.

When the SpeedBar Designer SpeedBar is displayed, you can select from eight different sets of standard buttons by making a selection from the button palette list box. Figure 16.13 shows the SpeedBar Designer SpeedBar and the eight sets of standard buttons.

Fig. 16.13

The SpeedBar Designer SpeedBar and the eight sets of standard buttons.

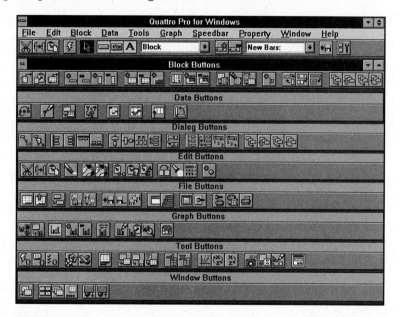

The SpeedBar Designer SpeedBar has the following buttons and controls:

> Cut, Copy, Paste, Test, Select, Push Button, Bitmap Button, Label Tool, Button Palette list, New SpeedBar, Remove SpeedBar, Custom SpeedBar list, and UI Builder.

The Block Buttons palette includes the following buttons:

> Block Move, Block Copy, Move Pages, Insert Rows, Delete Rows, Insert Columns, Delete Columns, Insert Pages, Delete Pages, Insert File, Fill, Create Name, Delete Name, Names From Labels, Reset Names, Table Of Names, Insert Break, Transpose, Values, Reformat, Bring Forward, Send Backward, Bring To Front, and Send To Back.

The Data Buttons palette includes the following buttons:

> Sort, Query, Parse, What-If, Frequency, Database Desktop, Table Query, and Data Modeling Desktop.

The Dialog Buttons palette includes the following buttons:

> Connect, Links, Align Left, Align Right, Align Top, Align Bottom, Vertical Center, Horizontal Center, Horizontal Space, Vertical Space, Resize To Same, Order Controls, Order From, Order Tab Controls, Order Tab From, Bring Forward, Send Backward, Bring To Front, and Send To Back.

The Edit Buttons palette includes the following buttons:

> Cut, Copy, Paste, Undo, Clear, Clear Contents, Paste Link, Paste Special, Paste Format, Goto, Search and Replace, Define Style, and Insert Object.

The File Buttons palette includes the following buttons:

> New Notebook, Open Notebook, Retrieve Notebook, Save Workspace, Restore Workspace, Save, Save As, Save All, Close Notebook, Close All, Print Preview, Page Setup, Printer Setup, Named Settings, and Print.

The Graph Buttons palette includes the following buttons:

> Graph Type, Graph Series, New Graph, Insert Graph, Delete Graph, Graph Titles, Edit Graph, Copy Graph, View Graph, and Run Slide Show.

The Tool Buttons palette includes the following buttons:

> Execute Macro, Record Macro, Macro Options, Debug Macro, Excel Macro Assistant, Define Group, Combine, Extract, Import, Invert Matrix, Multiply Matrix, Regression, Optimizer, Solve For, Scenario Manager, Consolidator, UI Builder, and SpeedBar Designer.

The Window Buttons palette includes the following buttons:

> New View, Tile, Cascade, Arrange Icons, Hide Window, and Show Window.

To add standard buttons from one of the button palettes to the new, blank SpeedBar, follow these steps:

1. If necessary, drag the button palette down until the new SpeedBar is completely exposed. You can also select **S**peedbar **T**ile to display both the new SpeedBar and the button palette.

2. Select a button to add to the new SpeedBar by clicking the left mouse button twice on the button (on the button palette) you want to add. The first click activates the button palette, and the second click selects the button.

3. Point to the position on the new SpeedBar where you want to place the button and click the left mouse button twice. The first click activates the SpeedBar, and the second click places the button. Figure 16.14 shows how the screen appears after you click the SpeedBar the first time. Figure 16.15 shows the SpeedBar after the File Retrieve button is added.

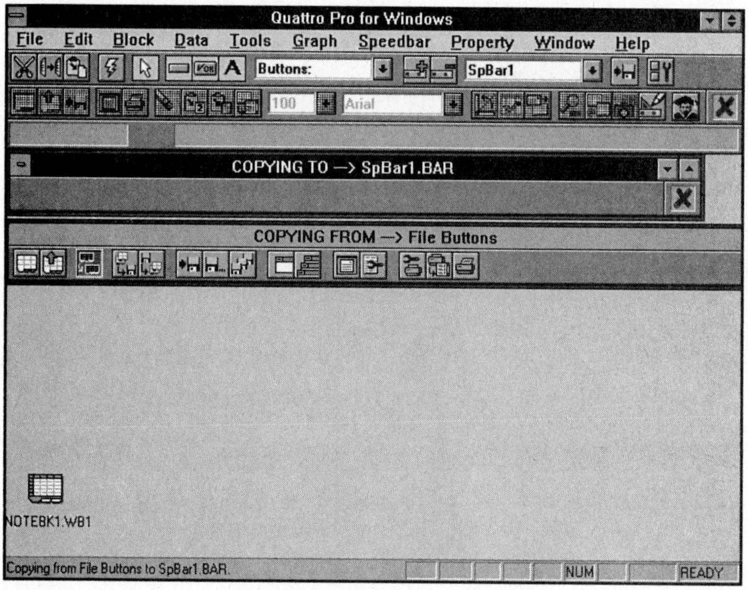

Fig. 16.14

Copy buttons from the button palettes to custom SpeedBars.

4. Continue adding buttons from any of the button palettes until your SpeedBar has the buttons you want.

5. Select **S**peedbar **S**ave or click the Save SpeedBar button to save the SpeedBar using the default name displayed in the SpeedBar title bar. You can also select **S**peedbar Save **A**s if you wish to enter a new name.

6. Select **S**peedbar **D**ock to add the new SpeedBar immediately below the existing SpeedBars and exit the SpeedBar Designer, or **S**peedbar Clos**e** All to exit the SpeedBar Designer without adding the new SpeedBar at this time.

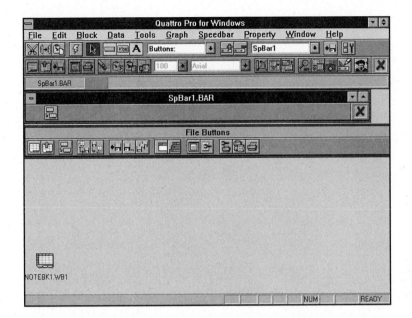

Fig. 16.15

The new SpeedBar with the File Retrieve button added.

You can use the new SpeedBar as is, or further modify it using the Dialog window commands discussed in the next section.

Using the UI Builder

While the SpeedBar Designer enables you to quickly create a new SpeedBar, you may want to also consider using the UI Builder if you want to create even more powerful SpeedBars. For example, if you want to add a drop-down list box for selecting from a group of choices, you must use the UI Builder. You can use the UI Builder to completely create a custom SpeedBar, or to modify one you started using the SpeedBar Designer.

When you are using the UI Builder, the Dialog window is displayed. If the Dialog window is not currently displayed, select **Tools** UI **Builder** or the UI Builder button on the SpeedBar Designer SpeedBar. When the Dialog window is active, you create a new SpeedBar by selecting D**i**alog **New** SpeedBar, as shown in figure 16.16. Figure 16.17 shows the blank default SpeedBar (the notebook and blank dialog box were minimized to emphasize the SpeedBar). To instead modify an existing custom SpeedBar, select D**i**alog **Open** Speed**B**ar.

Fig. 16.16

The Dialog menu.

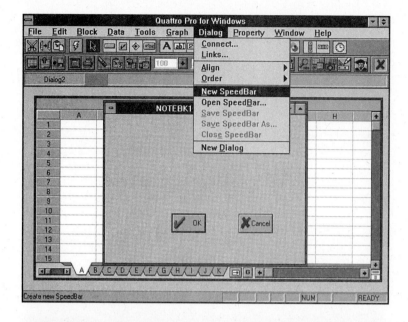

Fig. 16.17

A new blank SpeedBar.

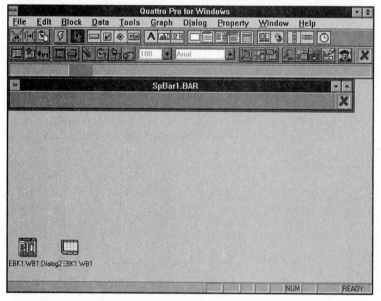

You can add controls to the SpeedBar that execute commands. Suppose, for example, that you want to add a push button to save quickly the active notebook. Although you can use one of the standard File

Buttons palette buttons, this exercise shows how to add a labeled button that performs this task. You easily can create a new SpeedBar control that performs this common task by following these steps:

1. Select the Push button tool and place a push button on the SpeedBar.

2. Point to the new push button and click the right mouse button to display the Button Object Object Inspector menu.

3. Select Label Text.

4. Type **Save Notebook**.

5. Select OK to confirm the dialog box. The SpeedBar now appears as shown in figure 16.18.

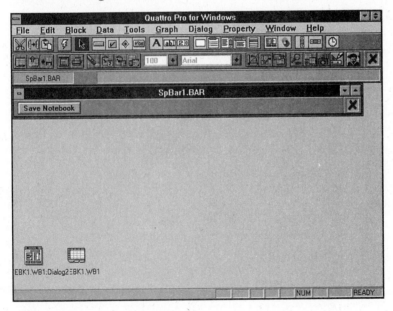

Fig. 16.18

The Save Notebook push button added to the SpeedBar.

Creating Object Links

To assign an action to a dialog box object, whether the dialog box is a dialog box associated with a specific notebook or a SpeedBar that can be displayed with any notebook, use the Dialog Links command. Quattro Pro 5.0 for Windows enables you to link notebook objects using many different types of links.

Here, you want to create a link that executes a command equivalent macro command to save the notebook when the button is clicked. To create a link that assigns an action to the push button, follow these steps:

1. Select the object to link—here, the Save Notebook push button.

2. Select the Dialog Links command. The Object Link dialog box appears, as shown in figure 16.19.

Fig. 16.19

The Object Link dialog box.

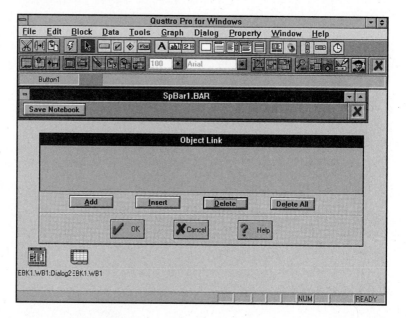

3. Select Add to create a new link, and a new default link appears, as shown in figure 16.20.

4. Point to the word Check at the left of the new link, hold down the left mouse button, and select Clicked to change the event that activates the link.

5. Point to the next word, RECEIVE, hold down the left mouse button, and select DOMACRO as the action the link performs when it is activated.

6. Type **{FILESAVE!}{ALT+R}** in the text box. This macro uses a command equivalent to tell Quattro Pro 5.0 for Windows to execute the File Save command and select Replace. The dialog box appears, as shown in figure 16.21.

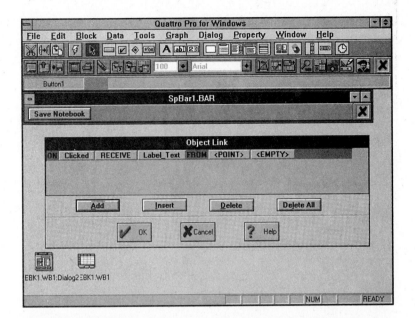

Fig. 16.20

A new default link.

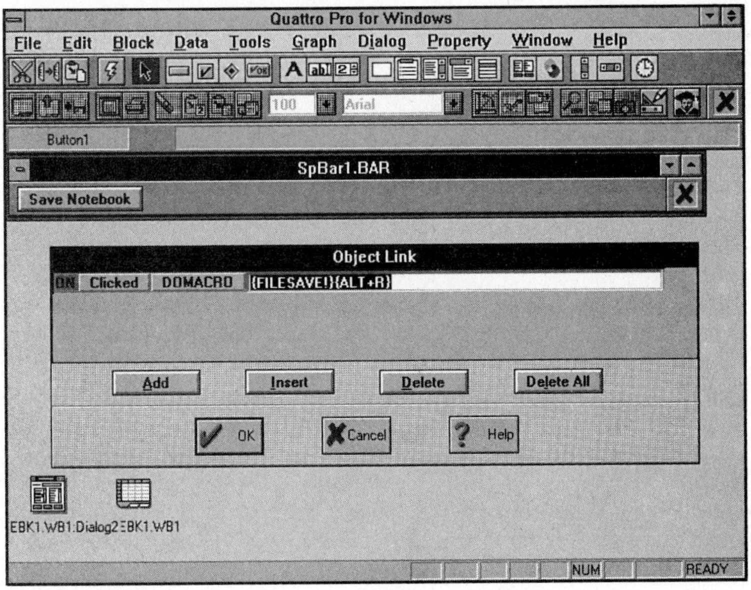

Fig. 16.21

The completed dialog box.

7. Select OK to confirm the dialog box and link the Save Notebook push button to the macro command.

8. Click the new SpeedBar outside the Save Notebook push button to deselect the push button.

9. Select Dialog Save SpeedBar As and type a name for the SpeedBar. In this case, type **QUEBAR_1**.

10. Select OK to save the SpeedBar.

11. Close the Dialog window by selecting Close from the window control menu or by pressing Ctrl+F4.

To display the new SpeedBar, follow these steps:

1. Point to the SpeedBar to which you want to append your custom SpeedBar and click the right mouse button.

2. Select Append.

3. Select the name of the custom SpeedBar or, if it is not already displayed, select <Browse> and select QUEBAR_1.BAR.

Quattro Pro 5.0 for Windows adds the new SpeedBar below the existing SpeedBar, as shown in figure 16.22.

Fig. 16.22

Quattro Pro for Windows adds the new SpeedBar below the existing SpeedBar.

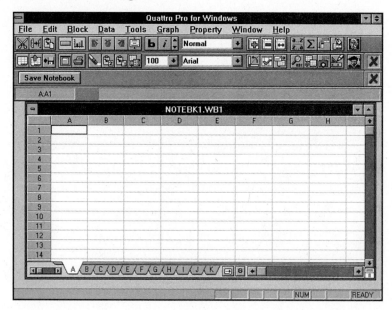

Testing the SpeedBar

Test the Save Notebook push button by pointing to it and clicking the left mouse button. Clicking the Save Notebook push button should have the same effect as executing the **File Save** command.

If you encounter any difficulties, select the Dialog window Dialog Open Speed**B**ar command to open the new SpeedBar. Use the same commands you used to create and link the Save Notebook push button to correct the problem.

Using a Secondary SpeedBar

Quattro Pro 5.0 for Windows includes sample SpeedBars you can add as additional SpeedBars. If you add an additional SpeedBar, it appears below the normal Quattro Pro 5.0 for Windows SpeedBar.

To add a sample SpeedBar as a secondary SpeedBar, follow these steps:

1. Point to the SpeedBar to which you want to append an additional SpeedBar, and click the right mouse button.

2. Select Append.

3. Select <Browse>, and choose the additional SpeedBar you want to add. You can choose BUDGTRAK.BAR in the QPW\SAMPLES directory.

Questions and Answers

Q: How should I decide whether to use SpeedButtons or a custom SpeedBar?

A: The choice depends on what you want to accomplish. Consider the following points in making your decision:

If the task is closely related to a particular notebook, a Speed-Button is a good choice because the SpeedButton is saved with the notebook. In addition, because the SpeedButton remains at the same location in the notebook, you can place the SpeedButton at the most convenient spot, such as immediately adjacent to the cell where you enter the final data for a report.

If the tasks are more general, such as saving notebooks, or are common to a number of related notebooks, a custom SpeedBar may be a better choice. Buttons on a SpeedBar are always visible, regardless of the cell selector location, so their functions are available through the notebook.

SpeedBars, however, use some of the available room on the screen, leaving less room to display notebooks. This can be a particular problem if your application requires displaying several notebooks at the same time.

Q: Why doesn't the full label appear on the face of my SpeedButtons?

A: You can only display a single line of text on SpeedButtons. The text does not wrap to a second line. Either change to a shorter label or make the SpeedButton wider. Remember, though, that it is better to have a short label that describes the button's purpose in a few words.

Q: Which control can I add to a dialog box or SpeedBar to allow the user to quickly select from a group of numbers?

A: The spin control is perfect for this use. The spin control displays an integer value, and it allows the user to click up- or down-arrows to increment or decrement the value. When you add a spin control, you can specify the default value, as well as the upper and lower limits.

Q: I want to add my own custom SpeedBar, but the SpeedBars take too much room from the screen. What should I do?

A: You might consider replacing the Productivity Tools SpeedBar with your custom SpeedBar. One good way to do this is to decide which controls on the Productivity Tools SpeedBar you really use, and then add those same controls to your custom SpeedBar. The SpeedBar Designer allows you to select from the standard SpeedBar buttons, and you can use UI Builder to add additional custom controls. There's no reason you can't build exactly the SpeedBar you want.

Summary

Quattro Pro 5.0 for Windows provides many powerful options that enable you to create SpeedButtons, custom dialog boxes, and SpeedBars.

You can use the linking options to create sophisticated Windows applications that previously could be created only by very advanced programmers. This chapter has provided several ideas that you can use to build your own applications.

The next part of the book covers some of the new and powerful advanced data management tools in Quattro Pro 5.0 for Windows. These tools enable you to perform extremely sophisticated data analysis functions quickly and easily, and make Quattro Pro 5.0 for Windows by far the most powerful spreadsheet program available.

Analyzing Data

PART

VI

OUTLINE

Using Analysis Tools and Experts

Spreadsheet programs such as Quattro Pro 5.0 for Windows have many very powerful capabilities. These capabilities enable you to perform extremely sophisticated data analysis—if you know how to use them. Unfortunately, actually taking advantage of the power of these features can be a difficult and complex task. For most spreadsheet users, it's too time-consuming to learn how to use much more than the program's basic features.

Instead of forcing you to spend hours learning to use its power, Quattro Pro 5.0 for Windows offers two new features designed to enable you to use sophisticated data analysis techniques easily: Experts and Analysis Tools. This chapter introduces these features and shows you how to quickly begin using them.

This chapter discusses the following subjects:

■ Using the Experts to create graphs, manage scenarios, consolidate data, improve notebook performance, and analyze data

■ Displaying the Analysis Tools SpeedBar

■ Using the Analysis Tools

Understanding Experts and Analysis Tools

Experts are like intelligent assistants who know all of the commands and procedures necessary to perform complicated tasks. They step you through a task, such as creating a graph, by asking you for the information needed to successfully complete the task. At each step, the Experts tell you the purpose of the step, and can provide a more in-depth explanation if necessary. Quattro Pro 5.0 for Windows has five main Experts, which are summarized in table 17.1.

Table 17.1 Experts

Expert	Description
Graph Expert	Helps you create graphs
Scenario Expert	Helps you create and manage scenarios— multiple groups of related data that enable easy what-if analysis
Consolidation Expert	Helps you combine data from different sources
Performance Expert	Helps you maximize the performance of notebook applications
Analysis Expert	Helps you use the Analysis Tools

Another Expert, the Parse Expert, works somewhat differently from these five, and is discussed in Chapter 13, "Understanding Advanced Data Management."

The Analysis Tools help you perform sophisticated statistical, engineering, and financial analysis functions. They provide an organized approach to specifying all the necessary data, and then apply the correct calculations to perform the desired analysis. Quattro Pro 5.0 for Windows has 19 Analysis Tools, which are summarized in table 17.2.

Table 17.2 Analysis Tools

Analysis Tool	Description
Advanced Regression	Performs multilinear regression analysis
Amortization Schedule	Generates a mortgage amortization schedule
Anova: One-Way	Performs a single-factor analysis of variance
Anova: Two-Way with Replication	Performs a two-factor analysis of variance using more than one sample for each group of data
Anova: Two-Way without Replication	Performs a two-factor analysis of variance using one sample for each group of data
Correlation	Shows the relationship between two or more data sets
Covariance	Generates a covariance matrix showing how much a change in one data set is related to changes in other data sets
Descriptive Statistics	Calculates a variety of statistics for one or more data sets
Exponential Smoothing	Finds the curve that best fits a data series
Fourier	Performs a fast Fourier transform on a block of data
F-Test	Compares the variances of two data sets to yield the F-satistic
Histogram	Calculates probability and cumulative distributions
Mortgage Refinancing	Generates a table of information relating to refinancing a mortgage
Moving Average	Returns a moving average for a series of values
Random Number	Returns random numbers using a specified type of distribution
Rank and Percentile	Computes the ordinal and percentile rank of each value in a sample
Sampling	Returns a periodic or random sample from a block of values

(continues)

Table 17.2 Continued

Analysis Tool	Description
t-Test	Tests the means of two small samples to determine whether the differences between them are significant
z-Test	Tests the means of two large samples to determine whether the differences between them are significant

The following sections describe how you can use the Experts and the Analysis Tools in Quattro Pro 5.0 for Windows.

Using Experts

Creating a graph, managing what-if scenarios, consolidating data from several sources, optimizing performance, and performing complex data analysis are all tasks that require you to perform a specific and often lengthy set of steps. Remembering all those steps, especially if the task is not one you perform very often, can be difficult.

Consider, for example, the task of creating a graph. In addition to specifying the data you want to chart, you must remember the commands for adding titles, legends, and labels. If you want to use a different type of graph, you have to remember how to select the graph you want. What do you do if the graph isn't showing the data the way you want— perhaps showing information graphed by quarter instead of by product?

When you use the Quattro Pro 5.0 for Windows Experts, you don't have to worry about remembering all the little details, because the Experts guide you through the task one step at a time. Each step is explained in clear detail, and you can even ask for more information about anything that seems unclear. Using the Experts is like having a knowledgeable and patient computer whiz always available to show you what to do.

Using the Graph Expert

To see how the Experts work, assume that the notebook shown in figure 17.1 contains sales data that you want to graph. This notebook shows the sales figures for one of your company's stores, and you want to compare each product line's contribution to the total sales for each quarter. Follow these steps to use the Graph Expert and create a 100% stacked bar comparison chart:

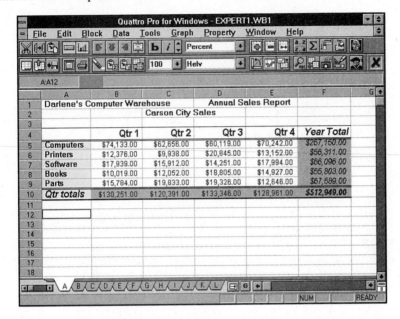

Fig. 17.1

Sales data to chart using the Graph Expert.

1. Click the Experts button to display the Experts dialog box, as shown in figure 17.2.

2. Click the Graph Expert button to display the Graph Expert dialog box, as shown in figure 17.3.

   If you prefer, you can also select **Help Experts Graph** to display the Graph Expert dialog box directly without first displaying the Experts dialog box.

3. The first step in creating a graph is to select the data you want to graph. For additional information on selecting the data to graph, ask the Graph Expert for an additional explanation by selecting (or clicking) the E**x**plain button shown in figure 17.4.

4. Select (or click) the E**x**plain button again to remove the additional explanation from the left side of the Graph Expert dialog box. After you select the data to graph, the left side of the dialog box displays a reduced size view of the graph, showing the progress as you complete each step.

Fig. 17.2

The Experts dialog box.

Fig. 17.3

The Graph Expert
dialog box.

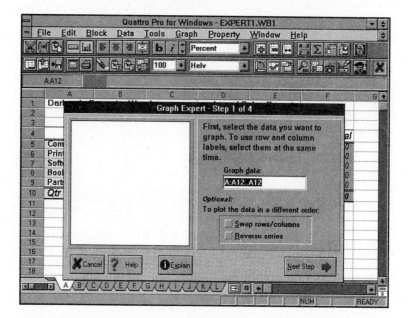

5. Specify the data to graph by either pointing to the notebook and highlighting the data, or by typing the addresses in the Graph **d**ata text box. In this notebook, column A contains the sales categories, and row 4 contains the time periods you want to graph. Because you will want to use the labels in column A and those in row 4 to identify the data, specify **A4..E9** as the data to graph.

After you specify the data to graph, the left side of the Graph Expert dialog box displays a small version of your data graphed as the default bar graph, as shown in figure 17.5.

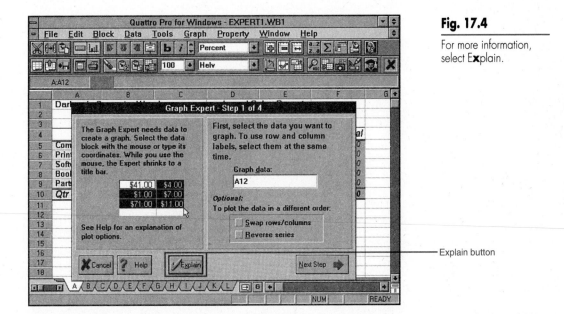

Fig. 17.4

For more information, select E**x**plain.

Explain button

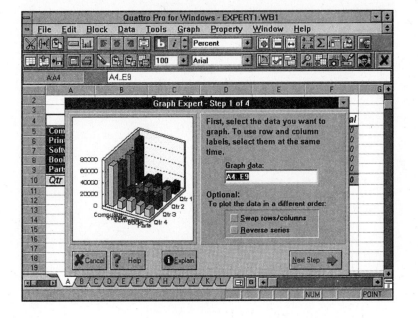

Fig. 17.5

The left side of the Graph Expert dialog box displays a small version of the graph.

The totals in row 10 and in column F are not included in the data to graph, because the 100% stacked bar comparison chart will already display each data set as 100% of the total. Including the totals in the data to graph would simply reduce the relative size of the other segments without adding additional information.

6. The default graph is charting the sales figures by item rather than by quarter. Since you want to see how each item's sales contribute to the total sales for each quarter, you will want to select **S**wap rows/columns to graph by quarter, as shown in figure 17.6.

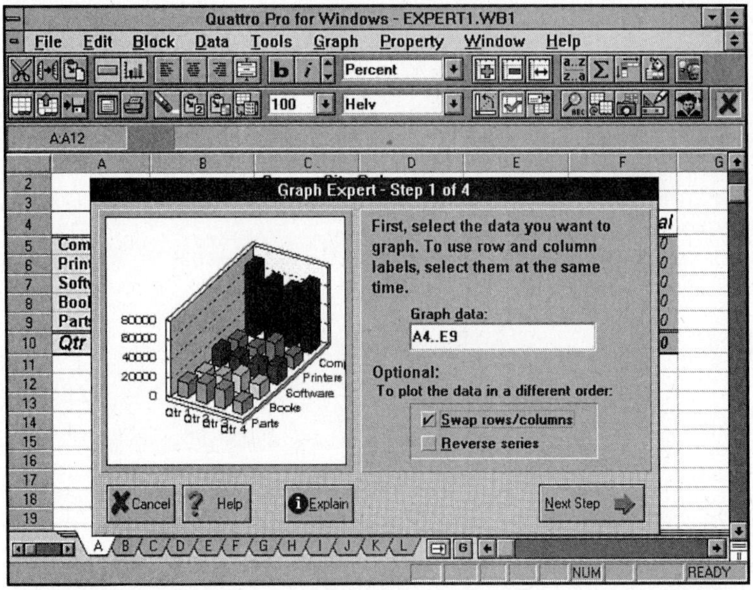

Fig. 17.6

Swapping rows and columns changes the focus of the graph.

7. Select (or click) the **N**ext Step button to continue.

8. Choose a general graph type by selecting one of the graph type buttons shown in figure 17.7. In this case, the 100% stacked bar comparison graph is a bar graph, the default, so you do not have to make a selection.

You can select the alternate types of graphs to see how they appear, but make certain Bar is selected before continuing.

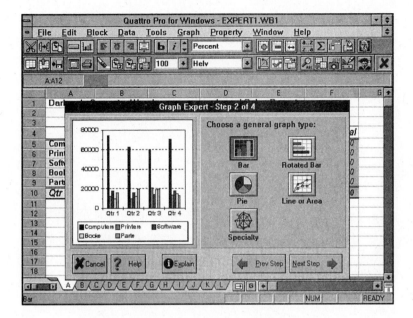

Fig. 17.7

Select the general graph type before continuing.

9. Select (or click) the Next Step button to continue.

10. Select the 100% stacked bar comparison chart (the second choice in the row labeled 100% Stacked). Figure 17.8 shows the change in the graph to the 100% stacked bar comparison chart.

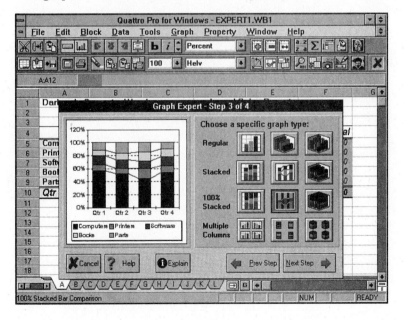

Fig. 17.8

Select the specific graph type.

11. Select (or click) the **N**ext Step button to continue.

12. The final enhancement to the basic graph is to add titles. Type a title such as **Departmental Sales** in the Title text box. Type **Compared to Total Sales** in the Subtitle text box.

13. To display the graph in the Graph Window, select the Graph Window radio button. When you select this button, the Notebook Page radio button is deselected, because you can only select one radio button in a group.

14. Select Create Graph to display the graph in the Graph Window, as shown in figure 17.9.

Fig. 17.9

The completed graph.

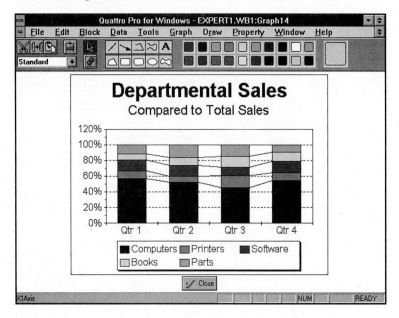

Using Other Experts

The Scenario, Consolidation, Performance, and Analysis Experts function in the same step-by-step manner as the Graph Expert. Each step is explained, and you simply fill in the requested information to complete each step of the task.

The Scenario Expert helps you create and manage multiple what-if scenarios. Figure 17.10 shows the first step screen that is displayed when you select the Scenario Expert. The Scenario Expert, like the Graph Expert, leads you through four steps as you create and define a what-if scenario.

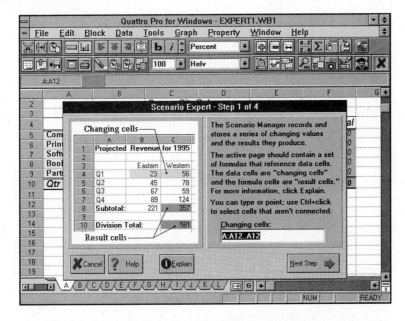

Fig. 17.10

The Scenario Expert helps create and manage multiple what-if scenarios.

The next Expert, the Consolidation Expert, helps you combine data from several sources—either in one notebook or in several. Figure 17.11 shows the first Consolidation Expert screen. This Expert also leads you through the four steps necessary to complete the task.

The Performance Expert analyzes several factors to help you decide whether or not the recalculation performance of the notebook would be improved by compiling the formulas. Figure 17.12 shows the first Performance Expert screen.

Compiling formulas may improve the speed at which formulas are re-calculated, but many factors are involved in determining whether or not you will see any improvement. These factors include the type of processor in your system, whether or not a numeric coprocessor is present, the available physical memory, the length of time currently needed to recalculate the formulas, the types of formulas in the note-book, and whether you spend more time entering data or editing note-book contents. By using the Performance Expert, you can be certain that all factors are given the correct emphasis, and your notebooks will recalculate at the highest possible speed.

Fig. 17.11

The Consolidation Expert helps combine data from several sources.

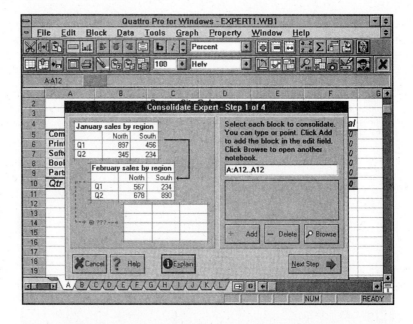

Fig. 17.12

The Performance Expert helps improve notebook performance.

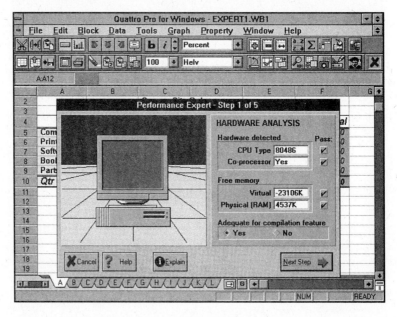

The Analysis Tools Expert helps you use the Analysis Tools by providing an in-depth explanation of each tool's requirements. Because each Analysis Tool is different, using the Analysis Tools Expert will involve a varying number of steps, depending on which tool you select. The Analysis Tools are discussed in the next section. Figure 17.13 shows the first Analysis Tools Expert screen.

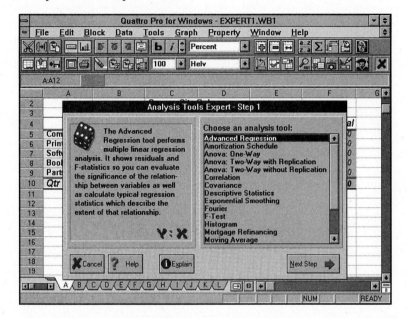

Fig. 17.13

The Analysis Tools Expert helps you use the Analysis Tools.

◀◀ "Creating Presentation Graphics," p. 313.

▶▶ "Consolidating Data and Managing Scenarios," p. 709.

FOR RELATED **INFORMATION**

Using the Analysis Tools

The Analysis Tools provide a straightforward method of performing complex statistical, engineering, and financial data analysis functions. They use dialog boxes to gather the information necessary to complete the analysis. This information includes the location of the data to analyze, the location to store the results, whether or not data labels are included, the order of the data, and so on.

You can use the Analysis Tools in two different ways. You can use the **T**ools **A**nalysis **T**ools command or the SpeedBar Object Inspector to add the Analysis Tools SpeedBar to the top of the screen. When the Analysis Tools SpeedBar is displayed, you can select any of the Analysis Tools by clicking its button on the Analysis Tools SpeedBar.

You can also use the Analysis Tools Expert, discussed in the previous section, to access the Analysis Tools. If you use the Analysis Tools Expert, you will see additional information about the selected Analysis Tool, as well as more information explaining each required input.

As an example, figure 17.14 shows the Descriptive Statistics Analysis Tool dialog box, and figure 17.15 shows the Analysis Tools Expert Descriptive Statistics dialog box. Both dialog boxes have the same input fields and selection options, but the Analysis Tools Expert Descriptive Statistics dialog box also includes information about the Descriptive Statistics Analysis Tool and its purpose.

Fig. 17.14

The Descriptive Statistics Analysis Tool dialog box.

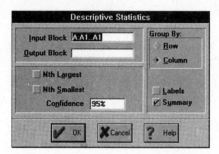

Whether you use the Analysis Tools by selecting the tool directly from the SpeedBar, or by using the Analysis Tools Expert, you provide the same information to complete the analysis.

Using the Mortgage Refinancing Tool

To see how the Analysis Tools function, we will use the Mortgage Refinancing Tool to examine the effects of refinancing a home mortgage at a lower rate. For this example, assume the current loan has a remaining balance of $97,000. There are 25 years remaining on the loan, and the current annual interest rate is 9.5%. Another lender is offering to refinance the loan for 30 years at 7.0%, but wants a 3% fee for making the loan. Because you may be transferred to another city in about five years, you want to know whether or not it is worthwhile refinancing now.

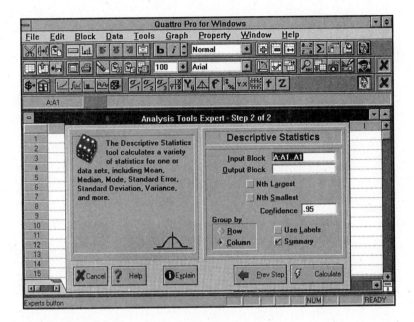

Fig. 17.15

The Analysis Tools Expert Descriptive Statistics dialog box.

To try this example, follow these steps:

1. Select the Mortgage Refinancing Tool on the Analysis Tools SpeedBar. The Mortgage Refinancing dialog box shown in figure 17.16 appears.

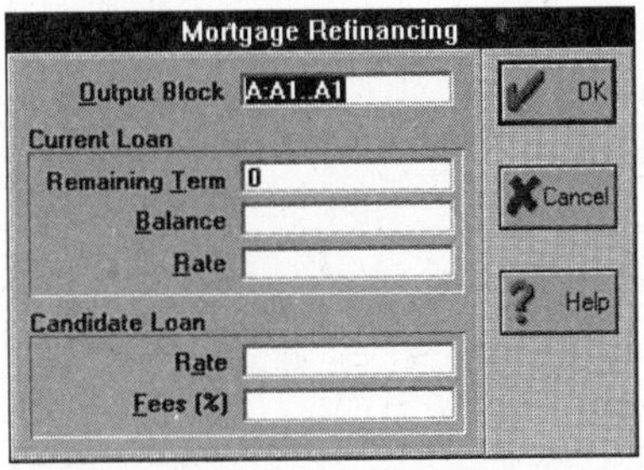

Fig. 17.16

The Analysis Tools Mortgage Refinancing dialog box enables you to specify refinancing terms.

2. Specify the **O**utput Block. If you are using a new, blank notebook, the default A:A1..A1 will be okay.

3. Select the Remaining **T**erm text box and enter **25**, the number of years left on the current loan.

4. Select the **B**alance text box and enter **97000**, the remaining balance on the current loan.

5. Select the **R**ate text box and enter **9.5%**, the interest rate on the current loan.

6. Select the **R**ate text box and enter **7%**, the interest rate on the candidate loan.

7. Select the **F**ees (%) text box and enter **3%**, the fees (points) on the candidate loan. Figure 17.17 shows the completed Mortgage Refinancing dialog box.

8. Press Enter or click OK to confirm the dialog box and start the mortgage refinancing calculations.

After you confirm the dialog box, Mortgage Refinancing Tool creates a table showing the effects of the refinancing. Figures 17.18, 17.19, and 17.20 show the table generated for this example (after adjusting column widths). In this case, the lower interest rate reduces the monthly payment by enough to offset the refinancing fees in 1.68 years (about 20 months). Because the payback period is considerably shorter than the time you intend to remain in the home, refinancing is definitely worthwhile.

Using Other Analysis Tools

Each of the other Analysis Tools functions in a manner similar to the Mortgage Refinancing Tool. Many of these tools are very specialized, and you may have little need for most of them. If you do perform the types of data analysis offered by the Analysis Tools, you will find they provide a very easy method of doing so.

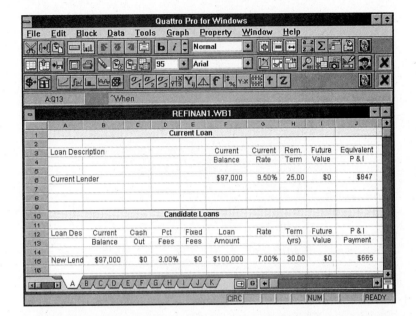

Fig. 17.18

Part 1 of the completed mortgage refinancing table.

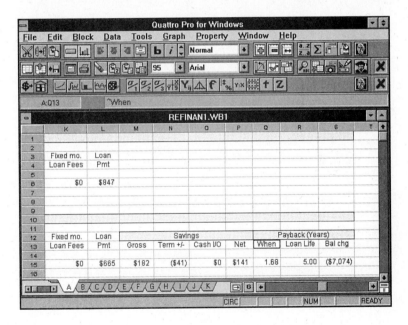

Fig. 17.19

Part 2 of the completed mortgage refinancing table.

Fig. 17.20

Part 3 of the completed mortgage refinancing table.

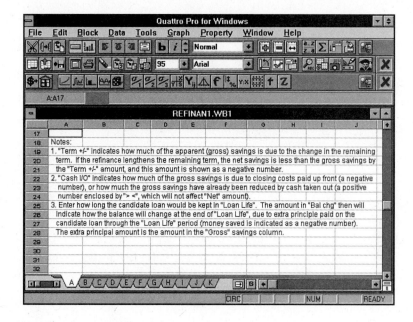

Questions and Answers

Q: I want to use the Analysis Tools, but I don't want to use a mouse. Where can I find the Analysis Tools on the Quattro Pro 5.0 for Windows menus?

A: To use the Analysis Tools without a mouse, you must use the **H**elp **E**xperts **A**nalysis Tools command to access the Analysis Tools Expert dialog box. You can then use the direction keys to select a tool.

Q: Even though I have a 486 processor in my system, the Performance Expert says I don't have a coprocessor. Don't all 486 systems have coprocessors?

A: No, the "coprocessor" the Performance Expert is referring to is a numeric (or math) coprocessor that is used to increase performance of certain mathematical calculations. The 486DX processor has a built-in numeric coprocessor, but other processors such as the 486SX and all 386 processors do not.

5.0
Mc
in
an
ba:

Fig
the
am
rep

Most systems that lack a numeric coprocessor have a socket on the system board for adding a numeric coprocessor. In some cases a numeric coprocessor is both easy and inexpensive to install, but you may want to check with your computer dealer for more information.

Summary

The Analysis Tools and the Experts make using Quattro Pro 5.0 for Windows very easy. In this chapter, you learned how to use these powerful new features to perform the most complex tasks without having to learn difficult procedures.

Chapter 18 introduces another new feature: the Data Modeling Desktop. With this powerful tool, you can examine the many different relationships in your data quickly and flexibly.

Understanding the Data Modeling Desktop's Window

When you first start the Data Modeling Desktop, the screen looks similar to figure 18.2. Several screen elements are similar to Quattro Pro 5.0 for Windows. The title bar shows the program title and the name of the current model. The menu bar has three familiar menus—File, Edit, and Help—as well as four new menus—Build, Gadget, Font, and Preferences. The third line has the Data Modeling Desktop SpeedBar. Below the SpeedBar is the Report Data Area, which has three parts. The Top Label Bar Area and the Side Label Bar Area are the areas where you place the field names of the data categories you want to tabulate. The Report Data Area is the area where you place the data to summarize. The Source Window holds the data you are transferring from Quattro Pro 5.0 for Windows.

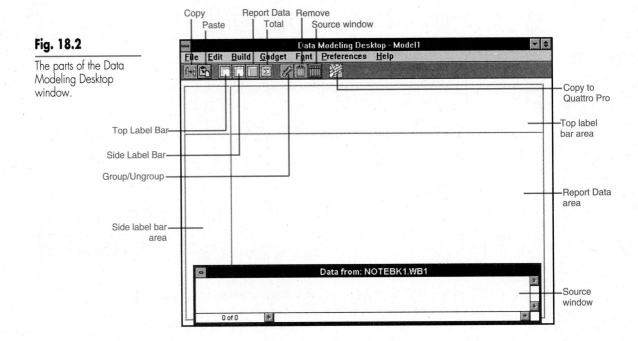

Fig. 18.2

The parts of the Data Modeling Desktop window.

Understanding the Data Modeling Desktop's Data Requirements

To analyze data using the Data Modeling Desktop, you must first organize that data in a fashion Data Modeling Desktop can use. Keep the following points in mind as you prepare data for transfer to the Data Modeling Desktop:

- Data must be in tabular format, using a layout identical to a typical Quattro Pro 5.0 for Windows notebook database.

- Each record must be in a single row.

- All values in each field (column) should be the same type of data.

- If possible, avoid empty rows in the data.

- Place the field names in the top row.

- Data should be related, otherwise a cross-tabulation analysis is meaningless.

Figure 18.3 shows part of a Quattro Pro 5.0 for Windows notebook database that will supply data for the Data Modeling Desktop examples in the balance of this chapter. This database shows the monthly sales for several part-time sales representatives at a computer store. Sales are shown for several major categories of items, along with each sales representative's total sales. As store manager, you want to analyze the sales in several different ways.

Using the Data Modeling Desktop

To begin using the Data Modeling Desktop, prepare your data in a Quattro Pro 5.0 for Windows notebook. If your data is already in a Quattro Pro 5.0 for Windows notebook database, you can use the existing database. If your data is in another type of database, first open the database file as a Quattro Pro 5.0 for Windows notebook or use the Database Desktop to transfer the data to a Quattro Pro 5.0 for Windows notebook.

FOR RELATED INFORMATION

◄◄ "Opening Files from Disk," p. 275.

Sending Data to the Data Modeling Desktop

Quattro Pro 5.0 for Windows and the Data Modeling Desktop share data by sending notebook data to the Data Modeling Desktop Source Window and by sending Data Modeling Desktop report data back to an empty location in the notebook. Because both Quattro Pro 5.0 for Windows and the Data Modeling Desktop support live (or *hot*) DDE links, you can specify that the two programs share data in a manner that automatically updates the data as changes occur.

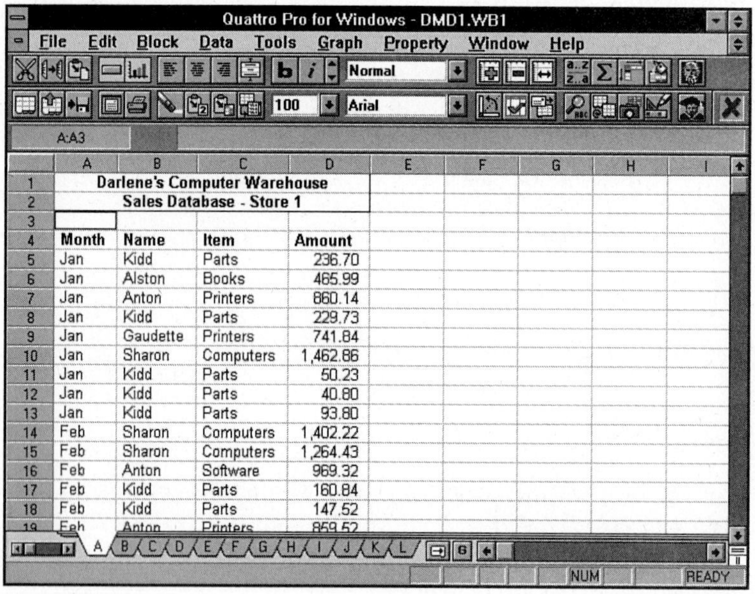

Fig. 18.3

A sales database to analyze using the Data Modeling Desktop.

To begin sending data to the Data Modeling Desktop, follow these steps:

1. Highlight the notebook database block. In figure 18.3, the database block includes cells A4..D110.

2. Next, choose the **D**ata Data **M**odeling Desktop command or click the Data Modeling Desktop button on the Productivity Tools SpeedBar to open the Send Data to Data Modeling Desktop dialog box (see fig. 18.4).

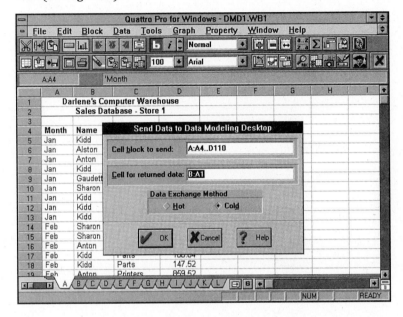

Fig. 18.4

The Send Data to Data Modeling Desktop dialog box.

3. If you did not specify the database block, type the database block address in the Cell **b**lock to send text box.

4. By default, the data returned from the Data Modeling Desktop to Quattro Pro 5.0 for Windows is placed at cell A1 of the first un-used notebook page. If you prefer another location for the re-turned data, specify the location in the **C**ell for returned data text box.

5. Choose **H**ot to create live DDE links between Data Modeling Desk-top and Quattro Pro 5.0 for Windows or choose Col**d** to transfer unchanging data.

If you choose **H**ot, any changes in the notebook data are reflected automatically in the Data Modeling Desktop report.

If you choose Col**d**, you must manually update the data. In most cases, the default Col**d** selection is acceptable.

6. Press Enter or click OK to display the Data Modeling Desktop window. If necessary, maximize the Data Modeling Desktop window so that you have a larger work area. Your screen should now be similar to figure 18.5.

Fig. 18.5

The sales data after transfer to the Data Modeling Desktop Source Window.

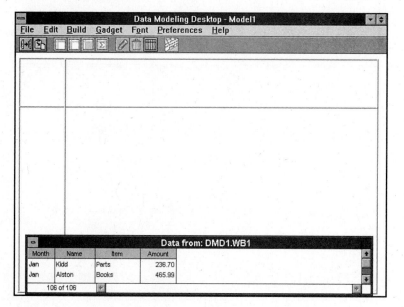

Building a Data Modeling Desktop Report

The Side Label Bar and Top Label Bar areas on the Data Modeling Desktop hold the categories of data you want to analyze. Usually, the data categories you add to the Side Label Bar or Top Label Bar areas contain labels or dates, such as a month, item, or sales representative's name.

The Report Data Area holds the summary data. In this case you want to summarize the sales for each month, showing which sales representatives sold which items. The data categories you add to the Report Data Area should contain numeric data that can be summarized mathematically, such as the sales totals.

To begin building the report, follow these steps:

1. Select the first field you want to add to the Side Label Bar or Top Label Bar by pointing to the field in the Source Window and clicking the left mouse button. In this case, select the *Month* field.

2. Copy the *Month* field to the Side Label Bar by dragging the field to the Side Label Bar area, by clicking the Side Label Bar button, or by choosing **B**uild Make **S**ide Label Bar. Your screen now should appear similar to figure 18.6.

3. Select the next field you want to add to one of the label bar areas and copy the field to the appropriate area. In this case, select the *Item* field and copy it to the top label area by dragging the field to the Top Label Bar area, by clicking the Top Label Bar button, or by choosing **B**uild Make **T**op Label Bar.

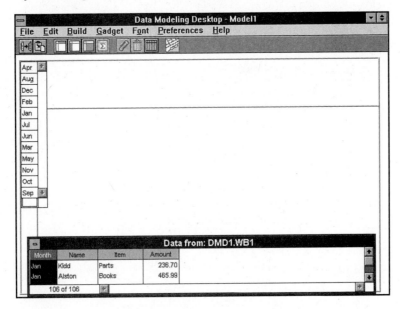

Fig. 18.6

First copy the *Month* field to the Side Label Bar area.

The Data Modeling Desktop now appears with an empty cross-tabulation grid similar to figure 18.7.

As you add fields to the side or Top Label Bar areas, an open box appears immediately below the field in the Side Label Bar area or immediately to the right of the field in the Top Label Bar area. This open box is the label bar *handle*, which you later use to move fields.

4. Select any other fields you want to add to the label bar areas and copy the fields to the appropriate area. In this case, select the *Name* field and copy it to the top label area. The top label area now contains two field labels, with the *Name* field displayed below the *Item* field.

Fig. 18.7

Next, copy the *Item* field to the top label area.

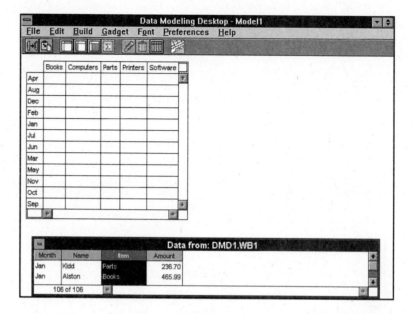

5. Finally, select the field containing the numeric data you want to summarize and copy the field to the report data area. In this case, select the *Amount* field and copy it to the report data area by dragging the field to the report data area, by clicking the Report Data button, or by choosing **B**uild Make **R**eport Data.

   The basic report now is finished and looks like figure 18.8.

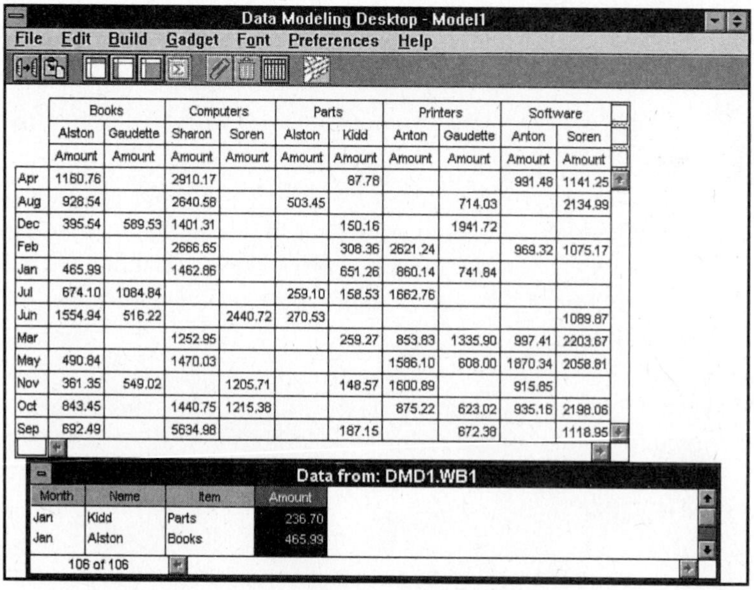

Fig. 18.8

The finished basic report.

		Books		Computers		Parts		Printers		Software	
		Alston	Gaudette	Sharon	Soren	Alston	Kidd	Anton	Gaudette	Anton	Soren
		Amount	Amount	Amount	Amount	Amount	Amount	Amount	Amount	Amount	Amount
Apr		1160.76		2910.17			87.78			991.48	1141.25
Aug		928.54		2640.58		503.45			714.03		2134.99
Dec		395.54	589.53	1401.31			150.16		1941.72		
Feb				2666.65			308.36	2621.24		969.32	1075.17
Jan		465.99		1462.86			651.26	860.14	741.84		
Jul		674.10	1084.84			259.10	158.53	1662.76			
Jun		1554.94	516.22		2440.72	270.53					1089.87
Mar				1252.95			259.27	853.83	1335.90	997.41	2203.67
May		490.84		1470.03				1586.10	608.00	1870.34	2058.81
Nov		361.35	549.02		1205.71		148.57	1600.89		915.85	
Oct		843.45		1440.75	1215.38			875.22	623.02	935.16	2198.06
Sep		692.49		5634.98			187.15		672.38		1118.95

If you want a less cluttered work area, you now can remove the Source Window from the screen because all the fields have been copied to the cross-tabulation report. To remove the Source Window, double-click the Source Window control menu or use the Source Window control menu **C**lose command. You can redisplay the Source Window at any time by clicking the Source Window button or by choosing **B**uild Source **W**indow. The remaining screens in this section have the Source Window removed to make the screens easier to understand.

Modifying the Report

Although the basic report shows the cross-tabulated data, the report certainly can use some improvement. Notice, for example, that the months listed in the Side Label Bar area are in alphabetical order rather than calendar order. In addition, some totals would be a useful addition. The next sections show you how to make these types of modifications. Later sections show you how to consolidate data into quarterly totals, change the cross-tabulation view by moving categories between label bar areas, and view other types of summaries.

Rearranging the Order of Data

When you copy a field to one of the label bar areas, the data items in the field are sorted automatically in alphabetical order. This order may be acceptable for fields such as the *Name* or *Item* field, but alphabetical order clearly is unacceptable for the *Month* field. To make the report easier to understand, you want to rearrange the months into standard calendar order.

To rearrange items in one of the label bar areas, point to the item you want to move, hold down the left mouse button, and move the item to its new position in the same label bar area. Continue moving the month labels until they are in standard, calendar order as shown in figure 18.9.

Adding Totals

To accurately assess the results, including totals in the report would be helpful. You easily can add both column and row totals to show the overall sales for each month and the sales for each item. Follow these steps to add totals to the report:

Fig. 18.9

The report after rearranging the months in the Side Label Bar area.

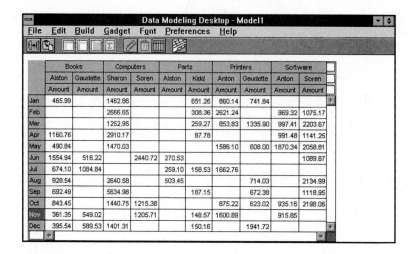

	Books		Computers		Parts		Printers		Software	
	Alston	Gaudette	Sharon	Soren	Alston	Kidd	Anton	Gaudette	Anton	Soren
	Amount	Amount	Amount	Amount	Amount	Amount	Amount	Amount	Amount	Amount
Jan	465.99		1462.86			651.26	860.14	741.84		
Feb			2666.65			308.36	2621.24		969.32	1075.17
Mar			1252.95			259.27	853.83	1335.90	997.41	2203.67
Apr	1160.76		2910.17			87.78			991.48	1141.25
May	490.84		1470.03				1586.10	608.00	1870.34	2058.81
Jun	1554.94	516.22		2440.72	270.53					1089.87
Jul	674.10	1084.84			259.10	158.53	1662.76			
Aug	928.54		2640.58		503.45			714.03		2134.99
Sep	692.49		5634.98			187.15		672.38		1118.95
Oct	843.45		1440.75	1215.38			875.22	623.02	935.16	2198.06
Nov	361.35	549.02		1205.71		148.57	1600.89		915.85	
Dec	395.54	589.53	1401.31			150.16		1941.72		

Data Modeling Desktop - Model1
File Edit Build Gadget Font Preferences Help

1. Click the handle of the Top Label Bar (which contains the item names) to select that label bar. When you select the label bar, you highlight all item names.

2. Add the TOTAL column by choosing **B**uild Add **T**otal Element or by clicking the Total button. The TOTAL column shows the total of the selected label bar, the items, for each month.

3. Next, click the handle of the Side Label Bar (which contains the months) to select that label bar.

4. Add the TOTAL row by choosing **B**uild Add **T**otal Element or by clicking the Total button. The TOTAL row shows the total of the items for each month. Figure 18.10 shows how the report now appears.

Deleting an Element

Deleting a report element you don't want, such as an unnecessary total, is as easy as adding a total. Suppose, for example, that you feel the TOTAL row at the bottom of the report is unnecessary and adds confusion rather than useful information. To delete the TOTAL row, follow these steps:

1. Select the TOTAL row. You can select this row by clicking the word TOTAL in the Side Label Bar area or by clicking the TOTAL row in the Report Data Area. If you click the TOTAL row in the Report Data Area, move the mouse until the pointer is in the TO-TAL row and the mouse pointer changes to an arrow pointing left.

2. Click the Remove button to delete the TOTAL row (no equivalent command is available—you must use the Remove button). The report now appears as shown in figure 18.11.

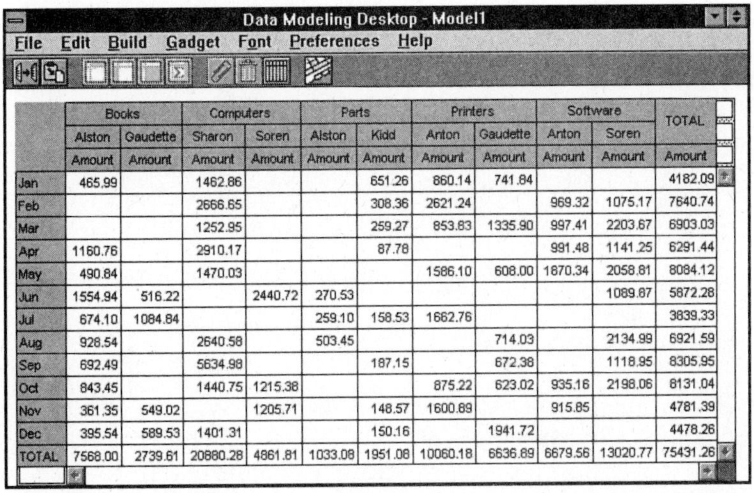

Fig. 18.10

The report now has totals added.

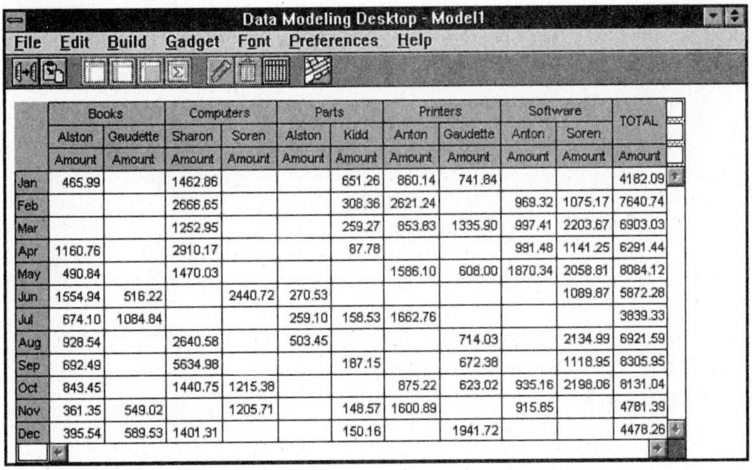

	Books		Computers		Parts		Printers		Software		TOTAL
	Alston	Gaudette	Sharon	Soren	Alston	Kidd	Anton	Gaudette	Anton	Soren	
	Amount	Amount	Amount	Amount	Amount	Amount	Amount	Amount	Amount	Amount	Amount
Jan	465.99		1462.86			651.26	860.14	741.84			4182.09
Feb			2666.65			308.36	2621.24		969.32	1075.17	7640.74
Mar			1252.95			259.27	853.83	1335.90	997.41	2203.67	6903.03
Apr	1160.76		2910.17			87.78			991.48	1141.25	6291.44
May	490.84		1470.03				1586.10	608.00	1870.34	2058.81	8084.12
Jun	1554.94	516.22		2440.72	270.53					1089.87	5872.28
Jul	674.10	1084.84			259.10	158.53	1662.76				3839.33
Aug	928.54		2640.58		503.45			714.03		2134.99	6921.59
Sep	692.49		5634.98			187.15		672.38		1118.95	8305.95
Oct	843.45		1440.75	1215.38			875.22	623.02	935.16	2198.06	8131.04
Nov	361.35	549.02		1205.71		148.57	1600.89		915.85		4781.39
Dec	395.54	589.53	1401.31			150.16		1941.72			4478.26
TOTAL	7568.00	2739.61	20880.28	4861.81	1033.08	1951.08	10060.18	6636.89	6679.56	13020.77	75431.26

Fig. 18.11

The TOTAL row deleted from the report.

	Books		Computers		Parts		Printers		Software		TOTAL
	Alston	Gaudette	Sharon	Soren	Alston	Kidd	Anton	Gaudette	Anton	Soren	
	Amount	Amount	Amount	Amount	Amount	Amount	Amount	Amount	Amount	Amount	Amount
Jan	465.99		1462.86			651.26	860.14	741.84			4182.09
Feb			2666.65			308.36	2621.24		969.32	1075.17	7640.74
Mar			1252.95			259.27	853.83	1335.90	997.41	2203.67	6903.03
Apr	1160.76		2910.17			87.78			991.48	1141.25	6291.44
May	490.84		1470.03				1586.10	608.00	1870.34	2058.81	8084.12
Jun	1554.94	516.22		2440.72	270.53					1089.87	5872.28
Jul	674.10	1084.84			259.10	158.53	1662.76				3839.33
Aug	928.54		2640.58		503.45			714.03		2134.99	6921.59
Sep	692.49		5634.98			187.15		672.38		1118.95	8305.95
Oct	843.45		1440.75	1215.38			875.22	623.02	935.16	2198.06	8131.04
Nov	361.35	549.02		1205.71		148.57	1600.89		915.85		4781.39
Dec	395.54	589.53	1401.31			150.16		1941.72			4478.26

Consolidating Data in the Report

Sometimes consolidating several report *elements*—the individual report items such as *Jan*, *Feb*, and so on—better summarizes the data in a report. In the sales report, for example, you may be more interested in quarterly totals rather than monthly totals. You easily can consolidate report elements by combining them into a group. After you create a group, you also may want to rename the group to better reflect the combination of elements in the group.

Grouping Report Elements

Grouping report elements causes individual items to combine into a single total. The following steps show you how to combine the month elements into quarterly groups:

1. Click the Jan label in the Side Label Bar to select the Jan element.

2. Hold down the shift key and click the Feb label, then the Mar label.

3. Choose **B**uild **G**roup Elements or click the Group/Ungroup button. The three elements combine to form a group with the label * Jan.

4. Repeat the process to group the Apr, May, and Jun elements, the Jul, Aug, and Sep elements, and the Oct, Nov, and Dec elements. The report now has four groups of elements in the Side Label Bar as shown in figure 18.12.

Fig. 18.12

The month elements combined into quarterly groups.

Data Modeling Desktop - Model1										
File Edit Build Gadget Font Preferences Help										
	Books		Computers		Parts		Printers		Software		TOTAL
	Alston	Gaudette	Sharon	Soren	Alston	Kidd	Anton	Gaudette	Anton	Soren	
	Amount	Amount	Amount	Amount	Amount	Amount	Amount	Amount	Amount	Amount	Amount
* Jan	465.99		5382.46			1218.89	4335.21	2077.74	1966.73	3278.84	18725.86
* Apr	3206.54	516.22	4380.20	2440.72	270.53	87.78	1586.10	608.00	2861.82	4289.93	20247.84
* Jul	2295.13	1084.84	8275.56		762.55	345.68	1662.76	1386.41		3253.94	19066.87
* Oct	1600.34	1138.55	2842.06	2421.09		298.73	2476.11	2564.74	1851.01	2198.06	17390.69

If you later want to view each month's data again, rather than the quarterly groups, use the **B**uild **U**ngroup Elements command or click the Group/Ungroup button to redisplay the months.

Renaming Report Elements

The labels that now appear in the Side Label Bar, * Jan, * Apr, * Jul, and * Oct, do not clearly identify the grouped elements as quarterly totals. To make the report easier to understand, you probably want to rename the groups as Qtr 1, Qtr 2, Qtr 3, and Qtr 4. Data Modeling Desktop uses *gadgets* to make this type of report modification.

Follow these steps to rename the group elements:

1. Click the group element labeled * Jan to select the element.

2. Choose **G**adget **N**ame to open the Name dialog box (see fig. 18.13). You also can point to the * Jan group element and click the right mouse button to open both the Name and Format gadget dialog boxes.

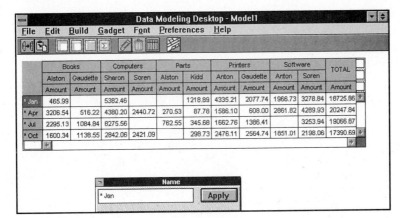

Fig. 18.13

Fig. 18.13

Use the Name dialog box to rename report elements.

3. Select the text box in the Name dialog box and type **Qtr 1** as the new name for the * Jan group element.

4. Click the Apply button to change the group element name. The Name dialog box remains on-screen.

5. Select the group element labeled * Apr.

6. Select the text box in the Name dialog box and type **Qtr 2** as the new name for the * Apr group element.

7. Repeat steps 5 and 6 to rename the * Jul group element as **Qtr 3** and * Oct as **Qtr 4**.

8. Close the Name dialog box by double-clicking the dialog box control menu or by choosing **C**lose from the dialog box control menu. The report now appears as shown in figure 18.14.

Changing Other Report Characteristics

In addition to the modifications you have seen already, you can make several other changes that affect the appearance of the report. Table 18.1 summarizes the commands you can use to change the appearance of the report.

Fig. 18.14

The Side Label Bar group elements are now renamed as quarters.

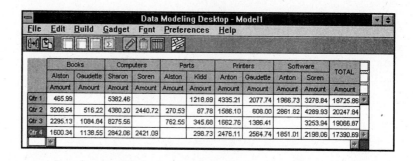

Table 18.1 Commands to Modify Report Appearance

Command	Description
Gadget **D**isplay	Changes the grid in the Report Data Area to display only horizontal lines, only vertical lines, no lines, or the default of both horizontal and vertical lines
Gadget **F**ormat	Changes the numeric format of the values displayed in the report
Gadget F**o**rmula	Changes the cross-tabulation summary formula to one of the following: Sum (default), Average, Count, % of Column, % of Row, % of Grand, Increase, % Increase, or String
Gadget **L**imit	Changes the cross-tabulation summary to include data that meets specified criteria: None (default), Equals, Not Equals, Less Than, Less Than or Equal, Greater Than, Greater Than or Equal, Begins With, Contains, Ends With, or Like
Font	Changes the size of the characters in the report
Preferences **R**esize All Cells to Fit	Adjusts report column widths to display all data

Figure 18.15 shows the effect of using the **G**adget F**o**rmula command to change the cross-tabulation summary formula to *Count*, which displays the number of data items rather than their totals.

If you want to limit the data in the report to include only data that meets certain conditions, use the **G**adget **L**imit command to specify those conditions. For example, to report on sales only over $100.00, specify the limit as Greater Than 100.

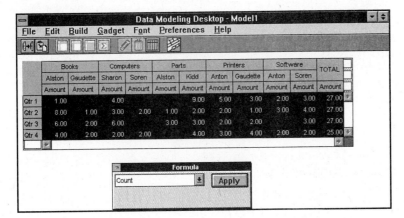

Fig. 18.15

Changing the formula to *Count* displays the number of data items.

Changing the Report by Moving Label Bars

So far, you have seen how to create a Data Modeling Desktop report and make some simple modifications in the report's appearance. The real power of the Data Modeling Desktop becomes apparent only when you learn how to rearrange the report by moving label bars. As you move the label bars, you change the entire basis of the report and can examine different types of relationships in the data.

You can move the label bars in two ways. You can *pivot* a label bar, changing it from a Side Label Bar to a Top Label Bar or from a Top Label Bar to a Side Label Bar. You also can change the *order* of the label bars in the top or Side Label Bar area. Both types of changes have a profound effect on the cross-tabulation report.

The ease of making these changes represents the major difference between the Data Modeling Desktop and Quattro Pro 5.0 for Windows (or any other spreadsheet program). Rearranging the cross-tabulation report to view different data relationships is simple in the Data Modeling Desktop, but this process is difficult and time-consuming in a standard spreadsheet program.

Pivoting a Label Bar to Change the Report

The report created in the earlier examples does a good job of summarizing the quarterly sales for each type of product, but the report does not summarize each sales representative's sales very well. Fortunately, with the Data Modeling Desktop, you can change the focus of the report quickly and easily. The first step is to pivot the label bar containing the sales representatives' names from the Top Label Bar area to the Side Label Bar area. Follow these steps to pivot the label bar:

1. Point to the handle for the Top Label Bar containing the sales representatives' names.

2. Hold down the left mouse button and drag the label bar handle to the Side Label Bar area. As you drag the label bar handle, a dotted line shows the label bar pivoting (see fig. 18.16).

Fig. 18.16

Drag the Top Label Bar containing the sales representatives' names to the Side Label Bar area.

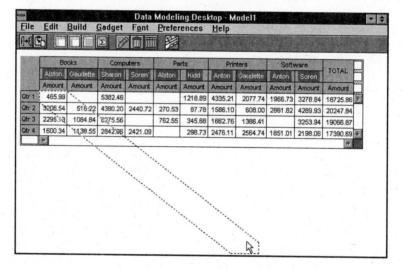

3. Release the mouse button when the label bar handle is in the Side Label Bar area. The report changes to reflect the new cross-tabulation summary generated by the new positions of the label bars (see fig. 18.17).

The new report shows the total sales for each sales representative for each quarter. You easily can see who had sales for each product line and who did not. This entirely new view of the relationships resulted from simply pivoting the label bar containing the names from the Top Label Bar area to the Side Label Bar area.

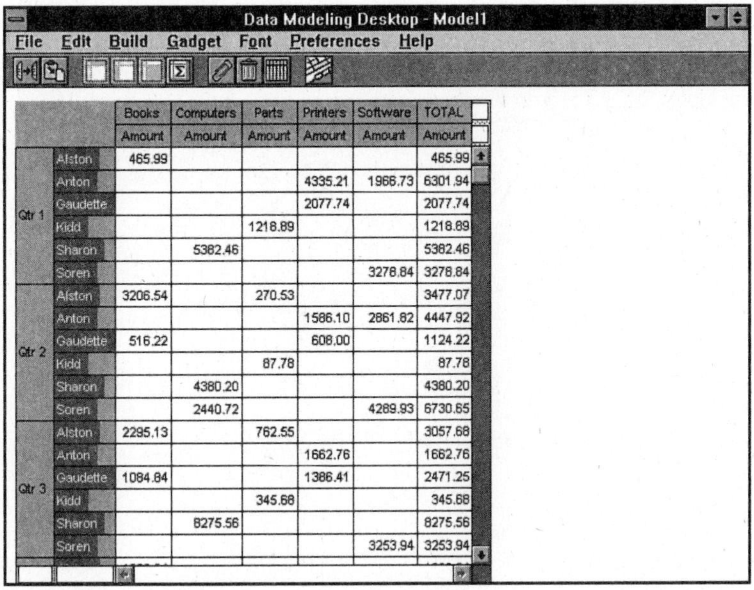

		Books Amount	Computers Amount	Parts Amount	Printers Amount	Software Amount	TOTAL Amount
Qtr 1	Alston	465.99					465.99
	Anton				4335.21	1966.73	6301.94
	Gaudette				2077.74		2077.74
	Kidd			1218.89			1218.89
	Sharon		5382.46				5382.46
	Soren					3278.84	3278.84
Qtr 2	Alston	3206.54		270.53			3477.07
	Anton				1586.10	2861.82	4447.92
	Gaudette	516.22			608.00		1124.22
	Kidd			87.78			87.78
	Sharon		4380.20				4380.20
	Soren		2440.72			4289.93	6730.65
Qtr 3	Alston	2295.13		762.55			3057.68
	Anton				1662.76		1662.76
	Gaudette	1084.84			1386.41		2471.25
	Kidd			345.68			345.68
	Sharon		8275.56				8275.56
	Soren					3253.94	3253.94

Fig. 18.17

The report changes to reflect the new cross-tabulation summary.

Moving a Label Bar in the Same Label Bar Area

The new report in figure 18.17 still does not focus on the individual results for each sales representative, but you quickly can move the label bar containing the names to change the cross-tabulation report again. Moving a label bar within the same label bar area changes the *level*, or importance, of the items in the label bars. In figure 18.17, quarterly sales have a higher importance than who sold the items. If you move the names label bar to the left of the quarterly groups label bar, sales are grouped by sales representative rather than by quarter, because the items in the names label bar become more important. To move the names label bar to the left of the quarterly groups label bar, follow these steps:

1. Point to the handle for the Side Label Bar containing the sales representatives' names.

2. Hold down the left mouse button and drag the label bar handle to the left of the quarterly groups label bar.

3. Release the mouse button when the label bar handle is at the left of the Side Label Bar area. The report changes to reflect the new cross-tabulation summary generated by the new positions of the label bars (see fig. 18.18).

Fig. 18.18

Changing the position of the label bar changes its importance in the report.

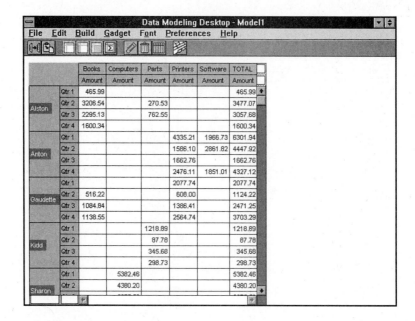

		Books	Computers	Parts	Printers	Software	TOTAL	
		Amount	Amount	Amount	Amount	Amount	Amount	
Alston	Qtr 1	465.99					465.99	
	Qtr 2	3206.54		270.53			3477.07	
	Qtr 3	2295.13		762.55			3057.68	
	Qtr 4	1600.34					1600.34	
Anton	Qtr 1				4335.21	1966.73	6301.94	
	Qtr 2				1586.10	2861.82	4447.92	
	Qtr 3				1662.76		1662.76	
	Qtr 4				2476.11	1851.01	4327.12	
Gaudette	Qtr 1				2077.74		2077.74	
	Qtr 2	516.22			608.00		1124.22	
	Qtr 3	1084.84			1386.41		2471.25	
	Qtr 4	1138.55			2564.74		3703.29	
Kidd	Qtr 1			1218.89			1218.89	
	Qtr 2			87.78			87.78	
	Qtr 3			345.68			345.68	
	Qtr 4			298.73			298.73	
Sharon	Qtr 1		5382.46				5382.46	
	Qtr 2		4380.20				4380.20	

Pivoting label bars and moving label bars within the same label bar area completely change the focus of the cross-tabulation. You can try any number of combinations to see the many different relationships contained in your data. The Data Modeling Desktop enables you to examine every possibility easily.

Narrowing the Report by Focusing on Labels

Sometimes you can improve a report by narrowing the scope of the report. A report showing the sales commissions paid to all sales representatives may be of interest to the sales manager, but you probably should not distribute the report to every sales representative, for example. Instead, separate reports showing only the commissions paid to individual sales representatives probably is a better idea. Likewise, you probably should limit a December sales contest report to showing sales made in December rather than the entire year's sales.

The following steps show you how to narrow the report by showing only sales for the fourth quarter:

1. Point to one of the Qtr 4 labels in the Side Label Bar and click the left mouse button to select all the Qtr 4 elements. You can point to any of the Qtr 4 labels to select the entire set.

2. Choose **B**uild **F**ocus on Labels to narrow the focus of the report to only the selected items. The report now appears as shown in figure 18.19.

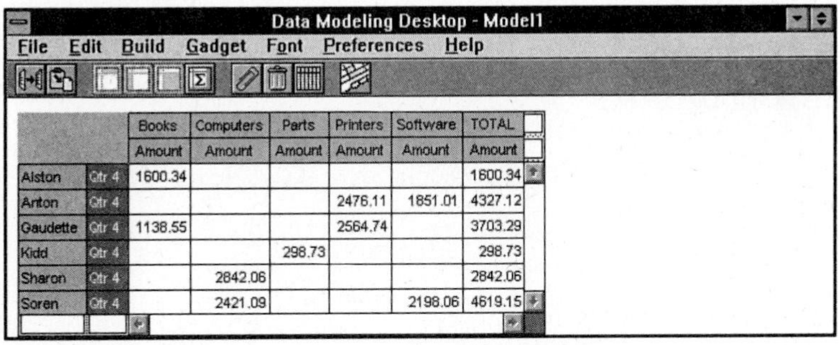

Fig. 18.19

Focus on selected labels to narrow the scope of the report.

Use the **B**uild **R**estore **L**abels command to redisplay all the hidden labels. You also can hide a selected group of labels using the **B**uild **H**ide Labels command.

Copying the Report to Quattro Pro

After you have created your cross-tabulation report in the Data Modeling Desktop, you copy the report to a Quattro Pro 5.0 for Windows notebook for formatting and printing. The report data copies to cells in the notebook, but any formatting (such as numeric format or lines) does not copy.

Use the **E**dit Copy to **Q**uattro Pro command or click the Copy to Quattro Pro button to copy the current report to the Quattro Pro 5.0 for Windows notebook (see fig. 18.20).

By default, copying a report to the Quattro Pro 5.0 for Windows notebook minimizes the Data Modeling Desktop and displays the notebook in the active window. You can use the **P**references **C**opy to Quattro Pro Options command in the Data Modeling Desktop to modify the type of copy performed. This command opens the Quattro Pro Copy Options dialog box shown in figure 18.21.

Fig. 18.20

Copy the report to a
Quattro Pro 5.0 for
Windows notebook for
formatting and printing.

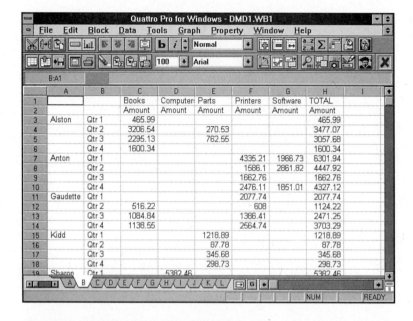

Fig. 18.21

The Quattro Pro Copy
Options dialog box.

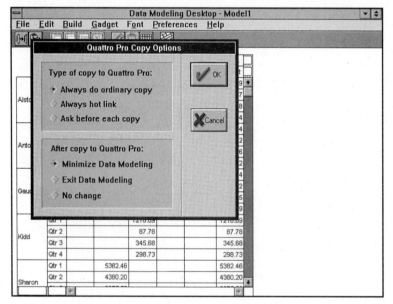

Use the Type of copy to Quattro Pro options to specify how Data Modeling Desktop copies a report to the notebook. Choose Always do ordinary copy to copy the report data only when you use the **Edit Copy** command. Choose Always hot link to establish a live DDE link between Data Modeling Desktop and the notebook. Choose Ask before each copy to be prompted before data copies.

Use the After copy to Quattro Pro options to specify how Data Modeling Desktop responds after a copy. Choose Minimize Data Modeling to make the notebook the active window but leave the Data Modeling Desktop in memory. Choose Exit Data Modeling to make the notebook the active window, closing the Data Modeling Desktop. Choose No change to return to the Data Modeling Desktop after a copy.

Questions and Answers

Q: My data is in a Paradox for Windows file. How can I use that data in the Data Modeling Desktop?

A: Open the Paradox file directly in a Quattro Pro 5.0 for Windows notebook or use the Database Desktop to extract the records you want and copy those records to the notebook. Then you can proceed as if you were analyzing a standard notebook database.

Q: Why does my label bar show numbers?

A: Keep in mind that the database fields you add to label bars should be fields containing labels, not numbers. You should add fields containing numeric data to the report data area, not to one of the label bars.

Q: How can I use a Data Modeling Desktop report in another program, such as Word for Windows?

A: Use the **Edit Copy** command to copy the report to the Windows Clipboard. You then can paste the report into any Windows program that has an Edit Paste command.

Summary

The Data Modeling Desktop is an extremely powerful yet easy-to-use data analysis tool. Data Modeling Desktop offers the flexibility of the stand-alone Lotus Improv program, but because it is a part of Quattro Pro 5.0 for Windows, Data Modeling Desktop offers much better value.

This chapter showed you how to use the Data Modeling Desktop, sharing data with Quattro Pro 5.0 for Windows. You learned how to quickly generate many types of cross-tabulation analysis reports and modify those reports for different purposes.

Chapter 19 introduces the Consolidator and the Scenario Manager, two important new tools you can use to combine and manage data from several sources as well as to play what-if games to learn even more about your data.

Consolidating Data and Managing Scenarios

Managing information is not always a simple task. Data may come from several sources and in different formats, and you may need to consolidate the data to produce meaningful results. Many optional scenarios may exist, each with its own outcome. To make sense of the vast maze of information, you need powerful tools to help you consolidate data and track changes.

Quattro Pro 5.0 for Windows offers two new tools, the *Consolidator* and the *Scenario Manager*, which reduce these types of tasks to simple projects. This chapter introduces these tools and shows you how to use them to manage your information.

In this chapter, you learn to perform the following tasks:

- Consolidate information from different sources, even when the source formats differ

- Analyze consolidated information using different consolidation options

- Create what-if scenarios with several data sets

- Track different versions of a notebook

The first part of this chapter shows you the Consolidator. Later in this chapter you learn about the Scenario Manager.

Understanding the Consolidator

Information often comes from many sources. Before investing in a company's stock, for example, you may read a company's annual report, scan articles in a financial newsletter, and consider a stock broker's advice. In a business, you may receive sales data from several departments, as well as from several stores, or even regional offices, all of which you combine to produce a summary of overall sales. A membership organization may have many local groups that all contribute to its total membership figures. Each of these examples demonstrates a different situation in which data from several sources must be consolidated to produce an accurate picture of the available information.

Combining data from several sources to produce a true, overall picture can be complicated, and unless you are very careful, can be an error-prone project. The Consolidator, one of the new tools in Quattro Pro 5.0 for Windows, simplifies the task and greatly reduces the chance of errors.

Two of the most common methods of combining data from several Quattro Pro 5.0 for Windows notebooks are using the **Tools Combine** command or linking notebooks with formulas. The first method, using the **Tools Combine** command, has several drawbacks. Not only do you need to issue the command for each notebook you want to combine, but you have no reliable method of checking for errors, such as forgetting to include a notebook or including a notebook more than one time. Linking notebooks with formulas at least enables you to audit the linking formulas to ensure that each source notebook is included exactly one time. But linking notebooks with formulas can be a complex task, especially if you must link many cells. Both methods also have considerable difficulty coping with notebooks that contain the same information but present the information in a slightly different format.

The Consolidator eases the task of combining data by enabling you to create and save a consolidation, which you easily can recall for later use. Source notebooks can contain related data in different formats, and the Consolidator can determine automatically which data to combine. You can consolidate data using your choice of nine analysis methods, and you can link data using live formulas or combine data as static data. Each subsequent data consolidation combines the data in the same way, with no chance of forgetting to include some data or including data more than one time.

FOR RELATED INFORMATION

◀◀ "Combining Data," p.280.

◀◀ "Linking Notebook Files," p.282.

Using the Consolidator

You can use the Consolidator to combine data from different blocks in the same notebook or from blocks in several notebooks. Figure 19.1 shows a sample notebook used in the examples throughout this chapter.

The sample notebook shows the quarterly sales for three stores, but each store in this example reports its data in a slightly different order. Store 1 reports departmental sales in the following order: Software, Books, Parts, Computers, and Printers. Store 2 reports sales by Computers, Printers, Software, Parts, and Books. Store 3 reports sales by Books, Computers, Parts, Printers, and then Software. Although you could go to the trouble to rearrange all the data in the same order, the Consolidator can combine the data correctly without requiring this extra work. If you consider how much work is involved in rearranging the data categories in several notebooks, you can gain a better appreciation for this capability.

Keep in mind, however, that the Consolidator can correctly find and combine data from blocks where the data is in a different order only if the same labels identify the data. In figure 19.1, the Consolidator can find all entries for *Books* in *Qtr 1* because the same labels are in every block. If Store 1 listed the category as *Computer Books* or used the term *Quarter 1*, the Consolidator could not identify the data correctly. Make certain that you use the same labels in all source blocks if you want to combine data that may be in a different order.

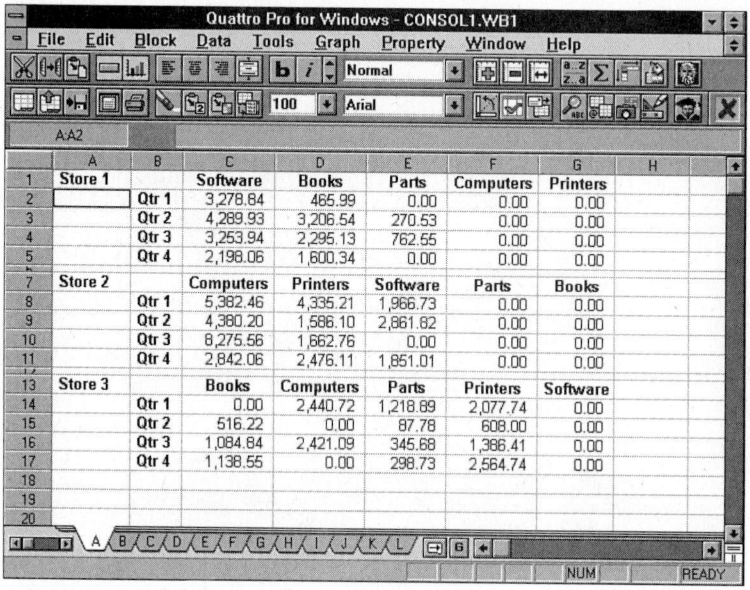

	A	B	C	D	E	F	G	H
1	Store 1		Software	Books	Parts	Computers	Printers	
2		Qtr 1	3,278.84	465.99	0.00	0.00	0.00	
3		Qtr 2	4,289.93	3,206.54	270.53	0.00	0.00	
4		Qtr 3	3,253.94	2,295.13	762.55	0.00	0.00	
5		Qtr 4	2,198.06	1,600.34	0.00	0.00	0.00	
7	Store 2		Computers	Printers	Software	Parts	Books	
8		Qtr 1	5,382.46	4,335.21	1,966.73	0.00	0.00	
9		Qtr 2	4,380.20	1,586.10	2,861.82	0.00	0.00	
10		Qtr 3	8,275.56	1,662.76	0.00	0.00	0.00	
11		Qtr 4	2,842.06	2,476.11	1,851.01	0.00	0.00	
13	Store 3		Books	Computers	Parts	Printers	Software	
14		Qtr 1	0.00	2,440.72	1,218.89	2,077.74	0.00	
15		Qtr 2	516.22	0.00	87.78	608.00	0.00	
16		Qtr 3	1,084.84	2,421.09	345.68	1,386.41	0.00	
17		Qtr 4	1,138.55	0.00	298.73	2,564.74	0.00	
18								
19								
20								

Fig. 19.1

The sample notebook data for the Consolidator examples.

To begin using the Consolidator, choose the **T**ools Co**n**solidator command to add the Consolidator SpeedBar to the top of the screen. Figure 19.2 shows the Consolidator SpeedBar.

Adding Source Blocks

The first step in building a consolidation is to add the *source blocks*—the notebook blocks containing the data you want to consolidate. Source blocks can be in the active notebook, or you can specify source blocks in another Quattro Pro 5.0 for Windows notebook.

If the source blocks contain data that is not organized in the same order, such as the source blocks in figure 19.1, the top row and the left column of each source block should contain identical labels that identify the data. If the row order is the same in each source block, as shown in figure 19.1, the labels in the left column of the source blocks are optional. Likewise, if the column order is the same in each source block, the labels in the top row of the source blocks are optional. See "Setting Consolidator Options," later in this chapter, for more information on row and column labels.

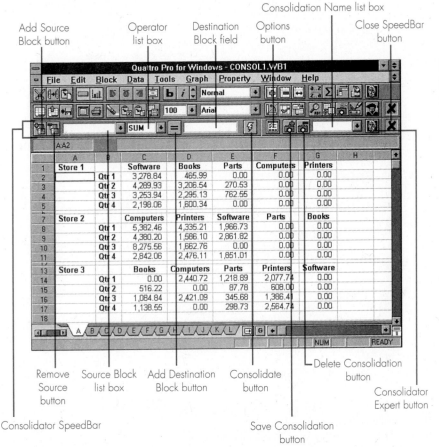

Fig. 19.2

Use the Consolidator SpeedBar to consolidate data.

To add the three source blocks to the consolidation, follow these steps:

1. Highlight the first source block, in this case B1..G5.

2. Click the Add Source Block button.

3. Highlight the next source block, in this case B7..G11.

4. Again click the Add Source Block button.

5. Highlight the final source block, in this case B13..G17.

6. Again click the Add Source Block button.

To add a source block that is not in the active notebook, click the down-arrow button on the Source Block list box and select < Browse >. Then select the source notebook and type the source block name or address.

NOTE ▶ Quattro Pro 5.0 for Windows makes certain you do not duplicate the same source block. If you try to add the same source block twice, a warning box appears and the duplicate entry is ignored.

To view the current source block list, click the down-arrow button on the Source Block list box. The list box drops down to display the current list of source blocks as shown in figure 19.3.

Fig. 19.3

The Source Block list box displays the current list of source blocks.

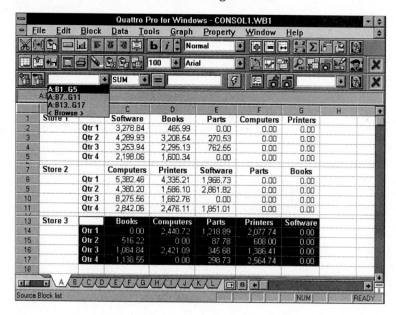

computer sales, plus store 3's first-quarter book sales. Clearly, this consolidation is not very useful. The next section shows you how to correct this problem.

Setting Consolidator Options

The Consolidator has three options you can use to adjust the consolidation methods. To choose Consolidator options, click the Options button on the Consolidator SpeedBar to open the Consolidator Options dialog box shown in figure 19.5.

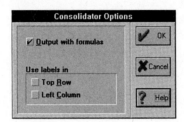

Fig. 19.5

The Consolidator Options dialog box.

Choose from the following options:

- **Output with formulas** (the default) includes formulas in the destination block. Deselect this option to include the results as values rather than formulas.

- Use labels in Top **R**ow matches source block data items using the labels in the top row of each source block to find matching data. Choosing this option also includes the row of labels in the destination block.

- Use labels in Left **C**olumn matches source block data items using the labels in the left column of each source block to find matching data. Choosing this option also includes the column of labels in the destination block.

In this case, because the three source blocks have the same row layout but a different column layout, you must choose Use labels in Top **R**ow to match the source block data items correctly. To make the destination block easier to understand, you may also want to choose Use labels in Left **C**olumn to include the left column of labels.

After you have chosen both of the Use Labels in options, specify B:A7 as the new destination block and click the Consolidate button again. Figure 19.6 shows how the new results in cells B:A7..F11 compare to the original results in B:B2..F5.

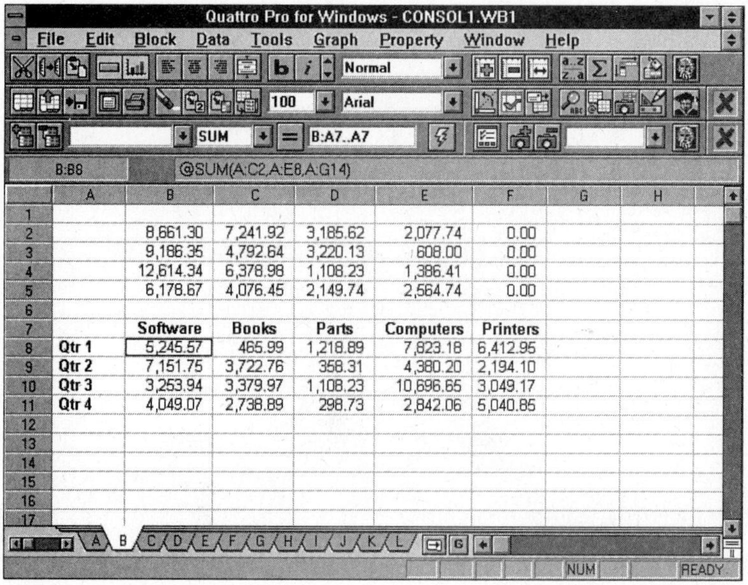

	A	B	C	D	E	F
1						
2		8,661.30	7,241.92	3,185.62	2,077.74	0.00
3		9,186.35	4,792.64	3,220.13	608.00	0.00
4		12,614.34	6,378.98	1,108.23	1,386.41	0.00
5		6,178.67	4,076.45	2,149.74	2,564.74	0.00
6						
7		Software	Books	Parts	Computers	Printers
8	Qtr 1	5,245.57	465.99	1,218.89	7,823.18	6,412.95
9	Qtr 2	7,151.75	3,722.76	358.31	4,380.20	2,194.10
10	Qtr 3	3,253.94	3,379.97	1,108.23	10,696.65	3,049.17
11	Qtr 4	4,049.07	2,738.89	298.73	2,842.06	5,040.85

Fig. 19.6

Consolidating data using labels produces correct results.

In the new destination block, the correct data items were consolidated. Consider the consolidation formula in cell B:B8:

@SUM(A:C2,A:E8,A:G14)

Compare this formula with the consolidation formula in cell B:B2 of figure 19.4. The new formula correctly sums the first-quarter software sales for each of the three stores.

In addition to including the correct consolidation formulas, the new destination block identifies the rows and columns of data, making the block much easier to understand. In most cases, choosing the Use Labels in Top **R**ow and Use labels in Left **C**olumn options improves the appearance of the output block, even if these options are not required to correctly consolidate the data.

Saving a Consolidation

To save a consolidation for reuse, name the consolidation, and then save the notebook.

To name a consolidation, follow these steps:

1. First build the consolidation by specifying the source blocks, the operator, the destination block, and any options.

2. Click the Save Consolidation button.

3. Type the name for the current group of settings in the Consolidation Name text box.

4. Press Enter or click OK.

Figure 19.7 shows a notebook with three named consolidations. These three consolidations show the sum, average, and maximum of the corresponding values; the names are SUM_1, AVG_1, and MAX_1.

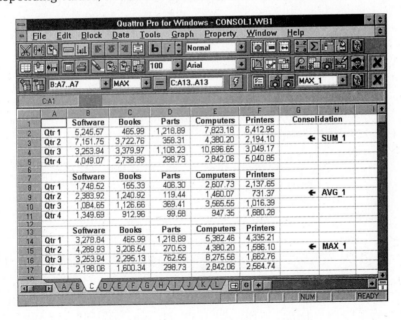

Fig. 19.7

Named consolidations enable quick reuse of the same consolidation settings.

To reuse a saved consolidation, choose the consolidation name in the Consolidation Name list box, and then click the Consolidate button. To delete a saved consolidation setting, choose the consolidation name in the Consolidation Name list box, and then click the Delete Consolidation button. Deleting a named consolidation does not remove the results from the destination block, but deleting does prevent you from reusing the named setting.

FOR RELATED **INFORMATION**

◄◄ "Using Functions," p. 213.

Understanding the Scenario Manager

Often, knowing where you are going is just as important as knowing where you have been. The Consolidator makes collecting existing data a simple process, and the Scenario Manager helps you with the planning process by enabling you to track the ways a model changes. Using the Scenario Manager, you easily can see the effects different sales growth projections may have on your costs and profits.

The Scenario Manager tracks changes in a notebook model. The Scenario Manager notes both cells in which you make a change plus cells that change value as a result of your changes. This information enables you to track what-if scenarios as well as follow version changes as you modify a notebook model.

In addition to tracking individual scenarios, you can save several scenarios in a group. You even can have several groups of scenarios in a single notebook. This flexibility enables you to track a broad range of changes.

Using the Scenario Manager

Before you use the Scenario Manager, build your notebook model with all its formulas and basic data. This step is important, because the Scenario Manager tracks any changes made between the time you create the *base scenario*—a snapshot of the notebook before you make any changes—and when you save another scenario. Each time you save another scenario, all the additional changes are noted. Because you want to know the effects of changing certain data assumptions, you must start with a completed model so that the reported scenario reflects only those changes you really want to track.

Figure 19.8 shows a model created to demonstrate the Scenario Manager. This model calculates the monthly payments and the total interest paid on a mortgage. The Scenario Manager tracks each change as you enter different interest rates and terms, reporting on each change.

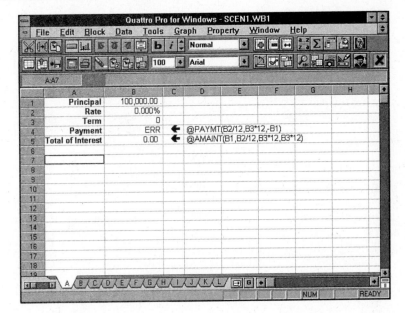

Fig. 19.8

A model created to demonstrate the Scenario Manager.

In this model, the initial interest rate and term are set to zero, which results in the formula for payment returning ERR. Although you could start by setting these two variables to actual values, using dummy values for the variables you want to track is better, because the Scenario Manager starts off by recording a base scenario. If you want a record of all values for the variables and the resulting calculations, start with values you will not use in the actual examples.

After you have created the model, choose **T**ools **S**cenario Manager to display the Scenario Manager SpeedBar (see fig. 19.9).

Fig. 19.9

The Scenario Manager SpeedBar.

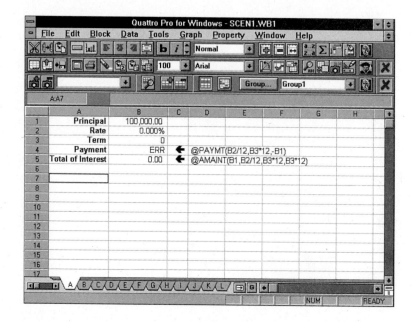

Recording the Base Scenario

You begin tracking changes by recording the base scenario. The base scenario is a picture of your notebook just before you begin making the changes you want to follow. To record the base scenario, follow these steps:

1. Click the Capture Scenario button to open the Capture Scenario As dialog box (see fig. 19.10).

Fig. 19.10

Record the starting point as your base scenario.

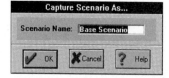

2. To change the name for the base scenario, type a new name in the Scenario Name text box. In this case, the default name, *Base Scenario*, is fine.

3. Press Enter or click OK to confirm the dialog box and return to the notebook.

Recording Additional Scenarios

You next make the first set of changes in the values of the variables. In this case, you want to track the changes that result from different interest rates and lengths of the loan. Follow these steps to create and capture the first changed scenario:

1. Enter the new interest rate in cell B2. For the first example, enter **7%**.

2. Enter the new term in cell B3. In this case, enter **15**.

3. Verify that the Scenario Manager has found all cells you changed by clicking the Find Scenario Cells button. On a color monitor, the variable cells are highlighted in yellow and the result cells are highlighted in green.

4. If some of the variable or result cells you want to track are not highlighted, select those cells and click the Add Scenario Cells button. In this example, cell B4 is not highlighted because it showed ERR in the base scenario.

5. If some cells are highlighted but you don't want to track their changes, select those cells and click the Remove Scenario Cells button. You might use this option if the notebook contains a number of intermediate formulas and you want to track only the final result.

6. Click the Capture Scenario button.

7. If you want to specify a different name for the scenario, type a new name in the Scenario Name text box.

8. Press Enter or click OK to confirm the dialog box and return to the notebook.

Repeat the above steps to capture any additional scenarios you want to track. For example, change the interest rate to **7.375%** and the term to **30**, and then capture the new scenario.

If the highlighting makes the notebook hard to read, you can use the Toggle Highlights button to temporarily remove the yellow and green highlighting. Click the Toggle Highlights button again to restore the highlighting.

Creating the Report

After you have captured several scenarios, you can see what changes Scenario Manager tracked. Follow these steps to create the Scenario Manager report:

1. Click the Report button to open the Scenario Report dialog box (see fig. 19.11).

Fig. 19.11

The Scenario Report dialog box.

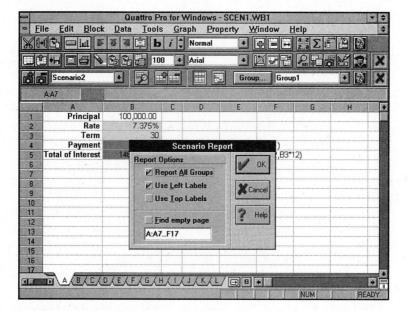

2. Choose Report **A**ll Groups to create a report showing all groups of saved scenarios.

3. Choose Use **L**eft Labels to identify report cells using the labels to their left. Make certain you choose this option in this example.

4. Choose Use **T**op Labels to identify report cells using the labels in the row above the cells.

5. Choose **F**ind empty page to create the report on the first empty notebook page.

6. Press Enter or click OK to confirm the dialog box and generate the report (see fig. 19.12).

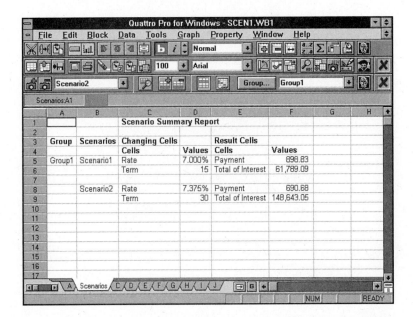

Fig. 19.12

The Scenario Manager report.

If you choose the **F**ind empty page option, the Scenario Manager places the report on the first empty page following any used notebook pages. The page automatically is named *Scenarios*, as shown in figure 19.12.

In this example, the Scenario Manager report shows that the 15-year loan at 7% interest has a much higher monthly payment than the 30-year loan at 7.375%. The report also shows that total interest on the longer term loan is over twice the interest on the shorter loan.

Saving Scenario Groups

In addition to saving individual scenarios, you can save groups of related scenarios. For example, you may decide to track several scenarios using a loan principal of $100,000 and another set using $125,000.

To save a scenario group, click the Group button to open the Scenario Group Control dialog box shown in figure 19.13.

`Group...`

Choose from the following options:

- **N**ew creates a new scenario group and enables you to access the Capture Area options (described later in this section).

- **R**ename changes the current group name.

- **O**ptions enables you to change whether the Scenario Manager tracks block moves.

- **D**elete removes a named group.

Fig. 19.13

The Scenario Group Control dialog box.

When you create a new scenario group, you can choose from the following Capture Area options:

- **N**otebook tracks changes in the entire notebook.

- **P**age (default) tracks all changes on the current page.

- **B**lock tracks changes in a specified block.

To reuse a saved scenario group, choose the group name in the Group Name list box.

In addition to tracking changing variables and formula results, you also can use the Scenario Manager to track the changes as you build a model or changes you make as you modify macros. Tracking these types of changes can provide valuable documentation, especially if you make a change that proves unsuccessful. By seeing the differences in the notebook between the version that worked and the version that did not, you probably can determine exactly where the problem lies.

Questions and Answers

Q: Why didn't the Consolidator combine the values from two identical data categories in two different source blocks?

A: When you use the Use labels in Top **R**ow or Use labels in Left **C**olumn options to match the data categories, the Consolidator combines data only if the labels are an exact match. If the labels have any differences, such as extra spaces, the Consolidator cannot determine that the data categories are an exact match and does not combine them.

Try copying the labels from one source block to the other. You should find that the Consolidator correctly identifies the data categories.

Q: Why didn't all the values appear in the destination block?

A: You probably specified a multi-cell destination block. The Consolidator fills only the specified block if you specify a multi-cell destination block, even if leftover values exist. To make certain the block shows all the values, specify a single-cell destination block or make sure the multi-cell destination block you specify is large enough to contain all the values.

Q: I tried to create a new consolidation using a different operator, but the new consolidation overwrote the existing one. What's wrong?

A: Don't forget to specify a new destination block. If you want to have multiple consolidations in a notebook, save each consolidation under a different name.

Q: How can I track the changes on two pages of my notebook using the Scenario Manager?

A: You have two choices. You can track each page separately or use the Group button to create a new scenario and change the Capture Area setting to Notebook. Note, though, that if you choose Notebook, Scenario Manager tracks all changes on any notebook page. If you choose this option, limit any changes between capturing scenarios to the two pages you want to track.

Q: Why doesn't the Scenario Manager report show my first set of values?

A: The report does not show the base scenario values. If you want to see these values and their formula results, start the base scenario with dummy values for the variables.

Summary

The Consolidator and the Scenario Manager help you combine data from several sources and track version differences. What formerly were tedious, manual tasks now are handled easily using these new tools. This chapter showed you how to use these tools to produce data summaries and create what-if scenarios projecting possible outcomes.

The next chapter introduces the Workgroup Desktop, a powerful new way to share data across a network or around the world.

Sharing Data Using the Workgroup Desktop

Sharing accurate, up-to-date data is one of the most important tasks in the world of business. Few businesses can survive if the information they use to make decisions is obsolete or inaccurate. Your ability to share information quickly can mean the difference between being a winner or loser in today's highly competitive business world.

Workgroup computing—the process of combining the talents and resources of two or more people using their computers to accomplish a task—is a highly effective method of sharing data. Workgroup computing can take many forms. In the past, computer workgroups consisted of terminal users connected to a mainframe or minicomputer. Today, however, computer users are much more likely to use PCs. Those PCs may be stand-alone systems, systems connected to a network, or even laptop systems with modems.

In the changed office place of today, sharing accurate, timely data across many different connections may be more complex than ever, but that sharing is just as important as ever. The *Workgroup Desktop*, one of the powerful new tools in Quattro Pro 5.0 for Windows, makes sharing data a simple, manageable, and reliable task. This chapter presents an overview of the Workgroup Desktop and shows how you can use it to stay on top of the information your business needs.

This chapter presents the following subjects:

- Setting up Workgroup Desktop accounts

- Creating an address book for data sharing

- Mailing, publishing, and subscribing to notebooks over networks or through data-sharing services

Understanding the Workgroup Desktop

The Workgroup Desktop is a tool that enables Quattro Pro 5.0 for Windows users to share notebooks or notebook pages across a network or through a service such as MCI Mail. The Workgroup Desktop uses a program called the *Object Exchange* (also called Obex) to handle all the details of sharing data. When you use the Workgroup Desktop to send a notebook page, the Object Exchange first stores the page, and then contacts the Object Exchange on the destination system. The Object Exchange on the destination system stores the received page, ready for the other Quattro Pro 5.0 for Windows users to access. If you update the page on your system, the copy on the destination also updates, making certain that everyone has timely data.

Three very important terms—*publishing, subscribing,* and *mailing*—define the Workgroup Desktop data-sharing process. Publishing creates a data-sharing relationship that effectively links the shared data to the source notebook. As new data develops, it becomes available to everyone who uses that data. Subscribing creates a link on the destination system that automatically obtains updated data when it becomes available. Mailing sends a one-time copy of a notebook or a set of data to other members of the workgroup. A single project usually uses some combination of all three processes.

Using the Workgroup Desktop, you can share data using MCI Mail, Novell's Netware Message Handling Service, NetWare Global Messaging, Microsoft Mail, Windows for Workgroups, and many other local area networks. After you create your *address book* showing the electronic addresses of users with whom you want to share data, the Object Exchange automatically handles the complexities of dealing with these many options.

Using the Workgroup Desktop

To use the Workgroup Desktop, you must first establish an *account* so that the Object Exchange can determine how to send and receive messages. You then can create and publish or mail notebooks and notebook pages, and you can subscribe to notebooks published by other users. You also can create electronic address books that the Object Exchange uses to determine where to send your messages.

The following sections show you how to establish your account and begin using the Workgroup Desktop.

Opening a Workgroup Desktop Account

You cannot send or receive data using the Workgroup Desktop until you establish your account. Opening your account is easy and automatic. If you open the Workgroup Desktop before you have established your account, you are prompted automatically to create your account before continuing.

To open the Workgroup Desktop and create your account, follow these steps:

1. Choose **D**ata Workgroup Desktop or click the Workgroup Desktop button on the Productivity Tools SpeedBar. If you have not yet established your account, the message box shown in figure 20.1 appears.

2. Press Enter or choose **Y**es to create your account. The New Account dialog box appears (see fig. 20.2).

3. From the **T**ransport list, select the type of network or messaging system you intend to use:

■ *MCI*. MCI Mail, an electronic mail service accessed through a modem.

■ *MHS*. Message Handling Service Versions 1.5 or 2.0, Novell's mail system for local area networks.

■ *LAN*. Local area networks such as Novell, Banyan, LanMAN, Lantastic, or NetWare Lite.

■ *MAPI*. Windows for Workgroups or other MAPI-compliant (Mail Application Programming Interface) messaging services such as Microsoft Mail.

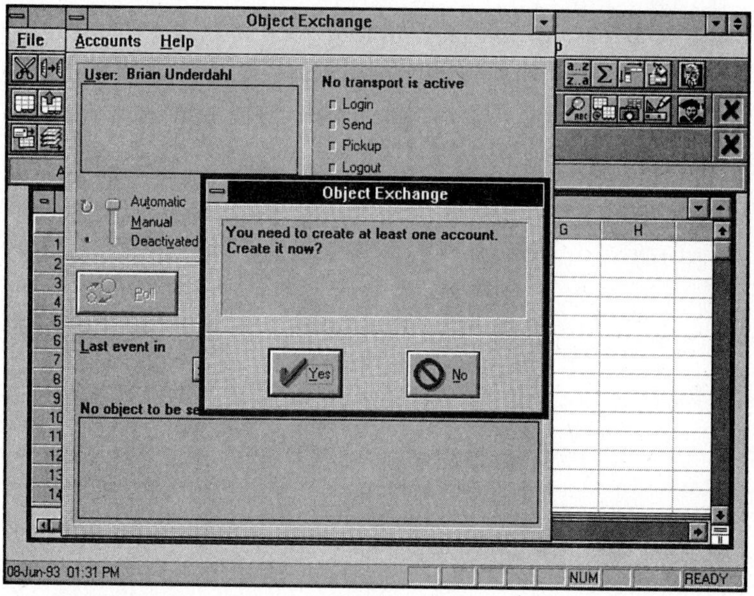

Fig. 20.1

You must create your account before you can use the Workgroup Desktop.

4. Press Enter or click OK to continue. The configuration dialog box for your selected network or messaging system appears. Figure 20.3 shows the Configure MAPI Account dialog box.

5. Enter your user account information. This information varies according to the type of system you use, but it always includes the account name and your user or mailbox name. You also may need to supply your account password, electronic post office location, and various modem setup information. If you do not know the correct information, ask your network administrator for assistance.

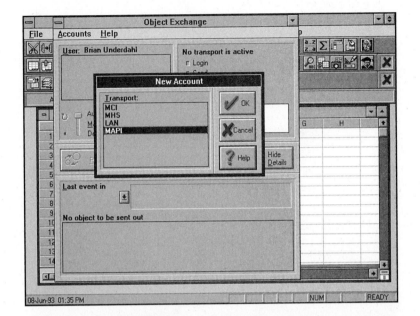

Fig. 20.2

The New Account
dialog box.

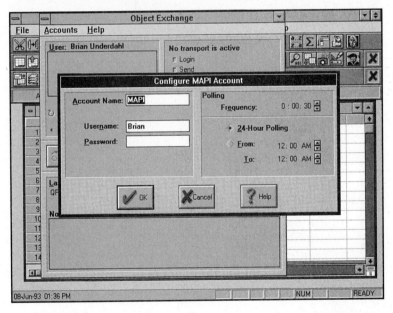

Fig. 20.3

The Configure MAPI
Account dialog box.

6. For the Polling Frequency, specify the time interval between attempts to seek updated data. Choose 24-Hour Polling to poll around the clock, or use the From and To settings to specify the time period in which to poll.

7. Press Enter or click OK to continue.

Figure 20.4 shows the Object Exchange dialog box, which appears after you have established an account. If your dialog box does not show the **Last** event in QPW section, click the Show **D**etails button (which becomes the Hide **D**etails button) so that you can view any pending events.

Fig. 20.4

The Object Exchange dialog box after an account has been established.

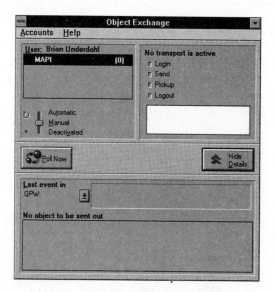

You now are ready to begin using the Workgroup Desktop. Press Alt+Tab (or click the Quattro Pro 5.0 for Windows window) to return to the notebook. The Object Exchange remains in memory. Figure 20.5 shows the Object Exchange SpeedBar.

Creating and Using Address Books

You use address books—special notebooks containing the electronic mail addresses of your workgroup members—as an electronic telephone book for the Workgroup Desktop. In fact, to publish or mail a notebook or a notebook page, you must first connect to an address book.

To connect to your address book, follow these steps:

1. Click the Address button on the Workgroup Desktop SpeedBar to open the Address Book dialog box (see fig. 20.6).

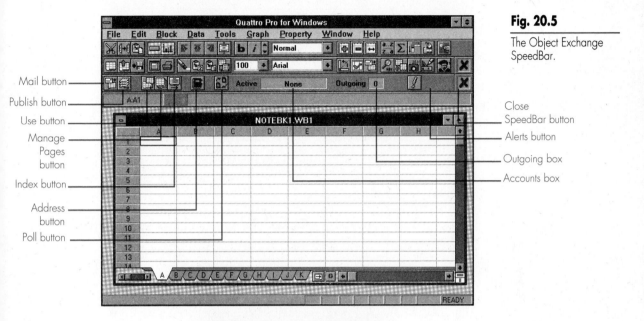

Fig. 20.5

The Object Exchange SpeedBar.

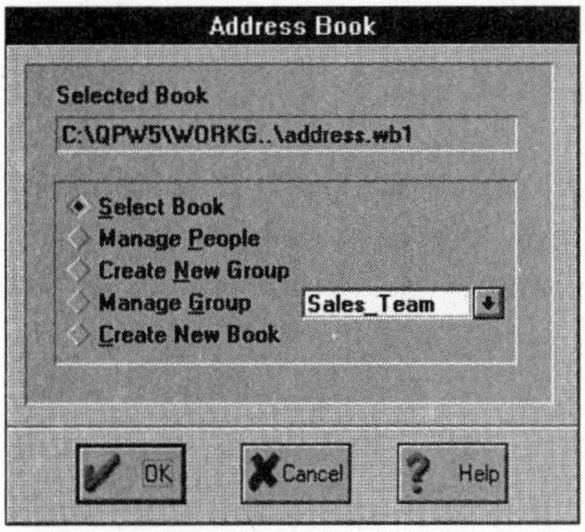

Fig. 20.6

The Address Book dialog box.

2. Click the **S**elect Book radio button.

3. Click OK.

4. Type the name of your address book in the File **N**ame text box.

5. Press Enter or click OK to confirm the dialog box and connect to your new address book.

Publishing and Mailing Data

After you have established your account and created your address book, you can send data to other members of your workgroup. You can send complete notebooks or selected notebook pages. You also can choose to mail the data or publish it. If you mail data, you send a one-time copy to the addressees. If you publish the data, it remains linked to your original notebook and updates automatically as needed.

Whether you choose to mail or publish your data depends on the importance of updating the data. Often a good approach is to mail the master notebook, and then publish pages containing the data that you frequently update. This method enables the other users in your workgroup to use their copy of the notebook and maintain timely data with minimal message traffic.

Figure 20.7 shows a notebook that converts currency rates. For anyone whose business involves cross-border trade, accurate currency conversions are very important. The currency conversion notebook is a good example of a notebook you could mail to your workgroup members, and you could publish the Rates page so that it is constantly updated.

Fig. 20.7

Publish the Rates page of the currency conversion notebook to maintain the current exchange rates.

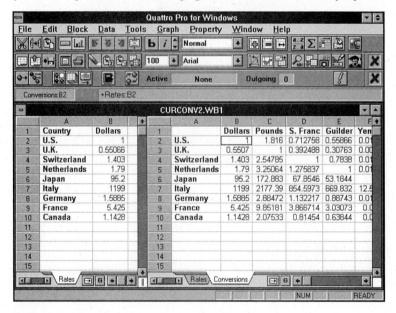

To mail the notebook, follow these steps:

1. Click the Mail button on the Workgroup Desktop SpeedBar to open the Mail dialog box (see fig. 20.8).

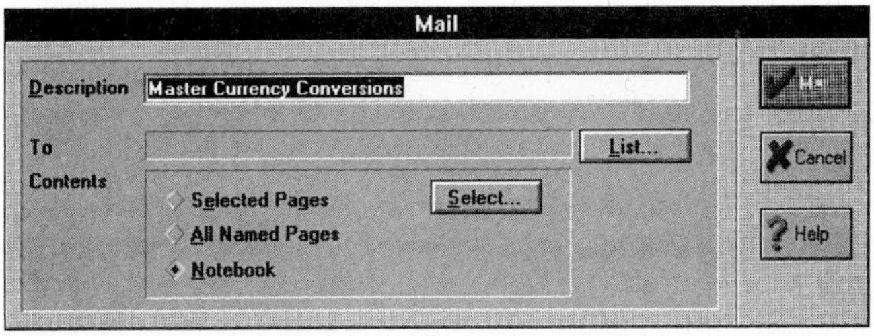

Fig. 20.8

The Mail dialog box.

2. In the **Description** text box, type descriptive text that explains the purpose of the notebook. In this case, type **Master Currency Conversions.**

3. Choose whether to send Selected Pages, All Named Pages, or the Notebook by clicking the appropriate radio button.

4. If you choose Selected Pages, click the Select button and choose the pages to send.

5. Click the **List** button to open the Select Names dialog box (see fig. 20.9).

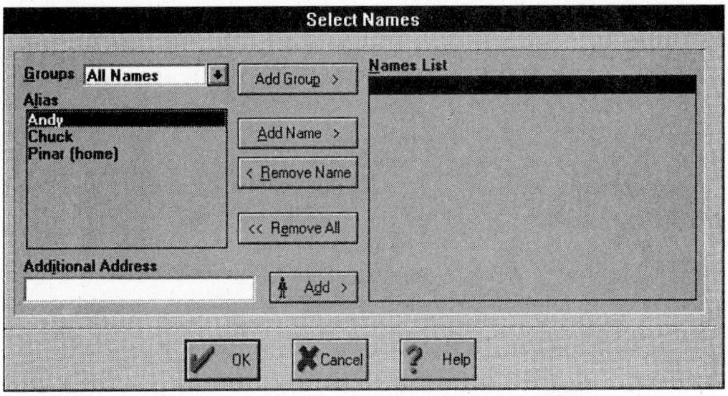

Fig. 20.9

The Select Names dialog box.

6. Select the names of the recipients using the Add Group, **A**dd Name, **R**emove Name, Remove All, and A**dd** buttons.

7. Press Enter or click OK to return to the Mail dialog box.

8. Press Enter or click Mail to send the data.

The value in the Outgoing box—which is on the SpeedBar—increases to show each message being sent.

After you have mailed the notebook, the members of your workgroup who receive the notebook can open their copy, save it, and use it like any other notebook. To maintain the changing data, however, you must publish the page containing the volatile data, in this case, the Rates page. To publish the Rates page, follow these steps:

1. Click the Publish button on the Workgroup Desktop SpeedBar to open the Publish dialog box (see fig. 20.10).

Fig. 20.10

The Publish dialog box.

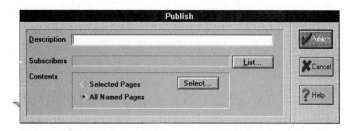

2. In the **D**escription text box, type descriptive text that explains the purpose of the published page. In this case, type **Changing Rates**.

3. Click the Select button to open the Select Pages dialog box (see fig. 20.11).

Fig. 20.11

The Select Pages dialog box.

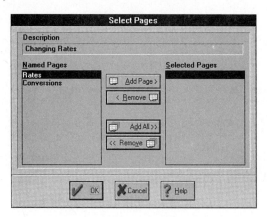

4. Select the pages in the Named Pages list you want to publish. In this case, select Rates.

5. Choose **A**dd Page to add the page to the **S**elected Pages list.

6. Press Enter or click OK to return to the Publish dialog box.

7. Click the **L**ist button to open the Subscriber List dialog box (see fig. 20.12).

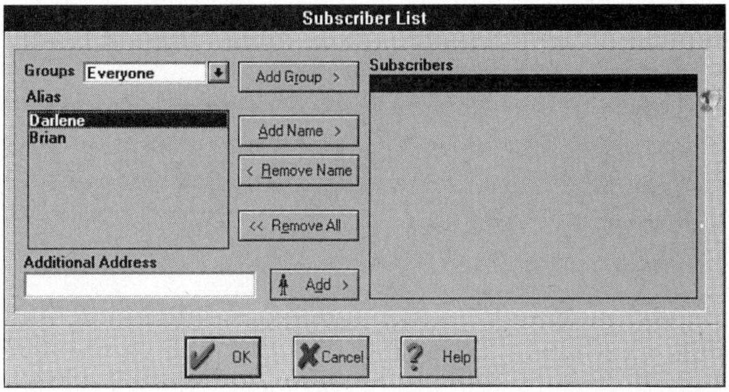

Fig. 20.12

The Subscriber List dialog box.

8. Select the names of the subscribers using the Add Group, Add Name, Remove Name, Remove All, and Add buttons.

9. Press Enter or click OK to return to the Publish dialog box.

10. Press Enter or click Publish to send the data.

After you have published a notebook or selected pages in a notebook, you can issue new versions of the publication as the notebook changes. You also can change the list of subscribers or cancel the publication. To issue a new version, follow these steps:

1. Click the Publish button on the Workgroup Desktop SpeedBar to open the Publication dialog box (see fig 20.13).

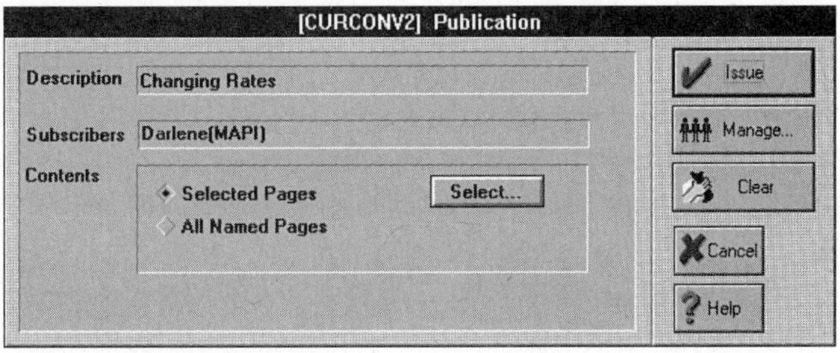

Fig. 20.13

The Publication dialog box.

2. To change the subscriber list, click the Manage button to open the Subscriber List dialog box (again see fig. 20.12). If you make any changes to the subscriber list, the Subscribers Modified dialog box appears after you press Enter or click OK (see fig. 20.14).

3. Return to the Publication dialog box and press Enter or click Issue to issue a new version of the publication.

Fig. 20.14

The Subscribers
Modified dialog box.

Polling Accounts

After you mail or publish a notebook, the Object Exchange holds the
notebook in queue until the next time polling occurs. If you set polling
to manual or if you want to send the notebook data immediately, click
the Poll button—located on the Workgroup Desktop SpeedBar—to
open the Poll Accounts dialog box (see fig. 20.15). Select the accounts
you want to poll and press Enter or click Poll.

Fig. 20.15

The Poll Accounts
dialog box.

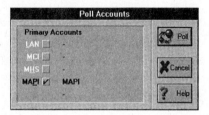

TIP

If you are working with data that changes frequently during the business
day, specify a short polling interval and use automatic polling on both
the publishing and subscribing systems.

Using Published and Mailed Data

When you receive published or mailed notebooks or notebook pages,
you insert the received notebook or page into a notebook on your system. You then save the notebook containing the inserted pages and you
can use the notebook.

If you subscribe to a published notebook or notebook pages, you create a link to the source notebook on the publishing system. Whenever the source issues a new version, your copy updates if polling is set to automatic. If polling is set to manual, your copy updates when you click the Poll button.

To subscribe to published notebooks or insert mailed notebooks or notebook pages, follow these steps:

1. Click the Use button on the Workgroup Desktop SpeedBar to open the Use Notebooks and Pages dialog box. The **D**escription box shows any objects available in the Object Exchange (see fig. 20.16).

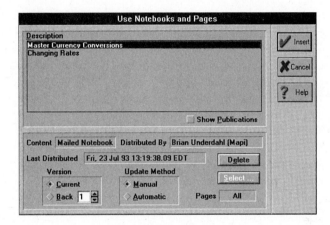

Fig. 20.16

The Use Notebooks and Pages dialog box shows any objects available in the Object Exchange.

2. Select the object you want to insert.

3. If you want to change the Update Method, choose **M**anual or **A**utomatic.

4. Choose **S**elect if you want to specify which pages to insert.

5. Press Enter or click Insert to insert the selected object.

Figure 20.17 shows the notebook after inserting the Rates page from the currency conversion notebook. The inserted data is linked using a DDE link. In figure 20.17, the following linking formula appears in the input line:

```
@DDELINK([OBEX¦C:\QPW2\NOTEBOOK\CURCONV2.WB12C15F5CA]"RATES")
```

Fig. 20.17

The inserted Rates page
from the currency
conversion notebook.

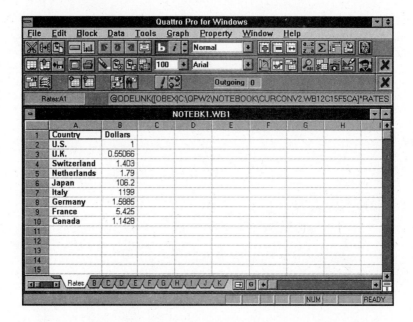

Data you subscribe to is protected from any change other than the automatic updates. You can use the data in your notebooks, but you cannot change the data or the formulas.

 If you want to remove, rename, or change the Update Method for inserted pages, click the Manage Pages button on the Workgroup Desktop SpeedBar. The Manage Inserted Pages dialog box appears (see fig. 20.18). After you have made any changes, press Enter or click Close to return to the notebook.

Fig. 20.18

The Manage Inserted
Pages dialog box.

When you insert pages into a notebook, a workgroup index is created automatically on the last page of the notebook. This index provides information on all inserted pages. To view the index, click the Index button on the Workgroup Desktop SpeedBar (see fig. 20.19).

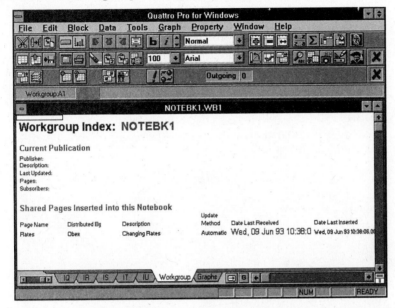

Fig. 20.19

The workgroup index provides information on all inserted pages.

To view any messages from the Object Exchange, such as login error messages, click the Alerts button on the Workgroup Desktop SpeedBar to open the Alerts dialog box (see fig. 20.20). These messages advise of any problems that exist.

Questions and Answers

Q: My LAN doesn't provide mail service. Can I still use the Workgroup Desktop?

A: Yes, in most cases you can. The Object Exchange provides the services needed in most cases.

Q: I work on the road but need up-to-date information. How can I use the Workgroup Desktop to make certain I have timely data?

A: MCI Mail may be a good choice for someone who uses a laptop PC but needs to have information updated regularly. Your office can use the Workgroup Desktop to publish new data as it is available and send the published pages to your MCI Mail account. Whenever you need to make certain you have the latest information, access your MCI Mail account, and your notebooks update automatically.

Q: How can I set up a notebook so that the members of my workgroup automatically receive the newly published pages?

A: Create the page you intend to publish first. Publish the page, sending yourself a copy. Insert the page into the master notebook you intend to share with the other workgroup members, and then mail the completed notebook to them. Because you already have inserted the published page, the other workgroup members don't need to add the page themselves, and you can be certain everyone's notebook uses the same formulas.

Fig. 20.20

The Alerts dialog box.

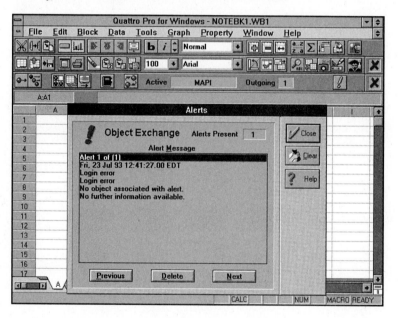

Summary

Sharing timely data can make the difference between being successful or watching your competitors win all the business. The Workgroup Desktop enables you to share data easily and automatically, whether across a small network or around the world. This chapter presented an overview of the Workgroup Desktop and showed you how you can mail, publish, or subscribe to Quattro Pro 5.0 for Windows notebooks, regardless of the size of your workgroup.

Part VII provides a comprehensive command reference you can use whenever you need to know more about the commands in Quattro Pro 5.0 for Windows.

PART

VII

OUTLINE

Quattro Pro 5.0 for Windows
Command Reference

Quattro Pro 5.0 for Windows Command Reference

Quattro Pro 5.0 for Windows Command Reference

File Commands

The File commands organize and maintain Quattro Pro 5.0 for Windows files. The File commands also enable you to print documents and control printer settings. Figure CR.1 shows the Quattro Pro 5.0 for Windows File menu.

Fig. CR.1

The File menu.

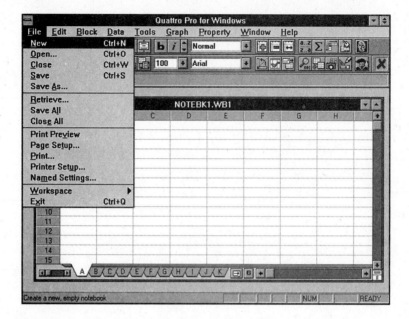

File New

Purpose

File New creates a new Quattro Pro 5.0 for Windows notebook file. **File New** does not close any existing open notebook files.

Procedure

Select **File New**.

Important Cues

- **File New** enables you to create a new notebook in addition to any notebooks currently open in memory. Existing open notebooks are not affected by the **File New** command.

- Use **File New** when you want to copy data or macros to a new, blank notebook file without making changes in the current notebook. Use **File New**, for example, when you want to create what-if scenarios that might produce large, difficult-to-reverse changes.

For more information, see File **O**pen, **F**ile **R**etrieve, and Chapter 8.

File Open

Purpose

File **O**pen retrieves an existing notebook file on disk without replacing any notebooks currently open in memory.

Procedure

1. Select File **O**pen (or click the Open Notebook button on the Productivity Tools SpeedBar). The Open File dialog box appears (see fig. CR.2).

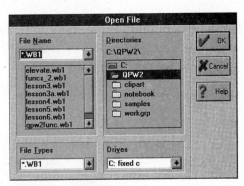

Fig. CR.2

The Open File dialog box.

2. To open a notebook file on another drive, select the **D**rives field and choose the drive letter.

3. To open a notebook file in another subdirectory, select the **Direc**tories field and choose the directory.

4. To open a different type of file, select the File **T**ypes field and choose the file extension.

5. Select the name of the notebook file to open from the File **N**ame list box.

6. Select OK or press Enter.

Important Cues

■ File Open retrieves an additional notebook file without replacing any notebook files currently open in memory. To replace all notebook files currently open in memory, choose File Retrieve.

■ Quattro Pro 5.0 for Windows can open many different types of files, including Quattro Pro for DOS, Lotus 1-2-3, Microsoft Excel, Paradox, and dBASE files. To open a file that has a different extension, such as DBF, type the file name (or a wild card) and the extension.

For more information, see File New, File Retrieve, and Chapter 8.

File Close

Purpose

File Close removes the active notebook file from the screen. All other open notebook files remain open.

Procedure

1. Select File Close.

2. If you haven't saved the latest changes, Quattro Pro 5.0 for Windows asks whether you want to save the changed notebook file (see fig. CR.3). Select Yes to save the notebook file with the same name, No to close the notebook file and discard any changes, or Cancel to abort the File Close command.

Important Cues

■ File Close removes the active notebook file from the screen, but leaves Quattro Pro 5.0 for Windows and any other notebook files open. Use File Close All to close all open notebook files in a single step.

■ Use **File Retrieve** instead of **File Close** and **File Open** to close the active notebook file and retrieve an existing notebook file in a single step.

For more information, see **File Save**, **File Retrieve**, and Chapter 8.

File Save

Purpose

File Save stores the currently active notebook file on disk with the same name.

Procedure

1. Select **File Save** (or click the Save Notebook button on the second SpeedBar). If you have not already saved the notebook file on disk, the Save File dialog box appears (see fig. CR.4).

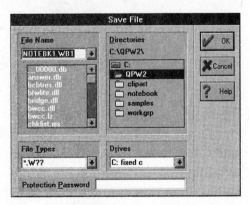

2. To save the notebook file on another drive, select the **D**rives field and choose the drive letter.

3. To save the notebook file in another subdirectory, select the **D**irectories field and choose the directory.

4. To save the notebook file as a different type of file, select the File **T**ypes field and choose the file extension.

5. Enter the name of the notebook file in the File Name text box.

6. To save the file using a password, select the Protection **P**assword text box and enter the password. The Verify Password dialog box appears (see fig. CR.5). Enter the password again using the same sequence of upper- and lowercase characters.

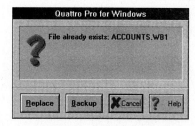

7. Select OK or press Enter.

If you previously saved a notebook file using the same name, Quattro Pro 5.0 for Windows displays the dialog box shown in figure CR.6. To replace the existing notebook file on disk, select **R**eplace. To save the existing notebook file on disk as a backup file, select **B**ackup.

Important Cues

■ The first time you save a notebook, selecting the File **S**ave command is identical to selecting File Save **A**s.

■ Also, use File **S**ave before making extensive changes to a notebook. This way you can use the File **R**etrieve command to return the notebook to the state prior to the changes.

> **CAUTION**
>
> Use the **F**ile **S**ave command often to prevent loss of data in the event of a power failure or system crash.

For more information, see **File Save As**, **File Save All**, and Chapter 8.

File Save As

Purpose

File Save **As** stores the current notebook file with a new name, in a different directory, on a different drive, or as a different file type.

Procedure

1. Select **File Save As**. The Save File dialog box appears (refer to fig. CR.4).

2. To save the notebook file on another drive, select the Drives field and choose the drive letter.

3. To save the notebook file in another subdirectory, select the Directories field and choose the directory.

4. To save the notebook file as a different type of file, select the File Types field and choose the file extension.

5. Enter the name of the notebook file in the File Name text box.

6. To save the file using a password, select the Protection **P**assword text box and enter the password. The Verify **P**assword dialog box appears (refer to fig. CR.5). Enter the password again using the same sequence of upper- and lowercase characters.

7. Select OK or press Enter.

Important Cues

- Use the File Save **As** command when you want to change the name of the currently active notebook file. Quattro Pro 5.0 for Windows assigns the new name to the currently active notebook file and uses the new name and destination when you later issue a File **Save** command.

■ Use the File Save **As** command when you want to make a backup copy of the active notebook file on another disk or in another directory.

For more information, see File **S**ave, File Save All, and Chapter 8.

File Retrieve

Purpose

File **R**etrieve retrieves an existing notebook file and replaces the current notebook in memory.

Procedure

1. Select File **R**etrieve. The Retrieve File dialog box appears (see fig CR.7).

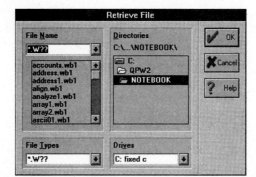

2. To retrieve a notebook file on another drive, select the Drives field and choose the drive letter.

3. To retrieve a notebook file in another subdirectory, select the **D**irectories field and choose the directory.

4. To retrieve a different type of file, select the File **T**ypes field and choose the file extension.

5. Select the name of the notebook file to retrieve from the File **N**ame list box.

6. Select OK or press Enter.

7. If the notebook file was saved with a password, type the password in the text box and click OK or press Enter.

Important Cues

■ File **R**etrieve retrieves a notebook file and replaces the current notebook file in memory. To open additional notebook files without replacing the currently open notebook in memory, choose **F**ile **O**pen.

■ If you make an error that destroys notebook data, do not save the active notebook. Use **F**ile **R**etrieve to reload the last copy you saved of the notebook file.

For more information, see **F**ile **N**ew, **F**ile **O**pen, and Chapter 8.

File Save All

Purpose

File Save All stores all currently open notebook files on disk without changing their names.

Procedure

1. Select **F**ile Save All. Depending on whether you previously saved the open notebook files, the Save File or the File Exists dialog box appears (refer to figs. CR.4 and CR.6).

2. To replace an existing notebook file on disk, select **R**eplace.

3. To save an existing notebook file on disk as a backup file, select **B**ackup.

Important Cues

■ Use the **F**ile Save All command often to prevent loss of data in the event of a power failure or system crash.

■ To preserve the layout of open notebook windows, use the **File Workspace** command in addition to File Save All. Because File Workspace doesn't save the current contents of the open notebooks, you must use both commands to save both the contents and layout of the currently open notebooks.

For more information, see **File Save**, **File Save As**, **File Workspace**, and Chapter 8.

File Close All

Purpose

File Close All removes all open notebook files from the screen.

Procedure

1. Select **File Close All**. If you haven't saved the latest changes, Quattro Pro 5.0 for Windows asks whether you want to save the changed notebook file (refer to fig. CR.3).

2. Select **Yes** to save the notebook file with the same name, **No** to close the notebook file and discard any changes, or Cancel to abort the Close All command.

Important Cue

File Close All removes all open notebook files from the screen, but leaves Quattro Pro 5.0 for Windows open. You then can use **File New** to create a new, blank notebook file or **File Open** to retrieve an existing notebook file.

For more information, see **File Save**, **File Retrieve**, and Chapter 8.

File Print Preview

Purpose

File Print Preview enables you to see how a report looks on the page before you actually print on paper. This command shows how the print block is positioned on a page with respect to the margins, headers, footers, and other page layout settings.

Procedure

1. If you don't want to include the entire active area of the current notebook page in the print block, or if the print block covers more than one notebook page, highlight the print block you want to preview.

2. Select File Print Preview (or click the Print Preview button on the Productivity Tools SpeedBar).

3. To examine an area more closely, press the plus key (+) or click the left mouse button to zoom in. To view a larger area of the page, press the minus key (–) or click the right mouse button to zoom out.

4. To change print settings, click the Spreadsheet Setup or Print Options buttons.

5. To view margin settings as dotted lines displayed on the page, click the Margins button.

6. To print the report using the current settings, click the Print button.

7. To return to the notebook without printing, click the End button.

Important Cues

- Use File Print Preview to make sure that the reports appear the way you want before printing.

- Use File Print Preview to make sure that page breaks occur where you want on multiple-page reports.

■ If the File Page Setup Print to fit check box is selected and File Print Preview shows the report excessively compressed with large blank areas on the page, check the print block settings to ensure that only the desired block is included.

■ If the notebook makes extensive use of color, but you are printing the report on a black-and-white printer, click the Color button to view the preview using the monochrome palette. Make sure that all data and graphics will print properly.

For more information, see File Page Setup, File Print, File Printer Setup, and Chapter 11.

File Page Setup

Purpose

File Page Setup controls the page layout of the printed report. With this command, you can specify a header, footer, margins, scaling, options, paper type, and orientation.

Procedure

1. Select File Page Setup. The Spreadsheet Page Setup dialog box appears (see fig. CR.8).

Fig. CR.8

The Spreadsheet Page Setup dialog box.

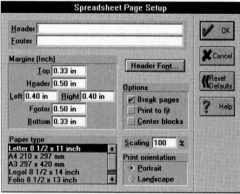

2. To include text at the top of each page, enter the text in the **He**ader text box.

3. To include text at the bottom of each page, enter the text in the **F**ooter text box.

4. To change the distance from the edges of the paper at which printing begins, enter new settings in the **T**op, **B**ottom, **L**eft, or **R**ight boxes.

5. To change the amount of space used to print headers and footers, enter the new settings in the Header or **F**ooter boxes.

6. To change the size of the paper, select the correct paper size in the Paper **t**ype list box.

7. Select Header Fo**n**t to change the font used for printing the report header.

8. Select the B**re**ak pages check box to print headers and footers.

9. Select the Print to **fi**t check box to instruct Quattro Pro 5.0 for Windows to compress the report automatically to fit on as few pages as possible.

10. Select **C**enter blocks to print the print blocks centered horizontally between the left and right page margins.

11. Select **P**ortrait or Lan**d**scape to change the orientation of the printed report.

12. To compress or expand the printed output by a specific factor, enter the percent of normal size in the **S**caling box.

13. Select Reset Defaults to return all settings to the Quattro Pro 5.0 for Windows default settings.

14. To confirm the dialog box, click OK or press Enter.

Important Cues

■ To determine the exact distance between the top of the page and the first line of the report, add the **T**op and Header margin settings.

■ To determine the distance between the last line of the report and the bottom of the page, add the **B**ottom and **F**ooter margin settings.

- Some printers don't support Landscape print orientation. If your printer doesn't support changing print orientation, this setting is ignored.

- If the Print to fit check box is selected and the report seems compressed more than is necessary to fit the page, verify that the print block is properly specified. If you don't select a print block, Quattro Pro 5.0 for Windows prints the entire active area of the active page. The active area may include cells you did not intend to print.

For more information, see File Print Preview, File Print, File Printer Setup, and Chapter 11.

File Print

Purpose

File Print prints one or more blocks to the destination printer.

Procedure

1. If you don't want to include the entire active area of the current notebook page in the print block, or if the print block covers more than one notebook page, highlight the print block you want to print.

2. Select File Print (or click the Print button on the Productivity Tools SpeedBar). The Spreadsheet Print dialog box appears (see fig. CR.9).

3. In the Print block(s) text box, specify additional blocks. Separate each block with a comma.

4. To print a range of pages, enter the page numbers in the From and to boxes. To print all pages, select the All pages radio button.

5. Enter the number of copies to print in the Copies box.

6. Select Options to change additional print options. In the Spreadsheet Print Options dialog box (see fig. CR.10), select the additional print options.

Specify notebook rows to include on each page in the **Top** heading text box.

Specify notebook columns to include on each page in the **Left** heading text box.

Select **C**ell formulas to print cell formulas instead of cell contents.

Select **G**ridlines to print the notebook grid.

Select **R**ow/Column borders to include specified rows or columns on each page.

To separate multiple print blocks, specify the number of Lin**e**s between blocks or check Pag**e** advance to print each block on its own page.

To separate print blocks that you placed on separate notebook pages, use the Li**n**es and Page **a**dvance settings in the Print between 3D pages section.

Select OK or press Enter to return to the Spreadsheet Print dialog box.

7. Select Print to print the report.

Procedure

1. Select all print setting options you want to include in the named setting.

2. Select **File Named Settings**. The Named Print Settings dialog box appears (see fig. CR.12).

Fig. CR.12

The Named Print Settings dialog box.

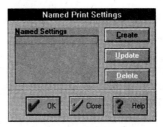

3. To create a new print setting, select **Create** and enter the name for the print setting.

4. To modify an existing named print setting using the currently selected settings, highlight the name of the print setting to modify and select **Update**.

5. To remove an existing named print setting, highlight the print setting name and select **Delete**.

6. Click OK or press Enter.

Important Cues

Fig. CR.1

The Printer box.

■ Use **File Named Settings** to ensure that the reports are printed using the same settings every time, or that reports printed by several different users have a consistent appearance.

■ You can store several different named print settings and recall them later as necessary.

For more information, see **File Page Setup**, **File Print**, and Chapter 11.

File Workspace

Purpose

Use **File Workspace** to save or restore the layout of open notebook windows.

Procedure

To save information about which notebooks are currently open and their size and location in the Quattro Pro 5.0 for Windows workspace, follow these steps:

1. Select **File Workspace Save**. The Save Workspace dialog box appears (see fig. CR.13).

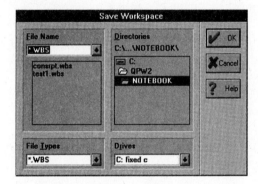

Fig. CR.13

The Save Workspace dialog box.

2. To save the workspace file on another drive, select the **D**rives field and choose the drive letter.

3. To save the workspace file in another subdirectory, select the **D**irectories field and choose the directory.

4. To save the workspace file as a different type of file, select the File **T**ypes field and choose the file extension.

5. Enter the name of the workspace file in the File Name text box.

6. Select OK or press Enter.

To open the notebooks contained in a previously saved workspace, follow these steps:

1. Select **File Workspace Restore**. Quattro Pro 5.0 for Windows displays the Restore Workspace dialog box (see fig. CR.14).

2. To load a workspace file on another drive, select the **D**rives field and choose the drive letter.

Fig. CR.14

The Restore Workspace dialog box.

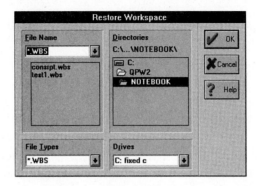

3. To load a workspace file in another subdirectory, select the **Directories** field and choose the directory.

4. To load a workspace file previously saved as a different type of file, select the File **Types** field and choose the file extension.

5. Enter the name of the workspace file in the **F**ile Name text box.

6. Select OK or press Enter.

Important Cues

■ The **F**ile **W**orkspace **S**ave command doesn't save the contents of the currently open notebook files. After you use File **W**orkspace Save, use **F**ile Save All to save the contents of each of the open notebook files.

■ The **F**ile **W**orkspace commands make working with linked or multiple notebook files much easier, because you can treat the notebook files as a single unit.

Quattro Pro 5.0 for Windows uses the WBS extension for workspace files to differentiate these files from notebook files, which use a WB1 extension.

For more information, see File **S**ave, File Save All, and Chapter 8.

File Exit

Purpose

File Exit quits Quattro Pro 5.0 for Windows and displays the Windows Program Manager.

Procedure

1. Select **File Exit**.

2. If you made any changes to open notebook files, Quattro Pro 5.0 for Windows asks whether you want to save the changes before exiting (refer to fig. CR.3). Be sure to save the work if you don't want to lose changes.

Important Cues

■ You can close all open notebook files without exiting from Quattro Pro 5.0 for Windows by using the **File Close** All command.

■ If you want to use another Windows application without exiting Quattro Pro 5.0 for Windows, press Ctrl+Esc to access the Windows Task List. Select the application you want and press Enter. You later can use the same steps to switch back to Quattro Pro 5.0 for Windows, which remains in the same state as you left it before you switched to the other application.

Edit Commands

The Edit commands enable you to move and copy data to another open notebook file or to another application using the Windows Clipboard. The Edit commands also enable you to create *DDE* (Dynamic Data Exchange) and *OLE* (Object Linking and Embedding) links between Quattro Pro 5.0 for Windows notebook files and other Windows applications. With these commands, you can undo actions in a notebook file, search for and replace text and numbers in a notebook file, and create named styles—sets of defined formats that can be applied quickly to notebook blocks. Figure CR.15 shows the Edit menu.

Fig. CR.15

The Edit menu.

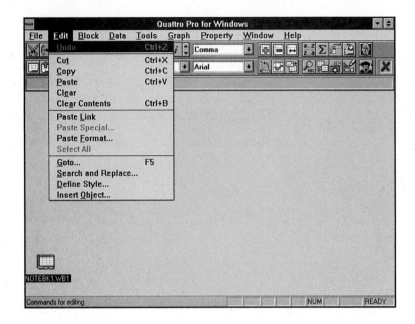

Edit Undo

Purpose

Edit Undo reverses the last change you made to a notebook. If you accidently delete a row or erase the wrong block, Edit Undo reverses the operation.

Procedure

To undo a mistake, select Edit Undo, press Ctrl+Z, or click the Undo button on the Productivity Tools SpeedBar.

Important Cues

■ Not all actions can be undone. Edit Undo can reverse only the last action that occurred in memory. Any command that saved a notebook file to disk or sent data to a printer cannot be undone.

■ Because **Edit Undo** can undo only a single action, use **File Save** to save the current notebook file before performing operations with several steps you might later want to undo. That way you can retrieve the original notebook file if you discover an error.

■ After you use the **Edit Undo** command, the **Edit** menu shows **Edit Redo** until you issue another command that can be undone. This tells you that you can undo the effects of the **Edit Undo** command.

Edit Cut

Purpose

Edit Cut deletes the data, with formatting and attributes, from the highlighted cells and moves the data to the Windows Clipboard.

Procedure

1. Highlight the data you want to cut (use the Shift and arrow keys or use the mouse).

2. Select **Edit Cut**, click the Cut button on the SpeedBar, press Ctrl+X, or press Shift+Del.

Important Cue

Data moved to the Clipboard by **Edit Cut** or **Edit Copy** can be pasted into most other Windows applications.

> The Windows Clipboard holds only the most recent data that was moved or copied to the Clipboard. If you use **E**dit Cut or **E**dit **C**opy again, all existing Clipboard data is destroyed.   **◄ CAUTION**

For more information, see **Edit Copy** and Chapter 5.

Edit Copy

Purpose

Edit Copy copies the data with format and attributes in the highlighted cells to the Windows Clipboard without removing the data from the highlighted cells.

Procedure

1. Highlight the data you want to copy (use the Shift and arrow keys or use the mouse).

2. Select Edit Copy, click the Copy button on the SpeedBar, press Ctrl+C, or press Ctrl+Ins.

Important Cues

■ When you need to make multiple copies of the same data, Edit Copy and Edit Paste are much faster than Block Copy because you have to specify the source of the copy just one time.

■ Remember that the Clipboard holds only the most recent data that was copied to the Clipboard.

For more information, see Edit Cut, Edit Paste, and Chapter 5.

Edit Paste

Purpose

Edit Paste inserts the contents of the Windows Clipboard into the current notebook, beginning at the current cell selector location.

Procedure

1. Use Edit Copy or Edit Cut to place the data you want to paste onto the Windows Clipboard.

2. Position the cell selector in the upper left cell of the destination block.

3. Select **Edit Paste**, click the Paste button, press Ctrl+V, or press Shift+Ins.

Important Cues

■ You can use **Edit Paste** to paste examples copied from the Quattro Pro 5.0 for Windows Help screens into the notebook files.

■ Use **Edit Paste** to quickly paste data copied from other Windows applications into Quattro Pro 5.0 for Windows notebook files.

For more information, see **Edit Copy**, **Edit Cut**, **Edit Paste Link**, Chapter 5, and Chapter 8.

Edit Clear (Del)

Purpose

Edit Clear erases the highlighted cells without moving them to the Windows Clipboard.

Procedure

1. Highlight the data you want to delete (use the Shift and arrow keys or use the mouse).

2. Select **Edit Clear** or press Del.

Important Cues

■ If you accidently clear a cell or a block of cells by pressing the Del key, restore the data by immediately selecting **Edit Undo** before issuing any other commands.

■ Because **Edit Clear** doesn't use the Windows Clipboard, existing data on the Clipboard is not affected by **Edit Clear**.

■ To remove the data from notebook cells without removing any special formatting, use **E**dit **Clear** Contents.

For more information, see **E**dit **Clear** Contents, **E**dit **Cut**, and Chapter 5.

Edit Clear Contents

Purpose

Edit **Clear** Contents erases the data in the highlighted cells without moving them to the Windows Clipboard and without removing any special formatting from the cells.

Procedure

1. Highlight the data you want to delete (use the Shift and arrows keys or use the mouse).
2. Select **E**dit **Clear** Contents or press Ctrl+B.

Important Cues

■ If you accidently clear a cell or a block of cells, restore the data by immediately selecting **E**dit **Undo** before issuing any other commands.

■ Because **E**dit **Clear** Contents doesn't use the Windows Clipboard, existing data on the Clipboard is not affected.

■ To remove the data and formatting from notebook cells, use **E**dit **Clear**.

For more information, see **E**dit **Clear**, **E**dit **Cut**, and Chapter 5.

Edit Paste Link

Purpose

Use the **E**dit **Paste** **Link** command to create a live data link to data copied to the Windows Clipboard from another Windows application.

Then, when you change data in the other application, the linked data is updated by default.

Procedure

1. In the source file of the other Windows application, copy the data to the Windows Clipboard.

2. In the Quattro Pro 5.0 for Windows notebook file, highlight the destination block you want to link the data to.

3. Select Edit Paste Link.

Important Cues

■ When you use Edit Paste Link, you can use "live" data from other Windows applications in the Quattro Pro 5.0 for Windows notebook file. Edit Paste Link ensures that the data in the Quattro Pro 5.0 for Windows notebook file remains current even when changed in the other application.

■ Edit Paste Link creates a DDE (Dynamic Data Exchange) link. To create an OLE (Object Linking and Embedding) link (in Windows 3.1 only), use Edit Paste or Edit Paste Format.

For more information, see Edit Paste Special, Edit Paste Format, and Chapter 8.

Edit Paste Special

Purpose

Edit Paste Special enables you to control how data copied to the Windows Clipboard from a Quattro Pro 5.0 for Windows notebook file is pasted into the current notebook file.

Procedure

1. Copy the data to the Windows Clipboard using Edit Copy or Edit Cut.

2. Highlight the destination block you want to paste the data to.

3. Select **Edit Paste Special.** The Paste Special dialog box appears (see fig. CR.16).

Fig. CR.16

The Paste Special
dialog box.

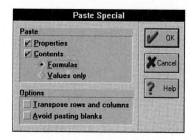

4. To paste the properties associated with the data on the Clipboard, select the **Properties** check box.

5. To paste the contents of the data on the Clipboard, select the **Contents** check box. If you are pasting the contents of the data, select the **Formulas** radio button to paste any formulas, or the **Values only** radio button to convert formulas to their current values.

6. To transpose the rows and columns when pasting the Clipboard data, select the **Transpose rows and columns** check box.

7. To prevent blank cells in the Clipboard data from overwriting notebook data, select the **Avoid pasting blanks** check box.

8. Click OK or press Enter.

Important Cues

■ **Edit Paste Special** is available on the **Edit** menu only when the Windows Clipboard contains data from a Quattro Pro 5.0 for Windows notebook. If the Windows Clipboard contains data from another Windows application, **Edit Paste Format** appears. **Edit Paste Special** is dimmed to show that this option is unavailable.

■ Avoid using the **Formulas** option along with the **Transpose rows and columns** option. Unless the formulas that were copied to the Clipboard used absolute addressing exclusively, the results are unlikely to be what you desire.

For more information, see **Edit Paste** and Chapter 8.

Edit Paste Format

Purpose

Edit Paste Format enables you to control the type of link created when you paste data that was copied from another Windows application to a Quattro Pro 5.0 for Windows notebook.

Procedure

1. In the source file of the other Windows application, copy the data to the Windows Clipboard.

2. In the Quattro Pro 5.0 for Windows notebook file, highlight the destination block you want to link the data to.

3. Select Edit Paste Format. The Paste Format dialog box appears (see fig. CR.17).

Fig. CR.17

The Paste Format dialog box.

4. Select the format of the link from the list box. The kinds of links available depend on the application that produced the data currently on the Windows Clipboard.

Important Cues

■ The text format, which is always one of the Edit Paste Format choices, simply copies the Clipboard data to the Quattro Pro 5.0 for Windows notebook without creating a link to the source application. You may have to experiment with other available link formats to determine which works the best.

■ Unless you have a special reason to control the type of link that is created, use **Edit Paste** instead of **Edit Paste Format**. **Edit Paste** creates the most complete version of the data possible.

For more information, see **Edit Paste**, **Edit Paste Special**, **Edit Paste Link**, and Chapter 8.

Edit Select All

Purpose

Edit Select All selects all elements in a graph.

Procedure

Select **Edit Select All**.

Important Cue

Edit Select All is only available when a graph window is the active window.

Edit Goto (F5)

Purpose

Edit Goto moves the cell selector to a specified cell or to the upper left corner of a specified block.

Procedure

1. Select **Edit Goto** or press F5. The Goto dialog box appears (see fig. CR.18).

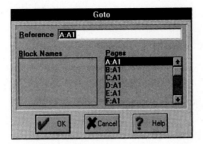

2. Enter the address or block name to which you want to move the cell selector in the **R**eference text box, or select the block name from the **B**lock Names list box.

3. To move the cell selector to cell A1 of another page, select the page in the **P**ages list box.

4. Click OK or press Enter.

Important Cues

■ The **Edit G**oto command enables you to move the cell selector quickly to remote areas of the notebook file, whether on the same or a different notebook page.

■ Create easy-to-remember block names for notebook areas to which you may often want to move the cell selector. Block names are easier to remember than cell addresses. To move the cell selector to a different notebook, select the notebook from the Window menu.

For more information, see **B**lock **N**ames **C**reate and Chapter 4.

Edit Search and Replace

Purpose

Edit Search and Replace finds or replaces characters in a block. Use this command to search databases quickly, to change cell or block references in a group of formulas, or to substitute one number for another throughout an entire block.

Procedure

1. Highlight the block to search.

2. Select **E**dit **S**earch and Replace. The Search/Replace dialog box appears (see fig. CR.19).

Fig. CR.19

The Search/Replace dialog box.

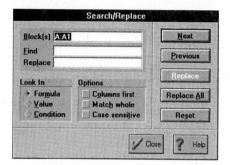

3. If necessary, add additional blocks to search in the **B**lock(s) text box. Separate multiple blocks with commas.

4. Enter the text to search for in the **F**ind text box.

5. Enter any replacement text in the Replace text box.

6. Select the For**m**ula, **V**alue, or **C**ondition radio button to specify where Quattro Pro 5.0 for Windows should search.

7. Select the Matc**h** whole check box to specify whether to match partial or whole words.

8. Select the **C**olumns first check box to specify the direction to search.

9. Select the Case sensi**t**ive check box to specify that the search string must exactly match the case entered in the **F**ind text box.

10. Select **N**ext to highlight the next matching occurrence, **R**eplace to replace the highlighted matching string, or Replace **A**ll to replace all matching strings. Select Re**s**et to return to the default settings. Select **P**revious to highlight the previous occurrence.

11. Select Close to return to the notebook.

Important Cues

■ Use **E**dit **S**earch and Replace to modify a block of formulas quickly to change incorrect cell or block references.

■ Use Condition to treat the find string as a conditional expression—that is, to search for the first cell in the block that satisfies the formula you enter as the find string.

For more information, see Chapter 5.

Edit Define Style

Purpose

Use **Edit Define** Style to create or modify named styles that can be used to apply a specified set of properties quickly to a notebook cell or block.

Procedure

1. Select **Edit Define** Style. The Define/Modify Style dialog box appears (see fig. CR.20).

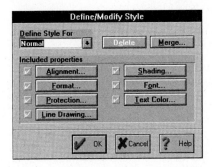

Fig. CR.20

The Define/Modify Style dialog box.

2. Select an existing named style or enter a new style name in the **Define** Style For list box.

3. Select the properties you want to define for the named style (**Alignment, Format, Protection, Line** Drawing, **Shading, Font,** or **Text** Color).

4. Select **Delete** to remove a named style.

5. Select **Merge** to add the properties for a selected cell or style to the current named style.

6. Click OK or press Enter.

Important Cues

- After you create or modify a named style, select the style from the style list box on the Quattro Pro 5.0 for Windows SpeedBar. Named styles enable you to quickly apply properties, including alignment, numeric format, protection, line drawing, shading, font, and text color to a cell or block.

- Create special named styles for different purposes in the notebook files. Named styles make it easier for several users to create notebooks with similar appearances.

- To copy a style to another notebook, copy and paste a cell formatted with this style into the new notebook. This style name then appears in the style list for the notebook. To make the style permanently available to the notebook, select **E**dit **D**efine Style OK. Otherwise, if you delete the cell with the format, the style list no longer displays this style in the list.

For more information, see Chapter 6.

Edit Insert Object

Purpose

The **E**dit Insert **O**bject command inserts an embedded OLE object into the active page.

Procedure

1. Select **E**dit Insert **O**bject. The Insert New Object dialog box appears (see fig. CR.21).

2. Select a type of object to insert.

3. Click OK or press Enter.

Important Cues

- **E**dit Insert **O**bject is available only if you use Windows 3.1 and you have OLE server applications available.

Fig. CR.21

The Insert New Object dialog box.

- When you choose an OLE server, it opens a window on top of Quattro Pro 5.0 for Windows, where you can create an object. When you finish work on the object and choose Exit or Update, the object is inserted at the position of the active cell in Quattro Pro.

- The size of the object is determined by the server application. You can resize the object by selecting one of the object's handles and moving the mouse pointer.

For more information, see Chapter 8.

Block Commands

The **B**lock commands manipulate rectangular areas (blocks) of notebooks. The **B**lock commands don't use the Windows Clipboard. Figure CR.22 shows the **B**lock menu.

Block Move

Purpose

The **B**lock **M**ove command reorganizes a notebook by moving blocks of labels, values, or formulas to different locations on the same or another spreadsheet page.

Procedure

1. Highlight the block to move.

Fig. CR.22

The Block menu.

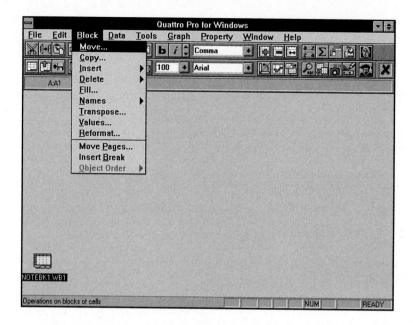

2. Select **B**lock **M**ove. The Block Move dialog box appears
(see fig. CR.23).

Fig. CR.23

The Block Move dialog
box.

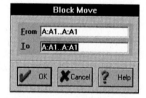

3. Select the destination for the block by selecting the **To** text box
and entering the cell address or block name, or by pointing to the
destination block.

4. Click OK or press Enter.

Important Cues

■ Because **B**lock **M**ove doesn't use the Windows Clipboard, you
can move a block without destroying the current contents of the
Clipboard.

■ To move a block by using the mouse, first select the block. Hold down the left mouse button until the mouse pointer changes to a hand, and then drag the block to a new location. Release the button to drop the block in its new position.

For more information, see **B**lock **C**opy and Chapter 5.

Block Copy

Purpose

Block **C**opy duplicates data from and to a cell or block without using the Windows Clipboard.

Procedure

1. Highlight the block to copy.

2. Select **B**lock **C**opy. The Block Copy dialog box appears (see fig. CR.24).

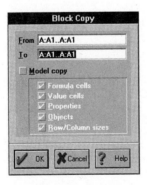

Fig. CR.24

The Block Copy dialog box.

3. Select the destination for the block by selecting the **T**o text box and entering the cell address or block name, or by pointing to the destination block.

4. If the **F**rom block contains formulas with absolute references that you want to adjust to the new location instead of continuing to refer to the same cells, select the **M**odel copy check box.

5. If you select **Model** copy, select the check boxes for the types of objects you want to copy.

6. Click OK or press Enter.

Important Cues

■ Because **Block Copy** doesn't use the Windows Clipboard, you can copy a block without destroying the current contents of the Clipboard.

■ If you select the **Model** copy check box, formulas that contain absolute references adjust to reflect the new position but remain absolute rather than relative references. The formula +$A$1, for example remains +$A$1 when copied from B1 to C3 if **Model** copy isn't selected, but changes to +$B$3 if **Model** copy is selected.

For more information, see **Block Move** and Chapter 5.

Block Insert

Purpose

Block Insert inserts rows, columns, pages, or files into the current notebook file.

Procedure

1. Move the cell selector to the area where you want to insert cells. To insert more than one row or column, highlight a block the size of the one you want to insert.

2. Select **Block Insert Rows**, **Block Insert Columns**, **Block Insert Pages**, or **Block Insert File**. Figure CR.25 shows the Insert Rows dialog box that appears if you select **Block Insert Rows**.

3. If you select **Block Insert Rows**, **Block Insert Columns**, or **Block Insert Pages**, select Entire or Partial to choose whether the inserted block should span the entire row, column, or page.

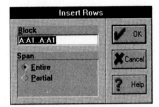

Fig. CR.25

The Insert Rows dialog box.

4. If you select **Block Insert File**, select the file from the **File Name** list box. If necessary, select a different file type, directory, or drive. In the **B**efore page text box, enter the name or letter of the notebook page that you want to follow the inserted file.

5. Click OK or press Enter.

Important Cues

■ Insert a partial row, column, or page when you need to reorganize part of a notebook quickly. A partial insertion adds a block equal in size to the highlighted block.

■ You cannot insert a block if the insertion would move data beyond the boundaries of the notebook. That is, if column IV on a notebook page contains data, you cannot insert entire columns on that page. You can, however, insert a partial column if the insertion doesn't move data off the page.

For more information, see **Block D**elete and Chapter 5.

Block Delete

Purpose

Block Delete deletes rows, columns, or pages from the current notebook file.

Procedure

1. Move the cell selector to the area where you want to delete cells. To delete more than one row or column, highlight a block the size of the one you want to delete.

2. Select **Block Delete Rows**, **Block Delete Columns**, or **Block Delete Pages**. Figure CR.26 shows the Delete Columns dialog box.

Fig. CR.26

The Delete Columns
dialog box.

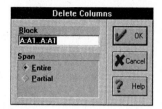

3. Select **Entire** or **Partial** to choose whether the deleted block should span the entire row, column, or page.

4. Click OK or press Enter.

CAUTION

Use care when deleting blocks. Formulas that refer to deleted blocks can produce incorrect results or return a value of ERR.

Important Cue

To remove data from a block without removing the block from the notebook, use **Edit Cut**, **Edit Clear**, or **Edit Clear Contents** rather than **Block Delete**.

For more information, see **Block Insert** and Chapter 5.

Block Move Pages

Purpose

Use **Block Move Pages** to reorganize the order of notebook pages.

Procedure

1. Move the cell selector to the page to move.

2. Select **Block Move Pages**. The Move Pages dialog box appears (see fig. CR.27).

3. Enter the destination page in the **To** before page text box.

4. Click OK or press Enter.

Important Cues

■ Use **B**lock **M**ove Pages after creating a complex notebook to place the pages you use most often at the top of the notebook. Move pages containing macros, sensitive formulas, and other data that should not be changed on lower notebook pages.

■ To move a page by using the mouse, point to the page tab of the page you want to move, hold down the left mouse button, and drag the tab down to slightly enlarge the tab. Drag the tab right or left until you place the tab to the left of the page to follow the moved page. Release the mouse button to complete the move.

For more information, see **B**lock **M**ove and Chapter 5.

Block Fill

Purpose

Block **F**ill enters a series of incremented numbers, dates, times, or percentages into a specified block.

Procedure

1. Highlight the block you want to fill.

2. Select **B**lock **F**ill. The Block Fill dialog box appears (see fig. CR.28).

Fig. CR.28

The Block Fill dialog
box.

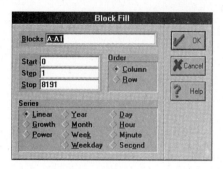

3. The block you highlighted is entered in the **B**locks text box. If not
   selected, select the fill block now.

4. Select St**a**rt and specify the value with which you want to begin
   numbering. The default value is 0. If you are filling a block with
   percentages, remember that you must divide the entries by 100.
   To start with 7.5 percent, for example, type **.075**.

5. Select St**e**p and specify the positive or negative number by which
   you want the values incremented. The default value is 1. For a
   Growth series fill, the Step value is used as a multiplier. For a
   Power series fill, the Step value is used as the exponent.

6. Select **S**top and specify the value at which to stop the fill. The
   default value is 8191. If the Stop value is too small, the entire block
   may not be filled.

7. Select **C**olumn to fill the block starting at the top of the first column and working down, and then filling the second column top to
   bottom, and so on. Select **R**ow to fill across rows, left to right.

8. Select the Series, or type of increment.

9. Click OK or press Enter.

Important Cues

■ Use **B**lock **F**ill to create incrementing date entries for table headings, incrementing percentage entries for mortgage calculations,
and growth entries for business expansion projections.

■ When filling a block with dates or times, remember to adjust the
Stop value to reflect the date serial number of the ending date or
time.

- If **B**lock **F**ill fills only part of the block or fills none of the block, make certain that the **S**top value is larger than the St**a**rt value plus the increment added by the selected Series.

For more information, see Chapter 5.

Block Names Create

Purpose

Use **B**lock **N**ames **C**reate to assign a name to a cell or block.

Rather than column-and-row cell addresses, use block names to make formulas and macros easy to read and understand. You also can use block names in commands, such as **E**dit **G**oto.

Procedure

1. Highlight the cell or block that you want to name.

2. Select **B**lock **N**ames **C**reate or press Ctrl+F3. The Create Name dialog box appears (see fig. CR.29).

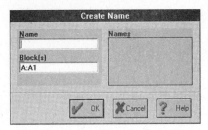

Fig. CR.29

The Create Name dialog box.

3. Enter the new block name in the **N**ame text box. The Name**s** list box displays existing block names, which you can examine to ensure that you don't accidently replace an existing block name.

4. Click OK or press Enter.

Important Cues

- Always use block names instead of cell addresses in macros. This ensures proper macro operation if the notebook is reorganized.

■ Create block names for notebook locations where you must frequently move the cell selector. Block names are easier to remember than cell addresses.

For more information, see **B**lock **N**ames **L**abels and Chapter 5.

Block Names Delete

Purpose

Block **N**ames **D**elete removes a block name but doesn't delete the data in the block.

Procedure

1. Select **B**lock **N**ames **D**elete. The Delete Name dialog box appears (see fig. CR.30).

Fig. CR.30

The Delete Name dialog box.

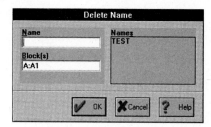

2. Select a block name from the Names list box, type the block name in the **N**ame text box, or enter the address in the **B**lock(s) text box.

3. Click OK or press Enter.

CAUTION

Be careful when deleting block names that may be used in macros. If you delete the name of a block used by a macro, the macro can no longer function properly.

Important Cue

Block Names Delete removes a single block name from the notebook. If you want to remove all block names from the notebook quickly, use **Block Names Reset.**

For more information, see Chapter 5.

Block Names Labels

Purpose

Block Names **L**abels assigns block names to single notebook cells, using the contents of the highlighted block.

Procedure

1. Highlight the block of notebook cells that contain the labels you want to use as block names.

2. Select **B**lock Names **L**abels. The Create Names From Labels dialog box appears (see fig. CR.31).

Fig. CR.31

The Create Names From Labels dialog box.

3. Select one of the following options:

Option	Description
Down	Uses the highlighted labels to name the notebook cells in the row below the labels
Left	Uses the highlighted labels to name the notebook cells in the column to the left of the labels

Option	Description
Right	Uses the highlighted labels to name the notebook cells in the column to the right of the labels
Up	Uses the highlighted labels to name the notebook cells in the row above the labels

4. Click OK or press Enter.

Important Cues

■ Blank notebook cells in the label block are ignored.

■ Block names can be up to 15 characters long.

■ Don't include spaces in block names. To connect two words as a block name, use the underscore (_) instead of the dash (-). Block names that include a dash may be misinterpreted by Quattro Pro 5.0 for Windows.

■ Although you can include numeric characters within block names, don't begin a block name with a number.

CAUTION

Be careful that you don't accidentally replace existing block names; Quattro Pro 5.0 for Windows doesn't warn you before making the replacement.

For more information, see **B**lock **N**ames **C**reate and Chapter 5.

Block Names Reset

Purpose

Block **N**ames **R**eset removes all block names in the current notebook file.

Procedure

1. Select **B**lock **N**ames **R**eset. The Reset Names confirmation box appears (see fig. CR.32).

Fig. CR.32

The Reset Names confirmation box.

2. Click **Y**es or press Enter.

Important Cue

To remove a single, specified block name, use **B**lock **N**ames **D**elete rather than **B**lock **N**ames **R**eset.

> Be careful with **B**lock **N**ames **R**eset. This command removes all block names in the current notebook.

CAUTION

For more information, see **B**lock **N**ames **D**elete and Chapter 5.

Block Names Make Table

Purpose

Block **N**ames **M**ake Table lists all block names in the current notebook file in a two-column table.

The first column of the block name table lists defined block names. The second column lists the corresponding addresses.

Procedure

1. Position the cell selector in a blank area of the notebook. The table requires two columns and as many rows as there are block names.

2. Select **B**lock **N**ames **M**ake Table. The Name Table dialog box appears (see fig. CR.33).

Fig. CR.33

The Name Table dialog box.

3. If you didn't pre-position the cell selector in the upper left corner of the block where the block name table should be placed, enter the starting cell for the table in the **B**lock text box.

4. Click OK or press Enter.

Important Cues

- Consider placing the block name table on a separate notebook page, which prevents the table from overwriting notebook data.

- Remember, you can use the **D**ata **S**ort command to sort the block name table.

- The block name table is not updated automatically when you add or delete block names. Use **B**lock **N**ames **M**ake Table again to create an updated table.

For more information, see **B**lock **N**ames **C**reate and Chapter 5.

Block Names Auto Generate

Purpose

Block **N**ames **A**uto Generate names blocks with more than one cell.

Procedure

1. Select the block containing the cells to name and the labels to use as names.

2. Select **Block Names Auto Generate**. The Generate Block Names dialog box appears (see fig. CR.34).

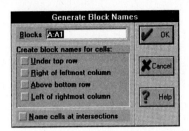

3. Select **U**nder top row to name the second row of cells.

4. Select **R**ight of leftmost column to name the second column of cells.

5. Select **A**bove bottom row to name the cells in the next-to-last row.

6. Select **L**eft of rightmost column to name the cells in the next-to-last column.

7. Select **N**ame cells at intersections to name the cells using a combination of row and column labels to name each cell.

8. Click OK or press Enter.

Important Cue

If you use **N**ame cells at intersections, use labels no longer than seven characters so that the complete labels can be used to name the cells. If the labels are too long, the block name will use a shortened version of the label.

Block Transpose

Purpose

Block Transpose copies data from one location and orientation in a notebook to another location and orientation.

Procedure

1. Highlight the block that you want to transpose.

2. Select **B**lock Transpose. The Block Transpose dialog box appears (see fig. CR.35).

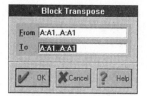

3. If you did not previously select a block, select the **F**rom text box and enter the address or block name.

4. Select the **T**o text box and enter the address or block name where you want the transposed data to appear. You only need to specify the upper left cell in the destination block.

5. Click OK or press Enter.

Important Cue

Use **B**lock **T**ranspose to swap the row and column orientation of a block of data. Rows of data in the source block become columns of data in the destination block. Columns of data in the source block become rows of data in the destination block.

CAUTION

If the block you want to transpose contains formulas, the formulas must use absolute addressing. If the formulas use relative references, the transposed formulas become meaningless.

For more information, see Chapter 5.

Block Values

Purpose

Block **V**alues converts formulas in a block to their current values.

Procedure

1. Highlight the block of formulas you want to convert to values.

2. Select **B**lock **V**alues. The Block Values dialog box appears (see fig. CR.36).

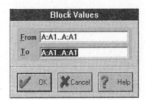

Fig. CR.36

The Block Values dialog box.

3. To place the values in another location in the notebook, enter the destination block address or name in the **T**o text box.

4. Click OK or press Enter.

Important Cues

■ To convert the formulas to values without changing their current locations, make certain the **T**o text box contains the same addresses as the **F**rom text box.

■ Use **B**lock **V**alues to *freeze* calculated data (to prevent data from changing) when other notebook data changes. To preserve the original formulas, make sure that you specify nonoverlapping **F**rom and **T**o blocks.

For more information, see Chapter 5.

Block Reformat

Purpose

Block **R**eformat fits text within a desired block by wrapping words to form complete paragraphs. **B**lock **R**eformat redistributes words so that each line is approximately the same length.

Procedure

1. Highlight the block in which you want the text to be justified. If you choose not to specify the number of rows in the block, highlight the width of the block in the top row only.

2. Select **B**lock **R**eformat. The Block Reformat dialog box appears (see fig. CR.37).

Fig. CR.37

The Block Reformat dialog box.

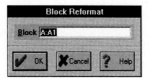

3. Click OK or press Enter.

Important Cues

■ If you specify a single row block for justification, data below the block in the first column included in the block may move up or down in relation to data in other columns.

■ If you specify a multiple row block, **B**lock **R**eformat moves no data not contained in the block. A multiple row block must, however, be large enough to hold all the text contained in the block.

For more information, see Chapter 5.

Block Insert Break

Purpose

Block Insert **B**reak enables you to control where Quattro Pro 5.0 for Windows separates printed report pages by inserting a page break symbol.

Procedure

1. Position the cell selector in the cell that you want to be the upper left corner of a new page.

2. Select **B**lock Insert **B**reak.

Important Cues

- **B**lock Insert **B**reak inserts a new row that contains only the page break symbol (|::). All data you add to this row doesn't print.

- The Print to fit option on the Spreadsheet Page Setup dialog box (refer to fig. CR.8) enables Quattro Pro 5.0 for Windows to compress printed reports to fit on fewer pages. You may find that this option eliminates the need to use **B**lock **I**nsert **B**reak.

Block Object Order

Purpose

Block **O**bject Order controls the relationship of overlapping floating objects. Floating objects include graphs, SpeedButtons, and OLE objects.

Procedure

1. Select the floating object whose position you want to adjust.

2. Select **B**lock **O**bject Order and choose one of the following options:

Option	Description
Bring Forward	Moves selected object up one level
Send Backward	Moves selected object down one level
Bring to **F**ront	Moves selected object to the top level
Send to Bac**k**	Moves selected object to the bottom level

Important Cues

- Use **B**lock **O**bject Order to control whether overlapping floating objects hide other floating objects.

- OLE objects you insert into a Quattro Pro 5.0 for Windows note-book are always floating objects.

Data Commands

The **Data** commands perform database tasks, including database selection and maintenance, data analysis, and data manipulation. The **Data** commands also assist with data input, both through keyboard input and through importation of external data files. Figure CR.38 shows the **Data** menu.

Fig. CR.38

The Data menu.

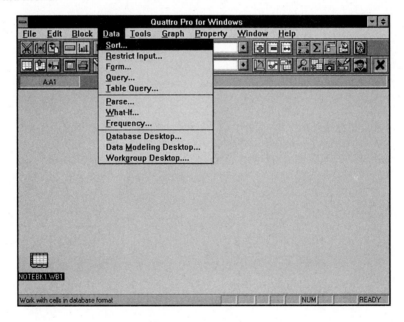

Data Sort

Purpose

Data Sort rearranges the records in a database in ascending or descending order, according to the entries in up to five fields.

Procedure

1. Highlight the block that you want to sort. If you are sorting a database, you must include every field (column) in the database, but not the field name row.

2. Select **Data Sort**. The Data Sort dialog box appears (see fig. CR.39).

Fig. CR.39

The Data Sort dialog box.

3. Select the key columns to control the order used to sort the data. You always must select the **1st** key; the **2nd** through **5th** keys are optional and are used to break ties in the higher level keys.

   To select a sort key, select the appropriate text box and point to the column in the notebook, enter the address of a cell in the column, or enter the name of a block (such as the field name) contained in the column.

4. Select ascending or descending sort order. In ascending sort order, A comes before B and 1 comes before 2; in descending order, B comes before A and 2 comes before 1.

5. Select **Numbers First** or **Labels First** to control whether numbers or labels appear at the top of the sorted data.

6. Select **D**ictionary or **C**haracter Code to determine whether the case of letters is ignored. In **D**ictionary sort order, upper- and lowercase letters sort together. In **C**haracter Code sort order, uppercase letters sort together before lowercase letters, if an ascending sort order is selected. In **C**haracter Code sort order, uppercase letters sort together after lowercase letters, if a descending sort order is selected.

7. Click OK or press Enter.

CAUTION ▶

If you sort a database without including all the fields, the data becomes meaningless because parts of one record become mixed with parts of other records.

Important Cues

■ Make certain that the **D**ata **S**ort block doesn't include the field name row. Quattro Pro 5.0 for Windows sorts the entire specified block, so if the field names are included in the **D**ata **S**ort block, these names are sorted into the records.

■ Returning a **D**ata **S**ort block to the pre-sort order can be difficult. To make returning the **D**ata **S**ort block to the pre-sort order easier, add an additional *record number* field to the **D**ata **S**ort block. Fill this field with ascending numbers by using the **B**lock **F**ill command. After sorting the **D**ata **S**ort block, you can return to the pre-sort order by re-sorting the data using the record number field as the 1st key.

For more information, see **B**lock **F**ill and Chapter 12.

Data Restrict Input

Purpose

Data **R**estrict Input restricts cell selector movement to unprotected cells in a block. Use **D**ata **R**estrict Input to create fill-in-the-blanks notebooks.

Procedure

1. Use the Object Inspector or select **P**roperty **C**urrent Object to unprotect notebook cells you want to use to accept data.

2. Highlight the block containing the input cells.

3. Select **D**ata **R**estrict Input. The Restrict Input dialog box appears (see fig. CR.40).

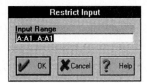

Fig. CR.40

The Restrict Input dialog box.

4. Click OK or press Enter. The mode indicator changes to INPUT.

5. Type the data in the input cells. Then use the direction keys to select the next input cell. The cell selector moves to the next unprotected cell in the input block.

6. Press Enter or Esc to return to READY mode.

Important Cues

- Organize the notebook so that the data input areas are together, and include descriptive labels to indicate the types of data the user should enter into each cell.

- Because both the Enter and Esc keys end the **D**ata **R**estrict Input command, you may find it easier to use macros than **D**ata **R**estrict Input to control input. This is especially true if you are creating a notebook application for other people to use.

For more information, see Chapter 5.

Data Form

Purpose

The **D**ata **F**orm enters and edits records in a database.

Procedure

1. Select the database block.

2. Select **D**ata **Fo**rm. The Database Form dialog box appears
(see fig. CR.41).

3. If you did not preselect the database block, enter the address in
the Input **R**ange text box.

4. Press Enter or click OK.

Important Cue

■ Make certain that the field name row is included in the selected
Input **R**ange.

Data Query

Purpose

The **D**ata **Q**uery command finds, extracts, and deletes records in a
database.

Procedure

Before you can use the **D**ata **Q**uery command, you must create a criteria table. The *criteria table* contains one or more of the field names from
the database, and it is used to select database records. The criteria
table contains two or more rows, depending on the desired search
conditions. To create the criteria table, follow these steps:

1. In a blank notebook area, enter the names of the fields you want
to use for record selection. You can type the names or copy them

from the field name row of the database. The names must match the field names in the database exactly, but you don't need to include all database fields in the criteria table.

2. In the rows immediately below the field names, enter the selection criteria. Selection criteria entered on the same row are combined in a logical AND condition. Selection criteria entered on different rows are combined in a logical OR condition. To select all records, leave the row below the field names blank.

3. Select **Data Query**. The Data Query dialog box appears (see fig. CR.42).

Fig. CR.42

The Data Query dialog box.

4. Select the **Criteria Table** text box. Enter the cell address or block name of the criteria table block.

5. Click Close.

Before you can use the **Extract** or **Extract Unique** options of the **Data Query** command, you must create an output block. The *output block* is an area you designate in the notebook to hold the extracted records.

To create an output block, follow these steps:

1. In a blank notebook area, enter the names of the fields you want to include for each extracted record. You can type the names or copy the names from the field name row of the database. The names must match the field names in the database exactly, but you don't need to include all database fields in the output block. The fields can be listed in any order and don't have to match the order of the fields in the database.

2. Select **Data Query**.

3. Select the **Output Block** text box. Enter the cell address or block name of the output block.

You can specify a single row output block or a multiple row output block. A multiple row output block can hold a specified number of extracted records—one less than the number of rows in the output block. A single row output block can hold as many records as the number of rows between the field name row and the bottom row (8192) of the notebook page. If you specify a single row output block, all data below the field name row in the columns included in the output block is erased when the **Extract** or **Extract Unique** options of the **Data Query** command are used.

4. Click OK or press Enter.

To specify the database block and find, extract, or delete records, follow these steps:

1. Highlight the database block, including the field name row.

2. Select **Data Query**.

3. If you haven't preselected the database block in the notebook, enter the block name or cell address in the **Database Block** text box.

4. Select an option from the following list:

Option	Description
Locate	Finds database records that match the selection criteria specified in the criteria table. Use for notebook databases only.
Extract	Copies full or partial records that match the selection criteria specified in the criteria table to the output block.
Extract Unique	Copies a single copy (no duplicates) of full or partial records that match the selection criteria specified in the criteria table to the output block—for example, to produce a single copy of each ZIP code in the database.
Delete	Eliminates database records that match the selection criteria specified in the criteria table.
Field Names	Creates block names using the database field names.
Reset	Resets **Data Query** options to defaults.

5. Click Close or press Enter.

Important Cues

■ Before deleting database records, create a backup copy of the notebook or extract the records to be deleted and store the extracted records in a separate notebook.

■ Use **Data Query** Extract **U**nique to create lists that show categories of database records such as postal codes or telephone exchanges.

For more information, see Chapter 12.

Data Table Query

Purpose

The **Data T**able Query command enables you to query an external database.

Procedure

1. Select **Data T**able Query. The Table Query dialog box appears (see fig. CR.43).

Fig. CR.43

The Table Query dialog box.

2. Select Query in **F**ile or Query in **B**lock from the Source of Query field.

3. Complete the **Q**BE file/block and **D**estination text boxes.

4. Select OK.

Data Parse

Purpose

Data Parse takes a single column of long labels (usually imported from an ASCII file) and separates the data into individual cell entries. **Data Parse** often is used when data is imported from mainframe files.

Procedure

1. Highlight the column of labels (the **I**nput block).

2. Select **Data Parse**. The Data Parse dialog box appears (see fig. CR.44).

Fig. CR.44

The Data Parse dialog box.

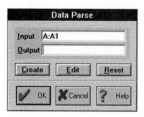

3. Select **Create**. Quattro Pro 5.0 for Windows creates a format line and inserts it into the notebook in a new line at the top cell of the **I**nput block. The format line has a vertical bar (|) label prefix, which indicates that this line is a nonprinting label.

4. You may need to edit the format line if a field is not the correct type. To change the format line, select **E**dit. If necessary, use the scroll bar in the dialog box to view the end of the format line.

   When you edit the format line, use symbols to indicate the first character of a label (L), value (V), date , or time (T). Specify additional characters of the same type with a greater than symbol (>), or add a blank space between fields with an asterisk (*). To skip a character, use S. Depending on the font in use, the symbols may not align with the characters in the sample input line, but the format line will still function properly if the symbols are the correct number of character positions from the beginning of the input line.

5. Select the **O**utput text box. Specify the block to contain the parsed data. You need to specify only the upper left cell of the block; Quattro Pro 5.0 for Windows automatically expands the block to include one column for each field and one row for each record.

6. Select OK.

Important Cues

- If the format line includes field markers breaking a multiple word field into multiple fields, edit the format line by changing the additional field markers into greater than (>) symbols, which continues the first field and includes the words that follow in the same field.

- Many Windows fonts are proportional fonts. As a result, format lines may not appear to match the field positions in the input block. Temporarily changing to a nonproportional font, such as Courier, may enable you to edit a format line more easily.

For more information, see **Tools Import** and Chapter 13.

Data What-If

Purpose

Data **W**hat-If generates a table showing the result of varying a single input value in one or more formulas, or of varying two input values in a single formula. This command is useful for generating *what-if* models that show the results of changing variables.

Procedure

A **O**ne free variable what-if table shows the results of changing a single variable in multiple formulas. To create a **O**ne free variable what-if table, follow these steps:

1. Starting in the second row of the first column of the what-if table block, enter the variables down the column.

2. Starting in the second column of the first row of the what-if table block, enter the formulas across the row.

3. Highlight the what-if table block.

4. Select **D**ata **W**hat-If. The What-If dialog box appears (see fig. CR.45).

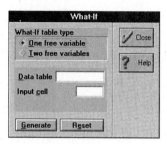

5. The block you highlighted is shown in the **D**ata table text box. If you didn't select the block, enter the block in the text box now.

6. Select the Input **c**ell text box and specify the input cell. The input cell is the variable cell to which the what-if table formulas refer. The variables down the first column of the what-if table are plugged into the formulas one at a time.

7. Select **G**enerate.

8. Click Close or press Enter.

A **T**wo free variables what-if table shows the result of changing two variables in a single formula. To create a **T**wo free variables what-if table, follow these steps:

1. Starting in the second row of the first column of the what-if table block, enter the first set of variables down the column.

2. Starting in the second column of the first row of the what-if table block, enter the second set of variables across the row.

3. In the upper left corner of the what-if table block, enter the formula.

4. Highlight the what-if table block.

5. Select **D**ata **W**hat-If.

6. The block you highlighted is shown in the **D**ata text box. If you did not select the block, enter the block in the text box now.

7. Select **T**wo free variables.

8. Select the **C**olumn input cell text box and specify the first input cell. The **C**olumn input cell is the variable cell that the variables down the first column of the what-if table are plugged into one at a time.

9. Select the **R**ow input cell text box and specify the second input cell. The **R**ow input cell is the variable cell that the variables across the first row of the what-if table are plugged into one at a time.

10. Select **G**enerate.

11. Click Close or press Enter.

Important Cues

■ Use a **O**ne free variable what-if table when you want to apply the same variables to different formulas. Use this table, for example, to calculate the interest and principal portions of a mortgage payment at different interest rates.

■ Use a **T**wo free variables what-if table when you want to assess the results of changing two variables in a single formula. Use this table, for example, to produce a table of payments based on different interest rates and payment periods.

For more information, see **B**lock **F**ill and Chapter 13.

Data Frequency

Purpose

Data **F**requency creates a frequency-distribution count of the number of values that fall within a numeric interval.

Procedure

1. Create the bin block. The bin block contains the value ranges by which you want the data separated.

2. Highlight the values block—the data you want to analyze.

3. Select **D**ata **F**requency. The Frequency Tables dialog box appears (see fig. CR.46).

Fig. CR.46

The Frequency Tables
dialog box.

4. Select the **B**in Block text box and enter the address of, or point to the bin block in the notebook.

5. Click OK or press Enter.

Important Cues

■ Use **D**ata **F**requency to analyze the data in a database block by providing a count of the number of records that fit into separate categories.

■ Use **D**ata **F**requency to produce data that can be graphed to show how factory production quality is distributed compared to nominal dimensions.

For more information, see **B**lock **F**ill, **D**ata **W**hat-If, and Chapter 13.

Data Database Desktop

Purpose

Data **D**atabase Desktop enables you to access the Quattro Pro Database Desktop, a program that queries external database files.

Procedure

Select **D**ata **D**atabase Desktop. The Quattro Pro Database Desktop screen appears (see fig. CR.47).

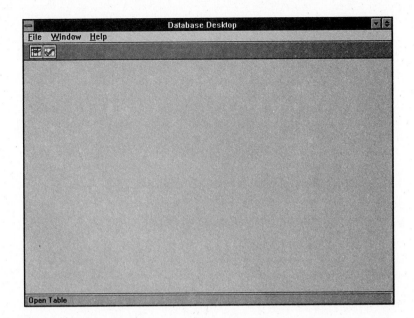

Fig. CR.47

The Quattro Pro Database Desktop.

When you finish querying an external database, you can copy the selected data to the Clipboard before you return to Quattro Pro 5.0 for Windows.

Data Data Modeling Desktop

Purpose

The **D**ata Data **M**odeling Desktop command enables you to access the Quattro Pro 5.0 for Windows Data Modeling Desktop, a program that allows you to perform sophisticated cross-tabulation analysis of data.

Procedure

1. Select the block of data you want to analyze.

2. Select **D**ata Data **M**odeling Desktop. The Send Data to Data Modeling Desktop dialog box appears (see fig. CR.48).

3. If you did not preselect the data block, enter the data block address in the Cell **b**lock to send text box.

Fig. CR.48

The Send Data to Data
Modeling Desktop
dialog box.

4. If you want to specify a location for the returned data, type the address in the **C**ell for returned data text box.

5. Specify **H**ot or Co**l**d as the Data Exchange Method.

6. Press Enter or click OK.

Important Cues

- The data you want to analyze must be in tabular format, with field names in the top row.

- Do not include any blank rows in the data block.

For more information, see Chapter 18.

Data Workgroup Desktop

Purpose

Data Workgroup Desktop starts the Object Exchange, enabling you to share data across a network or using a messaging service.

Procedure

Select **D**ata Workgroup Desktop. The Workgroup Desktop SpeedBar is appended to the lowest existing SpeedBar.

For more information, see Chapter 20.

Tools Commands

The Tools commands offer utilities that enable you to perform tasks, such as solve complex mathematical problems; create and use macros; group objects; combine, extract, or import data; and control links between Windows applications. The Tools commands also enable you to control and change the Quattro Pro for Windows user interface. Figure CR.49 shows the Tools menu.

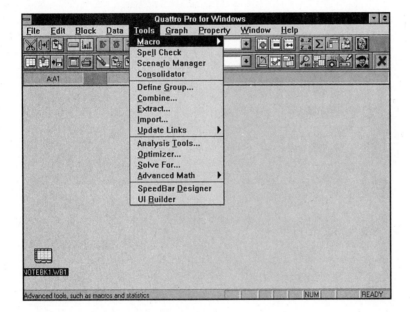

Fig. CR.49

The Tools menu.

Tools Macro Execute

Purpose

Tools Macro Execute enables you to select and run a macro.

Procedure

1. Select Tools Macro Execute or press Alt+F2. The Run Macro dialog box appears (see fig. CR.50).

Fig. CR.50

The Run Macro dialog box.

2. In the Macro Library list box, select the name of the notebook that contains the macro you want to execute.

3. Enter the cell address of the macro you want to execute in the **Location** text box, or select the name of the macro in the **Macros/Namedblocks** list box.

4. Click OK or press Enter.

Important Cues

■ You can begin macro execution at a cell other than the first cell of a macro. This technique is especially useful when you are debugging macros. To begin macro execution at a cell other than the first cell, in the **Location** text box, enter the address where you want execution to begin.

■ If you name a macro with a backslash (\ ) followed by a single letter, you can execute the macro by holding down the Ctrl key and pressing the letter.

For more information, see **T**ools **M**acro **R**ecord and Chapter 14.

Tools Macro Record

Purpose

Use **Tools Macro Record** to create macros that duplicate keyboard commands and mouse actions.

Procedure

1. Select **Tools M**acro **R**ecord. The Record Macro dialog box appears (see fig. CR.51).

2. In the Macro Li**b**rary list box, select the name of the notebook you want to use for recording the macro.

3. In the **L**ocation text box, enter the cell address where you want to record the macro.

4. Click OK or press Enter.

5. Enter the commands and mouse actions you want to record.

6. Select **Tools M**acro Stop **R**ecord.

Important Cues

- Use **Tools M**acro **R**ecord to quickly record macros that duplicate common notebook tasks. Save these macros in a separate note-book file so that you can use them with any of the notebooks.

- If possible, always record macros as logical rather than keystroke macros (see **Tools M**acro **O**ptions). This enables the macros to execute properly even if Quattro Pro 5.0 for Windows is displaying a menu other than the standard Quattro Pro 5.0 for Windows menu.

For more information, see **Tools M**acro **E**xecute, **Tools M**acro **O**ptions, and Chapter 14.

Tools Macro Options

Purpose

Tools Macro Options enables you to select how Quattro Pro 5.0 for Windows records macros.

Procedure

1. Select **Tools Macro Options**. The Macro Options dialog box appears (see fig. CR.52).

Fig. CR.52

The Macro Options dialog box.

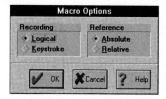

2. To record macros as logical command sequences, select **Logical**. To record macros as keystrokes, select **Keystroke**.

3. Select **Absolute** or **Relative** to control macro references as absolute or relative.

4. Click OK or press Enter.

Important Cues

■ By recording macros as logical command sequences, the macros execute properly regardless of the active menu. Macros recorded as keystrokes depend on a particular menu and may fail if you select a different menu tree.

■ When you execute macros that were recorded with **Relative** references, the cell selector moves relative to the cell it was in when the macro was started. If, for example, the cell selector is in A1 when you begin recording a macro and you move the cell selector to B3, the macro records cell selector movement as "right one column and down two rows."

For more information, see **Tools Macro Record** and Chapter 14.

Tools Macro Debugger

Purpose

Tools Macro Debugger finds errors in a macro by single-stepping through each macro instruction.

Procedure

1. Create the macro.

2. Select **Tools Macro Debugger**.

3. Execute the macro. The Macro Debugger dialog box appears (see fig. CR.53). Press the space bar to step through the macro.

Fig. CR.53

The Macro Debugger dialog box.

Important Cues

■ The **Tools Macro Debugger** command enables you to find errors in the macros quickly. Besides simply stepping through macros one instruction at a time, other options enable you to set **Breakpoints**, which halt macro execution when a specified instruction is reached, and **Conditional** cells, which halt macro execution when specified cells reach predetermined values.

■ Don't forget to select **Tools Macro Disable Debugger** to turn off the debugger after you test the macros.

For more information, see **Tools Macro Execute** and Chapter 14.

Tools Spell Check

Purpose

The **Tools** Spell Check command activates the Spelling Checker.

Procedure

Select **Tools** Spell Check. The Spelling Checker SpeedBar is appended below the last active SpeedBar.

Important Cue

■ Click the Remove SpeedBar button to remove the Spelling Checker SpeedBar when you are finished using the Spelling Checker. This frees up more space for notebooks.

For more information, see Chapter 5.

Tools Scenario Manager

Purpose

The **Tools** Scenario Manager command activates the Scenario Manager.

Procedure

Select **Tools** Scenario Manager. The Scenario Manager SpeedBar is appended below the last active SpeedBar.

Important Cue

■ Click the Remove SpeedBar button to remove the Scenario Manager SpeedBar when you are finished using the Scenario Manager. This frees up more space for notebooks.

For more information, see Chapter 19.

Tools Consolidator

Purpose

The Tools Consolidator command activates the Consolidator.

Procedure

Select Tools Consolidator. The Consolidator SpeedBar is appended below the last active SpeedBar.

Important Cue

- Click the Remove SpeedBar button to remove the Consolidator SpeedBar when you are finished using the Consolidator. This frees up more space for notebooks.

For more information, see Chapter 19.

Tools Define Group

Purpose

The Tools Define Group command enables you to create groups of notebook pages, which are linked for simultaneous editing.

Procedure

1. Select Tools Define Group. The Define/Modify Group dialog box appears (see fig. CR.54).

2. Select the Group Name text box and enter the name for the grouped pages.

3. Select the First Page text box and enter the page letter or assigned name of the top notebook page to include in the group.

4. Select the Last Page text box and enter the page letter or assigned name of the bottom notebook page to include in the group.

Fig. CR.54

The Define/Modify
Group dialog box.

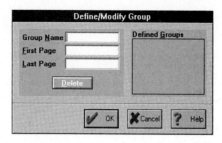

5. Click OK or press Enter.

Important Cues

■ Use **Tools** Define **G**roup to speed the process of setting up a series of notebook pages with identical properties.

■ To group pages temporarily, select a block on the first page, hold down the Shift key, and click the left mouse button on the page tab for the last page of the temporary group. Quattro Pro 5.0 for Windows displays a black line below the page tabs for temporary page groups. Temporary page groups disappear when the next block selection is made.

For more information, see Chapter 5.

Tools Combine

Purpose

Tools **C**ombine copies, adds, subtracts, multiplies, or divides values from notebook files on disk into the current notebook. You can combine values from any file that Quattro Pro 5.0 for Windows can read.

Procedure

1. Move the cell selector to the upper left cell of the block where the data is to be combined.

2. Select **Tools** **C**ombine. The File Combine dialog box appears (see fig. CR.55).

Fig. CR.55

The File Combine dialog box.

3. If necessary, select a different disk in the **D**rives list box.

4. If necessary, select a different directory in the **D**irectories list box.

5. To limit the displayed file types, select a specific file type in the File **T**ypes list box.

6. Enter the name of the file to combine in the File Name text box, or select the file in the list box.

7. In the Operation field, select one of the following options:

Option	Description
Copy	Copies data from a notebook file on disk to the active notebook file, replacing data in the active notebook, starting at the cell selector. Cells in the active notebook that correspond to blank incoming cells don't change. Otherwise, labels, formulas, and values in the active notebook are replaced.
Add	Adds numbers in the notebook file on disk to numbers or blank cells in the active notebook. Labels and formulas in the active notebook don't change.
Subtract	Subtracts numbers in the notebook file on disk from numbers or blank cells in the active notebook. Labels and formulas in the active notebook don't change.
Multiply	Multiplies numbers in the active notebook by numbers in the notebook file on disk. Labels, blanks, and formulas in the active notebook don't change.
Divide	Divides numbers in the active notebook by numbers in the notebook file on disk. Labels, blanks, and formulas in the active notebook don't change.

8. In the Source field, select **Entire File** to combine all the data in the notebook file on disk, or select **B**lock(s) to combine information in a specified block from a disk file. If you select **B**lock(s), enter the blocks in the text box.

9. Click OK or press Enter.

Important Cues

■ Use **Tools Combine** to consolidate data from several notebook files into a single notebook. You then need only update the single, consolidated notebook rather than keeping track of several different notebooks.

■ You also can link notebooks by using formulas. This technique is useful when several people must provide supporting notebook files.

CAUTION

Be careful when combining notebooks. Incoming data overwrites existing data in the active notebook.

For more information, see **Block Names Create**, **Tools Extract**, and Chapter 8.

Tools Extract

Purpose

Tools Extract copies data from part of the current notebook to a new notebook file.

Procedure

1. Highlight the block you want to extract.

2. Select **Tools Extract**. The File Extract dialog box appears (see fig. CR.56).

3. If necessary, select a different disk in the **D**rives list box.

Fig. CR.56

The File Extract dialog box.

4. If necessary, select a different directory in the **Directories** list box.

5. To save the extracted information as another file type, select a specific file type in the File **Types** list box.

6. Enter the name of the file to extract *to* in the **File Name** text box, or select the file in the list box.

7. In the Option field, select F**o**rmulas to extract formulas contained in the highlighted block as formulas, or select Values to convert formulas to their current values before extracting them.

8. To save the extracted data in a password-protected notebook file, select **P**assword Protection and enter the password. If you use a password, you must verify the password after clicking OK. The Verify Password dialog box appears.

9. Click OK or press Enter.

Important Cues

■ When extracting formulas, be certain that the block you are extracting contains all the data referred to by the formulas. If the extracted block contains formulas that refer to cells outside the extracted block, the formulas don't evaluate correctly.

■ The extracted data block begins at cell A:A1 in the new notebook file created by **T**ools **E**xtract, regardless of the location in the original notebook.

For more information, see **T**ools **C**ombine and Chapter 8.

Tools Import

Purpose

Tools Import combines data from text files into the active notebook.

Procedure

1. Position the cell selector in the upper left corner of the block where you want the imported data to appear.

2. Select Tools Import. The Import File dialog box appears (see fig. CR.57).

Fig. CR.57

The Import File dialog box.

3. If necessary, select a different disk in the Drives list box.

4. If necessary, select a different directory in the Directories list box.

5. By default, Tools Import imports text from files with a PRN extension. To import the information from another file type, select a specific file type in the File Types list box.

6. Enter the name of the file to import *from* in the File Name text box or select the file in the list box.

7. Select the type of text file from the choices in the Option field.

8. Click OK or press Enter.

Important Cues

■ After you import a text file, use **Data Parse** to break the lines of text into individual cell entries.

■ Often you can use **Edit Copy** and **Edit Paste** to import data directly from other Windows applications instead of creating a text file and using **Tools Import**.

For more information, see Chapter 8 and Chapter 13.

Tools Update Links Open Links

Purpose

Tools Update Links Open Links opens notebook files currently linked to the active notebook.

Procedure

1. Select **Tools Update Links Open Links**. The Open Links dialog box appears (see fig. CR.58).

Fig. CR.58

The Open Links dialog box.

2. In the **Hotlinks** list box, select the notebook file you want to open.

3. Click OK or press Enter.

Important Cues

■ When you open a notebook that has formula links to other notebooks, Quattro Pro 5.0 for Windows offers to open the supporting notebooks or update the links. If you did not choose to open the supporting notebooks or update the links, use **Tools Update Links Open Links** to open the supporting notebooks.

■ If you open all supporting notebooks and then save the workspace (**File Workspace Save**), Quattro Pro 5.0 for Windows automatically opens all supporting notebooks if you use **File Workspace Retrieve**.

■ If the notebook contains no links, you get an error message that states No (unopened) hotlinks.

For more information, see **Tools Update Links Refresh Links** and Chapter 8.

Tools Update Links Refresh Links

Purpose

Tools Update Links Refresh Links recalculates the values of the formulas in the active notebook based on the current values in the supporting notebook files.

Procedure

1. Select **Tools Update Links Refresh Links**. The Update Links dialog box appears (see fig. CR.59).

2. In the **Hotlinks** list box, select the notebook file that contains the data you want to update in the active notebook.

3. Click OK or press Enter.

The Update Links dialog box.

Important Cues

■ If you work on a network, use **Tools Update Links Refresh Links** to make certain that the active notebook contains the most recent data from supporting notebook files that may be updated by another user.

■ Unlike the option Quattro Pro 5.0 for Windows provides for opening the supporting notebooks or updating the links when you first open a linked notebook, **Tools Update Links Refresh Links** enables you to select the links to update.

For more information, see **Tools Update Links Open Links** and see Chapter 8.

Tools Update Links Delete Links

Purpose

Tools Update Links Delete Links removes links to supporting notebook files.

Procedure

1. Select **Tools Update Links Delete Links**. The Delete Links dialog box appears (see fig. CR.60).

Fig. CR.60

The Delete Links dialog box.

2. In the **H**otlinks list box, select the notebook file containing the link you want to delete.

3. Click OK or press Enter.

CAUTION

If you delete links to a supporting notebook file, Quattro Pro 5.0 for Windows changes the links to ERR. **E**dit **U**ndo cannot restore links removed with **T**ools **U**pdate Links **D**elete Links.

For more information, see **T**ools **U**pdate Links **O**pen Links and Chapter 8.

Tools Update Links Change Link

Purpose

Tools **U**pdate Links **C**hange Link enables you to change the name of the supporting notebook referenced in linking formulas.

Procedure

1. Select **T**ools **U**pdate Links **C**hange Link. The Change Link dialog box appears (see fig. CR.61).

2. In the Change Link **F**rom list box, select the notebook file that contains the link you want to change.

The Change Link dialog box.

3. In the **To** text box, enter the name of the notebook file you want to change the links to.

4. Click OK or press Enter.

Important Cues

■ Use **Tools Update Links Change Link** to correct the references in linking formulas if you change the name of a supporting notebook file.

■ The new supporting notebook file must use the same layout as the old one. Otherwise, the linking formulas are meaningless.

For more information, see **Tools Update Links Open Links** and Chapter 8.

Tools Analysis Tools

Purpose

The **Tools Analysis Tools** command activates the Analysis Tools SpeedBar.

Procedure

Select **Tools Analysis Tools**. The Analysis Tools SpeedBar is appended below the last active SpeedBar.

Important Cue

- Click the Remove SpeedBar button to remove the Analysis Tools SpeedBar when you are finished using the Analysis Tools. This frees up more space for notebooks.

- Use the Analysis Tools Experts to learn how to use the Analysis Tools.

For more information, see Chapter 17.

Tools Optimizer

Purpose

Tools **O**ptimizer analyzes notebook data and helps you solve problems that have several possible outcomes. **T**ools **O**ptimizer uses goal seeking to find optimal solutions to complex problems.

Procedure

1. Select **T**ools **O**ptimizer. The Optimizer dialog box appears (see fig. CR.62).

Fig. CR.62

The Optimizer dialog box.

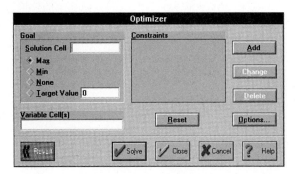

2. In the **V**ariable Cell(s) field, specify the cells that the Optimizer adjusts to solve the problem.

3. Select **A**dd to add a constraint. The Add Constraints dialog box appears (see fig. CR.63).

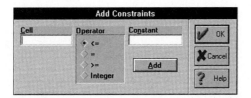

Fig. CR.63

The Add Constraints dialog box.

4. Enter the constraint cell and conditional relationship in the three text boxes. You can add more constraints by selecting **A**dd.

5. When all constraints are added, click OK or press Enter to return to the Optimizer dialog box.

6. Select **S**olution Cell and specify the cell that contains the value you want to minimize or maximize.

7. Select Ma**x**, **M**in, or **N**one.

8. If you want the **S**olution Cell to reach a specific value, select **T**arget Value and specify the value.

9. To begin solving the problem, select Solve.

10. Click Close or press Enter.

Important Cues

■ Select **T**ools **O**ptimizer **O**ptions **R**eporting to generate a report on the method used to solve the problem. The available reports may suggest areas where you can improve the problem definition to increase the viability of the solution.

■ For problems with a single variable, consider using **T**ools **S**olve For. You may also want to compare the results of the two methods to determine which solution best meets your needs.

For more information, see Chapter 9.

Tools Solve For

Purpose

Tools **S**olve For returns the value for a variable cell that is needed to produce a specified value in a target cell.

Procedure

1. Select **Tools Solve For**. The Solve For dialog box appears (see fig. CR.64).

Fig. CR.64

The Solve For dialog box.

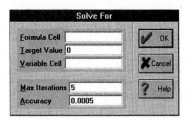

2. Select the **Formula Cell** text box and enter the address of the cell that contains the formula you want to equate to a specific value.

3. Select the **Target Value** text box and enter the value that you want to be the result of the formula.

4. Select the **Variable Cell** text box and enter the address of the cell **Tools Solve For** can change. The formula in the **Formula Cell** text box must refer to this cell directly or indirectly.

5. Click OK or press Enter.

Important Cues

- To find solutions to problems with multiple variables, use **Tools Optimizer**.

- If **Tools Solve For** is unable to find a solution, consider increasing the number of iterations or reducing the level of precision.

For more information, see **Tools Optimizer** and Chapter 9.

Tools Advanced Math Regression

Purpose

Tools Advanced Math Regression is used to analyze the relationship between a set of independent variables and a dependent variable.

Procedure

1. Prepare the data you want to analyze. Variables must be arranged in columns, and independent variables must be in adjacent columns.

2. Select **T**ools **A**dvanced Math **R**egression. The Linear Regression dialog box appears (see fig. CR.65).

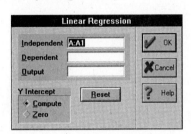

Fig. CR.65

The Linear Regression dialog box.

3. Select **I**ndependent and enter the block address or block name that contains the independent variables.

4. Select **D**ependent and enter the block address or block name that contains the dependent variables.

5. Select **O**utput and enter the block address or block name where you want Quattro Pro 5.0 for Windows to write the calculated results.

6. Select **C**ompute to allow Quattro Pro 5.0 for Windows to calculate the y-intercept value or **Z**ero to force the y-intercept value to be zero.

7. Click OK or press Enter.

Important Cue

If you change the data used in a regression analysis problem, you must reissue the **T**ools **A**dvanced Math **R**egression command to update the results.

For more information, see Chapter 13.

Tools Advanced Math Invert

Purpose

Tools **A**dvanced **M**ath **I**nvert performs an algebraic inversion on a matrix.

Procedure

1. Create the block of values you want to invert.

2. Select **Tools A**dvanced **M**ath **I**nvert. The Matrix Invert dialog box appears (see fig. CR.66).

Fig. CR.66

The Matrix Invert dialog box.

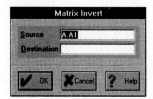

3. Select **S**ource and enter the block address or block name of the block you want to invert.

4. Select **D**estination and enter the block address or block name for the output of the inversion.

5. Click OK or press Enter.

Important Cues

■ The **S**ource block you specify for **Tools A**dvanced **M**ath **I**nvert must be square.

■ You can invert a matrix with up to 90 rows and columns.

For more information, see Chapter 13.

Tools Advanced Math Multiply

Purpose

Tools Advanced Math Multiply multiplies two matrices and creates a third matrix containing the results.

Procedure

1. Create the two matrices you want to multiply.

2. Select Tools Advanced Math Multiply. The Matrix Multiply dialog box appears (see fig. CR.67).

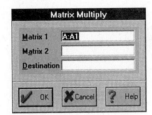

Fig. CR.67

The Matrix Multiply dialog box.

3. Select Matrix 1 and enter the block address or block name of the first (coefficient) matrix.

4. Select Matrix 2 and enter the block address or block name of the second (variables) matrix.

5. Select Destination and enter the block address or block name of the destination matrix.

6. Click OK or press Enter.

Important Cues

- The number of columns in matrix 1 must equal the number of rows in matrix 2.

- The destination matrix must have as many rows as matrix 1 and as many columns as matrix 2.

For more information, see Chapter 13.

Tools SpeedBar Designer

Purpose

Tools SpeedBar **D**esigner activates the SpeedBar Designer.

Procedure

Select **T**ools SpeedBar **D**esigner. The SpeedBar Designer SpeedBar replaces the notebook SpeedBar, and a blank SpeedBar appears. You can use this blank SpeedBar as the basis for designing a custom SpeedBar.

See Chapter 16 for more information.

Tools UI Builder

Purpose

Tools UI **B**uilder enables you to create custom dialog boxes.

Procedure

1. Select **T**ools UI **B**uilder. Quattro Pro 5.0 for Windows displays a new, sample dialog box and the Dialog window SpeedBar (see fig. CR.68).

2. Use the tools on the SpeedBar to add objects to the dialog box.

3. Use the Dialog menu commands to create and modify links to dialog box objects (see Dialog commands).

4. Press Ctrl+F4 to close the Dialog window and return to the notebook.

For more information, see Dialog Connect, Dialog Links, and Chapter 16.

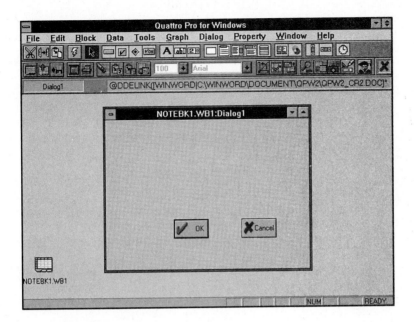

Fig. CR.68

A sample dialog box and the Dialog window SpeedBar.

Graph Commands

With the **G**raph commands, you can define the block for a new chart and manipulate existing charts. You can insert a graphic into a note-book block, import and export graphics files, and view a graph in a Graph window.

Some **G**raph commands and options are available in only a Graph window. The following sections cover all the **G**raph commands, and indicate commands available only in the Graph window.

Figure CR.69 shows the **G**raph menu as it appears when selected in the notebook window.

Graph Type

Purpose

Graph **T**ype enables you to select the type of graph used to display data.

Fig. CR.69

The Graph menu.

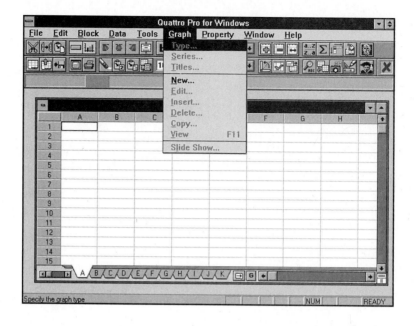

Procedure

1. **G**raph **T**ype is available only in a Graph window. If the graph is currently being displayed as a floating object in a notebook window, point to the graph and double-click the left mouse button to display the graph in a Graph window.

2. Select **G**raph **T**ype. The Graph Types dialog box appears (see fig. CR.70).

Fig. CR.70

The Graph Types dialog box.

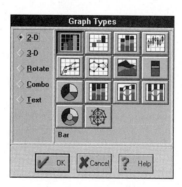

3. Select the category of graph; **2**-D, **3**-D, **R**otate, **C**ombo, or **T**ext.

4. Select the specific type of graph from the gallery of graph type icons in the right side of the dialog box. The name of the selected graph type appears below the graph type icons.

5. Click OK or press Enter.

Important Cues

■ Select a graph type appropriate to the data. A pie chart, for example, graphs a single data series. An *HLCO* (or high low) graph commonly is used to graph stock prices.

■ Use **Text** graphs to create freehand drawings that don't graph notebook data.

For more information, see Chapter 10.

Graph Series

Purpose

The **G**raph **S**eries command enables you to specify the data and legend blocks within a notebook.

Procedure

1. **G**raph **S**eries is available only in a Graph window. If the graph currently is being displayed as a floating object in a notebook window, point to the graph and double-click the left mouse button to display the graph in a Graph window.

2. Select **G**raph **S**eries. The Graph Series dialog box appears (see fig. CR.71).

3. Enter the data block addresses or names in the **1**st through **6**th Series text boxes.

4. Enter the address or block names of the **X**-axis labels in the **X**-Axis text box.

5. Enter the address or block name of the data legends in the **L**egend text box.

6. Select **R**everse series to reverse the order data is graphed.

7. If necessary, select Row/**c**olumn swap to match the order of data in the data block.

8. Click OK or press Enter.

Fig. CR.71

The Graph Series dialog box.

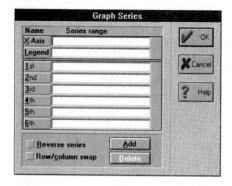

Important Cues

■ To save time, highlight the data you want to graph before creating a graph. If Quattro Pro 5.0 for Windows seems to graph the data incorrectly, select **G**raph **S**eries Row/**c**olumn swap to swap the rows and columns in the graphed data.

■ If the data blocks containing larger values hide those with smaller values, select **G**raph **S**eries **R**everse series to change the order the data appears on the graph.

For more information, see Chapter 10.

Graph Titles

Purpose

The **G**raph **T**itles command enables you to add a title centered above the graph and titles for each axis of the graph.

Procedure

1. **G**raph **T**itles is available only in a Graph window. If the graph is currently being displayed as a floating object in a notebook

window, point to the graph and double-click the left mouse button
to display the graph in a Graph window.

2. Select **G**raph Titles. The Graph Titles dialog box appears
(see fig. CR.72).

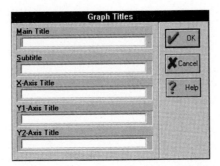

Fig. CR.72

The Graph Titles dialog
box.

3. Select **M**ain Title and enter the text for the main graph title or the
address of the cell that contains the text for the main graph title.

4. Select **S**ubtitle and enter the text for the second graph title or the
address of the cell that contains the text for the second graph
title.

5. Select **X**-Axis Title and enter the text for the x-axis title or the
address of the cell that contains the text for the x-axis title.

6. Select **Y**1-Axis Title and enter the text for the y-axis (left side) title
or the address of the cell that contains the text for the y-axis title.

7. Select **Y**2-Axis Title and enter the text for the second y-axis (right
side) title or the address of the cell that contains the text for the
second y-axis title.

8. Click OK or press Enter.

Important Cues

■ Specify cells containing string formulas as the source for graph
titles to create titles that automatically update to reflect current
notebook data.

■ For additional flexibility in creating graph text, use the Graph
window Text tool to create text.

For more information, see Chapter 10.

Graph New

Purpose

Graph New creates a new graph using the currently selected data.

Procedure

1. Highlight the block of data to graph.

2. Select **Graph New**. The Graph New dialog box appears (see fig. CR.73).

Fig. CR.73

The Graph New dialog box.

3. Select the **Graph Name** text box and specify the name for the new graph.

4. Enter the data block addresses or names in the **1**st through **6**th Series range text boxes.

5. Enter the address or block names of the X-axis labels in the **X-Axis** text box.

6. Enter the address or block name of the data legends in the **Legend** text box.

7. Select **R**everse series to reverse the order data is graphed.

8. If necessary, select Row/column swap to match the order of data in the data block.

9. Click OK or press Enter.

Important Cues

- Quattro Pro 5.0 for Windows creates names for graphs starting with GRAPH1, GRAPH2, and so on. Instead of using the default graph names, create descriptive graph names that denote the purpose of the graph.

- Create data legends and x-axis labels before selecting **Graph New**. Include these legends and labels in the highlighted data block so that Quattro Pro 5.0 for Windows automatically enters the **X-Axis** and **Legend** series in the text boxes.

- To add a new data series between two existing data series, select the data series text box that the new data series should follow. Choose **Add** to insert a text box for the new series. If there are more than six data series, use the scroll bars to access the text boxes for the additional data series.

For more information, see Chapter 10.

Graph Edit

Purpose

Graph Edit selects a graph to edit and opens the Graph window. When the Graph window is active, you have full access to all Quattro Pro 5.0 for Windows graph enhancement commands and options.

Procedure

1. Select **Graph Edit**. The Graph Edit dialog box appears (see fig. CR.74).

2. Select the name of the graph you want to edit.

3. Click OK or press Enter.

Important Cue

To quickly open the Graph window, point to the graph you want to edit and double-click the left mouse button.

For more information, see Chapter 10.

Fig. CR.74

The Graph Edit dialog
box.

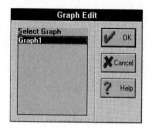

Graph Insert

Purpose

Graph Insert enables you to place an existing graph as a floating object
on a notebook page.

1. Select **G**raph Insert. The Graph Insert dialog box appears
   (see fig. CR.75).

Fig. CR.75

The Graph Insert dialog
box.

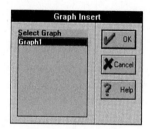

2. Select the graph you want to insert.

3. Click OK or press Enter.

4. Highlight the notebook area where you want the graph to appear.

Important Cues

■ Use **G**raph Insert to include graphs on the same notebook pages
as the data. Quattro Pro 5.0 for Windows can print graphs as part
of a notebook page or on a separate page.

■ You can easily resize or move a graph that you've inserted as a
floating object. Select the graph; then drag it to move it, or move
one of its handles to resize it.

■ After inserting a floating graph on a notebook page, use **File Print Preview** to make sure that the graph will be large enough to be easily visible on the printed page.

For more information, see Chapter 10.

Graph Delete

Purpose

Graph **D**elete removes a named graph from the active notebook.

Procedure

1. Select **G**raph **D**elete. The Graph Delete dialog box appears (see fig. CR.76).

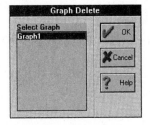

Fig. CR.76

The Graph Delete dialog box.

2. Select the graph you want to delete.

3. Click OK or press Enter.

> **Gr**aph **D**elete removes all settings for the selected named graph. Before you delete a graph, make sure that you no longer need it.   **CAUTION**

Important Cue

Make a backup of the notebook before you delete graphs so you can restore the graph, if necessary.

For more information, see Chapter 10.

Graph Copy

Purpose

Graph **C**opy enables you to copy a complete graph, the graph style, the graphed data, or objects added to a graph.

Procedure

1. Select **G**raph **C**opy. The Graph Copy dialog box appears (see fig. CR.77).

Fig. CR.77

The Graph Copy dialog box.

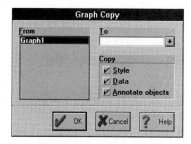

2. In the **F**rom list box, select the graph you want to copy *from*.

3. Select the **T**o list box and specify the name of the graph you want to copy *to*.

4. Specify what you want to copy by checking selections from the **S**tyle, **D**ata, and **A**nnotate objects check boxes.

5. Click OK or press Enter.

Important Cues

■ The **G**raph **C**opy **D**ata selection doesn't copy data from one notebook location to another. Instead, it creates a new graph of the same data.

■ Use the **G**raph **C**opy **S**tyle selection to create a new graph with the same properties as an existing graph, but based on a different set of data.

For more information, see Chapter 10.

Graph View

Purpose

Graph **V**iew displays a full page preview of a selected graph.

Procedure

1. Select **G**raph **V**iew or press F11. The Graph View dialog box appears (see fig. CR.78).

2. Select the graph you want to view.

3. Click OK or press Enter.

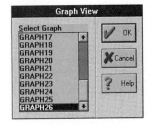

Fig. CR.78

The Graph View dialog box.

4. Press any key or click the left mouse button to remove the graph from the screen.

Important Cue

Graph **V**iew enables you to view a full page view of a graph without menus, SpeedBars, or the status line.

For more information, see Chapter 10.

Graph Slide Show

Purpose

Graph **S**lide Show executes a slide show that you previously created.

Procedure

1. Select **G**raph Slide Show. The Select Slide Show dialog box appears (see fig. CR.79).

Fig. CR.79

The Select Slide Show dialog box.

2. Select the name of the slide show you want to run.

3. Click OK or press Enter.

Important Cue

You must create a slide show in the Graph window before you can use **G**raph Slide Show.

For more information, see Chapter 10.

Property Commands

The **P**roperty commands enable you to select properties for a selected object, the current notebook page, the active notebook, or Quattro Pro 5.0 for Windows itself. Figure CR.80 shows the **P**roperty menu that displays when a notebook page is the active page.

Property Current Object

Purpose

Property **C**urrent Object enables you to set the properties associated with the currently selected object.

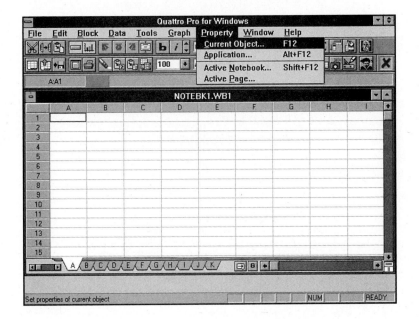

Fig. CR.80

The notebook page
Property menu.

Procedure

1. Select the block whose properties you want to set.

2. Select **P**roperty **C**urrent Object or press F12. The Active Block
   dialog box appears (see fig. CR.81).

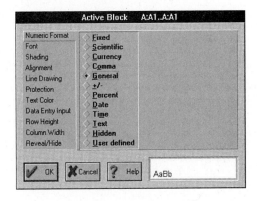

Fig. CR.81

The Active Block dialog
box.

3. Choose the properties you want to set for the selected block, and
   make the selections.

4. Click OK or press Enter.

Important Cues

- Use the right mouse button as a shortcut method of setting object properties. Point to the cell or selected block and click the right mouse button.

- Select different object properties in the Active Block dialog box by pointing to the property and clicking the left mouse button or by pressing Ctrl+PgDn and Ctrl+PgUp.

- Select as many object properties as you like before confirming the dialog box.

- If you find that you are often setting the same object properties, use **E**dit **D**efine Style to create a named style that you can quickly apply to selected blocks.

For more information, see Chapter 6.

Property Application

Purpose

Property **A**pplication enables you to establish default settings for Quattro Pro 5.0 for Windows.

Procedure

1. Select **P**roperty **A**pplication or press Alt+F12. The Application dialog box appears (see fig. CR.82).

Fig. CR.82

The Application dialog box.

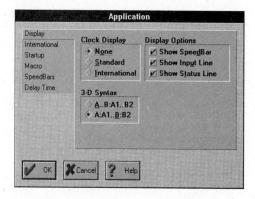

2. Select the properties you want to set for Quattro Pro 5.0 for Windows and make the selections.

3. Click OK or press Enter.

Important Cues

■ Use **P**roperty **A**pplication to control settings that apply to all Quattro Pro 5.0 for Windows notebooks.

■ To make certain that **E**dit **U**ndo is available, use **P**roperty **A**pplication Startup **U**ndo Enabled.

■ To quickly activate the Application dialog box, point to the Quattro Pro 5.0 for Windows title bar and click the right mouse button.

For more information, see Chapter 3.

Property Active Notebook

Purpose

Property Active **N**otebook enables you to specify properties for the entire active notebook.

Procedure

1. Select **P**roperty Active **N**otebook or press Shift+F12. The Active Notebook dialog box appears (see fig. CR.83).

2. Select the properties you want to set for the active notebook.

3. Click OK or press Enter.

Important Cues

■ Use **P**roperty Active **N**otebook to control settings that apply to the currently active Quattro Pro 5.0 for Windows notebook only. These property settings are saved with the notebook.

Fig. CR.83

The Active Notebook
dialog box.

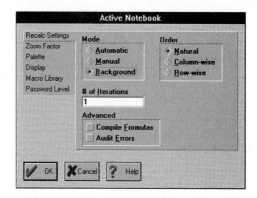

■ To quickly activate the Active Notebook dialog box, point to the notebook title bar and click the right mouse button.

For more information, see Chapter 3.

Property Active Page

Purpose

Property Active **P**age controls property settings for the current notebook page.

Procedure

1. Select **P**roperty Active **P**age. The Active Page dialog box appears (see fig. CR.84).

Fig. CR.84

The Active Page dialog
box.

2. Select the properties you want to set for the active page.

3. Click OK or press Enter.

Important Cues

■ Use **P**roperty Active **P**age to control settings that apply to the currently active Quattro Pro 5.0 for Windows notebook page only. These property settings are saved with the notebook.

■ To quickly activate the Active Page dialog box, point to the notebook page tab and click the right mouse button.

For more information, see Chapter 3.

Window Commands

The commands on the **W**indow menu control the appearance and position of the notebook windows. These commands enable you to create additional views of a single notebook, rearrange open notebook windows, hide or display selected windows, split windows, and keep titles on-screen as you scroll the notebook. Figure CR.85 shows the Window menu.

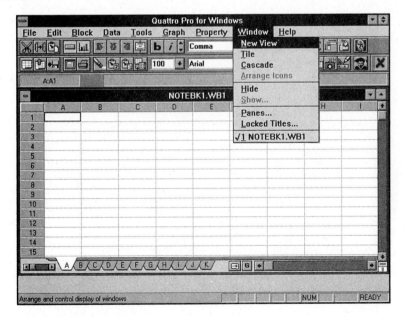

Fig. CR.85

The Window menu.

Window New View

Purpose

Window **N**ew View creates an additional window displaying the active notebook.

Procedure

Select **W**indow **N**ew View. Quattro Pro 5.0 for Windows creates an additional view of the active notebook, as shown in figure CR.86.

Fig. CR.86

Window **N**ew View adds an additional window that displays the notebook.

Important Cues

■ When you use **W**indow **N**ew View, each window title bar has the view number appended to the end of the notebook title. For example, the first view of NOTEBK1.WB1 becomes NOTEBK1.WB1:1, the second becomes NOTEBK1.WB1:2, and so on.

■ If you are displaying a single notebook in multiple windows, you can close one window without closing the others by using the notebook window Control menu **C**lose command.

■ File **Close** closes all open windows.

■ If you save a File with multiple windows open, all windows are open when the file is retrieved.

For more information, see Chapter 5.

Window Tile

Purpose

Window Tile rearranges the open notebook windows so that they don't overlap. If, for example, you have two open notebook windows, **Window Tile** places the two windows side by side in equal sized windows (see fig. CR.87).

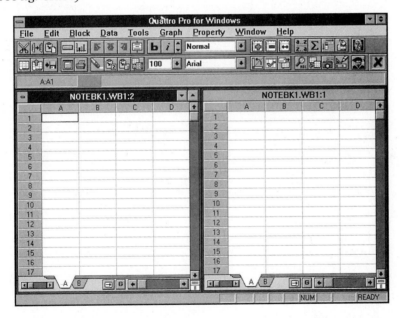

Fig. CR.87

Tiled notebook windows.

Procedure

Select **Window Tile.**

Important Cues

- Use **Window Tile** to see all open windows at the same time. This makes it easier to create formulas that link notebooks, or to copy or move data between open notebook files.

- **Window Tile** doesn't display hidden windows.

- Although **Window Tile** creates equal-sized windows, you can easily adjust the sizes of the displayed windows by using the mouse or the notebook window Control menu **Size** command.

For more information, see Chapter 5.

Window Cascade

Purpose

Window Cascade rearranges the open notebook windows to overlap one another. As shown in figure CR.88, each window is the same size and slightly offset so the window title bars are visible.

Fig. CR.88

Cascaded notebook windows.

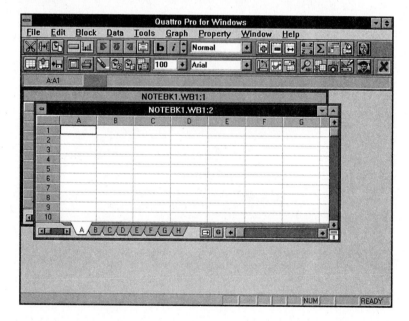

Procedure

Select **Window Cascade**.

Important Cues

- Use **Window Cascade** to display a larger view of the active window than that displayed by **Window Tile**, while still allowing easy access to all open windows.
- To quickly move between cascaded windows, point to the title bar of a window and click the left mouse button to make that window the active window.

For more information, see Chapter 5.

Window Arrange Icons

Purpose

Window Arrange Icons lines up icons for minimized notebook windows in rows of eight along the bottom of the screen.

Procedure

Select **Window Arrange Icons**.

For more information, see Chapter 5.

Window Hide

Purpose

Window Hide removes the active window from the display. The window remains open, but is hidden from view.

Procedure

Select **Window Hide.**

Important Cues

- Use **Window Hide** to hide a macro library notebook after verifying proper macro operation.

- Use **File Workspace Save** to preserve the display status of notebook windows.

For more information, see Chapter 5.

Window Show

Purpose

Window Show displays hidden notebook windows.

Procedure

1. Select **Window Show.** The Show Window dialog box appears (see fig. CR.89).

Fig. CR.89

The Show Window dialog box.

2. Select the hidden window you want to display.

3. Click OK or press Enter.

Important Cue

You don't need to display a notebook window in order to execute macros contained in the hidden notebook.

For more information, see Chapter 5.

Window Panes

Purpose

Window Panes splits the active notebook window horizontally or vertically into two panes.

Procedure

1. Select **Window Panes**. The Panes dialog box appears (see fig. CR.90).

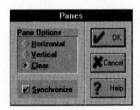

Fig. CR.90

The Panes dialog box.

2. Select **Horizontal** to split the window into two panes horizontally at the current cell selector position. Select **Vertical** to split the window vertically at the current cell selector position into two panes. Select **Clear** to return a split window to a single pane.

3. Select the **Synchronize** check box to force split panes to scroll together. To allow split panes to scroll independently, deselect the **Synchronize** check box.

4. Click OK or press Enter.

For more information, see Chapter 5.

Window Locked Titles

Purpose

Window Locked Titles locks rows or columns on-screen so that titles included in the notebooks remain visible when you move the cell selector to other areas of the notebook page.

Procedure

1. Position the cell selector in the row below and the column to the right of any titles you want to lock on-screen.

2. Select Window Locked Titles. The Locked Titles dialog box appears (see fig. CR.91).

Fig. CR.91

The Locked Titles dialog box.

3. Select from the following options:

Option	Description
Clear	Removes any locked titles from the notebook page
Horizontal	Locks rows above the cell selector
Vertical	Locks columns left of the cell selector
Both	Locks rows above the cell selector and columns left of the cell selector

4. Click OK or press Enter.

Important Cues

■ To move the cell selector into a block of locked titles, use **Edit Goto** (or press F5) and specify a cell address within the locked title block.

■ When titles are locked on a notebook page, pressing the Home key moves the cell selector to the upper left cell outside the locked block.

For more information, see Chapter 5.

Help Commands

With the **Help** pull-down menu you can display the following Help screens:

Option	Description
Contents	Displays an index of Help topics
Search	Enables you to search for Help topics by keyword
Experts	Activates the Quattro Pro 5.0 for Windows Experts
Functions	Describes how to use the built-in functions of Quattro Pro 5.0 for Windows
Interactive **T**utors	Displays the Interactive Tutors Catalog, and enables you to learn about various tasks
About Quattro Pro	Displays the Quattro Pro 5.0 for Windows version number and memory settings

Dialog Commands

The Dialog commands are used to create dialog boxes. The Dialog commands appear on the Quattro Pro 5.0 for Windows menu bar only when a Dialog window is active. Use the **Tools** UI **B**uilder command to access the Dialog window. Figure CR.92 shows the Dialog menu.

Fig. CR.92

The Dialog menu.

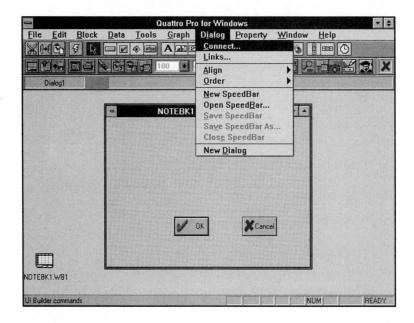

Dialog Connect

Purpose

You use the Dialog Connect command to produce a quick connection between a dialog box and a notebook cell. By connecting a dialog box and a cell, you create a link that enables the dialog boxes to interact with the notebook.

Procedure

1. Display the Dialog window by selecting Tools UI Builder.

2. Select the dialog box you want to connect to a notebook cell.

3. Select Dialog Connect. The Connection dialog box appears (see fig. CR.93).

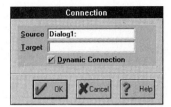

Fig. CR.93

The Connection dialog box.

4. In the Target text box, enter the cell address or block name of the cell you want to connect to the dialog box.

5. To copy any change in value to the cell, make certain that the Dynamic Connection check box is selected. If this check box isn't selected, the Target cell is updated only when the dialog box is closed.

6. Click OK or press Enter to confirm the dialog box.

Important Cues

■ Use Dialog Connect to make the dialog boxes display and change the value of a single notebook cell.

■ Use Dialog Links to make the dialog boxes display and change the value of multiple notebook cells.

■ To remove the connection between a dialog box and a notebook cell, use Dialog Links Delete.

For more information, see Chapter 16.

Dialog Links

Purpose

The Dialog Links command enables you to control the interactions between objects you create, as well as objects and notebook cells. Dialog Links also enables you to delete object links within the notebook.

Procedure

1. Display the Dialog window by selecting **Tools UI Builder**.

2. Select the object you want to connect to a notebook cell.

3. Select **Dialog Links**. The Object Link dialog box appears (see fig. CR.94).

Fig. CR.94

The Object Link dialog box.

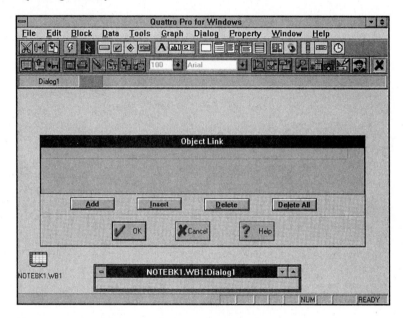

4. Select **A**dd to create a new object link.

5. Point to the word Init at the left of the text box, hold down the left mouse button, and select the event that triggers the link command.

6. Continue selecting each link argument until the text bar shows the link command correctly.

7. Click OK or press Enter to confirm the dialog box and create the link.

Important Cues

■ To connect an object to a single cell, use **Dialog Connect**.

■ Links respond to *events* (actions, such as a mouse click or exiting a dialog box). Use **Dialog Links** to control how dialog boxes respond to user input and manipulate notebook data.

For more information, see Chapter 16.

Dialog Align

Purpose

The **Dialog Align** command enables you to control the alignment of objects in dialog boxes you create.

Procedure

1. Display the Dialog window by selecting **Tools Dialog Builder**.

2. Create the dialog box and add any necessary objects.

3. Select **Dialog Align**, and select an option from the following list:

Option	Description
Left	Aligns dialog box elements to the left edge of the leftmost selected object
Right	Aligns dialog box elements to the right edge of the rightmost selected object
Horizontal Center	Centers dialog box elements between the left and right sides of the dialog box
Top	Aligns dialog box elements to the top edge of the topmost selected object
Bottom	Aligns dialog box elements to the bottom edge of the bottommost selected object
Vertical Center	Centers dialog box elements between the top and bottom of the dialog box
Horizontal Space	Horizontally spaces dialog box elements by the number of pixels you specify
Vertical Space	Vertically spaces dialog box elements by the number of pixels you specify
Resize to Same	Resizes dialog box elements to the same size as the first dialog box element you select

Important Cues

■ Use Dialog **Align** to improve the appearance of dialog boxes you create.

■ Use Dialog **Align Resize** to Same when you want similar dialog box elements to all have the same size—especially when you resize an object after adding it to the dialog box.

For more information, see Chapter 16.

Dialog Order

Purpose

Dialog **Order** determines the sequence of tabbing, returned values, and on-screen layering of dialog box objects.

Procedure

1. Display the Dialog window by selecting Tools UI **B**uilder.

2. Select Dialog **Order**.

3. Select the option from the following list:

Option	Action
Order Controls	Specifies the order in which the control settings appear in the notebook block.
Order From	Specifies the order in which the control settings appear in the notebook block. The first control you click determines the starting location; each subsequent control you click follows in sequential order.
Order Tab Controls	Specifies the order in which the controls are selected by pressing Tab.
Order Tab From	Specifies the order in which the controls are selected by pressing Tab. The first control you click determines the starting location; each subsequent control you click follows in sequential order.

Bring Forward	Moves the selected object in front of an overlapping object.
Send Backward	Moves the selected object behind an overlapping object.
Bring to **F**ront	Moves the selected object in front of all overlapping objects.
Send to Bac**k**	Moves the selected object behind all overlapping objects.

For more information, see Chapter 16.

Dialog New SpeedBar

Purpose

The **D**ialog **N**ew SpeedBar command creates a new SpeedBar.

Procedure

1. Display the Dialog window by selecting **T**ools UI **B**uilder.

2. Select **D**ialog **N**ew SpeedBar.

3. Add objects to the new SpeedBar by using the standard Dialog window tools.

For more information, see Chapter 16.

Dialog Open SpeedBar

Purpose

Dialog Open SpeedBar enables you to select a different SpeedBar.

Procedure

1. Display the Dialog window by selecting **T**ools UI **B**uilder.

2. Select D**i**alog Open SpeedBar. The Open SpeedBar dialog box appears (see fig. CR.95).

3. If necessary, make selections in the **D**irectories, D**r**ives, or File Types list boxes.

4. In the File Name list box, select the name of the file that contains the SpeedBar you want to add.

5. Click OK or press Enter to confirm the dialog box.

For more information, see Chapter 16.

Fig. CR.95

The Open SpeedBar dialog box.

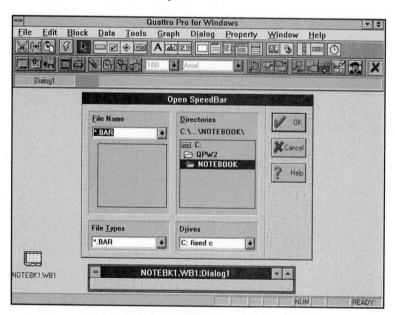

Dialog Save SpeedBar

Purpose

The D**i**alog **S**ave SpeedBar command saves a new SpeedBar.

Procedure

1. Display the Dialog window by selecting **Tools Dialog** Builder.

2. Select Di**a**log **S**ave SpeedBar.

For more information, see Chapter 16.

Dialog Save SpeedBar As

Purpose

Dialog Save SpeedBar As saves a SpeedBar with a specified name.

Procedure

1. Display the Dialog window by selecting **T**ools UI **B**uilder.

2. Select Di**a**log Save SpeedBar As. The Save SpeedBar dialog box appears (see fig CR.96).

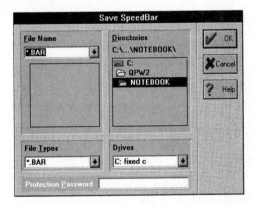

Fig. CR.96

The Save SpeedBar dialog box.

3. If necessary, make selections in the **D**irectories, **D**rives, and File Types text boxes.

4. Enter the name for the SpeedBar in the **F**ile Name text box.

5. Click OK or press Enter.

For more information, see Chapter 16.

Dialog Close SpeedBar

Purpose

The Dialog Close SpeedBar command closes the active SpeedBar.

Procedure

1. Display the Dialog window by selecting Tools UI Builder.
2. Select Dialog Close SpeedBar.

For more information, see Chapter 16.

Dialog New Dialog

Purpose

Dialog New Dialog displays a new, blank dialog box.

Procedure

1. Display the Dialog window by selecting Tools UI Builder.
2. Select Dialog New Dialog.

For more information, see Chapter 16.

Draw Commands

The Draw commands enable you to group and ungroup graph objects, control the relative positioning of graph objects, and import and export graphics in several different graphics file formats. The Draw commands are available only when a Graph window is active. Figure CR.97 shows the Draw menu.

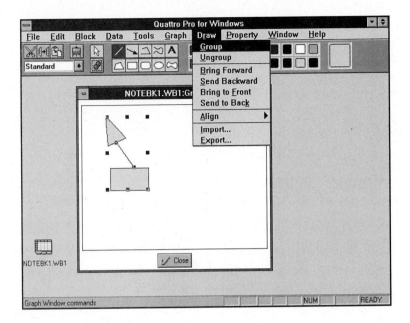

Fig. CR.97

The Draw menu.

Draw Group

Purpose

You use the Draw Group command to group several graph objects to protect them from accidental changes. When objects are grouped, you can select the group only as a whole, you cannot select the individual objects.

Procedure

1. Create the graph objects you want to group.

2. Select the objects you want to group.

3. Select Draw Group.

Important Cues

- Group graph objects that should not be changed individually. Grouping objects prevents them from being selected and changed.

- If you need to modify an object that was grouped, select **Draw Ungroup**.

For more information, see Chapter 10.

Draw Ungroup

Purpose

Draw Ungroup enables you to ungroup graph objects. After graph objects are no longer part of a group, you can select the individual objects and make changes to these individual objects.

Procedure

1. Select the group of graph objects.

2. Select **Draw Ungroup**.

Important Cues

- Ungroup graph objects so that you can change the objects individually. You don't need to ungroup grouped objects to change the color or style of grouped objects.

- After you create graph objects, select **Draw Group** to prevent individual objects from changing.

For more information, see Chapter 10.

Draw Bring Forward, Send Backward, Bring to Front, Send to Back

Purpose

Draw **B**ring Forward, Draw **S**end Backward, Draw Bring to **F**ront, and Draw Send to Bac**k** control the relative positioning of overlapping graph objects. Use these commands when one graph object that should be displayed is hidden by another graph object.

Procedure

1. Select the graph object you want to move.

2. From the following list, select the action you want:

Option	Description
Bring Forward	Moves the selected object one layer forward
Send Backward	Moves the selected object one layer backward
Bring to **F**ront	Moves the selected object to the top layer
Send to Bac**k**	Moves the selected object to the bottom layer

Important Cues

■ Any graph objects that disappear may be behind other graph objects that were added later.

■ After you position graph objects in the correct relative positions, use Draw **G**roup to lock them in these positions.

For more information, see Chapter 10.

Draw Align

Purpose

The Draw Align commands help you improve the appearance of the graphs by enabling you to control their alignments relative to each other.

Procedure

1. Select the graph objects you want to align.

2. Select the desired alignment option from the Draw Align menu:

Option	Description
Left	Aligns selected objects along their left sides
Right	Aligns selected objects along their right sides
Horizontal Center	Aligns selected objects along their horizontal center lines
Top	Aligns selected objects along their top edges
Bottom	Aligns selected objects along their bottom edges
Vertical Center	Aligns selected objects along their vertical center lines

Important Cues

■ You also can use the Property Graph Window Snap to Grid check box to control the positioning of graph objects as you create them.

■ After you position graph objects in the correct positions, use Draw Group to lock them in those positions.

For more information, see Chapter 10.

Draw Import

Purpose

Draw Import enables you to use graphics images that were produced by other applications in the notebooks.

Procedure

1. Select Draw Import. The Import graphics file dialog box appears (see fig. CR.98).

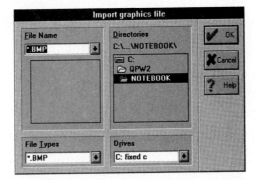

Fig. CR.98

The Import graphics file dialog box.

2. If necessary, select the **Directories, Drives,** or File **Types** list boxes and make the appropriate selections.

3. Select the graphics file to import in the **File Name** list box.

4. Click OK or press Enter to confirm the dialog box.

Important Cues

■ Many graphics images—especially bitmap images, such as those produced by scanners—appear distorted if not displayed at the same size as the original image. To see how the image appears when printed, use File Print Preview.

- Encapsulated PostScript (EPS) files don't always include a screen image, but usually print correctly.

- Windows wallpaper files are bitmap (BMP) images you can use as graph backgrounds and for object fills.

For more information, see Chapter 10.

Draw Export

Purpose

Draw Export enables you to export Quattro Pro 5.0 for Windows graphics for use in other applications.

Procedure

1. Select and, with the left mouse button, double-click the graph you want to export to an active Graph window.

2. Select Draw Export. The Export graphics file dialog box appears (see fig. CR.99).

Fig. CR.99

The Export graphics file dialog box.

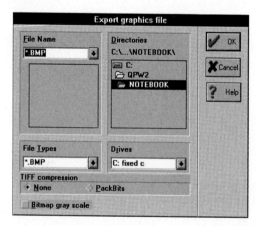

3. Enter the name of the file to create in the File name list box.

4. Select the type of graphics file to create in the File Types list box.

5. If you are exporting a Tag Image File Format (TIFF) file, select the image compression method.

6. Click OK or press Enter.

Important Cues

■ Programs that accept TIFF files may not be able to use some image compression methods. Be sure that you determine which methods your application program can use.

■ You can use Quattro Pro 5.0 for Windows to translate graphics image files between otherwise incompatible applications. Use Draw Import to import the image, and then use Draw Export to save the image in a different format.

For more information about exporting graphics files, see Chapter 10.

Installing Quattro Pro 5.0 for Windows

Installing Quattro Pro 5.0 for Windows is almost automatic; after you start the program, you follow simple on-screen instructions. You must install Quattro Pro 5.0 for Windows on a hard disk; you cannot run the program from floppy disks.

Installing Quattro Pro takes fewer than 15 minutes on most systems. When you are ready to begin, turn on the computer and follow the instructions in this appendix.

Quattro Pro 5.0 for Windows includes one set of disks, either 5 1/4-inch or 3 1/2-inch. Make certain that you have the correct set for your system. After you install Quattro Pro 5.0 for Windows, store the original disks in a safe location.

Before you install the program, make certain that you meet the following hardware, storage, and memory requirements:

- A system with 80286, 80386, 80486, or Pentium architecture
- An EGA, VGA, or IBM 8514 monitor

- Microsoft Windows Version 3 or higher, running with DOS Version 3.11 or higher

- 4M of random-access memory

- 10M of available hard disk storage

The following are optional, but highly recommended:

- Any printer supported by Windows Version 3 or higher

- A mouse

Using the Install Program

Because Quattro Pro 5.0 for Windows runs only under Microsoft Windows, the Windows Program Manager must be active before you install Quattro Pro 5.0 for Windows. Start Microsoft Windows and insert Disk 1 into drive A. (If you are installing from a different drive, substitute that drive letter.) Choose **File Run** from the Program Manager menu and type **A:INSTALL** in the **C**ommand Line text box (see fig. A.1). Then choose OK.

Fig. A.1

The File Run dialog box of the Windows Program Manager.

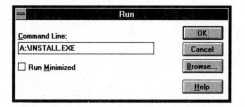

Registering Your Original Disks

To make the original set of disks usable, you must register them by entering and saving your name and your company name on Disk 1 (see fig. A.2). After you start the Install program, enter this information in the appropriate text boxes in the Install program dialog box.

Selecting Directories

By default, Quattro Pro 5.0 for Windows is installed in C:\QPW5, sample files are installed in C:\QPW5\SAMPLES, and certain files used by the Database Desktop are installed in C:\ODAPI. If you want to use different directories, select Directories to display the QPW Directories dialog box shown in figure A.3. After you have made any necessary changes, press Enter or click OK to return to the main screen.

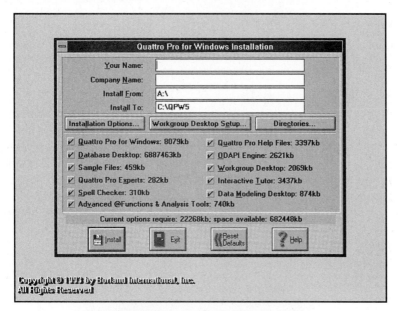

Fig. A.2

Begin by entering your name and selecting installation options.

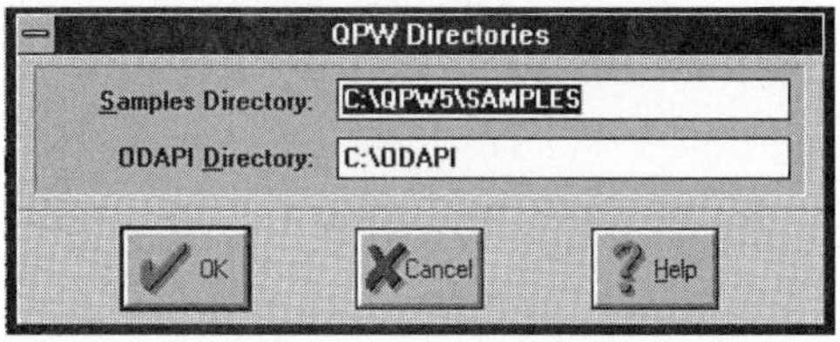

Fig. A.3

The QPW Directories dialog box.

Selecting Workgroup Desktop Options

The Workgroup Desktop enables you to share data with other Quattro Pro 5.0 for Windows users. To change the default directories used by the Workgroup Desktop, select Workgroup Desktop Setup from the Installation dialog box; the Workgroup Desktop Setup dialog box appears (see figure A.4). After you have made any necessary changes, press Enter or click OK to return to the main screen.

Fig. A.4

The Workgroup Desktop
Setup dialog box.

Selecting Installation Options

By default, the installation program creates a program group called
Quattro Pro for Windows to hold the program icons for the options you
install. In addition, the installation program modifies the PATH statement in AUTOEXEC.BAT to enable Database Desktop to function properly. If you prefer, you can select Installation Options and deselect
these two options (see fig. A.5). In most cases, however, you will want
to use the default settings. After you have made any necessary
changes, press Enter or click OK to return to the main screen.

Fig. A.5

The Installation Options
dialog box.

If you do not have enough available disk space, you may choose to skip
installing some of the optional features, such as Workgroup Desktop or
the sample and clip art files. To bypass installation of a feature, deselect its check box.

Select Install to begin installing Quattro Pro 5.0 for Windows.
Figure A.6 shows how your screen will appear shortly after beginning
the installation.

Because Quattro Pro 5.0 for Windows is distributed on several disks,
you will see several messages during the installation, such as the one
shown in figure A.7. Be sure to insert the correct disk and then press
Enter or click OK to continue.

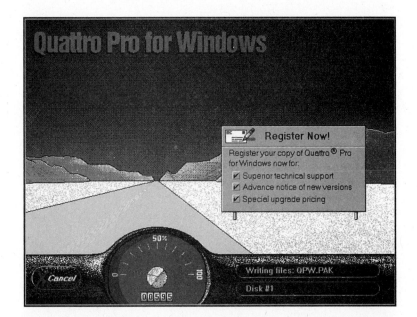

Fig. A.6

Installing Quattro Pro
5.0 for Windows.

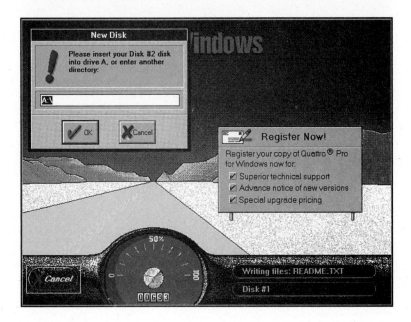

Fig. A.7

You are prompted to
change disks during
installation.

The Database Desktop uses the DOS program SHARE to make certain database files are properly shared between programs. If SHARE is already loaded on your system, the installation program will display the message shown in figure A.8. If you do not already have SHARE loaded, you will not see this message, but will want to modify your AUTOEXEC.BAT file to include the command **SHARE /F:4096 /L:400**.

Fig. A.8

SHARE must be loaded in order to control file sharing.

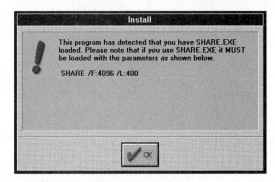

When the installation is complete, the Install program displays a list of the files that were installed or modified (see fig. A.9). You may want to examine this list so that you know which files were added to your system, and which files were changed. Press Enter or click OK to continue.

Fig. A.9

The Install program displays a list of the files that were installed or modified.

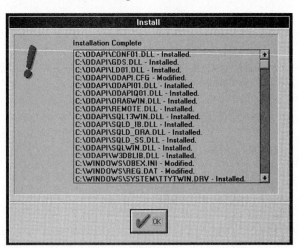

Next, the dialog box shown in figure A.10 asks whether you want to view README.TXT, the file containing late information about Quattro

Pro 5.0 for Windows. It is a good idea to view this file because it contains important information, such as new program features and any known problems, that became relevant after the final documentation was printed.

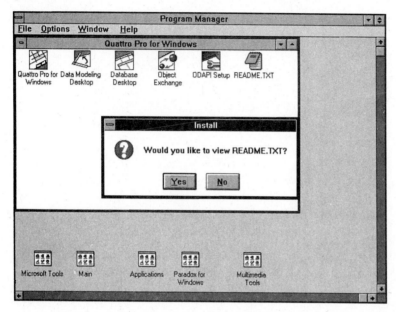

Fig. A.10

View README.TXT for last-minute information.

If you are attached to a network, you must next configure the ODAPI database engine—the optional portion of Quattro Pro 5.0 for Windows that enables sharing of network files. Figure A.11 shows the dialog box that asks whether you want to configure ODAPI, and figure A.12 shows the ODAPI configuration screen. In most cases, you can accept the default configuration, but you may want to consult with your network manager for further details.

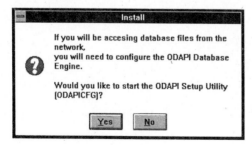

Fig. A.11

If you are attached to a network, you must configure the ODAPI database engine.

Fig. A.12

The ODAPI configuration screen.

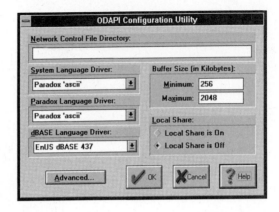

Summary

Installing Quattro Pro 5.0 for Windows is a simple process. All you need to do is make a few selections and follow on-screen instructions.

You may need to change the Windows configuration. If you purchase a new printer or video display, you must reconfigure Windows for the printer or video display. You can modify the configuration of Windows through the Program Manager Control Panel. For details, refer to the Windows documentation or *Using Windows 3.1,* Special Edition, published by Que Corporation.

Upgrading to Quattro Pro 5.0 for Windows

If you have used previous versions of Quattro Pro or Lotus 1-2-3, you may feel familiar with Quattro Pro 5.0 for Windows. While you are learning the new, easy-to-use, Quattro Pro 5.0 for Windows commands, you also can access a Quattro Pro for DOS compatible menu.

Quattro Pro 5.0 for Windows can directly read and write files in many different formats, including Quattro Pro for DOS, 1-2-3 for DOS Releases 2.x and 3.x, 1-2-3 for Windows, Excel, dBASE, and Paradox. Most Quattro Pro for DOS and 1-2-3 macros can be used without modification, although these older macros do not take full advantage of the powerful new features available in Quattro Pro 5.0 for Windows.

Many of the new features of Quattro Pro 5.0 for Windows are capabilities offered by Microsoft Windows. You can, for example, easily and quickly create reports that combine the best features of several different types of programs by using the Windows DDE and OLE capabilities. For instance, you can create a report in a Windows word processor that contains a table from a Quattro Pro 5.0 for Windows spreadsheet and detailed graphics from a Windows graphics program.

If you are an experienced Quattro Pro for DOS or 1-2-3 user, you may want to try Quattro Pro 5.0 for Windows right away. Before you do, however, read Chapter 3, "Using the Graphical User Interface." It contains important information new to Quattro Pro 5.0 for Windows and shows you how to manipulate windows, use the mouse, and move through the Quattro Pro 5.0 for Windows menus and dialog boxes.

This appendix presents a brief overview of the major enhancements and new features in Quattro Pro 5.0 for Windows.

What Is Quattro Pro 5.0 for Windows?

Quattro Pro 5.0 for Windows is a graphical spreadsheet application program that runs under the Microsoft Windows operating environment. Quattro Pro 5.0 for Windows enables you to create spreadsheets and graphs, analyze and store database information, and share information with other Windows applications.

In Quattro Pro 5.0 for Windows, spreadsheets are always three-dimensional, and the *notebook* metaphor is used to describe the organization of spreadsheets. A page tab appears at the bottom of each page; you can quickly move between pages by clicking the page tab. Each Quattro Pro 5.0 for Windows notebook has 256 spreadsheet pages and a graphs page.

Quattro Pro 5.0 for Windows is an object-oriented spreadsheet program. Each object, whether a selected block, a notebook page, a complete notebook, or the Quattro Pro 5.0 for Windows program itself, has a set of properties that you can control using the Object Inspectors feature. Object Inspectors, which you can access through menu commands or by pointing to the object and clicking the right mouse button, display only those settings appropriate to the selected object. Instead of trying to remember which menu you must use to find a particular setting, you use Object Inspectors to access all available object settings.

Quattro Pro 5.0 for Windows supports both DDE (Dynamic Data Exchange) and the newer, more powerful OLE (Object Linking and Embedding) available in Windows 3.1. Through these capabilities, you can share data between Windows applications and create compound documents that combine the best features of each application.

Quattro Pro 5.0 for Windows also adds many other new features that make it the most powerful and easy-to-use spreadsheet program available. These features include the following:

- Over 250 new @functions. Quattro Pro 5.0 for Windows has the broadest range of functions of any spreadsheet program, making it much easier to perform sophisticated calculations without the necessity of building complex formulas. The new @functions are discussed in Chapter 7, "Using Functions."

- Interactive Tutors, a new approach to learning the power of Quattro Pro 5.0 for Windows. The Interactive Tutors teach you how to use Quattro Pro 5.0 for Windows using your own, live data, instead of requiring you to follow a carefully scripted example. The Interactive Tutors are introduced in Chapter 4, "Learning Spreadsheet Basics."

- Analytical Graphs, which enable you to spot trends in your data without requiring you to be an expert in statistical analysis. Analytical Graphs are discussed in Chapter 10, "Creating Presentation Graphics."

- Experts—which are similar to the Wizards in Excel—help you perform complex operations by simply following along and answering simple questions.

- Analysis Tools, which make the power of extremely sophisticated data analysis techniques available to everyone—not just those with advanced degrees in statistical analysis. Experts and the Analysis Tools are discussed in Chapter 17, "Using Analysis Tools and Experts."

- Data Modeling Desktop, which integrates the power of a flexible cross-tabulation analysis tool, such as Lotus Improv, directly into Quattro Pro 5.0 for Windows. Unlike Lotus Improv, the Data Modeling Desktop was designed to make sharing data with Quattro Pro 5.0 for Windows easy and straightforward. Data Modeling Desktop is discussed in Chapter 18, "Using the Data Modeling Desktop."

- Scenario management, which enables you to try many different what-if options, and have each option quickly available for review.

- Data consolidation, which enables you to easily combine information from many different sources. Both the Scenario Manager and the Consolidator are introduced in Chapter 19, "Consolidating Data and Managing Scenarios."

■ Automatic data sharing across a network or around the world. The Workgroup Desktop automatically manages data sharing among Quattro Pro 5.0 for Windows users, making certain that everyone has the latest information at all times. For the first time, companies can have total confidence in the data sharing process, regardless of the location of the users of that data. The Workgroup Desktop is discussed in Chapter 20, "Sharing Data Using the Workgroup Desktop."

Using Compatible Menus

To help you upgrade from Quattro Pro for DOS, Quattro Pro 5.0 for Windows enables you to access menu trees compatible with Quattro Pro for DOS. By default, the slash key (/) activates the Quattro Pro 5.0 for Windows menu bar. You can use the Application Object Inspectors dialog box to specify a different action, however. Figure B.1 shows the Application dialog box, which appears when you select **Property Application** or point to the Quattro Pro 5.0 for Windows title bar and click the right mouse button. You then select Macro to choose the action initiated by pressing the slash key.

Fig. B.1

You can select a 1-2-3 or Quattro Pro for DOS menu.

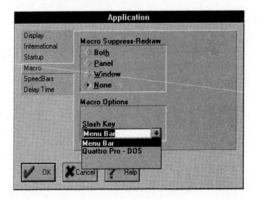

If you select Quattro Pro - DOS, the menu shown in figure B.2 appears when you press the slash key.

Although you can still use most Quattro Pro for DOS commands if you specify the appropriate Slash Key Menu, you soon will find that using the Quattro Pro 5.0 for Windows commands offers many advantages.

Generally, the Quattro Pro 5.0 for Windows menus have far fewer levels, and selections are often displayed in dialog boxes. Also, because Quattro Pro 5.0 for Windows fully supports the mouse, it is frequently much more efficient to use the mouse to make selections than to use the keyboard.

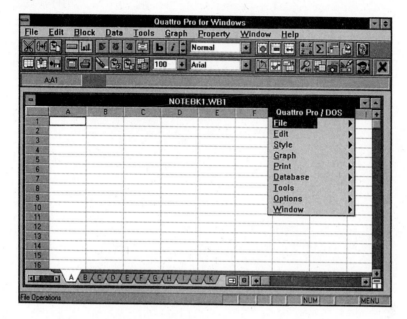

Fig. B.2

The Quattro Pro for DOS Slash Key menu.

Translating Files

File translation is a built-in feature of Quattro Pro 5.0 for Windows. When you retrieve a file created in another spreadsheet program, or a database file created by dBASE or Paradox, translation to Quattro Pro 5.0 for Windows is automatic.

Quattro Pro 5.0 for Windows also can save files in many different formats automatically. If you use the normal file extension used by another spreadsheet or database program, such as WK1 for Lotus 1-2-3 Release 2.x, Quattro Pro 5.0 for Windows converts the file to the other program's format as it saves the file. Of course, features unique to Quattro Pro 5.0 for Windows are lost in the conversion because of a lack of support in the other programs.

Summary

Quattro Pro 5.0 for Windows offers many new and exciting features not available in any DOS spreadsheet program or even any other Windows spreadsheet program. Throughout *Using Quattro Pro 5.0 for Windows, Special Edition*, you will find the tips and techniques you need to learn to master this program.

Symbols

A

I

M

R

radar graphs, 336-337
radio buttons, 77
    see also option buttons
@RAND function, 216
READ command (File menu), 596
reading
    file formats, 271
    files in different formats, 891
READLN command (File menu), 596
READY mode, 108, 113
real mode (Windows), 32
recalculation
    Automatic, 153-155
    column-wise, 154
    manual, 153-155
    natural order, 154
    row-wise, 154
Record Macro dialog box, 535
recording
    base scenarios, 722
    macros, 533-537
records
    databases, 414
        add, 421
        searching for, 429-443
        sorting, 423-429
    deleting, 422, 443
    entering in databases, 420
    extracting, 434-436, 442
    locating, 433-434
    search variations, 436-442
Rectangle tool, 357
Redo command (Edit menu), 21
references
    cells on other notebook
        pages, 108
    circular, 155
    links, 285
referencing cells outside the
    database, 438
Reformat command (Block
    menu), 22, 799-800
registering Quattro disks, 884

relational databases, 459
relational operators, 437
relative addressing
    command equivalents, 512
    copying formulas, 166
    macros, 535
renaming elements (Data
Modeling Desktop), 698-699
repetition factors (macros), 520,
529
Replace command (Edit menu),
169-171
replacing
    cell contents, 112
    data, 169-171
    existing data/moving data, 159
Report Output Blocks dialog
box, 301
reports
    Answer (Optimizer tool),
        303-304
    copying to notebooks, 705-707
    Data Modeling Desktop,
        689-701
        appearance modification
            command, 699-701
        consolidating data, 697-699
        deleting, 696-697
        grouping elements, 698
        modifying, 695-697
        pivoting label bars, 702
        rearranging data order,
            695-697
        rearranging with label
            bars, 701-704
        renaming elements, 698-699
        totaling, 695-696
    Detail (Optimizer tool),
        302-303
    fitting on one page, 395
    focussing on labels, 704-705
    multiple-page, printing, 391
    Optimizer tool, 301-304
    printing, 26, 381
    Scenario Manager, 724-726
    single-page, printing, 389-391